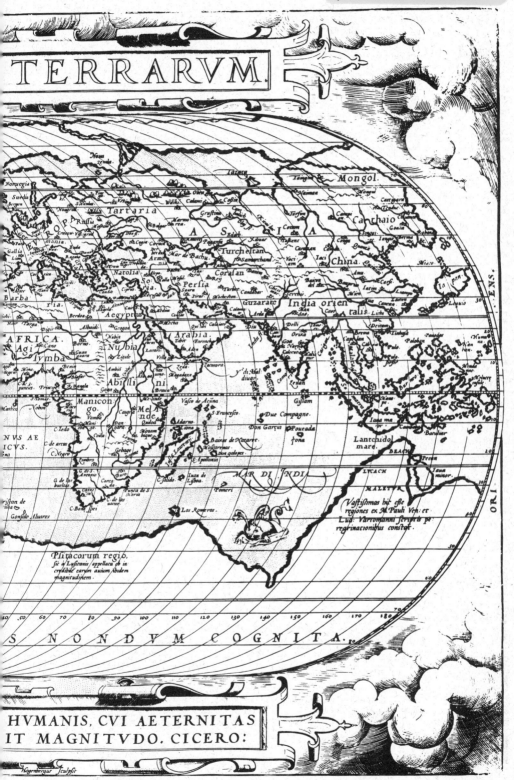

TERRARVM.

Norve gia

Noua Zembla

Tazata

Tangut   Mongol.

Suedia
Bergen

Nugrad   Wladi

Naman   Mongul

Cassogu

Tartaria

Grustina

Turfon

Cami   Tendur

E V R O P A

Rhllu

A   S   I   A

Tascent   Camul   Ergi mul   Brema

Carthaio

mania.
Galli...

Belgor

Penaria

Khaur

Congu

Singui

Tanguc

Quinsai

Natolia   Armi nia

Mar de Bachu

Turcheſtan

Samarchand   Veci   am   Iaci am   China   Olm

Cefi

So. Polle   Wfol

Persia   Saura   Siraz

Arde   Turcon   Candahar   Berrem   Bazbu   Paqu...   Quian   Iatim   Xa   Quanzu   Cauzu   Ochu   Ia. pon.

Ceolan   Barg...

Aegyptus

Coralan

Guzarate   Man Tan

India orien   talis. Lichi   Verinen   Curven

Mier

Laoiu   30

E   N   S.

AFRICA.
Agi
Iymba

Albaidi

Geogaa

Nubia   Borno   Ziquet

Arbia

Om bel   Calicut   Enroch   Adea   Len   Anian

Arabia.
Zibit

Diu   Delli   Yine   Oriza   Goa   Nar ſing   Bi ſna   Calecu   pur   Narſin   Driven   Pedir

Chi   Tisigai

Pole   Polohen   Pauxdar   Hainan   Hum   nan.

Benin   Aganh   Zua   Lacaori   Villa   Incoa

Nubia

Giu   Magadazo   Brauas

Abiſſi   ni

Indus   Con...   Zeilan

Banda   Timor   Vitu...   inſula

Manicon   go.   Melo nde   Vambu   Mani   Caugra   Dan guru   Badara   Adamo   iona   Don Garcia   Poueada   fona

Vasco de Acuna   S. Francesco   Due Compagne

Gaſſam   Iaua ma   iour

Lantchidol   mare.

Barulier

NVS AE ICVS.

C. Iedo
C. de arcus
C. Negro   Colua   Zembro   Gebage   nue   Naſcaruaas   Bassos de Mazaret   Don galopes   S. Apollonia   Baixos de Mazaret   MAR DI INDI

BEACH   Peron   Iaua minor.

LVCACH

MALETVR

G de S.
Antonio

C. ledo   Coroa   da...   Punta de S. Maria

Iuxa de Lisboa   Pomeri

Vaſtiſſimas hæ eſſe regiones ex M. Pauli Ven: et Lud: Varromanni ſcriptis pe: regrinationibus conſtat.

C. de lpe buelto
Capo   C. Bone ſſpei   Gonſalo Aluares

Los Romeros

Plitacorum regio, ſic a Luſitanis appellata ob in: credibilē earum auium ibidem magnitudinē.

O   R   I

10   20   30   40   50   60   70   80   90   100   110   120   130   140   150   160   170   180

40   50   60   70   80   90   100   110   120   130   140   150   160   170   180

S NONDVM COGNITA.

Hogenbergus Sculpsit

ASIA

IN THE MAKING OF EUROPE

ASIA

IN THE MAKING OF EUROPE

DONALD F. LACH

VOLUME

I

The
Century
of Discovery

BOOK ONE

THE UNIVERSITY OF CHICAGO PRESS

CHICAGO AND LONDON

Library of Congress Catalog Card Number: 64–19848

THE UNIVERSITY OF CHICAGO PRESS, CHICAGO & LONDON

The University of Toronto Press, Toronto 5, Canada

© *1965 by*
The University of Chicago
All rights reserved. Published 1965

Printed in the
United States of America

Endpaper. The World Map from Abraham Ortelius' *Theatrum orbis terrarum* (Antwerp, 1575). Courtesy of the University of Chicago Libraries.

To Alma and Sandy

Preface

The idea for this enterprise dawned upon me over a quarter of a century ago. It came while hearing my professors at West Virginia University, especially Dr. T. E. Ennis, lecture stirringly about the revolutionary impact of the West upon the traditional cultures of Asia. The question of how Asia had affected the West throughout history strangely seemed not to be a part of these considerations.

With all the optimism of youth, I then determined that I would prepare myself to study the impact of Asia upon the West. Throughout graduate study at the University of Chicago I plagued the professors with my questions, and they willingly read and criticized my pedestrian efforts. I am especially grateful to the late Harley F. MacNair and to Louis R. Gottschalk for their patient guidance and understanding through many weary years.

Once on an independent course, I decided to prepare what can euphemistically be called footnotes to this larger study. Most of these were embellishments on my doctoral dissertation and were published as articles and monographs. These earlier pieces related mainly to the German Enlightenment, a field in which I likewise have great interest.

While preparing smaller studies, learning languages, and traveling in Europe and Asia, I realized that my research would have to be pushed back to the beginnings of the expansion movement. Such a decision also required that I bring India, as well as the Far East, into the range of my vision. To learn a bit about the subcontinent and Ceylon required a further expenditure of time.

Throughout these preparatory years my colleagues, friends, and the Foundations have shown remarkable patience. For travel and research in Europe and Asia I have received grants from the Fulbright board, Merle and Louise Thompson of Elmira, New York, and the American Council of Learned Societies. Of equal importance were the generous grants-in-aid regularly awarded me by three groups of the University of Chicago: the Social Science

Research Committee, the Committee on South Asia, and the Committee on Far Eastern Civilizations. Without support from these generous patrons I would have been helpless.

The grants-in-aid were used to hire graduate assistants. Miss Zoe Swecker, now of Winona College, aided me loyally and ably for eight years and ended her tenure with an excellent dissertation reviewing the Iberian sources (1550–1600) for the history of East Asia. Her successor, Mrs. Carol Flaumenhaft, worked diligently with me for more than five years. She and Mrs. Margaret Woodward went through the anguish of putting the present study into shape for publication, and their work (as well as the index) was completed by Miss Linda Eichmeier. At many spots in this study I am indebted to my former assistants for insights and references which would certainly have escaped me.

Special research projects on individual topics were competently handled by Johanna Menzel, Harold Johnson, Diane Kelder, and Bentley Duncan. For aid with Chinese and Japanese materials I am indebted to Joseph Cha, Ch'en Min-sun, Nelson Chou, and Tamiko Matsumura. Finally, I want to mention without acknowledging them individually the numerous students who have worked in my seminar, and to thank in advance for their contributions those who are now writing doctoral dissertations on various phases of this field.

Each of these lengthy chapters has been read and criticized by specialists in various disciplines or periods of history, especially by Professor Earl H. Pritchard, now of the University of Arizona. William H. McNeill, chairman of my department, generously read several chapters and gave them a few of his unique touches. The materials on antiquity profited greatly from the erudite criticisms of my colleague Stuart I. Oost. Eric W. Cochrane, Francis H. Dowley, and Edward A. Kracke, Jr., also helped to polish the first two chapters. On the spice trade I have benefited from conversations with Earl J. Hamilton and from the careful reading of Robert M. Hartwell. The India chapter owes much to the specialized knowledge of J. A. B. van Buitenen, Milton B. Singer, and Father Cyriac Pullapilly, a priest of the Malabar Church. Professor C. C. Berg of the University of Leyden contributed greatly to the chapter on Southeast Asia, especially with regard to Malay and Javan terms and conceptions. Evett D. Hester, associate director of Chicago's Philippine Studies program, likewise gave freely and kindly of his specialized knowledge. My Japan colleagues, Joseph Kitagawa, Eugene Soviak, and Edwin McClellan, saw to it that I did not make too many errors in Japanese history, names, and terms. The China chapter owes much to my conversations with Herrlee G. Creel and to his reading of it; Ho Ping-ti, Y. C. Wang, and Robert M. Hartwell have also left indelible imprints upon it. When I had run out of ideas, Daniel J. Boorstin and Hans Morgenthau helped work out the titles for these volumes.

The reference librarians of the University of Chicago, especially Helen M. Smith, have served me patiently and well. I owe particular thanks also to Robert Rosenthal, curator of Special Collections at the University of Chicago, and to Fred Hall of the Greenlee Collection at the Newberry Library. Without the great resources in books and personnel of the University of Chicago and the Newberry Library I would never have undertaken a work of this magnitude.

Finally, to my parents, wife, and daughter I owe a deep debt of gratitude for their forebearance and encouragement over many years. To all those anonymous others who have lightened my load, I also give my thanks.

At this point the author traditionally relieves everybody else of responsibility for his errors. I do that too, but with a strong feeling that this book is what I am, and that I am what my family, friends, colleagues, and students have made me.

Introduction

What were the drives which first impelled the men of the Renaissance to push out into the unknown worlds beyond the sea frontiers of Europe? How did the expansion of Europe maintain its momentum for four centuries until there were no more continents left to conquer on this earth? Historians, fascinated and impressed by the uniqueness in world history of the European expansion movement, have spent a great deal of time trying to analyze and explain the cultural dynamism which lay behind the thrust into the overseas world. While unanimously hailing the discoveries as a triumph of European enterprise and ingenuity, many modern scholars have been bitterly divided along national and religious lines in their assessments and evaluations of the forces which motivated the overseas pioneers. Others, less concerned with causation, have produced extended narratives and analytical monographs devoted to describing the voyages, reconstructing the administrative structure of overseas trade, and probing the colonizing techniques of the empire-builders. Researchers of mission history have traced in meticulous detail the attempt to transplant Christian institutions and ideas to the pagan world. But very few students of European expansion have sought to investigate the significance of the discoveries for the development of Western civilization itself.

The expansion and resulting rise to world predominance of the European nations meant the obscuring of the ancient and brilliant cultures of the East by the newer and more dynamic civilizations of the West. Historians have usually attributed this eclipse of the East to the rapid industrial growth of the West and the failure of the East to keep pace with it. None of the great centers of Asian civilization, they point out, was able to mount an industrial revolution of its own comparable to that which transformed Europe after 1800 and gave to the West its decisive technical and military superiority.

Students in both Europe and Asia, in their preoccupation with the period and problems of Europe's world predominance, have all too often given the impression that the entire history of the intercourse between East and West is simply the story of how the Westerners got to the East, how they maintained themselves there, and how they contributed to the modernization, Westernization, and transformation of Asia's traditional cultures and modes of life. As a consequence these scholars have neglected to point out that an eclipse is never permanent, that this one was never total, and that there was a period in early modern times when Asia and Europe were close rivals in the brilliance of their civilizations.

From 1500 to 1800 relations between East and West were ordinarily conducted within a framework and on terms established by the Asian nations. Except for those who lived in a few colonial footholds, the Europeans in the East were all there on sufferance. This was related to the obvious but often overlooked fact that, while Europeans dispatched trading, diplomatic, and religious missions to Asia, Asian countries never sent similar missions to Europe on their own initiative. Although the Europeans traveled with seeming ease along the maritime routes of Asia, they penetrated the main continental states infrequently and with difficulty. And, in the sixteenth century, they were never in a position to force their will upon the imperial rulers of India or China; the great political and cultural capitals of the Asiatic continent in no way felt threatened by their arms. Still, it is surprising how much a handful of enterprising Europeans was able to do toward making East and West conscious of each other.

The revelation of Asia to preindustrial Europe did not transform or quickly modify the basic tenets of Western life, faith, or institutions. Europe's responses to the knowledge that high civilizations existed in Asia were ordinarily slow in developing, and shifting and scattered in impact. They are hard to identify with precision, but a few random examples will suffice to show how continual and varied the European reactions were from the time of Vasco da Gama to our own day.

The first travelers to the East, as well as sophisticated Humanists back home in Europe, were quick to recognize that in some facets of life the great civilizations of Asia were more advanced than their own. Secular and religious observers alike, some of them natives of the great Italian towns of the Renaissance, were openly astounded by the impressive cities and architectural monuments which they saw everywhere in continental Asia and Japan. They freely acknowledged that the Chinese, in particular, were gifted craftsmen from whom Europeans had much to learn. The German philosopher Leibniz was so impressed with the social and familial organization of China that he puckishly suggested that the Son of Heaven should send missionaries to the West to teach Europe about the precepts governing civil relationships. Voltaire called upon the kings of Europe to follow the example of the Ch'ien-lung emperor by studying and patronizing philosophy and the arts. The Society of Jesus presented printed copies of the most informative of the missionary letters from the East to the crowned heads and prelates of Catholic Europe, and in the eighteenth century, following the encyclopedic trend of the day, published a great multivolume collection of the missionary letters from China.

The Sinophilism of the Philosophes, Cameralists, literati, and artists of eighteenth-century Europe subsequently fell into disrepute along with many other highly esteemed ideas of the Enlightenment. The Westerners of the industrial age, impressed by their own technical and organizational achievements, no longer felt awed by what they saw in the Orient. Disillusionment with rationalism as the key to universal understanding also precipitated a reaction in Europe against China as the rational model of political and social organization. European and American thinkers of the nineteenth century increasingly looked upon the countries of the East as centers of retardation, as a potential menace to the world which the Westerners seemed divinely destined to make over in their own image, and as an irritating reminder of the fact that decay and disintegration ultimately overtake even the most brilliant and powerful of civilizations.

But at the same time, the uncompromising and optimistic materialism of the 1800's stimulated a number of disenchanted Westerners to extol the spirituality of Asian life. Ralph Waldo Emerson, an avid student of the Indian scriptures, looked at Hindu thought as an ancient and untouched treasury of truth. Merchants and missionaries in the field and scholars at home began around the same time to apply the new scientific techniques of the day to the study of Asian languages and literatures, institutions, and history. As scholarly penetration increased, the generalizers and popularizers made efforts to analyze and describe the peculiar racial and national characters of the Orientals. In the late nineteenth century, when it was fashionable in Europe to admire Japan, numerous Westerners sought, as their forebears had three centuries earlier, to uncover and describe the roots of the Japanese character and to emphasize the unsurpassed devotion of the Japanese, individually and socially, to simplicity, frugality, discipline, serenity, adaptability, and militarism. Even the Malays and the Javanese were celebrated by Europeans for artistic and spiritual accomplishments which, it was felt, had not been equaled in the West.

A self-conscious Asian historiography began to develop in the West during the nineteenth century contemporaneously with the overwhelming of traditional Asian cultures by the superior arms of the West. At first, the school of scientific history, as it developed in Germany, barely recognized the existence of the great Asian cultures. To give Ranke and his followers their due, they ignored Asia because they realized that they were not able to command the languages necessary to exploit the primary sources and were not even aware of the existence or location of the Asian annals. Hegel, who depended for his view of Asia upon earlier European sources and upon the merchant accounts of his day, postulated in his philosophical history a hypothetical Asia that was static and lifeless when compared to the dynamic and vital West.[1] The missionary

---

[1] Ernst Schulin, *Die weltgeschichtliche Erfassung des Orients bei Hegel und Ranke* (Göttingen, 1958); for nineteenth-century "Orientalism" see Raymond Schwab, *La renaissance orientale* (Paris, 1950).

historians, mainly economic liberals and Protestants, tended in the nineteenth century to denigrate the work of their mercantilistic and Catholic predecessors. Out of these currents of historical writing a nineteenth-century view emerged in the West which emphasized the backwardness of Asia and its stubborn resistance to the spread of the Christian and Western way of life.

Those few general historians of our day who have deigned to comment on the European reaction to the East have ordinarily played it down as a minor episode in the history of expansion. They have also tended to regard the European response to overseas cultures as a single and undifferentiated phenomenon. For example, they have not sought to distinguish between Europe's reaction to the primitive cultures of America and its response to the high cultures of Asia. All too often they have failed to grasp, and consequently to relay an understanding of, the sporadic and uneven growth of knowledge about the overseas world. Historians of various disciplines—art, literature, and technology—have characteristically treated the Asian impact upon their special fields in isolation. While students of art often relate the adoption of Asian techniques and embellishments to the European interest in Oriental crafts, they do not commonly point out that the philosopher and the painter were similarly attracted by the unconventional and exotic quality in the ideas being transmitted from the East. The best of the works by specialists are the splendidly documented volumes of Professor Joseph Needham of Cambridge which map out how scientific and technical ideas and devices have migrated from China to Europe throughout recorded history.[1]

Students of Asian history, by contrast, have focused most of their efforts in recent years upon mastering the languages of Asia necessary to the penetration of the native historical sources. In so doing they have often overlooked the Western materials or have been unable to command the languages of the European sources (especially Latin, Portuguese, and Dutch). This neglect of the European sources has been particularly noticeable among writers on India and southeast Asia. Historians of south Asia, both Westerners and natives, have depended too exclusively upon the voluminous materials readily available in English. For the period before 1600 particularly, the Latin and Iberian sources are often much more authoritative than the English materials, and for many periods, are more reliable for dates and statistics than the native documentation.

Clearly, the Europeans' view of Asia was not a static one. Europe responded to the various overseas cultures with constantly changing degrees of enthusiasm or revulsion. It follows that the techniques, art forms, and ideas from the East had different appeal in Europe at different times, and that Europe's own climate of opinion in a given epoch helped to determine the selections which Europeans made from the new cultures which were revealed to them. And perhaps most important of all, the knowledge that there existed in Asia several high cultures which owed nothing to the Graeco-Roman heritage or to the Christian

---

[1] J. Needham and Wang Ling, *Science and Civilization in China* (3 vols.; Cambridge, 1954–59).

revelation helped to produce a new sense of cultural relativism in Europe that was earth-rocking in its ultimate implications.

The present volume (in two books) is the first in the series of six which I contemplate. They are jointly entitled *Asia in the Making of Europe*, and will deal with the period from 1500 to 1800. I plan to devote two volumes to each of the three centuries under review. The first volume to deal with each century will include a summary of the European view of Asia prevailing at the time, the channels through which new information got to Europe and its dissemination there, and the composite and changing images which Europeans had of the individual Asian countries during the century in question. The second volume for each century will be concerned with the impact which knowledge of Asia had upon European institutions, arts, crafts, and ideas. While the various volumes will be independent studies, I hope that the series as a whole will provide a general background for the more intensive monographs of the specialists in the various disciplines.

The first volume, entitled *The Century of Discovery*, deals with what Europe had come to know about Asia by 1600. Asia, as used here, refers to the lands and civilizations east of the Indus. Europe is defined as the nations and peoples west of the Slavic world. The Levant, eastern Europe, and Russia will be treated, particularly in later volumes, as intermediaries in the transmission of knowledge about Asia to Europe. The Americas, as offshoots of western European civilization, will likewise figure in these volumes as intermediaries. Mexico, for example, was from the sixteenth century onward an important link in the chain which bound Manila to Madrid.

The terminal date (1600) of this first volume is not an arbitrary one, even though it happens to be a round number. The final years of the sixteenth century and beginning years of the seventeenth century saw fundamental changes both in Europe and Asia which altered basically their earlier relationships. In Europe the years around 1600 were marked by the end of the Iberian monopoly over the sea routes to Asia and the beginning of overseas activity by the Dutch and English under the auspices of their newly founded East India companies. The direct participation of the northern powers in Eastern trade after 1600 added new dimensions to Europe's knowledge of Asia, brought an end to the Roman Catholic monopoly of the Christian mission, and prepared the ground for a new set of responses to the East. In Asia the Hindu empire of Vijayanagar was suffering its death throes in 1600; in the north of India the empire of Akbar was at its apogee. And it was in these years that the Jesuits began to penetrate the interior of the two great Indian empires—a penetration which helped to produce a new view of the internal content of Indian civilization. China, the other great continental state which had previously kept its doors closed to the Europeans, was finally entered by the Jesuit, Matteo Ricci, who got to Peking early in 1601. The establishment thereafter of a Jesuit mission at the Ming capital enabled Ricci, like his fellow Jesuits at the court of Akbar, to perceive native life and culture more intimately than had ever been possible before. In Japan the end of the sixteenth century saw the achievement of political unification and the beginnings of the Tokugawa shogunate, a new political dispensation which would rapidly move to shut out the Europeans and close Japan to all but limited Western intercourse for more than two centuries. Thus, from the viewpoint of this study, 1600 may be taken as the date around which the terms for trade, diplomatic intercourse, and evangelizing in the East changed markedly, and as a date which heralded the end in Europe of the exclusive claims of Spain and Catholicism to the overseas world and the opening of new northern and Protestant channels of direct information about the East.

The present volume starts with a brief section (Part I) which surveys the evolution of Europe's knowledge of Asia from the time of the ancient Greeks to the opening of the route around the Cape of Good Hope. While most of the materials reviewed are well known, I felt a need to summarize them in order to set the stage for the changes which began to occur after 1500 and to help the reader adjust his own sight to the lenses through which Renaissance man saw Asia. In this preliminary section, unlike my treatment of the sixteenth century itself, I have not separated what was known about Asia from the influences of that knowledge. I justify this departure by concluding that knowledge of Asia before 1500 effected no fundamental alterations in Europe's own artistic, technological, or religious premises. Basic mutations, I believe, came only after Europeans in numbers began to live and work in Asia and were forced increasingly to compare their native practices and ideas with those which they found among the peoples of Asia. The heritage from the European past, while it certainly colored the new Western view of Asia, was seriously challenged and radically changed by the opening of cultural and geographical vistas far removed in space from the Mediterranean world.

How was it possible for the European public of the early sixteenth century to comprehend what was happening? Marco Polo in the fourteenth century had been scoffed at by men who could have known better. Mandeville in the fifteenth century had told many wild stories about Asia which were accepted at face value by men who should have known better. What changes had taken place by the sixteenth century which removed Asia from the realm of the mysterious and the exotic, placed it within the domain of man, and made it subject to the same natural and divine laws which obtained in Europe? The general awakening to the Asia of reality had to come, I contend, from a European public which had been roused out of its sleep by inescapable and concrete data testifying to the existence of flesh-and-blood Asians with skills and beliefs of their own which Europeans had to recognize even if they denied their worth or validity.

Neither disbelief in nor blind acceptance of an imaginary East was possible in Europe after 1500 and the opening of direct trade with Asia. The flow into European markets of spices from the East was nothing new, for regular trade had been carried on through intermediaries since antiquity. Now, however, for the first time in history, sailors, merchants, and missionaries from all parts of Europe sailed to the East themselves and returned to tell tales of the wonders they had personally seen or of the privations which they had individually suffered. But perhaps even more impressive than the stories of the returned travelers were the samples which they brought back of Asian ingenuity and skill in the arts and crafts. While such objects had appeared in Europe at an earlier date, they had come through intermediaries, and the ultimate purchaser could not always be certain of their place of origin. With the opening of direct trade the products of Asia were more correctly associated with the lands from which they initially came. The returned merchants and sailors meanwhile educated their fellow townsmen and friends about the cultivation of pepper, the manufacture of porcelain, and the quarrying of precious stones. In the face of such concrete testimony, it was hard for the legends of the past to remain alive. Whenever they did retain their appeal, the locales of the monstrous peoples and mythical animals of earlier times were usually shifted away from known places to those which still lay beyond the ken of most of the European overseas adventurers. And these unknown lands and continents were very few by 1600. Indeed, it would never again be possible for the leading civilizations of Asia and Europe to go their separate ways or to be utterly ignorant of each other.

The establishment of direct trade with the East also had the effect of reorienting commerce in Europe and of bringing the cities of the Atlantic seaboard directly in touch with the non-European world. The shift away from the Mediterranean and Adriatic entrepôts forced the interior market towns to develop closer commercial ties with the port cities of western Europe. This fundamental reordering of commerce was originally associated with the spice trade rather than with the exploitation of the New World. It was therefore Asia rather than America which had profound importance for the European mercantile community of the first half of the sixteenth century. I have consequently felt compelled to write a lengthy chapter (chap. iii) on the vagaries of the spice trade in Europe in order to show how it helped to give to the European public a sense of Asia as a real place inhabited by civilized peoples, and to bring out how this realization was extended even to interior parts of Europe through the activities of the traders, sailors, and bankers associated with the traffic in spices.

The art of printing in Europe came of age contemporaneously with the reorientation of commerce. The old and new centers of trade became after 1500 the home of prominent publishing houses. In the first half of the sixteenth century practically all the news of the East which got into print came off the presses located in the business capitals of Italy, France, and northern Europe. In Portugal, official control over information about the trade routes had the effect of discouraging the publication at Lisbon of pamphlets or books on current events in Asia. In the latter half of the century, as Portugal's control over the spice trade weakened, books on Lusitania's Asian empire (some of them classics of their kind) finally began to be printed on Portuguese presses at Lisbon, Coimbra, and Evora. A great stimulus likewise came after 1550 to the publication and diffusion of information on Asia from the books produced by the Jesuit presses which were established in many European towns and at a few mission centers in Asia. In chapter iv, I review the system of news control maintained by the Portuguese, study the appearance of printed books, and maps of Asia, and try to depict the general influence of the printed word upon Europe's slowly evolving image of Asia.

The growth of the Portuguese system of trade in the East was paralleled by the development of the religious *padroado* (patronage). While a complete history of the sixteenth-century Catholic mission in Asia has still to be written, I have recounted in brief (chap. v) its establishment in various Asian outposts, the nature of the secular and religious problems it faced, and the evolution of its methods for handling them. This account is long and detailed enough, I hope, to enable the reader to understand the missionary climate in which the Jesuit letters on Asia were penned. Such information and appreciation is necessary for even the most elementary appraisal of the Jesuit letters and letter-books as historical sources. Because the Jesuits were acute observers, untiring correspondents, and dedicated archivists, a vast literature of published and unpublished texts has been preserved for historians to exploit.

After tracing the three main channels (spice trade, printed materials, and the Christian mission) through which Europe obtained its information, in the last part of this first volume I try to summarize what Europe knew about India, southeast Asia, Japan, and China in the sixteenth century. The European images of these Asian regions described in chapters vi, vii, viii, and ix are based almost entirely on the extant *printed* sources. It should be understood, however, that the published materials now available are not completely representative of what was then in circulation. Manuscript and oral reports were probably every whit as influential as the printed matter in shaping Europe's view of Asia. But it is obviously impossible for a historian of today to know, except at second hand, what was being circulated by word of mouth. Given the present chaotic disarray of the multitude of manuscript sources still in existence, it would be impractical, and perhaps misleading as well, to include detailed study of them. The plans of men being always imperfect for the reconstruction of the past, my decision to exclude the manuscript sources exacerbated certain technical problems in the handling of the printed materials, particularly the Jesuit news-letters and the maps. Still, I think that the exclusion of the manuscripts enabled me to control my sources more effectively and to produce a more accurate, although more limited, depiction of what was generally known in Europe about the East. To facilitate my task of surveying the large number of European sources printed during the sixteenth century in Latin, Portuguese, Spanish, Italian, Dutch, and German, I have, whenever possible, used English translations of the originals.

Image-makers (and I am one of them) in their understandable eagerness to cast into a literary mold the attitudes of people in ages past have all too often created resemblances rather than likenesses, statues rather than beings. This is perhaps inevitable, for the historian turned sculptor must accept the limitations and conditions of the plastic arts. The sculptor, irrespective of his materials or his artistic talent, is limited to reproducing natural objects and imaginary conceptions in three dimensions only. He is forced to call a halt to time, and can at best merely suggest the possibility of change and the inner dynamics of his subject. The historian who works in the medium of the sculptor is similarly forced to freeze the moment, even when, in Lessing's language from the *Laokoon*, he is successful in selecting the "pregnant moment." The historical image he produces is at best therefore a stylized picture, and, as such, it ordinarily fails to give the viewer an acute sense of the confused and constantly changing reality of the past. It also bears the heavy imprint of the artistic preconceptions of the historical sculptor. To introduce a feeling of change, I decided to deal with an entire century and to try, even at the risk of too much repetition, to show in what a piecemeal and uneven way each image was created. About my personal preconceptions I can do very little except to say that I have had them, that many of them have changed while I was researching and writing this book, and that some of them now seem more firmly founded than they were when I started out.

Tracers of influence (and I am one of them) also have numerous pitfalls in their path. One of the worst of these is the tendency to look for a particular influence, to abstract it from the context, and then to give it proportions and stature which it may not have had in comparison with other influences upon the person, art motif, institution, or idea being examined. While not able to avoid this pitfall entirely, I have tried in what follows to assemble from published writings, maps, and illustrations what was generally available to an interested European reader of the sixteenth century. Without question very few, if any, European contemporaries were likely to have read all of the printed materials used in the preparation of the surveys which follow. My object in providing such a comprehensive review is to show what knowledge was available so that I might be able to assess in the second volume how well informed about Asia an interested reader could be. At the same time I have tried to give enough figures on printing generally to show, quantitatively at least, how large the works on Asia bulked in the total output of the European printing presses, and how many individuals were responsive to them. Although such a technique is cumbersome and admittedly not without pitfalls of its own, I hope that Europe's interest in Asia will emerge within its context rather than as something arbitrarily extracted from it.

While the accuracy of the materials published in Europe is certainly not of primary importance in image-making, it is of genuine concern to students of Asian history who might want to incorporate European materials into their own works. An estimate of accuracy, as well as attention to contradictions in the sources, likewise helps to establish the reliability of the European author being considered and contributes to our understanding of why certain books were more influential or had longer lives than others. We are also in a better position to judge the perspicacity of those later writers who have used the raw materials on Asia for their own purposes. Naturally, I have not always thought it desirable or worthwhile to track down obscure references. I have, however, made a serious effort to check the major writings of the sixteenth century against the best of modern scholarship. In the process I have learned to my surprise and gratification that the earlier writers are reliable about what they reported. They did not on all occasions report everything they knew, often because there were prohibitions against it.

No effort has been made in the present volume to assess the influence of Asia upon Europe during the sixteenth century. That will be the subject of the next volume in this series. It has become clear, however, in the preparation of this volume that the spread of knowledge about Asian beliefs, institutions, arts, and crafts was of genuine and serious interest to European rulers, Humanists, churchmen, government reformers, religious thinkers, geographers, philosophers, collectors of curiosa, artists, craftsmen, and the general public. To what extent this interest helped to bring about fundamental changes in European institutions, arts, sciences, and ideas is not yet entirely clear. Further research into European materials will, I am confident, reveal that the impact of Asia was not insignificant even in a Europe constantly beset by more immediate problems stemming from international wars, rapid economic change, rise of the national state system, fundamental religious cleavage, and the exploitation and colonization of the New World.

Contents

Contents

Contents

Contents

Illustrations

Macao, *ca.* 1600

Coins used in commerce in the East Indies, Cambay, Ormuz, Goa, Malabar, Coromandel, Bengal, and Malacca

The Bourse at Antwerp

The port of Lisbon in the sixteenth century

A small merchant ship, *ca.* 1532

Manuelina Naus. A painting of Portuguese ships executed *ca.* 1521 by Gregório Lopes

Leaves and berries of canella or "wild cinnamon" (*Ravensara aromatica*)

The clove tree

Leaves and berries of the pepper plant

East Indian trees

East Indian trees and plants

Animals of India

FOLLOWING PAGE 164

Woodcut of Indian warriors

Title page of Valentim Fernandes' Portuguese translation of *Marco Polo*, 1502

Title page of João de Barros, *Asia*, 1552

Title page of Volume I (revised second edition) of G. B. Ramusio, *Delle navigationi et viaggi*, 1554

Title page of Book I of the *Historia* of Fernão Lopes de Castanheda, 1551

Portrait of João de Barros; first printed in the 1615 edition of his *Décadas da Ásia*

Painting from life of Luis de Camoës, by Fernando Gomes

Facsimile of a copper engraving of Damião de Góis by Albrecht Dürer

Title page of first edition of *The Lusiads*

Title page of a sixteenth-century edition of António Galvão's *Tratado*

Title page of first edition, printed in Goa in 1563, of Garcia da Orta's *Colloquies*

Title page of Jan Huygen van Linschoten's *Itinerario*, 1596

Map of Asia, from A. Ortelius' *Theatrum orbis terrarum*, 1575

Map of eastern Asia and the East Indies, from Linschoten's *Itinerario*

Map of Eurasia and Africa from G. Mercator's World Map of 1569

FOLLOWING PAGE 260

Panoramic view of Goa in the sixteenth century

Chapel of Saint Catherine constructed in 1510 by Albuquerque and rebuilt in 1550 by Jorge Cabral

Cathedral of Old Goa

Dom Costantino de Braganza, Viceroy of Goa from 1558 to 1561

Alessandro Valignano, S.J. (1539–1606)

Coimbra in the sixteenth century

The ruins of the façade of the Church of Saint Augustine (Goa)

Matteo Ricci, S.J. (1552–1610)

Title page from a typical Jesuit letterbook

Akbar and Prince Salim

Title page from the Venetian edition (1589) of G. P. Maffei's *Historiarum Indicarum libri XVI*

Map of Asia, from G. B. Peruschi's *Informatione*, 1597

[xxvii]

Illustrations

PART

I

Heritage

Introduction

Europeans, in the first two millenniums of their history, saw Asia to the east of Mesopotamia as an unclear and constantly changing concept. This is not surprising if one recalls that "Europe" itself, before assuming its present delineation in the time of Charlemagne,[1] was regularly undergoing redefinition. From about 500 B.C. until the opening of the sea route to India at the end of the fifteenth century, the distant East, as distinct from the Levant, remained a shadowy image upon the European view of the world. Information about the vast eastern two-thirds of the Asiatic continent reached Europe by tortuous routes, in unrelated fragments, and at irregular intervals. Knowledge of the East was frequently relayed to Europe through Egyptian or Near Eastern intermediaries, a circumstance which also contributed to the mixing of myth with fact. Indeed, several centuries had to pass in antiquity before China and India were clearly identified as individual countries with independent civilizations. In the Middle Ages, much of the earlier knowledge, so slowly and painfully assembled, was lost sight of completely or transmuted into a stereotyped view of a fanciful East. This is not to say that Europeans were completely uninformed or always misinformed about the Asia of reality. Some learned men knew with surprising accuracy the more dramatic of Asia's geographical and topographical features. Merchants taught themselves through perseverance and hardship about the sources of spices and silks, the trade routes, ports, and marts in those distant places. Missionaries in the later Middle Ages made converts in India and China as they sought to spread Christianity among the pagans of Asia. Nevertheless, in the European popular imagination, and in many scholarly treatises as well, the mythical and the real about Asia often remained undifferentiated, even some of the most general geographical terms not being settled upon until later.

[1] For discussion of its evolution see Jürgen Fischer, *Oriens, Occidens, Europa: Begriff und Gedanke "Europa" in der späteren Antike und im frühen Mittelalter* (Wiesbaden, 1957).

The terms "Asia" and "East" are obviously imprecise as geographical conceptions. They are certainly no clearer when used in their adjectival forms to describe racial, religious, or cultural attributes. But before the great discoveries, these terms were used interchangeably and so broadly that Egypt was sometime pictured on maps as belonging to Asia. "India" often stood as a synonym for Asia, and, as late as 1523, Maximilian of Transylvania wrote that "the natives of all unknown countries are commonly called Indians." [2] But we shall use "India" here in its modern designation as referring exclusively to the subcontinent itself. "Further" and "Upper" India, as the areas east of Bengal were often called, will be replaced in most cases with later terms such as "East Indies" and "southeastern" or "eastern" Asia. Serica, Sinica, Cathay, and the various other names under which China was known before the sixteenth century were never used, as "India" was, in a general, undifferentiated sense synonymous with East. China will therefore figure in our account under its modern and earlier names, depending upon the historical period in which each was current. "Asia" and "East," as vague as they are, will nevertheless be employed, partly to reflect the uncertainty Europeans felt when talking about these distant places, and partly because their usage by contemporaries often makes it impossible for us to be more precise. To grasp the total problem better, one needs only to recall that the Abbé Raynal writing in the eighteenth century still continued to define the East Indies as including "all regions beyond the Arabian Sea and the kingdom of Persia." [3]

[2] *De moluccio* . . . as translated by H. Stevens in *Johann Schöner* (London, 1888), p. 116.
[3] *A Philosophical and Political History of the Settlements and Trade of the Europeans in the East and West Indies* . . . (2d ed., rev. & corr.; London, 1776), I, 40.

CHAPTER I

Antiquity
and the Middle Ages

In the dim obscurity of the Homeric age (pre-eighth century), the Greeks may possibly have heard tales of India and of the peoples farther to the east. The *Iliad* and the *Odyssey*, while not concerned primarily with faraway places, show a tendency to idealize as simple and uninvolved the lives of the peoples who dwell beyond the frontiers of the known world.[1] As Greek knowledge of the world expanded, the happy primitives as well as the monstrous peoples of mythology receded to places more and more distant from the Mediterranean heartland. Beginning in the sixth century the Persian empire stood to the east of the Greek world and India lay in the mists beyond it. Mediterranean merchants and soldiers, sometimes as associates or hirelings of the Persians, were nevertheless known to trade and fight in the East at this early date. From their reports, stories began to filter back to the West about the dimensions and placement of India. But since these itinerant informants were not primarily interested in objective description, the earliest materials relayed to Europe tended to be more fantastic than factual.

I

INDIA IN THE GREEK TRADITION

(600–100 B.C.)

The valley of the Indus was annexed by Darius of Persia around 515 B.C. Not long thereafter he sent Scylax of Caryanda, a Greek officer, on a mission of

[1] James Oliver Thomson, *History of Ancient Geography* (Cambridge, 1948), pp. 21–22. For greater detail see Edward Bunbury, *History of Ancient Geography* (2 vols.; 2d ed.; London, 1883).

[5]

exploration and reconnaissance into this easternmost province of Persia. Though Scylax sailed the entire length of the Indus and along the coast of Arabia, he, like many early Greek writers, was not always clear about directions.[2] In his report, he has the Indus run southeastward instead of southwestward, and he is equally mistaken about other geographical features. He was clearly much more interested in the wealth and developmental possibilities of Darius' new province than in its configuration. His "India," the most remote land to the east, is bountifully endowed with a numerous and fantastic people who pay an enormous tribute in gold. The people themselves include settled agriculturalists and wandering nomads. Their gold comes from great anthills found in the northern deserts.[3] To the south live people almost as black as Ethiopians who eke out an existence in the marshes and along the rivers; others even farther south are cannibals. While most of this matter seems to have a certain factual basis, Scylax interlards his report with a host of fabulous stories. Some of the Indians have feet so enormous that they sit on the ground and hold them over their heads as umbrellas; beasts, birds, and plants are both fantastic and recognizable. Of the land beyond his "India" there is no information, but it seems to be nothing but desert. So begins the traditional European view of the East as a mélange of fact and fantasy.

Herodotus (*ca.* 484–425 B.C.) relied in his *History* upon both oral and written reports of the East.[4] Where Herodotus actually traveled himself is a question which still vexes scholars; it is clear, however, that the "father of history" studiously compiled and sifted information of all kinds on the vast and uncharted areas east of Mesopotamia. He consulted earlier writings such as the *Arimaspea*, a poem by Aristaeus of Proconnesus, and tested its statements against those made by his contemporaries. For his physical description of India, Herodotus derived most of his information from Hecateus of Miletus, a geographer who wrote around 500 B.C. He disagrees, however, with Hecateus' proportions and challenges his depiction of a large Asia simply because he believes that Asia cannot be more extensive than Europe. From his sources Herodotus places the Indians at the easternmost point in the known world, shows the Indus as running southeastward, and apparently has no conception of India's peninsular shape. Beyond India he knows of nothing but uninhabited deserts of endless sand and rejects disdainfully Aristaeus' catalogue of the various

---

[2] They were often mistaken about directions much closer to home. Herodotus, for example, imagined that the pass of Thermopylae ran from north to south. See M. Cary and E. H. Warmington, *The Ancient Explorers* (London, 1929), pp. 6–7.

[3] This story of gold-producing ants is repeated by a number of Greek and Roman commentators. It may derive from an Indian fairy tale concerning "ant-gold" which the Greeks possibly heard through the Persians. See Thomson, *op. cit.* (n. 1), p. 80.

[4] On his sources see G. Rawlinson, *The History of Herodotus* (New York, 1859), pp. 38–42. A more recent appraisal may be found in J. E. Powell, *The History of Herodotus* (London, 1930). For comment on his knowledge of India see J. W. McCrindle, *Ancient India as Described in Classical Literature* (Westminster, 1901), pp. 1–5, and the *Cambridge History of India*, I, 396.

peoples said to be spread across continental Asia.[5] Like Hecateus, he depicts the Indians as including many nations and language groups with diverse customs. In the north live the fair Aryans; to the south, black, nomadic barbarians. The Indians on the Persian frontier are said to practice cannibalism. They gather wild cotton, which surpasses in beauty and quality the wool of the sheep, and make their clothing from it. He likewise refers to the gold-digging ants who supply the Indians with the tribute they pay to Persia. Lacking concrete materials, Herodotus, like lesser men, accepted uncritically a number of incredible stories which had acquired a veneer of authenticity through constant repetition.

The writings of Ctesias of Cnidus, a critic of Herodotus' work, enshrined for posterity a few concrete facts and a whole host of fantastic stories and marvels about Asia.[6] Around 400 B.C. Ctesias wrote treatises called *Persica* and *Indica* in which he sought to correct Herodotus on the East. While Ctesias is the first author to produce a separate work on India, his description is far less factual than Herodotus' more prosaic effort. Some writers of antiquity disputed Ctesias, but his imaginative descriptions of oriental animals and monsters attracted a numerous audience for a long time. His flights of historical fancy were taken up by later writers, many of whom apparently delighted in embroidering Ctesias' tales with fictions of their own.[7] Grossly exaggerating the size of India, he portrays the Indians as satyrs. The sun of India, he alleges, is extraordinarily hot, and so seems to be ten times larger than it is elsewhere. He becomes more factual in telling about the routes and distances between India and Ephesus and about the mountain barrier of northern India. But his facts are fewer than his fantasies. His accumulation of traditions and fables was relayed through Pliny to the writers of the Middle Ages, who often had their own embellishments to add.[8]

The latitudes of fact and fantasy were markedly broadened by Alexander's campaign into India from 326 to 234.[9] The great Macedonian conqueror, who

[5] It has been contended that Aristaeus may have had knowledge of the various peoples of continental Asia, even to the distant Hyperboreans or Chinese. See G. F. Hudson, *Europe and China* (London, 1931), chap. i. While Hudson buttresses his argument with Chinese sources, most classical scholars hold that the Hyperboreans belong to a fabulous and idealized set of peoples, and they are not yet ready to identify them with a known people. A recent summary of the status of the Hyperborean question may be found in Denis Sinor, "Autour d'une migration de peuples au Ve siècle," *Journal asiatique*, CCXXXV (1946–47), 37–50. But the controversy continues. For example, see the suggestion that the Hyperboreans were originally a religious group with Orphic tendencies before being designated as a mythical people in A. J. van Windekens, "Les Hyperboréens," *Rheinisches Museum für Philologie*, C (1957), Pt. II, 164–69.

[6] For the "reigning" editions of Ctesias see E. Manni, *Introduzione allo studio della storia greca e romana* (Palermo, 1951–52), pp. 201–2. For appropriate extracts from his texts see Georges Coedès, *Textes d'auteurs grecs et latins relatifs à l'Extrême-Orient depuis le IVe siècle avant J.C. jusqu'au XIVe siècle* (Paris, 1910).

[7] For example, see the discussion of the unicorn in chap. x of Charles Gould, *Mythical Monsters* (London, 1886).

[8] For example, see the version of Ctesias included by Photius (*ca.* 820–*ca.* 891), patriarch of Constantinople, in the codices of his *Myriobiblon.*

[9] Details in W. W. Tarn, *Alexander the Great* (Cambridge, 1948), Vol. I, Pt. II.

in his youth had learned from Aristotle something of the Asia of tradition, broke through the Persian wall separating the Greek world from Asia. The penetration of the Indus Valley and the success of Greek arms in northwestern India made a profound impression upon the ancient world. To Alexander, "Asia" may have been synonymous with the empire of Darius I, and "India" probably meant the country surrounding the Indus River. What lay eastward— the Ganges, the East Indies, and China—was apparently unknown to the Macedonian conqueror. Like Aristotle and the earlier writers, Alexander presumably visualized India as lying mainly to the *east* of Persia and but slightly to the south. Despite the limited extent of the Greek penetration of India, Alexander's conquest brought the subcontinent into direct communication with Asia Minor and the Greek world and laid the foundations for more direct intercourse between regions hitherto only remotely conscious of each other.

Alexander's death in 323 B.C. brought Macedonian expansion to a halt, and the scholarly debate over the great conqueror's exploits began. A daily record of Alexander's activities in Asia was kept to 327 B.C. by a court diarist. The philosopher, Callisthenes of Olynthus, who is often called a court historian, accompanied Alexander and wrote about his campaigns. But the diary, as well as the *History* of Callisthenes based upon it, ends before Alexander's departure from Bactria to India. It was only after Alexander's death that factual histories of the Indian phase of his expedition were written. Two of these were written by his associates, Aristobulus, an architect, and Ptolemy, a student of military operations and founder of the famous Egyptian dynasty which is named for him. The eyewitness accounts of these authors, while glorifying Alexander's achievements, significantly enlarged the body of concrete material on India available to the Greeks. Although the originals of these early and essentially factual histories were soon lost, their data are preserved for posterity in Arrian's *Indica* (*ca.* A.D. 150) and are the basis for the "historical Alexander" as we know him.[10]

Not long after Alexander's death, his exploits also became the subject of highly imaginative tales, some of which apparently originated in India. One of his contemporaries, Cleitarchus of Colophon, composed a romantic version of the conqueror's deeds. Bent upon telling a good story, Cleitarchus mixed fact and myth indiscriminately and it was from this source that the romance of Alexander began. But the main source for the legendary Alexander and his marvelous exploits was a nameless book written around A.D. 200 in Alexandria and falsely ascribed to Callisthenes.[11] The "pseudo-Callisthenes," as this book

[10] For a compact historiographical discussion see C. A. Robinson, Jr., "The Extraordinary Ideas of Alexander the Great," *American Historical Review*, LXII (1957), 326–27. For a review of these historical works as part of Greek literature see L. Pearson, *The Lost Histories of Alexander the Great* (London, 1960). For a recent summary of the unsettled problem of dating these histories see J. R. Hamilton, "Cleitarchus and Aristobulus," *Historia*, X (1961), 448–58.

[11] The most authoritative study of the Greek pseudo-Callisthenes is Reinhold Merkelbach, *Die Quellen des griechischen Alexanderromans* ("Zetamata; Monographien zur klassischen Altertums- wissenschaft," No. 9 [Munich, 1954]). The "reigning" text is the A version. It has been translated into English by E. H. Haight, *Essays on the Greek Romances* (New York, 1945).

is now called, is a farrago of reliable data, literary forgeries, market-place stories, and just plain gossip. It was mainly from the recensions of the pseudo-Callisthenes and from elaborations on them that the medieval world derived its stories of Alexander and many of its impressions of India.

The military and political successors of Alexander, in their struggle to take over control of his shaky dominion in Asia, began to fight among themselves. Seleucus Nikator emerged victorious from this internecine battle about two decades after Alexander's death. By 304 B.C. Seleucus felt strong enough in his possession of the Levant to resume Alexander's campaign in India. His forces crossed the Indus, but Seleucus found the early Maurya rulers too powerful to be overwhelmed. After concluding a treaty with Chandragupta, Seleucus sent Megasthenes as his ambassador to the Maurya court located in the Ganges Valley. During his residence at Pāṭaliputra (Patna), Megasthenes compiled the fullest and most reliable account of India known to the Greek world. Later classical writers depended heavily upon his sober and critical record of the geography, social life, and political institutions of India.

The works of the historians of Alexander and the account of Megasthenes set the image of India for the Greek world. Although the original books perished, their contents were preserved by being incorporated into the works of later writers, such as Strabo, Pliny, and Arrian. From these accounts emerges the picture of India as a land of gold and precious stones. Taking their lead from Megasthenes, later Greek authors remark upon the unusual natural phenomena to be observed in tropical India—the sun being directly overhead at midday, the shadows falling toward the south in summer and toward the north in winter, the absence of the Great Bear from the night sky, the rainy season, monsoons, and the extremes of temperature in the Punjab. They are also impressed by the numerous mighty and shifting rivers of India. They credit the heavy rains to the monsoons and to the exhalations of the great rivers. About southern India little is known except that it was reportedly the source of pearls.[12] The phenomena of two annual harvests, of rice and millet in the summer and of wheat and barley in the winter, astonished Greeks untutored in the great fertility of tropical lands. Sugar cane, the cotton plant, and precious spices and drugs helped to shape the Greek belief in the natural wealth of India. Wonderment at this strange world grew as stories were circulated of mighty banyan trees, enormous elephants, deadly snakes, and manlike monkeys.

Megasthenes also comments at length upon the customs and everyday life of the India he knew. His remarks on the palisaded capital of Pāṭaliputra and the palace of the king and its gardens "in which were tame peacocks and pheasants" lends to his account an atmosphere of reality. He was struck by the noble simplicity of the people, their cotton clothes sometimes in bright colors,

[12] The first direct notice of south India occurs in Megasthenes, whose "quaint account of the Pāndyan Kingdom seems to be a mixture of facts and of contemporary fables relating to that kingdom." This is the verdict of K. A. Nilakanta Sastri, *Foreign Notices of South India from Megasthenes to Ma Haun* (Madras, 1939), p. 4.

and their brilliant ornaments of gold and precious stones. He also notes their diet of rice and seasoned meats and the absence of wine from their regime. The people of India are thought of as being tall and slender, long-lived, and free from disease. The southerners are dark like the Ethiopians, but without woolly hair; the northerners remind the Greeks of Egyptians. According to Megasthenes, the people are divided into seven classes. The highest in rank and smallest in number are the "philosophers," a term he used to describe both the Brahmans and the ascetics. The cultivators, being the largest class, till the land and pay taxes. Herdsmen and hunters, his third class, live a nomadic life in the deserts and jungles. Traders, artisans, and boatmen, unless engaged in war work, pay taxes on the products of their industry. The fighting class performs no work except in war, and its members receive regular stipends even in peacetime. The sixth class is made up of secret government agents who report to the king or tribal headmen. The last class is that of the councilors or magistrates, a group that we might call an administrative caste. Presumably, a man remains in the class to which he was born unless he is able to qualify as a "philosopher."

Although he was an acute observer, Megasthenes was handicapped by his ignorance of the native languages.[13] Like many Europeans since his time, he was unable to penetrate deeply into the thought, literature, and history of the country simply by looking and listening or by using interpreters. He was also guilty of looking at India through Greek spectacles and he consequently posited parallels between the two cultures which were based on Greek tradition rather than on his own observations. While he understood that polygamy was commonly practiced, he knew little about the laws and customs governing the marital relationship. Still, his observations on legal customs constitute one of the few sources available for study of private law in ancient India.[14] Like many later observers, he was impressed by the rite of *sati* (widow-burning) but understood little of its meaning in religious or social terms. Nevertheless, he tried to discuss the practices and ideas of the "philosophers," and correctly asserted that the Brahmans had a "dogmatic system."

The geographical data accumulated in the century after Alexander's death was collated and analyzed by Eratosthenes in his *Geographica*. As librarian at Alexandria from *ca.* 234 to 196 B.C., Eratosthenes also collected Greek knowledge about geographical theory.[15] Although the three books of his *Geographica* are lost, they were summarized by Strabo along with the criticisms of them by Hipparchus. Eratosthenes, like the Pythagoreans, postulates a spherical earth which he measures and divides into zones. The known world he regards as an island surrounded by a continuous outer sea. In an effort to place the known portion on the globe he took the island of Rhodes as his center and calculated

---

[13] See T. S. Brown, "The Reliability of Megasthenes," *American Journal of Philology*, LXXVI (1955), 21. Also see the comments of G. L. Barber in *The Oxford Classical Dictionary* (Oxford, 1957), p. 553.

[14] For comment see Bernard Breloer, *Altindisches Privatrecht bei Megasthenes und Kautalya* (Bonn, 1928).

[15] See Thomson, *op. cit.* (n. 1), pp. 158–67.

distances along two lines which intersected there. At the extreme east of the known, temperate zone he started with the Ganges and proceeded westward in his identifications and calculations. Eratosthenes also computed the shape, size, and placement of India for his world map. Of the shape of India he made a remarkable quadrilateral projection which clearly shows for the first time the peninsular character of south India. But he mistakenly assumes, like most of the earlier commentators, that its extension is greater to the east than to the south. In his projection the Indus flows south but its length is badly overestimated. He shows the Ganges as a shorter river which flows eastward into the encompassing sea. Southwest of the peninsula he indicates the existence of the large island of Taprobane (Ceylon) which was known to the Greeks only by report. No evidence exists that he had heard anything about places or peoples to the east of India.[16]

Commercial relations also helped to extend the horizons of the classical world. Even before Alexander, Indian oddities were known in the Mediterranean countries, and colorful peacocks and parrots were introduced to Greece at an early date. In the time of Aristotle silkworms were known in Greece, though it appears that they were native to Asia Minor.[17] Trade in Indian ivory and spices began with Alexander's conquest.[18] In the time of disintegration following Alexander's death, the trade continued but its control fell into the hands of intermediary powers along the land routes, the Persian Gulf, and the Red Sea. As early as the second century B.C. merchants from India occasionally reached Alexandria.[19] The rulers of Egypt, as regular trading expeditions to and from India became more numerous, took official action to regulate the commerce. Finally, shortly before the beginning of the Christian era,[20] a Greek called Hippalus learned how to sail directly from Arabia across the open sea to India by catching the southwest summer monsoon.[21] Earlier, the northeast monsoon of winter had been used, by both the Arabs and the Greeks, in coasting westward along the shores of India, Persia, and Arabia. Even after Hippalus' "discovery," the Arabs, in their ships without nails, sewn together with hemp made of coconut fibers, probably felt unable to brave the turbulence of the open sea as the sailors of Greece and Rome were able to do in their sturdier

[16] For a reconstruction of his map of the East see *ibid.*, p. 135, or F. L. Pullé, *La cartografia antica dell'India* ("Studi italiani di filogia Indo-Uranica," Vol. IV [Rome, 1901]).

[17] See for the importation of peacocks, parrots, and many other exotics, Victor Hehn, *Kulturpflanzen und Hausthiere in ihrem Uebergang aus Asien nach Griechenland und Italien sowie in das übrige Europa* (5th ed.; Berlin, 1887). On the peacock specifically see pp. 286–94. It has often been mistakenly supposed that Aristotle's description indicated the migration of the silkworm to Greece from China. For a discussion of this problem see Thomson, *op. cit.* (n. 1), p. 86. R. Patterson in Charles J. Singer *et al.* (eds.), *A History of Technology* (5 vols.; Oxford, 1954–58), II, 197, remarks that silk was probably unknown in ancient Greece and Republican Rome.

[18] W. W. Tarn, *The Greeks in Bactria and India* (Cambridge, 1951), pp. 361–62.

[19] Sir Mortimer Wheeler, *Rome beyond the Imperial Frontiers* (London, 1954), p. 130.

[20] *Ibid.*, pp. 126–30, for an account of the difficulties in dating Hippalus accurately.

[21] See G. F. Hourani, *Arab Seafaring in the Indian Ocean in Ancient and Early Medieval Times* (Princeton, N. J., 1951), pp. 25–28.

craft.[22] So, before the period of Roman hegemony, trade became more regular between India and the Mediterranean, but only as uncertain political, economic, and sailing conditions permitted.

This limited commercial intercourse between India and the Mediterranean world seems to have affected the classical image of India only slightly. The Greek invaders, envoys, and merchants had mainly brought back knowledge of practical matters *relating to northern India only*. About the religious practices and deities of the Indians the Greeks have little to say. While points of resemblance have been noted between Pythagorean and Indian thought, no reliable evidence of borrowing has so far been produced.[23] Apparently the Greeks knew parts of Indian literature such as the Sanskrit epic, *Mahabharata*, but the question whether certain literary motifs were borrowed from India remains highly debatable.[24] Concerning the influence of Indian upon Greek art the evidence is equally obscure and conflicting. It must not even be assumed that Greek information on more concrete matters was a part of common knowledge.[25] We are constrained by the nature of our materials to talk about what a few elite and not overly popular writers have to say about the East. The populace at large evidently continued throughout Greek times and long thereafter to think of the world as a flat disc suspended somehow in the air. If they bothered to think about Asia at all, it was as a hazy, hot place beyond the eastern horizon, peopled by monstrous barbarians living in the kind of simple and just society ordinarily postulated for primitive tribes. Even the elite among Greek thinkers fail to evince great interest in the realistic delineations of India presented by Megasthenes and Eratosthenes. People of all classes continued to be primarily absorbed with matters closer to home.

2

THE EXPANDING HORIZONS OF THE GRAECO-ROMAN WORLD

(26 B.C.–A.D. 300)

The replacement of Greece by Rome as the arbiter of the Mediterranean basin set up a new center of authority and unification in the West during the first century B.C. The hegemony of Rome over Egypt and the Red Sea littoral made possible the resumption of direct trade and communication with the East and the elimination of certain of the tolls previously exacted by the middlemen of the south. A mission from Taprobane (Ceylon)[26] waited on Augustus in 26 B.C.,

[22] *Ibid.*, p. 28.
[23] H. G. Rawlinson, *Intercourse between India and the Western World* (Cambridge, 1916), pp. 156–58.
[24] Tarn, *op. cit.* (n. 18), pp. 380–81; and especially A. Berriedale Keith, *A History of Sanskrit Literature* (Oxford, 1928), pp. 352–57.
[25] See Thomson, *op. cit.* (n. 1), pp. 167–68.
[26] The idea of Taprobane being Sumatra in Strabo and Pliny is maintained by Pierre Paris, "Notes sur deux passages de Strabon et de Pline," *Journal asiatique*, CCXXXIX (1951), 13–27.

and others appeared later at the courts of his successors.[27] The autocracy of Augustus and his successors brought stability to the intermediate areas, reduced piracy, and stimulated the growth of a wealthy Roman ruling class. The demand for silk and spices by the Roman aristocracy moved Pliny the Elder to remark that "India is brought near by lust for gain."[28] A few Roman subjects even ventured to take trips to India on their own.

The development of the monsoon trade in the first century A.D. broke the monopoly of the middlemen of Yemen and forced the Parthians and Arabs who controlled the land routes of western Asia to adjust their prices so as to compete on the Roman market with the goods now being brought directly from India by sea. In these years a merchant could journey from Italy to India via Egypt in from four to six months, including the land voyage over Egypt. Should he desire to go as far as China, nothing stood in his way. Some Roman commercial missions evidently reached China in the second and third centuries. Meanwhile, Indian ships sailed westward to Egypt and eastward to China. The maritime routes of southern Asia, monopolized by no single power, were the highroad for all who braved their dangers.[29] At no time before had such easy intercourse been possible; and after the third century A.D. the Indian Ocean was not again to be traversed freely by Europeans until the Portuguese broke the Arab power there in the second decade of the sixteenth century.

The expansion of trade certainly made available new materials for geographical understanding at the beginning of the Christian era. Strabo (*ca.* 63 B.C.–A.D. 21), the author of six historical books on Asia in Greek,[30] shows himself to be aware of the trade but will not deign to learn from the merchants about distant places. While he incorporates materials derived from his own experiences in Asia Minor, he relies mainly upon Homer, Eratosthenes, Polybius, and Posidonius for his scattered and contradictory references to the East. In his selection of sources he favors the illusions of Homer while scorning the factual data of Herodotus. As a conserver of earlier geographers, Strabo has no

[27] On the Indian missions to the Roman emperors see E. H. Warmington, *The Commerce between the Roman Empire and India* (Cambridge, 1951), pp. 35–38. Also see Sastri, *op. cit.* (n. 12), pp. 46–48, who seems to think that the envoys to Augustus might have been a Pāndyan embassy. For the argument that it came from northern India see Osmond di Beauvoir Priaulx, "On the Indian Embassy to Augustus," *Journal of the Royal Asiatic Society* (London), XVII (1860), 317–18. For later embassies see Priaulx, "On the Indian Embassies to Rome from the reign of Claudius to the Death of Justinian," *Journal of the Royal Asiatic Society*, XIX (1862), 274–98; XX (1863), 269–312.

[28] For Pliny's account of the voyages to India see J. Bostock and H. T. Riley (eds. and trans.), *The Natural History of Pliny* (London, 1890), Bk. VI, chap. xxvi, pp. 60–65. All subsequent citations are to this same edition. For Pliny's sources on India, which he describes at some length, see D. Detlefsen, *Die Anordnung der geographischen Bücher des Plinius und ihre Quellen* (Berlin, 1909), pp. 129–32. For an example of a philosopher's visit to India based on Pliny and others, see Osmond de Beauvoir Priaulx, "The Indian Travels of Apollônius of Tyana," *Journal of the Royal Asiatic Society*, XVII (1860), 70–105.

[29] For a map of the world known to the Graeco-Romans see L. R. Nougier, J. Beaujeu, M. Mollat, *Histoire universelle des explorations* (Paris, 1955), I, 241. For details see P. Thomas, "Roman Trade Centers on the Malabar Coast," *Indian Geographical Journal*, VI (1931–32), 230–40. See also the colored reproduction of the Peutinger chart in Konrad Miller (ed.), *Die peutingersche Tafel* (Stuttgart, 1962).

[30] *Geographica*, Books 11–16. First printed in Latin translation by the Aldine Press in 1516.

peer; but as an original writer on Asia he does not go beyond Eratosthenes and is generally inferior. This may perhaps be accounted for by the fact that he was writing a general history of the inhabited world for the instruction of his contemporaries and was not intent upon compiling data about remote places.

Pomponius Mela, the first Latin geographer whose work is extant, has little to add to Greek learning about the East in the short treatise which he prepared *ca.* A.D. 40. Instead, he revives and embroiders many wild stories about griffons, Amazons, and headless peoples. His major claim to distinction is the vague mention which he makes of Chryse and Argyre to the east of India, the soil of the former being of gold and the latter of silver. Inexact though these terms are, they mark the beginning of an understanding in the West of the existence of prosperous lands east of India. They also provide the background for the conception of the Golden Chersonese (Malay Peninsula), a name and a hope which was to be prominently featured in geographical discourse throughout the following millennium.[31] A synonym for the Golden Chersonese was the biblical land of Ophir from which King Solomon commanded his sailors to fetch gold.[32] Later writers constantly seek to identify known or remote places with these lands of gold and presumably vast wealth. The Roman map-makers of Mela's time and later derive very few of their ideas from Hellenistic cartography; their representations of the world are generally flat, oval in shape, and with the East portrayed at the top. It is this oval map of Roman origin which formed the basis for most medieval depictions.

The best source for Roman trade in the East is the practical merchant handbook, originally written in Greek around A.D. 50, called the *Periplus* [Circuit] *of the Erythrean Sea* [Indian Ocean].[33] An anonymous work by a Roman subject from Egypt, the *Periplus* gives a clear, accurate, and comprehensive picture of Rome's trade with India. It describes India's coastal regions, especially the port towns, from the mouth of the Indus to the delta of the Ganges.[34] The *Periplus* also lists the commodities exchanged and indicates generally that the goods obtained in northwestern India were usually items that had been shipped into India from the Asian hinterlands, including China. Ceylon is known to its author only by hearsay, and the *Periplus* likewise gives some secondhand reports on the markets of eastern India.[35] Mention is also made of the island of Chryse

---

[31] Paul Wheatley, *The Golden Khersonese: Studies in the Historical Geography of the Malay Peninsula before A.D. 1500* (Kuala Lumpur, 1961), pp. 127–28. For an older and very general survey of the gradual revelation of continental southeast Asia in the West see Hugh Clifford, *Further India* (New York, 1904), chap. i.

[32] On the identifications of Ophir see Thomson, *op. cit.* (n. 1), pp. 29–30.

[33] Translated and edited by Wilfred Schoff (London, 1912).

[34] For a map showing the ports and markets of India in the first century A.D., see Wheeler, *op. cit.* (n. 19), p. 119.

[35] M. P. Charlesworth, "Roman Trade with India: A Resurvey," in P. R. Coleman-North (ed.), *Studies in Roman Economic and Social History* (Princeton, N.J., 1951), argues that no more than "an occasional Graeco-Roman boat got through to the eastern side of India until after the end of the first century." If this is so, then the author of the *Periplus* must have obtained his information on eastern India by report.

and of a region north of Chryse called "Thin" (possibly the first reference in European literature to China) where dwarfs engage in silent barter with their neighbors.[36]

Alexandria remained throughout this period the entrepôt for Eastern goods coming by the sea route. Antioch in Syria was a place of exchange for the goods arriving over the land routes from India and China.[37] In Italy the chief port for oriental wares was Puteoli (Pozzuoli) near Naples. Emperor Domitian in A.D. 92 constructed warehouses in Rome for storing the precious spices and silks, and later improved and shortened the highway from Rome to Puteoli. Very few material remains still exist to testify to the magnitude of Rome's commercial and political relations with India. Since most of the purchases were consumed or were perishable, such a deficiency is understandable. Even so, there was unearthed in 1939 at Pompeii an ivory statuette of Lakshmi, an Indian goddess of good fortune, which was evidently brought to Rome before A.D. 79.[38] But the demand for Eastern products in the first century of the Christian era is best attested through reference to the complaints of the Roman moralists about the drain of precious metals from Rome to pay for them.[39]

In the first two Christian centuries, Romans imported from the East a wide variety of commodities, from Indian female slaves to asbestos. Parrots and monkeys were domesticated and larger Asiatic and African animals, such as elephants and rhinoceroses, appeared in exhibitions. A white elephant, perhaps from Siam, provided a special attraction in the time of Augustus. Skins, furs, and hides from Tibet, Siberia, and Turkestan were used for rugs and apparel. Wool from Kashmir provided shawls for the Roman matron, who also used musk from India as scent. Ivory, pearls, and tortoise shell were also bought for decoration and personal adornment. Nearly all of the best precious stones came from India. The irascible Pliny waxed angry over the large sums of money spent on luxuries for the ladies. Apparently customers were also found for Chinese bronzes and earthenware.[40]

From distant China came about 90 per cent of the silks—the staple article of trade along the land routes. Silk became a fabric of distinction when Pompey returned to Rome in the first century B.C., wearing a robe of rich Persian silk. The great poet Vergil was responsible for perpetuating one of the commonest myths about silk production: the belief that silk was combed from the leaves of trees. While no conclusive evidence exists that any Roman subject reached China through its western portals, or that any Chinese ever came within the

[36] Sometimes regarded as a fable, even though there are many well-attested examples of silent trading from various parts of the world. For an attempt to treat this reference seriously see Wheatley, *op. cit.* (n. 31), pp. 130–31.

[37] For details on the routes see Hudson, *op. cit.* (n. 5), pp. 77–86, and Warmington, *op. cit.* (n. 27), chap. i.

[38] A. Maiuri, "Statuetta eburnea di arte indiana a Pompei," *Le arti*, I (1938–39), 111–15.

[39] A question is raised about the reliability of Pliny's figures on trade with India in Charlesworth, *loc. cit.* (n. 35), p. 137.

[40] L. Petech, "Rome and Eastern Asia," *East and West*, II (1952), 76, tells of a fragment of a wine goblet (*ku*) found in the Roman port of Ostia.

confines of Roman Italy by overland travel, the routes across continental Asia regularly bore caravans carrying quantities of raw and fabricated silk to the Levant for transshipment to Europe. Much of the Chinese silk was reprocessed in Syria and Egypt to satisfy the Roman taste for diaphanous and brightly colored fabrics; evidently the heavy, patterned Chinese silk fabrics had little appeal to the Romans. Cotton cloths from India also underwent refurbishing before they reached the Roman market.

Silk was the staple of the land trade; pepper and the other spices were the major items in the sea trade with India. An essential in cookery, pepper was also used in Europe for compounding medicines and drugs. Pliny wrote:

It is quite surprising that the use of pepper has come so much into fashion, seeing that in other substances which we use, it is sometimes their sweetness and sometimes their appearance that has attracted our notice; whereas, pepper has nothing in it that can plead as a recommendation to either fruit or berry; its only desirable quality being a certain pungency; and yet it is for this that we import it all the way from India! Who was the first to make trial of it as an article of food?[41]

Ginger apparently spiced the dried fish commonly found on Roman tables and, like pepper, was esteemed as a digestive. Cinnamon was prized as perfume, incense, condiment, and unguent. The Romans, however, were unaware of its oriental origin, believing that it grew in Africa. Frankincense and myrrh, two of the gifts of the Three Wise Men, were likewise thought to be products of India, though they were actually African and Arabian gum resins. Other such plant products formed the bases of dyes. Ornamental and fragrant woods as well as oriental timber for furniture and statuary were available on the Roman market. Seeds from oriental fruits and vegetables were experimented with, and it is possible that bananas were successfully grown in Rome. With all these imports it is little wonder that the Roman moralists decried the lavish expenditures on Eastern trade and warned of the unhealthy effects of an adverse balance of trade on the Roman economy.

The most influential of the geographers of antiquity, Ptolemy of Alexandria (active A.D. 127–60), derived his conception of India and eastern Asia from the Greek works and from the reports of merchants and navigators in his native city. Unfortunately, scholars are not agreed about the credit which should be given to Ptolemy himself for the extant texts and maps which ordinarily go under the name of the *Geographia*.[42] It is likely that the only parts preserved of Ptolemy's original work are his discourse on the theory of map-making and his list of cities.[43] Most of the narrative now extant seems to have been compiled from a number of later sources by an unknown Byzantine scholar of the tenth

---

[41] Bostock and Riley (eds.), *op. cit.* (n. 28), Bk. XII, chap. xiv. 112–13.

[42] The two critical texts of recent date are: J. Fischer (ed.), *Claudii Ptolemaei geographiae codex urbinas Graecas 82* (Leyden, 1932); Edward L. Stevenson (trans. and ed.), *Geography of Claudius Ptolemy: Based upon Greek and Latin Manuscripts and Important Late Fifteenth and Early Sixteenth Century Printed Editions* (New York, 1932).

[43] Following the excellent article of Leo Bagrow, "The Origin of Ptolemy's Geography," *Geografiska Annaler* (Stockholm), XVII (1945), 319–87.

and eleventh centuries. The maps which exist do not collate with the texts and appear to be of even later origin. In the past, historians have credited Ptolemy with a vast and detailed knowledge of India and south Asia, and have occasionally castigated him for gross errors.[44] From what we know now, it hardly seems just either to praise or attack him. It is quite impossible at this stage of scholarship to determine how he himself conceived of Asia and what new details he was able to add to the knowledge of that region. Nonetheless, the method which he adopted for measuring, dividing, and mapping the world was to provide modern Western cartography with its basic plan. And the elaborations of the original Ptolemaic system provided fifteenth-century Europe with its view of the world and its standard maps. In our discussion of the Renaissance we shall include a summary of the then prevailing conception of Asia, even yet appropriately called "Ptolemaic."

To what extent did the trade in Eastern wares affect Roman life and its image of Asia? Without question it extended the horizons of Western man eastward beyond India to southeast Asia and China. For example, in the first centuries of the Christian era China was known both as "Sinae" and "Serica,"[45] though more commonly by the latter name. When viewed as the terminus of the sea route, it is called Sinae. Northern China is referred to as the "land of silk" at the distant end of the land route and is called Serica by the poets of the Augustan age and by Pomponius Mela and Pliny. Mela asserts that the eastern extremity of Asia is populated by three peoples: Indians, Seres, and Scythians, a division roughly approximating the more modern designations of India, China, and Tartary.[46] The land of the Seres was identified mainly with silk, and the ancient writers agreed that it was a vast and heavily populated land at the end of the habitable world. Its peoples were civilized, just, and frugal. The Seres were thought to be reluctant to have close relations with other peoples but not unwilling to sell their silks, furs, and iron products to foreign merchants. Traders from the Seres may have reached Roman territory in the time of Augustus, but clearly no official Chinese missions visited the city of Rome.[47] Vague rumors of Confucian and Taoist ideas may have reached Rome, but no clear evidence of such transmission exists.[48]

Even though intercourse with India was closer, few Indians, except merchants, emissaries, and slaves, actually appeared in Latin Europe. While exotic and

[44] For example, see the following studies: S. R. Sastri (ed.), *McCrindle's Ancient India as Described by Ptolemy* (Calcutta, 1927); A. Berthelot, *L'Asie ancienne centrale et sud-orientale d'après Ptolémée* (Paris, 1930), chap. vii.

[45] Apollodorus (*ca.* 200 B.C.) is one of the first Western writers to use the term "Seres," but he does not use it to refer to a silk-producing people. See Tarn, *op. cit.* (n. 18), p. 110. In later times, the term was apparently also applied to peoples of Central Asia who produced silk. It would appear by the time of Pliny (first century A.D.) that the identification of the word Seres with silk and China was well established (Bostock and Riley [eds.], *op. cit.* [n. 28], Bk. IV, chap. xx, pp. 36–37).

[46] See H. Yule and H. Cordier, *Cathay and the Way Thither* (London, 1913), I, 15–17.

[47] *Ibid.*, p. 18.

[48] The opinion that such rumors "seem to have reached Europe" is held by J. Needham, *Science and Civilization in China* (Cambridge, 1954), I, 157.

useful oriental products were common in Rome, the great civilizations of Asia apparently made no deep imprint upon Roman institutions, crafts, or arts. Faint traces of Indian influence may perhaps be observed in Roman work with silver and ivory, or in Egyptian cotton and silk fabrics which were ultimately sold in Europe.

Indian ideas and stories probably affected Neo-Platonic and Manichaean thought. Indians were certainly present at Alexandria in the second century, but how much of Indian culture could be learned from them is debatable. The historians of Alexander had enlightened the West about some Indian ideas and beliefs, but they had added very little to the general statements on Brahmanical doctrine and Buddhist practices included in Megasthenes. Clement of Alexandria (d. A.D. 220) was the first to exhibit any real knowledge of Indian philosophy and to mention Buddha in his writings. Considerable force is added to the possibility of Indian influence upon Roman thought by examination of the *Philosophoumenos* (*ca.* A.D. 230) of Hippolytus, a writer of the early church. Long thought of as a simple summary of ideas current since Megasthenes, Hippolytus' work on closer examination appears to show remarkably direct textual knowledge of a poetic dialogue on metaphysics, the *Maitry-Upanishad*, a fact not fully appreciated until recently.[49] Nor is Hippolytus entirely alone. The witnesses are relatively numerous that disenchantment with Greek rationalism in the first three centuries of the Christian era led to the conviction that the eastern barbarians probably possessed secret ways of attaining a closer and purer knowledge of the divine than was known in the West.[50]

Indian influence upon Plotinus (*ca.* 204-70) and the Neo-Platonists has been a subject of intense controversy for the past generation and more. Plotinus' rejection of the Greek view of the ability of reason to distinguish between subject and object in an intelligible world, and his mystical insistence upon the absolute unity of the self and the infinite is attributed by some scholars to his knowledge of the *Upanishads*.[51] Others see an affinity between the Yoga doctrine of *patanjali* and the efforts of the Neo-Platonists to achieve through meditation a mystical union between the individual spirit and the supreme spirit.[52] All the commentators agree in emphasizing the difficulty of definitely establishing Indian influence, but even those who insist most rigidly upon intellectual self-sufficiency do not specifically exclude the possibility of external influence.[53] At any rate, the parallels between Plotinus and the *Upanishads* are

[49] See J. Filliozat, "La doctrine des brâhmanes d'après Saint Hippolyte," *Revue de l'histoire des religions,* CXXX (1945), 59-91; and the same author's "Les échanges de l'Inde et de l'empire romain aux premiers siècles de l'ère chrétienne," *Revue historique,* CCI (1949), 27-28.

[50] A. J. Festugière, *La révélation d'Hermes Trismégiste* (Paris, 1944), I, 20-26. This tradition also goes back to the Jewish philosopher Philo of Alexandria (A.D. 40), who suggested that Moses anticipated many of the best ideas of the Greeks. This argument was uncritically accepted and broadcast by Christian thinkers who hoped to win acceptance for their own faith by deprecating the pagan beliefs of the Greeks. See Thomson, *op. cit.* (n. 1), p. 349.

[51] Especially E. Bréhier, *La philosophie de Plotin* (Paris, 1928), pp. 107-33.

[52] H. G. Rawlinson, *op. cit.* (n. 23), p. 175.

[53] For example, A. H. Armstrong, "Plotinus and India," *Classical Quarterly,* XXX (1936), 23.

sufficiently striking to leave the question open until more reliable evidence is forthcoming.

The separation of Brahman from Buddhist traces in the ancient West, while next to impossible, has occasionally been attempted.[54] The clearest case of a Western response to Buddhist doctrine is to be found in Manichaeanism. The prophet of this religious syncretism, Mani, sojourned in India for a period in the third century, and he placed Buddha alongside Jesus, Adam, and Zoroaster in his pantheon of divine emissaries. Manichaeanism was sufficiently wide-spread in the Roman Empire for Diocletian (*ca.* 296) to proscribe it. In the formula of abjuration required by the Byzantine church for converts from Manichaeanism, a denunciation of Buddha is required in three different places. The introduction of Buddha to the West by the Manichaeans was, however, vague and relatively brief; few mentions of Buddha can be found in later Roman writers. Not until the eleventh century, when the Barlaam and Josaphat legend first appeared, did the Latin world add the Buddha story to its repertory of saints' lives.[55]

The Orient, whether India or China, was still too far removed physically and spiritually to make a deep impression upon the classical world. Factual knowledge, as illustrated by Eratosthenes and Pliny, was limited, and it was frequently impossible for the most sincere and critical commentators to separate myth from fact, or to distinguish clearly one Eastern area or people from another. India, as distinguished from China, was the scene of marvels and the habitat of monstrous animals and peoples. India was also looked to by the ancients as the source of the spices, as China was the land of silk. Greek writers like Megasthenes described northern India, while knowledge of the southern and eastern shores of the peninsula was later carried by merchants to Alexandria and Rome. That oriental products convinced the Greeks and Romans of the existence of rich oriental peoples there can be no doubt. But the traders who visited India and farther East were probably more concerned with quick and high profits than with learning about the religions, institutions, or customs of the oriental peoples with whom they dealt. Even if they had been differently motivated, their limitations of back-ground and language would have prevented them from making more than superficial observations. Nevertheless, to the third century A.D., knowledge about the East and its peoples became increasingly more profound and general. The effects of Brahmanism and Buddhism upon Neo-Platonism and Manichaeanism respectively, while debatable, tend to confirm the belief that ideas as well as products made their way westward. Once the Roman Empire began to decline, Europe's image of Asia, like its concepts about almost everything else, under-went a radical transformation.

---

[54] One of the most recent and most successful attempts is Henri de Lubac, *La rencontre du Bouddhisme et de l'Occident* (Paris, 1952), chap. i. See also for a history of the expansion of Manichaeanism the study by G. Messina, *Christianesimo, Buddhismo, Manicheismo nell'Asia antica* (Rome, 1947).

[55] Cf. below, p. 27.

3

THE MEDIEVAL VIEW OF ASIA
(300–1300)

From the time of Ptolemy until the return of Marco Polo to Venice more than one thousand years later, very little factual information about India, the East Indies, and China was added to Europe's store of knowledge. The pioneering efforts of Megasthenes were either forgotten altogether or so lost in a maze of fable that separating fact from fiction became next to impossible. In the Middle Ages the myths of antiquity, as expressed by Ctesias or the authors of the legend of Alexander, were Christianized and embellished with biblical allegories and newer geographical fantasies. The myth of Asia as a land of griffons, monsters, and demons, lying somewhere beyond the terrestrial Paradise, slowly enmeshed the popular imagination of medieval Europe and gradually penetrated the popular literature of the crusading era. It was to be many centuries after Marco Polo before the last of these fables would disappear from scientific and critical literature. Many of them still retain a place today in imaginative literature, poetic imagery, and artistic decoration.

Rome's incapacity to maintain its grip on the Red Sea region and the monsoon trade with India had become obvious by the third century. The contemporary expansion of the Abyssinian kingdom of Axum brought a new intermediary into the southern commerce which was to control the Isthmus of Suez until the seventh century. The interposition of the Axumites, and later the Arabs, constantly forced upward the cost of spices in Europe as more exactions were placed upon the trade. The monopoly was not broken when the Venetians came into the trade in the tenth century; it was merely extended by the addition of another middleman. Venice, in its economic relation to the rest of Europe, acted in much the same way as the middlemen of the Levant. Prices therefore continued to mount, and the spice monopoly of the Eastern powers remained effective until the discovery of the route around Africa. Spices in western Europe became so rare that at times (though not frequently) they were substituted for gold and silver in making payments.

Nor, after the third century, were the Europeans able to exercise the same measure of control as formerly over the land routes and the silk trade. In its last years imperial Rome was not even able to play off the Persian middlemen of the silk routes against the Axumite monopolists of the spice route. The intermediary powers ignored Rome's threats and enticements designed to get them to compete with each other: the Persians would not take over the spice trade and the Axumites refused to permit silks to traverse the sea route. Rome was therefore squeezed into paying constantly higher prices for silks as well as spices. Even in its temporary period of revival in the fourth century, Rome remained unable to launch a military expedition against the Axumites or force the Persians to be more tractable.

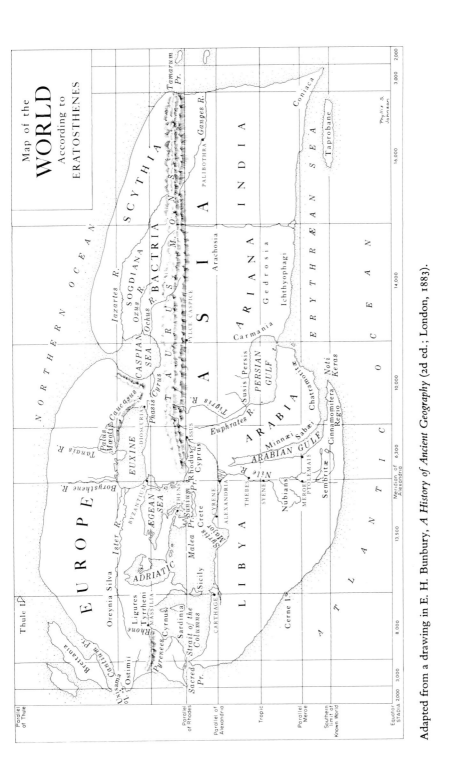

Map of the
WORLD
According to
ERATOSTHENES

Adapted from a drawing in E. H. Bunbury, *A History of Ancient Geography* (2d ed.; London, 1883).

Christ extending his divine power to all peoples, even the monstrous ones. Central
Tympanum, Church of St. Magdalen, Abbey of Vézelay, France. Twelfth
century(?).

Detail from Central Tympanum, Vézelay. Twelfth century.

Elephant. Reims Cathedral, France. Thirteenth century.

Seal of Grand Khan Kuyuk on a letter to Rome. From Paul Pelliot, *Les Mongols et la papauté* (Paris, 1923).

The pepper harvest. This and the two pictures on the facing page are colored illustrations in a fourteenth-century manuscript, Bibliothèque nationale, Paris (Codex 2810).

Dog-headed people of India.

Fantastic Indians.

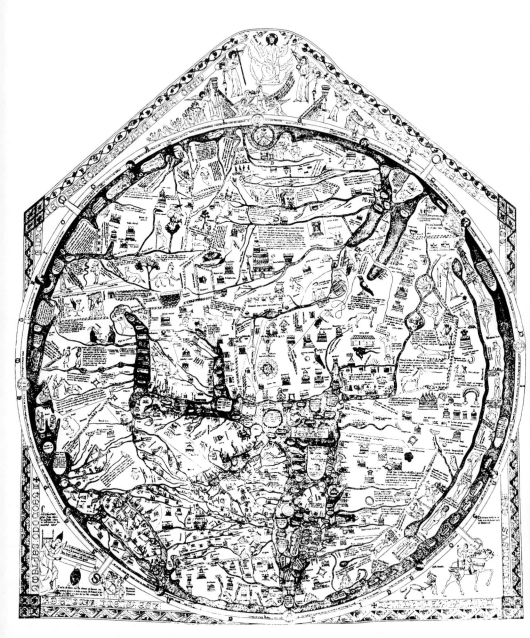

The Hereford (England) World Map, *ca.* 1276. A. E. Nordenskiöld, *Periplus: An Essay on the Early History of Charts and Sailing Directions* (Stockholm, 1897).

The establishment of imperial authority at Constantinople in A.D. 330 had the general effect of shifting the flow of eastern trade away from the sea route to the land routes. The eclipse of the imperial market of Rome helped to bring economic decline to Egypt and Alexandria and consequently increased the importance of Syria and Armenia as key economic centers. Although the volume of trade was reduced, the Byzantine Empire itself eventually became a monopolistic intermediary. By the fifth century the Mediterranean peoples were completely at the mercy of Byzantium when purchasing Indian spices and gems or Chinese silks, just as the Byzantines until the sixth century were at the mercy of the intermediaries farther to the east.

The demand for spices and silk among the upper classes of both Constantinople and Rome continued heavy despite mounting prices. Christian society was as devoted as earlier pagan Rome to ostentatious display and sumptuous living. Like Pliny, John Chrysostom (A.D. 345–407) denounced the frivolous society that lavished its wealth on imported silks while permitting barbarians to overrun large sections of the western empire. The barbarians themselves, as they took on a Roman coloration, acquired a taste for Eastern luxuries. Part of the ransom of Rome demanded by Alaric in 408 was to be paid in spices. In the fifth and sixth centuries the Byzantine court frequently bribed the barbarian chieftains or enticed them to compromise and co-operation with gifts of oriental goods. By this means silk and spices were taken into the service of the state and given high rank in the Byzantine diplomacy of overriding grandeur. As it became increasingly important to the state, the Eastern trade was removed from the control of private merchants and in the fifth century the importation of silk was declared a state monopoly in the Byzantine Empire. In 542 the state extended its monopoly to include the silk manufacturing industry, and shortly thereafter Emperor Justinian determined to learn the secret of making raw silk. By 553, a monk, it is said, had smuggled the eggs of the silkworm into Constantinople in a hollow stick, probably of bamboo.[56]

The "smuggled moth" apparently adapted well in its new environment. No more than a century later sericulture was somehow developed in Syria. The question that remains bothersome is that of the growth of silk technology. Who were the people who knew how to cultivate the eggs and reel and twist the silk from the captured cocoon?[57] Native production, however, soon became large enough to meet a good part of the demand for raw silk, though importation continued. The itinerant worm was shortly carried to Greece, Sicily, and Spain, and in the crusading age it finally arrived in Italy. By smuggling and native production, rather than control of the routes to Asia, medieval Europe was finally freed of its utter dependence upon China for silk. The Asiatic monopoly of spices, however, continued to operate effectively until the sixteenth century.

[56] For a review of this much-debated episode in the history of the spread of silk production see R. Hennig, "Die Einführung der Seidenraupenzucht ins Byzantinerreich," *Byzantinische Zeitschrift*, XXXIII (1933), 295–312. See also Thomson, *op. cit.* (n. 1), pp. 371–72.
[57] Question raised by Needham, *op. cit.* (n. 48), I, 186.

Although direct relations between East and West gradually ceased in the last years of the Roman Empire, individual merchants and travelers from the West continued on rare occasions to find their way eastward. In the time of Justinian, Cosmas Indicopleustes took the sea route to India, visited its west coasts, and stayed for a time in Ceylon. From the information gathered in his travels he prepared a geographical and theological treatise called *Universal Christian Topography* (*ca.* 540). Dismissing the Greeks as "windy babblers," Cosmas compiled a fantastic medley of hard facts and religious theory about the world's topography. Unlike Augustine or the Venerable Bede, Cosmas advocated the theory of a flat earth with Jerusalem at its center. He denied the existence of the antipodes and viewed the world as three continents forming a single land mass surrounded by a universal sea. He not only described India and Ceylon, the places he visited, but also gathered information on the countries east of India. Of the placement of China[58] he had a more accurate impression than the Romans. Apparently he understood that a ship sailing eastward from India would after a long journey have to turn northward to reach the China coast. From information collected in Ceylon he located the clove country between China and India and observed that Ceylon operated as an entrepôt in the trade between India and the Eastern countries.

The cessation of direct trade, followed as it was by the rise of Muslim power in the seventh and eighth centuries, forced a further narrowing of European horizons. Preoccupied with immediate problems brought on in part by the threat of Islam, Europe almost completely lost sight of the East as a land of reality. Even though pilgrims trekked to the Holy Land throughout the Middle Ages, knowledge of the East was not significantly broadened by their travel accounts.[59] Although the Egyptian Greek, Theophylactus Simocatta, writing around 628, presented an accurate description of China, his *History* had but a slight impact on a Europe that had almost forgotten about the "Seres." [60] The store of factual knowledge was not increased again until the crusaders began to return from the Levant with their tales.

During the first Christian millennium, the Bible increasingly became the main source of geographical knowledge. The accounts in Genesis of the Paradise located at the eastern edge of the world, of the division of the earth among the sons of Noah, and the existence of the enclosed peoples of Gog and Magog were important items in medieval speculation about the world east of Mesopotamia. The tradition of monsters and marvels inherited from the Greeks had been assembled and popularized by Solinus (third century) in his *Collectanea rerum memorabilium*. Even Augustine felt compelled to devote one chapter in the *City of God* to the fabulous races. While early medieval writers generally tended

---

[58] "Tzinitza" is the name he used for China. For discussion of the origins of this term see Yule and Cordier, *op. cit.* (n. 46), I, 28.

[59] On the pilgrimages see C. R. Beazley, *The Dawn of Modern Geography* (London, 1897), I, chaps. ii, iii, and iv.

[60] "Taugas" was the name he used for China. Yule and Cordier, *op. cit.* (n. 46), I, 29-32.

to forget about the classical delineation of the East, Chryse and Argyre continued to be mentioned as remote places of great wealth. For example, in the fifth century, Martianus of Heraclea, a disciple of Ptolemy, remarks in his *Periplus of the Outer Sea*:

In Trans-Gangetic India is the Golden Khersonese [peninsula] and beyond is the Great Gulf, in the middle of which is the frontier between trans-Gangetic India and the Sinai. Then comes the *Sinai* and their capital, called *Thinai*. It is the boundary between lands known and unknown.[61]

But Martianus' concrete information seems not to have affected to any significant degree the tendency of later medieval commentators to evolve their own view of the mythical lands of gold and silver to the east.

Among the earliest of the medieval encyclopedic works, the *Etymologiae* of Isidore of Seville (d. 636) quickly became a standard reference work on Asia. For his information Isidore relied upon the Bible and some of the later Latin purveyors of mythology. Numerous geographical myths inherited from antiquity were thus given the authority of the Scriptures, Augustine, and Isidore. The factual information that the early medieval commentators derived from the classical writers was often badly garbled or so confused with later myths as to be unrecognizable. Not all of the early Christian writers adopted the belief in a flat earth. The Neo-Platonists especially kept the idea of sphericity alive in the Middle Ages. Like Cosmas, however, most of the commentators of the patristic age and of the pre-crusading era believed in the universal, encircling sea and thought of Africa as having only a slight southward extension. Those who maintained the sphericity of the earth also kept alive the Greek conception of the antipodes, an idea regarded as heretical by the proponents of a flat earth. Practically all observers were agreed, however, that the equatorial zone was uninhabitable because of its extreme heat and the polar regions uninhabitable because of their extreme cold.

Asia was usually designated as the locale of the terrestrial Paradise, and various rivers, such as the Indus, Ganges, Nile, and Euphrates, were thought to have a common source in the Garden of Eden. Men were kept out of the forbidden garden, it was alleged, by an insuperable barrier. Far to the east and the north lived the sons of Japeth, horrible barbarians who would, according to the prophecy of Revelation (20:7), ravage the world on judgment day. Until the apocalypse the giants and their minions inhabiting Gog and Magog, would be prevented from overrunning the Christian world by being held behind the wall that Alexander the Great had allegedly built in the dim past.[62]

Before the crusading era, maps likewise reflected a scriptural and fanciful view of the world.[63] Most medieval world pictures made no use of the Hellenistic

---

[61] As translated by Wheatley, *op. cit.* (n. 31), p. 135.

[62] For the history of these mythical barbarians in European thought see A. R. Anderson, *Alexander's Gate, Gog and Magog, and the Enclosed Nations* (Cambridge, Mass., 1932).

[63] For a brief survey of medieval world maps see L. Bagrow, *Die Geschichte der Kartographie* (Berlin, 1951), pp. 28–36. Further illustrative material in J. G. Leithäuser, *Mappae mundi* (Berlin, 1958), chaps. ii and iii.

patterns of antiquity. Practically all knowledge of Ptolemy and his works had been lost, though John Scot Erigena, the eighth-century Platonist, may have read the *Geographia* in Greek.[64] In most of the medieval maps the Ganges is the world's eastern boundary and the Sahara desert its southern frontier. The inhabited world lies like an island surrounded by a universal sea. In the maps that survive, like the Beatus chart of the eighth century, the East is commonly placed at the top and is decorated with vignettes of Adam and Eve and the serpent. In the encircling sea, boats, fish, and demons are sketched in. While most of the map-makers designed similar representations, the Venerable Bede and a few other critical minds held to a cosmogony closer to the Greek views. It would seem, however, that Bede's conception of the physical world held little attraction for the map-makers, chroniclers, and poets of the era before Marco Polo.[65]

Medieval representations of the world were not altered materially by the geographers of the crusading age. Like their predecessors, they divided the known world into three parts—Asia, Africa, and Europe—and made Asia equal in size to the combined areas of Europe and Africa.[66] The writers of the crusading age had a more detailed knowledge about India than about China. As previously also, the term "India" continued to be used in describing the subcontinent, the East Indies, and everything in the distant East. In short, the Crusades themselves changed almost nothing in Europe's pictorial image of Asia and so, from this viewpoint, the period from the eleventh to the thirteenth centuries must be considered part of the medieval panorama. On the other hand, the dynamism released and stimulated by the Crusades helped to prepare Europeans for the new revelation of the East that was to come in the thirteenth century.

In the millennium after Ptolemy, three legends of European origin nourished and elaborated the view of the fabulous East. Medieval writers added stories from a variety of sources to the vast accumulation of great deeds performed by the mythical Alexander. This gossamer web of stories was interlaced in the first Christian centuries with traditions revolving around the saga of St. Thomas, the Apostle of India. The European belief in the existence of a cult of the apostle in India was reinforced in the twelfth century by the growth of the Prester John legend, a story about a powerful Christian ruler to the east of the Muslim world who could be counted upon to aid the crusaders in their fight

---

[64] J. K. Wright, *The Geographical Lore of the Time of the Crusades* (New York, 1925), p. 48. Masudi, the Arab geographer, is the first to refer to the Ptolemaic maps in 947. See Bagrow, *op. cit.* (n. 63), p. 345.

[65] Beazley, *op. cit.* (n. 59), I, 375–91; also A. P. Newton "The Conception of the World in the Middle Ages," in A. P. Newton (ed.), *Travel and Travellers of the Middle Ages* (London, 1926), pp. 4–7.

[66] In its most elementary form this division is clearly depicted in the world pictures (T-O maps) of the early Middle Ages. Two late medieval geographies which retain the description of the East for which Isidore had set the model are the *Imago mundi* of Honorius Inclusus (*ca.* 1100) and the anonymous *Semeiança del mundo* prepared in Spain in the latter part of the thirteenth century. See W. E. Bull and H. F. Williams, *Semeiança del mundo, a Medieval Description of the World* (Berkeley, 1959), pp. 2–4.

against Islam. Although these three stories had different sources, they tended with the passage of time to become intertwined and increasingly difficult to distinguish as separate traditions. While each of the traditions had a basis in historical fact, the composite form which they assumed in the late Middle Ages became the source for what might be called the medieval dream of the East.

The early church fathers in Europe, as well as the Christian community at large, believed that the Apostle Thomas had set out for the East immediately after the Resurrection of Christ.[67] In these distant regions the "doubting" disciple had preached the gospel in Parthia and India. After establishing Christian communities in India, he suffered martyrdom. The disciple's remains, according to the European tradition,[68] were then transported to Edessa (Urfa in southern Turkey) where they remained until 1142. Shortly thereafter they were taken to Europe and since 1258 they are said to have reposed in the cathedral of Ortona a Mare on the Adriatic coast of Italy. The earliest European writing which deals with the Apostle's mission in India is in the Acts of Thomas, an apocryphal book, apparently set down in the Syriac language at Edessa around the beginning of the third century. It was later translated into Greek, Latin, Ethiopic, and Armenian. Ecclesiastical writers of subsequent centuries repeat the assertion of the Acts that Thomas was assigned India when the apostles divided the world among themselves. None of them is specific about the particular district of India in which Thomas carried on his work of evangelizing. Evidently, the Europeans nonetheless believed that they could find his Christian colony in India. For, in 883, during the reign of King Alfred, the *Anglo-Saxon Chronicle* reports that two Englishmen, Sighelm and Aethelstan, were dispatched to India to visit the tomb of St. Thomas.[69] In his *Geography of the Known World*, based on the work of Orosius, Alfred discusses India and designates the Don River as the boundary of Europe and Asia. Though Alfred mentions Ceylon, he was apparently uninformed about the East Indies and China.[70] Whatever the facts may be, it was a universally accepted tradition in Europe before the crusading era that Thomas had preached in India, that a Christian community existed there, and that miracles occurred annually on the Apostle's feast day.[71]

With the Thomas tradition in the background, it was not difficult in the era of the Crusades to hope for and ultimately to believe in the existence of a great

[67] The Indian Christians of St. Thomas still hold to this traditional belief as an article of faith, and in December, 1952, all Syrian Christians celebrated the nineteen-hundredth anniversary of the Apostle's arrival in India. See L. W. Brown, *The Indian Christians of St. Thomas: An Account of the Ancient Syrian Church of Malabar* (Cambridge, 1956), p. 43.

[68] In the Malabar tradition his death occurred in A.D. 52 and his body is buried at Mylapore. *Ibid.*, pp. 54–60.

[69] See the careful discussion of this event in Robert Kerr (ed.), *A General History and Collection of Voyages and Travels* (Edinburgh and London, 1824), I, 18–20.

[70] Translation in *ibid.*, pp. 22–26.

[71] For a good summary of the most recent scholarship on the Thomas tradition in the European imagination see Francis M. Rogers, *The Travels of the Infante Dom Pedro of Portugal* (Cambridge, Mass., 1961), pp. 93–97. L. W. Brown, *op. cit.* (n. 67), p. 65, comments: "The only certain conclusion which can be drawn from an examination of the St. Thomas tradition is that at any rate such a visit was physically possible."

Christian nation of Asia which might be a potential ally in the fight against the Saracens. This belief was reinforced by the visit to Rome around 1122 of an oriental patriarch named John.[72] The anonymous narrator who describes John's visit also relates that the Eastern prelate created a sensation throughout Italy. His lectures to the Curia (Romana) on his native country of India and the St. Thomas Christians impressed another medieval writer enough to inspire him to comment on John's visit in a letter to Odo, the abbot of St. Remi in Rheims.[73] Nearly a quarter of a century later, Bishop Otto of Freisingen mentions in his chronicle the exploits in war against the Muslims of a fabulous Christian ruler of Asia whom he calls Prester John.[74] This is probably a reference to the defeat suffered by Muslim forces in 1141 near Samarkand at the hands of the Chinese.[75] From the middle of the twelfth century to the beginning of the fourteenth century at least, the belief was commonplace in Europe that somewhere in India (perhaps including Africa in this concept) a pious and fabulously wealthy king ruled who had waged successful war against the Medes and Persians and who might be induced, if he could be reached, to take up the sword against the Saracens.

The legend of Prester John acquired new credibility in 1165 with the reception in Europe of a letter[76] purporting to be from him and addressed in the surviving manuscripts to the pope and two of the lay rulers of Christendom. Actually its author was probably a European cleric who had possibly traded in the Levant and was well grounded in sacred and profane literature about the East.[77] This can easily be discerned by an examination of its contents. The letter describes in detail the opulence of the Prester's realm and remarks on his desire to deal a death blow to the enemies of the Cross. His empire reportedly includes the three Indias, presumably meaning the lands from India to the farthest East. Within his lands the body of St. Thomas reposes in state. Asia, according to the letter, appears to be populated by peoples of all beliefs except the Muslim faith. Some notion of the contemporary popularity of this letter may be gained by noting that almost a hundred manuscript copies of it survive and that several lengthy renderings of it were made into old German verse.[78] The travelers of

---

[72] V. Slessarev, *Prester John: The Letter and the Legend* (Minneapolis, 1959), pp. 7–9.

[73] For a summary of the source problem see *ibid.*, p. 10.

[74] On the origin of the name "Prester John" see *ibid.*, chap. vii.

[75] R. Grousset, *L'Empire des steppes* (Paris, 1939), pp. 218–20.

[76] The argument has been advanced that this letter should be looked upon as a political pamphlet of utopian character similar to Dante's *De monarchia*. See L. Olschki, "Der Presbyter Johannes," *Historische Zeitschrift*, CXLIV (1931), 13. For a summary of other viewpoints on the Prester as a historical figure see C. E. Nowell, "The Historical Prester John," *Speculum*, XXVII (1953), 436–37.

[77] Slessarev, *op. cit.* (n. 72), pp. 53–55.

[78] Friedrich Zarncke, *Der Priester Johannes* ("Abhandlungen der königlich sächsischen Gesellschaft der Wissenschaften, Philologisch-historischen Classe" [Leipzig, 1879], Vol. VII), pp. 947–1028. The author of a south German translation preserved in Vienna reports (p. 960) as follows on Prester John's statement about India:

> Wir haben in vnnserm lande
> ein michel tail der helphande,
> chamel vnd dromedary. . . .

The other poems also include fairly long descriptions of the physical features of India, its flora and fauna, and shorter sections about the people. For a summary of the French versions see Slessarev, *op. cit.* (n. 72), chap. iv.

the thirteenth century, including Marco Polo, looked in vain for this great Christian king in Asia. Odoric of Pordenone in the early years of the fourteenth century was the last commentator to place the Prester's land in Asia. Thereafter it migrated to Africa where it was first identified with Abyssinia by Giovanni da Carignano in a treatise which is now lost.

Medieval literature received from India a number of readily identifiable motifs and themes. Coming by circuitous routes through various intermediary languages and traditions, Indian fables were incorporated into European imaginative literature at an early date. Because of the obvious complications involved in studying the migration of literary themes, particularly if any effort is made to divorce, for example, Indian motifs from Persian ones, the only certain ground to stand on is that provided by the actual translations of Indian works into Western languages. The best example available is to be found in the story of the migration of the *Panchatantra*, a famous collection of Indian fables. It was translated into Syriac in the sixth century, into Arabic in the eighth century, and into Hebrew in the twelfth century. Between 1263 and 1278 the Hebrew version was translated into Latin by John of Capua. Other Indian tales probably entered Latin culture in similar fashion or through oral reports, but evidence for many suspected cases is either partial or lacking altogether.[79]

The spread of Indian literary themes to Europe was accompanied and paralleled by the diffusion of the Barlaam and Josaphat legend. This version of the life and parables of Buddha, derived in all probability from the *Bhagavan Bodhisattvascha*, migrated first to the Levant. In the ninth century it appeared in a Latin translation attributed to Anastasius Bibliothecarius. In the following century St. Euthyme d'Hagiorite produced a Greek version. In Europe, parables were generally read and reproduced in Latin, and Barlaam and Josaphat soon became saintly exemplars.[80] In the thirteenth century Vincent of Beauvais incorporated an abstract of the legend in his *Speculum historiale* and Jacobus de Voragine reproduced certain of its parables in his *Golden Legend*. The careers of Barlaam and Josaphat were introduced at an early date into the *Vitae sanctorum*, and were inscribed in the sixteenth century into the Roman martyrology where they still figure today on the date November 27. While these parables were widely celebrated from the ninth through the eighteenth centuries, they were divorced almost entirely from any ideas of India and Buddhism. The passage of time and the transfer to a new locale had the effect of Christianizing the stories. It was only long after the opening of the sea route to India that the Eastern origins of this legend became clearly appreciated in the West, even though it was regularly used as a literary and dramatic theme and as a historical source.

---

[79] Keith, *op. cit.* (n. 24), pp. 357–65.

[80] For the transformation of the name Buddha to Josaphat see Paul Peeters, "La première traduction latine de 'Barlaam et Joasaph' et son original grec," *Analecta Bollandiana*, XLIX (1931), 276–312; for the transformation of the name of the Hindu ascetic Bilahaur to Barlaam see P. Peeters, *Recherches d'histoire et de philologie orientales*, I, 19, n. 1. For a pedigree chart of the translations see J. Jacobs, *Barlaam and Josaphat* (London, 1896), facing p. 10.

Beginning in the eleventh century, the tales of Alexander began to be regularly employed as poetic themes in French romances. The great emperor's mythical adventures, originally compiled in Greek, had been translated during the early Middle Ages into a number of other tongues. The version of the pseudo-Callisthenes produced in the middle of the tenth century in Latin by Leo of Naples became the major source for those who took up these tales in the later Middle Ages and cast them into vernacular poems and stories. While the earliest adaptations appeared in France, the tales soon spread northward into England and Germany and southward to Spain. Wherever they went the Alexander poems helped inaugurate a departure in literary form and content. Italy, however, appears to have experienced an independent tradition, for there the tales are usually cast in prose form with many of the customary French embellishments missing. Generally, the romance of Alexander is of constant interest from about 1100 to 1500, the peak of its impact coming in the fifteenth century.[81]

An excellent example of the influence exerted by the Alexandrian romance and Isidore of Seville upon medieval literature and art can be found in the mythical travel accounts and picture books that were copied from country to country in western Europe.[82] These all seem to derive from a single archetype, but the earliest such manuscript known to us dates from ninth-century Beauvais. While purporting to be a travel account, this Beauvais manuscript (called "Fermes") is merely a collection of marvels translated into Latin from an unknown Greek original. Three other Latin manuscripts, beautifully illuminated, of the eleventh and twelfth centuries, appear to be descended from the "Fermes" as does an Anglo-Saxon version of the ninth century. In these manuscripts, references are made to India and Asia mainly for the purpose of providing a background for the dog-headed people and weird animals which were the major preoccupation of the writers and illustrators.[83]

From medieval works written in the vulgar languages for lay consumption, something of the popular image of Asia also emerges. Written before the appearance of the great travel accounts of the later thirteenth century, the long poem *L'Image du monde* (1245 or 1247)[84] describes the terrestrial Paradise and notes that India is on its further side. India has two summers and two winters each year, but the climate is so mild that plants stay green at all seasons. Located near Ceylon (Taprobane), India is the country of gold, precious stones, spices,

---

[81] For the transition from the pseudo-Callisthenes of the third century to the French romance see Paul Meyer, *Alexandre le Grand dans la littérature française du moyen âge* (Paris, 1886), Vol. II, chap. ii; also consult J. Storost, *Studien zur Alexandersage in der alten italienischen Literatur* (Halle a. S., 1935), pp. 305–7. A general summary of the medieval conception of Alexander is to be found in George Cary, *The Medieval Alexander* (Cambridge, 1956).

[82] R. Wittkower, "Marvels of the East," *Journal of the Warburg Institute*, V (1942), 179–80.

[83] See Montague R. James (ed.), *Marvels of the East: A Full Reproduction of the Three Known Copies...* (Oxford, 1929).

[84] See C. Langlois, *La connaissance de la nature et du monde au moyen âge d'après les écrits français à l'usage des laics* (Paris, 1927), pp. 80–89.

and coconuts. It is divided into twenty-four heavily populated regions inhabited in part, at least, by horned pygmies, who live in groups and become old in seven years. These pygmies inhabit the country of white pepper. Beasts and men with six toes or fingers are not oddities. The Brahmans of India commit suicide by throwing themselves into a fire; others eat their old parents to do them honor.

In *Le livre du trésor* (*ca.* 1266) of Brunetto Latini, Florentine diplomat and scholar, an account of China is given. The *Trésor*, based on Pliny and Marcellinus, describes the Caspian area as the country of Amazons beyond which "are immense snowy wastes and some deserts.[85] Further on live the Seres, a peaceable people among themselves but wary of foreigners.

They do not desire our goods and sell their own to our merchants without uttering a word; they put their goods down on a river bank with price labels attached; our merchants carry off their goods after having left the price indicated.[86]

This reference to mute exchanges appears to indicate some knowledge of Chinese reserve, or more likely of the inability of the traders to speak each other's language.[87] Certainly the merchants, even at a later date, brought little information to Europe besides fables and idle stories. Like the unlettered folk at home, the merchants and mariners learned much of their oriental lore from the legends and stories told or read aloud in the public square.

Neither the works of antiquity nor the accounts of Arab and Jewish travelers appear to have imparted a greater sense of reality to the popular image. The writers of this period, at least five hundred years after Byzantium acquired the secret of silk, continue to repeat the classical belief that raw silk was somehow combed from trees. References to the Seres were clearly derived from Pliny and Solinus. The *Lucidarius*, a kind of lay catechism that circulated widely in Germany from the twelfth century onward, and the *World Chronicle* of Rudolf von Ems of about the same period, both identify the land of the Seres as the place from whence the silk comes. For the poet, Wolfram von Eschenbach, India and China were part of the Alexandrian legend and he referred to them for distant and exotic effects.[88] The term "Seres" was little more than a name, while Prester John, the mythical king, was celebrated as a real and potential ally.

While Eastern products entered Europe through intermediaries, they did little to give substance to the medieval image of Asia. Exotic products tended to confirm rather than disprove the simple belief in Asia as a remote land of wonders. Erudite literature, even if fanciful, and trade, even if substantial, probably

[85] *Ibid.*, pp. 357–58.
[86] *Ibid.*, p. 359.
[87] On this point see L. Olschki, *Marco Polo's Precursors* (Baltimore, 1943), pp. 5–8. For a good summary of this "silent trade" in history see H. Hart, *Sea Road to the Indies* (New York, 1950), p. 21 n. The above may be derived from a comment of the Roman historian, Ammanius Marcellinus, who wrote *ca.* A.D. 330.
[88] E. H. von Tscharner, *China in der deutschen Dichtung bis zur Klassik* (Munich, 1939), pp. 8–9.

had less impact upon the medieval conception of Asia than the wonderful tales derived from the Alexandrian romance and the Prester John legend. For Christian missionaries it was even a question whether the monsters of India should be considered real men to whom they might teach Christianity. It appears from the tympanum of the central interior portal of the cathedral of Vezelay that the answer was affirmative. Completed around the middle of the twelfth century, it depicts a Christian teacher (Christ) addressing, and presumably instructing, cynocephalic Indians and other monstrous peoples.[89] Literary information, aside from the writings of antiquity, was to be found only in Arabic works not generally available in European tongues until the thirteenth century. While occasional European travelers and merchants visited India and places along the trade routes, no important account of Asia appeared in medieval Europe after the time of Cosmas. Chinese textiles, Indian spices, games, such as chess,[90] and perhaps technical devices of Asian origin continued to find their way to Europe throughout the Middle Ages, but always through intermediaries. Though oriental monsters and legends appeared in Europe's artistic and literary productions, most of them were quickly transformed, as in the case of the Barlaam and Josaphat legend, into the local artistic, literary, or religious idiom. Neither singly nor in combination, however, were any of these contacts sufficient to provide Europe with more than a sketchy and distorted picture of the India known to Alexander, or the Land of the Seres celebrated by the Romans.

4

THE REVELATION OF CATHAY
(1240–1350)

Europe's intellectual and spiritual isolation from the East of reality helped to delay its reaction to the rise of Mongol power in Asia. Early in the thirteenth century, reports from Nestorian missionaries in Asia about the activities of Jenghis Khan funneled into Syria, and warnings of hordes running wild in western Asia were relayed to Rome about 1220 by Syrian Christians and Latin

[89] J. F. Filliozat, "Les premières étapes de l'indianisme," *Bulletin de l'Association Guillaume Budé*, III (1953), 81; also Emile Mâle, *L'Art religieux du XIIᵉ siècle en France* (Paris, 1922), pp. 329–30.

[90] The game of knights, kings, and bishops seems to have been introduced into Europe between the ninth and eleventh centuries and to have enjoyed a popularity between the twelfth and fifteenth centuries which it would never attain again. It probably originated in India and passed into Europe through the Arab world by various routes. For the history of chess in Western literature see H. J. Murray, *A History of Chess* (Oxford, 1913), pp. 394–528. See also Helena M. Gamer, "The Earliest Evidence of Chess in Western Literature: The Einsiedeln Verses," *Speculum*, XXIX (1954), 734–50. On the diffusion of Asian textiles to Europe see especially A. Geijer, *Oriental Textiles in Sweden* (Copenhagen, 1951).

missionaries in Hungary. Though they bemoaned the depredations of the khan, these reports also aroused hopes in Europe. They indicated that the Mongol ruler was not intolerant of Christians and that he even took Christian priests into his service and confidence. So the knowledge that the khan was constructing a huge Asian Empire appeared not unduly to trouble the pope or the lay rulers of Christendom. Still bewitched by the Prester John legend, Pope Honorius III apparently believed that the Mongols might became an ally and help to rescue the Holy Land.[91] Little note was evidently taken of Mongol activities in the Volga region or of their threat to move westward. It was not until the Mongols appeared in eastern Europe that Christendom awakened for the first time to the immediacy of the danger from the "barbarian" frontier to the east.

Two Mongol columns struck at Poland and Hungary in 1240. Without much difficulty the northern army sacked Cracow and went on to defeat a joint Polish-Silesian army near Liegnitz on April 9, 1241. After devastating Silesia and Moravia, the northern army moved into Hungary to join forces with other Mongol legions. Meanwhile the southern army had crushed the Hungarians and poured westward to the Adriatic. The victorious Mongols made no effort to occupy or annex the ravished lands of eastern Europe. Their raid completed, they retired eastward without attacking the heart of Christendom—perhaps because of the death of the Grand Khan.

Had they realized how many divisions existed within Christendom, the Mongols might have continued their westward drive. Only after central Europe seemed doomed did Pope Gregory IX preach a crusade against the Mongols. Emperor Frederick, at war with the papacy, was suspected in Rome of having a secret understanding with the Tartars. In Germany an army was mobilized hastily, and appeals for assistance were dispatched to France and England. Fortunately for Europe the Mongols retired without engaging the German forces and without seeking to drive into Italy. The full measure of the devastation wrought in Hungary, Poland, and Silesia by the "scourge of God" was not fully realized until after the Mongol withdrawal.

The leaders of Europe still persisted, even after the Mongol onslaught, in believing that salvation might come from the East. The mortal enemy of Christendom, despite the Mongol depredations, remained the infidel Muslims. Although unwilling to negotiate with Islam, the pope possessed no scruple about dealing with the pagan Mongols. In 1245, from the Council of Lyons, Innocent IV[92] dispatched two embassies to Mongolia. A Franciscan, John of Plano Carpini, accompanied by the Polish Friar Benedict as interpreter, was to

[91] Letter of June 20, 1221, as quoted by S. Runciman, *A History of the Crusades* (Cambridge, 1954), III, 246. For the Mongol attack and Europe's reaction see Giovanni Soranzo, *Il Papato, l'Europe Cristiana e i Tartari* (Milan, 1930), chap. ii.

[92] A Genoese who was elected pope in 1243. "He introduced into papal policy the diplomatic methods of his own city, directing it towards the spiritual conquest of Asia." Olschki, *op. cit.* (n. 87), p. 31. Also see Soranzo, *op. cit.* (n. 91), chap. iii. For a summary of the missions dispatched by the Council see R. Streit, *Bibliotheca missionum* (Aachen, 1928), IV, 2.

journey to the headquarters of the Grand Khan through Poland and Russia. Another Franciscan, instructed to travel via Armenia, was never heard from again, but after a two-year voyage to Mongolia, Friar John returned to Lyons in the autumn of 1247.

Although the Mongols had carried many European slaves into Asia,[93] John is the first European on record to proceed east of Baghdad and return to tell his tale. He visited the Mongol camp pitched not far from Karakorum and eventually was permitted to deliver the pope's letter. Although John felt that the Grand Khan Kuyuk was favorably inclined toward Christianity, he failed to convert him or even to impress him with the strength of Christendom; in the brief letter John carried back to the Council of Lyons, Kuyuk replied haughtily to the pope's overtures, invited him to do homage, and showed little disposition to co-operate with the Holy See against the Muslims.[94]

Of greater moment in Europe was Friar John's report of his mission entitled *History of the Mongols*. This book marks something of a transition in medieval literature on Asia, for it is primarily an itinerary and a factual description of what he and his companion saw, heard, and surmised. He does not quote earlier writers except for Isidore, or incorporate in his narrative many of the traditional fables about Asia. He heard about Cathay,[95] learned that it bordered the sea, and was apparently informed about its language, religion (somewhat mistakenly), and arts. The good friar himself was clearly conscious of the unusual character of his account, for he prefaces it with the following admonition:

But if for the attention of our readers we write anything which is not known in your parts, you ought not on that account to call us liars, for we are reporting for you things we ourselves have seen or have heard from others whom we believe to be worthy of credence.[96]

Before John died in 1252 he circulated manuscript copies of his book and apparently talked with many who expressed incredulity or requested further information.[97] A few years after his death, the *History of the Mongols* was incorporated into the encyclopedic *Speculum historiale* of Vincent of Beauvais.

The Council of Lyons, shortly after Friar John's departure, proclaimed that missions to Mongolia should be undertaken on an international basis as part of Christendom's joint effort to win a powerful Asiatic ally for the struggle against

[93] Cf. L. Olschki, *Guillaume Boucher, a French Artist at the Court of the Khans* (Baltimore, 1946), pp. 1–9.

[94] For the French translation of this letter of 1246 based upon the Persian and Latin texts see Paul Pelliot, *Les Mongols et la papauté* (Paris, 1923), pp. 16–21.

[95] For a discussion of the origin of this word for China, see Yule and Cordier, *op. cit.* (n. 46), I, 146.

[96] As translated in Christopher Dawson, *The Mongol Mission* (New York, 1955), p. 4.

[97] Olschki, *op. cit.* (n. 87), p. 33, n. 4. There are extant five manuscripts of Friar John's work. C. R. Beasley (ed.), *The Texts and Versions of John of Plano Carpini and William de Rubruquis* (London, 1903), p. vii.

the Muslims.[98] The dispatch of King Louis IX of France to the Levant in 1248 to wage war against the Saracen stronghold in Egypt helped to promote intercourse between the Christians and the commanders of the Mongol armies operating in Asia Minor. Christian hopes for an effective alliance against the Muslims reached a peak with the destruction of Baghdad by the Mongols in 1258. Henceforward Egypt alone would have to carry the burden of defending Islam against the attacks of the crusaders. And the Mamelukes soon showed themselves equal to the double task of stalemating the Mongols in Syria and protecting Islam against the forces of Louis IX. Although unable to defeat the Saracen, Latin Europe from its outposts in the Levant established relations in this period with the Mongol commanders in the Near East. Two doors to the Mongol empire were thus opened by the middle of the thirteenth century: one in northern Europe through Poland and the "barbarian frontier" and the other through Syria and the old trade routes of southwestern Asia.

One of the first to use the southern gate was Andrew of Longjumeau who in 1249 was dispatched to Karakorum, the Mongol capital, by Louis IX.[99] As emissary of the king of France, he was received at the Mongol court as a legate bearing tribute from a vassal king. Andrew returned with nothing for his pains but a patronizing letter admonishing Louis IX to send tribute every year. While only fragments of his report remain, Andrew appears not to have viewed Asia with the same objective attitude of Friar John. His fanciful descriptions conform much more closely to the prevailing literary traditions. Andrew and other Dominican travelers in Asia also persisted in reporting the conversion to Christianity of leading Mongol princes. It appeared from this and various other references that members of the court had already accepted the teachings of the Nestorian missionaries.

Dismayed by the treatment accorded his emissary, but encouraged by reports of Christian successes in the Mongol empire, Louis IX dispatched the Flemish Franciscan, William of Rubruquis, to the Grand Khan's court in 1253, not as an avowed diplomatic representative but as a missionary. William's efforts during his eight months (December, 1253–August, 1254) at the Mongol court to win the conversion of the Grand Khan and his chieftains were utter failures. Apparently he was more graciously received by the European slaves of the khan, one of whom sent greetings to Louis IX as well as a girdle set with precious stones. The letters written as a report to Louis IX on William's return to Antioch in 1255 added substantially to Europe's knowledge of the Mongol empire.

Before leaving the Levant, William had read Friar John's account, and it would seem probable from the observations made in his own report that he had also studied the major Roman writers on Asia. Karakorum appeared to William to be "not as big as the Parisian suburb of St. Denis." Like Friar John, William was a keen observer of landscape and peoples. While he comments at length on animal life, his observations of vegetation were inconsequential,

[98] Olschki, *op. cit.* (n. 87), p. 46.
[99] For a detailed study see Pelliot, *op. cit.* (n. 94), pp. 151–220.

though he does remark admiringly on the natural beauty of the landscape.[100] Perhaps because of his religious objective he paid more attention than others to the numerous creeds of Asia, at least in their surface aspects. Although he abhorred the pagan doctrines, he described in some detail the temples, idols, and rites. Apparently he also engaged in religious controversy with the priests.

About the other peoples of the East, William was well informed, even commenting on the Tanguts and Tibetans. He never visited China himself, but he deduced that Cathay and the Land of the Seres were but different names for the same place. "The best silk stuffs," he reported, "are still got from them." The Cathayans "are first-rate artists in every kind of craft." They show "an admirable skill in diagnosis by the pulse" and transact their business with "a common money" made of "pieces of cotton paper." His observations about Chinese writing were even more perceptive than those made later by Marco Polo. "They do their writing," he stated, "with a brush such as painters paint with, and a single character of theirs comprehends several letters so as to form a whole word."[101] After returning to Paris, Friar William discussed his report with Roger Bacon, who included information from it in his *Opus maius*. Not letter perfect on the main aspects of Chinese civilization, he accepted some traditional stories as true. Friar William clearly learned, however, a number of things from his informants about China that probably were not known to the writers of antiquity or to his predecessors of the thirteenth century.

The opening of the land routes from Europe to Mongolia in the mid-thirteenth century was followed in 1264 by the extension of Mongolian hegemony into China south of the wall. In that year Kublai Khan took up residence at "Cambaluc" (Peking) and established his summer retreat at "Xanadu" (Shang-tu) in the hills northwest of the capital. Among his first visitors from Latin Europe were the Polo brothers, Nicolo and Maffeo. These two Venetian merchants had left the Crimea after 1260 and had followed the trade routes to Cambaluc.[102] Received in audience by Kublai, they were closely questioned about Europe. Apparently they were unable to satisfy the khan's curiosity. So they were sent as his emissaries to Europe bearing a request to the pope to send one hundred learned men to Cambaluc to instruct the Tartars about Europe and debate with savants of other lands assembled at Kublai's court.

Upon their arrival at Acre in 1269, the Polos forwarded the khan's message to Rome. The Eternal City was then host to a conclave called for the election of a new pope. After a considerable delay, the Polos were appointed Apostolic delegates to the khan's court. When they set out again for Cambaluc in 1271, they were accompanied by Nicolo's young son, Marco, and two Dominican

---

[100] For some provocative remarks on the medieval attitude toward nature see W. Ganzenmüller, *Das Naturgefühl im Mittelalter* (Leipzig and Berlin, 1914).

[101] As quoted in Yule and Cordier, *op. cit.* (n. 46), I, 158–61.

[102] For what is known of their activities see A. C. Moule and P. Pelliot, *Marco Polo: The Description of the World* (London, 1938), I, 22–28. A detailed study of the itinerary is in the introduction to N. M. Penzer, *The Most Noble and Famous Travels of Marco Polo . . .* (London, 1929).

friars deputed to represent Western learning at Peking. In Little Armenia the two friars turned back, but the intrepid Polos braved the perils of the road and in 1275 had the satisfaction of being greeted by Kublai at his summer palace.

Like many foreigners then in Cambaluc, the Polos were immediately taken into the khan's service. The Mongols made a practice of bringing foreigners into their complex government as part of a studied policy designed to maintain the khan's autocratic power by preventing any single national group, especially the Chinese, from becoming dominant in the imperial administration. In various capacities the Polos served the Mongol administration for seventeen years. Young Marco in particular, if his account is to be accepted, was entrusted with missions which took him from one end of China to the other. On his trips to remote areas of China, such as Yunnan, Marco took notes for the khan on topography and peoples. Other Europeans lived and worked in China during the thirteenth century, but Marco Polo was the only one, so far as is known, to travel and work there and to write an account of his experiences. For the first time in history Europe possessed a detailed narrative about China and its neighbors based upon more than hearsay and speculation.[103]

Once back in Venice in 1295, Marco quickly won a reputation for himself as a teller of tall stories. Perhaps personal wealth as well as his fantastic stories earned him the name of *Il Milione*[104] by which title both he and his book are still known in Italy. *The Description of the World*, which is a title that explains what his book really is about, was not committed to writing until 1298–99. The occasion for the recording of his narrative was the period of his enforced sojourn in Genoa, where he was taken as a prisoner after having been captured in a naval battle in September, 1298. He dictated his story to a fellow prisoner, Rustichello of Pisa, a writer of popular romances.

Like most of his other stories, Rustichello's version of Marco's narrative was written in Old French generously sprinkled with Italianisms. The *Livre des diversités*, as Rustichello entitled the Polo story, was immediately popular.[105] Ramusio, the great sixteenth-century collector of travel literature, remarked that "all Italy in a few months was full of it." While this was probably an exaggeration, certainly it appears likely that Marco's book was widely circulated, translated, and adapted even before the author's death in 1324. There are 119 manuscript versions extant of *The Description of the World* in various languages, no two of which are exactly alike. The text read and enjoyed in our

---

[103] The most systematic study of Marco's knowledge of Asia is L. Olschki, *L'Asia di Marco Polo* (Florence, 1957); this book was translated into English by John A. Scott and revised by Olschki as *Marco Polo's Asia: An Introduction to His "Description of the World" Called "Il Milione"* (Berkeley, 1960). The references which follow are to the English translation.

[104] Moule and Pelliot, *op. cit.* (n. 102), I, 33, conclude that "The real meaning of the name was not certainly known even in the fourteenth century, and until further evidence is found we must be content to remain uncertain ourselves." But his reputation for great wealth is a part of the legend of Marco Polo perpetuated mainly by writers of popular literature. One of the most recent examples is the play by Eugene O'Neill called *Marco's Millions* (1927).

[105] Moule and Pelliot, *op. cit.* (n. 102), I, 40. Olschki, *op. cit.* (n. 87), pp. 13–15, argues that the Venetian dictated his work as a romance "for the enjoyment of his contemporaries."

era is actually a scholarly restoration based upon certain manuscripts considered primary.

While many of his contemporaries doubtless suspected the accuracy of Marco's account, he reportedly asserted on his deathbed that he had not told one-half of what he knew. Perhaps the selective character of the events related in his narrative helps to account for a number of the omissions noticed by later commentators. Although he generally describes accurately most of what he saw, his failure to mention commonplace characteristics of life in China, such as tea cultivation, the fishing cormorant, foot-binding, and printing of books, has frequently been remarked.[106] Perhaps these omissions occurred because he usually met and associated with foreigners and evidently had only a limited knowledge of the Chinese language.[107] On the other hand, if his treatment had been exhaustive, the "book" might have strained the credulity of contemporaries even more than it did.[108]

Marco Polo provided Europe with the most comprehensive and authoritative account of the East produced before 1550. No criticism of the khan's policies can be found in his survey of those vast dominions, and indeed the reader is struck by his sympathy and deference for the Tartars and for Kublai Khan himself.[109] Being so young, Marco had no trouble learning enough spoken Mongol and Chinese for his work, even though he talks little of their peculiarities as languages. He knew only a smattering of Chinese, but his thorough, though restrained, account of Cathay as the largest, wealthiest, and most populous land of the thirteenth century is most impressive. He vividly describes the cities,[110] canals, rivers, ports, and industries of a China far more advanced in internal organization than Europe. Like later European visitors to Asia, he was much more impressed by architectural masterpieces than by any other phase of Asian artistic activity. Particularly rich and informative are the stories of his experiences within the political system maintained by the khan.[111] Being primarily an administrator, Marco carefully noted natural resources, plants, and animals. Marco achieved no intimate understanding of Chinese civilization, possibly because his interest was not great. He paid little heed to the moral and religious tenets of Taoism or Confucianism, but does mention some Buddhist

[106] For example see H. Yule, *The Book of Ser Marco Polo* (New York, 1903), I, 110–11.

[107] He knew enough Persian and Mongol to get along in official circles. It is not known precisely how much he understood of other languages, but possibly he knew enough about spoken and written Chinese to conduct his daily affairs in China. See Olschki, *op. cit.* (n. 103), p. 100, n. 8.

[108] Cf. the fascinating article of R. Wittkower, "Marco Polo and the Pictorial Tradition of the Marvels of the East," in *Oriente Poliano* (Rome: Istituto italiano per il medio ed estremo Oriente, 1957), pp. 155–72. Wittkower here endeavors to show, by examining the illustrations in the Marco Polo manuscript prepared at the beginning of the fifteenth century for John the Fearless, Duke of Burgundy, that the illustrator tried to "correct" Marco's text by supplying it with traditional artistic conceptions of the East such as the dog-headed people of India (especially pp. 160–61).

[109] For a discussion of his idealized portrait of the khan see Olschki, *op. cit.* (n. 103), pp. 397–413.

[110] For a comparison of Marco's accurate description of Hangchow with contemporary Chinese sources see Etienne Balazs, "Marco Polo dans la capitale de la Chine," in *Oriente Poliano*, pp. 133–54. Also A. Moule, "Marco Polo's Description of Quinsai," *T'oung pao*, XXXIII (1937), 105–28.

[111] See Olschki, *op. cit.* (n. 103), chap. vi.

practices.[112] In speaking of Ceylon on his way back to Europe, Marco recounted the life of Buddha and, astonishingly for a man of his times, declared that if the Buddha had been Christian, "he would have become a great saint in the company of Our Lord Jesus Christ."[113]

Marco, who had lived in the East during his most active years, admired the customs, wealth, and tradition of the lands in which he had been successful and well-treated, even though he generally understood little of their inner workings. He reflects the Mongol attitude of contempt toward those peoples subject to the khan, and the Christian attitude of superiority to the pagan religions.[114] He contrasted the civilization of Cathay and Mangi (Mongol name for South China) with the aboriginal societies of the Tibetans and natives of southwestern China whom he visited. Although Korea is not mentioned, he added descriptions of the peoples of southeastern Asia and for the first time in history informed Europe of the existence of Japan ("Cipangu"). Dependent upon hearsay for his knowledge of Japan, he placed it at too great a distance from the China coast and reported that "they have immense quantities of gold . . ., pearls in abundance . . .," and are "so rich that no one can tell their wealth."[115] It is hardly to be wondered at that later writers and cartographers placed the "golden islands" and the Land of Ophir to the east of China.[116]

On leaving China in 1292, Polo traveled by sea from Zayton[117] (Ch'üan-chou near Amoy) in Fukien province to Sumatra, Ceylon, and the Malabar coast of India.[118] On this trip Marco evidently continued his practice of making careful observations, of gathering information from other merchants and travelers, and of making notes. He describes in detail the junks used in Asiatic waters and asserted that in the sea east of China (the Ocean-Sea) there are 7,448 islands, "the majority of which are inhabited,"[119] In describing the course of his voyage to the southwest he indicates roughly the geographical outlines of southeastern Asia and provides data on the navigation of the southern seas from the Straits of Formosa to the Persian Gulf. He certainly visited Champa (southern Indochina), but it is more than doubtful that his comments on Java and the Lesser

[112] See Paul Demiéville, "La situation religieuse en Chine au temps de Marco Polo," in *Oriente Poliano*, pp. 193–234.

[113] E. D. Ross and E. Power, *The Travels of Marco Polo* (London, 1931), p. 321.

[114] Olschki, *op. cit.* (n. 103), pp. 138–40.

[115] Ross and Power, *op. cit.* (n. 113), pp. 270–77. He erroneously referred to Japan as a single island, a mistake which was repeated in Europe by some observers until the end of the sixteenth century (see below, pp. 709–10).

[116] For a detailed evaluation of his remarks on the wealth of Japan see K. Enoki, "Marco Polo and Japan," in *Oriente Poliano*, pp. 25–27.

[117] Variously spelled in medieval renditions, "Zayton" was evidently an Arabic transliteration of the Chinese *Tz'u-t'ung*. See D. H. Smith, "Zaitun's Five Centuries of Sino-Foreign Trade," *Journal of the Royal Asiatic Society* (London), 1958, p. 165. On the medieval names of this city and its history see Needham, *op. cit.* (n. 48), I, 180.

[118] For evaluation of his relatively few references to India see K. A. Nilakanta Sastri, "Marco Polo on India," in *Oriente Poliano*, pp. 111–20.

[119] It is conceivable that this reference, like many other comments on "islands" made by late medieval writers, properly belongs to the literary convention described as "insular romanticism." For a discussion see L. Olschki, *Storia letteraria delle scoperte geografiche* (Florence, 1937), pp. 34–42.

Sundas are derived from personal experience. A stay of five months in north-western Sumatra enabled him to record a number of details about the topography and ways of life prevailing there. In his progress westward he touched on Ceylon and a number of towns along the west coast of India as far north as the Persian Gulf. He discourses on the beauty of Pagan, the ancient capital of Burma, but it is not likely that he actually visited it or the interior towns of India to which he alludes. Sumatra and other neighboring islands are clearly identified as the sources of the valuable spices, a simple fact that was nonetheless not clearly understood or fully appreciated in Europe until the Portuguese took Malacca in the sixteenth century.

The literature on Marco Polo is vast, but few efforts have been made to catalogue his impact on his contemporaries.[120] That some doubted the credibility of his work or were bewildered by its revelations cannot be questioned. For a long time it was classified by bibliographers and editors as a romance. So far, only five independent, contemporary references to the man and his "book" have been uncovered for the period before his death. In 1307, Thiebault de Cepoy, on a mission from France to the Venetian Republic, received an adaptation in literary French of *The Description of the World* from Marco's own hands. Jacopo da Acqui, a Dominican contemporary, in his chronicle called *Imago mundi*, related a story about Marco's imprisonment which has since become a source of scholarly controversy. A notice of Polo's later activities was recorded by Friar Francesco Pipino, the Dominican translator of the standard Latin version (*ca.* 1315–20) which first appeared in print in 1485 at Antwerp. Pipino was entrusted with this task by his Order, which was then beginning to be seriously interested in undertaking missionary activities in the Orient. The historian of Florence, Giovanni Villani (*ca.* 1275–1346), when discussing the Tartars, referred to the author of the *Milione* as one "who recounts much of their power and their rule, inasmuch as he was for a long time among them."[121] Marco was also visited by Pietro d'Abano (*ca.* 1250–1316), physician of the University of Padua, who sought from the much-traveled Venetian some practical support for his attack upon the prevailing geographical hypothesis of an uninhabitable equatorial zone. In his conversations with Marco, the Paduan scholar received reliable substantiation for his belief that man could live in an equatorial climate, and in his *Conciliator* (1303) he records Marco's celestial observations in the tropics.[122]

In the generation after Marco Polo, Long John of Ypres, a great medieval collector of travel literature, noted in a chronicle written after 1350 several references to the voyages of the Polos into Tartary. Marco's incidental contributions to the geography of Asia seem not to have been incorporated into the maps of the period until the construction of the Catalan map of 1375. In the following century, Prince Henry the Navigator and Columbus were both

---

[120] The best summary is in Yule, *op. cit.* (n. 106), I, 116–40.
[121] As quoted in H. Hart, *Venetian Adventurer* (Stanford, Calif., 1942), p. 255.
[122] Olschki, *op. cit.* (n. 103), pp. 34–36.

students of his book. Numerous other references, direct and indirect, to this epoch-making work of medieval literature will be noted in the following pages.

In 1287, while the Polos were on their way back to Europe, a mission from the western Mongols reached Rome. The leader of this legation was Bar Sauma, a Nestorian born in Peking, and the first identified Chinese to reach Europe. Unable to obtain an immediate response to his request for an alliance against the Saracens, Bar Sauma traveled to Genoa, Paris, and southern France. In the diary of his voyage he relates that he met King Philip IV in Paris, and King Edward I of England in Gascony. He failed, however, to obtain the alliance he sought and thereafter the western Mongols apparently abandoned their efforts to co-operate with the Latin world.[123]

While Bar Sauma traveled back to the Levant, John of Monte Corvino was on his way to China. Commissioned by the Supreme Pontiff in 1289 to carry the gospel to the Grand Khan, Friar John made his way to China through India and the Straits of Malacca—the route taken by the Polos on their return journey. Upon his arrival at Cambaluc in 1294,[124] he immediately set to work and soon converted a Tartar prince, a near relative of the khan. The lone Roman friar had serious difficulties, however, with the Nestorians, and his life was repeatedly in jeopardy. In spite of the tremendous odds against him, he succeeded before the end of the thirteenth century in building a church with a bell tower on it.[125] Realizing that he would require a native clergy, he "bought one hundred and fifty boys," baptized them, and taught them Latin and liturgy. After 1303, he was aided in his apostolic duties by Friar Arnold of Cologne. John's successes and his hopes for the future of the China mission led him in 1305 to write a letter to his brother Franciscans for relay to the pope. Though he felt that Timur, the Grand Khan, "had grown too old in idolatry," he evidently believed also that if he had had "but two or three comrades" Timur might have been prevailed upon to accept baptism.[126] In a second letter of 1306 he told of a European merchant, Peter of Lucolongo, who helped him establish his church by purchasing the land for it.

Of the Eastern regions John reported only a few facts confirming what Marco Polo had already written. After thirteen months in India, he declared that he saw no monstrous peoples along the Coromandel coast. He apparently

---

[123] For his own account of Europe see the translation from the Syriac by E. A. W. Budge, *The Monks of Kûblâi Khân, Emperor of China* (London, 1928), pp. 170–96; and James A. Montgomery (ed.), *The History of the Yaballaha III, Nestorian Patriarch, and of His Vicar, Bar Sauma, Ambassador to the Frankish Courts at the End of the Thirteenth Century* (New York, 1927).

[124] Date given by A. Van den Wyngaert, *Sinica Franciscana* (Quaracchi, 1929), I, 346; also accepted by Yule and Cordier, *op. cit.* (n. 46), III, 5; for some unstated reason G. F. Hudson, *op. cit.* (n. 5), p. 153, gives "1292 or 1293."

[125] The remains of this first Roman Catholic Church, supposed for a long time to be built in China, have just recently been uncovered between Inner and Outer Mongolia. See N. Egann, "Olon-Sume et la découverte de l'église catholique romaine de Jean de Montecorvino," *Journal asiatique*, CCXL (1952), 155–67.

[126] Letter translated in Yule and Cordier, *op. cit.* (n. 46), III, 45–51.

understood almost nothing of the inner workings of Indian culture.[127] His main interest was in bestirring the papacy to continue and expand its proselytizing efforts in eastern Asia. He foresaw a rich harvest of souls in India and reported that the Grand Khan, who "has heard much about the court of Rome and the state of the Latin world, desires greatly to see envoys arriving from those regions." Friar John's plea was carried by Tommaso da Tolentino directly to Pope Clement V. Under pressure from the Franciscans, in 1307 the pontiff dispatched a group of missionaries to China with orders to consecrate John Archbishop of Cambaluc and Patriarch of all the Orient, and to remain there as his suffragans. Three of the missionaries sent out died in India, but Gerard Peregrini of Castello and Andrew of Perugia joined the Mongol mission. In 1311 three more suffragans were sent to join the little group of Franciscans in China. Two years later a bishopric dependent on Cambaluc was created at Zayton (Ch'üan-chou), the great entrepôt in Fukien province.[128]

Of the Franciscan friars traveling on apostolic duties to India and China, none left a more complete account than Odoric of Pordenone. Little is known about the exact circumstances of his life except for what can be deduced from his narrative. Apparently he started on his wanderings between 1316 and 1318, sojourned in western India during 1321, and went via southeast Asia to China, where he arrived in 1322 and stayed for at least three years. He returned to Italy in 1330 with a petition from Peking to the pope asking that fifty missionaries be dispatched to China. Shortly before Odoric's death in 1331, he dictated his narrative to a brother of his Order. The large number of Odoric manuscripts still extant (seventy-three) testifies to the importance of his work for the diffusion of knowledge about Asia in fourteenth-century Europe. While its authenticity has frequently been questioned, modern scholars accept it as essentially reliable, even though the author himself was probably somewhat gullible in accepting at face value stories related to him by others.[129] To the end of his account he appends an affidavit testifying to its veracity.

In his excursion along the Malabar Coast, Odoric describes the cultivation of pepper and notes that in this region "is grown better ginger than anywhere else in the world." He also comments on Sumatra, Java, and Champa in his description of the voyage from India to China, although he has but little to add to Polo's discussion of these places. The "Mangi" (South China) of Marco Polo he calls "Upper India," a term that was still current as late as the seventeenth century. Here he was told there are "two thousand great cities . . . of such magnitude that neither Treviso nor Vicenza would be entitled to be numbered

---

[127] See Filliozat, *loc. cit.* (n. 89), p. 82.

[128] See Smith, *loc. cit.* (n. 117), pp. 165–71, for a brief review of "Zayton's" place in the international trade of the Far East from the tenth to the fifteenth centuries. Smith also summarizes (pp. 171–77) the results of the archeological research conducted at "Zayton" in 1954 by Professor Chuang Wei-chi. Among the stones uncovered, there are several bearing Latin inscriptions. Smith (p. 167) reports that there is the possibility that one of these is "the actual tombstone from the grave of Bishop Andrew of Perugia."

[129] Yule and Cordier, *op. cit.* (n. 46), II, 23–25. Subsequent citations are to this recension.

among them."[130] Canton is "as big as three Venices" and "indeed all Italy hath not the amount of craft that this one city hath." Zayton has a "great plenty of all things that are needful for human subsistence," and is "twice as great as Bologna." He protests that he would not dare to describe Hangchow, "the greatest city in the whole world," had he not already heard about it "at Venice from people in plenty who have been there." He observes that, like Venice, "this city is situated upon lagoons," and that its bridges are numerous. Of the Chinese mores, those that particularly impressed him were the habits of foot-binding among the women and the male custom of letting the finger-nails grow inordinately long as "a mark of gentility."

Odoric identifies the Yangtze as "the greatest river that exists in the world" being "some seven miles in width." Clearly he understood that it divided "Mangi" from Cathay. He traveled up the Yangtze and voyaged on canals to the Yellow River which "passeth through the very midst of Cathay, and doth great damage to that country when it breaks its banks, just as the Po does by Ferrara." At Lin-tsin in Shantung province he comments on the abundance of silk and its low cost. The physical size of Cambaluc and the splendor of the khan's palaces left Odoric wide-eyed in astonishment. Evidently the Franciscans were welcome at the khan's court and during his three years in Cambaluc Odoric had an opportunity to observe from close range the ceremonies of the court, the imperial method of traveling in a great procession, the efficient courier system, and the khan's hunting matches and festivals. On his departure from Cambaluc he traveled westward by overland caravan and, as earlier mentioned, was the last of the medieval travelers to place the land of Prester John in Asia, though he remarks "as regards [the Prester] not one hundredth part is true of what is told of him." Tibet he correctly places "on the confines of India proper" and remarks on a few of the unusual customs prevailing there. Second only in popularity to Marco Polo's, Odoric's book was widely circulated in the Renaissance era. Mandeville relied heavily upon Odoric's narrative in preparing his *Travels*.

By the time Odoric returned to Italy in 1330, Archbishop John of Cambaluc had been dead for two years. The Latin community in China, although it numbered several thousands at John's death, was never to enjoy such prosperity again. Andrew of Perugia, Bishop of Zayton, was apparently called to his reward before 1330. Although Pope John XXII formally appointed a successor in 1333, he seems never to have reached China and so the mission began to fail for lack of leadership. A Mongol mission of sixteen persons arrived at Avignon in 1338 to petition the pope for another legate. Under the leadership of Andrew the Frank, this Tartar embassy was probably lionized in France and Italy while awaiting the papal answer. Pope Benedict XII responded by dispatching a

---

[130] The descriptions of cities, monuments, and edifices of the medieval travelers sometimes seem highly stylized. The image of Byzantium derived from the pilgrims and crusaders perhaps established a literary convention for the treatment of the metropolis. For a discussion of this viewpoint see Olschki, *op. cit.* (n. 119), pp. 107–32.

Franciscan mission of four persons to the East under the leadership of John da Marignolli.

No complete account of Marignolli's mission has yet come to light. What we know of it has been disinterred painfully from the *Chronicle of Bohemia*, a manuscript prepared around 1355 by Friar John after his return from the East.[131] As reconstructed from numerous but scattered remarks, the story commences at Avignon in 1338. At Naples the papal envoys joined the Tartar embassy for the voyage from Italy to Constantinople and then made the long trek across the land road to Cambaluc, where they arrived in the spring of 1342. Marignolli remained in the khan's capital for three or four years, traveled southward to Zayton, and set sail in 1346 or 1347 for India. Of Zayton he wrote:

... a wondrous fine seaport and a city of incredible size, where our Minor Friars (Franciscans) have three very fine churches, passing rich and elegant; and they have a bath also and a *fondaco* (factory) which serves as a depot for all the merchants.[132]

Almost nothing is known of his voyage westward. After visiting the shrine of Thomas the Apostle on the Coromandel coast of India, his ship was apparently forced by gales to take refuge for a period in Ceylon. Eventually he made Ormuz on the Persian Gulf and by 1353 had returned to Avignon with another letter from the khan requesting more missionaries.

The missionary accounts of the Mongols and Cathay were not without their effect on contemporary scholars in Europe. Aside from the work of Vincent of Beauvais already mentioned, the *Opus maius* (*ca.* 1266) of Roger Bacon incorporated material on Asia from the account of William of Rubruquis. In this work Bacon urged the pope to undertake a complete and accurate survey of the world and insisted upon the habitability of the Southern Hemisphere. He also indicated his belief that the Indies might be reached by sailing westward. An interesting work on the geography of Asia and the history of the Mongol khans was dictated in France in 1307 by Prince Hayton, an exile from Armenia. This work was taken down at Poitiers by Nicholas Faulcon of Toul, who put it into Latin.[133] Around 1330 another work appeared called *The Book of the Estate of the Great Caan*.[134] The author, who is supposed to have been the Dominican John de Cora, was particularly impressed by the extent of the khan's domains, the size of Cathay's cities, the system of grain storage in times of abundance for use in lean years, the courier system, the use of paper money, "the greater variety of merchandize than in Rome or Paris," and the khan's tolerance of Christianity.

As far as is known, Marignolli was the last of the Franciscan papal envoys to visit China in the era of Mongol dominion. Even during his visit to Cambaluc, signs of the approaching downfall of the Tartar regime could clearly be

[131] Yule and Cordier, *op. cit.* (n. 46), III, 199–207.
[132] *Ibid.*, p. 229.
[133] For a bibliographical rundown of Hayton's work see Streit, *op. cit.* (n. 92), IV, 42–43.
[134] Yule and Cordier, *op. cit.* (n. 46), III, 89–103.

perceived. Travel along the land routes had become increasingly hazardous in the mid-fourteenth century as the Mongols found it ever more difficult to maintain control over their sprawling Asiatic empire. In Europe, too, the problems of this period were gravely intensified by the decimation caused by the Black Death of 1348. While the papacy continued until 1426 to name Bishops of Cambaluc, none of them was able to reach his see. The Franciscan *Annals* written before 1369 comment about the Asian mission: "Owing to the subsequent lack of zeal here and there on the part of those whose duty it was to promote this enterprise, it hardly made any progress."[135] Meanwhile, the overthrow of the Mongols in China in 1368 made doubly certain that the curtain between China and Europe, raised for a brief century, would be lowered once again.

The other Latin Catholic missions in Asia had also fallen upon evil days by the middle of the fourteenth century. In 1321, a French Dominican, Jordan of Severac, had sought to establish a Catholic mission on the Malabar Coast of India. This enterprise started inauspiciously, inasmuch as four of Jordan's companions were martyred at Tana on the Gulf of Cambay by Muslims. Jordan pleaded for aid in his letters from India, but it was not forthcoming. In 1329 Pope John XXII created a bishopric at Quilon for Jordan. In his *Book of Marvels* (*Mirabilia, ca.* 1340) Jordan adds significantly to the descriptions of India recounted by Marco Polo, Odoric of Pordenone, and John da Marignolli. He describes the coastal region from Sind to the Malabar frontier accurately, noting the oppressive heat, its long rainless seasons, its black, rice-eating people, and its fauna and flora. He tells also of some religious and social practices of the Hindus, describes the burial customs of the Parsis, comments on the practice of *sati*, and deplores the great freedom enjoyed by the Muslims in India. Strangely enough, his description of the Malabar Coast, which he presumably knew at first hand, and his depiction of the interior of India are not sketched with clarity or fidelity.[136] Nevertheless, his is the best and fullest account of India produced in the late Middle Ages.

From the accounts of the travelers on missions it is learned, by incidental references only, that Italian merchants, especially Genoese, were active in India and China during the first half of the fourteenth century. As early as 1224 a society had been organized in Genoa for the promotion of commerce with India.[137] The merchants themselves, except for Marco Polo, have left but few records of their activities in the East.[138] John of Monte Corvino relates that

---

[135] As quoted in P. M. D'Elia, *The Catholic Missions in China* (Shanghai, 1934), p. 30.

[136] Beazley, *op. cit.* (n. 59), III, 227–29.

[137] Pullé, *op. cit.* (n. 16), II, 65. For the foundations of Genoa's Eastern trade see E. H. Byrne, "Easterners in Genoa," *Journal of the American Oriental Society*, XXXVIII (1918), 176–87.

[138] For review of Italian merchants in the Far East from *ca.* 1250 to 1350, based in part upon records of the notarial archives of Genoa, Venice, and Lucca see R. S. Lopez, "Nuove luci sugli italiani in Estremo Oriente prima de Colombo," in *Studi colombiani* (International Meeting for Studies on Columbus, Genoa, 1951), III, 337–98. As an appendix to this article the author includes transcriptions of the relevant notarial documents.

land for his church in Cambaluc was purchased by a European merchant, Peter of Luculongo. Bishop Andrew of Zayton, in a letter of 1326, talks of "Genoese merchants" in his see. Marignolli, as noted above, observed that a factory for the Genoese traders was set up at Zayton. Friar Odoric comments on the numerous trades practiced in Canton and notes how inexpensive silk could be to merchants willing to buy directly on the China market.

Information about silk and the sources of the spices must also have been current in the mercantile world of Italy, even though contemporary commercial documents contribute but little to our understanding of the trade between East and West. The mercantile interest of Marco Polo in jewels and spices is slight, but his contemporaries on the Rialto probably had what information they needed from other merchants. Venetians must have journeyed far and wide within the Mongol domains, for Friar Odoric heard of Hangchow in Venice "from people in plenty who have been there." So far, however, study of Venetian commercial documents, many of which were destroyed over the years, has yielded little data on the infiltration of medieval Venetian traders into the regions east of Persia, Egypt, and Arabia.[139]

In the spice trade the Venetians had become a party to the Egyptian monopoly in the tenth century. Generally, however, their activities were confined to the purchase of spices in Alexandria for resale in Venice. Muslim dealers in linen and spices dominated the southern trade from Spain to India and usually viewed Christian interlopers with an eye something more than jaundiced. The commercial revolution in the Mediterranean world from the twelfth to the fourteenth centuries was accompanied in Europe by a steady increase in population and consequently by an expansion of the European market. The Crusades had helped to extend the horizons of Europe and had given the growing population of southern Europe a commercial frontier in the eastern Mediterranean region. The returned crusaders also added their names to the customer lists of those selling oriental and African commodities.

This growing demand in Europe was accompanied by increased purchasing power won from moneylending, piracy, and the looting of Muslim towns. Much of the capital so accumulated apparently was used to buy spices, raw silks, and furs from Asia. With the passage of time the prices on oriental commodities constantly mounted, since Egypt and Venice retained their tight monopoly of the spice trade. The Byzantines and the Muslims found it relatively easy, for a time, to pass on price increases to Venice, but with the later decline of earnings in western Europe the Venetians found it increasingly difficult to pass rising prices on to the ultimate consumers. Given such difficult conditions, it is not to be wondered at that the European merchants were quick to take advantage of the land routes opened by the Mongol conquests. In their drive to gain direct access to the emporiums of Asia, the Genoese apparently led the

---

[139] R. S. Lopez, "European Merchants in the Medieval Indies," *Journal of Economic History*, III (1943), 164–65.

way, for they, unlike the Venetians, had everything to gain by outflanking the monopolistic intermediaries.

Practically all the Christian missionaries, as well as the Arab traveler, Ibn Batuta, agree that Genoese merchants were active in India and China during the first half of the fourteenth century, Boccaccio refers to the Genoese as the best witnesses to consult in verifying one of his stories that allegedly happened in China. One would suppose therefore that the thousands of Genoese commercial documents for this period still extant might yield valuable confirmatory information on Eastern trade. Such is not the case. From the Genoese, posterity has not received a single general account of the trade and very few incidental records. The silence of the Genoese sources may perhaps be accounted for by the desire of the merchants to keep their business secrets to themselves or even by the traditional taciturnity of the Genoese.[140]

The only general account of the trade extant is that of the Florentine merchant, Francesco Balducci Pegolotti. Little is known of the author except that he was a factor for the Bardi banking house and that he wrote a manuscript between 1310 and 1340, the years of his active business carreer, called "La practica della mercatura" ("The Practice of Commerce"). Although Pegolotti traveled widely in Europe, he apparently had no personal experience east of the Levant. His account is therefore not a personal document but rather a compilation of data from various sources designed as a handbook for the practicing merchant. For the instruction of the itinerant trader he describes one of the routes that could be followed across Asia from the Levant to Peking. "The road . . . is perfectly safe, whether by day or by night, according to what the merchants say who have used it."[141] He gives the stages of the journey, the necessary equipment for the caravan, and the merchandise to carry for sale in China. For example, "Anyone from Genoa or from Venice wishing . . . to make the journey to Cathay should carry linens with him."[142] Pegolotti even gives the prices in Genoese currency that the merchant might expect to pay for silk in China. He also appends a list of 288 spices and drugs commonly traded in Europe, most of which came originally from the East.[143]

For Pegolotti the most important produce of China was silk. As already indicated, China had continued to export silk to Europe, even after sericulture had been introduced to the Mediterranean countries through Byzantium.[144]

[140] *Ibid.*, pp. 166–68. See also Lopez's more detailed work, *Storia delle colonie Genovesi nel Mediterraneo* (Bologna, 1938). Also compare the Portuguese policy of secrecy on the spice trade. See below, pp. 151–54.

[141] Yule and Cordier, *op. cit.* (n. 46), III, 152.

[142] *Ibid.*, p. 154.

[143] R. S. Lopez and I. W. Raymond, *Medieval Trade in the Mediterranean World* (New York, 1955), pp. 108–14.

[144] R. S. Lopez, "China Silk in Europe in the Yüan Period," *Journal of the American Oriental Society*, LXXXI (1952), 72–73. On Genoa see R. di Tucci, "Lineamenti storici dell'industria serica Genovese," *Atti della Società Ligure di Storia patria*, LXVIII (1948), 22–24. See especially the detailed account of E. Sabbe, "L'importation des tissus orientaux en Europe occidentale en Haut Moyen Age (IXe et Xe siècles)," *Revue belge de philologie et d'histoire*, XIV (1935), 811–48, 1261–88.

The thriving industries of the Levant, Sicily, and Spain evidently were not able to fulfil the demand for raw silk in Constantinople and the Latin countries. The silk industry of northern Italy also expanded rapidly in the era that followed. In Florence the *Arte di* Seta began functioning in 1193 and within the city it soon rivaled the *Arte di Lana* in wealth and prestige.[145] By the thirteenth century Lucca had become Europe's greatest silk production center, with Genoa as its principal port. While China silk probably had been relayed to the Italian merchants through Muslim intermediaries before, the minute books of the Genoese notaries record the appearance of Chinese raw silk (*seta catuya*) for the first time in January, 1257. The Genoese merchants also sold China silks at the fairs of France as well as on the market of Lucca. Among the wares delivered by the Frescobaldi at the port of London in 1304 was a bale of "silk called Cathewy."[146]

Chinese raw silk brought a lower price in European markets than similar products from Persia. Pegolotti observed that the silk from Cathay was usually worn from travel and handling upon arrival in Florence. Evidently the business was nonetheless profitable because of the low purchase price of silk in China. The Genoese merchants obviously found that it paid them to make the long journey, with all of its risks, to carry back raw silk that brought three times its purchase price when sold in Italy. Perhaps the availability of silk in unlimited quantity as well as hopes for future business also encouraged the Genoese to persist in their efforts to control the direct trade in raw silk between China and Europe in the era of the "Mongol peace." The consumption of silk certainly increased throughout the period of the commercial revolution (twelfth to fourteenth centuries) and the manufacture of silk materials spread in the fourteenth century from Lucca to Genoa and Bologna. Clearly the Genoese merchants hoped to control China's unlimited quantities of silk to feed the expanding industry of northern Italy as it sought to make silk products available to more than the few wealthy lay and ecclesiastic purchasers who had previously been its only consumers.[147] Chinese patterned silks, brocades, and damasks were also purchased in Europe and a few from this period are still preserved in European churches and museums. Chinese motifs in textiles designed in Europe reinforce the other examples of technological and artistic borrowings of the late Middle Ages.[148] But the expulsion of the Mongols from China in 1368 brought the direct trade to an end and consequently reduced the possibility of additional borrowing.

As a consequence both of the prosperity of Europe in the era of the commercial revolution and of the disturbances attending the decline of Mongol

[145] G. R. B. Richards, *Florentine Merchants in the Age of the Medici* (Cambridge, 1932), p. 44.

[146] Lopez, *loc. cit.* (n. 144), p. 74.

[147] *Ibid.*, pp. 75–76.

[148] For an example of a Chinese design in European ornamentation other than in textiles see Lewis Einstein, "A Chinese Design in St. Mark's at Venice," *Revue archéologique*, Ser. V, Vol. XXIV (1926), 28–31. See also below, pp. 71–74 for more details on art.

power in Asia, slavery in Italy grew rapidly in the fourteenth century. Marco Polo brought his slave, Peter the Tartar, back to Venice and in 1328 Peter was granted citizenship. The decimation caused by the Black Death of 1348, supposed by one contemporary to have been "brought back from China in bales of silk by Genoese merchants returning to Caffa"[149] produced a need for additional labor in Europe. Prosperous nobles and merchants increasingly found it necessary or fashionable to add "Tartar" slaves to their expanding households. In 1363 the priors of Florence permitted "the unlimited importation of foreign slaves of either sex—provided only that they were infidels not Christians."[150] The slaves sold to Venetian and Genoese merchants were of many different peoples and the records indicate that at least one was of Chinese background.[151] Between 1366 and 1397 over two hundred Tartars were sold in the slave market of Florence. Slaves, like foreign animals, were added to the courts of the more affluent princes to provide exotic atmosphere. As will be seen later, Italian artists depicted the foreign slaves in their paintings and frescoes. It would be hard to claim, however, that the slaves from distant places contributed directly to Europe's information about Asia, though intelligent people may have been piqued by curiosity to inquire about the lands of their origin.

The long century of the "Mongol peace" brought Europe and eastern Asia into closer touch than ever before. Europeans for the first time on record traversed the Eurasiatic continent to the Pacific. Some of them sailed all the way from China to Persia through the eastern seas and the Indian Ocean. The first hand observations of missionaries and merchants helped to dispel the myths about Prester John, the uninhabitability of the tropical and equatorial regions, and some of the misinformation previously current about the sources of spices and the production of silk. Other myths and legends remained very much alive and were even substantiated by supposed direct observation. The realm of Prester John was shifted to Africa, Gog and Magog were placed in eastern Siberia, and the terrestrial Paradise was moved to India. For Europe in the fourteenth century, Cathay was of greater moment than India, both as a mission field and as a center of commerce. This was true primarily because the Muslims were not so important there either as potential religious enemies or as commercial competitors.[152] And perhaps India remained more fabulous to Europeans than Cathay because more was known about the life and peoples of eastern Asia. The cities of Cathay, its crafts, and its material wealth excited great curiosity and skepticism. While myth and disbelief continued to cloud Europe's view of the East, the contacts established in the period of relative freedom of communication added a dimension of reality to the European image which

---

[149] As quoted in I. Origo, "The Domestic Enemy," *Speculum*, XXX (1955), 324.
[150] *Ibid.*, pp. 324–25.
[151] *Ibid.*, p. 329.
[152] Cf. the way in which the Portuguese and the Jesuits of the sixteenth century sought to work in lands where the Muslims were not firmly entrenched.

previously had been wanting. While some of this factual knowledge was to be forgotten or obscured by myth again in the following century, the revelation of Cathay in the late medieval period was to provide subsequent generations with materials for speculation and with a stimulus to outflank the Muslim control of the sea and land routes to southern Asia and China.

CHAPTER II

The Renaissance
before the Great Discoveries

The break in Europe's relations with Asia cannot be attributed simply to the decline of the Mongols, the rise of the Ming, and the expansion of the Muslims. In Europe itself, the mid-fourteenth century was catastrophic. The epidemic of the Black Death decimated crowded urban areas, estimates of deaths varying from 35 to 65 per cent of the total population. Destruction and dislocations attending the Hundred Years' War and the civil wars in Castile and southern Italy accelerated the rapid economic decline of western Europe and retarded its efforts to carry forward a more forceful policy in the Levant. And, in this connection, it should be remembered that the general economic rise of the West was really something new, for the Orient had remained dominant, even in Roman times, in its trade contacts with the West. Not until the nineteenth century would Europe be able to claim economic and political primacy in its relations with Asia.[1]

The intermediary states of the Near East had also suffered from the Mongol invasions and from the depredations of the Turks. To make up for its losses Egypt increasingly sought to exact higher tribute from trade.[2] In 1428 the Mameluke sultan, in an effort to recoup his fortunes, created a state monopoly of the export of pepper which raised its price in Alexandria by more than 60 per cent. The decision to establish a fixed price for pepper was accompanied by other monopolistic measures that increasingly became a burden to the Venetian merchants trading at Alexandria. Because of the weakened state of the

[1] See the excellent review article by Robert S. Lopez, "Les influences orientales et l'éveil économique de l'Occident," *Journal of World History*, I (1953–54), 594.

[2] For an example of the multiple exactions imposed by Egypt upon the trade see R. S. Whiteway, *The Rise of Portuguese Power in Asia* (London, 1899), pp. 7–8.

European economy, it apparently was not possible for the Venetians to pass on these new exactions to the ultimate consumer. While pepper prices constantly mounted in Europe, the profits of the Venetians correspondingly declined. The Venetians and other Italians suffered further serious reversals of fortune when the Turkish capture of Constantinople in 1453 brought an end to the extraordinary privileges they had earlier enjoyed in Byzantium and cut them off from direct access to their Black Sea colonies.

Such losses in the Levant left the Italians more dependent than ever upon trade at Alexandria and thereby gave the sultan an even better opportunity to tighten the vise of exaction. When (*ca.* 1480) the Venetians sought to boycott the pepper market at Alexandria, the sultan threatened the lives of their factors and the safety of their establishments. Caught in this trap, the Venetians and other Europeans sought desperately to break or to outflank the Muslim monopoly. While the Portuguese looked for a route around Africa, the Italians vainly tried through diplomatic negotiation and war to break the stranglehold of Egypt and the Turks. From the occasional merchant who managed to slip into the East through the Muslim blockade, the Italians and Portuguese sought information on trade routes, entrepôts, and prices as part of a program that they hoped might produce some concrete means for dealing with the monopolists.

I

TRADE, EXPLORATION, AND DIPLOMACY

The spice trade was not the sole economic motive for the activities of the Europeans, but it was the most universal one. Gold, ivory, slaves, and malagueta pepper from nearby Africa had long been sold by Muslim traders at high prices to the European merchants doing business in the Mediterranean region. The gold from Africa was then frequently used by the Europeans to pay for oriental imports. In this way, much of the precious metal available in the West had been steadily drained toward the East over a long period before 1500. And in the late Middle Ages and Renaissance, the European powers contested among themselves for control of the Mediterranean trade in gold and spices, as they would continue to do for a full century after the return of Vasco da Gama.

The rise of Catalonia in the fourteenth century as a Mediterranean commercial power presented a threat to the primacy of Venice and Genoa in the trade with North Africa. Employing Arab and Jewish agents of their own, the Catalans sought first of all to bypass the European monopolists. When they found that Egypt and Venice acted together in defense of their common interests in the monopoly, the Catalans sought, as the Genoese had earlier, to outflank North Africa by sailing through the Pillars of Hercules and southward down the African coast. Neither the Genoese attempt of the thirteenth century nor the

Catalan effort of the fourteenth was successful. The outflanking of the Muslim area of trade control was left for the Portuguese of the fifteenth century to accomplish. [3]

Prince Henry the Navigator (1394–1460) was the guiding genius in the systematic and continuous exploration of the African west coast launched by the Portuguese in the early fifteenth century. In no way does it detract from the magnitude of Henry's achievements to remark that his discoveries were in many ways the logical consequences of Portugal's geography and history. Rugged mountains, barren stretches of land, and the river barriers which lie between it and the rest of the Iberian Peninsula enabled Portugal to develop an independent history beginning in 1095. Most of Portugal's subsequent history has actually been enacted along the five-hundred miles of its coastline and in the narrow hinterland that helps to support its port cities. Expansion on land has been blocked to Portugal ever since the consolidation of the other Iberian states under Castile. Forced to face the sea, Portugal has concentrated on the conquest of it and on association with maritime states like Great Britain and Brazil.

Another theme in Portugal's early history was the crusade against the Moors. From the early years the Moors were continually driven southward until Lisbon and the fertile Tagus Valley were finally won in 1147. The rulers of Portugal had meanwhile constantly to guard their isolated kingdom against attack from Leon or Castile. In their struggles against both the Moors and the Spanish, the Portuguese were aided from time to time by crusaders from northern Europe. These early crusading relations with the maritime powers of the Atlantic were soon transmuted into economic ties, as for example in the commercial treaty of 1294 with England. These commercial ties were soon extended by the conclusion of marriage and military relations, as Portugal sought outside support in its efforts to remain independent and to unify itself politically.

Portugal's bonds with England were strengthened in 1385–86 by the military defeat of the Castilians with English aid and by the conclusion of a treaty sealed by a marriage alliance between John of Avis and Philippa of Lancaster. The third son of this marriage was Prince Henry, a boy who saw the Spanish wars finally end in the peace of 1411 and who himself was soon caught up in the enthusiasm for carrying the war against the Moors into Africa.

Like most such enterprises, the fifteenth-century Portuguese crusade against the Moors was inspired by a mixture of religious and commercial motives, and, perhaps, a desire for adventure and conquest. Some of the early chroniclers suggest that the southward military drive was undertaken to provide gainful employment for those who had been occupied for most of their lives in frontier

[3] On Portugal see Damião Peres and Elentério Cerdeira, *História de Portugal* (Barcelos, 1931), Vol. III; also Charles E. Nowell, *A History of Portugal* (New York, 1952); H. V. Livermore, *A History of Portugal* (Cambridge, 1947). For a convenient collection of documents of the Portuguese discoveries to 1460 see Vittorino Magalhães Godinho, *Documentos sobre a expansão portuguesa* (3 vols.; Lisbon, 1945–46).

raids against Spain.[4] The first Portuguese military success in Africa was the capture of the fortress and trading center of Ceuta in 1415. Although only twenty-one years old at this time, Prince Henry soon took over the leadership of the Portuguese effort to outflank the Muslims and gain direct access to the gold of Timbuktu.

For his Atlantic and African explorations, Prince Henry established in 1419 a headquarters in the Algarve at Sagres, on the southern tip of Portugal, and gradually developed the neighboring port of Lagos as his harbor. From Lagos, Henry then regularly sent out small expeditions into the Atlantic and down the African coast. Earlier voyagers from Genoa and Catalonia had touched the Atlantic islands before and may even have sailed south of Cape Bojador on the African coast. So it was not long before the Canary Islands were rediscovered; by 1420 the Madeira Islands were located and opened to settlement; and between 1427 and 1432 even the distant Azores were gradually being uncovered. But progress southward along the African coast was not so swift. The first Portuguese explorers hesitated for some time before daring to brave the treacherous currents and reefs of Cape Bojador, about 1,000 miles south of Lagos. Finally, in 1434, Gil Eannes sailed around Bojador and two years later the Portuguese had landed on the African continent south of the area of Muslim control.

The achievements of Henry's captains did not come alone from their personal courage and determination. Behind them they had the directing force of the prince himself, the wealth and prestige of the Order of Christ,[5] and the best information and instruments available. At Sagres, Henry had constructed a special site for his exploration enterprise that came to include an observatory, a chapel, and an academy. The group of international specialists which he gathered here had at their command most of the geographical and astronomical knowledge that could be found in books, charts, and correspondence. Much of the scholarly stimulus behind the effort appears to have come from Prince Pedro, Henry's older brother, who had collected books and charts while traveling about Europe (1425–28).[6] The traditionally close ties between Portugal and Florence also enabled the Portuguese to hear news of India, Cathay, and Tartary through its representatives at the ecclesiastical Council of Ferrara-Florence (1438–41).[7]

---

[4] See H. V. Livermore, "Portuguese History," in H. V. Livermore (ed.), *Portugal and Brazil: An Introduction* (Oxford, 1953), p. 59.

[5] Prince Henry was apostolic administrator of the Order of Christ, the Portuguese version of the crusading Knights Templar. He acquired this office in 1420 and with it undoubtedly went an increase in his personal independence and the right to communicate directly with Rome on matters concerning the Order.

[6] See Charles E. Nowell, "Prince Henry the Navigator and His Brother Dom Pedro," *Hispanic American Historical Review*, XXVIII (1948), 62–67. Pedro got as far east as Hungary but apparently did not make a pilgrimage to the Holy Land. In his travels to eastern Europe he almost certainly learned about the Tartars and Indians. In Venice he acquired a manuscript of Marco Polo. For his itinerary see Francis M. Rogers, *The Travels of the Infante Dom Pedro* (Cambridge, Mass., 1961), chap. iii.

[7] Rogers, *op. cit.* (n. 6), pp. 65–66.

Martyrdom of the Franciscans at Ceuta, by Ambrogio Lorenzetti, 1332(?).
San Francesco, Siena.

Ecclesia militans, by Andrea da Firenze, *ca.* 1365. Spanish Chapel, S. Maria Novella, Florence.

Parement de Narbonne, silk altar hanging, *ca.* 1375. Louvre, Paris.

Winged creatures, from an illustration in *Heures de Rohan*, *ca.* 1420. Bibliothèque nationale (Lat. 9471, fol. 159).

Madonna in a mandorla of exotic angels, by Gentile da Fabriano, *ca.* 1420. Uffizi, Florence.

Adoration of the Magi, by Gentile da Fabriano, *ca.* 1423. Uffizi, Florence.

Sketch of a Mongol archer, by Antonio Pisanello, *ca.* 1440. Louvre, Paris.

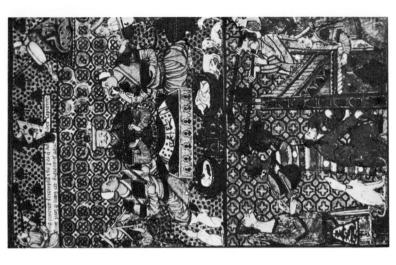

Illuminated Titus Livius manuscript of Charles V, ca. 1370. Bibliothèque Sainte Geneviève, Paris (777, fol. 7).

Gluttony. Treatise on the Vices, attributed to the "Monk of Hyeres," a Genoese miniaturist of the Cybo family, ca. 1400. British Museum (Add. MS. 27695, fol. 13).

Ptolemy's map of Asia. Adapted from a drawing in E. H. Bunbury, *A History of Ancient Geography* (2d ed.; London, 1883).

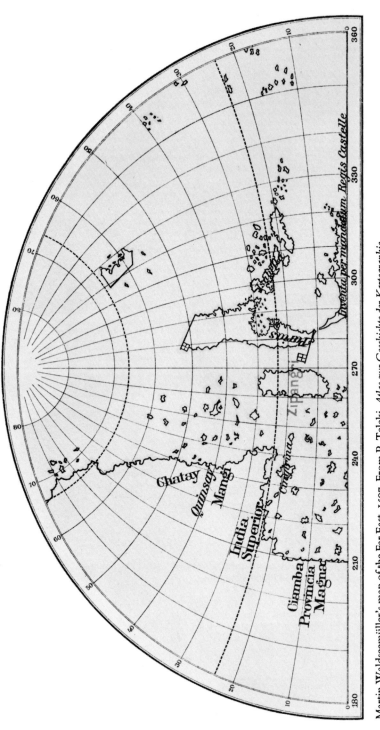

Martin Waldseemüller's map of the Far East, 1507. From P. Teleki, *Atlas zur Geschichte der Kartographie der Japanischen Inseln* (Budapest, 1909).

In addition to the information gathered in Europe, the specialists at Sagres were able to avail themselves of the observations brought back from the overseas voyages, as Henry sought systematically to collect accurate records of winds, tides, and sailing directions. His aides also concentrated on problems of ship design in an effort to adapt their vessels, originally intended for travel along the coasts or inland seas, to sailing on the open ocean. New navigational instruments had also to be developed, for the inadequacies of the old compass and sextant were soon obvious, particularly in the determination of latitude. Perhaps most important of all, however, was the zeal and determination with which Henry's group strove to overcome what must have seemed at the beginning an overwhelming number of insoluble problems.

Direct trade with Africa south of the Sahara was meanwhile inaugurated in 1441 when Henry's captains brought back to Lagos a few slaves from the region around the Rio de Oro. Henry was granted a complete monopoly of this trade and was exempted by the new regent, the interested Dom Pedro (1439-47), from paying any part of his profits to the crown. From this time forward the prospect of a lucrative trade in slaves and gold aroused general interest in Portugal about activities at Sagres and Lagos. Almost a thousand slaves were brought back to Portugal in the next five years. Meanwhile, Henry apparently expanded his business activities to find more capital and income for the voyages of exploration. In 1443, a private merchant group formed a company which received a monopoly on coral fishing and in 1456 another such syndicate obtained a cork monopoly.[8] In both these groups Italian merchant interests were represented.

Agents of Venice and the other trading cities of Italy hurried to Lagos in the mid-fifteenth century to learn the meaning of the new discoveries for European trade.[9] Interest in African commerce was stirred further by the knowledge that slaves numbering in the thousands were sold on the Lagos market in the first five years of the trade, by the rounding of Cape Verde in 1445, and by the establishment in 1448 of the African fort and trading center of Arguim, just south of Cape Blanco. The search for slaves, the gold country, and a route to

---

[8] See Richard Konetzke, "Entrepreneurial Activities of Spanish and Portuguese Noblemen," *Explorations in Entrepreneurial History*, VI (1953), 116–18.

[9] See Tito Augusto de Carvalho, *As companhias portuguesas de colonização* (Lisbon, 1902), chap. ii. The real story on foreign participation in Portuguese trade and on the growth of trading companies in the time of Prince Henry has been obscured by a shortage of documentary material and by scholarly divisions of opinion. In the *Vierteljahrschrift für Sozial- und Wirtschaftsgeschichte* for 1931 (XXIV, 282–98) and for 1932 (XXV, 209–50), M. A. Hedwig Fitzler published, respectively, her "Überblick über die portugiesischen Überseehandelsgesellschaften des 15.–18. Jahrhunderts" and her "Portugiesische Handelsgesellschaften des 15. und beginnenden 16. Jahrhunderts." Much of her data and many of her citations, allegedly based on Portuguese archival materials, have been challenged. See Virginia Rau and B. W. Diffie, "Alleged Fifteenth-Century Portuguese Joint-Stock Companies and the Articles of Dr. Fitzler," *Bulletin of the Institute of Historical Research* (London), XXVI (1953), 181–99. For a somewhat milder indictment of Dr. Fitzler and for a modification of the Rau-Diffie assertions about the meaning of the word "company" see Charles Verlinden, "La colonie italienne de Lisbonne et le développement de l'économie metropolitaine et coloniale portugaise," in *Studi in onore di Armando Sapori* (Milan, 1957), pp. 617–28.

Prester John led the Portuguese to explore the rivers and hinterlands of Africa and for a time halted their progress southward. The attention of the rest of Europe was meanwhile being temporarily shifted away from the African discoveries by a series of momentous internal happenings.

The end of the Hundred Years' War, the Turkish conquest of Constantinople, and the invention of printing were mid-century events which had both immediate and long-term effects. At the very time when Europe itself was developing closer internal ties and improved means of communication, the last of the older ties with Asia and the Muslim world were severed—or radically changed. Not only were trade and intercourse severely limited at Constantinople, but relations between Muslim and Christian also worsened because of the determined efforts of the rulers of Castile to drive the last remnants of the Moorish community from Spain. In terms of contacts with the outside world, Europe was perhaps more isolated in the second half of the fifteenth century than it had been since before the Crusades. Nor was the barrier of isolation to be cracked until the opening of the sea route, despite the best efforts of the Italian cities, particularly Venice, to reopen the older connections. [10]

Little progress was made in the period immediately after mid-century in the exploration of Africa. Henry's captains ventured into the interior along the Senegal and Gambia rivers, but after the prince's death in 1460, King Afonso took only a mild interest in further exploration. His main concern was in receiving assured revenues from the exploitation of that part of Africa already discovered. In 1469, the king leased the whole Guinea Coast to a concessionaire, Fernão Gomes, a wealthy Lisbon merchant, on condition that he pay a substantial yearly rental to the crown and explore southward at least one hundred leagues each year. During the five years of his contract, Gomes' captains rounded the great bend of Africa and proceeded eastward and then southward across the equator almost to the mouth of the Congo River. Trade also received stimulus with the discovery of the Gold Coast and the Ivory Coast, and with the uncovering of the main sources of malagueta pepper.

The management of the overseas monopoly was apparently beyond the capacities of a private individual. Foreigners from Europe soon began to appear in the area of the Portuguese discoveries in spite of the fact that the government and its concessionaire tried to preserve their monopoly and to suppress news about the discoveries. [11] In 1474, the king transferred the concession from Gomes to Prince John, the heir apparent. Occupied by problems at home and by war with Castile, John accomplished little toward the further exploration of Africa until he became king in 1481.

[10] A. H. Lybyer, "The Ottoman Turks and the Routes of Oriental Trade," *English Historical Review*, XXX (1915), 577–88, argues convincingly that the Turks were willing and eager to trade. Nevertheless, the disruptions and changes attending the rise of the Ottomans helped to dislocate the older system at a critical time.

[11] See below, pp. 151–54.

In the meantime war had broken out on the Iberian Peninsula in 1475 over the question of the Castilian succession. This issue was complicated by conflicting claims over the discoveries, and especially over the Canary Islands, which the Spanish had started colonizing in 1402. Castile also looked with envy upon the advances of the Portuguese in Africa. By the Treaty of Alcáçovas of 1479, King Afonso renounced his claim to the kingship of Leon, and Portugal relinquished all claim to the Canary Islands. In return, Ferdinand and Isabella promised "never to disturb the King and Prince of Portugal and their heirs in their possession or quasi-possession . . . in Guinea . . . or in any other islands, coasts, or lands, discovered or to be discovered, found or to be found. . . ." While this was later interpreted to mean that Castile had made a blanket concession of the whole overseas world to Portugal, the intent of this clause almost certainly was to give Portugal carte blanche only in Africa. Such a renunciation in Portugal's favor was sanctioned, as were earlier Portuguese claims, by papal bull. The purpose of the *Aeterni regis* of 1481, for which both Castile and Portugal appealed to the papacy, was to make certain that the church and the European world at large would clearly understand and perhaps help to maintain the terms of the treaty.[12]

From the viewpoint of the discoveries, the beginning of the reign of King John II in 1481 opened the golden century of expansion. It found Portugal ready to launch a new and final drive in its lengthy project of rounding the tip of Africa, the necessary first step on the road to India. Although initially troubled by an anarchical nobility, King John dealt firmly with their uprisings, even beheading the mighty Duke of Braganza in 1483. Once domestic problems were brought under control, the king was able to proceed at a faster pace with his projects of trade and exploration in Africa. The building of São George da Mina in 1482 as fort, mart, and first white settlement on the Gold Coast, was followed by a series of voyages that culminated in Bartolomeu Dias' epoch-making trip around the Cape of Good Hope in 1487. In the course of these voyages the crown tightened its hold upon the whole enterprise of trade and exploration by systematically wiping out interlopers, both Portuguese and foreign; by throwing the resources and credit of the royal treasury behind the project; by accumulating more detailed information on geography, navigation, and trade; by establishing special committees at Lisbon to assess the new information and to co-ordinate it; and by imposing a strict policy of secrecy on all aspects of the undertaking.[13]

It was in this atmosphere that Christopher Columbus proposed to King John in 1483–84 his project of sailing westward. Columbus' overtures were rejected

---

[12] Texts of the various pertinent treaties and bulls in Vol. I of F. G. Davenport (ed.), *European Treaties Bearing on the History of the United States* (Washington D.C., 1917). For a discussion of the role of papal authority and for the conditions established by the treaty see G. E. Nunn, *The Diplomacy Concerning the Discovery of America* (Jenkintown, Pa., 1948).

[13] Details in John W. Blake, *Europeans in West Africa* (London: Hakluyt Society, 1942), I, 3–63. On the policy of secrecy see below, pp. 151–54.

by the king, perhaps because the Portuguese, as some authorities now claim, had already discovered America. [14] Without entering into the question of the pre-Columbian discovery of America, it can easily be argued that the Portuguese court was too much involved in the African enterprise to sponsor a westward voyage whose expense would be high and whose outcome unpredictable. Africa was already a paying proposition and even in 1483 the prospects of further revelations and greater successes were excellent. When Columbus again went to Lisbon, in time to see the triumphant return of Dias in 1488, his hopes of Portuguese support for his westward voyage suffered a final blow.

The question that has helped to stimulate certain aspects of the Columbus controversy relates to the lapse of ten years between the return of Dias and the sailing of Vasco da Gama. Perhaps this hiatus can most readily be explained by the illness of the king, lasting from 1490 to his death in 1495, by the military expeditions of Portugal in Morocco, by the long delay in receiving news from Pero da Covilhã[15] on the routes and marts of India and East Africa, and by the difficulties of outfitting and manning a fleet for such a dangerous and lengthy adventure. Divided counsels within Portugal probably also contributed to the delay, since most of the people concerned very likely suspected that the establishment of a direct sea route to India would involve the Portuguese nation in international complications of a type not previously experienced.

Such international complications were not long in coming. The success of Columbus' first voyage westward revived the hostility between Portugal and Castile that the Portuguese, at least, believed they had settled by the Treaty of Alcáçovas. In 1493, when Columbus landed in Lisbon and announced the success of his first voyage, King John laid claim to his discoveries, presumed to be islands off the eastern coast of Asia, under the terms of the Treaty of Alcáçovas and the papal bull *Aeterni regis*. In the ensuing dispute, Castile contended that, although it had relinquished all rights south of Cape Bojador in the agreement concluded thirteen years before, it had in no sense yielded all rights in the Atlantic. To reinforce their claims, Ferdinand and Isabella appealed to Pope Alexander in Rome. Their Catholic Majesties knew that the pope would be inclined in their favor, since he was a Spaniard and well aware of Castile's strength in Italian and ecclesiastical affairs. Without consulting Portugal, the Borgia pope published four bulls in 1493, within a period of several months, the materials for which had been furnished him through the Castilian envoy in Rome. The last of these revoked all earlier papal grants in Portugal's favor

[14] For a summary discussion of this much disputed question see S. E. Morison, *Portuguese Voyages to America in the Fifteenth Century* (Cambridge, Mass., 1945), and for a summary of the Columbus question consult Charles E. Nowell, "The Columbus Question," *American Historical Review*, XLIV (1939), 802–22; see also Nowell, "The Rejection of Columbus by John of Portugal," *University of Michigan Historical Essays* (Ann Arbor, 1937), pp. 25–44.

[15] For an account of this expedition and the question of the report see below, p. 64.

and recognized Castile's dominion over all territories not already effectively occupied by a Christian power.[16] Portugal was thus to be limited to Africa and her Atlantic possessions at a time when Lisbon was excited about the prospect of reaching India by the sea route.

Of primary concern in the direct negotiations between Castile and Portugal that followed were their conflicting claims to Asia. Despite the papal bulls, the rulers of Castile clearly recognized the superiority of Portuguese naval power in the Atlantic and realized that an unappeased Portugal might readily block the route from Cadiz westward. The decision of King John in 1493 to prepare a fleet for crossing the Atlantic also caused alarm in Castile. The position of Castile was further weakened by the growing power of France, which threatened her position in the western Mediterranean and Italy. Lisbon, on the other hand, was not anxious for a renewal of war with Castile, for after 1492 the Castilians were no longer distracted by problems with the Jews, Moors, and Granada, and were in a position to act more effectively in the looming contest with Portugal.

It was therefore in an atmosphere of mutual desire for peace that a series of compromises was worked out at Tordesillas in June, 1494.[17] Both sides accepted the principle of demarcation, which was defined in greater detail than it had been in the papal bulls. The circular line of division was to extend from pole to pole and to pass through a point 370 leagues west of the Cape Verde Islands. The ships of Castile were granted the right to sail through Portuguese seas by the course that would take them most directly to their destination. But the Portuguese were not given the right to sail west of the demarcation line. Geographical knowledge being uncertain, and in process of being radically revised, the interested parties held differing concepts of the world and particularly of the possibility of sailing westward to India.[18] Evidently the Portuguese held the view, probably derived from Pierre d'Ailly, that a sea road across the Atlantic and then southward around eastern Asia to India was not possible and that land travel across Asia to the marts of India was impractical. By insisting that the demarcation line be moved westward, the Portuguese (assuming that they did not know of Brazil), apparently believed that they were giving water to Castile in return for a larger portion of Asia. On their side, the Castilians probably believed that Columbus had reached, or was close to reaching, the fabled "gold land" of "Cipangu" (Japan) on which Marco Polo had remarked, and that from there they might sail southward, even as the Venetian traveler had, around southwestern Asia to India.

In 1494 neither side had any idea that Columbus had discovered a New World,

[16] See Hermann Vanderlinden, "Alexander VI and the Demarcation of the Maritime and Colonial Dominions of Spain and Portugal, 1493–94," *American Historical Review*, XXII (1916), 18–19.

[17] Details in C. E. Nowell, "The Treaty of Tordesillas and the Diplomatic Background of American History," in *Greater America: Essays in Honor of Herbert Eugene Bolton*, ed. A. Odgen and E. Sluiter (Berkeley, 1945), pp. 1–18.

[18] Nunn, *op. cit.* (n. 12), pp. 12–13.

and both sides, under the influence of the Ptolemaic tradition,[19] overestimated the eastward extension of Asia and underestimated the circumference of the globe. But from Portugal's viewpoint the treaties of 1494 guaranteed that Castile would not interfere with her plans for sending an expedition around Africa to India. Papal confirmation for the shift in the demarcation line was sought immediately, but the arrangements of Tordesillas did not receive Rome's approval until 1506.

The northern European powers bordering the Atlantic Ocean studiously ignored this division of the overseas world between the Iberian powers. For example, the Cabots sailed from England to the Americas in 1497 and 1499 and colonization projects were designed in the years immediately following without any apparent regard for the exclusive claims of the Spanish and Portuguese. The Cabots, like Columbus on his first voyage, clearly believed that they had uncovered the eastern shores of Cathay.[20] King Henry VII evidently was convinced that in 1498 he had won a part of Asia. The chroniclers of these events, primarily Italian merchants doing business in London, heralded the achievements of the Bristol mariners as great triumphs. At no time do they mention the fact that these voyages violated the intent of the bulls of 1493. The English king, like his French contemporary, was not disposed to recognize the papacy's right to sanction the division of the world. The northern powers, even those which remained Catholic, continued throughout the sixteenth century to deny the right of the papacy to adjudicate overseas claims.

Even before the departure of John Cabot for America, Columbus and his sponsors had become disillusioned about reaching Asia by sailing westward. When Columbus returned in the summer of 1496 from his second voyage without positive proof that he had reached Asia, the court of Castile was bathed in gloom. Meanwhile, in Lisbon, King John had died in 1495 and had been replaced by King Manuel I, dubbed "the Fortunate." One of the first acts of Manuel's reign was to convoke his council in December, 1495, for a series of meetings to decide whether or not the long-delayed expedition to India should be sent out.[21] Those who favored pursuing the enterprise were encouraged by the determination of the new king to throw the full power of the state and its treasury into the project. The majority of the king's advisers warned of the vast expenditures that would be required and expressed their fear that profound international complications might result. While many of their fears were borne out by later events, the advocates of the proposal to send out an expedition won the day. So Portugal was launched on an adventure that was to alter its entire history as well as that of western Europe and the rest of the world.

---

[19] Cf. below, pp. 67–69.

[20] J. A. Williamson, *Maritime Enterprise* (Oxford, 1913), pp. 54–58.

[21] The chronicler of the reign of Manuel, Damião de Góis, tells of these meetings. See the translation from his work cited in H. Hart, *Sea Road to the Indies* (New York, 1950), pp. 84–85.

2

TRAVEL ACCOUNTS OF INDIA

While the Portuguese prepared for the conquest of the sea route to India, Europeans still occasionally made their way to India along the old routes. Some of them lived to record their experiences for their contemporaries and posterity. But in the century and a half between the end of the Mongol sway over Eurasia and the circumnavigation of Africa, no European appears to have penetrated to Cathay. If merchants or sailors did somehow manage the journey to eastern Asia, no undisputed accounts of their travels are known to us today. Reports of travel during this period refer only to India and the East Indies, and are generally short and not substantially different from those produced earlier. Still, the Renaissance accounts do corroborate and supplement the stories of the older travelers, and they helped to keep alive the revelation of the East which reached Europe during the Mongol era.

An example of Europe's state of knowledge about Asia in the mid-fourteenth century is provided by the *Book of Knowledge of All the Kingdoms, Lands and Lordships in the World* written by a Spanish Franciscan. Whether the good friar was actually a traveler or merely a compiler is of little moment for our purposes.[22] He claims to have traveled to India, the East Indies, Cathay, and Tartary. His remarks on these distant lands combine, at times bewilderingly, the factual with the fanciful. He is factually accurate, though vague, about the sea east of China, describing it as "full of reefs and islands, and to the eastward there is no news of any lands, only waters as in the western sea." In his description of Gog and Magog he appears to combine myth with rumor and claims to have "lived for some time in that castle of Magot." He shows specific knowledge of "two certain roads to Catayo," and remarks of Tartary that it is a land "entirely inhabited by tribes with flocks." While the friar occasionally takes liberties with the facts, his knowledge of geography, his accurate naming of cities, and his information on the land and sea routes show a respect for the concrete particulars that was not always characteristic of his contemporaries—his concern with particulars is perhaps carried to an extreme when he concocts flags that he claims to be the devices of Prester John and of the rulers of Java and Cathay!

Not until almost a century later did a new and important account of Asia appear. In 1441, after twenty-five years in the East, Nicolò de' Conti, a Venetian, returned to his native Italy. This merchant traveler came back in the company of Near Eastern delegates to the Council of Florence. At this ecumenical council the European delegates, including those from Portugal, had the opportunity to learn from representatives of the Greek church and from Conti about the

---

[22] For a discussion of this disputed matter see C. Markham (trans.), *Book of Knowledge . . .* ("Hakluyt Society Publications," Ser. II [London, 1912]), pp. x-xi. The quotations that follow are extracted from Markham's translation.

"Christian Indies" (Ethiopia, India, and Cathay).[23] While traveling in the Muslim world, Conti had been forced to renounce the Christian faith to insure the safety of his family and himself. On his return to Italy he asked Pope Eugene IV for absolution, a petition that was quickly granted. Fortunately for posterity, Conti was closely questioned about his Eastern travels by the papal secretary and Humanist, Poggio Bracciolini.[24]

Conti's recollections were evidently of great scholarly interest to Poggio and the pope. Poggio's introductory comment reflects the state of his own knowledge about Asia, and presumably that of his papal master. The great Humanist wrote:

His [Conti's] accounts bore all the appearance of being true, and not fabrications. He went farther than any former traveller ever penetrated, so far as our records inform us. For he crossed the Ganges and travelled far beyond the island of Taprobana [Taprobane], a point which there is no evidence that any European had previously reached. . . .[25]

Such a statement betrays the fact that Poggio knew next to nothing about the other writers on India or that if he did he considered their works fabrications. While showing knowledge of Greek and Roman contacts with India, the papal secretary appears to be completely unaware of the Indian mission or the fourteenth-century writings of Jordanus. By textual comparison it has been concluded that he must have known the writings of Marco Polo and Hayton.[26] His assertion about the uniqueness of Conti's experiences is particularly difficult to understand when one recalls that Mandeville's *Travels* was circulating widely in Poggio's day, that the *Catalan Atlas* had been prepared in 1375, and that Genoese merchants had at least indirect contacts with India.

Conti's itinerary took him to widely scattered places in India. He describes the jewels of Cambay; he remarks on the extent and wealth of the then great metropolis of Vijayanagar; and he comments on the tomb of St. Thomas at Mylapore while observing that numerous native Christians practice traditional rites. He wildly exaggerates the size of Ceylon, but presents a remarkably accurate description of the cinnamon tree. Aside from this reference, he has little to say about spices and their sources. On Sumatra and the Andaman Islands he observed the cannibalistic rites of the natives and notes a few of the islands' products. From here he voyaged to continental southeast Asia, where he observed the fauna, particularly elephants. From Tenasserim he proceeded to the mouth of the Ganges, voyaged up it for three months, and noted the large and wealthy cities lining its shores. A trip in which he touched on Burma and

[23] Rogers, *op. cit.* (n. 6), pp. 65–67. On the background see Joseph Gill, S.J., *The Council of Florence* (Cambridge, 1959), chaps. i–iii.

[24] English translation in R. H. Major (ed.), *India in the Fifteenth Century* ("Hakluyt Society Publications," Ser. I, Vol. XXII [London, 1857]). The quotations that follow are from Major's translation.

[25] *Ibid.*, p. 4.

[26] W. Sensburg, "Poggio Bracciolini und Nicolò de Conti in ihrer Bedeutung für die Geographie des Renaissancezeitalters," *Mitteilungen der K. K. geographischen Gesellschaft in Wien*, XLIX (1906), 283.

Malaya was followed by a visit to Java and perhaps as far east as Sumbawa in the Lesser Sunda chain. He then returned to the continent and Cochin-China.[27] Thereafter he apparently brought his long-suffering family back to India and eventually returned to Europe with two of his children.

From his lengthy experience in Asiatic waters Conti was able to comment empirically and intelligently about geographical and nautical matters. Without paying Ptolemy (whom he may not have known, though Poggio certainly did) the deference of rebuttal, he posits an open Indian Ocean and comments graphically on its environs. He pays no attention to previous topographical descriptions of India, but divides it into three major sectors based on the natural divisions created by the Indus and the Ganges. He was certainly among the first to refer to the islands of the Sunda archipelago east of Java, whether he visited Sumbawa or not. Of seagoing ways he observes, perhaps incorrectly, that the Arab and Indian sailors "are not acquainted with the use of the compass," but "steer their vessels for the most part by the stars of the southern hemisphere." Like Marco Polo, he describes their vessels as being built without nails and depicts vividly the hazards of the sea as well as land journeys for the itinerant European.

In reply to a series of questions put to him by Poggio, Conti presents the most lucid account of Indian manners and customs to be prepared by a European since Megasthenes. His insights were sharpened by the length of his stay in south Asia, the extent of his travels, his knowledge of Asian languages, and perhaps by the fact that he was married to a woman who was apparently of Indian origin and who enabled him in the course of his travels to live a relatively settled life. On costume Conti's remarks might well describe modern Indian modes:

The style of dress is different in different regions. Wool is very little used. There is a great abundance of flax and silk, and of these they make their garments. Almost all, both men and women, wear a linen cloth bound round the body, so as to cover the front of the person, and descending as low as the knees, and over this a garment of linen or silk, which, with the men, descends to just below the knees, and with the women to the ankles.[28]

Unlike most of the earlier commentators, Conti stresses regional differences in Indian customs and practices. Monogamy, he asserts, is a characteristic practice in central India and among the Nestorian Christians; "in the other parts of India polygamy prevails very generally." Funeral rites vary from place to place also, and in this connection he recounts vividly the practice of *sati*, and

---

[27] Because Conti comments on Cathay, its people, and some of its customs, it has been argued that he might have visited there. See H. Yule and H. Cordier, *Cathay and the Way Thither* ("Hakluyt Society Publications," Ser. II, Vols. XXXVII–XLI [London, 1913–15]), I, 174–76; Sensburg, *loc. cit.* (n. 26), pp. 304–7, concludes that, while Conti shows knowledge of Chinese customs and practices, the evidence now available does not substantiate the assertion that Conti visited China. At the end of Conti's report Poggio also gives a brief account by another person who had come "from Upper India towards the north," perhaps Cathay. Possibly this was the mysterious delegate to the Council of Florence who represented the Christians of Cathay. See Rogers, *op. cit.* (n. 6), p. 264.

[28] Major, *op. cit.* (n. 24), p. 22.

describes realistically a number of different modes of displaying bereavement. He notes that the Indians use the ox as a beast of burden, but "consider it a great crime to kill or eat" it. Throughout all India "there is a class of philosophers called Brahmins, who are men of superior cultivation, and are distinguished by a greater sanctity of life and manners."

Of religious and superstitious practices and of festivals and holidays in India Conti says much and in detail. They divide the year "into twelve months, which they name after the signs of the Zodiac." He notes that currencies vary from place to place and that "some regions have no money, but use instead stones which we call cats' eyes." He comments on war implements, armor, and siege machinery. Paper, he asserts, is used only in Cambay, while "all other Indians write on the leaves of trees, of which they make very beautiful books." While noting that the Indians have many dialects and languages, he also remarks that they write "perpendicularly, carrying the line from the top to the bottom of the page." Of the people he contends that they are not tormented by pestilence or "those diseases which carry off the population in our own countries." Like any modern Westerner in India, he feels that "the number of these people and nations exceeds belief."

Conti's account of India exhibits certain notable similarities to that of Megasthenes—particularly the notion that the Indians, unlike the Europeans, are relatively free from disease and pestilence. Conti adds a number of striking details to the tradition of India inherited from the ancient Greek, perhaps because he visited southern as well as northern India. He also had the advantage of seeing Indian culture in relation to the cultures of Malaya, Java, and Sumatra. Of the Renaissance travelers to India, Conti was the first to travel extensively in the interior of the peninsula, and to identify and describe the multitude of cities in the Ganges Valley. His account is remarkably free of the European popular beliefs about India—its insular character, its dog-headed peoples, its demons and monsters—with which Megasthenes' story had been embellished over the centuries. From Poggio's comments it is clear that he questioned Conti closely and that he probably omitted from the narratives those tales which he considered incredible. Conti himself probably felt inclined, in replying to the skeptical papal secretary, to stick as closely as possible to the unvarnished truth as he understood it.

From about 1431 to 1447 Poggio gathered material for his dialogue entitled *Historia de varietate fortunae*. Divided into four books, this work of the great Humanist summarizes what was known of the outside world in his day. His description of India (Book IV) is based principally, but not exclusively, on his interrogation of Conti. Poggio wrote the first Latin manuscript summarizing Conti's travels in 1447 or 1448, apparently from notes that he had taken in Italian during his conversations with the traveler. A writing-house then prepared a number of copies of his Latin manuscripts and some copies of an Italian translation. The oldest manuscript known contains all four books and is dated 1448. About forty manuscript versions, partial and complete, dating from the mid-fifteenth century, are still extant.[29] Portions of Conti's account first appeared in print in the second edition (1485–86) of the *Supplementum chronicarum* of Jacopo Filippo Foresti da Bergamo, an Augustinian friar.[30] The first complete printed edition known appeared in Cremona in 1492 under the title *India recognita*.[31] A Latin chapbook, the first of a long series on the East, was likewise published around 1492. The anonymous compiler of this work, entitled *De ritu et moribus Indorum*, was mainly concerned with the medieval letters from Prester John, but he also extracted supporting information on India from Foresti da Bergamo's *Supplementum* which was derived originally from Poggio. Ten years after its first appearances in print, Conti's account was published at Lisbon in a Portuguese translation.[32] Although three Spanish translations appeared shortly thereafter, it was the Portuguese version that Ramusio used in 1550 when he prepared the Italian translation and adaptation for his great collection of voyages.

Without question Conti's account influenced contemporary thought on geography. The fact that so celebrated a person as Poggio brought it out almost guaranteed it general attention. Aeneas Sylvius Piccolomini, a contemporary and acquaintance of Poggio, drew heavily upon Conti's account for the chapters on India in his geographical work published in 1461.[33] Toscanelli, a personal friend of Poggio and the first geographer who sought to establish a realistic picture of Asia by rectifying Ptolemy and Strabo in the light of later information, used Marco Polo and Conti as his main postclassical sources. The cartographers of the fifteenth century also placed Conti's geographical information on their maps.[34] Poggio himself helped to spread Conti's information further, through his relations with Portuguese ecclesiastics. The Regent of Portugal, Dom Pedro, followed closely the proceedings of the Council of Florence and he probably learned all he could about the East from Italian informants.[35] Most of the great discoverers, including Columbus, knew Conti's account, either directly or indirectly, through writings and maps which incorporated materials from it.[36]

Direct travel between Christian Europe and the East became highly impractical after the Turkish capture of Constantinople in 1453. Of the European states Venice stood to lose most heavily from the Turkish efforts to control the Levantine trade, even though the Turks themselves were probably eager to continue trading on their own terms. As part of Venice's effort to counter the Turkish

---

[29] Sensburg, *loc. cit.* (n. 26), p. 261. For an analytical description of Poggio's book see Francis M. Rogers, *The Quest for Eastern Christians: Travels and Rumor in the Age of Discovery* (Minneapolis, 1962), pp. 44–49.

[30] Sensburg, *loc. cit.* (n. 26), p. 261.

[31] *Ibid.*, pp. 266–67.

[32] The connection with Poggio is made by Rogers, *op. cit.* (n. 29), pp. 78–86. Conti's account is included as an appendix to the Portuguese edition of Marco Polo prepared by the German printer Valentim Fernandes. Cf. Sensburg, *loc. cit.* (n. 26), pp. 268–69.

[33] See below, pp. 70–71.

[34] See below, p. 69.

[35] Rogers, *op. cit.* (n. 29), chap. iii, esp. p. 59.

[36] Sensburg, *loc. cit.* (n. 26), pp. 35–70.

advance, the Seignory sought to establish an alliance with Persia against the common enemy. To further this end, several Venetian ambassadors were dispatched to the Persian court. Merchants from the Island Republic also continued, despite the danger, to voyage to Persia for commerce in Eastern wares. When Josafat Barbaro, one of Venice's emissaries, returned to his homeland in 1478, he reported news of Cathay, described the emporium of Ormuz, and remarked on a city "called Calicuth, of verie great fame, being, as it were, a staple of merchants of various places." [37]

Like the Venetians, the Portuguese sent emissaries over the land routes into the East. Beginning in 1419, the Portuguese, as we have seen, had made a systematic and continuous enterprise out of exploring the African coast in an effort to outflank the Muslims. While gathering information on Eastern trade from all sources (particularly Italian), the Portuguese sought to keep their own discoveries in Africa and their ambition to capture the Eastern trade a close secret. In 1487, the year that Dias rounded the Cape, King John sent Pero da Covilhã and Afonso de Paiva on an inland trip across north Africa to seek out the trade routes to the East, to learn about the origin of the spices, and to carry a letter to Prester John. Assuming Muslim garb, they accompanied a caravan to Aden. At this point they parted company, Covilhã embarking on an Arab dhow sailing for India. De Paiva was never heard from again, but Covilhã sent a report back to Lisbon in 1490 after exploring most of the great Muslim trading centers. This report contained a summary of the commodities available in India, a discussion of the Arab trade, and remarks on how the Arab sailors took advantage of the monsoons. [38] After dispatching his report from Alexandria, Covilhã proceeded to Ethiopia to carry his royal master's letter to "Prester John." He remained at the court of the Lion of Judah for the rest of his life.

The Genoese also sought and obtained information on the Eastern trade from travelers and merchants. Around 1493, Girolamo da Santo Stefano left Egypt for Calicut and points to the East. His trip was evidently made as a private, speculative enterprise. In the course of his wanderings this Genoese merchant reached Ceylon, the eastern coast of India, Pegu, Sumatra, the Maldive Islands, Ormuz, and finally returned to Syria in 1499. Here he dictated by request of his associates in the business world the narrative of his trials and tribulations, a woeful story of personal hardship and financial disaster. [39] Of the pepper and ginger grown around Calicut he gives a detailed description and stresses that in the city itself "are as many as a thousand houses inhabited by Christians." He stayed only one day in Ceylon, but he remained on the Coromandel coast of India for seven months. Here he observed that "the red sandalwood tree grows in such

---

[37] As quoted in B. Penrose, *Travel and Discovery in the Renaissance* (Cambridge, Mass., 1955), p. 26.

[38] While there is reason to think that this report actually reached Portugal, no clear proof of its arrival exists. See Charles F. Beckingham, "The Travels of Pero da Covilhã and Their Significance," in *Resumo das communicações*, International Congress for the History of Discoveries (Lisbon, 1960), p. 94.

[39] In Major (ed.), *op. cit.* (n. 24), pt. I.

abundance that they build houses of it." Little new information could be gathered from his account, however, as he concentrated primarily upon his personal misfortunes. The clearest conclusion that could be drawn from his experience is the one he makes himself. Once, after being requested to undertake further commissions east of the Levant, he remarked tersely: "As the roads were not safe, I declined going."

Of those whom we know something about, the last of the independent land travelers before the opening of the sea route was the Italian gentleman Ludovico di Varthema. Since his travels took place after the opening of the sea route and are related to the Portuguese in India, they will be treated in detail later.[40] Like his predecessors of the land routes, he was forced to travel in disguise and as part of his masquerade to learn enough colloquial Arabic to conduct everyday affairs. While Varthema's account published in 1510 had a wide circulation in his own day and after, his predecessors of the fifteenth century, except for Conti, received no such acclaim. Their remarks seem generally to have been intended for a limited audience. Venetians, Florentines, Genoese, and Portuguese all sought specific information on the Eastern trade after the Turkish victory at Constantinople. It would appear that the Italians, like the Portuguese, sought to keep to themselves such information as they were able to acquire. Caution, for example, may account for Conti's failure to talk at greater length about the spices and their sources. By comparison with the fourteenth century, the amount of new factual information added to Europe's store of knowledge about Asia was limited indeed. What new material came to light dealt primarily with India and the East Indies. Almost nothing was added to Europe's image of Cathay (China) in the fifteenth century, a time when the Ming dynasty was coming to full flower.

3

CARTOGRAPHY AND GEOGRAPHY

The conception of the world inherited from the Bible, classical antiquity, and the earlier Middle Ages continued throughout the Renaissance to influence the thought of even the most critical scholars. Created by the arbitrary act of God, the earth was still generally believed to stand in the cosmos as a small and immobile disc. The idea of the flat earth with Jerusalem as its center, though a popular belief until the opening of the sea route, was not generally accepted either by the Schoolmen or the interested Humanists. The globe's surface was thought to be divided into five zones, two of them being temperate and habitable. The two polar zones and the equatorial zone were generally thought to be uninhabitable, but, as we have already seen, certain inquiring minds

---

[40] See below, pp. 164–66.

became convinced in the fourteenth century that men lived and worked in the equatorial zone.

Fable still vied with concrete information to form the European conception of the world beyond the *oikumene*. The fantasies of the Alexandrian romance and the tradition of St. Thomas continued to shape the popular view of Asia. Among informed people, however, some of the old fables were shifted to still unknown locales or were banished from their minds. The cartographic representations of the world prepared before 1300 generally followed the convention of placing the East at the top of the map as the scene of the terrestrial Paradise. The world east of the Levant was practically a closed book until it was opened by travelers of the Mongol era. When the book was closed again in the mid-fourteenth century, a recollection of what had been seen persisted, although somewhat uncertainly, until the Portuguese rounded Africa.

Vincent of Beauvais and Roger Bacon had helped to preserve in their encyclopedic works some of the factual information relayed to Europe by the early missionaries to the Grand Khan. The Schoolmen also, from their study of the Arabic writers, had begun to obtain geographical information of a more realistic type derived from Ptolemy or from the experience of Muslim traders and travelers.[41] European sailors in the Mediterranean and the Black Sea had meanwhile begun to prepare portulan charts accurately outlining the shorelines of these two great regions. The earliest portulan still extant dates from around 1300; similar charts, it may be assumed, were prepared at an even earlier date. Unlike the medieval maps, the portulans were not simply graphic symbols of the world but practical charts with comments prepared by seamen for everyday use. Adopting the techniques evolved in the portulans, geographers of the fourteenth century became increasingly interested in depicting the known world as accurately as possible. This concern for scientific map-making of known regions soon caused the more critically minded to suspect that their maps of the unknown must be faulty and vague if not entirely mythical.

Production of "true" maps for the first time in a thousand years involved assembling the portulan charts and using them as the basis for modifying the depiction of the known world. The maps of Marino Sanuto and Pietro Vesconti, prepared in the early fourteenth century, combined portulans for the Mediterranean world with earlier depictions of the outer regions of the pre-portulan type. The growing tendency to base maps on empirical data led gradually to the inclusion on the more ambitious maps of information from the travel accounts of Marco Polo and his successors. The Laurentian portulan of 1351 is the earliest map still extant to include data derived from Marco Polo's description of his sea voyage from China back to Europe. India here begins to appear as a peninsula and something resembling southwest Asia emerges in vague outline.

No map produced before the sixteenth century gives so comprehensive a picture of Asia as the celebrated *Catalan Atlas* prepared in 1375 for King Charles V

[41] On Ptolemy see below, pp. 67–69.

of France.[42] The work of Abraham Cresques, a Jew of Majorca, this series of maps painted on boards is preserved in the Bibliothèque Nationale in Paris (Ms. Espagnol 30). The peninsular shape of India, though hinted at by the Laurentian portulan, here emerges clearly for the first time in the history of cartography and is truer than that found on some other maps prepared a century later. Southeast Asia is somewhat less accurately depicted, an authentic description of Sumatra being spoiled by the presence far to the east of a totally mythical "Taprobana." The representation of continental Asia and China shows Cresques' familiarity with the writings of Marco Polo and Friar Odoric. The chief divisions of the Mongol empire, the lakes and rivers of central Asia, and the cities of India and central Asia are placed according to the cartographer's understanding of the travel accounts and are roughly correct. Cresques' *mappemonde* shows the semicircular coastline of China and locates most of the cities immortalized by Polo and his successors. A striking fault is the failure of the author to divide the Chinese empire into Cathay and Mangi. Like many of his contemporaries, he paid only slight heed to the exact course of inland waterways and to major topographical features such as mountain ranges. On the map all the rivers of eastern Asia rise in the region around Peking, and in the south the mountain ranges which give the rivers their character and direction are completely omitted. Mythology also has its place in this otherwise remarkably accurate atlas: north of Cathay live the giants of Gog and Magog, while between Cathay and India the pygmies reside. Nonetheless, no better portrayal of the Eastern Hemisphere was available in Europe until the production of the world maps of the sixteenth century.

Greek and Latin manuscript versions of Ptolemy's *Geographia* began to circulate in western Europe in the fifteenth century. More than forty of these manuscripts, in whole or in part, are extant. What happened to the original work of Ptolemy between its completion in the second century A.D. and the transmission of the first manuscripts from Byzantium to Rome is a matter for scholarly conjecture.[43] The older school generally holds that there is nothing to be explained about this period of more than 1,300 years: Ptolemy had himself prepared the text and the maps to go with it. Thereafter the text was presumably copied many times and the maps redrawn and revised by later cartographers. Finally, one of the manuscripts on parchment reached Rome in the fifteenth century and adaptations of it were soon made. Long before the twentieth century, certain scholars felt dissatisfied with this explanation but were hardly prepared to do much about it.[44] After World War I, a systematic attack

---

[42] See Henri Cordier, *L'Extrême-Orient dans l'Atlas Catalan de Charles V, roi de France* (Paris, 1894); Francesco L. Pullé, *La cartografia antica dell'India* ("Studi italiani di filologia indo-iranica," Vol. V [Florence, 1905]), Pt. II, chap. xii; and A. Kammerer, *La Mer Rouge . . . et la cartographie des portulans du monde oriental* (Cairo, 1952), III, 52.

[43] The best summary of the results of several centuries of scholarly ingenuity and industry may be found in Leo Bagrow, "The Origin of Ptolemy's Geographia," *Geografiska Annaler*, XXVII (1945), 319-87.

[44] For example, J. C. Gatterer, in his *Allgemeine Welthistorie* (Göttingen, 1792), p. 148.

began to be made on the origins of the *Geographia* in a series of pioneering papers. These culminated at the end of World War II in Leo Bagrow's article in the *Geografiska Annaler* which concludes[45] that neither the texts nor the maps in the *Geographia* in the form extant are Ptolemy's original work throughout. It is, rather, a work of compilation based on Ptolemy's theory of map-making and his list of excellent cities. The compiler, or compilers, are believed to be unidentified Byzantine scholars of the tenth and eleventh centuries. The extant maps (probably of the thirteenth century) are of a later date than the extant texts (the earliest is of the eleventh century), and the maps include data from Arab and Byzantine sources. The geography of the individual countries and such features as the southern land-bridge and the enclosed Indian Ocean, are now considered to be post-Ptolemaic in origin and un-Ptolemaic in their relation to his original plan.[46] Finally, if this analysis is accepted, it is impossible to date anything by its appearance in the *Geographia* until much more study, particularly by Byzantinists, has been undertaken.

It is only in the fifteenth century that we move to surer ground in studying Ptolemaica. In this century, Greek versions, and probably Latin adaptations of them, were circulated in manuscript form, primarily from Rome. A Latin translation, accompanied by maps, was first printed in 1475,[47] and it was shortly followed by a number of other printed editions. In 1533 Erasmus published at Basel an edited version of one of the Greek manuscripts. Because of the knotty problems produced by variant texts, all these earlier editions are replete with errors, no matter how critical the editor happened to be. The best text of Book VII, chapters i–iv, the part which deals with India and the Far East, was established by L. Renou only in 1925.[48] Many other modern editions and translations are less carefully done. It is still next to impossible to find a fully satisfactory critical edition of the whole of this famous work.[49]

The *Geographia* in the extant versions consists of eight books. The first, which appears to be mainly the work of Ptolemy himself, is a discussion of the theory and principles of map-making. The next five books and part of the seventh list the latitudes and longitudes of more than eight thousand places arranged in crude regional divisions.[50] In the final portion of Book VII this information is reviewed in connection with a discussion of the dimensions of the known world. The last book explains how to divide the map of the world into twenty-six regional maps. The authors of these books are essentially interested in cartography and scorn the kind of descriptive and historical matter which makes the

[45] *Op. cit.* (n. 43), p. 387.

[46] For discussion, as part of an effort to modify Bagrow's earlier published article, see Erich Polaschek, "Ptolemy's Geography in a New Light," *Imago mundi*, XIV (1959), 34–35.

[47] Often misdated 1462. It is entitled *Claudii Ptolem. Cosmographiae libri primi capita.*

[48] *La Géographie de Ptolemée, l'Inde*, Bk. VII (Paris), chaps. 1–4.

[49] The best version in English, though the translation and editing leave much to be desired, is Edward Luther Stevenson, *Geography of Claudius Ptolemy* (New York, 1932).

[50] For aid in identifying Ptolemaic and other placenames used in the Renaissance see Ivar Hallberg, "L'Extrême-Orient dans la littérature et la cartographie de l'Occident des 13e, 14e, et 15e siècles," *Göteborgs kungl. vetenskaps- och vitterhets- samhälles Handlingar*, 4th ser., VII–VIII (1906), 1–573.

general geographies of the Renaissance more readable and appealing! It was perhaps because of its vast list of place names and its severe dedication to the careful compilation of cartographic data that the *Geographia* became the proto- type for all similar endeavors until the end of the sixteenth century.

The *Geographia* was not only the most detailed gazetteer available to Renais- sance cartographers; it also came to them imprinted with the name of one of the most celebrated mathematicians and astronomers of antiquity. In an age devoted to the resurrection and adulation of the classical past, Ptolemy's work was widely admired as one of the greatest treasures found in the rich storehouse of Greece. So, despite the contrary evidence of Marco Polo and the portulans, many of the learned and not-so-learned of the fifteenth century showed almost no hesitation in adopting the Ptolemaic view of the world. There were always, however, those exceptional individuals who refused to accept the Ptolemaic conventions uncritically, particularly when they knew from local sources that the *Geographia* was incorrect in many of its identifications in the Mediterranean area.

For our purposes the most important of the Ptolemaic conventions are those which have to do with the underestimation of the world's circumference, the extent of the Eurasian continent, the enclosed Indian Ocean, the truncated India, the Golden Chersonese (Malay Peninsula), and the Sinus Magnus (Great Bay). The *Geographia* vastly overestimated the eastward extension of Asia, and indicated the existence of unknown land (not ocean) to the east of China, thus leading Columbus, among others, to believe that Asia could be reached by a relatively short voyage westward. It postulated, possibly on the basis of the antipodes idea of the Greeks, a huge southern continent which ran from south Africa to southeastern Asia enclosing the Indian Ocean and thereby making impossible the circumnavigation of Africa. It makes the Indian peninsula too short and Ceylon too large. And the Sinus Magnus, at the eastern end of the southern land-bridge, looks like an elongated Indochinese peninsula, which could be said to make it doubly impossible to reach China by sailing eastward. Other lesser points on which Ptolemy disagrees or agrees with the findings of the discoverers will be taken up in the appropriate places.

The world maps of the latter half of the fifteenth century make their most significant additions to the picture of the East with respect to India and the Indian Ocean. The celebrated planisphere of Fra Mauro (*ca.* 1459) seems to follow written sources as well as the Ptolemaic maps. Working in Venice, Fra Mauro depended heavily on Conti's narrative, less on Marco Polo, and possibly on a written book of sailing instructions in Arabic.[51] While pushing the mythi- cal islands to the eastern extreme of the Indian Ocean, Mauro's world map shows the Maldives, Andamans, and Nicobars in a more realistic fashion than do its predecessors. The outline of southern Asia seems to be derived from the

[51] G. R. Crone, "Fra Mauro's Representation of the Indian Ocean and the Eastern Islands," in *Studi colombiani*, Papers read before the International Meeting for Studies on Colombus (Genoa, 1951), III, 57–64. The author also gives a list of identifications of the cities on the west coast of India mentioned on the map.

Ptolemaic maps, and so India's peninsular character is not as pronounced as it was shown to be in the *Catalan Atlas*. Its vast coast likewise follows the old convention of running too much in an east-west direction. The depiction of Sumatra, Java, and the spice islands of Banda and the Lesser Sundas depends almost completely upon Conti's account, and it is spoiled by the north-south direction given to the larger islands. Mauro gives very little guidance on the true configuration of eastern Asia, but he does show an island in the extreme east called "Zimpagu," the first time Japan is definitely shown and named on a Western map.[52]

The crude map prepared by Henricus Martellus, a German who worked in Italy from about 1489 to 1492, represents a further step backward in the true comprehension of Asia. Following Ptolemy slavishly, Martellus completely omits the empirical data of the travelers, presents a truncated India, and an enclosed Indian Ocean. The celebrated world globe of Martin Behaim (d. 1506), prepared in 1492 as a summary of the geographical knowledge of his day, adds nothing of significance on the Eastern Hemisphere, depending as it does primarily on Ptolemy and the accounts of Marco Polo and Mandeville.[53] Like his predecessors, Behaim preserved in his map of the East many fabulous relics of archaic and medieval cartography.

The first serious attempt at a world geography after the writings of the Schoolmen was the *Imago mundi* by the French cardinal, Pierre d'Ailly (1350-1420); it was prepared originally at the beginning of the fifteenth century and was first printed in 1483 at Louvain. Although he probably knew about the travelers to Asia, D'Ailly makes no reference to their descriptions. He derives his account of India and the other regions of Asia from Pliny, Solinus, and Isidore of Seville. In his chapter on the marvels of India he soberly and without qualification reports on the activities of griffons, pygmies, and "beasts of frightful shapes." From Roger Bacon he learned of Aristotle's belief in the possibility of a short passage to India by sailing westward from Spain.[54] In all probability Columbus derived both inspiration and confirmation from D'Ailly for his own hopes of reaching Asia by sailing westward. Like Bacon, D'Ailly also believed in the open Indian Ocean, insular Africa, and a habitable tropical zone.

Perhaps the closest and most critical student of Ptolemy was Pope Pius II (in office, 1458-64), better known as Aeneas Sylvius Piccolomini. His *Historia rerum ubique gestarum* (1461), digests Ptolemy and adds information about China and eastern Asia derived from Marco Polo and Odoric of Pordenone. Unwilling to accept the theory of the enclosed Indian Ocean, he leaned upon Conti's

[52] W. E. Washburn, "Japan on Early European Maps," *Pacific Historical Review*, XXI (1952), 222-23.

[53] For the suggestion that the world maps of Martellus and Behaim had a common origin see G. R. Crone, "Martin Behaim, Navigator and Cosmographer: Figment of Imagination or Historical Personage," in *Resumo das communicações*, International Congress on the History of the Discoveries (Lisbon, 1960), p. 20.

[54] More generally associated with Plato and the legend of Atlantis. See J. Oliver Thomson, *History of Ancient Geography* (Cambridge, 1948), pp. 90-92.

account for his description of India's land and waterways. Pius II lent the support of his learning and the prestige of his office to the idea that India might be reached by sailing around Africa. His geographical theories, like those of Marco Polo and Pierre d'Ailly, apparently influenced Columbus and his contemporaries in their estimate of the possibility of finding a sea route to India.

The maps and geographies of the fourteenth and fifteenth centuries, though few in number, brought together the materials of the past, including the Ptolemaic maps and names, and the best of them modified the traditional image of the East with data taken from Marco Polo and his precursors and successors. If anything, the information available on China was fuller and more accurate than that on India and other parts of Asia, despite the real contributions made by Conti. Much that was fabulous, particularly about India, continued to detract from the significant advances that had been made in the acquisition of a truer picture. Many points of issue remained outstanding and would not be settled until the voyages of the sixteenth century finally penetrated the oceanic barriers between Europe and the outside world. Even after 1500, however, the ideas of the past cast their shadow over places and peoples actually observed and upon information relayed to Europe for the use of cartographers and geographers. It was not until the seventeenth century that Cathay was generally accepted as being the Serica of Roman times. It was not until the eighteenth century that the last cartographical conventions inherited from the Ptolemaic atlas and the romance of Alexander were dropped from the European maps of Asia.

4

FINE ARTS

The Renaissance, like the Middle Ages, was intrigued by the riches, mysteries, and monsters of the East. Whether their ideas derived from the Alexandrian romance, Marco Polo, or the *Catalan Atlas*, the writers and artists of western Europe, clearly felt the attraction of a different, exotic world. Products from the East, as in Roman times, excited curiosity and wonder. Frequently the Europeans mistakenly identified products as being of East Asian origin when they actually came from the Levant or Africa. As with the geographers, a mythical East existed for the artists along with certain notions that were more solidly founded. Both strains contributed to their vision of the East and are inextricably intertwined, as with the oriental exoticism of this or any other historical period. To separate the genuinely oriental from the pseudo-oriental in either their knowledge of products or their artistic creations is practically impossible and perhaps not entirely necessary. What they mistakenly thought of as characteristically oriental was every whit as important as the genuine in guiding their ideas and shaping their creations.

One of the most intricate of the visual arts to deal with in this connection is painting. A number of modern scholars have sought to show an affinity between Renaissance Tuscan and oriental painting in terms of spiritual and philosophical content and by reference to the similar means employed to express artistically similar ideas or emotions.[55] Madonnas of the Sienese school, it is pointed out, are sometimes given hands and fingers of extraordinary length and diaphanous texture which make them look oriental, but, without additional evidence it does not necessarily follow that such resemblances are derived from imitation of Buddhist images. They may simply be another aspect of the Gothic desire to invest the human body with an unworldliness transcending the corporeal. Though curiosity about the East certainly existed in the Tuscan towns during the *trecento*, it overtaxes the imagination to conceive of deep cultural and spiritual affinities between Italian and oriental art. In the absence of concrete data, one can hardly claim more on this point than that affinities exist between different cultures in their artistic expressions of ecstatic religious feeling.[56]

Still, certain painters of the early Renaissance, like their predecessors of the Middle Ages, clearly incorporated oriental or pseudo-oriental subjects and motifs into their works to achieve unusual or striking effects. The earlier exotic tradition had found religious inspiration in Byzantine art and had borrowed decorative motifs from Near Eastern and Islamic art. To be sure, certain motifs borrowed from western Asia were already permeated, before their adoption by Europeans, with exotic themes from the Far East and south Asia. Such migrations in art (and in literature) were certainly common and they remain discernible. By the time they reached Europe, however, the various Asiatic themes had become inseparably intermingled and conventionalized. In early exoticism, for example, the fantastic is usually depicted by employing orientalized European figures displaying stock gestures, clothing, and physical features.

Painters in the thirteenth, fourteenth, and fifteenth centuries, motivated in part at least by the descriptions of the travel accounts and by the presence of oriental slaves in Italy, began to deal more realistically with oriental figures and increasingly brought identifiable Tartars and Chinese into their works. A remarkable number of Orientals appear in the representations of Giotto, Duccio, the Lorenzetti, Gozzoli, Andrea da Firenze and Gentile da Fabriano. Realistic ethnical representations of Chinese figures can be discovered in the Crucifixion scene of the famed *Parement de Narbonne* (1373–78) and in the seated personage entwined in foliage on a decorative page in a Flemish *Livre d'heures*

---

[55] Especially B. Berenson, *A Sienese Painter of the Franciscan Legend* (London, 1909); G. Soulier, *Les influences orientales dans la peinture toscane* (Paris, 1924); Josef Strzygowski, *Influences of Indian Art* (London, 1925); I. V. Pouzyna, *La Chine, l'Italie et les débuts de la Renaissance, XIIIe–XIVe siècles* (Paris, 1935).

[56] The best critical essay on this subject is Leonardo Olschki, "Asiatic Exoticism in Italian Painting of the Early Renaissance," *Art Bulletin*, XXVI (1944), 95–108.

(*ca.* 1460). Careful and convincing pictures of Asians also appear in Ambrogio Lorenzetti's (d. 1348?) "Martyrdom of the Franciscans at Ceuta" and in the "Ecclesia militans" of Andrea da Firenze (*ca.* 1365), two paintings commemorating the church's missionary activities in the East. Even more realistic is Pisanello's "Mongol Archer" (*ca.* 1440), a figure portrayed with such physical exactitude that we may surmise he used as a model one of the numerous Tartar slaves held in Italy. That such paintings introduced a new realism into European portrayals of Orientals can readily be discerned by comparing the works mentioned above with the highly imaginative depictions in the fourteenth-century illuminations found in the *Decades* of Titus Livius or those in the *Gluttony* of a Genoese artist of the same period.[57]

Renaissance iconography may have been enriched by the more numerous contacts with the East, though in its details this subject remains obscure and open to conjecture. New demonic figures appeared during the fourteenth and fifteenth centuries throughout Europe, as for example the winged tenebrous creatures in the Campo Santo fresco at Pisa (*ca.* 1350) and those in the Flemish tapestries (*ca.* 1378). Perhaps the association in religious and popular literature of the Tartar with antichrist and evil helped to produce additions to demonology of flying creatures from the Orient. Certainly in ancient, medieval, and even Renaissance literature about the East, the chimera of the Orient was as readily associated with evil and fantasy as with civilization and luxury. The repertory of Buddhist painting is replete with half-human, half-animal, and multilimbed creatures symbolizing demonic forces which bring to mind particularly the creations of Hieronymus Bosch, unexcelled in the Renaissance as a painter of the devil. Such associations, however, are merely suggestive of the variety of impressions about the East that may have been current in Renaissance Europe.

Like the devil himself, oriental exoticism could assume numerous forms and pervade various arts. The importation of Chinese silk textiles and their distribution to the princes and nobility of Europe helped to produce an interest in oriental design among European weavers. From about 1300 to the end of the fifteenth century, Islamic and Chinese designs were freely mingled by European weavers with more traditional European and Byzantine designs to produce exotic effects. On other occasions oriental designs were simply copied in detail. Gradually, however, the weavers of Italy fused Chinese decoration with Gothic design to produce an original textile genre that became more popular than the imported varieties by the end of the fifteenth century.[58]

The Asian impact on the visual arts of the Renaissance was largely indirect and from a host of intermingled sources. Europe and Asia merged most fully in Persia, and it was this commingled art, dubbed "migration art" for want of a better name, that was of primary moment in forming the artist's image of

[57] Both examples taken from J. Baltruvaitis, *Le Moyen Age fantastique* (Paris, 1955).
[58] See Otto van Falke, *Kunstgeschichte der Seidenweberei* (Berlin, 1913), pp. 19–34, and A. F. Kendrick, *Italian Silk Fabrics of the Fourteenth Century* (London, 1905–6).

Asia.[59] But we should also not ignore the fact that actual contact appears to have given this *orientalisme* a more realistic dimension, as in the depiction of oriental figures in painting and the introduction of Eastern designs to textiles. Oriental motifs also increased the linear richness of manuscript and painted compositions and rendered more opulent their abstract calligraphic effects. Such realistic influences were overshadowed, however, by a personalized exoticism that was perhaps also a phase in the decaying courtly art of medieval Europe. About all that can be said positively is that an oriental imagery helped to create for art a new exotic repertoire and interest which were not to have their full impact until the eighteenth century.

5

LITERATURE

As in art, the migratory themes in literature are difficult to isolate and their precise influence upon Western authors virtually impossible to determine. Many students of comparative literature seem convinced that oriental tales and stories had migrated to Europe in antiquity and the Middle Ages. But no more than a few fables of Indian origin seem to have reached Europe through oral transmission before the tenth century.[60] With the Islamic conquests in India, the tales of the *Panchatantra* and other such Indian collections were translated into Persian, Arabic, and Hebrew, and were then relayed in written form to the Christian world through the Byzantine empire, Italy, and Spain. Reference has already been made to the career of the Alexandrian romances and the legend of Barlaam and Josaphat in medieval Europe. To these might be added the appearance in Spanish translation from Arabic in the thirteenth century of the Indian tale called "Kalilah and Dinnah."[61] Clearly by the time of Dante a variety of romances, tales, fables, and travel accounts of Asia were current in Europe and many of them had been incorporated in standard collections such as *Le livre du trésor* of Brunetto Latini.

The great Florentine poet, Dante, was a disciple of Brunetto Latini and a contemporary of Marco Polo. Perhaps it reveals something of Dante's thought and work to observe that in his view of Asia he seems to be indebted to the literary and scholarly tradition represented by Latini and not at all to Polo's essentially factual account. The corollary of this observation is that he shows much greater interest in India than in the Tartars and none at all in Cathay. In the *Divine Comedy*, written between 1300 and 1321, the year of his death, Dante talks about the Ganges, the "Oriental sapphire," and *asvattcha*, the great

---

[59] C. Münsterberg, "Leonardo da Vinci und die chinesische Landschaftsmalerei," *Orientalisches Archiv* (1910–11), p. 93.

[60] Theodor Benfey, *Pantschatantra: Fünf Bücher indischer Fabeln, Märchen und Erzählungen* (Leipzig, 1859), I, xxii–xxiii.

[61] T. Benfey, "Die alte spanische Uebersetzung des Kalilah und Dinnah," *Orient und Occident*, I (1862), 497–507.

Indian fig tree celebrated by the classical writers. His references to the Tartars are indirect and reveal clearly that either he had not read Polo or had rejected the Venetian traveler's account as a creation of the imagination not worthy of being ranked with the *Composizione del mondo* of Ristoro d'Arezzo, a work with which he was undoubtedly familiar.[62]

Efforts have been made repeatedly to show Dante's indebtedness to oriental ideas and themes. The allegory of the "forest of life" at the beginning of the *Divine Comedy*, where Vergil rescues Dante from "ferocious beasts," has been likened to an allegory in *Mahabharata*, the Sanskrit epic.[63] Indian and especially Buddhist sources have been credited with inspiring his representations of various levels of the *Inferno*, as well as his delineation of Lucifer.[64] In locating the terrestrial Paradise in Ceylon, Dante clearly departs from the medieval tradition of placing it vaguely in the East, but the reasons for this innovation are not clear.[65] Dante's conception of the Tartars appears to go little beyond incoherent popular ideas. He mentions the Tartars in his *Convivio* (II, 8), for their belief in the immortality of the soul. Probably he merely wished to indicate by this reference that the idea had spread to the very end of the earth. A mention in the *Inferno* (XVII, 17) of the ability of the Tartars to weave cloth artistically was probably an equally vague reference to the East; all rich materials of oriental origin then widely used by the church and the aristocracy of rank and wealth were described as being "Tartar cloths."[66]

Dante's image of Asia was founded upon the learned tradition deriving from Pliny, Solinus, and Isidore—perhaps through the medium of the vulgar versions included in the writings of Latini and Ristoro. Like his contemporaries, he must have known something of the Alexander romances, the "history" of St. Thomas the Apostle, and the story of Prester John as they had been popularized in poems, songs, and artistic decoration. Embracing all that it knew, the mind of Dante transmuted some of the older ideas into something quite different. Seen against the setting of his time and his work, none of his references to the East seems either fabulous or exaggerated.[67] His personal image of Asia, though admittedly limited, retained few of the utterly fantastic elements that he could have derived from the scholarly and literary sources upon which he depended.

That the Tartars were a matter of actual interest in Dante's day and after is well illustrated by some comments made in 1373 by Giovanni Boccaccio. In a

[62] L. Olschki, "Dante e l'Oriente," *Giornale Dantesco*, XXXXIX (1936), 68. Also see the same author's "Marco Polo, Dante Alighieri e la cosmografia medievale," in *Oriente Poliano* (Rome, 1957), pp. 45–66.

[63] E. Levêque, *Les mythes et les legendes de l'Inde et la Perse dans Aristophane . . . Dante, Boccace, Ariste, etc.* (Paris, 1880), pp. 503–6.

[64] H. Baynes, "Oriental Characteristics in the *Divina Commedia*," *Transactions of the Royal Society of Literature*, 2d ser., XXVI (1918), 187–200.

[65] *Ibid.*, pp. 185–86.

[66] Paget Toynbee, "Tartar Cloths," *Romania*, XXXIX (1900), 559–60. Cf. also "The Knight's Tale," in Chaucer's *Canterbury Tales*, vss. 2160–61.

[67] Olschki, *loc. cit.* (n. 62), p. 82.

public lecture dealing with an obscure passage in Dante's *Inferno* (I, 105) (translated as "Twixt Feltro and Feltro shall his nation be,") Boccaccio expatiates on an interpretation advocated by some of his contemporaries. They apparently contended that "Feltro" refers to the "felt" used as ceremonial wrappings at the death of a Tartar emperor. The phrase "Twixt Feltro and Feltro" is then construed to mean that the events being described by Dante will take place in Tartary "during the reign of one of those emperors who rules between the one felt used at the death of his predecessor and the other which will be used after his own death." [68] Particularly remarkable in this passage from Boccaccio's lecture is a reference to the "Empire of the Middle," a possible direct translation of the Chinese *Chung kuo*. If this is indeed a reference to the "Middle Kingdom," it is the earliest such mention known.

Boccaccio might have learned the term "Middle Kingdom" from travelers or merchants of his day who had been there. That he knew such people is clear from his tale of Mitridanes and Nathan (*Decameron*, 10th Day, story 3), where he remarks, "if we may believe the report of certain Genoese and other folk who have been in those regions." Unfortunately for this explanation, he refers at this point to China as Cathay, and so far as is known makes no further references to the "Empire of the Middle." That the name Cathay was then being kept alive in Italian literary circles is clearly brought out by the poet M. M. Boiardo (1434–94). In his *Orlando Innamorato* (X, 18) he wrote of King Galafron:

> il qual nell'India estrema signoreggia
> Una gran terra ch'ha nome il Cattajo.

Meanwhile, Giuliano Dati (1445–1524), a Florentine priest, in his *Cantari dell'India* (1493–95) was keeping alive the tradition of the marvels of India and the glories of Prester John at the very time when Columbus made his first great discoveries. [69]

Boccaccio was particularly under the influence of the collections of Indian stories that had been coming over into European languages since the tenth century. Like Dante, he was more indebted to the learned tradition than to the travelers, merchants, and missionaries of the thirteenth and fourteenth centuries. The Latin translation of the *Panchatantra* probably furnished him with the germ of his plot in story 2 of Day 2 in the *Decameron*. [70] Others of Boccaccio's stories may contain elements derived from the Barlaam and Josaphat legend, the

[68] As quoted in L. Olschki, *The Myth of Felt* (Berkeley, 1949), p. 8; Olschki does not accept this explanation of the disputed passage. He posits rather an original and plausible explanation based upon astrology (pp. 39–42). The twins, Castor and Pollux, who are traditionally depicted wearing felt caps, are identified as the Feltri. Thus the passage reads "Twixt May and June," the months of Castor and Pollux between which Dante himself was born in 1265.

[69] L. Olschki, "I 'Cantari dell'India' di Giuliano Dati," *La Bibliofilia*, XL (1938), 289–316. For discussion of the edited versions of the two poems descriptive of the wonders of the East see Francis M. Rogers, "The Songs of the Indies by Giuliano Dati," in *Resumo das Comunicações*, International Congress of the History of the Discoveries (Lisbon, 1960), pp. 280–83. Also see Rogers, *op. cit.* (n. 29), pp. 94–104.

[70] Benfey, *Pantschatantra*, I, 15; also A. C. Lee, *The Decameron, Its Sources and Analogues* (London, 1909), pp. 25–26.

drama in verse of Kalidasa (A.D. fifth century?) called *Sakuntala or the Ring*, and from the ancient Sanskrit epic, *Ramayana*. Thus, it can be seen that Boccaccio, too, was more moved by the mythical and legendary tradition of India than by the really astounding wealth of fact, if he recognized it as such, available on Tartary and Cathay.

Chaucer, too, exhibits a traditional and vague knowledge of India. In the "Knight's Tale" he refers to "the great Emetrius, the king of Inde."[71] Perhaps Chaucer also knew some of the Buddhist parables that had migrated to Europe through the Levant. The "Pardoner's Tale" is similar to a parable from the *Vedabba Sataka*. Scholars disagree about whether or not Chaucer knew and used the writing of Marco Polo; if so, they were probably the source of some of the imagery in the "Squire's Tale." The suggestion has been advanced that the visit to London of the Armenian King Leo in 1385–86 may have awakened Chaucer's interest in the Tartars. Certainly it is hard to believe that Chaucer would have written so vaguely of Tartary had he had a copy of Marco Polo before him. It seems much more likely that he depended upon the tales of the Alexandrian romance and upon the common talk about Asia attending such events as the visit of King Leo.[72]

The man who most fully utilized the travel and mission accounts for literary purposes was Boccaccio's contemporary, the author of the *Travels of Sir John Mandeville*. Modern scholars are not certain of the author's identity, but the original claim that he actually was an Englishman called Sir John Mandeville now seems to be the most acceptable identification. While most commentators have accepted Liége as the place where the romance was written, a reasonable case can be made equally well for England.[73] The author claims that he had himself visited the lands he discusses, but it seems certain that he never traveled much outside western Europe. Nevertheless, many of his contemporaries accepted his claims at face value and his book was so widely read that it was translated into every major European language before 1500. Even the critical Samuel Purchas in the early seventeenth century called Mandeville "the greatest Asian traveller that ever the world had."[74] Was it that the European audiences

[71] Line 2156 of the *Canterbury Tales*. Also see Robert Sencourt [pseudonym of Robert E. G. George], *India in English Literature* (London, 1925), p. 34.

[72] See J. H. Manly, "Marco Polo and the Squire's Tale," PMLA, XI (1896), 350, 262; further discussion in H. Braddy, "The Oriental Origin of Chaucer's Canacee-Falcon Episode," *Modern Language Review*, XXXI (1936), 19.

[73] The most recent summaries of scholarly opinion are presented in Malcolm Letts, *Sir John Mandeville: The Man and His Book* (London, 1949), and Josephine Waters Bennett, *The Rediscovery of Sir John Mandeville* (New York, 1954). On the question of authorship, Letts holds the view that it was an Englishman "Mandeville who wrote the book" and not Jean de Bourgogne as has frequently been asserted. Bennett (in chap. xiii) summarizes in detail the available data on authorship, rejects the attribution to Bourgogne, and concludes that it is probable "that there was such a person [Sir John Mandeville] as the author of the *Travels* represents himself to be" (pp. 203–4). While Liége has usually been accepted as the place where the book was written, Bennett (p. 176) argues that it was probably written in England. Letts has edited *Mandeville's Travels* for the "Hakluyt Society Publications," Series II, Vols. CI and CII (London, 1953).

[74] As quoted in Letts, *Sir John Mandeville*, p. 35.

of Mandeville's day were better prepared to accept eagerly his fictional description of the East than were the Europeans of sixty years earlier to accord Marco Polo's factual book any more than a cool and skeptical reception? Or was Mandeville more acceptable and credible simply because he included many more of the conventionalized ideas of Asia which Europe had inherited from the distant past?[75]

Mandeville's book certainly owes much of its popularity to the sheer artistry displayed by the author in weaving the available sources into a rich backdrop for his fictional, personal narrative. The armchair traveler must have had at hand the huge encyclopedic *Speculum mundi* of Vincent of Beauvais, especially the two sections entitled, respectively, "Naturale" and "Historiale." From the former he was able to glean odd items of natural history that lent his work both authority and interest; from the historical portions of Vincent's work he extracted fantasies and facts from Pliny, Solinus, Isidore of Seville, the Alexander romances, the early bestiaries, and most importantly from John of Plano Carpini. His main source for the description of the countries east of the Levant was the account of Odoric of Pordenone—to which he fails to give even casual acknowledgment. The two accounts are so similar that scholars thought for a time that the authors had traveled together. Purchas even accused Odoric of being the plagiarizer.[76] Mandeville also used Hayton's *Fleurs des histoires d'Orient* freely and extensively for information about the Mongols and the Grand Khan. Other materials on Asia he derived from the account of William of Rubruquis, Ricold of Monte Croce (d. 1320), and from the famous forged "letter" sent to Europe by Prester John. How much Mandeville relied upon Marco Polo is an open question, but the books have a number of features in common and cover much the same ground.[77] It is hard to believe that Mandeville, a meticulous researcher, did not know Polo's book. Perhaps it was because Polo was so generally known, and not so rich in marvels, that Mandeville purposely relied upon the less widely diffused and more fantastic travel accounts to give his own romance a greater semblance of originality and a larger selection of colorful stories.

On the whole, Mandeville's picture of India remains quite traditional.

In India are many divers countries; and it is called India because of a water that runs through that land, the which men called Inde. . . . In India are more than five thousand isles that men dwell in, good and great, without others that men dwell not in. And in ilk one of those isles are many cities and towns and mickle folk.[78]

---

[75] Cf. R. Wittkower, "Marco Polo and the Pictorial Tradition of the Marvels of the East," in *Oriente Poliano* (Rome, 1957), p. 156.

[76] Letts, *Sir John Mandeville*, p. 35. For a thoroughgoing summary of his sources see Bennett, *op. cit.* (n. 73), chap. i.

[77] See the "comparative table showing passages common to Mandeville and Marco Polo" in Letts (ed.), *Mandeville's Travels*, I, 1. Also see Bennett, *op. cit.* (n. 73). p. 38.

[78] This quotation and those which follow are extracted from the Egerton text (between 1410 and 1420) as edited and reproduced in Letts (ed.), *Mandeville's Travels*, I, 1. Notice that India is still conceived of as a host of islands (cf. above, chap. i, n. 119).

He notes that "men go through India by many countries unto the great sea Ocean." He refers to the Christians, the tomb of St. Thomas, and the terrible heat of southern India. Pepper, he reports, "grows in manner of wild vines beside the trees of the forest, for to be suppoweld [supported] by them." He goes into detail to describe the three types of pepper (long, black, and white) and even notices, like Isidore, how the merchants "sophisticate [adulterate] pepper when it is old." Like Odoric, he observes that the "best ginger" comes from southern India. The worship of the "sacred cow" and the many rituals related to it he comments upon at length. He notes the practices of cremation and *sati*.

Odoric provided Mandeville with most of his material on the East Indies— "fifty-two days journey" from India he finds Sumatra. Here women, land, and "all things" are common property. From Sumatra it is not possible to see the Pole Star, but navigators rely upon "another star which is called Antarctic." Of Java he comments as we might today: "In the isle of Java is wonder mickle folk; and there grow divers manners of spicery in more plenty than in other places, that is to say ginger, cloves, canell, nutmegs, mace and many other." The king of Java is so great that "he has oftimes discomfited the Great Khan of Cathay in battle...."[79] About the island of Borneo and on Champa in Indochina he is less specific. He also embellishes Odoric's account by extracting from Vincent of Beauvais stories of other distant islands and peoples which he arbitrarily places east of Java.

But in leaving the islands "by sea towards the east many days journey men find ... Mancy [South China]. ... It is the best land and most liking and plentifulest of all goods that is in the power of man." Canton he describes as being "more than Paris" and notes, as might the traveler today, the great addiction of the Cantonese to feasting. Hangchow is "bigged [built] on the same manner as Venice ... and upon a side of the city runs a great river." Nanking "was first the see of the king Mancy" and it is the river "Dalay" (Yangtze) that separates "Mancy" from the "Great Khan's land" (Cathay). Of the "Caremoran" (Yellow River) he correctly reports that it "oft-times does great harm to the country by overflowing when it is great."[80]

Cathay for Mandeville is Utopia, and his hero is the Great Khan. The ruler of Cathay is far more impressive to him than Prester John, whose "land is good and rich, but not so rich as the land of the Great Caan. ..." Of northern China he states:

The land of Cathay is a great country, fair and good and rich and full of good merchandise. And thither come merchants ilk a year for to fetch spicery[81] and other manner of merchandise more commonly than til other countries. And ye shall understand

---

[79] Certainly a reference to the Mongol invasion of 1293 sent by Kublai Khan. See for details the account in D. G. E. Hall, *A History of South-East Asia* (London, 1960), pp. 70–72.

[80] The names which he uses for the Yangtze and Yellow Rivers are transliterations of the Mongol names recorded by Polo and Odoric.

[81] See the vast number of items included under this term by Pegolotti, above, p. 45.

that merchants that come from Venice or Genoa or other places of Lombardy or Romany, they travel by sea and by land eleven months or twelve ere they come to Cathay. . . .

For the history of the Mongol rulers Mandeville follows Hayton generally, though his lengthy description of Cambaluc derives from Odoric and some lesser items are clearly extracted from Carpini. Like his sources, Mandeville talks wonderingly about the philosophers at the khan's court, the elaborate festivals, the summer residences of Shangtu, the courier system, polygamy, and paper money. As if testifying to China's fascination for him, he ends the *Travels* with a story of a wealthy Chinese who is served "at his meat and his bed" by fifty damsels with bound feet who must serve him constantly since he has "so long nails on his fingers that he may hold nothing with them." To lend greater authenticity to his account Mandeville included alphabets for a number of languages including Cathayan. It goes without saying that the Cathayan alphabet contributed nothing to Europe's understanding of Chinese or the Tartar tongues![82]

Of the popularity of Mandeville's *Travels* there can be no doubt. The extant versions in manuscript number around 300 as compared to the 119 Marco Polo manuscripts now available. Sixty-five of the 300 Mandeville manuscripts are in German, testifying to his popularity in northern and central Europe. Versions also remain in English, French, Spanish, Dutch, Walloon, Bohemian, Danish, and Irish. With the introduction of printing in the mid-fifteenth century, still other versions appeared, some of them profusely illustrated. The illustrations most generally reproduced are those which were originally prepared for the German translation of 1481, printed in Augsburg.

More than any other single work, the *Travels* of Mandeville set the stylized half-realistic, half-fanciful image of the East that predominated in western Europe during the Renaissance. Unlike Dante and Boccaccio, Mandeville utilized the travel and mission accounts to their fullest and sought to integrate this newer knowledge with the more traditional materials. Since his veracity was generally unquestioned until the seventeenth century, his work helped to mold significantly the learned and popular view of Asia. Even his monsters and marvels could apparently be accepted as long as they were relegated to places still relatively unknown. The fact that we know today that Mandeville did not make the trip as he pretended in no way detracts from the importance of his book in helping to integrate knowledge of the East and in shaping the Renaissance view of the "worlds" beyond the Muslim world.

---

[82] On the sources of his alphabets and on their evolution in the various versions of Mandeville see Bennett, *op. cit.* (n. 73), pp. 65–66. Cf. the fanciful alphabet which Sir Thomas More contrived for his Utopians. Not all of Mandeville's alphabets are of his own invention, as for example the Syrian and Greek letters.

6

TECHNOLOGY AND INVENTION

To the modern eye, accustomed to seeing the flow of technology in the opposite direction, the idea that the Eastern countries might have been technologically superior to the West comes as something of a shock. But, as research in the history of technology and technological diffusion progresses, it becomes increasingly evident that many mechanical techniques and a number of fundamental inventions were known in the East before they were adopted or independently developed in Europe. The generalization may be made that before 1500 the Levantine countries were probably superior in skill and inventiveness to Europe, and that China, especially, was more creative than either.[83] The Spanish knight, Ruy de Clavijo, who went on a diplomatic mission to Tamerlane's court in 1403–5, remarked that "the craftsmen of Cathay are reputed to be the most skilful by far beyond those of any other nation. . . .[84]

We have already noted the migration of the silk industry across the land routes of Asia to Egypt and Syria and thence to Sicily, Spain, Italy, and France. The details of this history have never been thoroughly worked out, and, because of their complexity, perhaps they never will be. It has been suggested quite reasonably, however, that not only the silkworm and the technique of cultivating it traveled from China to the West, but that mechanical contrivances necessary to the manufacture of silken goods probably also spread to the West through the barbarian frontier, the Arab world, and Byzantium.[85] Before the fourteenth century the rotary reel and the spindle wheel had possibly migrated to Europe, and in fourteenth-century Italy water power was applied to spinning mills as it had been in China at a much earlier date.

Like silk, the delicate porcelains of China, despite their fragility, were carried across the land routes to the Levant and Europe. At the end of the twelfth century Saladin presented the Sultan of Damascus with a gift of forty pieces of Chinese porcelain. Marco Polo singled out the porcelain of Fukien province for special mention and brought samples of the Chinese ware back to Italy. Other travelers remarked with wonderment on the *porcelain dorée* and in the fifteenth century European royalty and nobility began to collect it. Especially prized was the translucent blue and white Ming ware that seemed to combine the qualities of both glass and pottery, materials well known to the craftsmen of Italy.

European artisans tried to imitate the delicate and highly prized porcelains of China. In fifteenth-century Italy the workshops of Faenza, Gubbio, Urbino,

---

[83] C. Singer, "East and West in Retrospect," in Singer *et al.* (eds.), *A History of Technology* (Oxford, 1956), II, 755; for a diametrically opposed view on Chinese technical competence see L. Olschki, *Guillaume Boucher: A French Artist at the Court of the Khans* (Baltimore, 1946), p. 61.

[84] *Embassy to Tamberlane* (London, 1928), p. 289.

[85] See the table in J. Needham, *Science and Civilization in China* (Cambridge, 1954), I, 242. Also see R. Patterson, "Spinning and Weaving," in C. Singer *et al.*, *op. cit.* (n. 83), II, 208.

Pesaro, Venice, and Florence sought to discover the secret of porcelain manufacture known in China since the second century B.C.[86] Despite their best efforts, the artisans of Italy were unable to duplicate the Chinese product. Florence produced a tin-glazed earthenware called *maiolica* which fused Chinese ornamentation with Western patterns of coiled foliage in monochrome blue. Long renowned for their glass, the Venetians produced a varicolored glass that failed to approach porcelain in composition, texture, or color. Orientalized patterns were as close as the Renaissance Italians could come to providing a substitute for the Chinese ware. The development of a "true" hard-paste porcelain in Europe would not come until the early years of the eighteenth century.

Like silk and porcelain, gunpowder may have been carried to Europe before 1500. True gunpowder, a pyrotechnical compound of saltpeter, sulfur, and charcoal, was manufactured in China in the late Mongol period; it was also known in Europe at about the same time. Iron cannon seem also to have been developed in both Europe and China shortly after the development of gunpowder. On the basis of information now available it is not certain whether gunpowder and the cannon were first invented in Europe or China. Dogmatic statements about transmission in either direction are thus worthless at the present stage of scholarly investigation.[87] Needham, however, promises to produce a "veritable time-table" to illustrate gunpowder's transmission from East to West.[88]

While Western military and naval techniques were being revolutionized by the development of firearms, navigation also underwent profound changes with the introduction of the magnetic compass. This instrument was fully described in a Chinese work of the eleventh century and may have been transmitted to Europe through the Arabs. By the thirteenth century it was in use in Europe. Although a good case based on circumstantial evidence can be produced for the migration of the compass from China to Europe, it might be well to recall that Nicolò de'Conti remarked that Arab sailors with whom he traveled were "not acquainted with the use of the compass." The case for the compass is usually accompanied by assertions that the stern-post rudder, the fore and aft rig, and a number of other nautical innovations were diffused from the Far East to Europe.

The impact of gunpowder on military techniques and of the compass upon navigation was followed by the adoption of the art and craft of printing in Europe, an achievement that revolutionized intellectual communication. As with the other migratory techniques, the question debated most in the history of printing is that of cultural diffusion versus independent discovery. The idea that European printing might owe a debt to China goes back at least to 1546. In that year an Italian historian surmised, after examining Chinese books

---

[86] J. Davillier, *Les origines de la porcelaine en Europe* (Paris, 1882), chap. ii; and A. Lane, *Italian Porcelain* (London, 1954).

[87] See J. R. Partington, *A History of Greek Fire and Gunpowder* (Cambridge, 1960), pp. 287–88; see also A. R. Hall, "A Note on Military Pyrotechnics," in Singer *et al.*, *op. cit.* (n. 83), II, 377.

[88] *Op. cit.* (n. 85), I, 231.

brought back by the Portuguese from Canton, that the art of Gutenberg was derived from China.[89] More recent scholarship[90] asserts that the Chinese invented paper, the necessary prerequisite for the development of printing, and that paper-making techniques were transmitted to Europe through the Islamic world. It was not until the fifteenth century that paper became common in Europe. The art of block printing was probably relayed to fourteenth-century Europe through the introduction of printed playing cards, through the importation of the paper money commented on so frequently by the travelers, and through religious image prints. So far no reliable evidence has been brought forward to show that movable type of the kind employed in Europe by Gutenberg and others was influenced by the typography of China or Korea. Indeed, it is worth observing that the Indians apparently first learned about printing from the Europeans rather than from the Chinese and that paper was not generally used in India until after the sixteenth century. The invention of typography in Europe around 1440, almost a century after the cessation of direct contact with China, appears to have been an independent discovery.[91] Certainly, in fifteenth-century Europe no reference to China is made by those who comment on the new art of typography. But a number of the voyagers of the sixteenth century remarked with astonishment that the Chinese possessed printed books in large numbers.

Before 1500, western Europe steadily received the impress of the superior technological civilizations of the Far East. While it is hard to construct a time-table of diffusion for each idea or contrivance, there is now no question about the diffusion of silk and paper from China to Europe. Qualifications about the transmission of gunpowder, the compass, and block printing are still retained by some scholars, because the evidence in these cases is largely circumstantial. Until proof emerges to the contrary, the majority of observers tend to accept the idea that the invention of movable type in Europe was an independent discovery. The suggestion that a number of other devices, such as canal lock-gates, the segmental arch-bridge, and the wheelbarrow, might have migrated from China into Europe reinforces the case for diffusion.[92] Irrespective of the merits or limitations of individual cases, the evidence that is being piled up on the westward flow of techniques is impressive. The realization that numerous techniques and contrivances might have passed from East to West also tips the balance slightly in favor of accepting the cases that are largely based on "what must have been."[93]

[89] T. C. Carter and L. C. Goodrich, *The Invention of Printing in China and Its Spread Westward* (New York, 1955), p. x.

[90] *Ibid.*, pp. 241–42.

[91] A stimulating rationale for independent development is clearly set forth in Pierce Butler, *The Origin of Printing in Europe* (Chicago, 1940); on the other hand, Needham (*op. cit.* [n. 85], I, 231, 241–42) appears to favor a diffusion hypothesis.

[92] Cf. Needham's table in *op. cit.* (n. 85), I, 242; for a good theoretical study of diffusion see R. B. Dixon, *The Building of Cultures* (New York, 1928), esp. chap. vii.

[93] See the suggestive, if somewhat superficial, article by B. F. Cressey, "Chinese Traits in European Civilization," *American Sociology Review*, X (1945), 604.

While inventions and perhaps ideas for invention penetrated the barrier between Europe and Asia, more abstract scientific ideas were certainly not relayed in either direction before 1500. They came rather as isolated phenomena and were generally, though not always, unrelated to the other impressions that Europe received from Asia. Moreover, no real consciousness existed in the West that these were ideas or inventions of Asian origin. While knowledge of the place of origin of silk may have been general, the relatively slow growth of the silk industry in the Levant and Europe contributed little to the idea that the West owed this expanding enterprise to China. Nor did the European mariner who learned to depend upon the magnetic compass either know or care about its origin—any more than the American farmer cares that the soybeans from which he makes a large part of his income were originally imported from Manchuria! The transmission of technical devices, unaccompanied by the related complex of Chinese scientific ideas and methods, appears to have had almost no effect in either enlarging or modifying the European's image of Asia.

7

SUMMARY

The last decade of the fifteenth century was one of the most momentous in Europe's history. In that short span of time Europeans were able to demonstrate that the oceans were not impassable and that "New Worlds" of unforeseen dimensions and promise lay open to those with the courage to seek them out. The decade during which America and India were discovered was also the critical period in the diffusion of the Italian Renaissance to northern Europe and the Iberian Peninsula. Teachers and Latin secretaries initiated in the ways of Humanist thought transmitted the "new learning" of Italy to France, Germany, England, and Iberia. German printers likewise began to set up shop and publish books in the great mercantile, political, and cultural centers of the Continent. While collectors continued for a time to prefer manuscripts for their libraries, printed materials steadily increased in number and soon contributed materially to the dissemination of information. Knowledge of the classical past, stripped of many of its medieval accretions, was thus becoming more widely known in western Europe, contemporaneous with information about the maritime discoveries. The revelations of the classical past and of the East were related events, not only because they were spread simultaneously, but also because they both helped to unsettle traditional attitudes and to bring about the intellectual orientation which we call "modern."

One of the main concerns of the *quattrocento* was to revive the classical past through the translation into Latin of the corpus of Greek literature. The

Schoolmen had revived Aristotle in the thirteenth century; the Humanists of the fifteenth century rediscovered Plato. To many luminaries of the intellectual world the rediscovery of Greece seemed as thrilling as, and perhaps more important than, the discoveries then being made by the Portuguese in the Atlantic and down the African coast. Steeped in classical learning, even universal minds like Poggio were not always aware of new information from non-classical sources, and when they were, they were frequently skeptical about it. The diffusion of the Ptolemaic texts, for example, helped to raise questions about the new geographical information which sometimes brought the old and the new knowledge into direct conflict. It should not be surprising therefore that knowledge of the East from classical sources continued to leave its imprint upon men who, often rightly, distrusted the more recent and sometimes conflicting information contained in the accounts of the missionaries and travelers.

Many private libraries, particularly in Italy, included in their collections the classical works on geography of Strabo, Pomponius Mela, and Ptolemy along with the medieval travel accounts of Marco Polo and John of Plano Carpini. While collectors sought to acquire Greek texts, most of the books on their shelves, including the geographical studies, were in Latin and vernacular versions.[94] Long before the great discoveries, scholars like Ramond Lull had begun to call for the serious study of Greek, Arabic, and other Eastern tongues. This trend had been encouraged by the efforts being made before the mid-fifteenth century to reunite the Greek and Latin churches and to bring the distant Christian groups of Asia into closer communion with the European church. Florentine Humanists of the fifteenth century freely speculated, as Plato had almost two thousand years earlier, about the possibility of finding new lands and the sources of the spices by sailing westward.[95]

But, in the Renaissance, the lands that lay beyond the Mediterranean world were still remote from the main concerns of educated and uneducated alike. Certainly exceptional figures such as Abraham Cresques, the author of the *Catalan Atlas*, or Prince Henry the Navigator, or Aeneas Sylvius Piccolomini sought to reconcile the geographical learning of the past with the practical experiences of more recent voyagers. Fundamentally, however, as Mandeville's book indicates, the European image of Asia in the fifteenth-century was still compounded of a mixture of fact, theory, and myth. Uncritical use of the available materials from the classical heritage sometimes even increased the number of fanciful notions. At the same time, some of the myths and legends that came in with the Middle Ages continued to enjoy respectability long after

94 Pearl Kibre, "The Intellectual Interests Reflected in Libraries of the Fourteenth and Fifteenth Centuries," *Journal of the History of Ideas*, VII (1946), 293. A library of 800 to 900 items was considered a collection of fair size in the fifteenth century (*ibid.*, p. 258). Most of the lists analyzed reveal that theological and scholastic interests remained paramount and that most of the books were still in Latin. The Humanists, though mainly concerned with the rehabilitation of Greek studies, sometimes also collected codices in Hebrew, Aramaic, and Arabic (*ibid.*, p. 217).

95 Thomas Goldstein, "Florentine Humanism and the Vision of the New World," in *Resumo das comunicações*, International Congress for the History of the Discoveries (Lisbon, 1960), p. 133.

other vestiges of medieval life had been discarded. A process of synthesis, however, was going ahead in the fifteenth century that sought to reconcile the old and the new. And, it should not be forgotten that when a New World finally was discovered, it did not take the Europeans long to adjust their minds to its reality and to begin speculating even more freely than before about the worlds beyond their own.[96]

The changes effected in Europe's life and viewpoints up to 1500 derive mainly from the buoyant commercial civilization of the Mediterranean region and from the humanistic revival of the classical past. While literary themes, artistic motifs, and technical devices certainly were imported into Renaissance Europe from Asia, their impact did not fundamentally alter the European way of life. The Christian tradition in scientific thought was not visibly affected by the adoption of new technical instruments wherever they originated. The mainstreams of European artistic and literary growth were not diverted by the new knowledge of Asia acquired after the thirteenth century. Embellishments were added to achieve unusual effects in both literary and artistic creations, but basic forms and styles were not materially changed. While certain Indian ideas may have been incorporated into Manichaean and Neo-Platonic thought in Roman times, the Christian and European tradition of the post-scholastic period refused, with few exceptions, to admit alien philosophical and religious ideas. Although conscious of Asia, Europe in no way felt required to alter its basic religious, philosophical, artistic, or institutional traditions in the light of this knowledge. It was only after the opening of the sea route around Africa that consciousness of Asia began to affect a number of Europe's traditional ways of thought and activity.

[96] See the suggestion about the possible influence of the discoveries upon the speculations of the sixteenth century regarding the plurality of worlds and an infinite universe in W. G. L. Randles, "Le nouveau monde, l'autre monde, et la pluralité des mondes," in *Resumo das comunicações*, International Congress for the History of the Discoveries (Lisbon, 1960), pp. 162–63.

PART

II

*New Channels
of Information*

Introduction

One of the most neglected aspects of the history of geographical discoveries is the story of how Europe as a whole came to learn about the rest of the world. In recent years, however, scholars have become increasingly aware of the importance of the opening of new vistas for Europe itself. This awareness has been stimulated by the growing realization that the history of expansion is best interpreted as an enterprise which involved commodities, people, and money from most of the nations of western Europe. Such an emphasis is not meant to detract from the acknowledged achievements and great sacrifices which the Iberian nations made as they led the way across uncharted seas to unknown lands. It is designed to show that enterprising people from many countries were quick to sense the revolutionary implications of the Portuguese and Spanish explorations, were anxious to be a part of the great enterprise, and were eager to profit from it. The Portuguese adventure in the East was especially interesting to outsiders because the Lusitanians, unlike the Castilians, seemed to have found a direct route to the cherished spices and to have established permanent contacts with the rich and powerful civilizations of an opulent East.

General participation in overseas activities produced general effects throughout the Continent which radiated to the other nations by way of Portugal. The channels through which Europe acquired its knowledge of the East were as numerous as the thousands of individuals who participated in the opening of the overseas world. To trace every channel of information to its source is clearly neither possible nor necessary. In our effort to understand what the European public might have known about the East, we have limited our examination to materials actually *published* in the sixteenth century. For this reason we have had to refrain from detailed analysis of certain types of news, such as Portuguese official sources, because the reports of overseas administrators, soldiers, and sailors were not readily available to the general public of this period. What was known of the Portuguese empire came to general attention through the publications after mid-century of the great Portuguese chronicles and the European travel collections. The Christian mission, as contrasted to the Portuguese political establishment, was much more international in its composition, less inclined to secrecy, and a major purveyor in the sixteenth century of information about non-commercial and non-political aspects of life in Asia. We will therefore examine its history in some detail as background necessary to the understanding of the viewpoints and biases of ecclesiastical commentators and historians. With these considerations in mind we have limited discussion to three major channels of new information: the operation of the spice trade and Europe's general involvement in it; the growth of widespread interest in the printed routiers, chapbooks, letterbooks, maps, travel accounts, and compilations, and the histories of the discoveries in Asia; and the Christian mission in Asia with the diffusion in Europe, through published letterbooks, of news about its successes and failures. The spice trade in Europe is discussed first to illustrate how fundamental it was in preparing Europeans to receive and disseminate printed accounts of the East.

CHAPTER III

The Spice Trade

The mere fact that after 1498 Europeans came increasingly into personal contact with Asian civilizations added a dimension of reality, slow as it was in coming, to the European view of Asia and enabled Westerners more easily to compare themselves to alien peoples at similar levels of achievement. The presence of Asian products, in quantity as well as in exotic samples, helped to create an atmosphere in which travel accounts and oral reports became more credible. No longer were impressions of Asia limited to the fables of antiquity, the sometimes unreliable stories of Muslim and Jewish traders, or isolated accounts of Christian missionaries and merchants. After the opening of the sea route to India, events taking place on the Malabar Coast, in Malacca, and the Spiceries became commonplace gossip in the trading centers of southern and western Europe. Tales were compared, reports challenged, and information sold on all aspects of Asian trade. Spice movements had become a vital facet of business activity and news from Asia often followed the trade routes within Europe.

Italians, Germans, French, Spanish, English, and Dutch, whether sailors, merchants, or statesmen, watched closely the vagaries of the spice trade and the arrivals at Venice and Lisbon. The papacy likewise kept in close touch with the expansion of the Portuguese trade, collected information on it from Portuguese embassies to Rome, and sent missionaries to the waiting harvest of souls in Asia. Bankers in Antwerp, Venice, and Augsburg anxiously watched from afar the struggle for control of the pepper trade between those who counted upon the revival of the old Levantine route and those who had cast in their lot with the Portuguese. For example, the Fuggers and other commercial banking establishments of central Europe collected information of all kinds relating to Eastern exploration and trade in order to keep abreast of developments both in Asia and in Europe.[1] It may be assumed that the Fuggers in Augsburg communicated pertinent information to their numerous branch offices and to business associates in other firms. Similar informal news services were maintained by other large business establishments with interests in overseas trade.[2] While these reports normally went unpublished in the sixteenth century, they helped to promote interest in and provide background for the readier comprehension of news about the East. The design of what follows is to show in detailed fashion how the Atlantic spice trade developed, how it helped to produce a reorientation of European commerce, and how it stimulated a general and lively interest in matters Eastern.

I

THE FIRST VOYAGE OF VASCO DA GAMA

The decade separating Dias' return in 1487 from the departure of Vasco da Gama's fleet was one of dramatic change and nervous activity in the history of both Portugal and Lisbon. Under King John II (1481–95) Lisbon had steadily become the center of administration, planning, and merchandising for the African trade, as the king and his advisers supervised commerce and navigation with increasing vigilance. Little is known about the early evolution of the organizations constituted in Portugal to regulate the African trade,[3] but sometime before 1415 the Casa de Ceuta was set up in Lisbon to govern trade with North Africa. Under Prince Henry, the Casa da Guiné was established at Lagos in the middle of the fifteenth century. Around the beginning of King John's reign the Casa da Guiné was moved to Lisbon where it functioned thereafter in conjunction with the Casa de Ceuta and those trading organizations originally set up to supervise Portugal's commerce with St. Thomas, the Madeiras, and the Azores. The Casa da Guiné moved to Lisbon at about the same time that the expedition was sent to Africa in 1480 to build the Castel de São Jorge da Mina.

[1] The Fugger newsletters which are extant were collected by Count Philip Edward Fugger (1546–1618) and relate mainly to the last generation of the sixteenth century. See Viktor Klarwill (ed.), *Fugger-Zeitungen: Ungedruckte Briefe aus das Haus Fugger aus den Jahren 1568–1605* (Vienna, 1923); the English translation is Pauline de Chary, *The Fugger News-Letters* (New York, 1924). For additions see L. S. R. Byrne, *The Fugger News-Letters, Second Series* (New York, 1926).

[2] For example, see the letters written from Lisbon to the Ruiz of Medina del Campo from 1563 to 1568 in J. Gentil da Silva (ed.), *Marchandise et finances. Lettres de Lisbonne* (Paris, 1959); on the history of the Ruiz family see H. Lapeyre, *Une famille de marchands: les Ruiz* (Paris, 1955) See also Valentin Vasquez de Prada (ed.), *Lettres marchandes d'Anvers* (Paris, 1960–62), Vols. II–IV.

[3] Some of the material relating to the history of these early commercial organizations was destroyed in the Lisbon earthquake of 1755. It is surprising, however, how much of this early history can be reconstructed from other archival sources, especially those in Spain. The best general work so far to appear is Francisco P. Mendes da Luz, *O Conselho da Índia* (Lisbon, 1952), pp. 30–39. For details of the archival problem in Portugal, see Pedro Augusto de S. Bartolomeu de Azevedo and António Baião, *O Archivo da Torre do Tombo: sua história, corpos que o compoem e organisação* (Lisbon, 1905).

Thereafter and until the end of the century it was known either by its older name or by the newer appellation of Casa da Guiné e Mina.

The organization of African trade set the administrative pattern for the regulation of Portugal's commerce with India. Indeed, after 1499, the Casa da Guiné e Mina came to be known simply as the Casa da India. From what can be pieced together from the available sources (diplomas, charters, writs, etc.), it appears that a warehouse and offices were erected in Lisbon in the early fifteenth century to serve as the headquarters of the Casa de Ceuta. The first caravels sent out to Guinea were probably outfitted and provisioned through the Casa de Ceuta, even though the West African trade soon came to have its own organization at Lagos. In 1455 Fernão Gomes was appointed *recevedor*, or collector of revenue, at Lagos for the Casa da Guiné, and all persons trading to Guinea were thereafter required to clear their exports and imports through that office and the adjacent warehouse. Another official of the Casa was the *escrivão*, or secretary, who kept the records and supervised the movement of goods and disbursements. All European products destined for overseas commerce and all imports from Africa were registered in quantities by the *escrivão* so that corresponding duties might be collected for the royal treasury on everything except those goods on the king's account. Most of the precious commodities from Guinea were declared royal monopolies in 1470, and all private traders were thereafter barred from trafficking in them. In 1486, five years after the Casa was moved to Lisbon, a separate section was constituted to handle the slave trade, an enterprise that was naturally different in technique and needs from other aspects of commerce. Foreigners were officially excluded at all times from direct participation in the African trade in either slaves or commodities.

It must not be concluded, however, that foreigners were uninterested in the Portuguese trade or completely dissociated from it. Italian merchants had been active in Portugal since the end of the thirteenth century. The Genoese seem to have taken the lead in the Italian colony of Lisbon during the fourteenth century and the early years of the fifteenth century.[4] For two centuries before Vasco da Gama's voyage, Florentine galleys had put into Lisbon on their voyages to and from Flanders.[5] The Genoese and Florentines had become prominent enough in Portugal by the middle of the fifteenth century to be singled out for repeated criticism by the Portuguese Cortes. The Italians were charged with sending precious metals out of the country, with interfering in retail trade, and with relaying information abroad about Portugal's exploration activities. The king, even if he agreed with the charges of the Cortes, could not break his affiliations with the Italians, for he needed their financial support in international dealings and their experience in foreign trade as intermediaries.

Bartolommeo Lomellini, a Genoese who resided in Lisbon in 1424, founded

---

[4] Virginia Rau, "A Family of Italian Merchants in Portugal in the Fifteenth Century: The Lomellini," *Studi in onore di Armando Sapori* (Milan, 1957), I, 717–22.

[5] W. Heyd, *Histoire du commerce du Levant au moyen-âge* (2d ed; Leipzig, 1886), II, 512.

one of the families that soon became prominent in trading and financial circles in both Portugal and the Madeiras. The Florentine commercial family, the Marchionni, seems to have had interests in Lisbon as early as 1443.[6] Bartolommeo Marchionni was obviously important in Lisbon banking circles by 1486 when he made the credit arrangements for the overland expedition of Covilhã and Paiva. The illustrious Florentine banking house of Bardi had a branch in Lisbon by 1471, and apparently it continued to function there throughout the era of great discoveries.[7] In 1485, Jakob Fugger opened a countinghouse in Lisbon and the following year he dispatched Cristóbal de Haro, a Spanish merchant, as his agent to Portugal.[8] Before the discovery of the New World, the Affaitadi of Cremona were engaged in the lucrative sugar trade which ran from the Madeiras to Portugal, Italy, and the Low Countries. Giovanni Francisco Affaitadi represented this interest in Lisbon.[9] The main channels of domestic business appear to have been controlled before 1496 by Jewish and New Christian merchants, only some of whom were natives of Portugal. Other foreigners directly associated with the discoveries, and frequently with the trade, were experts on arms and cartography.[10] Printers from Germany and Flanders, attracted by the opportunities opening in this once remote seaport on the Iberian coast, also assembled at Lisbon either as servitors of the crown or as free-lancing enterprisers. Thus, in the century before the opening of the route to India, it can be seen that Lisbon was rapidly becoming a European entrepôt of consequence and a meeting place for the representatives of some of the largest commercial and banking firms then operating in western Europe.

When King Manuel came to power in 1495, his first major act was to expel the Jews from Portugal. Following the lead of Spain, Manuel sought to break the hold of the Jews and Moors upon the economy and trade of Portugal through state action. In spite of warnings from members of his council that such a drastic measure would be followed by economic difficulties, the king in 1496 ordered all unbaptized Jews and Muslims to leave the kingdom within ten months.[11] Apparently, the privileges and businesses of the exiled Jews and Moors were then seized by the crown and turned over to the administration of the Knights of Christ, who in turn leased some of them to Italian businessmen and bankers. In this manner Manuel may have accumulated part of the capital and credit required for the outfitting of the fleet that, even before issuing his

[6] Prospero Peragallo, *Cenni intorna alla colonia italiana in Portogallo nei secoli XIV, XV e XVI* (Genoa, 1907), pp. 100–106.

[7] *Ibid.*, pp. 36–37.

[8] *Ibid.*, pp. 27–28; also J. Denucé, *Inventaire des Affaitadi* (Antwerp, 1934), p. 7.

[9] Denucé, *op. cit.* (n. 8), pp. 166–67.

[10] See W. F. K. Stricker, *Die deutschen in Spanien und Portugal und den spanisch und portugiesischen Ländern von Amerika* (Leipzig, 1850), pp. 192–93; on the German and Flemish *bombardeiros* employed by Portugal see P. E. Peiris and H. Fitzler, *Ceylon and Portugal* (Leipzig, 1927), I, 295–306.

[11] Alexandre Herculano, *History of the Origin and Establishment of the Inquisition in Portugal*, trans. John C. Branner ("Stanford University Publications in History and Economics," Vol. I, No. 2 [Stanford, Calif., 1926]), pp. 252–53.

decree against the Jews and Moors, he had determined at the end of 1495 to send to India.

Precisely what part was played by the Florentine merchants in encouraging and aiding the king to send out the expedition has not been fully determined. They may have achieved financial pre-eminence after the expulsion of the Jews and they may have supplied part of the capital for the outfitting of the fleet. It is possible that the German bankers and merchants, who had long purchased spices at Venice, were also taking more than a casual interest in the march of events at Lisbon. Certainly, Cristóbal de Haro, the Spanish representative of the Fuggers, was present and active in Lisbon while the final preparations for Vasco da Gama's fleet were being made on the banks of the Tagus.[12]

The construction of the fleet destined for India apparently commenced between the return of Columbus in 1493 and the death of King John in 1495. Though some disappointment was felt in Lisbon that Dias' discovery of the tip of Africa had uncovered only an almost barren land,[13] he was nevertheless put in charge of constructing the two leading vessels of the new fleet, the "São Gabriel" and "São Raphael."[14] Work apparently started in 1494 after suitable timber had been brought to Lisbon from the royal forests. After his own experience with the three-masted caravel rigged with lateen sail, Dias seems to have decided that it was not as practical for lengthy expeditions at sea as the heavier and more commodious square-rigged vessels called *naus*. The *naus* were also designed to insure greater safety and comfort for their crews during the long voyage to India. Meanwhile, scientific preparations were also being made, books and data collected, instruments readied, and personnel trained in the use of the available equipment.[15] And, after Manuel's decision in 1495 to proceed with the expedition, two smaller vessels were purchased from private owners in Lisbon to complete the fleet. Fernão Lourenço, factor of the Casa da Mina, was then summoned by the king and ordered "to equip the armada and provide it with every thing necessary, as speedily as ever he could."[16]

While the Portuguese vessels were small and few even by prevailing standards, they were constructed with the greatest care and bountifully supplied for the long voyage ahead. In the words of Duarte Pacheco Pereira written about 1507–8:

The best and most skilful pilots and mariners in Portugal were sent on this voyage, and they received, besides other favours, salaries higher than those of the seamen of other

---

[12] For further details see C. M. Parr, *So Noble a Captain* (New York, 1953), pp. 50–51. Unfortunately, Parr's work is not sufficiently well documented for us to be able to accept his conclusions, logical as they may be, without qualifications. Denucé (*op. cit.* [n. 8], p. 7) likewise seems to believe that the Italians played a major role in encouraging the king to push ahead, but he also gives no details.

[13] The sentiments of a contemporary, Duarte Pacheco Pereira, as quoted in H. Hart, *Sea Road to the Indies* (New York, 1950), p. 84.

[14] See account in E. G. Ravenstein (ed.), *A Journal of the First Voyage of Vasco da Gama* (London, 1898), p. 159. This is Vol. XCIX (O.S.) of the "Hakluyt Society Publications."

[15] *Ibid.*, pp. 166–67, also K. G. Jayne, *Vasco da Gama and His Successors* (London, 1910), pp. 36–38.

[16] As quoted in Hart, *op. cit.* (n. 13), p. 88.

countries. The money spent on the few ships of this expedition was so great that I will not go into detail for fear of not being believed.[17]

Clearly the king hoped to make certain that nothing would be left undone to insure the success of this expedition of discovery, and he entrusted its fate to a courtier and expert navigator, Vasco da Gama.

The details of the journey need not concern us. Of primary moment for the purposes of this study is some understanding of what its success meant to Portugal, Venice, and the rest of Europe. Nor do we need speculate whether Vasco da Gama's mission was primarily that of discoverer or ambassador.[18] It is enough to remark that he was both an experienced seaman and a seasoned diplomat, and that he acted in both these capacities during his first voyage. From either viewpoint, Da Gama's first voyage was essentially a reconnaissance mission.

The "Berrio," under the command of Nicolas Coelho and perhaps flying the flag of the House of Marchionni.[19] returned to the estuary of the Tagus on July 10, 1499. Da Gama himself, delayed in the Azores by the death of his brother, probably arrived in Lisbon on August 29. Ten days later he made his triumphal entry into the city and officially confirmed the reports of his successful expedition that were already circulating far and wide. Spirits were somewhat dampened, however, by the realization that but two of the four vessels sent out had returned. Clearly the voyage was possible, but it was equally apparent that the dangers were great.

King Manuel was not slow to understand the momentous implications of the discovery of the sea route. He immediately sent an announcement of this great achievement to all Portuguese cities. In a letter of July, 1499, written just after the arrival of the "Berrio," the king triumphantly relayed his news posthaste to King Ferdinand and Queen Isabella, his recently acquired parents-in-law:

... We learn that they did reach and discover India and other kingdomes and lordships bordering upon it; that they entered and navigated its sea, finding large cities, large edifices and rivers, and great populations, among whom is carried on all the trade in spices and precious stones. ... Of these they have brought a quantity, including cinnamon, cloves, ginger, nutmeg, and pepper, as well as other kinds, together with the boughs and leaves of the same; also many fine stones of all sorts, such as rubies and others.[20]

He also informed the rulers of Castile that the people of Calicut were Christian, an error of the past that Vasco da Gama persisted in believing for a long time,

[17] *Esmeraldo de situ orbis*, trans. and ed. George H. T. Kimble ("Hakluyt Society Publications," Ser. II, Vol. LXXIX [London, 1937]), p. 166.

[18] Ravenstein (ed.), *op. cit.* (n. 14), pp. xiv–xv, stresses his discovery objectives; E. Prestage, *The Portuguese Pioneers* (London, 1933), p. 249, emphasizes his diplomatic mission, as does Vicente Almeida d'Eça, *Normas economicas na colonização portuguesa até 1808* (Coimbra, 1921), pp. 51–52.

[19] Parr, *op. cit.* (n. 12), p. 52, claims that it was privately owned by Marchionni.

[20] As adapted from the translation in Ravenstein (ed.), *op. cit.* (n. 14), pp. 113–14.

even though he was struck at the outset by the strangeness of their religious practices.[21] While recognizing "that they are not as yet strong in the faith," Manuel felt that "once they shall have been . . . fortified in the faith there will be an opportunity for destroying the Moors of those parts" and for diverting the trade in spices and precious stones into Christian hands.

Once Da Gama himself returned in the "São Gabriel" at the end of August, 1499, King Manuel sent off a letter to the Cardinal Protector, D. Jorgé da Costa, in Rome.[22] Enclosed in this letter was also "the draft of a letter" to Pope Alexander VI, a document that has never been found. Of particular interest is Manuel's salutation in which he uses, for the first time so far as we know, his new title, "Lord of Guinea and of the Conquests, Navigations and Commerce of Ethiopia, Arabia, Persia, and India." The king's main object in sending this letter was to obtain papal confirmation of this title and his overseas claims.[23] He also informed the cardinal that the people of Calicut were Christian, that Pliny's Taprobane was Ceylon, and that Da Gama had returned with "five or six Indians," a Jewish merchant, and a young Moor of Tunis. The Moor was shortly baptized, adopted by Vasco da Gama, and given the distinguished Portuguese name of Gaspar da Gama.

Although these reports on India set off a chain reaction of curiosity and speculation in Europe, the commodities brought back by the fleet were but samples of what was generally available in East Africa and on the Malabar Coast. The Portuguese on this first expedition had almost nothing to trade for Indian wares, some of the sailors being literally reduced to exchanging the shirts off their backs for curios. Even if the Portuguese had been able to buy more, they could not have carried any great quantity in their two, heavily manned ships. Nevertheless, they brought back enough to give all the participants a share of the cargo. Vasco da Gama himself received ten quintal (hundredweight) of pepper, the heirs of his brother inherited five quintal, Nicolas Coelho got one quintal of all the "drugs," and each pilot and sailor was given one-half quintal of spices.[24] Even though the quantities were small, the prices of such commodities at Lisbon were high and so the returns were considerable.[25]

For the crown the greatest reward was the promise of future profitable ventures and the enhancement of its financial credit with the mercantile and

---

[21] This error persisted in some quarters for much longer than now seems reasonable. For example, Albuquerque remarks that the Brahmans "have knowledge of the Trinity, whereby it appears that anciently they were Christians" (Walter de Gray Birch [trans.], *Commentaries of the Great Afonso Dalboquerque* [London, 1875], I, 78). Cf. the persistence of the belief in Prester John and the old dream of Eastern Christians.

[22] *Ibid.*, pp. 114–16.

[23] A bull of 1497 had granted him the right to hold all countries conquered from infidels, and had required him to do his utmost to propagate the faith in them.

[24] Heyd, *op. cit.* (n. 5), II, 510, n. 1.

[25] F. C. Danvers, *The Portuguese in India* (London, 1894), I, 63–64, gives some of the contemporary prices in Lisbon and estimates that the value of the cargo "was sixty times the cost of the voyage." This is a generalization difficult to accept, for we have no accurate appraisal of the cost of the voyage.

banking houses of Europe. Optimism for future trade ran high, even though Da Gama's reception at Calicut was not all that had been hoped for, since the Zamorin (literally, captain of the sea or ruler) of Calicut, under the influence of the powerful Muslim merchant group that saw its trade supremacy threatened by the new arrivals from Christian Europe, failed to respond affirmatively to Da Gama's proffer of a treaty.[26] Nevertheless, India had been reached, and it was known that the products so much desired in Europe could be obtained there for a fraction of their current European price. Valuable information for future navigation of the South Atlantic and the Indian Ocean had been gathered, and it had been determined that points along the East African coast could be used as ports of call on the long voyage to India. Finally, Da Gama learned that even if peaceful trade should not be possible, the Portuguese vessels with their artillery were more than a match for the frail and unarmed vessels that plied the routes of the Indian Ocean. And from the natives and Arab pilots brought back to Portugal, it was learned that numerous possibilities for trade existed that had been hitherto unappreciated. Many of the Portuguese also persisted in believing, despite Gaspar da Gama's contention to the contrary, that the Indians were Christians and so would prefer to trade with other Christians rather than infidels. (It is only right to recall that the St. Thomas Christians were important participants in the pepper trade and that originally they were vitally interested in closer relations with the European Christians. See below, pp. 231-32.) In other parts of Europe the prospects for Portugal's trade with India stirred both hopes and fears. But as for King Manuel, he was jubilant, and so began in the fall of 1499 to prepare a new fleet and to embark upon an extensive program of public works in Lisbon to prepare the city for its new place in the sun.

2

THE BEGINNINGS OF TRADE BETWEEN PORTUGAL AND INDIA, 1499–1503

Manuel's exuberant reaction to the discovery of the sea route to India, his determination to make Lisbon the center of the spice commerce, his ambitious program of public works, and his decision to focus his own efforts and those of the state upon trade can only be understood by appreciating how expensive and scarce spices were at the end of the fifteenth century. At Venice in 1499, the absolute price of pepper was as much as 80 ducats per hundredweight. On the Rialto at Venice it had almost doubled (from 42 to 80 ducats) in less than five years, and other spices had mounted correspondingly in price. In distant Antwerp prices had similarly increased. Da Gama meanwhile learned that pepper could

[26] For an Indian viewpoint see K. M. Panikkar, *Malabar and the Portuguese* (Bombay, 1929), p. 33.

be purchased at Calicut for as little as 3 ducats. In Venice certain of the spices were apparently not available at all during the final years of the fifteenth century.[27]

These dramatic price increases and scarcities were not attributable alone to the desire for higher profits on the part of the intermediary powers. Actually, a general political crisis in the eastern Mediterranean appears to be the main reason for the chaos afflicting the spice traffic at the turn of the century. The Turkish Empire around 1496 experienced a decline of about 16 per cent in returns from trade. In Egypt a succession crisis beginning in 1496 made it impossible for the central authority to keep the trade routes open, and at Cairo the bazaars dealing in spices were forced to suspend business. Meanwhile, in Italy, a number of the banking houses went bankrupt, and the normal course of commercial life was interrupted by the French invasions, conquests, and exactions. The situation in the eastern Mediterranean was rendered even more chaotic in 1498 by the outbreak of war between Venice and Turkey over control of the Dalmatian coast. For this complex of reasons the Venetians, it would appear, imported no spices at all in 1499–1500 from Alexandria or Beirut. The Catalans, French, and Genoese meanwhile took advantage of Venice's involvement in war to seize for themselves whatever part of the spice trade in the eastern Mediterranean they could get. Spices remained scarce and prices abnormally high in western Europe for several years after Da Gama's ships returned to the Tagus in 1499.[28]

King Manuel sought to take advantage of this situation with all possible dispatch. At the waterfront in Lisbon the king's activity was most noticeable. Plans were laid for moving the Casa da India and the *armazem* (warehouses) right down to the quay.[29] Wharves were also constructed to take care of the increased traffic expected on the Tagus. Possibly to beautify and clean up the city, the king decreed that space should be cleared around the city walls and ordered that many of the olive trees cluttering the monastic gardens should be removed. At Restello, just a few miles downriver from Lisbon, Manuel bought lands and buildings from the Brothers of Christ. It was here in the small chapel erected by Prince Henry that Vasco da Gama had made his peace with God before setting sail, and it was now presumed that future commanders would be doing likewise. Late in 1499 work commenced on the Monastery of the

---

[27] The following statistics on prices (absolute and comparative) will illustrate the point. Short pepper in 1498 sold at 30 Brabant *groten* per *pond* (roughly equivalent to one British pound), and by 1500 at 55.5. See Charles Verlinden *et al.*, *Dokumenten voor de geschiedenis van prijzen en lonen in Vlaanderen en Brabant (XVᵉ–XVIIIᵉ eeuw)* (Bruges, 1959), pp. 332–33. In 1500 a whole sheep carcass, for example, cost 42 *groten* at the slaughterhouse in Antwerp (*ibid.*, p. 311). At Venice the price rise was relatively even greater. See especially the summary data compiled in the tables included in Vitorino Magalhães-Godinho, "Le répli vénitien et égyptien et la route du Cap, 1496–1533," *Eventail de l'histoire vivante* (Paris, 1953), pp. 287–89. Cf. Pierre Sardella, *Nouvelles et spéculations à Vénise au début du XVIᵉ siècle* (Paris, 1948), pp. 30–37. For these and other prices of pepper, the leading spice imported from India see the tables in the appendix to this chapter.

[28] Magalhães-Godhino, *loc. cit.* (n. 27), pp. 284–92.

[29] Julio de Castilho, *A ribeira de Lisboa* (Lisbon, 1941–48), II, 140–42.

Jerónimos, and its environs were renamed Belém (Bethlehem). For the next half-century, work continued on the monastery that stands today as one of the greatest monuments of the Manueline style of architecture and as a symbol of the great material upsurge that swept Lisbon at the beginning of the sixteenth century.

But the king was not entirely occupied with public works. He was also busy with the preparation of a new and larger fleet. While the king and many contemporaries were convinced of Portugal's divine mission in India, there were still those who advised caution and pointed out the great expenses and risks involved in such a gigantic enterprise for a small nation. The entire country had an estimated population of only 1,100,000, and Lisbon itself probably boasted no more than 50,000 inhabitants.[30] To outfit an expedition of twelve hundred men and thirteen ships, and to provide them with a cargo for trade was a large undertaking for Portugal, even though the gold from Mina, sugar from the Madeiras, and confiscations from the Jews and Moors had given the crown a recent influx of wealth.

Utmost care was taken in the selection of the personnel for this first great commercial voyage. Pedro Alvares Cabral, a young navigator of noble lineage, was assigned to command the fleet, and many of his captains were enlisted from Portugal's leading families. Franciscan missionaries were also sent as part of this expedition. A factor was put in charge of the cargo, for one of Manuel's main objectives was to set up a factory in Calicut that would acquire merchandise for the fleets that he hoped to send out to India on a regular schedule. Finally, on March 8, 1500, Cabral's fleet of thirteen ships set sail from Restello after appropriate religious ceremonies and the king's last-minute instructions to the young commander.[31]

On the way to India, Cabral made himself immortal by "discovering" Brazil. From there he sent a supply ship back to Portugal to let the king know of his good fortune. But Cabral's fortunes were soon to change. The trip across the South Atlantic and around the Cape was disastrous to the fleet, and Cabral arrived at Calicut with but seven vessels of his original thirteen. At Calicut itself Cabral also ran into difficulties. The factory and mission that he tried to set up were soon destroyed, and the Portuguese ended up by bombarding the

[30] These are the estimates given in A. de Sousa Silva Costa Lobo, *História da sociedade em Portugal no século XV* (Lisbon, 1903), p. 32. This figure for Lisbon's population seems to receive confirmation in the scientific demographic study of Roger Mols, *Introduction à la démographie des villes d'Europe du XIVᵉ au XVIIIᵉ siècle* (Gemblaux, 1954–56), II, 47, 424, 518–19. Mols indicates that Lisbon certainly had over 20,000 inhabitants at the beginning of the fourteenth century and that by 1629 its population numbered 110,800. He also indicates that it perhaps trebled in size during the sixteenth century, the greatest period of urban expansion on the Iberian Peninsula in early modern times. It should also be remarked, however, that the population of Portugal was more than that of Florence (700,000) but less than that of Venice with its possessions (1,700,000). More simply put, a nation of one million was relatively not so small in 1500 as it seems today, when Lisbon itself has a population of about 800,000.

[31] Details in William B. Greenlee (ed.), *The Voyage of Pedro Alvares Cabral to Brazil and India* ("Hakluyt Society Publications," Ser. II, Vol. LXXXI [London, 1938]).

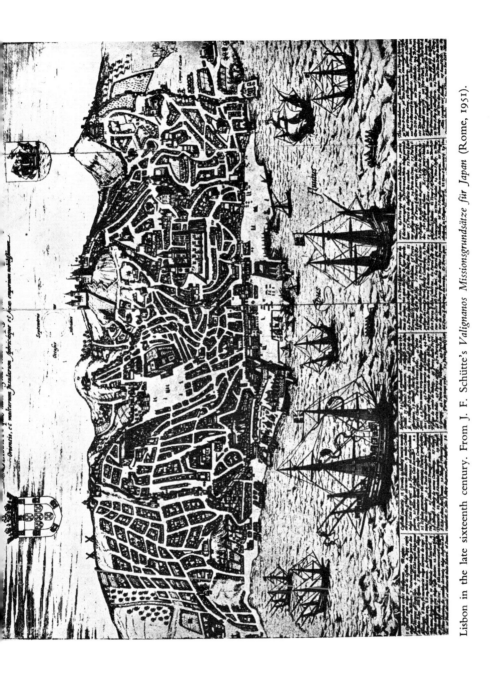

Lisbon in the late sixteenth century. From J. F. Schütte's *Valignanos Missionsgrundsätze für Japan* (Rome, 1951).

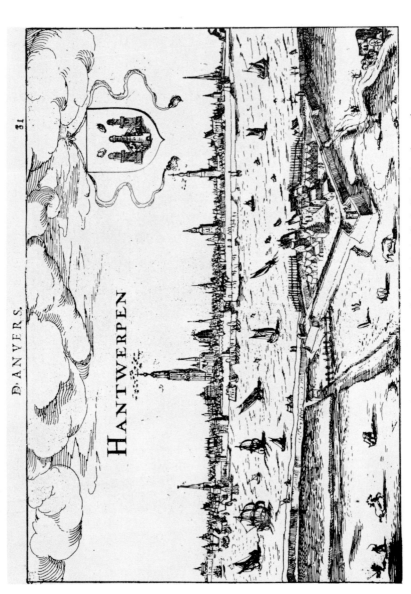

B. ANVERS.

HANTWERPEN

Antwerp in the middle of the sixteenth century. From Lodovico Guicciardini's *Description de touts les Pays-Bas* (Arnhem, 1593). Courtesy of the University of Chicago Libraries.

The Fortress of Malacca, *ca.* 1630. From the *Journal of the Malayan Branch of the Royal Asiatic Society,*

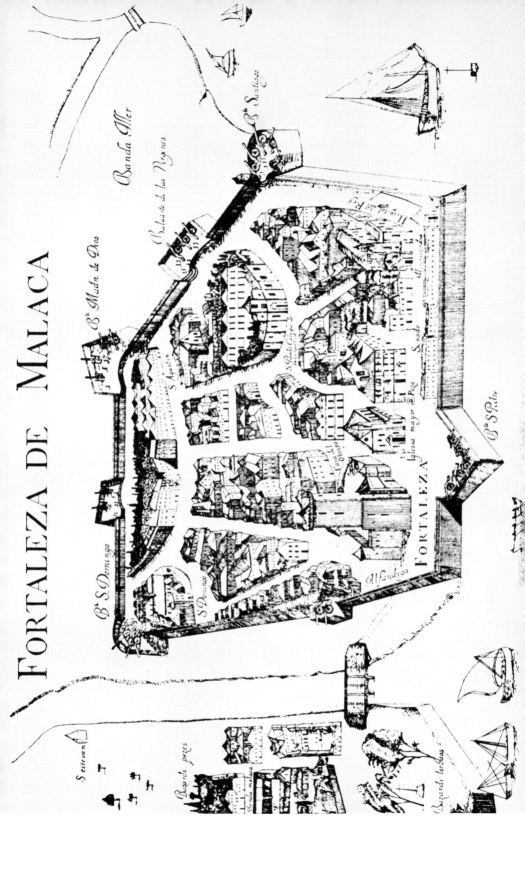

FORTALEZA DE MALACA

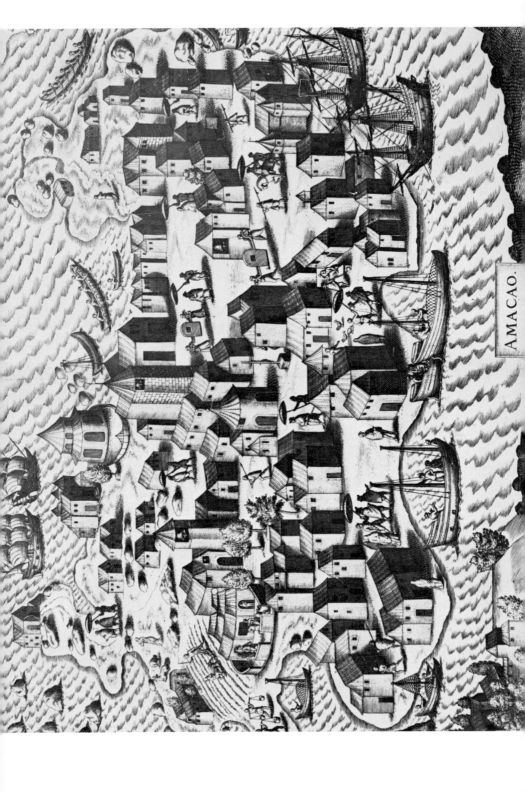

AMACAO.

Macao, *ca.* 1600. From Theodor de Bry's *Indiae orientalis* (Frankfurt, 1607).

Coins used in commerce in the East Indies, Cambay, Ormuz, Goa, Malabar, Coromandel, Bengal, and Malacca. From Theodor de Bry, *Indiae orientalis* (Frankfurt, 1599).

BORSE

S . P . Q . A.
Inuſu negotiatorum cui
uſcuq, Nationis acliguæ ur
biſq adeo ſuæ ornamenhun
Anno M D X X X I.
A ſolo exti u cur .

Mundi anima ut rerum mode-
retur Nummus habens Ter-
raſq, et tractus conclubtmarium
Diſce hoſpes toto quamvis
diviſis ab orbe:
Hậc tibi ſi Nummus non
peregrinus eris

The port of Lisbon in the sixteenth century. An engraving which originally appeared in the work of Hans Staden, *Wahrhaftige Historia und Beschreibung einer Landschaft der . . . Menschenfresserleuten in . . . Amerika* (Frankfurt, 1592). Merely an artist's conception of Lisbon and not a true depiction, this engraving is an interesting portrayal of a typical sixteenth-century European seaport. From Albino Forjaz de Sampaio's *Historia da literatura portuguesa* (Paris, 1929–32).

A small merchant ship, *ca.* 1532. A washed drawing by Hans Hans Holbein the Younger. Original now in the Frankfur am Main City Museum. From G. S. Clowes, *Sailing Ships* (London, 1936). For scholarly discussion of this drawing see *ibid.*, II, 19.

Manuelina Naus. A painting of Portuguese ships executed *ca.* 1521 by Gregório Lopes. From Forjaz de Sampaio's *Historia da literatura portuguesa illustrada.*

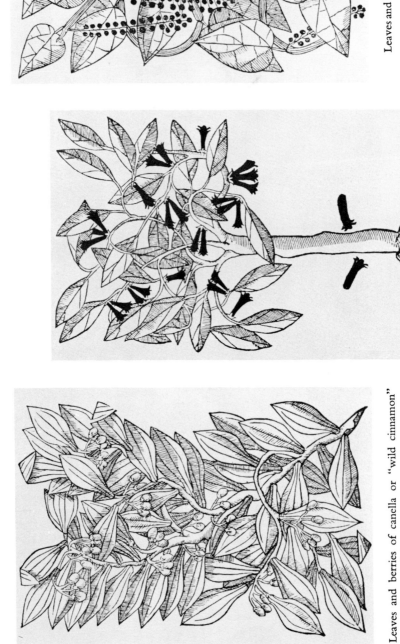

Leaves and berries of the pepper plant.

The clove tree.

Leaves and berries of canella or "wild cinnamon" (*Ravensara aromatica*).

These drawings are by Cristobal de Acosta. They are reproduced here from Sir Clements Markham (ed. and trans.), *Colloquies on the Simples and Drugs of India*, by *Garcia da Orta* . . . (London, 1913).

IDEA LANTOR, ASSA, PIMEN-
TA DEL RABO, TALASSE, MANGO.
stans, & Piperis.

ANTORÈ Coquos seu nucum Indicarum classe est, folia proferens porrectioriori longitudine, quibus Papyri loco indigene utuntur. Pimenta del Rabo (seu cubebæ,) unarum modo in arbore quadam proueniunt: quas Indi in tanto habent pretio, ut non nisi coctas eas in terras alienas exportent.

Simul additur arbor Tamarindi seu Assaß, ut & herba Talasse, in Iaua celebris: nec minus fructus aliud Mangostans, & rotundi nigri piperis in Iaua prodeuntis, quod Sabang incolæ vocitant.

DE ALGA SEV ARVNDINE
INDICA, BAMBVS DICTA, ITEM DE
arboreradicosa: & tandem de arbore
Duryoens.

ARVNDINIS quædam in India genus prouenit, quod Indi Bambus vocant, crassitiem femoris virilis occupans. Arbor quoque alia ibidem prouenit, Arbore de Rays i. de radicibus nuncupata, è cuius ramis filamenta plurima descendunt, quæ terram attingentia illi se denuò insinuant, & radice tagentia ramos vicissim alio sursum pariuntur, qui & insulatius propagati tandem arborem constituunt, ambitu suo quartam partem milliaris cenius complexam.

Hi quoque tantùm aspici cernitur alia quædam arbor, quæ fructum Duryoens dictum fert, in sola Malacca cognita. Fructus iste à gustantibus fructuum omnium, quos vonuerfus terrarum orbis gignit longè optimus & suauissimus censetur. De qua re uberius historiæ tradidimus.

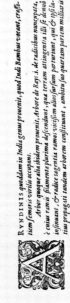

East Indian trees.

East Indian trees and plants.

Both from Theodor de Bry's *Indiae orientalis* (Frankfurt, 1601).

CONTRAFACTVRA QVO-
RVNDAM ANIMALIVM, IN INDIA
celebrium.

LEPHANTI in India frequentiſſimi, maxime tamen in Æthiopia apud Caffres reperiuntur: vbi cauſa dentium, quos Luſitanis vendunt, occidi ſolent. Illorum certa copia quoque in Bengala eſt:nec minor in Pegu, vbi tanto numero & multitudine vagantur, vt vna vice locoque interdum duo millia cogant, ex quibus optimos quoſque ſeligunt, & cæteros ad ſpeciei augmentum liberos iterum dimittunt.

Rhinoceros animal & ipſum in India, ſed in Bengalæ ſaltè Patanæɋ terminis reperitur, in quibus iuxta Gangem fluuium magna copia vagantur.

In flumine prædicto Crocodili quoɋ numeroſi ſunt, qui piſcatoribus infeſtatione crebra valde moleſti ſunt: vt ex hiſtoria fuſius patebit.

Animals of India. From Theodor de Bry's *Indiae orientalis* (Frankfurt, 1601).

city and seizing Muslim vessels standing in the harbor. With this action, the war between Muslims and Portuguese was carried into the Indian Ocean and to India itself as each sought to hold a monopoly of the spice trade.

After venting his wrath on Calicut, Cabral, following his orders, sailed southward to Cochin, a smaller state on the Malabar Coast whose ruler was perennially at odds with Calicut. For two weeks the fleet was anchored at Cochin to negotiate with its king and to load spices. In the meantime the Zamorin of Calicut had gathered a fleet of eight vessels to follow and attack the Portuguese ships. On the appearance of this armada, Cabral hastily beat a retreat and determined to sail back to Europe, after stopping for one day at Cannanore. Here he loaded more spices and took aboard an ambassador from the king of Cannanore who returned with him to Portugal.

The first of the vessels to arrive back at the Tagus was the one commanded by Nicholas Coelho, who reached Lisbon with news of the fleet on June 23, 1501; about one month later the other vessels made port. On learning that Cabral had returned with a substantial cargo of spices, the king held a feast in the palace, ordered that the bells of the city ring out the good news, and called for ceremonial processions throughout the land.[32] Six days later King Manuel dispatched a letter[33] to the rulers of Castile that remains one of the best contemporary sources for Cabral's voyage. Aside from a bare recital of Cabral's experiences, the king commented on the Indian custom of writing on palm leaves and on the numerous uses of the cocopalm and its fruit. Of Cochin he remarks that they found there "many true Christians of the conversion of St. Thomas," and records that Cabral brought two Malabar Christian priests back with him. Actually Priest Joseph was the only one to make the trip to Rome and Jerusalem, and from there back to India.[34] Cabral also is supposed to have heard news of China, where "there are such fine vases of porcelain that a single one of them is worth a hundred cruzados."

Of the returns from the voyage itself the king has little to say. Many more details on the economic results of the voyage can be found in the anonymous narrative probably written by an educated Portuguese member of the expedition.[35] This unknown commentator frankly states also that the Zamorin "is an idolater, although others [Vasco da Gama and his aides] have believed that they [the Indians of Calicut] are Christians." He remarks on the custom of chewing betel nut and notes "that those who do not do this are men of low degree." He comments at length on matrimonial customs and the tradition of matrilineal heritage. He also notices differences in color in the merchants who come from other parts of India and stresses how their customs differ from those of the Malabars. He observes that at Cranganore, near Cochin, there were Christians, presumably of the Malabar church, and that it was from here that

---

[32] As reported in the contemporary letter of Giovanni Matho Cretico, translated in *ibid.*, p. 122.
[33] Text translated in *ibid.*, pp. 43–52.
[34] On Joseph's account and his travels see below, pp. 157–58.
[35] Translation in Greenlee (ed.), *op. cit.* (n. 31), pp. 66–94.

the two priests originally came who wanted to go to Rome and Jerusalem. And he relates that in Cabral's hasty departure from Cochin, he took with him two hostages that he had on board as surety for the safety of the seven men whom he had sent ashore. Unlike the king, the anonymous author gives a list of the cost of spices and drugs in Calicut as well as a list of the sale prices of European products such as lead, copper, silver, alum, and coral. He also gives a comprehensive list of the places from which the spices marketed in Calicut originally came. This commercial information, which the Portuguese were evidently trying to keep to themselves as much as possible, was of particular interest to the Venetian and other Italian mercantile representatives in Lisbon.[36] To Rome the religious information about the Malabar Christians came as a welcome surprise.[37]

Even before the return of Cabral another Portuguese fleet of four vessels had departed for India in the spring of 1501 under the command of João da Nova.[38] Through a letter relayed to him in Africa by one of Cabral's men, Nova learned of Portugal's trouble with Calicut and so proceeded directly to Cochin. Here he loaded his vessels with spices. At Cannanore he took on more cargo and seized a ship of Calicut. From the captured vessel he removed the pilot, three silver navigational instruments, and a collection of 1,500 pearls. Nova returned to Portugal in September, 1502, with this loot and 1,550 hundredweight of pepper.

After hearing about the difficulties experienced by Cabral, King Manuel concluded that he would have to make a display of military and naval might in the East. He was also eager to strike against the Moorish centers of trade and fleets, before Egypt should have time or opportunity to put an armed fleet of its own into the Indian Ocean. An armada of twenty-five vessels was accordingly prepared and placed under the command of Vasco da Gama, whose glory in Lisbon was then exalted above that of Alexander the Great.[39] Twelve of the vessels belonged to the king and thirteen to the merchants. The first squadron of ten vessels was under the immediate authority of Da Gama, the second, of five ships, was commanded by his uncle, Vicente Sodré, and the third by his nephew, Estavão da Gama. On his flagship the admiral had in his company the ambassador of the king of Cannanore and the two captives from Cochin. Gaspar da Gama, who had been baptized by this time and admitted as a cavalier to the king's household, acted as interpreter on the flagship.[40]

Once the fleet had sailed around the Cape, Da Gama used his superior force to intimidate the rulers of East Africa. At Cannanore he began to look for Arab

---

[36] See below, pp. 105–7.

[37] See below, pp. 160–61.

[38] Details in Danvers, *op. cit.* (n. 25), I, 74–77.

[39] See the description by Alberto Cantino, diplomatic agent of the Duke of Ferrara, of the ceremony preceding Da Gama's departure. Translated in Hart, *op. cit.* (n. 13), p. 222.

[40] For biographical details see Greenlee (ed.), *op. cit.* (n. 31), pp. 179–80.

ships and pirated them whenever he could. Here he also loaded spices. Meanwhile, a squadron under the admiral proceeded to Calicut to punish that city for its refusal to co-operate in the Portuguese program. Other vessels were sent to Cochin to load cargo. Commercial agreements were signed at both Cochin and Cannanore and factories set up. Fixed rates of weights, measures, and prices were established by treaty in 1502. An agreement was also entered into with Quilon, a town just south of Cochin. In December, 1502, ten vessels under Da Gama set sail for Portugal and seven of them arrived at Lisbon in the following September with a rich spice cargo and gifts of jewels, a silver candelabrum, and cotton cloth for the king. Vicente Sodré was left in India with the remainder of the Portuguese vessels to protect the factories and to patrol Indian waters. By these forceful means the Portuguese secured footholds on the Malabar Coast and in so doing made certain that they would have an assured supply of spices at fixed prices. Muslim and Indian merchants, excluded from the Malabar trade, began to go eastward to Indonesia in search of other sources of spices.[41]

3

THE REORIENTATION OF COMMERCE IN EUROPE, 1500–1515

It is not until the voyage of Cabral that we have much information on the activities of the international financial and commercial interests operating in Portugal. That the financial groups must have been interested in a new European source of spices goes without saying when one recalls the high prices and scarcity of spices around 1500. Further support is given this assumption by King Manuel's decree of January, 1500, that permitted any private individual (and presumably group) to send licensed trading vessels to India with the simple proviso that the crown should receive one-fourth of the value of the cargo with which such private vessels returned.[42]

The Florentine merchants in particular had the confidence of King Manuel and they were more prominent at Lisbon in 1500 than any other foreign group. The elimination of their merchant fleet in 1494 by the Pisans forced the Florentine merchants to look abroad for investment opportunities, and they were not slow in trying to meet the commercial and financial needs of Portugal after the expulsion of the Jews and the discovery of the Cape route. Since the Portuguese were well aware of the hostility with which the Venetians might be expected to view their intervention in the spice trade, it was only natural that

---

[41] For a study of the changing character of the pepper trade in Asia see John Bastian, "The Changing Balance of the Southeast Asian Pepper Trade," in *Essays on Indonesian and Malay History* (Singapore, 1961), pp. 19–29.

[42] Danvers, *op. cit.* (n. 23), I, 74. In his diary for September, 1501, the Venetian Girolamo Priuli mentions the king's share as being 29 per cent. As translated in Greenlee (ed.), *op. cit.* (n. 31), p. 138.

they first looked for aid from and gave preference to the Florentine group which had nothing to lose and a great deal to gain from active support of the Portuguese economic program. At the same time King Manuel encouraged merchants from all over Europe to come to Lisbon for spices.

Of Cabral's thirteen vessels, ten were owned by the crown. One was owned by a partnership of Marchionni and the Portuguese nobleman, Dom Alvara de Bragança; another was the property of Girolamo Sernigi, a Florentine merchant, in company with a Genoese, probably Antonio Salvago; a third vessel was owned by a combine headed by Dom Diogo de Silva Meneses, the Count of Portalegre. The first of Cabral's fleet to return to Lisbon was the "Annunciada," the caravel commanded by Nicolas Coelho for the Marchionni interests and the fastest of the ships in the fleet. So, in the summer of 1501 a large number of people with differing interests awaited the results of Cabral's voyage.

Contemporary commentators generally agree that Cabral returned in June, 1501, with but four vessels. He had lost one well-laden ship of the original five to attempt the return voyage. The four caravels that returned had their holds filled with 2,000 hundredweight of pepper, 600 of cinnamon, and 400 of ginger, as well as smaller quantities of cloves, lac, and benzoin. The "Annunciada," according to Marchionni's own report,[43] carried 300 hundredweight of pepper, 160 of cinnamon, 60 of lac, and 14 of benzoin. Its crew also returned with "two parrots of different colors" and stories of many other animals and birds. In a letter written after the return of Cabral, Marchionni ruminated on the meaning of the Portuguese success for the eastern Mediterranean states. The Portuguese, he concluded, "must give great trouble to the Venetians, and on the route more to the Sultan who enjoys the traffic down there [India], because by this route they [the spices] come at rather small expense and more easily."[44]

The Venetians themselves, preoccupied with their efforts to win support from the other Christian powers for their war against the Turks, were rather slow to comprehend the full meaning of the Portuguese accomplishment. The first news of the arrival of Portuguese ships at Calicut reached the Queen City of the Adriatic in August, 1499, through Cairo and Alexandria. The diarist Girolamo Priuli recorded receipt of this information, but doubted its accuracy.[45] Since Venice had no legation in Lisbon at the time, it was somewhat difficult for the Republic of St. Mark to verify the report. It was only in 1500 that the Venetian Seignory commissioned Domenico Pisani, a recently appointed envoy to Spain, to undertake a side visit to Lisbon. He was sent there primarily to enlist King Manuel's aid in the war against the Turks.[46] While Pisani received assurance of continuing support from Portugal, letters arrived in Venice during March, 1501, from the emissary and from Manuel himself,

---

[43] Marchionni's letter to Florence of June 27, 1501 as translated in Greenlee (ed.), *op. cit.* (n. 31), p. 148.

[44] *Ibid.*, p. 149

[45] Heyd, *op. cit.* (n. 5), II, 515–16.

[46] Donald Weinstein, *Ambassador from Venice: Pietro Pasqualigo in Lisbon* (Minneapolis, 1960), p. 10.

telling of the discovery of the sea route to the spice marts of India. In response to this direct news, the Venetian Senate quickly appointed Pietro Pasqualigo as ambassador extraordinary to the Portuguese court. The new envoy arrived at Lisbon in time to witness the return of the first ships of Cabral's fleet, and to dispatch a report to his superiors in Venice informing them officially of the discovery of Brazil and the beginnings of the spice trade by the Atlantic route. This report was probably prepared by Giovanni Camerino, formerly a reader of Greek rhetoric at Padua and nicknamed *Il Cretico*, who had acted as secretary to Pisani and had remained in Lisbon in 1500 to watch the course of events there.[47]

Il Cretico's report apprised the Seignory of the events of Cabral's voyage, of Manuel's elation, and his joyous admonition that "I should write to Your Serenity that from now on you should send your ships to carry spices from here."[48] Of the spices he remarked that "they took on a heavy cargo . . . at a price I fear to tell. . . ."[49] and commented that Manuel "feels that he has India at his command." He also let the Seignory know that the Portuguese king "would forbid the Sultan to go for spices." The Venetians in Lisbon also had an opportunity to talk with the emissaries of the kings of Cochin and Cannanore, whom they sought to convince that a poor country like Portugal could never hope to take away control of the spice trade from the established commercial powers.[50] But these efforts to denigrate the Portuguese were all in vain.

Even though Manuel lived up to his promise to send a fleet to aid Venice against the Turks in the summer of 1501, the Venetian diarists[51] record the alarm felt on the Rialto at the Portuguese intervention in the spice trade. Priuli, in July, 1501, spoke of the news from Portugal as being "of greater importance to the Venetian state than the Turkish war, or any other wars which might have affected her." Of the profits he estimated that "from one ducat [investment] they can make more than one hundred," in spite of the severe losses to Cabral's fleet. Priuli predicted also, "There is no doubt that the Hungarians, Germans, Flemish and French, and those beyond the mountains, who formerly came to Venice to buy spices with their money, will all turn towards Lisbon, for it is nearer to all the countries, and easier to reach." Evidently he meant to say that Lisbon is more centrally located and more readily accessible by sea to the main entrepôts of western Europe than Venice. Because of his belief in the ability of the Portuguese to exploit their gains, Priuli foresaw "the ruin of the Venetian city." Unable to persuade Portugal to give greater aid to the Venetian crusade, Pasqualigo was recalled from Lisbon as the

[47] *Ibid.*, p. 29.
[48] Greenlee (ed.), *op. cit.* (n. 31), p. 114.
[49] *Ibid.*, p. 121.
[50] Heyd, *op. cit.* (n. 5), pp. 516–17.
[51] On Priuli and Marino Sanuto, the two who give greatest attention to the opening of the sea route, see the discussion in Greenlee, *op. cit.* (n. 31), pp. 130–31. For the story of the Portuguese fleet sent to aid Venice see Weinstein, *op. cit.* (n. 46), pp. 70–71.

Seignory turned its back on Portugal to face the more immediate menace of the Turks.

Just at the time when Portugal began to tap the spice trade in earnest, the Venetians were left without official representation in Lisbon. Over the next two years their only apparent source of information was the letters of the merchant Giovanni Francisco Affaitadi of Cremona. During this period Cremona was under the control of Venice, and so the Affaitadi representative in Lisbon kept the Seignory informed of developments in the trade with India. From his writings and those of others, we learn that though the financial returns from the first three Portuguese voyages were modest, the second venture of Vasco da Gama finally set to rest any doubt that might have persisted about the feasibility of the sea route. The ten vessels that returned in 1503 brought 35,000 hundred-weight (corresponding in modern terms to a little more than 1,900 metric tons) of spices, mostly pepper.[52] Thirty per cent of this went directly to the king in addition to what was on his account. Among the private investors, the Affaitadi realized a return on their investment of 150 per cent.[53] Presumably most of the other private investors netted a neat profit, or had cause to think they would when finally the spices were marketed. In the fleets sent out in 1503–4, the merchant syndicates still played a prominent role. In Albuquerque's fleet of 1503, for example, four ships were owned and outfitted by the Florentine syndicate.

The shortage and high cost of spices in Venice moved the Seignory to appoint at the end of 1502 an extraordinary council (*Additio Specierum*) to deal with the problems of the spice trade.[54] After Pasqualigo's failure to bring Portugal around to Venice's point of view, the new council decided to work more closely with the Sultan of Egypt in making the Indian ocean unsafe for Portuguese trading vessels. While refusing to give direct military support to the Egyptians, the Venetian emissaries in Cairo threatened to go to Lisbon to buy their spices if the Sultan would not reduce prices and guarantee supplies. The frustrated Mameluke ruler, being unable to sweep the Indian Ocean clear of the Portuguese interlopers, sent word to the papacy and to the secular rulers of Europe that he would attack the Holy Places if the Portuguese persisted in their penetration of India. While Egypt vainly threatened, the Portuguese doggedly continued to make their annual voyages and to prepare facilities for the expansion of trade at Lisbon.

Venice concluded a treaty with the Turks in 1503, both contestants being in need of a breathing spell to handle other problems. In July, 1504, the spice council in Venice secretly sent Leonardo da Ca'Masser to Lisbon to obtain detailed information on the spice trade and its prospects for future development. Although the Portuguese knew that they had a spy in their midst, Ca'Masser was allowed to carry on his work in Lisbon for the next two years. On his

[52] Gino Luzzato, *Storia economica dell'età moderna e contemporanea* (Padua, 1938), I, 157.
[53] Denucé, *op. cit.* (n. 8), p. 19.
[54] Weinstein, *op. cit.* (n. 46), p. 77.

return to Venice in 1506 he reported in comprehensive detail on the Portuguese voyages to date and on deliveries, commercial organization, and efforts to eliminate the Arabs from the spice trade in the East.[55] While he concluded that the Portuguese would certainly be able to continue and expand the trade, he considered it unlikely that they would find it possible with their limited resources to exclude the Muslims from participation, or maintain a monopoly over the marts of Asia. He also mentioned parenthetically that even greater riches were to be found east of India for those able to sail there and return. Still confronted with major problems in Italy and the eastern Mediterranean, Venice for the moment was left with no choice but to renew her old ties with the Islamic purveyors and to work subterraneanly against the Portuguese.

At Alexandria, Cairo, and Beirut, spices meanwhile had almost disappeared from the market. In 1505, a hundredweight of pepper at Cairo cost 192 ducats, the highest price it was to reach in the period from 1496 to 1531.[56] On the Lisbon market, contrariwise, prices began to fall, and in 1504 they dropped from 40 to 20 ducats. This was still a good price, however, for the pepper could be purchased in India at the price of about 3 ducats fixed by the treaties. In an effort to bring the spices and their purchasers closer together, Portugal had begun as early as 1501 to send spices to Antwerp for sale. Tomé Lopes, the Portuguese factor at Antwerp after 1498, began in 1503 to undertake the sale of spices on a regular basis at Antwerp in return for copper, silver, and other goods. This trade was made possible by a charter granted in 1502 permitting the Portuguese to export silver from Antwerp. From five to six thousand hundredweights of copper were supplied to the Portuguese fleets annually through the Affaitadi and their agents during the first decade of the sixteenth century. Antwerp took in return about one-quarter of the spices annually brought to Europe in the Portuguese fleets. Already, by 1503, the price of pepper at Antwerp had declined to the same level which had prevailed in 1945, or in the period before the great price rise at the end of the fifteenth century.[57] From these figures it can easily be seen that in the period from 1499 to 1505 the Portuguese had replaced Syria, Egypt, and Venice as spice monopolists, had begun to work out a new system for distributing the spices to northern Europe through Antwerp, and had found a means of obtaining in Europe the metals so highly prized in India.

The main trade at Antwerp was with the Germans, and for a few years the Affaitadi agents as middlemen controlled the exchange of Portuguese spices for central European metals. The German merchants themselves, who had traded at Venice for a long time, were forced in 1499–1500 to take their business

[55] Text in G. Scopoli (ed.), "Relazione di Leonardo da Ca'Masser . . .," *Archivio storico italiano*, Ser. I, Appendix 2 (1945). On the possible relation between his mission and the Portuguese policy of secrecy see below, p. 152 n.
[56] See the table compiled by Magalhães-Godinho, *loc. cit.* (n. 27), p. 294. Also consult appendix.
[57] Verlinden *et al.*, *op. cit.* (n. 27), pp. 332–33.

elsewhere. In 1501, under the leadership of the Fuggers, four German commercial houses tried unsuccessfully to enter directly into the Mediterranean spice trade through Genoa. At about the same time, Lucas Rem, until then a representative at Lyons of the Welsers of Augsburg, began to concern himself with events in the Iberian Peninsula. At the end of 1502, in company with Simon Seytz and Scipio Löwenstein, Rem went to Spain. Seytz and Löwenstein, leaving Rem behind in Spain, continued on to Lisbon. In May, 1503, Rem joined them in the Portuguese capital.[58]

Even before Rem's arrival in Lisbon, Seytz sought to get a contract from the king that would entitle the German houses to participate in direct trade with Lisbon. The Germans were apparently aided in their negotiations by Valentim Fernandes, a printer from Moravia who was influential in court circles and well informed on the latest developments in the spice trade. On February 13, 1503, an agreement was concluded between the Germans and the king which required the German houses to put up 10,000 ducats as surety. It was also agreed that Fernandes should act as their broker. Wood, pitch, and tar from north Germany, items in short supply in Lisbon and essential to ship construction, were to be admitted to Portugal at a duty of 10 per cent or less. The spices and other commodities purchased by the Germans at Lisbon might be exported duty-free from Portugal. Manuel was particularly anxious to have good relations with the German houses, for they ultimately controlled the production and distribution of most of the silver, copper, and lead produced in Europe.[59]

Not content simply to trade at Lisbon, the German merchants also pressed for permission to invest in the fleets and to send their agents directly to India. It was common knowledge in Lisbon that the Italian merchants had been permitted to invest heavily in the fleets of 1503 and that they had sent their own representatives to India. Early in 1504, Welser agents came to Lisbon through Antwerp with letters from Emperor Maximilian and Archduke Philip the Fair. They also brought with them the princely amount of 20,000 ducats' worth of metal and merchandise. Two of the younger Welser merchants came to Lisbon for the specific purpose of going out to India. On their arrival they saw the fleet of Lopo Soares lying in the Tagus being prepared to sail. The new arrivals from Germany wanted to invest in the fleet and to send the two young merchant-apprentices to India with it. The king refused their offer, saying that he intended in the future to reserve the trade exclusively to the crown.[60]

The principle of crown monopoly of overseas trade was nothing new in Portugal. As already indicated, from the time of Prince Henry, royal monopolies in the domestic economy had helped to pay for overseas activities, and

[58] For details see R. Greiff (ed.), *Tagebuch des Lucas Rem aus den Jahren 1484–1541* (Augsburg, 1861), pp. 48–49.

[59] Further details in F. Hümmerich, *Die erste deutsche Handelsfahrt nach Indien* (Munich, 1922), pp. 12–16.

[60] See K. Häbler, *Die überseeischen Unternehmungen der Welser* (Leipzig, 1903), pp. 14–18.

with the growth of the African trade the monopolistic economic practices of the crown were extended to the Portuguese overseas possessions and trade.[61] King Manuel, apparently in need of capital, permitted the Italian merchants to play a large role in the outfitting of the first Portuguese fleets, and most of the private investors, both Portuguese and foreign, seem to have profited considerably from their participation. By 1504, however, a series of events conjoined to convince the king that he would have to act directly and quickly if the crown were to reserve to itself the profits of the spice trade.

The appearance of the Welsers at Lisbon early in 1504 coincided with the beginning of a sharp drop in the prices of the spices on the Lisbon market. The great success of Vasco da Gama in returning in 1503 with 35,000 hundred-weight of spices apparently oversupplied the market, and pepper prices dropped from 40 to 20 ducats and seemed destined to go even lower. The fleet of Lopo Soares de Albergaria was outfitted entirely at the king's expense, the only private investors being the commander of the fleet and the captains of each vessel.[62] Shortly after the departure of Soares' fleet, the king apparently was placed under great pressure by Rem and other Germans in Lisbon. In August, 1504, he signed a contract with Rem by which he agreed to let a German-Italian syndicate of merchants send three ships of their own to India in the fleet of the next year. The syndicate was also permitted to send its own agents to buy spices, though they were to be under the supervision of the royal factor. Apparently the merchants felt, on the basis of the Italians' experiences, that the royal factor purchased the best spices for the king's account and assigned the inferior grades to the private accounts. On returning to Lisbon with their goods, the merchants were to deposit their cargoes in the warehouses of the Casa da India and turn over 30 per cent of their spices to the king.[63]

The privileges granted by the crown in the contract of 1504 ran counter to the other policies that the king was simultaneously trying to put into force. For at about the same time he proclaimed a royal monopoly of pepper, and by successive decrees likewise imposed controls on a number of the other important spices. Manuel forbade the merchants, on pain of being excluded from trading at Lisbon, to sell pepper for less than 20 ducats. As each successive fleet returned after 1503, the spices continued to accumulate at Lisbon despite the king's best efforts to market them. On January 1, 1505, the king decreed that the merchants could no longer dispose of their wares freely after having paid the king's share. Hereafter the merchants' spices, like those belonging to the king, could be sold only through the comptroller (*vedor*) of the Casa da India at the fixed price. The table on page 110 shows something about the price structure prevailing after the monopoly was enforced.

---

[61] M. A. H. Fitzler, "Portugiesische Handelsgesellschaften des 15. und beginnenden 16. Jahrhunderts," *Vierteljahrschrift für Sozial- und Wirtschaftsgeschichte*, XXV (1932), 247–49.
[62] Heyd, *op. cit.* (n. 5), II, 528–29.
[63] Häbler, *op. cit.* (n. 60), p. 17.

The story of the fleet of 1505, in which the German-Italian syndicate owned three vessels, illustrates the crown's difficulty, even at the beginning, in maintaining its monopolistic policies. The king had been forced to make concessions to the merchants because of his financial inability in 1504–5 to outfit from his own resources alone the fleet of twenty-two ships under Francisco de Almeida.

SPICE PRICES IN 1505[64]

Commodity	Fixed Price in India (in ducats per cwt.)	Fixed Price at Lisbon (in ducats per cwt.)
Pepper	3.00	22
Ginger	0.75	19
Cinnamon . . .	3.50	25
Cloves	7.50	60–65
Nutmeg	4.00	300
Camphor . . .	2.75	100

The total cost of the fleet and its cargo was estimated at 250,000 ducats.[65] The German-Italian syndicate invested a total of 65,400 ducats, Marchionni and his Genoese associates putting in 29,400. Of the 36,000 ducats invested by the Germans, the Welsers put in 20,000, the Fuggers and Höchstetters 4,000 each, the Imhofs and Gossembrods 3,000 each, and the Hirschvogels 2,000. The syndicate owned three vessels and sent out two agents with them. On the return of these vessels with their cargoes in the last months of 1506, a battle ensued between the king and the German merchants over the legality of retroactively applying the royal monopoly decrees to the returns from this voyage, particularly since the merchants' vessels returned before those outfitted by the king and carried two-thirds of the fleet's total cargo.[66]

When the ships dropped anchor in the estuary of the Tagus their personnel were not permitted ashore until the ship, its officers, and its men had been thoroughly searched for contraband goods, particularly jewels. The cargo and sea charts were then unloaded into the warehouses, each ship being assigned a separate warehouse on which the royal port officials posted its identifying insignia. At the gate the seamen were permitted to collect their non-taxable personal belongings. Those who owned taxable goods were given a receipt to enable them to collect their wares after payment of taxes. The percentages of the duties apparently fluctuated widely in these early years, but in 1506–7 goods carried on a royal vessel had to be divided between the king and the purchaser, with 60 per cent going to the king. Of those wares carried in their own vessels, the merchants had to give 25 per cent to the king and 5 per cent to the support of Bélem, a total of 30 per cent. Once the king had taken his shares from the private cargoes the remainder, according to the decree of January 1, 1505, had

[64] Adapted from Luzzato, *op. cit.* (n. 52), I, 161.
[65] G. Scopoli, (ed.), *loc. cit.* (n. 55), pp. 19–20.
[66] Hümmerich, *op. cit.* (n. 59), pp. 135–39.

to be sold out of the warehouses by the king's officials at the fixed price. Previously the merchants had been permitted to sell their own wares freely and remove them from the warehouses at will. It was this change in the regulation of selling procedure that the German-Italian syndicate objected to most vehemently in and after 1506,[67] because it was commonly known that the spices had been piling up higher in the warehouses as each fleet returned after 1503. By the time all of Soares' fleet had returned in May, 1506, about 40,000 hundredweight of spices, it is estimated, was standing in the warehouses.

With the return of the merchant vessels in 1506, the king and the merchants reached a deadlock over the question of whether the merchants, by virtue of their contract, had the right to withdraw and sell the spices freely. The king clearly feared that the merchants in their eagerness to convert their cargo into cash would sell below the fixed prices. Should they do so, it was obvious that the crown would then be unable to dispose of its wares and would have to borrow from the merchants again to outfit the fleet of the next year. Such an eventuality ran directly counter to the crown's effort to free itself from dependence upon the merchant-bankers. But on their side the merchants contended that the king was unilaterally setting aside the contract of 1504 and so instituted suit against the crown in the hope of obtaining a judicial order to release their merchandise. The crown's response to this gesture was to ordain that sale of the spices belonging to the merchants should not begin until there were no royal spices left in the Casa da India.

Still the merchants held the higher trumps, for they anticipated that the king would not be able to outfit the fleet of the following year unaided and would find it particularly difficult to obtain precious metals without their help. Finally the whole matter was compromised in 1507 through the establishment of a new system of selling. The crown thereafter consigned its pepper to a group of private commercial contractors (*contratadores*) who were given a greater degree of freedom in selling the pepper. They were bound to keep to the fixed price as their minimum sale price but were permitted to add about 2.3 ducats per hundredweight as service fees. They were also permitted to accept payment partly in cash and partly in goods, especially those goods essential to the outfitting and cargoes of the fleets being prepared to sail for India. In the context of this new procedure, the merchants were also permitted to remove their own goods in small lots from the warehouse and to dispose of them freely.[68]

Despite such difficulties, the German merchants participating in the fleet of 1505–6 realized a net profit of between 150 and 175 per cent.[69] Although the German merchants were not again permitted to send their own agents to India, they continued to invest in later fleets. And, in the following years, the south German commercial houses maintained branch offices in Lisbon to sell minerals, grain, armaments, ships' stores, and textiles. From the Portuguese they purchased

[67] *Ibid.*, pp. 136–37.
[68] *Ibid.*, pp. 137–42.
[69] *Ibid.*, p. 142.

olive oil, wine, fruits, African ivory, sugar, and spices from the East. At Antwerp, too, the merchants of Augsburg and Nuremberg did business with the Portuguese. But in both places they were gradually forced to deal with the king's factors on Portugal's terms. While Manuel's monopoly was not watertight it was efficient enough for him to be able to exclude from direct participation those groups whom he chose to eliminate. The Italians, meanwhile, continued to have good relations with the king, but they too were increasingly forced to realize that in the spice trade Manuel intended to make the rules.

The king's determination to monopolize the spice traffic, even though he had regularly been realizing about 300 per cent profit, is more understandable when it is recalled that he had to bear all the heavy and permanent expenses connected with the trade. The maintenance of an armed fleet in Indian waters, fortresses and soldiers in India, and a commercial administration that was constantly expanding had all to be paid for from the royal treasury. Meanwhile the threat of Moorish counterattack in the Indian Ocean was constantly growing. Hostile sentiment was at a high pitch in Egypt, particularly after a unit from Vasco da Gama's second fleet invaded the Red Sea in 1503. The Venetians had suspected ever since 1499 that their Egyptian informants were purposely belittling the successes of the Portuguese in India, and the emissaries of the Seignory had repeatedly urged that Egypt should strike back.[70] Finally, in 1502, the sultan began to build a fleet and to make the threats, already mentioned, that he would destroy the Holy Places. In the meantime Manuel went ahead with his plans, while reassuring Pope Julius II that the sultan would never destroy the Holy Places because he derived important revenues from the pilgrims who visited them. In 1505, Manuel sent an embassy of obedience to Rome to announce the discoveries and to give publicity to Portugal's conquests in India.[71]   Rumors meanwhile circulated to the effect that the spices of the Portuguese were inferior in quality, and some cities even legislated against purchasing them.[72]

In India, Portugal made ready to meet the Egyptian counterattack that was being prepared. The fleet of 1505 under Almeida, who was to remain in India as governor, included eleven war vessels and fifteen hundred fighting men. In the following year Afonso de Albuquerque was sent to India to help carry out Manuel's program of capturing the trading centers of Aden, Ormuz, and Malacca before the Egyptians could muster effective resistance. In 1507 Ormuz fell to Albuquerque and in the same year the Portuguese erected a fortress on

---

[70] Heyd, *op. cit.* (n. 5), II, 515–16.

[71] Discussion in P. MacSwiney de Mashanaglass, "Une ambassade portugaise à Rome, sous Jules II," *Revue d'histoire diplomatique*, XVII (1903), 51–63.

[72] Heyd, *op. cit.* (n. 5), II, 534, n. 5. This allegation was probably correct, for the producers in India quickly learned that the inexperienced Portuguese, unlike the seasoned Muslim merchants, could easily be duped. Moreover, the sellers of the spices, who were forced to deliver their goods to the Portuguese at the fixed price, clearly favored buyers whom they could charge whatever the market would bear. See below, p. 472.

Mozambique. And in 1507 Almeida met and defeated a large Egyptian fleet at Diu. The Mamelukes were never again able even to threaten the Portuguese in India, for thereafter Egypt was set upon by the Ottoman Turks to whom it finally fell captive in 1517.

After a lengthy contest for supremacy with Almeida, Albuquerque took over the governor's seat in 1509 and in the next year he captured Goa and began to develop it as the center of Portuguese India. Meanwhile, Diogo Lopes de Sequeira sailed east of India to Malacca in 1509 on an exploratory and reconnaissance voyage. This was followed in 1510 by a second squadron of Portuguese vessels which carried eastward two Florentine commercial agents.[73] Anxious to control the spice traffic at every stage, Albuquerque himself sailed to Malacca and captured that city in 1511. Not long after his conquest of this vital nexus of trade, Portuguese ships began to sail directly to the Spice Islands, the source of the valuable cloves and nutmegs. Meanwhile, other Portuguese vessels were dispatched northward to make direct contact with China; the first Portuguese were conveyed by Chinese junks from Malacca to the islands off the coast of southern China in 1514. Seeing that continued resistance against such an enterprising foe was hopeless, the Zamorin of Calicut agreed to sign a treaty[74] with Albuquerque in 1513 and to send two ambassadors to King Manuel. Thus by the time of Albuquerque's death in 1515, Portugal had established her hegemony over the sea lanes from Malacca to Calicut, to Goa, to Mozambique, and back to Lisbon itself. Aden alone, among the great distribution centers, had withstood the onslaughts of the Portuguese. In the eastern waters the Portuguese position seemed secure and the future very bright. Even direct trade with China now seemed possible.

In Europe meanwhile, the Portuguese sought to tighten their monopoly. The dispatch of a Portuguese embassy to Rome in 1513–14, with an elephant as a present to Pope Leo X, dramatized Portugal's new dominance of the spice trade.[75] The repeatedly promised competition from Venice failed to materialize in these years. Spices were in exceedingly short supply in Syria and Egypt, particularly as the Turks began to expand in the Levant. In 1512, a Venetian agent, in conversation with the Sultan of Egypt, let it be known that money was abnormally tight in Italy. Two years later the conditions of the spice trade had changed so radically that a vessel loaded in India returned via Lisbon and went on to Venice to unload its cargo. Meanwhile, Venetian agents continually addressed themselves to King Manuel for permission to accompany the fleets to India. But though Manuel permitted the citizens of other Italian states to sail in his fleets, he evidently had no intention of letting the Venetians go out to India or of selling the spice monopoly to the city of Venice as had repeatedly

---

[73] These two agents were Giovanni da Empoli (see below, pp. 168–69) and Leonardo Nardi. The former represented the Gualterotti and the latter the Marchionni. For Nardi's career see Peragallo, *op. cit.* (n. 6), pp. 114–15.

[74] Terms of the treaty in Danvers, *op. cit.* (n. 25), I, 283–84.

[75] A. S. de Ciutiis, *Une ambassade portugaise à Rom* (Naples, 1899).

been suggested by agents of the Seignory in Lisbon.[76] The Venetians, whenever peace prevailed, had to content themselves by doing business with the Turks.

4

THE CONFLICT OVER THE MOLUCCAS, 1519–29

Portugal's enjoyment of her far-flung monopoly did not long remain untroubled. The German merchants, particularly the Fuggers, were never satisfied with the organization of the spice trade after the creation of the Portuguese monopoly. Of the Fugger agents, none worked more assiduously against it than Cristóbal de Haro. Even before the departure of Da Gama, the Fugger agent had begun seriously to explore the possibilities of reaching the Spice Islands by the westward route. He may even have helped to finance the voyage of John Cabot. Upon the failure of Cabot's enterprise, De Haro evidently centered his attention upon Lisbon again and urged the Welsers and other south German merchants to compete with the Italians for the favor of King Manuel. The story of the fleet of 1505 has already been told in connection with the creation of the monopoly. It was not, however, until 1516 that De Haro finally broke openly with the king and fled to Seville.[77]

De Haro's flight meant a victory for the Florentines at Lisbon and a shifting of Fugger attention to Spain, especially since his appearance in Seville coincided with the accession of Charles I to the Spanish throne. In Seville, De Haro sought refuge with Juan Rodriquez de Fonseca, Bishop of Burgos and Prince President of the Supreme Council of the Indies. For a long time, Fonseca had advocated the development of a southwest passage to India while others were looking for a passage through the New World. De Haro, brimming over with information on the South Atlantic that he had acquired in Portugal, helped to strengthen Fonseca's resolution to send a fleet out for the express purpose of seeking a southwestward route to the Spiceries.

Ever since Columbus' fourth voyage, the court of Castile had sent out fleets to explore Brazil and the Caribbean area in the search for a passage to Asia. The discovery of the Pacific Ocean by Balboa in 1513 had stimulated this movement greatly. Since most contemporaneous estimates of the circumference of the earth were usually off by about 6,000 miles, the belief was common that continental Asia lay just beyond the recently discovered lands and that the westward route, provided that it could be found, must be much shorter than the way around Africa. Until late in the sixteenth century, some European cartographers continued to believe that North America was really an extension of Asia.[78] Moreover, Portugal's conquest of Malacca in 1511 was followed by

[76] Heyd, *op. cit.* (n. 5), II, 550–51.

[77] Account of De Haro's activities based on Parr, *op. cit.* (n. 12), pp. 172–81.

[78] For example, see map of Franciscus Monarchus in L. C. Wroth, "The Early Cartography of the Pacific," *Papers of the Bibliographical Society of America*, XXXVIII (1944), 267.

explorations of the East Indies that revealed to Europe (in spite of the gross underestimate of distance by the Portuguese commentators)[79] how great a distance the clove islands were from India by the eastward route. With the dissemination of this information in Europe the possibility seemed likely indeed, when one recalls the state of geographical knowledge, that the Moluccas would be found to lie within the Spanish demarcation. As evidence of Portugal's concern lest Castile might have a legal claim to the Indies, King Manuel, through letters and an embassy to Rome, prevailed upon Pope Leo X in 1514 to issue the bull *Praecelsae devotionis* limiting the demarcation line to the Atlantic and upholding Portugal's claim to all Indies wherever, whether known or unknown.[80]

In their search for a captain to lead a southwestern expedition, Fonseca and De Haro finally settled on Ferdinand Magellan. Like Columbus and Cabot, Magellan was one of the drifting professional explorers of the Renaissance— *condottieri* of the sea. Of Portuguese origin, Magellan had spent his early life working in the Casa da India at Lisbon. Then he left for India in the fleet of 1505, participated in the capture of Malacca in 1511, and after eight arduous years in the East returned to Lisbon in 1513. Dissatisfied with his treatment upon returning home, Magellan, along with several other Portuguese sailors, deserted to Spain. After his arrival at Seville in 1517, Magellan began to negotiate a contract with Fonseca and the king for a southwestward voyage to the Moluccas.

The voyage of Magellan (1519–22), like the other Spanish voyages of this period, was stimulated by a group of private investors. Charles I soon became a party to the syndicate being set up by Fonseca, and readily agreed to the conclusion of a generous contract with Magellan. Unlike other contracts concluded hereafter, this one guaranteed that Magellan and his co-captain should be the *adelantados* (governors) of the lands which they discovered and should have one-twentieth of the royal revenues from them.[81] Charles himself put up about three-fourths of the capital that went into Magellan's voyage, though he apparently borrowed about ten thousand ducats from the Fuggers for this purpose.[82]

The fate of Magellan's expedition is so well known that it hardly bears recounting. Magellan himself was killed in the Philippines. Of the five ships in his original fleet, three were lost and the "Trinidad" was unable to continue

---

[79] See below, p. 154.

[80] Text of the bull in F. G. Davenport (comp.), *European Treaties Bearing on the History of the United States and Its Dependencies* (4 vols.; Washington, 1917–37), I, 115–17.

[81] Charles's "capitulation" is printed in D. Martín Fernandez de Navarrete (ed.), *Colección de los viages y descubrimientos* (Madrid, 1837), IV, 116–21.

[82] Much of the information on the background of Magellan's voyage comes from evidence introduced into a lawsuit of 1539 instituted by the Fuggers. See J. T. Medina (ed.), *Colección de documentos inéditos para la historia de Chile* (Santiago, 1889), II, 324–56; also J. Denucé, "Magellan, la question des Moluques et la première circumnavigation du globe," *Académie royale de Belgique, Mémoires*, IV (1908–11), 214–18.

after the battering voyage across the Pacific, its crew remaining at the island of Tidore in the Moluccas. Only the "Victoria" returned to Seville to complete the circumnavigation of the globe. Aside from nominal amounts of cinnamon and mace, its hold carried a cargo of 524 hundredweight of cloves, the principal spice grown in the Moluccas. For the investors as well as for Magellan, the expedition was disastrous. At a time when similar fleets sailing from Lisbon were recording a profit of 400 per cent, the most that could possibly have been realized from the Magellan expedition was 4 per cent.[83] Despite the great loss of men and the poor financial return, the voyage of Magellan was of indirect profit to the crown inasmuch as it showed the existence of a southwestern route to India and it strengthened Charles's claim to the Spice Islands. That such an event should have become known to Europe so shortly after Charles's election as Holy Roman Emperor in 1519 helped to produce an impression, especially in Lisbon, that the new emperor and his banker friends, the Fuggers, had menacing designs upon both Europe and the overseas world.

King John III of Portugal sent a protest to Charles immediately after the return of the "Victoria." The Portuguese monarch charged that it had sailed illegally through Portuguese waters, that Magellan's men had invaded Portuguese territory (the Moluccas), and asked that Charles refrain from sending out any further expeditions until the thorny question of ownership of the islands could be resolved.[84] While recognizing that the Portuguese would seek to prolong the negotiations to establish themselves more firmly in the Moluccas, Charles was forced by a lack of funds to delay the dispatch of another India fleet until 1525. In the meantime Hernán Cortés, who had already made plans to explore the Pacific, urged that Mexico should be outfitted as a base for trade with the East Indies.[85] But Fonseca and others apparently feared that Cortés would thereby gain too much control over the spice trade if it should be allowed to develop through Mexico. Also anxious over the fate of the trade, the Cortes at Valladolid petitioned Charles in 1523 to hold "the spicery" in the name of Castile and "with all diligence the armada be prepared and finished to go there." Although Charles had already considered the possibility of selling Castile's claim to Portugal, he ultimately promised the Cortes to "keep the spicery for these realms."[86]

The emperor, on this occasion, was as good as his word. In April, 1524, the first of a series of conferences between the representatives of Castile and Portugal was held at Badajoz-Elvas. The twenty representatives divided into two commissions, one to determine ownership and the other to establish possession. In the ownership commission the discussions were based on the Treaty of Tordesillas as the assembled "specialists" sought to place the Moluccas

[83] Medina (ed.), *op. cit.* (n. 82), II, 235.

[84] Antonio de Herrera y Tordesillas, *Historia generale de los hechos de los castellanos en las islas i tierra firme del mar oceano* (Madrid, 1726–27), Década IV, Libro V, p. 93.

[85] *Ibid.*, Década III, Libro III, p. 105.

[86] Petition and reply in *Cortes de los antiguos reinos de Leon y de Castilla* (Madrid, 1882), IV, 388.

on a blank globe.[87] But the experts, like their royal masters, were unable to agree on location, the first step in the establishment of ownership. The discussions of the commission on possession also ended in deadlock. On May 30, 1524, the negotiations were broken off.[88]

Now Charles moved ahead again with his original plan of sending annual fleets to the Moluccas. The first to depart after the Badajoz-Elvas conference was that commanded by Esteban Gomez which made a vain attempt to find a northwest passage. Another armada of seven vessels under Garcia de Loaisa was outfitted at Coruña, the home of the Casa de Contratación for the Spiceries.[89] Magellan's fleet had been financed by a few large investors; the risk was more widely spread in the subscription to Loaisa's fleet. A number of relatively small Spanish investors were permitted to put money into it. Loaisa's expedition was even less fortunate than Magellan's. Only one of his vessels was able to make the incredible sea journey around South America and across the Pacific. This vessel struggled to the island of Tidore where its crewmen joined the survivors of the "Trinidad" from Magellan's fleet in their hopeless war against the Portuguese in the Moluccas.

In 1526 another fleet was dispatched southwestward under Sebastian Cabot.[90] Its shareholders were few and mainly foreigners, though no French or Portuguese investors were permitted to subscribe. Actually the Cabot fleet never attempted to cross the Pacific, for it ran into trouble off the coast of South America. Cabot contented himself with exploring the coast of Argentina. In the meantime, Charles ordered Hernán Cortés in 1527 to dispatch a fleet from Mexico into the Pacific to recover the goods and men from Loaisa's fleet. Only one of the three vessels sent out by Cortés actually reached Tidore, and it was forced to stay there because of its inability to sail eastward against the adverse winds and currents of the southern Pacific. It was not until 1565 that the Spanish learned that they had to sail to 43° north latitude before attempting to make an easterly crossing of the Pacific Ocean.

After Badajoz-Elvas and the losses suffered by his fleets, Charles was of two minds about the Moluccas. He had made an effort to fulfill his promise of 1523 to the Cortes, but with little success. The crown had lost prestige, money, and time in its fruitless efforts to gain the Moluccas. Moreover, this policy had aroused the enmity of Portugal at a time when Charles needed all the friends he could find for his struggle against France and the papacy. As the beginning of a rapprochement with Portugal, Charles married the Portuguese infanta at Seville in 1526. On that occasion a draft treaty was drawn up.[91] Though the treaty was not signed, the discussions of 1526 seemed to indicate that Charles

[87] Clements Markham (ed.), *Early Spanish Voyages to the Straits of Magellan* ("Hakluyt Society Publications," Ser. II, Vol. XXVIII [London, 1911]), pp. 11–15.

[88] Navarette (ed.), *op. cit.* (n. 81), IV, 355–72.

[89] *Ibid.*, V, 193–207.

[90] J. T. Medina, *Sebastian Caboto al servicio de España* (Santiago, 1908), I, 420–28.

[91] Text in Davenport, *op. cit.* (n. 80), I, 131–45.

would be willing to pawn his claim to the Moluccas. Despite the protests of the Cortes of 1528, Charles went ahead with his decision to abandon them.

On his way to Italy, Charles and his court stopped at Saragossa and on April 22, 1529, signed a treaty with Portugal there. The exact meaning of the Treaty of Saragossa[92] is hard to determine, for it is essentially a pawn of Charles's claim to something to which nobody was sure he actually had the right. Apparently both rulers felt that by the terms of the Treaty of Tordesillas (1494) the Moluccas should properly fall within their demarcation. But then nobody was exactly certain how the division of the world of 1494 should be applied to lands discovered thereafter. Aside from many juridical points that obscured the precise meaning of this new treaty, it in effect set aside Charles's claim to the Moluccas in return for 350,000 ducats. It also asserted that a line "must be determined from pole to pole . . . two hundred and ninety-seven and one-half leagues east of the Moluccas" to separate the Castilian from the Portuguese domains in the Pacific region. It provisionally recognized the monopoly of Portugal over the maritime spice trade to Europe until the time when the Pacific demarcations of the two powers could be accurately determined and the question of ownership finally clarified. Throughout the treaty the question of ownership was left open, though a proviso read that if ownership should eventually be decided in favor of Portugal, Charles would then have to return the 350,000 ducats. On their side the Portuguese promised not to fortify the islands any further, pending the settlement of the question of ownership.

Although many of Charles's Spanish subjects objected vehemently to his capitulation, the emperor's motives seem not too difficult to understand. His diplomacy in 1529 was directed toward the general "pacification" of Europe. In contrast to his main objective, the financial and patriotic interests of his Spanish subjects could hardly have weighed heavily in the balance. Furthermore, the claim to the Moluccas had deteriorated badly in the six years following his promise to the Cortes. Not only had the southwestern route proved too arduous, but Spain's preoccupation with it diverted money, energies, and interest from fully exploiting the wealth of the New World. And France, Charles's enemy, was also beginning to launch overseas enterprises in defiance of the claims of the Iberian powers to complete overlordship in the non-European world. The Moluccas might easily have seemed more of a burden than an asset to a ruler who, in 1529, was occupied with the problem of bringing peace to his widely scattered empire and with promoting its economic prosperity by concentrating on importing gold and silver from the New World.

Nor was everything to run smoothly for the Portuguese after 1529 in their possession of the spice sources and markets. Affonso Mexia, captain of Cochin, in 1530 wrote a long letter to the king in Lisbon deploring the privateering activities of the Portuguese in the East. He reported:

[92] Text in *ibid.*, I, 169–98.

The trade is also much more profitable for the captains and Portuguese officers there than for Your Majesty, as the Malacca trade is entirely carried on by junks and native craft which are controlled by these very Portuguese, who pay your Majesty no duties or taxes. The trade and revenue of your Majesty's factory is thereby on the decline, and your Majesty's revenues from Malacca will be almost *nil* as long as these captains remain there.

And then, almost as if to frighten the king about the wisdom of his bargain, Mexia wrote that "matters are going from bad to worse, and were it not for your Majesty's instructions to remedy the evils there, it would almost appear advisable to abandon those islands." [93] So, even though Portugal's fight for the Moluccas was won in Europe, an uphill battle remained to be fought if the crown were to be successful in exploiting the Spiceries for its own profit.

5

THE CONDUCT OF TRADE AT LISBON AND ANTWERP, 1509–48

While the eastern end of the spice monopoly was being fortified and protected against the intrusions of Castile, Portugal continued its policy of trying to retain exclusive control over the sale and distribution of spices in Europe. In the decade after 1505, Portuguese vessels annually brought into Lisbon spice cargoes averaging from 25,000 to 30,000 hundredweight. [94] Generally about two-thirds of the yearly arrivals was pepper. During the same decade (1505–15) not more than 75,000 hundredweight arrived in Venice, for in most of the years no fleets at all went from Venice to either Beirut or Alexandria. [95] In other words, over four times the quantity imported by Venice came into Portugal during this decade. But even so the Portuguese monopoly was far from being as effective as the crown wanted it to be. For the Portuguese were not able at any time to shut off Venice's spice supply entirely, though it does appear that pepper, on which the Portuguese concentrated, was usually hard to obtain on the Rialto. For example, in 1512 and 1513 the retail merchants of Vienna complained in a petition to Emperor Maximilian that not enough pepper could be obtained from Venice and that he should permit importations from Antwerp and other European cities. [96] In 1514 the Venetians themselves bought pepper in Lisbon. [97]

Although not entirely secure either in India or Europe, the Portuguese monopoly became increasingly more effective after 1505. The Germans continued, though to no avail, to badger the king to reconsider his stand against merchant participation in the fleets. Finally, in 1509, Lucas Rem left Lisbon,

[93] Danvers, *op. cit.* (n. 25), I, 409; also cf. the report to Charles V of 1537 by Urdaneta, a participant in Loaisa's expedition, as reproduced by Markham (ed.), *op. cit.* (n. 87), pp. 84–89.
[94] Luzatto, *op. cit.* (n. 52), I, 161.
[95] Magalhães-Godinho, *loc. cit.* (n. 27), p. 287.
[96] Heyd, *op. cit.* (n. 5), II, 550.
[97] *Ibid.*

and thereafter the Fuggers took over the leadership of the German group and inaugurated the common German policy of purchasing at Lisbon and doing little else.[98]

King Manuel meanwhile sought to work out detailed regulations for the conduct of the trade in the East and at the Casa da India in Lisbon. In 1507 the fleet of Fernão Soares carried to India a complete *regimento* pertaining to the fleets, their preparation, organization, and conduct.[99] These regulations sought to anticipate and prearrange the problems of trade, and to prescribe the methods of purchasing, the procedures for loading, and the types of cargo which should be sent to India. The crew members, each according to his rank, were to have the right of investing in the spices though they also had to make their purchases through the factor in India. As part of their *quintalados* (space on the ship for a quintal or hundredweight of merchandise), the sailors were permitted to import in their sea chests some of the rarer spices and jewels. From these regulations it can be concluded that all purchases had to be made through the factors in India, that they had in most cases to be paid for in money, and that the complete cargo from each ship was supposed to be deposited directly in the Casa da India upon arriving at Lisbon.

The organization of the Casa was itself the subject of a *regimento* of 1509.[100] After 1500 an independent Casa da India gradually came into being as the India trade outstripped the other parts of Portugal's overseas trade in importance and potential, but its organization still apparently left much to be desired. The *regimento* prescribes special rules, duties, and hours for each staff. It also makes clear that all three sections (India, Guinea, and the slave trade) were subordinate to a single factor, who came generally to be known as the factor of the Casa da India. While such an organizational chart is clear enough, it appears that in practice the spices and drugs from Brazil and Africa were handled through the Casa da India as was all the royal trade with Antwerp. Clearly the position of the factor was one of vast responsibility, since he was in effect the superintendent of practically all Portugal's overseas trade.[101]

The functions of the Casa were primarily commercial. On the arrival of vessels the factor was charged with informing the king of the size and composition of the cargo and with forwarding immediately any correspondence that might have come. All receipts and disbursements of spices were entered in an account book, and a register was kept of all contracts made by the factor in the king's name. The factor also had charge of all overseas correspondence, of keeping lists of all the ships and their crews, and of checking on the factors in the overseas world. A legal officer attached to the factor's office was in charge of examining and approving legal documents and of prosecuting thefts or other

[98] Häbler, *Die Geschichte der Fuggerschen Handlung in Spanien* (Weimar, 1897), pp. 24–26.

[99] Vicente Almeida d'Eça, *op. cit.* (n. 18), pp. 54–60.

[100] Damião Peres (ed.), *Regimento das Cazas das Indias e Mina* (Coimbra, 1947) publishes the text. Until the publication of this document the greatest confusion prevailed in our understanding of the organization of trade at Lisbon (pp. x–xi). See above, p. 93 for background discussion.

[101] See Mendes da Luz, *op. cit.* (n. 3), pp. 42–43.

crimes committed during the voyages or in the Casa. As for the building itself, it appears to have been a grandiose edifice for that epoch, judging by the large amounts of money spent on its construction between 1507 and 1514.[102] Even so, a new and larger building was constructed in the middle of the sixteenth century which stood until destroyed by the Lisbon earthquake of 1755.

The *armazems* (warehouses), though indirectly connected with the Casa, had separate buildings, staff, and functions. The official in charge was the *provedor* who had his own treasurer, scribes, and workmen. Among the main functions of his office were the outfitting, provisioning and arming of the fleets, the recruiting of the crews and other non-commercial personnel, and the issuing of the necessary navigational instruments, charts, and information. As time went on, the *provedor's* duties were extended to include the administration of the water front, the wharves, and the arms warehouse. But it seems that all financial affairs were handled through the Casa.[103] Both the factor and the *provedor* seem to have been responsible to King Manuel's celebrated secretary, Antonio Carneiro, who was unofficially the Secretary of State for India.[104]

To make the monopoly as tight as possible, it was clearly necessary for Manuel to tie the Portuguese factory at Antwerp into the system of control that he was evolving.[105] The first Portuguese ships carrying pepper had arrived in the estuary of the Scheldt River in 1501. Two years later, Tomé Lopes, the Portuguese factor at Antwerp, sold spices to an Antwerp merchant who hoped to develop the spice trade between the Netherlands and Germany. In his letters to King Manuel, written at a time when the Welser syndicate was negotiating with the crown for direct trade privileges, Lopes stressed the importance of the northern market to the future of the spice trade and evidently argued in favor of having the Germans buy at Antwerp rather than Lisbon. Flanders had long maintained land connections with Cologne, Frankfurt, and Nuremberg and was a great center of trade for the Hanseatic and English merchants who came by sea.

The traffic concentrated at Antwerp in the first decade of the sixteenth century[106] helped that city quickly to replace Bruges as the major entrepôt of northwestern Europe and to enjoy a period of heretofore unparalleled prosperity. Soon it came to be known as the "mistress of European cities."[107] Until 1514 the Affaitadi and Gualterotti combine retained the exclusive right to sell spices at Antwerp. But the south German merchants, especially the

---

[102] *Ibid.*, pp. 46–47.

[103] *Ibid.*, pp. 59–69.

[104] *Ibid.*, p. 72.

[105] The two best works dealing directly with the Portuguese factory at Antwerp are Anselmo Braamcamp Freire, *Noticias da Feitoria de Flandres* (s.l., 1920) and J. A. Goris, *Etude sur les colonies marchandes méridionales à Anvers de 1488 à 1567* (Louvain, 1925). For a summary of more recent scholarship see De Prada, *op. cit.* (n. 2), I, 89–95.

[106] See above, p. 107.

[107] See the hymn of praise to Antwerp as a spice center in A. Govea, *Histoire orientale des grands progrès de l'église*, cited in G. Atkinson, *Les nouveaux horizons de la Renaissance française* (Paris, 1935), p. 132.

Fuggers and Welsers, gradually became a part of the monopoly at third hand. Practically all the spices sold in northern Europe had to be bought in Antwerp at the factory of the syndicate. From the Portuguese viewpoint, the syndicate was necessary as a purveyor of precious metals and as a responsible agency that would, in the interests of their common monopoly, co-operate with the king in his determination to maintain a minimum price. Around 1515 it is estimated that the royal revenues from pepper were increased by marketing it at Antwerp where the prices were from 10 to 13 per cent over those of Lisbon.[108] The city of Antwerp itself sought to protect the trade by an ordinance of 1515 which imposed stiff penalties upon sellers who adulterated the spices.

The main complaint about Antwerp as the spice center came from the Germans, who had great difficulty transporting the spices safely from Flanders to the German states. Bands of irate knights or starving peasants regularly attacked the spice wagons and their convoys as they took their precious wares to Frankfurt, Nuremberg, or Augsburg and to cities beyond. By 1521 Germany was "empty of spices,"[109] despite the fact that spices from Venice, when available, competed effectively in Germany with those that came through Antwerp. Criticism of the great trading families and of their monopolistic practices had been growing in Germany since the beginning of the sixteenth century. In 1512, the Imperial Diet of Cologne formally condemned these practices. Ulrich von Hutten and other powerful noblemen were forthrightly hostile to the wealth and ostentatious living of the great merchants and their families. The Fuggers, in contriving the election of Charles V through open bribery, let it be seen clearly that the merchant could be a king-maker. The reformers Luther and Zwingli inveighed against the methods by which the monopolists manipulated money, people, and markets to increase their profits.

In 1522 at the Imperial Diet of Nuremberg the question of abolishing the companies was discussed at length. But it was pointed out on this occasion that abolition of the companies would not eliminate monopoly or co-operative buying and selling. The commercial interests argued that only the large merchant combines had the capital and the connections to operate effectively in the great international markets. They also urged the Diet to legislate against fraudulent wares, to provide greater security along the trade routes, and to eliminate a number of the tolls and duties levied on trade. They pointed out that Venice, Portugal, and Flanders had grown prosperous from merchandising, and that Germany would only weaken its international economic position by withdrawing from competition. To the complaint that too much metal was leaving Germany to pay for pepper, the merchants replied that only one-twentieth of the pepper purchased through Portugal was actually sold in Germany. To the suggestion that the king of Portugal could deliver his wares to Germany as well as to Antwerp, the merchants pointed out the importance of having a

---

[108] J. Denucé, "Privilèges commerceaux accordés par les rois de Portugal aux Flamands et aux Allemands (XVe et XVIe siècles)," *Arquivo historico portugues*, VII (1909), 313–14.

[109] Goris, *op. cit.* (n. 105), p. 197.

common meeting-place for trade in all types of commodities. Despite such protests and arguments, spices apparently continued to be abnormally high in price in the German states.[110]

At Antwerp there was also discontent with the conduct of the spice trade. In 1518 the Venetians stopped trading at Antwerp by sea and ordained at home that spices imported from the *ponente* (West) should be subject to a special tax. In 1522 the Spanish sent spices to Antwerp from the cargo carried by Magellan's only returning vessel. Around 1525 the *maranos* (Portuguese "New Christians") began to operate independently of the consortium in Antwerp and soon found themselves in trouble with the authorities. They were accused of numerous religious and commercial infamies.

But despite all such efforts to break it, the Portuguese-merchant syndicate relationship at Antwerp retained its hold on the sale and distribution of the spices in northern Europe. From year to year the syndicate, no matter who its shareholders were, contracted with the king through agents in Lisbon, for all the spices and drugs to be sent to Antwerp. The contract stipulated that the king should not sell to other merchants, Flemish or foreign, who might be operating in Antwerp. The consortium sold the spices through the intermediacy of a number of merchant houses especially enfranchised by the chiefs of the monopoly. Until 1530, the course of trade at Antwerp ran smoothly and absolute pepper prices for the decade of the twenties remained higher than earlier and relatively steady.[111] The conditions of Portuguese trade at Antwerp were upset after 1530 by the wars between Francis I and Charles V, by the omnipresent threat of effective competition from Venice, and by the speculative practices of the merchants in spices who did business on the Antwerp bourse. Shortly after 1530, pepper prices in Vienna and England jumped by about 20 per cent. After 1532, the cost of pepper in northern Europe declined steadily for four years, and then once again advanced by 10 per cent in the years from 1536 to 1544. But at no point in this period is there any dramatic change to be observed in the records of pepper prices which are available to us and the price of pepper seems to have corresponded closely to general price levels for the decade.

Meanwhile, Charles V, as part of his general program of "imperial peace," strove to elevate the Low Countries to the position of middle power between Germany and France. Initially, the result of Charles's policy was to help make Antwerp the freest port in the world and Flanders the greatest exchange of transferable wealth. Around 1530, as precious metals from the New World began to flow into Castile in large quantities, the emperor began to pay less attention to Antwerp and the general health of its economy. As time went on, Charles's wars against France, resumed again in 1536, led Francis I to encourage

---

[110] August Kluckhohn, "Zur Geschichte der Handelsgesellschaften und Monopole im Zeitalter der Reformation," *Historische Aufsätze dem Andenken an Georg Waitz gewidmet* (Hanover, 1886), pp. 666–703.

[111] See appendix to this chapter.

systematic attack on the carrying trade between Portugal and Flanders as part of his policy designed to develop the Atlantic ports of northwestern France as trading centers.[112]

During the first third of the century, merchant fleets had come into Antwerp with great regularity and on the average of about two each year. Under good conditions even a large trading fleet could make the run from Lisbon to Antwerp in about two weeks. The fastest overland coaches took twelve days to travel from Brussels to Madrid, and then they carried no wares at all. Until 1530, the Spanish and Portuguese vessels had a virtual monopoly on the carrying trade from Antwerp to the south. Thereafter they were harassed by Breton pirates, who operated against the trade with the unofficial sanction of Francis I. To protect the trade and to increase the number of ships available for it, the Portuguese more frequently began to use neutral vessels. The introduction of the intermediary carriers on the Lisbon–Antwerp run after 1530 cut into the profits of the Portuguese. Between 1540 and 1550 the Dutch gradually took over as carriers and at mid-century transported more tonnage between Antwerp and the south than all the other competing vessels combined. By 1560 Amsterdam was beginning to rival Antwerp as a trading center.

It has often been assumed that the Portuguese monopoly was not effectively challenged by the spices from the Levant until the last third of the sixteenth century. Certainly it appears that, throughout the first third of the century, spices were not coming into Venice in quantities comparable to the imports of Lisbon. The prices of pepper in Cairo were also considerably higher in this period than the prices prevailing in either Lisbon or Antwerp.[113] But it appears that many Venetian spices, with the possible exception of pepper, continued to compete seriously in European markets.[114] The story of the spice trade at Lyons forms a particularly significant case in point.[115] Italian merchants had brought pepper from Venice and Genoa to the fair of Lyons, the principal center of distribution for France, throughout the last quarter of the fifteenth century. The main traffic from Italy to Lyons was in silken goods of Italian manufacture, and the spice trade developed in conjunction with it. Most of the goods were carried overland through the Alps by convoyed wagon-trains from the north Italian towns. The Venetian spices coming in by this route were sold in Lyons at a price 20 per cent lower than those brought in through the Languedoc ports. Both the Languedoc towns and Lyons were quick to realize that the opening of the Atlantic route could have grievous consequences for their own position

---

[112] C. A. Julien, *Les voyages de découverte et les premiers établissements (XVe–XVIe siècles)* (Paris, 1948), p. 72, n. 5.

[113] Magalhães-Godinho, *loc. cit.* (n. 27) tables on pp. 287–88, 294.

[114] K. O. Müller, *Welthandelsbräuche (1480–1540)* (Stuttgart, 1934), p. 78.

[115] Based on R. Gascon, "Un siècle du commerce des épices à Lyon. Fin XVe–fin XVIe siècles," *Annales. Économies, sociétés, civilisations*, XV, No. 4, 638–66. He bases his account on the "Carnets du garbeau," a continuous series of tax lists which names the importers and the nature and the quantities of the wares, as well as on a more limited series (1523–35) of "Carnets des Cinq Espèces," which gives the quantities which passed through the gates of the city or entered at port towns.

in the spice commerce. What were at first vague fears began to take more definite shape with the initial appearance of spices from Antwerp at the Easter
Fair of Lyons in 1508.

Once the Portuguese spices began coming into Lyons, the quantities apparently increased at a rapid rate. But even in the peak years (1525–35) for Antwerp
spices, the deliveries made at Lyons constituted no more than one-third of its
total spice imports. Mediterranean, as opposed to Atlantic, spices were imported
in the next decade in even greater quantities as Francis I sought by political
pressure to break the entrepôt at Antwerp.[116] French freebooters, with the
unofficial sanction of the king, preyed, as we have seen, on the spice ships sailing
from Lisbon to Antwerp. Entrepreneurs at the royal port of Marseilles were
encouraged to sail directly to the Levant themselves. A royal edict of January 4,
1540, forbade spices to be brought into France except through royal ports.
While the royal command was successful in cutting off imports from Antwerp,
it did not have the desired effect of forcing the spices to come into France
through its Atlantic ports. The royal decree did, however, force most of the
spice trade through the port of Marseilles which hereafter became a partner with
Lyons in the merchandising of spices imported into France—still mainly by
merchants from Florence and Genoa.

At Antwerp, the great merchants were still able, around 1540, to maintain
the fixed price on pepper, though the price of other spices declined. Probably
as part of an effort to maintain price levels at Antwerp, no spice fleets from
Lisbon appeared in the Scheldt during 1543. In the following year Francis I
limited the importation of spices to Lyons, Rouen, and Marseilles. And two
years later, the Venetian ambassador reported that the spices no longer came into
France from Antwerp, but directly from Portugal.[117] Thus, while the carrying
trade was being taken over by the French and the Dutch, the persistent
competition of Venice and the growth of Marseilles as a Mediterranean spice
center, contributed to the undermining of the Portuguese position in
Antwerp.[118]

Of all the commodities traded at Antwerp, pepper and other spices were
those most commonly involved in speculation.[119] The factors of Portugal,
particularly after 1520, often sold the cargoes of vessels still at sea for advance
payments by the merchant syndicate. Prices in pepper usually fluctuated more
than others, and pepper quotations were regarded as the barometer of the
bourse's temper. War, peace, supply, demand, and the machinations of the
large syndicates combined to make speculation in spices one of the riskiest

---

[116] For a collection of documents relating to the preoccupation of Francis I with maritime trade,
see Louis Bigard (ed.), *Le trafic maritime avec les Indes sous François I er* (Paris, 1939).

[117] As quoted by Joseph Billioud in Gaston Rambert (ed.), *Histoire du commerce de Marseille*
(Paris, 1951), III, 440. See also the table (p. 450) on spice distribution through Marseilles between
1578 and 1592.

[118] On the growth of the competing market in spices at Marseilles see Florence E. De Roover, "The
Market for Spices in Antwerp," *Revue belge de philologie et d'histoire*, XVII (1938), 212–21.

[119] R. Ehrenberg, *Das Zeitalter der Fugger* (Jena, 1896), II, 14.

investments on the bourse. That the spice trade fell into the hands of the merchants can be accounted for in large part by the persistent need of the Portuguese kings for ready cash. Practically all the leading merchants at one time or other advanced money to the king, especially the Affaitadi, who were generally the largest shareholders in the pepper syndicate. In 1543 the Antwerp debt of the Portuguese king was estimated at two million ducats, a sizable part of which was in advances for pepper still to be delivered.[120] Although the king promised high interest rates to those who invested in Portuguese obligations, customarily neither the interest nor the face value of the bonds was paid off at the stipulated time. As a result, the credit of the crown steadily declined in the middle years of the sixteenth century. In the last months of 1548, King John, on the advice of his ambassador to Charles V, decided to close the Portuguese factory at Antwerp, perhaps because the expenses of supplying it over dangerous sea routes were deemed excessive.[121] At this juncture the Cortes at Valladolid petitioned the emperor to transfer the administration of the spice trade at Antwerp to Castile. Like the earlier Spanish demand of 1529, it was denied by the emperor.[122]

King John made every possible effort to find a solution to his serious financial predicament. After 1549 the spices were sold at Lisbon directly from the Casa da India. They were then carried to Antwerp and other distribution centers at the risk and expense of the private contractors.[123] Pope Julius III, meanwhile, by a special bull of 1551, permitted the Order of Christ with all its overseas holdings to be taken over by the Portuguese crown. Perhaps the king saw already at this period what John Wheeler, secretary of the Society of Merchant-Adventurers, at the end of the century described so graphically in *A Treatise of Commerce*. Wheeler wrote:

First for the *Portingal*, we know that like a good simple man he sailed every year full hungerly (God wot) about three parts of the Earth almost for spices, and when he had brought them home, the great rich purses of the *Antwerpians*, subjects of the King of Spain, engrossed them all into their own hands, yea oftentimes gave money for them beforehand, making thereof a plain *Monopoly*; whereby they only gained and all other Nations lost. For that the spices, being in few men's hands, were sold at such rate as they listed, to their own private lucre and gain, and to the hurt and damage of all others.[124]

---

[120] *Ibid.*, II, 52. For a contemporary account of the indebtedness of the Portuguese king see Ludovico Guicciardini, *Description de touts les Pays-Bas* ... (Arnhem, 1573), p. 150. By 1552, it was three million ducats and in 1560 the Casa da India was ordered to cease paying the interest on the king's loans. After 1560, the crown paid only 5 per cent and it was paid by the royal department of the creditor's choice. See H. V. Livermore, *A History of Portugal* (Cambridge, 1947), p. 247.

[121] Goris, *op. cit.* (n. 105), p. 236.

[122] Francisco Lopez de Gomara, "The Debate and the Stryfe between the Spanish and the Portuguese for the Division of the Indies and the Trade of Spices" in E. Arber, *The First Three English Books on America* (Birmingham, 1885), p. 274.

[123] J. Lucio de Azevedo, *Epocas de Portugal económico* (Lisbon, 1947), p. 132.

[124] J. Wheeler, *A Treatise of Commerce*, ed. George B. Hotchkiss (New York, 1931), p. 352.

6

The Revival of Eastern Mediterranean Trade, 1548–70

At Antwerp the conditions of trade deteriorated badly after the formal closing of the Portuguese factory. The merchants doing business at the Scheldt metropolis were caught up in the whirlpool of hostilities occasioned by the preparations that Charles V was making for the disposition of his vast empire and by the swirling currents of the Reformation. On his visit to Flanders in 1549, Prince Philip, the heir apparent, managed to obtain recognition from the Estates as Charles's successor. But almost immediately, opposition began to mount in the Low Countries against the foreign prince. Philip's stern devotion to Catholicism stimulated fear among both Protestant and Jewish merchants that the Inquisition and the Jesuits would soon enter Antwerp. Their fears were soon realized, and it was not long before new taxes and restrictions were placed upon trading operations as well. The marriage of Philip to Mary of England in 1554 aroused hope for a time in the war-weary Low Countries that a lasting peace might be rendered possible through an English alliance with Spain. But these hopes were soon dashed. After Philip was invested with sovereignty over the Burgundian Netherlands in 1555, it was not long before war with France was resumed. Once the Treaty of Cateau-Cambrésis (1559) brought the war between France and Spain to an end, Philip's financial exactions and his determination to stamp out heresy in the Netherlands triggered civil strife.[125]

Shortly after the Portuguese closed their factory, an emigration of merchants from Antwerp began that was to continue throughout the second half of the century. The first to leave were the *maranos*, shortly to be followed by the German, Baltic, and English Protestants. As business slowed down at Antwerp, the Catholic merchants of France, Italy, and Germany sought new bases for their trading operations. Most of those who left Flanders transferred their activities to Hamburg, the Rhenish cities, Zurich, Rouen, or Lyons. In 1560 the Affaitadi, who had been the chief spice contractors at Antwerp, were forced into bankruptcy. But as late as 1565 Ludovico Guicciardini was able to wax ecstatic about the thriving metropolis on the Scheldt. Though other business evidently continued, the complete collapse of the spice trade at Antwerp was clearly foreshadowed. Most of the foreign merchants were gone by 1567, and several years later Guicciardini himself was thrown into prison for protesting too vehemently against the Spanish policies. With the dispersion of the merchants to their homelands or to friendlier trading centers, Antwerp's period of prosperity ended, and in the general financial crisis of 1569 King Sebastian of Portugal suspended all payments at Antwerp. Europe was never again to have a single city which was so much the commercial and financial axis, since

[125] For details see Jervis Wegg, *The Decline of Antwerp under Philip of Spain* (London, 1924).

[127]

the dispersion of the merchants involved also the dispersion of trade and banking to a number of western and central European cities.[126]

With the failure of the Portuguese factory the problem of distributing spices in Europe was left to others. But in India, King John III still had the problem of holding the strategic centers upon which the trade depended. The citadel of Diu in northwestern India had been under constant pressure, the latest siege having just been lifted in 1546 after a protracted expenditure of effort on the part of the Portuguese. And just three years earlier the Portuguese had arrived in Japan, thus presenting the king with the challenge of extending his lines of communication and his ambitions even farther to the east. At Malacca and other Portuguese entrepôts the king's revenues steadily declined in the decade 1540–50, the customhouse of Malacca being reformed in 1543.[127] In the same decade St. Francis Xavier began his missionary activities in Asia, and the Jesuits began to establish a working arrangement with the king to be the mainstay of their missionary position in the Portuguese empire. The responsibilities of the Portuguese were also stretched farther to the south and west as French, Dutch, and English interlopers challenged the monopoly of the trade with Africa and Brazil. Both to make the sea lanes to the east more secure and to prevent colonial encroachments by the northern Europeans, the Portuguese government after the mid-sixteenth century sought to strengthen its hold upon Brazil by undertaking a more active colonizing and development policy there. The concentration at Lisbon of the African, Asian, and Brazilian trade seemed to be the best means by which Portugal could devote full attention to Asia, preserve her monopoly there, and restore her credit in Europe.

But such an estimate failed to take into account the resurgence of the Mediterranean spice trade. For the difficulties experienced by Portugal in the East at mid-century can be attributed in part to the revival of the Levantine trade with India via Persia and Egypt—a revival made possible by the stability re-established in the Near East through the authority of Suleiman the Magnificent. The prescient Fuggers, for example, closed shop in Lisbon in 1558 and in the following years began to purchase at Alexandria from whence, via Ragusa and Fiume, they transported pepper directly into central Europe.[128] From Lourenço Pires de Tavora, Portuguese ambassador to the papal court and onetime captain of a fleet of six "Indiamen," news was relayed to Lisbon in 1560 that 40,000 hundredweight of spices, mainly pepper, was entering Alexandria annually. Pires concluded that "there being so much which comes to the dominion of the Turks, it is no wonder that so little comes to Lisbon."[129]

---

[126] Goris, *op. cit.* (n. 105), pp. 599–602. In 1569 the Portuguese resident in England suggested that the spice staple should be moved to London, Bristol, or Southampton. See V. M. Shillington and A. B. Chapman, *The Commercial Relations of England and Portugal* (London, 1907), p. 142.

[127] R. S. Whiteway, *The Rise of Portuguese Power in India, 1497–1550* (Westminster, 1899), pp. 291–95.

[128] F. C. Lane, "The Mediterranean Spice Trade," *American Historical Review*, XLV (1939–40), 588.

[129] As quoted in *ibid.*, p. 585.

Around 1560, the quantities of spices arriving at Lisbon were just about equal to those entering Alexandria.[130] The Venetians, as earlier, still controlled most of the trade with Syria and Egypt, and for a time spice imports reached figures rivaling those of the pre-Portuguese period.[131] But Venice was now beginning to meet sharp competition in the Levant trade from the French, Genoese, and Ragusans. The French even tried at this time to go directly to Guinea for the purchase of malagueta pepper. From 1560 to 1563, as things were going from bad to worse at Antwerp, a new outbreak of hostilities in the Indian Ocean cost Portugal further losses. To compound Portugal's economic problem, the fleet of 1561 missed the monsoon. In India the Portuguese continually had trouble with their own administrators and personnel.[132] By 1563 Portuguese fortunes were everywhere on the decline, as the Levantine counterrevolution became a concrete fact, and as Venice once again threatened to become the major spice staple. It would appear that spice supplies in Europe were probably greater than at the beginning of the century, although they were still not adequate to meet the demand.[133]

Prices reflected this seesaw battle for supremacy in the spice trade. The decade of 1550 to 1560 was a particularly unstable one for pepper prices. In Vienna, where stocks could be obtained either through Venice or Antwerp, prices showed a 10 per cent decline over the decade. At Antwerp pepper prices fluctuated occasionally, but the absolute prices moved upward at a fairly steady rate. In England, with its almost complete dependence upon the Lisbon-Antwerp supply line, the price of pepper rose by about 25 per cent.[134] Such a contrast serves to set the stage for the battle of Atlantic (Portugal) versus Mediterranean (Venice) spice routes that was to be of continuing importance throughout the remainder of the sixteenth century. As in many such battles, both of the contestants lost.

The revival of the spice trade in the eastern Mediterranean between 1560 and 1566 may be accounted for in several ways[135]—first and foremost perhaps by the decline of Portugal's fortunes in both Europe and Asia. The retention of the

---

[130] Fernand Braudel, *La Méditerranée et le monde méditerranéen à l'époque de Philippe II* (Paris, 1949), p. 492.

[131] Gino Luzzato, "La decadenza di Venezia dopo le scoperte geografiche nella tradizione e nella realtà," *Archivio veneto*, Ser. 5, LIV–LV (1945), 168–70.

[132] Danvers, *op. cit.* (n. 25), I, 522–28.

[133] Lane, *op. cit.* (n. 128), p. 587, assumes that "evidently the consumption of spices, or at least of pepper, increased greatly in Europe during the sixteenth century."

[134] See appendix to this chapter.

[135] E. Hamilton, *American Treasure and the Price Revolution in Spain* (Cambridge, Mass., 1934), pp. 232–33, mentions the possible influence on prices of the Legazpi expedition of 1564 to the Philippines. But whatever hopes the Spanish might have had about developing the Philippines as a spice production center must have been dashed by Legaspi's declaration of 1569: "The Philippines ought to be considered of little importance, because at present the only article of profit which we can get from them is cinnamon" (as quoted in W. L. Schurz, *The Manila Galleon* [New York, 1959], p. 23). Hamilton (p. 231) also remarks that "because of the inveterate predilection of the Spaniard for the highly seasoned food . . . spice prices are plentiful in sixteenth- and seventeenth-century accountbooks."

monopoly depended upon the ability of the Portuguese to continue blocking the Red Sea trade and to secure their own markets and sea lanes, and this had proved too much for them to do. Because the prices of spices in Europe steadily mounted, the Levantine spice trade could be revitalized whenever the Portuguese interference was eliminated. The corruption of the Portuguese officials in the East and their self-aggrandizement at the expense of the crown gave the Muslim traders an opportunity to carry on trade again in the spice centers of India in defiance of the Portuguese monopoly. The inability of the Portuguese to sweep the Indian Ocean clean of Arab traders and to throw an effective blockade around the Persian Gulf let the spices flow again into the Levantine and Egyptian marts, where they could be bought by European suppliers at prices apparently lower than those obtaining in markets serviced through Lisbon.[136]

But the revival of the Mediterranean trade was destined to be short-lived, even though Alexandria and Aleppo continued to receive spice shipments until the end of the century. Revolts broke out after 1566 in Arabia and Yemen as a result of the difficulties that swept the Ottoman Empire for a short time following the death of Suleiman. The outbreak of war in 1570 between Venice and the Turks over control of Cyprus brought to an end a generation of peaceful relationships between the two foremost powers of the eastern Mediterranean.[137] In May, 1571, a Triple Alliance of the Venetians, the papacy, and Spain was organized to carry the war to the Turks. After the naval setback administered to the Turks at the Battle of Lepanto in 1571, the Christian allies at once began to fight among themselves over the distribution of the spoils. Taking advantage of these divisions among the Christians, the Turks rapidly prepared a new fleet. Deserted by her allies, Venice was forced in 1573 to conclude peace with the Porte and relinquish Cyprus. But within the Ottoman Empire the outbreak of disorders after the death of Sultan Selim II in 1574 marked the beginning of a long period of decline from the strength and stability achieved under Suleiman. Trade with the East was not entirely severed as a result of difficulties along the land and sea routes of the eastern Mediterranean region, but spices seem not again to have come into the Levantine and Eastern marts in quantities comparable to those of the period of 1560–66.[138]

The eastern Mediterranean was not the only region to which Philip II was sending Spanish wealth, arms, and ships in these years. His efforts to Hispanicize the Netherlands had met increasingly stiff national and religious resistance. The dispatch of the Duke of Alba to Brussels in 1567 was shortly followed by an outbreak of civil war. In the course of this war, engagements

136 For the quantities arriving at Alexandria from 1560 to 1564 see Aldo Stella, "La crisi economica veneziana della seconda metà del secolo XVI," *Archivio veneto*, Ser. 5, LVIII (1956), 42.

137 For a discussion of the way in which Marseilles exploited this opportunity to go to the Levant for direct purchases and for the resulting increase in French supplies, see Gascon, *loc. cit.* (n. 115), pp. 648–50.

138 For an analysis of the decline of the spice traffic at Venice during the 1570's, see Stella, *loc. cit.* (n. 136), pp. 43–44.

were fought on land and sea between the Spanish and the insurgent Netherlanders which made trade extremely difficult in the Low Countries. The first sack of Antwerp in 1576 by the "Spanish Fury" drove the last traders away from the Scheldt city. In the northern Netherlands meanwhile, an independent state was being formed under the leadership of Holland and the Prince of Orange. With the proclamation of the Union of Utrecht in 1579, Philip II was faced with the rise of a new Protestant state that enjoyed international support.

The preoccupation of the Spanish during the years 1566–80 permitted the Portuguese to regain some of their losses, both in Europe and overseas. The French likewise were involved in their own religious wars, and so their ability to continue poaching upon Portugal's preserves was limited. But in the East the Portuguese continued to have difficulty maintaining their footholds. For instance, Goa was heavily besieged in 1569–70 for about fourteen months. For five years the Portuguese fortress on Ternate in the Moluccas was besieged until it fell to the Muslims in 1574.[139] In Lisbon a devastating plague played havoc with commerce. And the British, taking advantage of the preoccupation of the continental powers with war, expanded their maritime activities to the point where, in 1572, Portugal felt compelled to throw open the Guinea trade to them.

7

THE NEW ERA OF CONTRACT TRADE, 1570–98

When King John III closed the Antwerp factory in 1549, Lisbon was declared to be "an open port for all purchasers."[140] Trade continued to be brisk at times in Lisbon, but generally it seems to have declined from 1549 to 1568. The great merchant syndicates which bought and distributed the spices apparently speculated with them constantly. In the regency set up in 1557 on the death of King John, confusion reigned at the court of the young King Sebastian, and private profiteering on the spice trade, both in Portugal and the East, increasingly became the order of the day. Despite the strict prohibitions against illicit trade, Portuguese subjects violated the crown's monopoly more freely with each passing year. Private individuals amassed huge fortunes while the crown bore the burden of administering and protecting a huge trade empire. Certain Portuguese even sold spices to the Arabs, or carried them to ports other than Lisbon in Portuguese bottoms.

---

[139] See Bernard H. M. Vlekke, *Nusantara: A History of the East Indian Archipelago* (Cambridge, Mass., 1945), p. 97.
[140] As quoted in Mendes da Luz, *op. cit.* (n. 3), p. 57.

In recognition of his inability to halt these illegal activities and in an effort to reduce the crown's obligations, King Sebastian in 1570 promulgated a new and fundamental *regimento* for the regulation of the trade.[141] The preamble states that under the new rules all subjects of the king might trade privately in the products of India, though with the proviso that all colonial goods should be brought to Lisbon for payment of duties. Certain ports on the Malabar Coast were designated as legally open to private traders. Malacca was proclaimed a free port, and it was ordered that spices bought there should not pay duties or fees on being transshipped in India. The Portuguese sailors and vessels patrolling Indian waters were to have the right of confiscating to themselves all pepper and other merchandise that was being carried illegally. Duties were to be paid at Lisbon in cash—pepper being taxed at a rate almost equal to the former fixed price. In the following year an additional law was promulgated that sought to regulate more rigorously navigational and shipping practices under the new dispensation.[142]

Still, according to the report of the Venetian ambassador, Sigismondo Cavalli, Lisbon around 1570 continued to be one of the most active ports of Europe.[143] In comparison with the fleets sent out at the beginning of the century, the vessels of this period were fewer in number but greater in tonnage. The cargoes brought back, over and above the king's spices, were more diverse and larger than those imported earlier in the century. From 1500 to 1560 the annual European imports of spices had increased markedly.[144] Around 1572, it is estimated that the king made a net profit annually from the trade of about one-half million ducats. But despite such returns, the young king's other expenses were evidently so heavy that he, like his predecessors, had constantly to be searching for new loans. In the process a system of contracting the pepper trade developed. Around 1575 private contractors began bidding to purchase the rights of distribution and sale in Europe[145] and later the right of purchase in the marts of Asia was also sold.[146]

King Sebastian clearly had no desire to follow his predecessors in their roles as merchant monarchs. After throwing open the spice monopoly to private enterprise, he embarked in 1574 upon a crusade against Morocco. This fruitless enterprise absorbed all the energies of the royal knight-errant for the next four years until he met his death in battle. Along with the king, many of Portugal's leading nobles either died or were taken prisoner in Morocco. The portable wealth of a number of Portugal's leading families was thereafter paid out as

[141] Details in Vicente Almeida d'Eça, *op. cit.* (n. 18), chap. ii.

[142] Mendes da Luz, *op. cit.* (n. 3), pp. 73–74.

[143] Original in E. Alberi (ed.), *Relazioni degli Ambasciatori al Senato* (Florence, 1839 ff.), Ser. I, Vol. V; also see comments in Luzzato, *op. cit.* (n. 131), I, 162–64.

[144] Lane, *loc. cit.* (n. 128), pp. 586–87, estimates that 1.5 to 2 million pounds of pepper were imported annually around 1500, and over 3 million pounds around 1560.

[145] See below, p. 134.

[146] T. A. de Carvalho, *As companhias Portuguesas de colonização* (Lisbon, 1902), chap. iv, tells of a monopoly given to Sebastião Pero da Cunha of the trade of Cochin China.

ransom for the captured *fidalgos*.[147] And in the meantime Spanish influence was growing in Portugal, and Philip II was taking an increasing interest in the spice trade.[148]

The ineffectiveness of the Portuguese monopoly was clearly apparent, as Spain's interest in the Portuguese spice trade mounted swiftly after 1570. Pepper prices in western Europe began declining around that time, and by 1580 had fallen by 25 per cent in England, 11 per cent in New Castile, and 8 per cent in Vienna. The price levels of other commodities such as grain were meanwhile rising precipitously.[149] In the eastern Mediterranean Venice and Turkey had embarked upon their three years' war. All of Venice's commercial rivals, especially Spain, her temporary ally, saw an opportunity to profit by the Seignory's involvement. In 1575, Mariano Azaro, a Carmelite monk, suggested, perhaps at Philip's solicitation, that Spain combine with the papacy and some of the other Italian rulers to replace Venetian with Portuguese pepper in Spain's Italian provinces and to establish at some Italian port a staple comparable to Antwerp.[150] From 1576 to 1578 the Grand Duke Francis of Tuscany, through Bardi agents, sought to obtain the contract for the spices coming from India to Portugal, the Italian agents apparently realizing that King Sebastian needed ready cash for his Moroccan campaign.[151] Venice itself was reduced in 1577 to setting aside for two years its prohibition of 1519 on the importation of spices from the *ponente*, so as to allow free entry to several spice ships from Portugal.

Desiring to profit by the involvements of Venice, Philip II apparently had in mind the establishment of a Spanish-Portuguese trading bloc. Such a combination would strengthen his hold in Portugal and would enable him to prevent the spice monopoly from falling into the hands of Italian or German middlemen. It would also strengthen his hand with the rebellious Netherlanders, who continued to trade at Lisbon. The initial negotiations with the Italians were not crowned with success; in 1575 the Germans once again became prominent in the spice trade. Apparently in an effort to thwart the designs of Spain and her Fugger associates, the Portuguese court rejected the initial overtures of the south German merchants for the "European contract" of pepper distribution. The great south German banking houses, which held and discounted Portuguese paper, were reckoned too powerful to be trusted with the pepper contract. In 1578 the Fuggers alone held Portuguese notes in the amount of 40,000 ducats.[152]

---

147 Details on the Moroccan campaign in J. M. Queiroz Veloso, *Dom Sebastian, 1554–1578* (Madrid, 1943).

148 On the growth of the Spanish party in Portugal, see Alfonso Danvila y Bourguero, *Felipe II y el rey Don Sebastian de Portugal* (Madrid, 1943), chaps. xxxii and xxxiii.

149 See appendix. For comparative prices see G. Wiebe, *Zur Geschichte der Preisrevolution des XVI. und XVII. Jahrhunderts* (Leipzig, 1895), p. 113.

150 Braudel, *op. cit.* (n. 130), p. 435.

151 *Ibid.*, pp. 435–36. On Francis' interest in India, see below, p. 476.

152 K. Häbler, "Die Fugger und der spanische Gewürzhandel," *Zeitschrift des historischen Vereins für Schwaben und Neuburg*, XIX (1892), 40.

The commercial world was astonished in the last months of 1575, when the pepper contract was awarded for five years to Konrad Rott, an Augsburg merchant who had long been doing business in the Iberian Peninsula but who was not one of the really great merchants.[153] Rott pledged himself to buy 12,000 hundredweight of pepper in the first year and 20,000 thereafter at 34 ducats per hundredweight. As part of his contract he had to go surety for an immediate loan to Portugal of several hundred thousand ducats at a moderate rate of interest. The loan was to be repaid in pepper deliveries during the last years of the contract. Up to one-fifth of his five years of payments could be met with old Portuguese notes. To help himself with this part of his obligation, Rott in 1576 bought at Madrid the promissory notes held by the Fuggers for 20,000 ducats, or at half price.[154] He was also permitted to pay the king in ships' stores and materials for shipbuilding, presumably from Germany.

Soon realizing that this enterprise was beyond his capacity to carry alone, the intrepid Rott sought a partner. After being turned down by the great south German houses, he sold three-eighths of his contract to Giacomo dei Bardi and Company of Florence. As if his obligations were not already overwhelming, the daring Augsburg merchant entered an India contract in 1578 with King Henry that looked toward the establishment of a world pepper monopoly. In other words Rott hoped to operate a monopoly that the kings of Portugal had found it impossible to maintain. The combined value of his contracts Rott divided into thirty shares, keeping twelve and a half for himself. Of the remainder he sold ten to Portuguese firms and seven and a half to Italian firms. Once his enterprise was organized in southern Europe, Rott entered into negotiations with the Elector Augustus of Saxony in 1579 to establish a staple in Leipzig from whence pepper would be sold to Germany, the Netherlands, the Baltic states, and Poland. To this end the elector's aides organized what was known as the Thuringian Company, a concern that would take pepper from Rott in exchange for copper and tin. Like Rott's scheme, the hopes of the elector to control the spice trade of northern Europe through Leipzig soon collapsed. By 1580 this grandiose enterprise had been abandoned and Rott had become bankrupt. Hereafter Rott's India contract was taken over by Giovanni Rovellasca, an Italian merchant from Milan.

The bankruptcy of Rott coincided with the union of the crowns of Spain and Portugal under Philip II. The childless Cardinal Henry, who had become king in 1578, had been blocked by Philip in his efforts to be released by the papacy from his vows so that he might, even though seventy-seven years old, father a legitimate heir to the throne. Meanwhile, in Lisbon, Philip was disbursing money generously in the hope of winning support from the Portuguese for the

---

[153] K. Häbler, "Konrad Rott und die thüringische Gesellschaft," *Neues Archiv für sächsische Geschichte und Alterthumskunde*, XV (1895), 179–81.

[154] Häbler, *loc. cit.* (n. 152), p. 41.

day when he would take over. Upon the old king's demise in 1580, Philip's army moved into Portugal and in the following year the Habsburg king was proclaimed by the Cortes. In terms of empire and commerce Philip now had the possibility of controlling within his realm the riches of Asia, Africa, and America along with some of the finest ports in Europe. His Dutch subjects, however, continued their successful resistance and were supported after 1580 by England and France.

According to the terms of the Agreement of Union made at Tomar in 1581, the Spanish and Portuguese colonial empires were to be kept separate and each administered by its own officials. And it is true that during the reign of Philip II the Secretary of State for India continued to operate as a separate administrative agency at Lisbon,[155] and the Casa da India to control the sale and distribution of Eastern goods. But it was not long before Philip II extended to Portugal the centralizing program that he had been evolving for the rest of the Iberian Peninsula. This effort was based primarily upon his plan to control as closely as possible the finances of his Portuguese possessions through an administration of his own creation. By a decree of November 20, 1591, he finally abolished the old Portuguese financial offices and created a new Council of Finance made up of men of his own choice. The Casa da India and the spice trade were placed under its jurisdiction and it soon became the center around which all the agencies of Portugal's metropolitan and overseas government had to revolve.[156] In the Far East, Spanish traders and missionaries from Manila began to invade the Portuguese monopolies in Macao and Japan.

To the powers of northern Europe the union of Spain and Portugal appeared as a threat comparable in long-range importance to the Turkish capture of Constantinople in 1453. Torn by religious wars, France was in no position to respond immediately to the danger posed by the new Iberian union. The Dutch, however, reasserted their independence despite forebodings that their revolt against the colossus of the south might have even less chance of final success. The English, who had been seeking a northern route to Cathay and the Indies since 1553, were cheered in 1580 by the return of Francis Drake from his hazardous trip around the world. In the course of his circumnavigation, Drake had halted at Ternate in the Moluccas and, like Sebastian del Cano before him, successfully evaded the Portuguese patrol vessels to complete the trip back to Europe. Although Philip called upon Queen Elizabeth to punish the bold marauder, Drake was instead knighted by the doughty queen. Clearly Elizabeth was preparing to challenge the international monopoly that had once divided the overseas world between the Iberian powers and which now sought to claim exclusive jurisdiction over the southern seas for the Habsburg ruler of Spain and Portugal.

The spice trade naturally reflected the reorientations and realignments that

---

[155] Mendes da Luz, *op. cit.* (n. 3), pp. 75–76.
[156] *Ibid.*, pp. 81–82.

followed the creation of the Iberian union. The Indian part of the contract originally concluded by Konrad Rott had been taken over by Rovellasca after 1580. Rovellasca, supported by the Italians and perhaps by a Spanish branch of the Fuggers,[157] managed the Indian contract until 1585. In the first five years of Philip's administration of the spice trade, it would appear that Portuguese pepper was replaced gradually in Italy by Levantine pepper. During 1582–83, very few Eastern commodities, aside from silk, were brought to Italy from Egypt and Syria and the price of pepper constantly mounted at Marseilles.[158] In Old Castile the prices of spices lagged behind the general price levels,[159] possibly owing to the fact that Portuguese pepper was being undersold elsewhere on the European market by that of Near Eastern origin. At Leghorn, for example, from 1578 until 1583 most of the pepper imported came from Portugal, but thereafter there were alternating periods of ascendancy for Mediterranean pepper and Atlantic pepper.[160]

With the expiration of the Rott-Rovellasca contract in 1585, Philip II apparently hoped to conclude a new arrangement for the distribution of spices in Europe. Plagued with continuing war in the Netherlands and the outbreak of war with England, Philip, in need of money, began as early as 1581 to negotiate with Venice to take the Portuguese pepper.[161] In 1585 he offered to sell to the Venetians 30,000 hundredweight per year at the low price of 30 ducats per hundredweight delivered at Lisbon.[162] Possibly Philip hoped by such means to deprive the northern powers, with whom he was on bad terms or at war, of the pepper that they regularly bought at Lisbon. The Spanish offer was refused, probably because Venice feared reprisals from the Turks against other aspects of her valuable Levantine trade and against her Near Eastern colonies. Similar offers were subsequently made to Milan, Genoa, and Florence. These were also refused. Individual merchants apparently continued to buy their pepper and other spices at Lisbon. For example, Simon Ruiz of Medina del Campo was attracted to the Lisbon market after 1580 and his business records, perhaps like those of other Spanish merchants, show a constantly greater interest in the purchase of spices and in the insuring of the India vessels.[163] Elsewhere in Europe, pepper prices rose sharply between 1580 and 1585, and then declined somewhat less sharply until about 1592.

Throughout the history of the staple at Lisbon, the traffic in spices was mainly a transit trade. As silver flowed through Castile, so the spices passed through Portugal. The use of pepper in Portugal and its colonies was estimated by

[157] F. Döbel, "Ueber einen Pfefferhandel der Fugger und Welser, 1586–91," *Zeitschrift des historischen Vereins für Schwaben und Neuburg*, XIII (1886), 125.

[158] Braudel, *op. cit.* (n. 3), pp. 442–43.

[159] Hamilton, *op. cit.* (n. 135), pp. 232–33.

[160] F. Braudel and R. Romano, *Navires et marchandises à l'entrée du porte de Livourne* (Paris, 1951), p. 96; also tables on pp. 118–19.

[161] Braudel, *op. cit.* (n. 130), p. 437.

[162] The price to the *contractadores* at this period was 36 to 38. *Ibid.*, p. 438.

[163] Lapeyre, *op. cit.* (n. 2), pp. 71, 238.

Konrad Rott[164] in 1579–80 at a mere 1,500 hundredweight per year, or about one-fifteenth of the annual amount imported. In this same estimate Spain and the British Isles were considered to be good prospects for 300 hundredweight each. Italy was scheduled for 6,000 hundredweight and France for 2,500. Rott evidently hoped to sell 12,000 hundredweight in the Low Countries, the German states, Bohemia, and Poland. With the bulk of the pepper imports going to northern Europe, it is little wonder that the south German merchants were constantly involved in the spice trade. Beginning in 1570, the Portuguese monopolists sought, with low risk, to make the maximum profit through the contracting system by bringing pepper into the Casa da India at the lowest possible price and selling it to the holders of the European contract at the highest possible price. In effect, the Casa da India during the last generation of the sixteenth century operated like a toll station that exacted as much profit from the spice trade as the traffic would bear.

While seeking to find a buyer for the European contract, Philip II concluded a new Indian contract in 1586. Giovanni Rovellasca, with his Italian backers, continued to be the principal interested party, though the negotiations in Spain were conducted by Giraldo Paris, a noble of Limburg and a copper trader. In the agreement signed at Valencia on February 15, 1586, the "contractors" stipulated that for a period of six years they would equip five vessels each year to sail to Malacca carrying 170,000 ducats for the purchase of pepper. They agreed to deliver 30,000 hundredweights of pepper to Lisbon each year. By article 28 of their agreement with the king, Rovellasca and Paris were permitted to bring associates into their enterprise. It was not long before the Welsers took a five-twelfths' interest. In the following year, Octavian and Philip Edward Fugger, secretly at first, bought a one-quarter interest in the Indian contract. The south German bankers evidently hoped through participation in the pepper trade to inform themselves more fully on the finances of Philip II so as to realize whatever they could from the debts he still owed them.[165]

The term of the new contract (1586–91) coincided with a period of turbulence in the Portuguese East and catastrophe in the fortunes of Philip II. In 1586, Malacca itself was under siege from the Achinese of Sumatra and a fleet had to be sent to its relief from India. Although the Portuguese succeeded in relieving the siege of their invaluable entrepôt, they were challenged repeatedly in the years immediately after 1586 in their possession of a number of other points in southern Asia vital to the spice trade.[166] In the meantime the "contractors" had their agents operating in India. In 1583, Filippo Sassetti arrived in Cochin to superintend the commercial operations being carried on there by Rovellasca.

---

[164] See the chart in Hermann Kellenbenz, "Der Pfeffermarkt um 1600 und die Hansastädte," *Hänsische Geschichtsblätter*, LXXIV (1956), 33. This same article, with revisions and additions, is entitled in French, "Autour de 1600: le commerce du poivre des Fugger et le marché international du poivre," *Annales. Économies, sociétés, civilisations*, XI (1956), 1–28. Future references to this article will be to the French version.

[165] *Ibid.*, p. 2.

[166] Details in Danvers, *op. cit.* (n. 25), II, 69–79.

Sassetti's reports and letters to friends in Florence are among the most urbane and informative of the merchant accounts of this period.[167] At Goa, the Fuggers and Welsers were represented by Ferdinand Kron of Augsburg and an accountant. The announcement at Goa in 1587 that the trade with India had been handed over to the contractors became the occasion for disturbance and unrest as the Portuguese there apparently felt their interests threatened.[168]

In Europe, meanwhile, the outbreak of war between Spain and England in 1585 merged the interests of England and the Dutch, the two greatest maritime powers of northern Europe, against the Iberian states. Trade between the Protestant countries and the Iberian states was forbidden by both belligerents, though the Dutch merchants continued to do a limited business at Lisbon through vessels flying neutral flags.[169] The estuary and facilities of the Tagus were meanwhile being used almost exclusively for the preparation of the Spanish Armada. Vessels returning from India were in constant dread of being captured in the south Atlantic by English or Dutch corsairs. And, with the defeat of the Armada in 1588, the Turks and Arabs in both the Mediterranean and the Indian Ocean took advantage of Philip's setbacks to renew their attacks.[170]

The turbulence of the international situation interfered seriously with the ability of the "contractors" to make good their pepper deliveries to Lisbon. In no single year were they able to bring in the stipulated 30,000 hundredweight of pepper. In 1587 only one-third of the amount called for in the contract arrived at the Casa, and in 1593 none came in at all. During the years 1588–91 a total of 65,000 hundredweight arrived safely, or only slightly more than one-half of the quantity contracted for. In 1592 a single vessel returned to Europe only to be captured by the English. Over the entire contract period less than one-half of the stipulated amount of pepper was delivered to the Casa da India.[171]

The uncertainty in the supply of spices at Lisbon and the troubles attending their distribution in Europe had the effect of making pepper prices unstable. In England and Alsace the price of pepper mounted constantly and fluctuated wildly, partly because of the international situation and partly because of the speculative practices of the merchants.[172] In 1588 the Welsers opened a branch in Venice to deal in spices and they were shortly followed there by Fugger representatives. By 1592 pepper at Venice could be bought once again in quantity and at lower prices than those prevailing at Lisbon.[173] For eight years,

---

[167] See below, pp. 475–77. The Fugger newsletters also include informative letters from India for this period.

[168] Danvers, *op. cit.* (n. 25), II, 80. On Philip II's effort to organize a Portuguese East India Company in 1587 see T. A. de Carvalho, *op. cit.* (n. 146), chap. iv.

[169] Danvers, *op. cit.* (n. 25), II, 104–5.

[170] On the relationship of the Arab revival in East Africa and the Persian Gulf to Philip's interests in south Asia see M. A. Hedwig Fitzler, "Der Anteil der Deutschen in der Kolonialpolitik Philipps II. von Spanien in Asien," *Vierteljahrschrift für Sozial und Wirtschaftsgeschichte*, XXVIII (1935), 251–58.

[171] Kellenbenz, *op. cit.* (n. 164), chart on p. 3.

[172] Wiebe, *op. cit.* (n. 149), p. 137.

[173] Kellenbenz, *op. cit.* (n. 164), p. 4.

after 1592, when deliveries to Lisbon practically ceased, pepper prices mounted at a fantastic rate. It is also true, however, that grain prices were mounting steeply in western Europe during the last decade of the century.

Philip II's losses following the defeat of the Armada could be made up only in part by the large quantities of silver coming in from the New World during the last decade of the sixteenth century. In 1589, and again in 1591, the king was forced to pay some of his debts in pepper.[174] At the same time the king ordered the reorganization of the administration of trade at Lisbon. He abolished the old system of *vedores* by a decree of November 20, 1591, and, as we have seen, created a Council of Finance to oversee all matters relating to the royal revenues, including the sale of spices and the other operations of the Casa da India.[175] Such a move was evidently related to the determination of the Iberians to take back the Indian contract themselves on the expiration of the syndicate's pepper contract in 1591.[176] It may well be that Philip wanted to make certain that no international group should ever gain a measure of control over both the Indian and European sides of the pepper trade.

In an effort to regularize the distribution of pepper in Europe and in the hope of collecting the debts owed them, a group of the king's creditors agreed in March, 1591, under pressure from the crown, to form a syndicate for the purpose of signing a European contract with the king. Of the thirty-two shares into which the contract was divided, twelve belonged to André Ximenes, a Portuguese merchant and banker doing business at Lisbon and Antwerp. The remainder were divided as follows: Fugger (7), Welser (5), Rovellasca (4), and the Spanish merchants Francisco and Pedro de Malvenda of Bourgos (4).[177] The king, who bought the pepper at 16 ducats per hundredweight, sold it to the syndicate at 36, thus making a handsome profit on the transaction.

Among themselves the merchants agreed to sell the pepper at from 40 to 42 ducats per hundredweight, but the "common" price was impossible to maintain. The great merchants sold their stocks at reduced prices to smaller contractors at Lisbon and elsewhere. Other shipments were delivered by the merchants after 1591 to Lübeck, Middleburg, Amsterdam, and Danzig, for northern Europe continued to be the greatest market for pepper. But of all the northern cities, Hamburg in the last decade of the sixteenth century became the most important point of distribution and sale for the pepper trade.[178] Evidently, Hamburg was one of the safest places for the merchants to operate during the disruption attending the Anglo-Dutch-Spanish war. Although the contractors had sent spice ships to Leghorn and other Italian ports, the Mediterranean was evidently more dangerous for trade than the Atlantic. And, perhaps more importantly, the lower price and the big stock of pepper in Venice after 1592

[174] *Ibid.*, p. 5.
[175] Mendes da Luz, *op. cit.* (n. 3), pp. 81–83.
[176] Kellenbenz, *op. cit.* (n. 164), p. 19.
[177] *Ibid.*, p. 5. Also see Fitzler, *loc. cit.* (n. 170), p. 267, who implies that with the conclusion of the European contract a world spice monopoly was held by the syndicate.
[178] Kellenbenz, *op. cit.* (n. 164), pp. 9–11.

kept Portuguese pepper out of Italian markets. The situation in Asia and Africa had meanwhile become quieter, thus also contributing to the revival of Venice and to the decline of trade relations between Italy and the Iberian states.[179]

The last five years of the sixteenth century were marked by modest prosperity in Venice and the disappearance of the last remaining vestiges of the Portuguese monopoly. The growing naval strength of the Dutch and English made the trading activities of the Iberian states constantly more hazardous. The high price of pepper at Lisbon after 1592, along with an understandable desire for direct access to the wealth of Asia, inspired Dutch and English merchantmen to encroach with ever greater boldness on the overseas preserve that Philip II sought to keep as his monopoly.[180] An attack on Cadiz and Philip's navy by the Protestant powers in 1596 was followed by a blockade of Lisbon. The adherence of France to the Anglo-Dutch combination further weakened Spain's hopes of recovering her former position of preponderance in Europe. The Peace of Vervins between France and Spain in 1598 was followed in the same year by the death of Philip II at the Escorial. While the war with England and the United Provinces continued, Spain after 1598 was no longer powerful enough to prevent the northern powers from invading the colonial world to stake out claims and to conduct commerce on their own.

For Portugal the sixteenth century was a heroic epoch in expansion, conquest, and trade; it was also a period of disappointment and decline. Over the century as a whole seven hundred and sixty-eight ships sailed from Lisbon to the East, or an average of almost eight each year.[181] Up to 1579 only about 10 per cent of the ships were lost; between 1580 and 1612 only 63 per cent got back safely. With the growth of the empire, the crown, by its monopolistic practices, succeeded in forcing the Eastern trade through a small number of key entrepôts: Goa, Ormuz, Malacca, Macao, Lisbon, and Antwerp. Despite the severe restrictions imposed by the system of monopoly, it was a far from perfect device for controlling the trade or for guaranteeing the crown a return commensurate with its investment. In Asia, the Muslim traders continuously sought

[179] Braudel, *op. cit.* (n. 130), pp. 445–47.
[180] For general studies of the beginnings of the northern trade, see W. Foster, *England's Quest for Eastern Trade* (London, 1933), and K. Glamann, *Dutch-Asiatic Trade, 1620–1740* (Copenhagen and the Hague, 1958).
[181] Statistics in text from R. Ehrenberg, "Ostindische Handelsgesellschaften," in *Handwörterbuch der Staatswissenschaften*, VI (1910), 949–50. Cf. the following table taken from Whiteway, *op. cit.* (n. 127), p. 43:

Period	Ships That Left Portugal	Ships That Stayed in India	Remain To Be Accounted For	Returned to Lisbon
1497–1579	620	256	364	325
1580–1612	186	29	157	100

to run the Portuguese blockade and almost at every period did so with some success. But the most serious breaches on the Asian side of the royal monopoly apparently were caused by the Portuguese officials, sailors, and merchants who conducted trade with all comers to fatten their private purses.[182] Nevertheless a practical monopoly, excluding other European powers, operated in Asia until 1580.

The monopoly was likewise seldom complete in Europe, probably because of the king's dependence upon foreign markets, raw materials, and capital. Both the Portuguese and Spanish efforts to monopolize the spice trade failed because of the general indebtedness of their rulers to the merchant-bankers of Italy and Germany. It is worth observing that when Portugal was finally divested completely of her control of the spice trade her successors were European states even further removed from the spice regions. Although the Muslims and Venetians made repeated efforts, some successful, to re-establish their monopoly, they too were doomed ultimately to failure. The appearance of fleets of Dutch and English merchantmen in Asian waters in the last decade of the sixteenth century was as much of a setback to Venice as it was to Portugal. Henceforward, the maritime states of northern Europe were to control larger shares of the Eastern trade, but there was never again any real effort on the part of any single European nation to control the trade completely. Portugal's failure had clearly shown how impossible it was for any single nation, far removed geographically from the East, to control the spice trade simply through blockade, fortified footholds, and patrol fleets.

In no sense can it be alleged that the consequences of the discoveries were revolutionary only in the Iberian Peninsula or in southern Europe. Throughout the Middle Ages, the spice trade had been of Continental proportions, and in the sixteenth century the leading agents of business and government from all parts of western Europe shared, to a degree at least, in the successes and failures of the Europeans who braved the seas and adventured into strange lands. For the purposes of our study, a review of pepper prices illustrates how difficult it is to show concretely the extent of the influence of trade on the European view of Asia. But even though the whole subject is admittedly amorphous, the conclusion is inescapable, as we shall see in later chapters, that the shift in the spice commerce—especially in the pepper trade—forced the European merchant community to leave the beaten tracks of the past and reorient their practices to an entirely different situation. In the process they were forced increasingly to learn about the vagaries of commerce conducted at a great distance and without the interposition of a large number of intermediaries. In so doing, they not only had to re-evaluate their practices in Europe, but they were required to learn about commercial practices, markets, and a host of other matters which had a bearing on the trade in Asia.

---

[182] See the reports of Simon Botelho that were submitted to the King of Portugal in 1554 as summarized in Ehrenberg, *op. cit.* (n.181), pp. 292–95.

The discoveries had demonstrated not only the interdependence of the European states; they had also highlighted the relationships of Europe to Africa, Asia, and America, and had made apparent the need of Europe for free access to the resources and markets of the outside world. The shift in the center of Europe's own economic gravity from the ports of the Mediterranean to those of the Atlantic seaboard, it has been shown, was neither immediate nor permanent following the return of Vasco da Gama. At the end of the century, the Dutch and British cracked the maritime monopoly of the Iberian powers, proceeded directly to the Indies, and soon managed to replace the Venetians and Portuguese as the purveyors of spices and other oriental commodities in Europe.

While trade on both land and sea was being revolutionized, the attitude in Europe toward Asia was also undergoing rapid transformation. The products of the Orient, being available in quantities so much larger than ever before, were more widely known and desired. This rapid democratization of oriental products had the effect of making information and ideas from the East more generally acceptable and credible in Europe. From Portugal, travel accounts, navigational and commercial handbooks, geographical charts, and Jesuit letters penetrated the heart of Europe. Often such information followed or accompanied the traders who sold spices. Travelogues were translated into a variety of languages for the commercial information contained in them or simply out of interest in the adventures they related. It was through these business channels that information was disseminated to western Europe by word of mouth, official pronouncements, and published books.

APPENDIX

Pepper Prices in the Sixteenth Century

The history of the price of pepper in Europe during the sixteenth century is a fascinating and elusive phase of economic history. Practically all the generalizations regularly made about it in the literature are only partially correct or of limited application. What is most perturbing about this problem is the fact that so far we have relatively few wholesale prices and practically no runs of figures at all incorporating the quantities reaching the various mart cities where pepper was commonly sold. Whenever we have continuous runs of pepper prices, it is generally for those cities not central to the trade. The sole exception to this generalization is the case of Antwerp. It is particularly distressing that we do not yet have a series covering the whole century for any of the permanent centers of distribution, such as Cairo, Venice, and Lisbon. And even when we do have long runs, such as those for Vienna or England, they are marred by breaks or so presented as to make accurate generalizations extremely dubious.

It is nevertheless possible to see from the limited data available that the *absolute* price of pepper mounted constantly from 1450 to 1600. In the period from 1450 to 1495 the prices rose steadily with the high point coming in the mid-1480's and with a perceptible break occurring in the mid-1490's. At Venice, from 1495 to 1520, the supplies of pepper were short and the prices extremely high. At Lisbon, meanwhile, the price of pepper which was 80 ducats in 1499, fell to 40 by 1502, and by 1504 was selling at 20 and below. In the following year the price at the Casa da India was fixed at 22. For a time the crown had difficulty maintaining the fixed price, but apparently after 1515 the monopoly entered upon its halcyon days. After the factory at Antwerp was shut down in 1549, the price at Lisbon appears to have risen slowly until it shot up steeply in the early 1590's. A similar pattern of prices seems also to emerge at Antwerp. Between 1495 and 1600 the price of pepper more than quadrupled. On Antwerp there is enough documentation on general prices and wages to show by comparative study that real prices mounted sharply before 1546 and declined thereafter to 1585 under the influence of the importation of precious metals from America. For places not central to the trade where we have continuous runs, it is clear that the absolute price of pepper in terms of silver mounted constantly. At Vienna, for example, the absolute price of pepper more than doubled (from 43.8 to 112.5) between 1500 and 1600.

But though the rise in the price of pepper was broadly continuous over the whole of

[143]

the sixteenth century, a closer analysis of prices shows considerable variation from decade to decade and from place to place. Such variations were often true only of a particular market and reflected its dependence upon either Lisbon or Venice for its supplies of pepper. For example, Vienna, Lyons, and Florence took pepper from both entrepôts, while England was almost entirely dependent upon the Lisbon-Antwerp line. For that reason the English markets were probably much more sensitive to disturbances within the Portuguese empire. Also, variations were introduced into pepper prices by local hostility toward the new Portuguese pepper which was sometimes thought of as being malagueta rather than true pepper and was also considered to be adulterated or inferior in quality to Mediterranean pepper—or by regional preferences for different varieties, such as long, black, or white.

The problem of quantities imported can be even less satisfactorily dealt with than prices on the basis of available materials. From 1496 to 1498 Venice imported between 5 and 7 million pounds of spices annually, more than one-fourth of which was probably pepper.[1] Thereafter the quantities brought in from the Levant fell off sharply, and in some years at the beginning of the century no spices were imported at all. In Lisbon after the consolidation of the monopoly (*ca.* 1515) the deliveries of pepper alone amounted to around three million pounds annually, though apparently it was not always possible to guarantee delivery of that quantity. Venice meanwhile resumed, particularly in 1516, 1520, 1530, and 1531, bringing in large quantities of spices, though the proportion of pepper in the Venetian spice importations was evidently smaller than before 1499 and therefore much less important than the amounts being imported by the Casa da India. Throughout the remainder of the century the major market for pepper, though not necessarily the other spices, was Lisbon. But by 1592, when the Dutch and English entered the maritime commerce in earnest, the supplies in Lisbon evidently fell off sharply for the remaining years of the century. If it is possible to generalize at all on quantities, it can be suggested that Europe received annually during the period from 1496 to 1592 about three million pounds of pepper, a modest figure when compared with the annual harvest in India alone.[2]

Now what is the relation between the supplies of pepper and its price? The low price of pepper at Lisbon at the beginning of the century before the monopoly was fully established can probably be accounted for by the oversupplying of an entrepôt that had not yet developed its machinery of distribution. The dramatic rise in prices after 1592 can probably also be accounted for in part by the cessation of deliveries at Lisbon. But as for the constant price rise throughout the century, no firm relationship can be established between supply and price.[3] For it would seem that the supplies were fairly constant from *ca.* 1515 to 1592, and that pepper nevertheless continued to mount in price in terms of silver.

Now what is the relation between pepper prices and the general commodity prices of the sixteenth century? This is almost impossible to determine on the basis of available

[1] F. C. Lane, "Venetian Shipping during the Commercial Revolution," *American Historical Review,* XXXVIII (January, 1933), 228.

[2] F. Döbel, Über einen Pfefferhandel der Fugger und Welser, 1586–91," *Zeitschrift des historischen Vereins für Schwaben und Neuburg,* XIII (1886), 128.

[3] For a conservative view of this problem in Spanish trade of the sixteenth century see H. and P. Chaunu, "A la recherche des fluctuations cycliques dans l'économie des XVIe et XVIIe siècles: crise de tonnage, crise de fret," *Eventail de l'histoire vivante; hommage à Lucien Febvre* (Paris, 1953), II, 392.

Year	Vienna Burger-Spital*	Vienna Kloster-neuburg*	Cairo †	Venice †	Old Castile Leon ‡	Valencia ‡	New Castile ‡	Andalusia‡	Antwerp §
95	23.1	23.1	..	42, 45, 46, 49½	..	..	..	..	30.0
96	..	24.3	66–68	49, 49, 42	..	..	..	..	30.0
97	..	23.2	74–75	42½, 48½	..	..	..	..	30.0
98	..	27.5	61, 78, 81	56, 57	..	..	..	..	30.0
99	..	25.8	..	70, 69–70, 70,	..	..	..	..	31.5
.	..	..	..	75, 80	..	..	..	..	..
00	..	43.8	..	87, 90–100,	..	..	..	..	55.5
.	..	..	..	88–92,	..	..	..	..	..
.	..	..	..	98–110, 120	..	..	..	..	..
01	..	42.5	90–102,	131, 102–70,	..	..	..	..	51.0
.	..	..	100	80, 75½, 75	..	..	..	..	..
02	..	..	140	100, 94, 90	..	..	..	..	39.0
03	..	..	105	100, 91, 80, 88	..	..	..	..	30.0
04	..	52.5	..	..	..	..	..	..	30.0
05	..	..	192	..	..	..	..	..	30.0
06	..	31.2	..	..	..	..	..	..	30.0
07	..	34.8	..	..	..	..	..	..	..
08	..	31.7	..	..	..	..	..	..	27.75
09	..	29.7	..	..	..	..	..	..	26.62
10	..	30.7	..	..	..	..	..	..	27
11	..	..	..	..	..	..	..	..	..
12	..	29.7	..	..	..	4.5	..	..	..
13	..	28.6	120	..	..	4.2	..	..	..
14	..	27.1	..	..	..	4.2	..	..	..
15	..	34.0	..	..	..	4.9	..	..	..
16	..	33.0	..	..	..	6.5	..	..	..
17	..	33.8	..	..	..	5.1	..	..	..
18	..	38.4	..	..	115.0	5.8	..	..	..
19	..	42.9	..	..	120.0	6.0	..	..	..
520	..	43.9	90	..	128.0	..	..	..	..
21	..	37.0	..	..	145.0	..	..	..	..
22	..	50.5	..	..	142.0	6.0	..	..	..
23	50.9	52.4	..	..	127.0	8.0	..	..	..
24	..	52.6	98	..	134.0	7.3	..	..	..
25	..	52.3	90	..	136.0	6.0	..	..	..
26	..	44.6	..	..	136.0	7.0	..	..	48
27	41.8	44.1	63	..	..	..	..	..	..
28	..	55.0	..	..	130.0	6.4	..	..	..
29	45.0	..	..	..	125.0	..	..	..	48
530	..	45.0	95	..	128.0	..	..	..	..
31	..	48.0	130, 100	..	..	8.0	..	..	..
32	..	55.3	..	..	..	6.5	..	..	..
33	48.1	48.1	..	..	170.0	..	..	..	..
34	47.8	..	..	..	..	6.0	..	..	..
35	47.5	..	..	..	..	6.0	..	..	..
36	47.5	..	..	..	127.6	6.0	..	..	..
37	..	..	..	..	125.0	..	..	..	..
38	45.0	..	..	..	138.9	..	..	..	..
39	..	..	..	..	123.3	..	..	..	..
540	41.3	..	..	..	113.4	..	..	..	..
41	45.0	..	..	..	136.0	..	..	..	..
42	45.0	..	..	..	140.0	..	..	..	..
43	..	..	..	..	136.0	..	..	..	..
44	43.3	..	..	..	..	..	..	..	..
45	55.0	..	..	..	136.0	6.5	..	..	..
46	45.7	..	..	..	136.0	7.3	..	..	41.5
47	71.9	..	..	..	136.0	7.7	..	..	..
48	47.5	..	..	..	140.0	7.6	..	..	..
49	47.5	47.0	..	..	129.5	7.3	..	..	..
550	..	..	..	..	136.0	7.8	..	..	54

For notes to table see p. 147.

Year	Vienna Burger-Spital★	Vienna Kloster-neuburg★	Cairo †	Venice †	Old Cas-tile Leon‡	Valencia ‡	New Cas-tile ‡	Andalusia ‡	Antwerp §
1551	..	..	..	..	160.0	..	9.8	..	42
52	..	..	..	..	141.8	..	12.0	..	39
53	54.5	..	..	..	160.0	..	8.0	..	42
54	50.4	..	..	..	155.0	..	..	..	43.5
55	51.3	..	..	..	165.0	..	..	152.8	43.5
56	49.3	..	..	..	150.0	..	12.0	..	..
57	49.6	..	..	..	147.5	..	8.0	..	..
58	48.9	..	..	..	136.0	..	..	..	..
59	50.4	..	..	..	155.0	..	..	..	..
1560	..	..	..	..	238.0	..	..	..	..
61	..	..	..	..	204.0	..	13.5	..	..
62	..	..	..	..	209.7	..	15.9	..	58.5
63	57.3	..	..	..	238.0	..	19.8	..	60
64	..	..	..	..	272.0	..	21.5	..	..
65	..	..	..	..	221.0	..	23.9	..	..
66	56.3	..	..	..	272.0	..	16.0	..	..
67	56.3	..	..	..	221.0	..	12.5	..	..
68	56.3	..	..	..	..	..	16.0	..	..
69	56.3	..	..	..	..	..	16.0	195.3	..
1570	56.3	..	..	..	..	..	18.0	..	..
71	56.3	..	..	..	..	..	14.0	..	..
72	55	..	..	..	..	..	10.0	..	..
73	52.5	..	..	..	..	..	10.0	140.0	..
74	56.3	..	..	..	..	..	13.8	..	..
75	52.5	..	..	..	..	..	14.0	..	..
76	56.3	54.6	..	..	..	..	15.0	140.1	..
77	..	..	..	..	..	..	13.1	..	..
78	52.5	..	..	..	..	..	12.5	..	..
79	..	..	..	..	..	..	13.0	..	..
1580	..	..	..	..	..	..	18.0	187.0	..
81	..	..	..	..	..	..	16.0	..	..
82	52.5	..	..	..	..	..	..	187.0	..
83	68.0	..	..	..	238.0	..	14.0	..	..
84	67.5	..	..	..	238.0	..	17.5	204.0	..
85	75.0	..	..	..	204.0	..	15.5	238.0	..
86	75.0	..	..	..	255.0	..	19.0	..	..
87	75.0	..	..	..	272.0	..	..	272.0	..
88	63.8	..	..	..	263.5	..	16.1	255.0	..
89	63.8	..	..	..	249.3	..	15.0	272.0	..
1590	64.0	..	..	..	233.8	..	..	..	..
91	64.0	..	..	..	225.3	..	12.7	238.0	96.0
92	57.0	..	..	..	244.4	..	14.8	243.7	..
93	66.0	..	..	..	225.3	..	12.3	246.5	91.5
94	66.0	..	..	..	240.8	..	18.0	250.3	94.5
95	..	..	..	..	247.9	..	17.5	260.7	..
96	..	..	..	..	246.5	..	16.0	255.0	99.0
97	..	..	..	..	235.9	..	16.0	..	133.5
98	..	..	..	..	265.6	..	20.0	289.0	..
99	105.0	..	..	..	398.6	..	31.7	408.0	..
1600	112.5	..	..	..	289.0	..	22.7	306.0	..
01	75.0	..	..	..	..	..	..	..	..
02	70.0	..	..	..	..	..	..	..	..
03	52.5	81.2	..	..	..	..	..	..	..
04	45.0	55.6	..	..	..	..	..	..	..
05	..	53.8	..	..	..	..	..	..	..
06	..	52.5	..	..	..	..	..	..	..
07	..	60.0	..	..	..	..	..	..	..
08	..	48.0	..	..	..	..	..	..	..
09	..	48.8	..	..	..	..	..	..	..
1610	..	..	..	..	..	..	..	..	..

data. In Old Castile general spice prices lagged behind the general commodity indices to about 1546, and in the following decade the spices moved on about the same level as general prices. From 1558 to 1563 the spice prices rose sharply, and then declined abruptly to 1570. After 1584 the spice indices fell far below the level of general commodity prices.[4] In France, Spain, and Florence general prices quadrupled between 1520 and 1590 with spices following but lagging considerably behind general price increases.[5] But even this analysis tells us little about pepper prices specifically and nothing about price relationships elsewhere in Europe.[6] The data being inconclusive, we can only surmise that pepper prices generally mounted in concord with other prices, except where local conditions of disruption or speculation temporarily brought about abrupt changes.

All of the above pepper prices have been gathered from published sources. These are fairly numerous and represent price movements in a number of different countries, cities, and regions. No effort has been made to go beyond the raw data in drawing our tentative conclusions, and prices are cited in the original currencies. Additional research is required to obtain the continuous series of prices for specific markets which are required for firmer conclusions. Sources used in the compilation of the price data are listed below.

[4] E. H. Hamilton, *American Treasure and the Price Revolution in Spain* (Cambridge, Mass., 1934), pp. 232–33.

[5] G. Parenti, *Prime ricerche sulla rivoluzione dei prezzi in Firenze* (Florence, 1939), pp. 158, 36.★

[6] For some discussion on English and Alsatian prices, see F. Simiand, *Recherches anciennes et nouvelles . . . des prix . . .* (Paris, 1932), diagrams III and V.

★ Alfred Francis Pribram, *Materialien zur Geschichte der Preise und Löhne in Österreich* (Vienna, 1938), Vol. I: Vienna B., pp. 280–81 (item 416); Vienna K., pp. 459–60 (item 636).

† Vitorino Magalhães-Godinho, "Le repli vénetien et égyptien et la route du Cap, 1496–1533," *Eventail de l'histoire vivante, hommage à Lucien Fébvre* (Paris, 1953), Vol. II: Cairo, p. 294; Venice, p. 289.

‡ Earl J. Hamilton, *American Treasure and the Price Revolution in Spain, 1501–1650* (Cambridge, Mass., 1934): Old Castile-Leon, pp. 323–27 (item 29), 348–53 (item 33); Valencia, pp. 328–34 (item 26); New Castile, pp. 341–47 (item 45); Andalusia, pp. 335–39 (item 35).

§ Charles Verlinden, *Dokumenten voor de geschiedenis van prijzen en lonen in Vlaanderen en Brabant (XVᵉ–XVIIIᵉ eeuw)* (Bruges, 1959): Antwerp, pp. 332–33.

CHAPTER IV

The Printed Word

The invention of the printing press in the mid-fifteenth century occurred at a time when the Italian Renaissance was in full flower, when literacy was rapidly increasing among the gentry and the urban middle classes, and when the Portuguese exploration of the coast of Africa was beginning to provoke general interest in overseas affairs. In the fourteenth century the book trade had been secularized; in the fifteenth century professional copyists turned out a wide variety of manuscript books in constantly increasing numbers: devotional works, Latin and vernacular Bibles, chronicles, romances (Mandeville's, discussed before, for example), and educational textbooks. The manufacture of paper, a technique originally imported into Europe from the East, began to develop in Spain in the twelfth century, and by the first decade of the fifteenth century paper mills were to be found in many countries of western Europe. Paper, a much cheaper material for book manufacture than parchment, gradually stimulated innovation in bookmaking techniques. The most successful of the new experimenters in book manufacture was Johann Gutenberg of Mainz, the European inventor of movable type.[1]

The first great achievement of the Gutenberg process was the completion of the forty-two-line Bible in 1456. During the following two decades, this mechanical technique of manufacturing books spread rapidly to other parts of Germany and to Italy, France, and Spain. In 1487 the first book to be printed in Portugal by movable type came off a press. The printing process was diffused so rapidly in western Europe because it was essentially an extension of processes already being developed in the existing great centers of book manufacture. In the last half of the fifteenth century, the cradle period of printing, books

---

[1] For a summary of the evolution of the mechanical process of book production, see Pierce Butler, *The Origin of Printing in Europe* (Chicago, 1940). The latest data on Chinese paper and its transmission to Europe is in T. H. Tsien, *Written on Bamboo and Silk* (Chicago, 1962), pp. 135–42.

normally were produced in numbers roughly equivalent to what the manuscript factories were turning out. Ordinarily editions of particular titles ranged from 200 to 1,000 copies, and these figures increased only slowly during the sixteenth century.[2] Aside from the single sheets on which proclamations and indulgences were often printed, it is estimated that 30,000 editions of incunabula were printed before 1500 by presses in more than two hundred different cities and towns in western Europe.[3] Italy, which had usurped the lead in printing that Gutenberg's invention had originally given the Germans, produced about one-third of these early editions. It should be noticed, however, that German and Flemish printers were acknowledged masters of the new technique and that their services were in demand in both old and new centers of book production for a full century after the invention of printing.

The growing literacy of western Europeans during the sixteenth century helped to stimulate innovations in book production and manufacture; in return the increase in the availability of books, particularly for schools, helped to promote the spread of literacy. While most of the books produced before 1500 were religious works of many varieties, readers also began to have at hand in printed form the classics of antiquity and the writings of the Humanists. Exhaustive research has long been devoted to the study of the incunabula. Scholars have not given similar attention to the printed books of the sixteenth century. Latin works, produced in all countries for international consumption in the sixteenth century, remain the great *terra incognita* of Renaissance literary history.[4] Fortunately, except for the chapbooks and the later Jesuit letter collections, practically all the printed materials dealing with expansion into Asia appeared in the vernacular languages.

Before 1501, Venice printed more books than any other European city, and was rivaled in Italy only by Rome.[5] Paris and Lyons were the two major centers of printing in France, and London accounted for 90 per cent of the books printed in England. Most German books came from the presses of Cologne, Strassburg, and Augsburg, while Antwerp dominated book manufacture in the Netherlands. Seville was the foremost of several great printing establishments in Spain and the one which produced a majority of the books about the discoveries. Practically all Portuguese books were printed at Lisbon until after mid-century, when Coimbra began to rival it by producing scholarly works and Jesuit letterbooks. With the passage of time many other cities were added to this list of major book-producing centers as the printer's art continued to spread.

[2] A few best-sellers, like the works of Erasmus, were produced in larger quantities. But individual printings of more than 1,000 to 1,500 copies were uncommon throughout the sixteenth century. See below, pp. 182–84.

[3] See P. Fumagalli in R. A. Peddie (ed.), *Printing: A Short History of the Art* (London, 1927), pp. 38–39.

[4] See the valuable essay by Paul von Tieghem, "La littérature latine de la Renaissance," *Bibliothèque d'humanisme et renaissance*, IV (1944), 177–418.

[5] J. M. Lenhart, O. M. C., *Pre-Reformation Printed Books: A Study in Statistical and Applied Bibliography* (New York, 1935), p. 32.

Before the end of the century, Madrid and Amsterdam had become important publishing centers.

The names of Venice, Lisbon, Seville, Antwerp, Lyons, and London were every whit as important in publishing as they were in trade. This is not surprising when one recalls that book distribution was a valuable facet of commerce and that its centers changed with the shift in the centers of trade. Throughout the sixteenth century, annual book fairs of international interest were held at Frankfurt, Mainz, and Lyons. With the passage of time books became somewhat cheaper and more compact. In Venice, Aldus began producing the small octavo in the early years of the sixteenth century. At mid-century the printers of Paris and Lyons reduced the octavo by half, and by the end of the century the printers of Antwerp and Leyden had again halved the size of some of their books. It was possible to decrease the price, size, and weight of books by using the lower-priced papers that were available and by substituting pasteboard for wooden covers. Books in handy sizes and at popular prices stimulated book buying and reading.

The reading public, as it grew in size, had available a constantly increasing number of books on Asia. Those in print were of several different types. First came the official Portuguese pronouncements usually made through royal letters to the monarchs and prelates of Europe. The accounts of ordinary participants—merchants, navigators, and officials mainly—detailed in letters or other short accounts both rumors and accurate information about the route to India, the marts of Asia, and incidental curiosa about geography, language, and religion. Such unofficial narratives were relayed, sometimes at great risk, to most of the countries of western Europe in short order, as firsthand news of the East was at a premium in the beginning years of the century. Outside Portugal, enterprising printers, whenever they were able, tried to publish both the official and unofficial accounts, either separately or in collections. Until 1550, the date when Ramusio's great collection of voyages began to appear, the available materials were few in number and generally of untested veracity. But in the latter half of the century a literary deluge fell upon Europe as the books, travel collections, and maps dealing with Europe's great adventure in the East rapidly appeared in print. A substantial number of the narrative accounts, both primary and secondary, which were published after mid-century, came from the pens of European missionaries, especially Jesuits. Printed maps, prepared generally from the manuscripts of Portuguese cartographers and from existing world maps, were soon added to the narrative accounts or included in the great atlases of Ptolemy, Ortelius, and Mercator. The interests of the religious writers, whether in Europe or in Asia, were often different from those who wrote on Asia from a secular viewpoint, the latter generally making material considerations their main concern. Our objective in this chapter is to show how secular literary materials on Asia gradually appeared and circulated in Europe, how they contributed to the growth of interest in secular literature, and how they helped to build Europe's many-sided image of Asia. The letters and histories of the missionaries will be taken up in the following chapter in connection with the Christian mission.

I

PORTUGAL'S CONTROL OF INFORMATION

That the Portuguese sought to keep to themselves the details of their overseas discoveries beginning in the time of Prince Henry is neither a new observation nor a remarkable fact. But much has been written about it in recent years as part of an effort to explore such debated questions as the pre-Columbian discovery of America, the superiority of Portuguese nautical science in the fifteenth century, the authenticity of and the lacunae in the Portuguese chronicles of discovery, and, most important for our purposes, the *suppression and distortion of news about the recently discovered lands.* Since any survey of this policy necessarily touches on numerous questions which cause scholarly and nationalistic tempers to flare, there exist wide divergences of opinion on the geographical areas to which the policy was presumably applied, on how premeditated and official it really was, and on how effectively it operated. But none of the commentators, as far as I know, denies the existence of a system for controlling news of overseas activities even though they may hold sharply differing viewpoints on one or the other of its ramifications.[6]

What are the undisputed facts in the matter and to what degree do they affect the theme of our work? First of all, Prince Henry, with the consent of his royal brother, Pedro, inaugurated a system of discovery and commerce that was in essence exclusive and monopolistic.[7] What Henry considered to be the

[6] The great exponent of the secrecy policy was the Portuguese historian, Jaimé Cortesão. See his "Do sigilo nacional sobre os descobrimentos. Cronicas desaparecidas, mutiladas e falseadas. Alguns dos feitos que se calaram," *Lusitania*, I (1924), 45–81; a more limited version of his same argument may be found in his article, "The Pre-Columbian Discovery of America," *Geographical Journal*, LXXXIX (1937), 29–42. Cortesão's final effort, written shortly before his death, deals primarily with the origins of the policy and its application to fifteenth-century works. See the little book in *Colecção henriquina* entitled *A política de sigilo nos descobrimentos* (Lisbon, 1960). See also, "A historiografia oficial e o sigilo sobre os descobrimentos," *Primeiro congresso da historia da expansão portuguesa no mundo* (Lisbon), II (1938), 203–31. For the application of the "policy" to the understanding of Portuguese historiography see H. M. A. Kömmerling-Fitzler, "Fünf Jahrhunderte portugiesische Kolonialgeschichtsschreibung," *Die Welt als Geschichte*, VII (1941), 105–13. In his article on "The Alleged Pre-Columbian Discovery of America," *Geographical Journal*, LXXXIX (1937), 456–57, the British scholar G. R. Crone argues that the "influence" of the policy "has been exaggerated" and that in any case "it was not successful." Another British scholar, George H. T. Kimble, argues for the effectiveness of the policy of suppression by reference to the failure of Martin Behaim's globe to show accurate and detailed information on West Africa (see pp. xxviii–xxx of his introduction to the *Esmeraldo de Situ Orbis*, "Hakluyt Society Publications," Ser. II, Vol. LXXIX [London, 1937]). Samuel E. Morison in chap. ii of *Portuguese Voyages to America in the Fifteenth Century* (Cambridge, Mass., 1940) attacks the Cortesão thesis, particularly with regard to the pre-Columbian discovery of America. But even Morison admits (p. 82): "In a sense, it is true to say that a Portuguese policy of secrecy did exist with regard to Africa [but not America]." But then he goes on to remark: "Yet this policy differed only in degree from the exclusive colonial policies of other countries."

[7] On the question of Henry's monopolistic practices see above, chap. ii, p. 53.

geographical extent of his monopoly is of no concern here, and it seems unlikely that the commentators really know anyway. Through a series of papal bulls issued in the fifteenth century, Henry and his successors sought to obtain international sanction for Portugal's exclusive right to explore and develop its discoveries in Africa. In 1455 the bull of Nicholas V called *Romanus Pontifex* prohibited all Christians, under pain of excommunication if a person, and under threat of interdict if a state, from intruding upon the Portuguese area of discovery "toward the southern and eastern shores of the ocean sea" which might, in the words of the bull, "become navigable as far as to the Indians who are said to worship the name of Christ."[8] While such papal declarations were valuable as bases for argument, this bull did not prevent Spaniards and other foreigners from invading Portugal's overseas preserve. Indeed, the Portuguese themselves hired foreign navigators, arms-makers, map-makers, printers, and commercial agents as aides in their maritime and trading activities. This policy, the opponents of secrecy argue, would hardly have been followed if the government in Lisbon wanted to suppress news of the discoveries.

But there is another side to this story. In the time of King John II (1481–95), the crown sought by all the means in its power, including oaths and unusual and cruel punishments, to prevent the national secrets from becoming general knowledge.[9] At the outset of John's reign, in 1481, the Portuguese Cortes petitioned the king to forbid foreigners, especially Genoese and Florentines, to settle in his kingdom because they stole the royal "secrets as to Africa and the islands."[10] But apparently King John needed both the skills and money of the Italians and so did not heed the Cortes' warning. Finally, on November 13, 1504, King Manuel, who was then busy working out details of the pepper monopoly, decreed that complete secrecy, under pain of death, should be kept with regard to southeastern and northeastern navigation.[11] Thereafter, it would appear, all the charts, maps, and logs concerning the routes to Africa, India, and Brazil were housed in the royal chartroom and placed under the custody of D. Jorgé de Vasconcelos.[12] Clearly, throughout the first century of the discoveries, fear fought with need in Portugal's determination to employ foreign aid while trying to preserve the discoveries for her own exploitation.

While the facts are few on the official control of information, the inferences therefrom are numerous. In this account we shall try to confine our attention to those inferences pertinent to our discussion of the dissemination of infor-

[8] Text of this bull of January 8, 1455, in F. G. Davenport (ed.), *European Treaties Bearing on the History of the United States and Its Dependencies* (4 vols.; Washington, 1917–37), I, 13–26.

[9] Cortesão, *loc. cit.* (n. 6, "Do sigilo nacional . . ."), p. 50.

[10] Cortesão, *loc. cit.* (n. 6, "The Pre-Columbian Discovery . . ."), p. 31.

[11] Text in Academia das Sciencias de Lisboa, *Alguns documentos do Archivo Nacional da Torre do Tombo . . .* (Lisbon, 1892), p. 139. For the suggestion that this royal order might have been issued as a reaction to the arrival in Venice during October, 1504, of the Venetian agent, Leonardo Ca'Masser, see Donald Weinstein, *Ambassador from Venice, Pietro Pasqualigo in Lisbon, 1501* (Minneapolis, 1960), p. 104, n. 10.

[12] C. M. Parr, *So Noble a Captain* (New York, 1953), p. 151. See below, pp. 218–19.

mation about Asia in Europe. Of particular moment is the problem of the Portuguese chronicles and of the role of Ruy de Pina, the official chronicler from 1479 until his death in either 1519 or 1523. It is alleged by Jaimé Cortesão and others that some of the first chronicles relating to the discoveries were intentionally left uncompleted by their authors and were probably also truncated and mutilated by later compilers like Ruy de Pina. In his *Asia*, João de Barros bewails, in the prologue addressed to King John III, the limited attention paid by ṭhe earlier chroniclers to recording the great deeds of discovery.[13] Damião de Góis, the chronicler of John II's reign, could not, it is further argued, tell the whole story of the discoveries of the late fifteenth century because of the disputes with Castile over ownership still going on when he was writing in the latter half of the sixteenth century. His chronicle, it is pointed out, does not even mention the dramatic voyage of Dias. It is also fairly certain that his chronicle of Manuel's reign was "revised" after it first appeared in 1566.[14]

That a policy of suppressing news about African discovery and trade was carried out by the Portuguese crown in the sixteenth century seems fairly certain. When King Manuel's decree of 1504 is recalled, it is probable that the policy of secrecy extended to information on India and the Far East. It is hard to believe that chance alone is sufficient to account for the fact that not a single work on the new discoveries in Asia is known to have been published in Portugal between 1500 and mid-century. The numerous chapbooks in which the royal letters joyously announced the progress of the Portuguese conquest were seemingly all published in other countries.[15] Portuguese cartographers, beginning at an early date, sold their services and their information on the overseas world to foreign princes who could not get news by more direct means.[16] The *Suma oriental* of Tomé Pires and the *Book* of Duarte Barbosa, both written before 1520 on the subject of Portugal's eastern empire, were not published, even in part, until the Italian compiler Ramusio put their texts into print in 1550. Even then, Ramusio did not know Pires' name and was unable to acquire that portion of his book which dealt with the Spiceries.[17] Treatises on Portugal's military and political establishments in the East were left unpublished, many of them not being printed until recent times. It seems highly likely that the chroniclers feared or were forbidden to include information in their accounts which was classified as a state secret. Castanheda, who began publishing his famous chronicle in 1552, was forced to recall the first volume even after it was

[13] Hernani Cidade and Manuel Múrias, *Ásia de João de Barros* (Lisbon, 1945), I, 4–5.

[14] Irrespective of whether or not the chronicles were intentionally mutilated, the suggestion of Cortesão (*loc. cit.* [n. 6, "Do sigilo nacional . . ."], p. 81) that they should be edited and published anew in critical editions is worthy of being followed up by interested scholars and groups.

[15] Only *one* of the king's letters, *Carta das novas que vieram a el Rey nosso Senhor do descobrimento do preste Joham* (Lisbon, 1521), was printed in Portugal and it dealt primarily with the discovery of the Christians of Ethiopia. It was apparently withdrawn from circulation almost at once, and today exists in a lone exemplar discovered in 1935. See Francis M. Rogers, *The Quest for Eastern Christians. Travels and Rumor in the Age of Discovery* (Minneapolis, 1962), p. 115.

[16] Cf. below, p. 222.

[17] Cf. below, p. 186.

in print, to "revise" it, and to present a more orthodox account of Manuel's reign.[18] As late as 1565 materials on the Moluccas in private hands had to be turned over to state officials.[19] In official materials, even the distances from Goa to Malacca and from Malacca to Ternate were minimized in order to place the Moluccas beyond all doubt within the Portuguese demarcation.[20] Further evidence of news control will be mentioned in the chapters following.

From the available evidence on suppression it must be concluded that Portugal sought before 1600, through imposing oaths of silence, severe punishments, close official control of source materials, and tight censorship, to prevent Europe and the Levantine countries from learning in detail her secrets of navigation, trade, and military and political establishments in Asia. In the first half of the sixteenth century, the monopoly on news was so effective that interested persons in other countries had to rely entirely for their information about Asia upon the ancient writers, the medieval travelers, official announcements, and the sketchy written and oral reports of merchants, sailors, and spies. This rigid control broke down around mid-century, a time when it had become apparent that Portugal would be unable to continue monopolizing the spice trade and when uncertainty and indecision about the future of the mercantile empire began to hang over Lisbon like a dark cloud. The beginnings of the systematic publication of the Jesuit letterbooks around mid-century may, likewise, have helped to undermine whatever independent efforts the Portuguese continued making to keep information on Asia from circulating abroad. It has been suggested that some of the comprehensive histories and biographies prepared by the Jesuits in Asia were not published in the sixteenth century out of deference to the wishes of the Portuguese authorities.[21] Aside from the chronicles which dealt mainly with the first half of the century, very few books on contemporary topics appeared in print except for poems extolling the victories of the Portuguese. Lisbon's control over information, like many of its other policies in the uncertain days preceding its submission to Philip II in 1581, was wavering and ambiguous. Once the country became subject to the personal rule of the Habsburg monarch, a blight settled upon literary production and upon many other activities of the proud Lusitanian nation.

2

CIRCULATION IN EUROPE OF THE FIRST REPORTS, 1500–1520

The first accounts circulated in Europe contained materials of differing types and of varying degrees of authority. First of all, there were the general pronouncements of the Portuguese king to his fellow monarchs

[18] Cf. below, p. 188.
[19] Cf. below, p. 195.
[20] Cf. below, p. 604.
[21] See below, p. 805.

and the papacy. As a rule the king's carefully framed letters were more tantalizing than informative. The reports of the Venetian spies and the letters of the Italian merchants doing business in Lisbon were largely concerned, as we have seen, with matters relating to the spice trade. The route to India, though classified as a state secret, was the subject of several of the early accounts written by participants of foreign background. The Portuguese themselves prepared detailed surveys and maps for the information of the court. Although these were not published at the time, some of the new knowledge that they contained was smuggled out in the letters prepared by the informants and agents of the German and Italian merchant houses. Despite the difficulty of obtaining general information on India and other parts of Asia, a hazy picture of the East could be reconstructed by those who were interested in doing so. The new materials, fragmentary as they were, could be and were used to test and supplement the accounts and maps inherited from the prediscovery era.

The return of the first vessels of Da Gama's fleet was announced, as we have seen,[22] by the king himself. But Manuel was not the only contemporary to relay this momentous news abroad. The Florentine merchant, Girolamo Sernigi, wrote a lengthy letter[23] in July, 1499, to a colleague at Florence, summarizing the information on India brought back by Coelho and his men. In this document, first published in 1507, there are many more details on trade routes, commercial practices, and local customs than the king saw fit to include in his letter to Spain. Calicut is reported to be "bigger than Lisbon, and peopled by Christian Indians." The Zamorin of Calicut "keeps regal state" and he received the diplomatic overtures of Vasco da Gama "most graciously." Even though the Zamorin is held to be wealthy, he is also alleged to be in the hands of the Moors who control the trade and government. Sernigi clearly understood that not all the spices grow in Calicut but some are carried there "as to a staple" and especially from Ceylon. Rich cloths, fancy brocades, brass, and tinware apparently attracted the attention of the Portuguese, who stayed in Calicut for about three months. In the harbor they also saw frail vessels from many places and noticed that "they carry neither arms nor artillery." Sernigi quotes a few Calicut prices and observes that "in payment they [the Calicut merchants] only take gold and silver; coral and other merchandise of our parts they esteem but little, linen-cloth excepted. . . ." He also comments on the trade of Calicut with East Africa and Egypt and even notes that eighty years earlier "certain vessels of white Christians" visited the Malabar Coast regularly.[24] Grain, rice, and fruit are described as being abundant, and the practice of not eating meat,

<hr>

[22] Above, p. 96.

[23] First published in the collection of Fracanzano da Montalboddo (ed.), *Paesi novamente retrovati* (Vicenza, 1507). Text in English translation in E. G. Ravenstein (ed. and trans.), *A Journal of the First Voyage of Vasco da Gama* ("Hakluyt Society Publications," Old Series, Vol. CXIX [London, 1898]), pp. 123–26.

[24] Sernigi suspects that these "strangers" may have been Germans or Russians, but most later commentators agree that they were probably Chinese merchants (see Ravenstein [ed.], *op. cit.* [n. 23], pp. 131–33, n. 5).

especially oxen, is dwelt upon at some length. The use of domesticated elephants for transportation and war seems to have piqued the curiosity of the Europeans. "All or most of these people," Sernigi writes, "are clothed in cotton-cloths from the waist down to the knee, but from the waist upwards they go naked." The Moorish navigators "do not guide themselves by the Pole in navigating this gulf [Indian Ocean], but trust to quadrants of wood." The people of Calicut also "have some knowledge of Prester John, but not much, as he is far away." They are literate, and justice in the city "is strictly administered." While remarking that Calicut is not a walled city, Sernigi observes that it is regularly laid out and "with many good houses." Even the arts come in for comment, and he notices that "there are many excellent painters . . . of figures as well as of other subjects." Since no one in Europe knew much at first hand, most of the early reports range like this one over a wide variety of topics—perhaps because nobody could really tell what might become important in future relations or perhaps just because there existed a genuine curiosity about this remote and reputedly wealthy and Christian land.

Another Sernigi letter of 1499 was written to his brother in Florence.[25] Apparently this was also prepared before the return of Da Gama himself, for in it he reports without qualification that the people of Calicut are Christians. In most regards, it follows his first letter, though it includes many more details and in some way contradicts the earlier one. Among the additional details, he observes, for example, that the Indians are neither black nor white, the implication being that they are somewhere in between. He states categorically that pepper grows at Calicut, though not in great quantity and of a quality inferior to that which comes from afar. Here he claims that the Indians want no form of payment other than gold, silver, and coral.

Sernigi again got busy with his pen after the arrival of Da Gama's vessel with its captives from India.[26] The Portuguese and Sernigi were shortly put right by Gaspar da Gama on a number of matters. Cinnamon of the best quality, Sernigi learned, comes from Ceylon, but "the pepper and cloves come from more distant parts." Both Jews and Christians are few in number in India and "the supposed churches and belfries are in reality temples of idolaters." On this news Sernigi remarks: "To me this seems more probable than saying that there are Christians but no divine administrations, no priests, and no sacrificial mass." Apparently dissatisfied with what he had earlier learned about the navigational practices of the Moors, Sernigi questioned Gaspar in detail. Again, he was told that "in those seas they navigate without compasses but with the aid of quadrants of wood."[27] Gaspar also threw "much light" on

---

[25] An abstract of it was found among the papers of Conrad Peutinger, the German Humanist and antiquarian of Augsburg, who apparently took notes from a copy that he saw in Rome. Published in G. Greif (ed.), *Briefe und Berichte . . . aus Dr. Conrad Peutingers Nachlass* in *Sechs-und-zwanzigster Jahresbericht des historischen Kreisvereins von Schwaben* (Augsburg, 1861), pp. 115–18. For a few excerpts translated into English see Ravenstein (ed.), *op. cit.* (n. 23), pp. 141–42.

[26] Ravenstein (ed.), *op. cit.* (n. 23), pp. 137–41.

[27] On the other hand, the rutter of Da Gama's voyage contends that they had "Genoese needles." See *ibid.*, p. 26.

"the articles of merchandise most suitable for that country," naming especially coral, copper kettles, and thin plates of copper, tartar, spectacles, coarse linens, wine, oil, thin brocades and cloths. Sernigi also informed his Florentine correspondent "that precious stones are plentiful [in Calicut] but dear in comparison with other merchandise."

Shortly after Cabral's return in July, 1501, King Manuel again dispatched a letter to Castile, and, as we have mentioned earlier, an anonymous narrative of this voyage, apparently written by a Portuguese, reached Italy shortly thereafter. A number of private letters relating mainly to trade were sent at the same time to Venice and Florence. But perhaps the most unique and informative account came from Priest Joseph, one of the two Syro-Malabar Christians whom Cabral took aboard at their request at Cochin. Priests Mathias and Joseph wanted to make a mission to Rome and Jerusalem. Mathias died either en route or shortly after arriving at Lisbon. After a stay of six months in Portugal, Joseph journeyed to Rome in 1502 for an audience with Pope Alexander VI. He also visited Venice, and returned to India either by way of Jerusalem and the Levant or through Lisbon.[28] In the cities of Europe he was apparently interrogated at great length about his homeland. A man of about forty, Joseph was considered "ingenuous, truthful, and of the highest integrity" by his Italian questioners and his replies were published in various places beginning in 1505.[29]

Joseph's description of Cranganore, the town from which he came, was apparently accepted without question even though he bluntly asserted, contrary to European beliefs of the time, that his king was an idolater like most of the people. Of their faith he remarks: "These Gentiles [Idolaters] worship one single god, creator of all things, and they say that he is one and three, and in his likeness they have made a statue with three heads (representing Brahma, Vishnu, and Siva)." His mention of the Indian religious texts is the earliest extant report of Indian religious practices to come to Europe with the authority of a native spokesman as intermediary. Joseph also gives some detail on Indian social customs. The gentiles are divided into three classes: gentlemen or *naires* (Nāyars), farmers or *canes* (Kaniyans?),[30] and fishermen or *nuirinan* (Mukkuvans?).[31] Each group is described as having its own temples, the women worshiping in temples apart from those used by the men. The fishermen are badly treated by the other two classes. The king and "all the other Gentiles" have many wives. They cremate their dead, and "the wives, in perfect possession of their faculties, voluntarily burn themselves alive eight days after the death of their husbands."

[28] For details see W. B. Greenlee (ed.), *The Voyage of Pedro Alvares Cabral to Brazil and India* ("Hakluyt Society Publications," Ser. II, Vol. LXXXI [London, 1938]), pp. 95–97.

[29] Translation of text in *ibid.*, pp. 97–113. Extracts first published at Rome in 1505 in the chapbook printed by John of Besicken. See below, p. 164. The best known and fullest text of his responses to the questions put to him in Italy is to be found in Book VI of the compilation of 1507 prepared by Montalboddo, *op. cit.* (n. 23).

[30] According to Duarte Barbosa (below, p. 367) the Kaniyans were a polluted caste of craftsmen.
[31] Cf. below, p. 367.

Aside from such matters, Joseph also presented in Rome a detailed account of the social and religious practices of the Malabar Christians, and evidently answered numerous questions, some of which were directed to him by Pope Alexander VI himself. He also informed the papal court of trading conditions at Calicut, where "almost all of India comes together." Like a number of other contemporaries, Priest Joseph insists that the Cathayans, who had earlier come to Malabar, were "white Christians." [32] And when the Indian priest was asked "whether any mention of our region is made in that place," he replied that "none are mentioned except Rome, France, and Venice."

While Europe learned about India from the letters of the king and the merchants as well as from Priest Joseph, an effort was made in Portugal to acquaint the nation's literate population with some of the great accounts of the East inherited from the past. In 1502, the Moravian printer Valentim Fernandes published at Lisbon a splendid folio volume in Portuguese[33] that included a translation of Marco Polo from the Latin edition by Pipino, the travels of Nicolò de' Conti, and a letter of Girolamo da Santo Stefano. In his dedicatory epistle to King Manuel, Fernandes chose as his text, Luke 5:26 ("We have seen strange things today"). A favorite at court since his arrival there in 1495 as a squire of the late king's widow, Fernandes lavishes praise on his royal patron whose name, he avows, is now known in the most remote regions of Africa and Asia. Lisbon, he asserts, has become not only the most prominent port of Europe but is also frequented by peoples from the most distant places. King John II he describes as the Moses who saw the promised land only from afar; it was left for King Manuel to become the Joshua who was granted the privilege of enjoying its fruits. The wealth pouring into Portugal is proclaimed to be greater than that rained upon King Solomon, and King Manuel's influence is held to be more universal than that of Alexander or the Romans. Among all Christian kings none, Fernandes holds, has ever before had an equal opportunity to aid in the spreading of the Gospel. Even after allowing for conventional exaggerations, Fernandes' preface conveys some of the exuberance and triumph that swept Portugal as the full significance of the discoveries came to be appreciated by more than a select few. It also helped to give the reading public the background information necessary to aid it in appreciating the meaning of the discovery of India.

Fernandes published nothing that gave concrete information on the Portuguese achievements. Perhaps as a reflection of the policy of secrecy in effect in Lisbon, he asserts in his introduction to Marco Polo that the Venetians had kept the traveler's work hidden in their archives and that it was not until it was

---

[32] For a thorough discussion of the European belief in a Christian East which lay beyond the world of Islam, and for this point in particular see Rogers, *op. cit.* (n. 15), pp. 118–19.

[33] Entitled *Marco paulo, Ho livro de Nycolao veneto. O trallado da carta de huum genoves das detas terras.* For an excellent analysis of his work see Max Böhme, *Die grossen Reisesammlungen des 16. ahrhunderts* (Strassburg, 1904), pp. 4–14. For a complete listing of Fernandes' publications see A. J. Anselmo, *Bibliografia das obras impressas em Portugal no século XVI* (Lisbon, 1926), pp. 155–60. For a reproduction of its frontispiece and for an evaluation of Fernandes' role in preparing the translation of Marco Polo for publication see King Manuel [II] of Portugal, *Early Portuguese Books (1489–1600) in the Library of His Majesty the King of Portugal* (London, 1929), I, 110–57.

presented as a gift of welcome to Prince Pedro, the brother of Henry the Navigator, that it became known in Portugal. Fernandes claims to have translated Marco Polo into Portuguese during his leisure for the purpose of instructing the laity and the uneducated about the new lands now being ruled over by their king.[34] The potential contribution of the discoveries to Portugal's internal prosperity and international importance is emphasized throughout the account provided always that the king's program should enjoy the unqualified support of all elements in the population. Thus, aside from being the first compilation of travel literature to appear after the discovery of the sea route, Fernandes' book like Hakluyt's work at the end of the century, was designed to inform the public of the great opportunity at hand and to proclaim full support for the king's overseas policy as a national duty.

Fernandes' influence was not limited to Portugal. His volume became the inspiration for a similar compilation produced at Seville in 1503 by Rodrigo de Santaella,[35] and Fernandes himself unofficially acted as intermediary between the German merchants in Lisbon and the Portuguese government. Like many go-betweens before and since, he found himself in a position that was both strategic and embarrassing. In his connections with the Welsers at Lisbon, Fernandes probably acted not only as a translator and agent but also as an informant about India. He helped in preparing for the German participation in the fleet of 1505, and thereafter continued to compile information on India and dispatch it to Germany. For example, on August 16, 1505, Fernandes wrote to Conrad Peutinger the Humanist, a relative of the Welsers, reporting on the sailing of Almeida's fleet.[36] In the three ensuing years, despite some embarrassed reluctance on his part, he sent a series of manuscripts to Augsburg which Peutinger bound together between wooden covers and entitled *De insulis et peregrinationibus Lusitanorum*.[37] Nor were these all that Peutinger received. In a letter to his fellow Humanist, Sebastian Brant, Peutinger wrote on April 7, 1507, of having in his possession a talking parrot from India and other curiosities.[38] A letter of Fernandes, unpublished until recently, was

[34] It has been asserted that Fernandes, contrary to what he says in the introduction, did not translate Marco Polo. Presumably this was the work of some earlier translator. See Böhme, *op. cit.* (n. 33), p. 10. He certainly did not use the manuscript given to Dom Pedro, for he indicates that he did not know the exact location of this manuscript.

[35] For a thoroughgoing comparison of the two books and a review of their place in the early literary tradition of India see Francis M. Rogers, "Valentim Fernandes, Rodrigo de Santaella, and the Recognition of the Antilles as 'Opposite-India,'" *Boletim da sociedade de geografia de Lisboa*, LXXV (1957), 279–309.

[36] Erich König (ed.), *Konrad Peutingers Briefwechsel* (Munich, 1923), pp. 56–58.

[37] J. Schmeller, "Ueber Valentin Fernandez Alema und seine Sammlung von Nachrichten über die Entdeckungen und Besitzungen der Portugiesen in Afrika und Asien bis zum Jahre 1508 . . .," *Abhandlungen der philosophischphilologischen Classe der königlichen Bayerischen Akademie der Wissenschaften*, Pt. III (1847), IV, 1–73. On his "reluctance" to send out these materials see W. Heyd, "Valentin Fernandez Aleman," *Sitzungsberichte der philosophisch, philologischen und historischen Classe der königlichen Akademie der Wissenschaften zu München*, Jahrg. 1872, II, 497–83. Many Fernandes' materials have been edited and published by Gabriel Pereira in *Revista portuguesa colonial e maritima*, VI (1900), 92–102, 155–64, 219–28, 283–90, 347–56.

[38] König (ed.), *op. cit.* (n. 36), pp. 77–78.

addressed on June 26, 1510, to a correspondent in Nuremberg summarizing events which had taken place in Asia from 1506 to 1509, including the Portuguese arrival in Ceylon.[39]

Other informants were also supplying data about the sea route and its possibilities. At Antwerp in 1504, shortly after the arrival there of the first spice shipments from Lisbon, a newsletter appeared in Dutch called *Calcoen* (Calicut), probably written by a Dutch sailor who had been on Vasco da Gama's second voyage.[40] He comments favorably on the "good Christians" of the Malabar Coast and notes that "they had just sent priests to the pope at Rome to know the true faith." After commenting on Ceylon and Malacca as sources for spices, he talks of the people of Calicut and their habit of chewing betel "wherever they go." He also describes the civet cat and notes that the musk obtained from it is very dear. He remarks on pearl-fishing and its techniques as practiced in south India. Clearly the author of this book received little more than a series of surface impressions, almost all of which were known from the writings about India that appeared before the opening of the sea route. It is nonetheless indicative of the deep interest existing in Europe at this time that such a superficial account of India should have found a publisher.

King Manuel himself sent news to Rome of progress in India by dispatching an embassy in 1505 to the pope under Diogo de Sousa, Bishop of Oporto. In an oration of obedience before Pope Julius II, Diogo Pacheco, an eminent Portuguese lawyer, gave the first official report of the discoveries and the commercial and religious possibilities of the Portuguese enterprise in the East.[41] The Portuguese mission was a huge success, and in 1506 the pope issued three bulls favoring the Portuguese commercial and missionary activities and bestowed the consecrated golden rose upon King Manuel. By the bull *Ea quae* the pope enjoined the heads of the church in Portugal and Spain to confirm the Treaty of Tordesillas, hitherto unrecognized by the papacy, and to cause it to be inviolably observed.[42] By the other two bulls *Sedes apostolica* and *Militans ecclesia* the conditions under which the Portuguese might trade with infidels were mitigated and the Order of Christ was officially recognized as the Catholic spearhead in the religious crusade against the Moors.[43]

It was probably in connection with the Portuguese embassy to Rome that

[39] António Brásio, "Uma carta inédita de Valentim Fernandes," *Boletim da biblioteca da universidade de Coimbra*, XXIV (1960), 338–58.

[40] J. P. Berjeau (ed. and trans.), *Calcoen* . . . (London, 1874). There is also another contemporary account of this voyage by an unknown author. It exists in Portuguese and German manuscript versions in the National Library at Vienna and came originally from the collection of Philippine Welser. See Christine von Rohr, *Neue Quellen zur zweiten Indienfahrt Vasco da Gamas* (Leipzig, 1939). This author also translates the account of Tomé Lopes into German (pp. 52–87).

[41] Published in a four-page chapbook at Rome as *Obedienta Potentissimi Emanuelis Lusitaniae Regis . . . ad Iulium II. Ponti. Max. Anno Domini M.D.V.* In 1956, a copy was offered at 40,000 frs. (about $133.00) by Chaumont in Paris.

[42] Text in translation in Davenport (ed.), *op. cit.* (n. 8), pp. 110–11.

[43] See P. MacSwiney de Mashanaglass, "Une ambassade portugaise à Rome sous Jules II," *Revue d'histoire diplomatique*, XVII (1903), 62–63.

John of Besicken, a printer in the Eternal City, published a chapbook purporting to be a copy of a letter sent by the king of Portugal to Castile, describing the progress made in uncovering India until 1505.[44] Actually this pamphlet was a compilation of materials derived from Manuel's letter of 1501, the anonymous narrative, and the account of Priest Joseph. Still, as far as we know, it was the first printed summary of the Portuguese successes to appear, and was probably compiled and issued at the behest of members of the embassy then in Rome. Certainly no other rationale has as yet been advanced that accounts for the appearance of this broadside at Rome on October 23, 1505. It was reprinted in Milan somewhat later in 1505 by P. M. di Mantegazzi and was reissued at Rome in Latin in 1506 by Besicken.[45] Manuel's letters recounting the glorious and gory deeds of the Portuguese in the Orient under Almeida were the subject of five more chapbooks published from 1506 to 1508. Over the next five years (1508–13) great events took place in the East, including the capture of Goa, but no official word appears to have been issued from Lisbon about Albuquerque's early triumphs. News of the conqueror's first victory at Goa was contained, however, in a Spanish compilation prepared by Martin Fernández de Figueroa of Salamanca on the basis of what he had learned during a sojourn with the Portuguese in the East between 1505 and 1511.[46]

In Nuremberg and Augsburg, attention was also focused on Lisbon, where the German merchants were preparing in the winter and spring of 1505 to sail with Almeida's fleet to India. The account of Amerigo Vespucci's alleged third voyage began to circulate in Germany in 1505 in both Latin and German versions, and was apparently the first newsletter on the discoveries to make a wide impression.[47] At Nuremberg a small pamphlet appeared in printed form later in 1505 from, it is believed, the press of Johann Weissenburger. It was called *Den rechten veg auss zu faren von Lissbona gen Kallakuthrichten vo meyl zu meyl*....[48] Perhaps one of the most striking features in this newsletter is

[44] Translated by Sergio J. Pacifici in *Copy of a Letter of the King of Portugal Sent to the King of Castile Concerning the Voyage and Success of India* (Minneapolis, 1955). This work was also printed in an edition limited to twenty-five copies by A. C. Burnell (ed. and trans.), from the version in the Marcian Library at Venice, in London in 1881. There are in all four copies extant. For the arguments as to why it is improbable that this was a copy of a letter actually dispatched from Lisbon to Castile see Greenlee (ed.), *op. cit.* (n. 28), p. 42, n. 1.

[45] The only known copy of the Milan edition is in the James Ford Bell Collection at the University of Minnesota. See John Parker (comp.), *A List of Additions, 1951–1954* (Minneapolis, 1955), p. 6.

[46] Entitled *Conquista de las indias de Persia & Arabia que fizo la armada del rey don Manuel de Portugal* (Salamanca). See Rogers, *op. cit.* (n. 15), pp. 126–27.

[47] L. Gallois, *Les géographes allemands de la Renaissance* (Paris, 1890), pp. 38–39. The fact that the *Mundus novus* has now been established as a forgery in no way invalidates its importance for diffusion of news. Indeed, the forgeries lend support to the idea that news of the discoveries was widely sought, and that in some cases overly ambitious people tried to make money from selling it. For a discussion of the forgeries, see F. Pohl, *Amerigo Vespucci, Pilot Major* (New York, 1944), chap. x.

[48] The English translation is from the copy in the James Ford Bell collection at the University of Minnesota. It was prepared by Alvin E. Prottengeier and John Parker and is entitled *From Lisbon to Calicut* (Minneapolis, 1956). For further details on this newsletter see also *A Selection of Extremely Rare and Important Printed Books ... Catalogue 77, Offered for Sale by William H. Robinson Ltd. London*, pp. 20–22.

The Printed Word

the reproduction of the globe according to Ptolemy on which Nuremberg, Lisbon, and Calicut are roughly located. The itinerary of the anonymous author is relatively accurate, and his comments on the spices have a firsthand quality. For example, he remarks:

It is also to be observed how all spices grow in India. Pepper grows like grapes in clusters, just as do elderberries. At times they bring to Lisbon green peppers just as they come from the tree. Cinnamon quills come also from large trees resembling the willow tree growing here.

It may be conjectured that this newsletter was part of a promotional campaign conducted by the south German commercial houses to stimulate interest in their Indian activities. It was apparently not known in 1505 that Manuel would shut off the Germans from direct access to India. Indeed, the high hopes of the Germans died only slowly. This tract, for example, was reissued, apparently around 1508, by Georg Stuchs, another printer of Nuremberg.[49]

The best example of the sentiments felt in Augsburg in 1505 is contained in a letter of January 13 from Peutinger to Blasius Höltzl, secretary to Emperor Maximilian and a member of the Augsburg circle of younger Humanists. Writing before the sailing of Almeida's fleet, Peutinger remarks on the imminence of its departure and notes that "to us Augsburgers goes the praise for being the first Germans to visit India."[50] Nor was this merely an idle remark on Peutinger's part, for the Augsburg Humanist had been called upon by his Welser relatives to get letters of introduction from the emperor for those Augsburgers sent to India. By August, 1505, Valentim Fernandes, as we have seen, had sent news both to Augsburg and Nuremberg about the sailing of Almeida's fleet.[51]

The two Germans who went to India as commercial agents returned in 1506 with a story to tell. But short accounts of Almeida's successes and activities were published in newsletters before the Germans were able to get their more detailed accounts into print. Their newsletters were also anticipated by being issued after the publication of a series of Manuel's letters to the pope.[52] Hans Mayr, factor on the "Raphael," kept a diary in Portuguese which was evidently sent to Peutinger by Fernandes shortly after the return of the German envoys. It was never published.[53] An account of the experiences of the Germans with Almeida's fleet was eventually published at Augsburg by Balthasar Springer, the other Welser agent, in 1509, and was called *Die Merfart uñ Erfarung nüwer*

[49] The copy in the Library of Congress is by Stuchs. The library card gives the date of this impression as *ca.* 1505. It is more likely, however, that it was issued in 1508. See Prottengeier and Parker, *op. cit.* (n. 48), pp. 7–8.

[50] König (ed.), *op. cit.* (n. 36), p. 50.

[51] *Ibid.*, p. 57 and n. 1; also above, p. 159.

[52] The first of these was published by Besicken at Rome in 1506 as *Gesta proxime per Portugalenses in India, Ethiopia et aliis Orientalibus terris*. For the titles of those which quickly followed see Rogers, *op. cit.* (n. 15), pp. 188–89.

[53] Viktor Hantzsch, *Deutsche Reisende des 16. Jahrhunderts* (Leipzig, 1895), pp. 3–4.

Schiffung und Wege zu viln overkauten Inseln und Künigreichen....[54] In this short narrative of fifteen pages Springer records his experiences aboard the "Leonhard" and in India, from March 23, 1505, to his return on November 15, 1506. It would seem that Springer kept a diary en route which he fashioned into a Latin narrative either on the return voyage or after arriving back in Europe.[55] A Flemish version of his account appeared at Antwerp in 1508 that was adapted apparently from the Latin version by the publisher Jan van Doesborch. The German edition produced at Augsburg has thirteen pages of woodcuts by the famous Augsburg engraver, Hans Burgkmair, and is the most full and interesting of the various Springer publications.

A man who had spent his life in trade, Springer shows no particular knowledge of the writers of antiquity but relies almost entirely on his own observations and the oral reports of others.[56] His references to the topography and climate of India are few, though he does observe that "when it is winter in our land, it is summer in India" and that it is hottest on the Malabar Coast around Christmas. He shows great interest in plants and animals and is much impressed with the use of elephants as draft animals. The people of the Malabar Coast are brownish-black in color and both men and women have long, black hair. He contrasts the relative nudity of the native population with the flowing robes and turbans of the Arab merchants. He calls each of the Malabar cities the residency of a king and describes a ceremonial procession of the king of Cochin which he evidently saw. He also comments on the king's despotism and notes that common farmers are taxed by being required to pay a portion of their harvest to the ruler. On other matters he confirms reports of earlier writers.

While the south Germans thus learned something of India, the Italians continued to accumulate as much information on the discoveries as possible. The forgeries of 1504 attributed to Vespucci were followed, as we have seen, by the publication at Rome and Milan in 1505 of the letter allegedly written by King Manuel to Spain. In both instances, the materials in these compilations were based in part on authentic accounts and were probably the product of an effort on the part of some enterprising printers to make a bit of easy money. Finally in 1507 a serious collection of materials on the discoveries was compiled and published at Vicenza called *Paesi novamente retrovati*. . . . After considerable controversy it has been established that this collection was brought together and edited by Francanzano da Montalboddo, professor of literature at Vicenza.[57] In the original Italian version this first of the notable travel collections appeared in quarto in 166 unnumbered pages, divided into 6 books and 142 continuously numbered chapters.[58]

The introduction states that in compiling the book the editor had a double

[54] Text reproduced in Franz Schulze, *Balthasar Springers Indienfahrt 1505-06* (Strassburg, 1902).
[55] *Ibid.*, p. 12.
[56] *Ibid.*, pp. 4–8 for biographical details.
[57] Böhme, *op. cit.* (n. 33), pp. 22–23.
[58] Reproduced in facsimile as Vol. VI of the *Vespucci Reprints, Texts and Studies* (Princeton, 1916).

purpose. Montalboddo wanted to show, it appears, that Pliny's stories of marvels unknown to Europe could be substantiated by observers who had but recently returned from the most remote parts of the world. But the main purpose of the book was to give pleasure to the zealous reader, an objective that the modern scholar is often prone to slight as he laboriously tries to decide on the basis of external and internal evidence how accurate the accounts may really be. The *Paesi* brings together a number of widely divergent accounts which begin chronologically with the Italian voyagers in the service of Prince Henry. Aside from materials on the westward discoveries, the *Paesi* contain Marchionni's description of the first voyage of Da Gama, the anonymous narrative by a Portuguese telling of Cabral's voyage, some of the letters written by the Venetian spies in Lisbon in 1501–2, and the report of Priest Joseph.

The first edition (1507) of the *Paesi* was published by the Venetian printer, Enrico di Sant' Orso, and it was reprinted unchanged at Venice in 1517 and 1521 and at Milan in 1508, 1512, and 1519. A somewhat careless Latin translation, *Itinerarium Portugalensium . . .*, was prepared by Arcangelo Madrignano and printed at Milan in 1508. At Nuremberg, Jobst Ruchamer, friend of Willibald Pirckheimer, translated the Italian text into German in 1508 as *Newe unbekanthe landte*. Ruchamer appended a note of his own to the end of the introduction in which he exaggeratedly reports that the king of Portugal has sent out an armada of "fifty well-equipped vessels." The German translator further expresses the hope that the religious enterprises of the missionaries will fare well so that the "dark and wrong hearts of the unbelievers" might be turned to God. A little later in 1508, Ruchamer's translation was put into Low German by Henning Ghetelen of Lübeck. Around 1511 an English work was printed at Antwerp by Jan van Doesborch called *Of the newe lands and of ye people founde by the messengers of the kynge of portyngale named Emanuel*. It was a compilation of material drawn from the *Paesi* collection and illustrated with woodcuts previously published in similar Dutch publications.[59] The oldest dated French translation is of 1515 and is in popular French. Over the next several decades, the *Paesi* was retranslated in most of the major languages of western Europe and reissued in numerous abridgments.[60]

At Rome, meanwhile, the *Itinerary* of Ludovico di Varthema of Bologna had appeared in Italian in 1510.[61] Unlike most of the commentators of the sixteenth century, Varthema went to the East over the land routes of the Levant, learned colloquial Arabic, and acknowledged Islam. He apparently left Venice for Egypt and Syria around 1502, arrived at Cambay in India around October 10, 1504, and then journeyed inland and southward to Vijay-

[59] Edward Arber (ed.), *The First Three English Books on America* ?1511–1555 A.D. (Birmingham, 1885), pp. xxv–xxi. Earlier commentators had ascribed this little book to the year 1522. See H. Harrisse, *Bibliotheca Americana vetustissima* (New York, 1866), p. 199.

[60] For further details on the translations and reprints see Böhme, *op. cit.* (n. 33), pp. 25–47.

[61] The best recent English edition is that of J. W. Jones and Sir Richard Temple, *The Itinerary of Ludovico di Varthema of Bologna from 1502 to 1508* (London, 1928).

Woodcut of Indian warriors. Illustration in Balthasar Springer's *Meerfahrt* (published 1509) attributed to Hans Burgkmair, the famous Augsburg engraver. Reproduced here from Franz Schulze, *Balthasar Springers Indienfahrt* (Strassburg, 1902).

Title page of Valentim Fernandes' Portuguese translation of *Marco Polo* (Lisbon, 1502).

Title page of João de Barros' *Asia* (Lisbon, 1552).

Title page of Volume I (revised second edition) of G. B. Ramusio, *Delle navigationi et viaggi* (Venice, 1554).

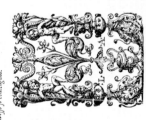

Title page of Book I of the *Historia* of Fernão Lopes de Castanheda (Coimbra, 1551).

Portrait of João de Barros; first printed in the 1615 edition of his *Décadas da Asia*. From A. Forjaz de Sampaio, *Historia da literatura portuguesa illustrada* (Lisbon, 1929–32).

Painting from life of Luis de Camoës, by Fernando Gomes. From Forjaz de
Sampaio, *Historia da literatura portuguesa illustrada*.

DAMIANVS A GOES.

Thucydides gentis enarrat gesta Pelasgæ
Romanis claret Liuius in Deca σιν
Hic, alia vt taceam serâ data scripta senectâ,
Æthiopvm accepit nomen ab Historia.

Facsimile of a copper engraving of Damião de Góis by Albrecht Dürer. A copy is in the Albertina Museum in Vienna. From Forjaz de Sampaio, *Historia da literatura portuguesa illustrada.*

Title page of first edition of *The Lusiads*. From Forjaz de Sampaio, *Historia da literatura portuguesa illustrada*.

OS

LVSIADAS

de Luis de Ca-
moés.

COM PRIVILEGIO
REAL.

Impreſſos em Liſboa, com licença da
Sanêta Inquiſição, & do Ordina-
rio em caſa de Antonio
Gõçaluez Impreſſor.
1572.

TRATADO.

Que compôs o nobre & no-
tauel capitão Antonio Galuão, dos
diuersos & desuayrados caminhos,
por onde nos tempos passados a pimenta & especearia veyo da India ás
nossas partes, & asi de todos os des
cobrimentos antigos & modernos,
que são feitos ate a era de mil & qui-
nhentos & cincoenta. Com os nomes
particulares das pessoas que os fi-
zeram : & em que tempos &
as suas alturas, obra cer
to muy notauel &
copiosa.

Foy vista & examinada pela santa Inquisição.

Impressa em casa de Ioam da Barreira impres-
tor del rey nosso senhor, na Rua de sã Mamede

Title page of a sixteenth-century edition of
António Galvão's *Tratado*. From Forjaz de
Sampaio, *Historia da literatura portuguesa
illustrada*.

Coloquios dos simples, e
drogas he cousas mediçinais da India, e
assi dalgũas frutas achadas nella onde se
tratam algũas cousas tocantes amediçina,
pratica, e outras cousas boas, pera saber
cópostos pello Doutor garçia dorta : fisico
del Rey nosso senhor, vistos pello muyto
Reuerendo senhor, ho liçençiado
Alexos diaz : falcam desenbar-
gador da casa da supricaçã
inquisidor nestas
partes.

Com priuilegio do Conde viso Rey.

Impresso em Goa, por Ioannes
de endem aos x dias de
Abril de 1563 annos.

Title page of first edition, printed in
Goa in 1563, of Garcia da Orta's,
Colloquies. From Forjaz de Sampaio
*Historia da literatura portuguesa
illustrada*.

ITINERARIO,

Voyage ofte Schipvaert / van Jan Huygen van Linschoten naer Oost ofte Portugaels In-

dien inhoudende een corte beschryvinghe der selver Landen ende Zee-custen/ met aen-
wysinge van alle de voornaemde principale Havens/Rebieren/hoecken ende plaetsen/ tot noch
toe vande Portugesen ontdeckt ende bekent: Waer by ghevoecht zijn / niet alleen die Conter-
feytsels vande habyten/drachten ende wesen/ so vande Portugesen aldaer residerende/ als vande ingeboornen Indianen/ ende huere Tempels/Afgoden/Huysinge/met die voornaemste
Boomen/Druchten/kruyden/Speceryen/ende diergelijcke materialen/ als oock die
manieren des selfden Volckes/so in hunnen Godts-diensten / als in Politie
en Huyf-houdinghe: maer oock een corte verhalinge van de Coophan-
delingen hoe en waer die ghedreven en ghebonden worden/
met die ghedenckweerdichste geschiedenissen/
voorghevallen den tijt zijnder
residentie aldaer.

Alles beschreven ende by een vergadert, door den selfden, seer nut, oorbaer,
ende oock vermakelijcken voor alle curieuse ende Lief-
hebbers van vreemdigheden,

t'AMSTELREDAM.

By Cornelis Claesz. op't VVater, in't Schrijf-boeck, by de oude Brugght.

Anno CIↃ. IↃ. XCVI.

Map of Asia. From Abraham Ortelius' *Theatrum orbis terrarum* (Antwerp, 1575). Courtesy of the University of Chicago Libraries.

Map of eastern Asia and the East Indies. From Linschoten's *Itinerario*. Courtesy of the Newberry Library.

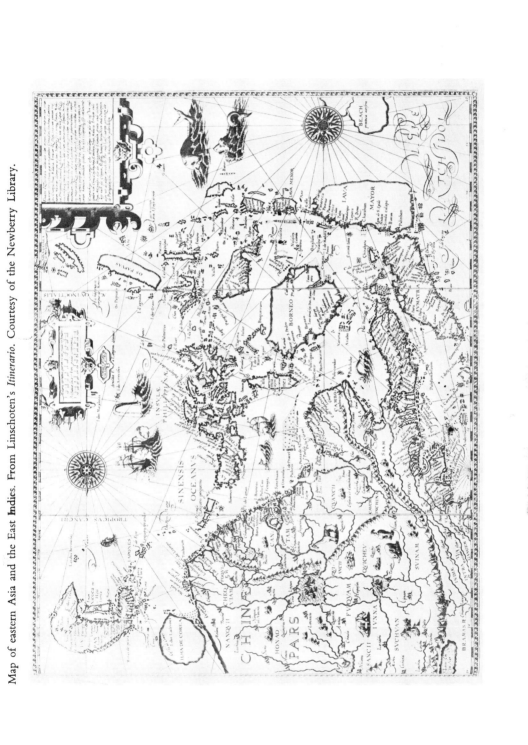

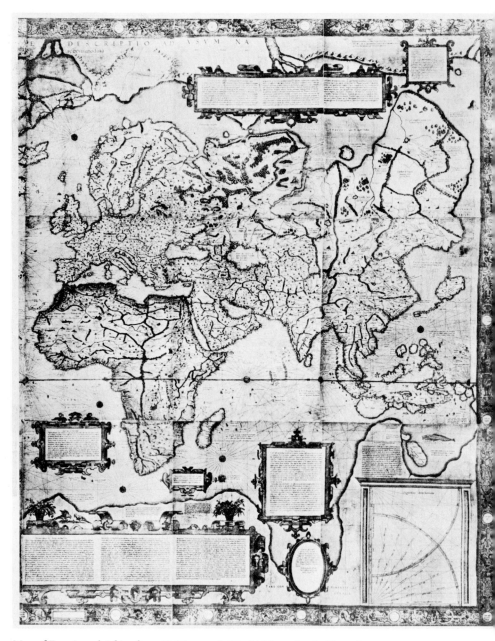

Map of Eurasia and Africa from G. Mercator's World Map of 1569. From *Imago mundi*, Vol. XII (1955).

anagar, and finally wound up in Calicut at the beginning of 1505. He then proceeded southward, rounded Cape Comorin by sea and perhaps then traveled northward along the eastern coast of India. It is at this point, however, that his *Itinerary* becomes vague and his descriptions inaccurate. It is about his travels east of Cape Comorin that later writers have long disputed.[62] If Varthema actually went where he said he did, he then touched at several places on the east coast of India and visited Tennasserim, Pegu, Malacca, Sumatra, the Moluccas, and Java. From this extended journey, he probably arrived back in Calicut on August 27, 1505. After a series of escapades in Calicut, he deserted his Muslim companions and took employment with the Portuguese at Cochin. For his work in India he was knighted by the Portuguese and returned to Lisbon in 1508 aboard the "Santo Vicentio," one of Marchionni's trading vessels. Late in 1508 he arrived in Rome where he made preparations to publish the account of his travels.

No matter how questionable Varthema's account might seem to later readers, it was an immediate success at the time of its publication in 1510. Varthema's contemporaries evidently shared the viewpoint which he set forth in the dedication of his *Itinerary*. He asserted that:

... not having an inclination (knowing myself to be of very slender understanding) to desire [to know distant places] by study or conjectures, I determined, personally, and with my own eyes, to endeavour to ascertain the situation of places, the qualities of peoples, the diversities of animals, the varieties of the fruit-bearing and odoriferous trees of Egypt, Syria, Arabia Deserta and Felix, Persia, India, and Ethiopia, remembering well that the testimony of one eye-witness is worth more than ten heard-says.[63]

And since the copyright was his to hold for ten years by special mandate of Pope Julius II, Varthema may even have enjoyed a financial profit from his book. From 1510 to 1535 the original Italian edition was issued on two separate occasions in each of three cities: Rome, Venice, and Milan. A Latin translation was prepared in 1511 and German versions began appearing in 1515. A Spanish translation was published in 1520 and was followed by three others in the course of the sixteenth century. No further translations are recorded until

---

[62] Garcia da Orta, the Portuguese naturalist, was the first important scholar to cast doubt upon the credibility of Varthema's account. Many others have since questioned its veracity, basing their assertions primarily on the vague character of his narrative after he leaves Cape Comorin for places farther to the east. Sir William Temple in Jones and Temple, *op. cit.* (n. 61), has examined Varthema's statements in the light of these doubts, and, on the basis of his personal experience in the area allegedly traversed by Varthema, has concluded "that it is possible for Varthema to have made the journeys that he says he made" (p. xxxiv). But the argument still goes on. B. Penrose, *Travel and Discovery in the Renaissance, 1420–1620* (Cambridge, Mass., 1955), p. 31, challenges Temple's timetable and asserts without citation that Armando Cortesão, the famous Portuguese scholar, "roundly denies the voyage and even states that Varthema never got east of India." Personally, I am inclined to accept Varthema's account as credible, though undeniably vague and inaccurate, on his activities east of India. For an impressive listing of his misstatements see O. Warburg, "Wer ist der Entdecker der Gewürz-Inseln (Molukkan)?" *Verhandlungen der Gesellschaft für Erdkunde zu Berlin*, XXII (1896), 106–35.

[63] Jones and Temple, *op. cit.* (n. 61), p. 5 of the *Itinerary*.

the latter half of the century, when the French (1556), Dutch (1563), and English (1577) versions made their appearance.

Like most of the other writers of this period, Varthema devotes more attention to Calicut and the Malabar Coast than to any other part of the East. He calls the town "a poor sort of place" and was evidently unimpressed with its houses and buildings. The Zamorin of Calicut, he asserts is "a pagan and worships the devil." He gives a fairly clear outline of the caste system, matrilineal succession, and polyandry. Like the writers of antiquity, he was most favorably impressed by the administration of justice. He also comments at length on the building of ships at Calicut and observes that "the Pagans do not navigate much, but it is the Moors who carry the merchandize." Of plants and fruits he provides detailed and accurate descriptions. And he notices that

the men of Calicut, when they wish to sow rice, . . . they plough the land with oxen as we do, and when they sow the rice in the field they have all the instruments of the city continually sounding and making merry.[64]

He describes too the custom of secretly making bargains by touching hands and fingers under a cloth, a practice "which is current [today] among the Eastern people from the Abyssinians to the natives of India and the Farther East."[65]

In the account of his disputed voyage east of Calicut, Varthema mentions pearl-fishing on the Coromandel Coast, the jewels of Ceylon, and the custom of writing on "paper like ours" in Tenasserim. From his comments on religion it appears that he knew nothing about Buddhism though he appears to think that the religion of Pegu (Burma) is peculiar. In commenting on Malacca he describes its location and government in generally correct terms and notices the infertility of the surrounding countryside. He identifies Sumatra with the Taprobane of antiquity and makes most of his comments on the island from hearsay. At Banda he notices the nutmeg tree and, apparently from his experience in the Moluccas, he is able to give a description of the clove tree. He also relates what was told him by an Arab sailor about the lands, climates, and peoples south of Java.[66] Thus, Varthema brought into European literature an appreciation of the area east of India, whether he had actually traveled there or not, which it had previously not received from the sea-travelers and which confirmed by firsthand observations many of the statements made earlier by Marco Polo and the writers of antiquity.

It was not until 1511, the year after the original publication of Varthema's account of the East, that the Portuguese captured the great entrepôt of Malacca and began to penetrate farther eastward. News of Albuquerque's victory became known in Europe in the spring of 1513, and Manuel quickly dispatched

[64] See *ibid.*, p. xviii, and H. Cordier, "Deux voyagers dans l'Extrême-Orient . . . Essai bibliographique. Nicolo De'Conti-Lodovico de Varthema," *T'oung pao*, X (1899), 390–404.

[65] Comment of Sir William Temple in Jones and Temple, *op. cit.* (n. 61), p. lviii.

[66] For further elucidation on this matter see *ibid.*, p. lxxvi.

letters to Rome informing the papacy of Portugal's progress.[67] Manuel's speedy proclamation of the capture of Malacca had certain specific objectives apart from his understandable desire to let the world know of his distant conquests. The question had already been raised in Spain whether the Moluccas were not within the Spanish demarcation, and a project was being considered in 1512 for advancing a claim to and taking possession of the Spice Islands.[68] Ever watchful as to the security of his demarcation claims, Manuel immediately set to work to obtain papal support and recognition for Albuquerque's advances into southeastern Asia. And it was Manuel's good fortune that a pope had been elected in March, 1513, who was likely to receive the news cordially.

Pope Leo X (Giovanni de' Medici) was the second son of Lorenzo the Magnificent and the real ruler of his family and the Republic of Florence. The traditional good relations between Portugal and the Florentine merchants and navigators certainly did no harm to Manuel's cause in the eyes of the urbane Medici pope. Moreover, a strong case could be made in Rome for confirming Manuel's claims inasmuch as the Portuguese were regularly defeating the Muslims and constantly enlarging the field of possible Christian missionary enterprise. In fact, public celebrations of thanksgiving were held in Rome shortly after the news of Albuquerque's conquest of Malacca arrived.[69]

It was in such a favorable atmosphere that Manuel dispatched another embassy of obedience to Rome in the spring of 1514. The chief of this splendid delegation was Tristão da Cunha, who had been one of Portugal's most successful commanders in the East. He was accompanied by three of his sons and two eminent professors of law, Diogo Pacheco and João de Faria. On March 20, 1514, Pacheco delivered an oration in which he tendered Manuel's obedience to the Holy Father and itemized his great successes in the East. Shortly thereafter the oration appeared in print.[70] But the greatest sensation in Rome was caused by the valuable and curious presents which were paraded before the pope and the populace. Indian slaves, Persian horses, two leopards, a young panther, colorful parrots, and a trained elephant were among the gifts brought from Asia. A rhinoceros intended as the highlight of this exotic parade perished en route from Portugal to Rome,[71] but the trained elephant caused a

[67] Salvatore de Ciutius, *Une ambassade portugaise à Rome au XVIᵉ siècle* (Naples, 1899), pp. 4–8, prints the text of Manuel's letter of June 8, 1513. For the titles of these letters and adaptations of them as they appeared in chapbooks published during 1513–14, see Rogers, *op. cit.* (n. 15), p. 190.

[68] J. T. Medina, *Juan Diaz de Solis* (Santiago de Chile, 1897), Vol. I, chap. vi; Vol. II, docs. 22, 30, 31.

[69] W. Roscoe, *The Life and Pontificate of Leo X* (London, 1827), II, 299–300. Also see Mashanaglass, *Le Portugal et le Saint-Siège* (Paris, 1898), I, 21–29. Manuel's letter of June 8, 1513 (see Roscoe, *op. cit.* [n. 69], pp. 496–500) was published in short order at Rome, Vienna and Nuremberg.

[70] Entitled *Emanuelis Lusitan: Algarbior: Africae Aethiopiae Arabiae Persiae Indiae Reg. Invictiss. Obedientia.*

[71] See the amusing book of A. Fontoura da Costa, *Les déambulations du Rhinocéros de Modofar, roi de Cambaye, de 1514 à 1516* (Lisbon, 1937). Also see Lúis de Matos, "Forma e natura e costumi del rinoceronte," *Boletim internacional de bibliografia Luso-Brasileira*, I (1960), 387–98.

sensation as it bowed three times before the pope and squirted water from its trunk over the admiring multitude. Even the poets sang its praises.[72]

The popular approval won by the embassy was but one aspect of its success. Its more concrete achievements were the papal pronouncements made in Portugal's favor after the departure of the emissaries. On June 7, 1514, a papal bull gave to Portugal "the patronage of ecclesiastical benefices in Africa and *in all other places beyond the sea*, acquired or to be acquired from the infidels, and subjected them to the spiritual jurisdiction of the Order of Christ."[73] The bull *Praecelsae devotionis* of November 3, 1514, confirmed and renewed the earlier papal bulls of Nicholas V and Sixtus IV in Portugal's favor and "for great security" granted also

All unfrequented [by Christians] places, recovered, discovered, found, and acquired from the aforesaid infidels, by the said King Emmanuel and his successors, both from Capes Bojador and Nao to the Indies, and in any place or region whatsoever, even although perchance unknown to us at present. . . .[74]

Such a concession seemed to indicate that Leo X regarded the demarcation line as applying only to the Western hemisphere and as leaving the entire East open to Portuguese control and development. The confusion over the problem of the eastern demarcation was compounded, as we have seen,[75] in the controversy over the Moluccas that followed Magellan's expedition of 1519–22. In the rest of Europe, outside Italy and Portugal, it was generally considered that the pope had exceeded his authority as head of the Christian church in making such sweeping concessions to Portugal.

News of events in the East was meanwhile being relayed to Italy, especially Florence, through the correspondence of merchants. Particularly important were the letters of Giovanni da Empoli, who had first sailed for India in 1503 as agent of the Gualterotti-Frescobaldi syndicate. In 1509 he again went to the East with Albuquerque on his Malaccan expedition, returning to Portugal in 1512. Three years later he visited Sumatra. He then went to China along with Fernão Peres d'Andrade's mission of 1516 and is presumed to have died there early in 1518.[76] The accounts of his first two voyages were addressed respectively to his Florentine employers and to his father. They were not published until Ramusio included them in his collection at mid-century, but like so many

---

[72] For descriptions see Ciutius, *op. cit.* (n. 67), pp. 19–28; Ludwig von Pastor, *History of the Popes . . .*, trans. R. F. Kerr (London, 1908), VII, 74–78; and W. Roscoe, *op. cit.* (n. 69), II, 300–303. And for samples of poems celebrating the occasion by Aurelio Severio, Giovanni Capito, and others, see Pastor, *op. cit.* (n. 72), Appendix C, pp. 501–3. For a study of the elephant as an exotic animal see Luis de Matos, "Natura, intelletto, e costumi dell'elefante," *Boletim internacional de bibliografia Luso-Brasileira*, I (1960), 44–55.

[73] Davenport (ed.), *op. cit.* (n. 8), I, 112. Italics mine.

[74] *Ibid.*, pp. 116–17.

[75] Above, pp. 114–19.

[76] On Empoli's career see Pietro Amat di S. Filippo, *Gli illustri viaggiatori italiani . . .* (Rome, 1885), pp. 143–47. Also see Angelo de Gubernatis, *Storia dei viaggiatori italiani nelle Indie Orientali* (Leghorn, 1875), p. 16.

other letters of the time they were circulated to people who, for one reason or another, were interested in the opening of the East.[77] The same generalization probably applies also to the letter of Pietro Strozzi, another Florentine, who wrote from Quilon in 1510, and to a longer, anonymous letter from Lisbon, written in 1513.[78] Indeed, we know that the two long letters of Andrea Corsali, a Florentine writing from Goa in 1516 and 1517, were circulated to members of the Medici family.[79] Like some of the other letters of the period, Strozzi's were published at the time they were written, long before Ramusio brought them to more general attention.[80]

The best illustration that we have of the informal circulation of such letters on India is the case of Valentim Fernandes' letter written at Lisbon in May, 1515, and sent to the merchants of Nuremberg. The original was probably in Latin or German, but the only copy extant is in Italian.[81] In this epistle, which was probably relayed from Nuremberg to Florence, he announced the arrival in Lisbon of a rhinoceros as a gift from the king of Cambay and displays his humanistic erudition by comparing the conduct of the real animal with the descriptions given by Plato and Strabo. The mention of Cambay also leads him to speak generally about India, its extent, divisions, and products.[82] Since there is nothing especially newsworthy about this letter, we conclude that the other more informative letters of this period, many of them the observations of eyewitnesses, were probably also circulated to interested parties.

Thanks to Manuel's announcements, the letters of the foreigners in Portuguese service, and the presumably clandestine letters of Fernandes, the rest of Europe was able in the years before 1520 to gather bits and pieces of written information on Portuguese activities in the East. A number of books actually printed in Iberia kept alive the dream of finding an eastern Christian empire. When Abyssinia was finally reached in 1520, the realization grew that a Christian Utopia was not going to be found in the East. Thereafter, over the next two decades, interest in east Africa gradually waned.[83] Even though news seeped out from time to time, the system of control over the more detailed data relating to actual discoveries in Asia, was surprisingly watertight. For we now know that, in the years shortly before 1520, two of the most detailed and informative accounts on the East were in existence and were presumably in Lisbon in manuscript copies. Tomé Pires, an apothecary by training and a

---

[77] For the published versions of Empoli's letters see Amat di S. Filippo (ed.), *Bibliografia dei viaggiatori italiani* (Rome, 1874), pp. 46–47. His letter on Malacca is reproduced and edited by Iacopo Graberg da Hemsö, "Lettera di Giovanni da Empoli a Leonardo suo padre intorno al viaggio da lui fatto a Malacca . . .," *Archivio storico italiano, Appendice*, III (1846), 35–91.

[78] Both are reproduced in Gubernatis, *op. cit.* (n. 76), pp. 372–73.

[79] Amat di S. Filippo, *op. cit.* (n. 76), pp. 149–70.

[80] Amat di S. Filippo, *op. cit.* (n. 77), p. 48. See also Renato Lefevre, "Una corrispondenza dal Mar Rosso di Andrea Corsali nel 1516," *Il libro italiano*, IV, Pt. 2 (1940), 433–48.

[81] Text in Gubernatis, *op. cit.* (n. 76), pp. 389–92.

[82] See Heyd, "Valentin Fernandez Aleman," *loc. cit.* (n. 37), pp. 482–83.

[83] Rogers, *op. cit.* (n. 15), chap. viii.

supervisor of the spice trade in Malacca, between 1512 and 1515 wrote the *Suma oriental*,[84] a full and authoritative account of the Eastern regions from the Red Sea to Japan. His account of Malacca is original and one of the best contemporary records that we have of Malaya in its relationship to the neighboring lands of southeast Asia. Most of his information about the archipelago was apparently gathered from merchant informants and from Javanese traditions and maps. His materials on India are slighter and relatively much less valuable than his precise information on southeast Asia. Another important work dating from around 1517 is the *Book* of Duarte Barbosa.[85] He had probably not traveled east of India, but for the complex of east Africa, Arabia, and western India he presented the best account prepared in the first half of the sixteenth century. To illustrate how authoritative Barbosa's *Book* was considered to be by contemporaries, it is of utmost interest to note that it was taken to the conference of Badajoz–Elvas in 1524 as one of the Portuguese exhibits. The Spaniards evidently received a copy of it in some way or other, for it was used extensively in the preparation of the so-called Second Borgia map of 1529.[86] Ramusio, in 1550, was the first to publish even extracts from these two highly valuable Portuguese reports, written by knowledgeable and inquiring observers from the field.

It may be concluded that in the first two decades of the sixteenth century the policy of secrecy operated with a fair measure of success. Information on the spice trade, some details on the navigational problem, and notices of the Portuguese activities in the vast southern region from the Red Sea to China filtered into Spain, the Italian cities, the Low Countries, and the commercial towns of south Germany. The presses of Portugal published nothing at all on the discoveries in Asia except for the retrospective collections of travel literature by Fernandes. Most of the written accounts, dealing with actual discoveries, whether published or not, were short, cryptic, and undetailed. For all practical purposes, almost as much was learned from the Portuguese official pronouncements as became available through the newsletters and the correspondence of the merchants and sailors. In the first decade of the century, a whole spate of chapbooks appeared in Italy, Germany, and the Netherlands which dealt with the opening of Asia. From 1516 to 1522 almost nothing new was published on the eastward progress of the Portuguese. Like the spice monopoly, the policy of control of information operated effectively until the dispatch of Magellan's voyage and the death of King Manuel in 1521, even though a certain amount of information was passed out of the country by spies, foreign navigators,

---

[84] The complete account was published in 1944 for the first time from a Portuguese manuscript found in the Bibliothèque de la Chambre des Députés in Paris. See Armando Cortesão (ed. and trans.), *The Suma Oriental of Tomé Pires* . . . (2 vols.; "Hakluyt Society Publications," Ser. II, Vols. LXXXIX, XC [London, 1944]).

[85] The most recent edition in English is that of Manuel L. Dames (ed. and trans.), *The Book of Duarte Barbosa* (2 vols.; London, 1918–21).

[86] *Ibid.*, I, liii–lviii.

seamen, merchants, and Portuguese who went abroad to work or study.[87] But these reports by themselves were only enough to give the interested foreign observer a general notion of what the Portuguese were about and very few specific insights into how they operated the spice trade, administered their outposts, waged war against the Muslims and heathens, or what they expected to extract from Malacca and hoped to gain from relations with distant China.

3

THE WIDENING CIRCLE, 1521–50

King Manuel was able to die secure in the thought that no other European ships had appeared in India to challenge the Portuguese monopoly of the sea route. There had been a few threats, particularly from Spain, but none of these had materialized before Manuel's demise in 1521. Not only had his efforts been crowned with success; they had also received the sanction and praise of two popes. He had even had the pleasure in 1518 of refusing Venice's request to act as Portugal's middleman in the distribution of spices. The Spanish fleet which sailed west in 1519 to find a passage to the Spice Islands under the Portuguese renegade, Magellan, seemed to have vanished from the face of the earth. In 1521 all of Manuel's eastern projects gave the appearance of being in excellent condition to be entrusted to the untried hands of young King John III.

Throughout his reign (1521–57), John III fought stubbornly to maintain and extend the imperial system inherited from his father. Perhaps a part of the failure which finally came to Portugal may be attributed to his determination to concentrate attention on Lusitania's eastern and American enterprises while paying only minimum heed to Africa. For with the passage of time the vulnerability of the Portuguese position in the East and America became constantly more apparent. It became particularly difficult to keep the ships of other European monarchs from the sea lanes and from intruding in Portugal's preserves. What was perhaps most distressing of all was the return in September, 1522, of the "Victoria," one of Magellan's ships, with twenty-three survivors, including four East Indians.[88] By its very return the "Victoria" proved not only that the world could be circumnavigated but that it could be done in spite of the Portuguese. It also raised to the level of public discussion the validity of the claims of the Iberian powers to exclusive demarcations in the overseas world.

[87] See above, p. 154. Also consult Luis de Matos, *Les portugais à l'université de Paris entre 1500 et 1550* (Coimbra, 1950). For example, see the story of Damião de Góis who was a student at Padua and then at Louvain as described in H. de Vocht, *History of . . . the Collegium Trilingue Louvaniense* (Louvain, 1951), III, 50–71.

[88] See Charles E. Nowell (ed.), *Magellan's Voyage around the World: Three Contemporary Accounts* (Evanston, Ill., 1962), p. 268.

The first report of the Spanish success to be published in Europe was the account of Maximilian of Transylvania. The natural son of the Archbishop of Salzburg, the young Maximilian was attached to the court of Charles V then in Castile. Maximilian was being tutored by Peter Martyr, the great chronicler of Spain's activities in America. At the suggestion of Peter, Maximilian interviewed Juan Sebastián del Cano,[89] the captain of the "Victoria," and his men, and addressed an account of their adventures and stories to his father. Maximilian's Latin report, *De Moluccis insulis* . . ., was sent northward in short order and in the course of 1523 was published at Cologne and Rome. Of his informants the young scholar wrote:

I have taken much care in obtaining an account of the facts from the commanding officer of the squadron and from the individual sailors who have returned with him. They also made a statement to the emperor [at Valladolid], and to several other persons, with such good faith and sincerity, that they appeared in their narrative not merely to have abstained from fabulous statements, but also to contradict and refute the fabulous statements made by ancient authors.[90]

The youthful author also sought to place his story in the perspective of the eastward progress of the Portuguese as he knew of it. He announced that the Portuguese had penetrated China "where they found a fair-complexioned and tolerably-civilized people, like our folks in Germany."[91] He also noted that Cristóbal de Haro, the Spanish merchant and Fugger agent, had through his representatives "for many years carried on trade with those Eastern countries and more recently with the Chinese."[92]

About the East Indies Maximilian's account is informative, factual, and precise. He tells of Magellan's slave, "whom he had formerly bought in Malacca," acting as an interpreter for the Spaniards. He states correctly that the Moluccas are five in number "situated partly to the north, partly to the south, and partly on the equator."[93] The people who live in palaces are Muslims while the ordinary folk are heathen. They want to trade, because their islands produce very little except for the spices. And, like many of the other "noble savages" discovered by Europeans in the sixteenth century and later, the Moluccans are praised for their simplicity and contentment.

They live on sago-bread, fish, and sometimes parrots; they live in very low-built cabins; in short, all they esteem and value is peace, leisure, and spices. The former, the greatest

---

[89] Maximilian's report was published under the title *De Moluccis insulis, itemq; alijs pluribus miradis, quae novissima Castellanorum Sereniss. Imperatoris Caroli V. auspicio suscepta, nuper inuenit.* . . . A report was also prepared by Peter Martyr to inform the papacy of the Spanish success, but this was apparently lost in the Sack of Rome of 1526. For an English translation of Del Cano's testimony at the official inquiry see Appendix B of Mairin Mitchell, *Elcano: The First Circumnavigator* (London, 1958), pp. 178–82.

[90] As translated by H. Stevens from Maximilian's *De Moluccis* . . . and included in *Johann Schöner* . . . (London, 1888), p. 107.

[91] *Ibid.*, p. 110.

[92] *Ibid.*, p. 111.

[93] *Ibid.*, pp. 138–39.

of blessings, the wickedness of mankind seems to have banished from our part of the world to theirs; but our avarice and insatiable desire of the luxuries of the table has urged us to seek for spices even in those distant lands.[94]

He also tells of a few of the curiosities brought back, especially the exotic birds, one of whose plumages he evidently sent to his father along with his letter.[95]

The other major contemporary source for Magellan's expedition is the account of Antonio Pigafetta, which was not published in its entirety until fairly recent times.[96] From our viewpoint, Pigafetta's impact upon his contemporaries must be looked for both in his peregrinations in Europe and in the epitomized versions of his work which appeared in the sixteenth century.[97] The son of a noble family of Vicenza, and a Knight of Rhodes in his own right, Pigafetta was a man of education and distinction. With the approval of Charles V and the Grand Master of Rhodes, he accompanied Magellan on his great adventure, as a chronicler of the voyage. In his own words, Pigafetta was determined "to experience and to go and see those things for myself, so that I might be able thereby to satisfy myself somewhat, and so that I might be able to gain more renown for later posterity."[98] It would perhaps be safe to conclude that his interest had been aroused by the *Paesi* and other accounts of the newly discovered lands that had circulated in Italy before his departure for Spain.[99] In order to keep as accurate a record as possible, Pigafetta seems to have kept a diary during the entire three years of his absence from Europe.[100]

As soon as the "Victoria" returned, news of its successful circumnavigation of the globe was relayed to Portugal, Italy, Germany, and France. A considerable share of the interest aroused was related to the general knowledge that Pigafetta had kept a diary of the voyage and that he had presented an oral summary based on it, or even a copy of it, to the emperor at a reception held at Valladolid. Shortly after this presentation, the ambassador to Castile from Mantua wrote

[94] *Ibid.*, p. 139.

[95] *Ibid.*, p. 143. Also see below, p. 598.

[96] The most authoritative version is Andrea da Mosto, *Il primo viaggio intorno al globo* (Rome, 1894) in *Raccolta di documenti e studi publicati dalla R. Commissione Colombiana*, Pt. V, Vol. III; and for the English translation see the three volumes of J. A. Robertson, *Magellan's Voyage around the World* (Cleveland, 1906).

[97] The oldest surviving edition is in poor French and is apparently the one from which all the other editions and translations of the sixteenth century were made. It is called *Le voyage et nauigation faict par les Espaignolz es isles de Mollucques* (Paris, ca. 1525). According to Ramusio, it was edited by J. Fabre and published by Colines. For an English translation of Ramusio's remarks see Nowell (ed.), *op. cit.* (n. 88), pp. 271–72.

[98] Robertson, *op. cit.* (n. 96), I, 23. It has also been suggested (Parr, *op. cit.* [n. 12], p. 255) that Pigafetta was "probably sent by the Seignory of Venice." Perhaps a variant reading (cited by Robertson, *op. cit.* [n. 96], I, p. 201, n. 8) helps to support this opinion. It reads: ". . . so that I might satisfy the wish of the said gentlemen, and also my own desires. . . ." At any rate it is known in support of Parr's contention that he reported back to the Doge of Venice shortly after his return to Europe, though he did not go directly there.

[99] Mosto, *op. cit.* (n. 96), p. 19.

[100] He refrains, purposely it seems, from mentioning Del Cano even once and apparently did not use him or his other companions on the voyage for checks on his own memory (see Mitchell, *op. cit.* [n. 89], pp. 93–94).

to the Marchesa Isabella d'Este on October 21, 1522, that the voyagers had returned with a beautiful book that contained a day-by-day report of the voyage and of the countries visited.[101] Three weeks later he sent a short extract to Mantua summarizing "the book that has been brought from India." [102]

From the court of Charles V, Pigafetta journeyed to Lisbon, where he was received by King John III. His reception here was not entirely cordial,[103] even though he told the king in detail about his adventures. After a very short stay in Portugal, he journeyed back across Spain to France where he was received by Marie Louise of Savoy, mother of King Francis I. In Paris he evidently recited the story of his adventure and left a version of his diary account with the Queen Mother. Early in 1523, Pigafetta was received graciously at Mantua by Isabella d'Este, the famous patroness of the arts, on the recommendation of Francesco Chiericati, a Venetian papal nuncio who was assigned to Spain when Magellan's ships left.[104] In his conversation with her, Pigafetta promised to prepare an extended narrative of his experiences.

To make good his promise to the Marchesa, Pigafetta retired to the quiet of his home at Vicenza to prepare his manuscript. The next notice we have of him is his appearance in Venice on November 7, 1523, before the Seignory and the Doge. Of this event the diarist Marino Sanudo wrote:

There came before the College a gentleman of Vicenza called the Knight Errant, who has been three years in the Indies to see what was to be seen. And he by word of mouth recounted all those matters and all the College gave great attention in listening to him. And he got through half his journey. And after dinner he was with the Doge [Andrea Gritti], and spoke for long upon these matters so that his Serenity, and all who heard him, were astonished at the things which are in India.[105]

After this triumphant occasion, Pigafetta apparently returned to Vicenza and to his labors of composition. While so occupied, he received in December, 1523, a dispatch from Rome which ordered him in the name of the newly elevated Pope Clement VII (Giulio de' Medici) "to come immediately to His Holiness and postpone everything else." [106]

Pigafetta left for Rome with his manuscript still uncompleted. On the road to the Eternal City he met Filippo Villiers de l'Isle Adam, Grand Master of the Knights of Rhodes, to whom he told his story. Like Isabella, the Grand Master

---

[101] Text in Guglielmo Berchet (ed.), *Fonti italiane per la storia della scoperta del nuovo mondo* (Rome, 1892), in *Raccolta di documenti e studi publicati della R. Commissione Colombiana . . .*, Pt. III, Vol. I, p. 172.

[102] *Ibid.*, p. 173. The summary was not attached to the letter, and it has not been located elsewhere.

[103] This is the judgment of Mosto, *op. cit.* (n. 96), p. 25.

[104] *Ibid.*, pp. 25–26. Apparently, Chiericati had seen a copy of Pigafetta's relation presented to Charles V. This was later sent to Germany. See also the reference to Chiericati at the very beginning of Pigafetta's account; Pigafetta had been attached to Chiericati's retinue before his departure with Magellan.

[105] *Diarii*, xxxv, 97 verso. Translation taken from H. F. Brown, *The Venetian Printing Press* (London, 1896), pp. 102–3.

[106] *Ibid.*, p. 26.

urged Pigafetta to prepare a narrative from his notes and reminiscences. In Rome, as in many of the royal courts he had already visited, Pigafetta told of his adventures. Pope Clement VII, himself an amateur of arts, letters, and sciences, granted Pigafetta the right to print his book wherever he would and to enjoy the returns therefrom. While in Rome, Pigafetta continued to communicate with the court of Mantua through Baldassare Castiglione, its renowned ambassador to the Holy See.[107] The Knight of Rhodes abandoned the papal court in the spring of 1524 and evidently returned to Vicenza and his writing.

His manuscript being completed, Pigafetta started in the summer of 1524 to look for a publisher and some financial backing. In July he appeared in Venice armed with a letter from the Marchesa to the Doge. Here he also received help from Giovanni Battista Malatesta, Mantua's representative in Venice. At the end of July or the beginning of August, the Venetian Council

granted to Antonio Pigafetta, Knight of Jerusalem, who voyaged with the caravels of his Caesarean Majesty to find the islands where the spices of the new Indies grow, inasmuch as he has circumnavigated the whole world, and has composed a work which he wishes to have printed, therefore it be conceded to him that no other except himself be allowed to have it printed for xx years, under the penalty of 3 lire per copy.[108]

But no record exists of the complete manuscript being published in Pigafetta's lifetime, or at any time in the sixteenth century. Perhaps he was never able to find the initial sum of money that the printer required.[109]

Four manuscripts of Pigafetta's relation are extant.[110] Our modern texts are derived from these manuscripts rather than from the epitomized versions published in the sixteenth century and circulated widely in the latter half of the century in the collections of Ramusio and Eden. Aside from being the only narrative published by a participant in the first expedition of circumnavigation, the account of Pigafetta is the first European work to depict the immense breadth of the Pacific Ocean and to describe in some detail the ways of life in Borneo and in certain of the Philippine Islands. His stories of gold being found in the Philippines helped to inspire the later expeditions that the Spanish sent westward from Mexico.[111] He tells of the trade of Cebu with China, India, and Siam, and stresses that the people love "peace, ease and quiet."[112] In connection with the mass baptisms of the Cebuans, he remarks categorically that "the Moros are much harder to convert than the heathen."[113] He concludes his

---

[107] *Ibid.*

[108] As translated from Sanudo's *Diarii* in Robertson, *op. cit.* (n. 96), II, 272–73 (cf. pp. 239–40). On the question of the exact date of this decree see, besides Robertson, Brown, *op. cit.* (n. 105), p. 103.

[109] Mosto, *op. cit.* (n. 96), p. 28.

[110] For their locations see Robertson, *op. cit.* (n. 96), I, 201.

[111] W. L. Schurz, *The Manila Galleon* (New York, 1939), p. 46.

[112] Robertson, *op. cit.* (n. 96), I, 149.

[113] *Ibid.*, I, 157.

account of Cebu with a short vocabulary of Bisayan words, most of which can be distinguished in modern dictionaries of that language and of Tagalog.[114] In commenting on the trade of Palawan he describes the Chinese porcelain he saw there as being made "of exceedingly white earth."[115]

After visiting the islands of the Philippine archipelago, the Spaniards touched on Borneo and cruised for a long time in the Sulu Sea. They finally arrived at Tidore in the Moluccas on November 8, 1521, where they were given a cordial reception by the local sultan, an enemy of the Portuguese. On the basis of information received from a Portuguese whom he met in the Moluccas, Pigafetta asserts that "the king of Portagalo had enjoyed Malucho already for ten years secretly, so that the king of Spagnia might not learn of it."[116] Pigafetta made a deliberate and careful investigation of the clove tree and sought to learn as much as he could about its cultivation. He also described in detail the bartering that went on to get the precious cloves. And as he had done in the Philippines, Pigafetta compiled a vocabulary of the terms used by the merchants on Tidore. This collection of forty-seven words is of considerable linguistic interest, since it is accurate and one of the oldest extant specimens of the Malay language,[117] the earliest surviving Malay manuscripts being dated from around 1500 to 1550. It would seem that by the time he left the archipelago, Pigafetta had acquired a working knowledge of two of the most important dialects of the Indonesian languages. Of the other islands of the East Indies, and he touched on many of them, Pigafetta gives only superficial comments or reports stories heard from others. Most interesting are the reports he heard of China "whose king is the greatest in all the world."[118]

No matter how skeptical the Portuguese might have felt about the reports they heard from Seville indirectly and from Pigafetta personally, a confirming letter arrived in Lisbon early in 1524 from António de Brito, the Portuguese captain at Ternate, which told of the Spanish expedition that had touched on neighboring Tidore.[119] This is the only other written relation extant of the Spanish activities in the East Indies put down by a contemporary who was actually in the field. Apparently it was this document which convinced the Portuguese of the accuracy of Pigafetta's story and led King John III to

[114] *Ibid.*, I, 183–93; 269–73; also see below, p. 636.

[115] *Ibid.*, II, 39.

[116] *Ibid.*, II, 83.

[117] In the accounts published during the sixteenth century only about one-tenth of Pigafetta's compilation was published (cf. G. B. Ramusio, *Delle navigationi et viaggi* [Venice, 1554], I, 408 verso). His complete vocabulary of Malay includes 450 words (Robertson, *op. cit.* [n. 96], II, 117–47). Also see John Crawfurd, *A Descriptive Dictionary of the Indian Islands and Adjacent Countries* (London, 1856), p. 352. The question as to how he was able to get this vocabulary together during his short stay in the East Indies has perplexed many students of Pigafetta's work. For a recent summary of the scholarship on this subject see C. C. F. M. Le Roux, "Nogmaals Pigafetta's Maleische woorden," *Tijdschrift voor Indische taal-, land- en volkenkunde*, LXXIX (1939), 446–51.

[118] Robertson, *op. cit.* (n. 96), II, 174–75.

[119] Translated into French and edited by Emile Eudi, "La lettre d'Antonio de Brito, capitaine de la fortresse de Ternate, au roi de Portugal Dom João III (6 mai 1523)," *La géographie*, XLIX (1928), 1–17.

undertake the negotiations with Charles V which culminated in 1529 in the Treaty of Saragossa.[120]

While Portugal negotiated with Castile over their conflicting claims in the East Indies, French corsairs increasingly intruded in the overseas area staked out by Portugal. The cities of Provence had engaged in the Mediterranean spice trade since the end of the seventh century and the medieval city of Montpellier had owed its prosperity to this traffic. Such French cities found that their trade, like that of Venice, was at least temporarily disrupted by the Portuguese effort to monopolize the spice traffic. Even the crown, fearing that France might soon be emptied of gold, began as early as 1517 to forbid the importation of spices and drugs except through the old marts related to the Mediterranean trade.[121] But such prohibitions failed in the long run to prevent the semi-independent French commercial cities and merchants from making their own accommodations to the changing trade picture. And after the election of Charles V in 1519, King Francis I was forced to concentrate his attention upon finding allies wherever possible, even in infidel Turkey.[122] The Atlantic ports of France, whose commercial importance had risen steadily after the end of the Hundred Years' War, then became more prosperous and relatively more independent of royal control. The maritime cities of western France thereupon took the initiative, sometimes contrary to the king's wishes and policies, in preying upon Portuguese trade in the Atlantic and on the west coast of Africa, and taking whatever part of it they could for themselves.[123]

Around 1520, the Norman town of Dieppe was one of the leading centers of French commercial activity on the Atlantic. The older ports at the mouth of the Seine had silted up, Rouen was too far upstream, and Le Havre was just being built. A leading spirit in commercial and overseas enterprises at Dieppe was Jean Ango, viscount, governor, and petty merchant-prince of great vigor. It was largely owing to his initiative that the Tuscan navigator Giovanni Verrazano was hired in 1523, shortly after the return of the "Victoria" from the Moluccas, to sail westward in the hope of finding a northern passage to Cathay.

In this enterprise the financing was evidently provided by a group of bankers from Florence and Lyons.[124] Although Verrazano failed to find the passage, his voyage encouraged the Normans to expand their activities to Brazil and the south Atlantic. While Portugal protested, the Normans persisted and became ever bolder in their encroachments. As early as 1527, ships from Dieppe were sailing the Indian Ocean as far north as the island of Diu. Two years later, while Portugal was winding up its arrangements with Castile, two vessels were outfitted at Dieppe to sail out "beyond the end of Asia,"[125] or to China.

---

[120] Cf. above, p. 118.

[121] See C. Julien, *Les voyages du découverte et les premiers établissements* (Paris, 1948), pp. 53–54.

[122] Cf. the viewpoint of C. D. Rouillard, *The Turk in French History, Thought and Literature* (Paris, 1938), pp. 105–7.

[123] Julien, *op. cit.* (n. 121), pp. 66–73.

[124] *Ibid.*, p. 80; for Italian commercial relations with Lyons see above, pp. 124–25.

[125] As quoted in *ibid.*, p. 100.

The commanders of the two vessels belonging to Jean Ango were Jean and Raoul Parmentier; their chief navigational aides and astronomers were Pierre Crignon and Pierre Maucler; and they took along two interpreters of the Malay language.[126] The Dieppe vessels ran the Portuguese blockade and finally made the Maldive Islands. On October 1, 1529, they landed at Ticon, a port of west Sumatra. Hardheaded as the Normans were reputed to be in trade, they met their match in the merchants of Sumatra. The physical conditions were also difficult, and the Parmentier brothers both died of fever. One of the Dieppe ships returned safely in 1530, but with little to show for the investment and effort. Hereafter the French were content to let the Portuguese do business in the East without further challenge. The corsairs of the French maritime cities, as already noted,[127] with the connivance of certain figures at court, after 1530 began systematically to prey upon the Iberian vessels carrying spices to Antwerp and silver on their return voyages.[128]

One of the consequences of the French voyage was the publication at Paris in 1531 of a collection of poems by the classical scholar, sailor, and poet, Jean Parmentier. His *Description nouvelle des merveilles de ce mode* was put together by the astronomer Pierre Crignon, who returned to Dieppe safely.[129] Crignon also kept a journal of his own during the voyage, but this was not published until the nineteenth century.[130] In 1534, however, he published a *Perle de cosmographie* of which there are apparently no extant copies.[131] Something of a mystery also shrouds the account of this expedition as Ramusio published it,[132] for it would now appear that it was not extracted from Crignon's journal as has been thought for a long time. Since it is not possible to determine whether or not it was extracted from Crignon's *Perle . . .*, we must remain content with the identification of Ramusio himself and conclude that it was written in 1539, a decade after the event.[133] Thus, the public at large learned but little about the French expedition or about Sumatra until the publication of Ramusio. But in the meanwhile the Portuguese, through their agents and emissaries in France and their war vessels on the high seas, fought against the growing threat from the French corsairs. Despite the representations of the French about the freedom

---

[126] One was a Portuguese and the other was named Jean Masson, possibly one of the Malay-speaking survivors of Magellan's expedition.

[127] Above, pp. 123–24.

[128] For a summary of some of Portugal's troubles with Jean Ango *ca.* 1530 see the introduction to J. D. M. Ford (ed.), *Letters of John III, King of Portugal, 1521–27* (Cambridge, Mass., 1931).

[129] Original from the Bibliothèque Nationale in Paris has been reproduced in the Massachusetts Historical Society photostat series of Americana. Copies of this reproduction are in the Library of Congress and the Newberry Library of Chicago. For further discussion see Kurt Graf von Posadowsky-Wehner, *Jean Parmentier (1494–1529). Leben und Werk* (Munich, 1937).

[130] See Louis Estancelin, *Recherches sur les voyages et découvertes des navigateurs normands* (Paris, 1832).

[131] Albert Anthiaume, *Cartes marines: Constructions navales: Voyage de découvertes chez les Normands, 1500–1650* (Paris, 1916), I, 164.

[132] Published in *Navigationi, op. cit.* (n. 117), Vol. III, fols. 423–34, as "Discorso D'un Gran Capitano di mare Francese. . . ."

[133] For details on the conclusions recorded here see George B. Parks, *The Contents and Sources of Ramusio's Navigationi* (New York, 1955), pp. 39–40.

of the seas, King John denied its applicability wherever it seemed to threaten Portuguese trade.[134]

A few published newsletters about the Portuguese progress in the East are extant for the period after 1530. André de Resende, who was attempting a massive history of Portugal, published in 1531 at Louvain in the Netherlands a Latin summary of the activities of the Portuguese in India during the year 1530.[135] From Evora in 1536 King John sent a letter to Pope Paul III about Portugal's conquests in northern India at the expense of Cambay. Shortly thereafter, this letter was published in Latin, possibly at Vienna.[136] Damião de Góis, Humanist and friend of Erasmus, was mainly preoccupied in these years with learning about Ethiopia. He nevertheless found time in 1539 to publish at Louvain a commentary, following the style adopted by Resende, which summarized the deeds of the Portuguese in western India during the year 1538.[137] Around 1545 King John dispatched another letter to the pope, this one about the conversion of four Indian princes. Sometime thereafter it was published in Italian, possibly at Milan, and in 1546 a French translation was printed at Paris.[138] Such progress reports kept Europeans abreast of the major Portuguese triumphs, both military and religious, in India, but they did not mention the setbacks suffered by both the secular and the religious arms in the East. As in the time of King Manuel, the royal letters and other semiofficial reports about contemporary events in Asia continued to be published outside Portugal itself.

As the circle of interest in the overseas world widened in Europe, the early accounts of the voyages and the descriptive narratives of the East were republished. For example, at Basel in 1532 a compilation was issued entitled *Novus orbis regionum ac insularum veteribus incognitarum.* . . . Many of the narratives reproduced in this work were gathered together by Johann Huttich of Mainz and Sebastian Münster,[139] and they were printed by Hervagius (Johann Herwagen). The preface was written by Simon Grynaeus,[140] a noted intellectual and the friend of Luther, Calvin, and Melanchthon. In addition to the older accounts of the East derived from Marco Polo and Hayton, the compilers published Varthema's relation and Manuel's letter of June 8, 1513, to Pope Leo X. Section VIII includes an account by M. de Miechow, Canon of Cracow, which brings together numerous fabulous travel tales and a remark to the effect that the king of Poland has been watching with interest the conquests of Portugal in Africa and India. In the subsequent editions published at Basel in 1537 and

---

134 Cf. Julien, *op. cit.* (n. 121), pp. 113–15.

135 Entitled *Epitome rerum gestarum in India a Lusitanis, anno superiori.* . . . On Resende's career see Aubrey F. P. Bell, *Portuguese Literature* (Oxford, 1922), p. 215.

136 See Rogers, *op. cit.* (n. 15), p. 193.

137 Entitled *Comentarii rerum gestarum in India citra Gangem a Lusitanis anno 1538.*

138 See Rogers, *op. cit.* (n. 15), p. 193.

139 Böhme, *op. cit.* (n. 33), p. 54. For further details see Harrisse, *op. cit.* (n. 59), pp. 291–96.

140 It has been claimed that Grynaeus took Fernandes' preface to the 1502 edition of Marco Polo as his model and point of departure. See Manuel II, *op. cit.* (n. 33), I, 125.

1555, the account of Maximilian of Transylvania was added, as well as materials on the New World and Land of Ophir. At Strassburg in 1534, a free German translation was made by Michael Herr, a physician who had studied at Basel, and this work in turn was translated into Dutch in 1563.

From the evidence it would appear that *Novus orbis* was published for the express purpose of making money.[141] It contains nothing that had not already been published before. The intended audience was clearly the learned public, for in the preface Grynaeus berates Marco Polo and Hayton for not having written in Latin, the language of "this compilation," so that their writings might have been more easily read and appreciated by the Humanists. Even the folio format of the book and its heavy binding were apparently designed to attract purchasers of means. The preface also stresses the convenience to the reader of the new compilation, for it gave him an opportunity to read and compare accounts, hitherto published mainly as separate books or pamphlets in various languages, simply by studying this Latin compendium at his leisure. It also includes a map engraved by Hans Holbein the younger on the basis of the cartography of the Paris professor, Orontius Finaeus. Clearly travel accounts had entertainment appeal to the learned public in an age when the novel and short story had not yet come into their own.[142]

A similar but original collection of voyages appeared at Venice in 1543. A product of the famous Aldine Press, it bore the title *Viaggi fatti alla Tana....* The work of compilation, as indicated in the preface, was done by Antonio and Paolo Manuzio. All five accounts that comprise the book are travelogues of Venetian emissaries and merchants who had journeyed to Asia via the eastern Mediterranean. Obviously one of the purposes of the book was to glorify Venetian enterprise. Just two of the five accounts, those in Folios III and V, relate to India. The earlier of these accounts[143] narrates the story of two trips to Calicut. The first was made overland in 1529 to the Persian Gulf and from there by water to the Malabar Coast. Shortly after returning to the West, the author evidently secured passage on a Portuguese vessel that took him in 1532 around Africa to Calicut. The second of these accounts[144] relates how the author, captive of a Turkish fleet, voyaged in the Indian Ocean between 1537 and 1540 as the Muslim ships harassed Portuguese shipping and installations there. In neither of these accounts is the author's identity made entirely clear and certain. It would appear that both accounts were prepared to give Venetians trustworthy (i.e., written by compatriots) news of Portuguese activities in the East. Both authors stress trade statistics, products, distances, and the importance of Goa and Malacca as the anchors of Portugal's eastern trading system. Implicit in the organization and tone of the book is a simple message: Venice has long had direct contact with Asia overland and there is no reason why these relations

---

[141] Böhme, *op. cit.* (n. 33), pp. 66–69.

[142] A survey of Venetian copyrights reveals that after 1533 travel literature of all sorts becomes of much more general interest. See Brown, *op. cit.* (n. 105), p. 102.

[143] Called *Viaggio di Colocut descritto per Messer Aloigi di messer Giovani Venetiano.*

[144] *Viaggio di Alessandria nelle India.*

should not be expanded and extended, particularly as the Portuguese seem to be having difficulties just holding their own in India. That the work was of more than passing local interest is borne out by the fact that it was reissued in 1545.[145]

The descriptions of Asia published in the generation from 1520 to 1550 were primarily the work of non-Iberians and most of them were published in Italy and northern Europe. Maximilian was Belgian or Hungarian, Pigafetta Italian, Parmentier and Crignon French, the group of Grynaeus German, and the authors of the *Viaggi fatti alla Tana* Venetian. And these were all accounts of independent experiences. Of the five collections of travel literature (Fernandes, Santaella, *Paesi, Novus orbis*, and *Viaggi fatti alla Tana*) compiled and published by mid-century, only one originated in Portugal. This is not to say that the Portuguese were idle about preparing materials on their trade empire. A few brief chronicles and royal letters were prepared by the Portuguese themselves for printing at foreign presses. Within the country this was a period of great, but silent, productivity. It needs only to be recalled that João de Barros was busy collecting in these years the vast store of material that was to be published shortly after mid-century in his encyclopedic *Ásia*.[146]

Until the closure of the Portuguese factory at Antwerp and the decision forced upon the crown to permit greater latitude to northern European states and merchants in the distribution of the spices, the Portuguese policy of news control apparently operated with moderate success. Nothing came off the presses of Portugal before mid-century to elucidate systematically the great discoveries which had been made since the first voyage of Vasco da Gama. It seems that few, if any, manuscript accounts filtered through to the rest of Europe in the second generation of Portugal's eastern enterprise. The effectiveness of the official system of news control may have been greatly enhanced by the establishment in 1536 of the national Inquisition in Portugal and by the dominance in education acquired shortly afterwards by the Society of Jesus. But even such new instruments of control were not sufficient after mid-century to keep the censorship intact, and indeed the Society of Jesus, once it sent missionaries to Asia, quickly became the agency which provided some of the most important and widely circulated sources of information on the East.[147]

4

THE IBERIAN COMMENTATORS AND LINSCHOTEN

The publication history of the great Portuguese and Spanish accounts (excluding the missionary writings) of the East is limited to a relatively few names and a short span of time.[148] Beginning with the publication of Ramusio's first

---

[145] For a further discussion see Böhme, *op. cit.* (n. 33), pp. 71–72.

[146] For this story see below, pp. 190–92.

[147] See below, pp. 314–31.

[148] For a general survey see Zoe Swecker, "The Early Iberian Accounts of the Far East" (Ph.D. dissertation, University of Chicago, 1960).

volume in 1550, the story of the earlier Iberian discoveries and conflicts in Asia was relayed to Europe through the works of fourteen major authors and a number of lesser lights who had their works printed during the latter half of the century. The greatest chroniclers (Oviedo, Gómara, Castanheda, and Barros) published their massive descriptions between 1548 and 1563. The books published thereafter no longer take the discoveries as their theme, but deal with Asia in connection with the biography of King Manuel, with special topics such as the sieges of Malacca, or in relation to China for which there was a growing appreciation. Linschoten's work, which appeared close to the end of the century, may be considered either a description of the Portuguese East by an interested outsider or the first of the great Dutch works which helped to stimulate the early Dutch voyages to the East.

Books began to be printed in Portugal around 1487 by German and Flemish printers, one of whom (after 1495) was the influential Valentim Fernandes. Of the forty-eight books still extant published by these printers between 1489 and 1539 just one, the compendium of Fernandes already discussed, deals with the East.[149] In this early period in the history of printing, it was not customary anywhere in Europe, including Spain and Portugal, to produce more than one thousand copies of even the most widely circulated materials in print.[150] Over the remaining years of the century the number of books issued at each printing seems not to have expanded markedly. At mid-century, however, a sharp rise occurs in the total number of titles being published and in the percentage of them which deal with the East. Of one hundred and seventy-five books published between 1540 and 1569, fifteen are on Eastern subjects and eleven are chronicles (including the great studies of Castanheda and Barros) with various sections of differing proportions on the East.[151] Between 1570 and the end of the century, at least one hundred and ninety titles were published; of these sixteen deal directly with Asia and fourteen are chronicles including Eastern matters.[152]

Most of the books dealing with the East were written in Portuguese, and probably enjoyed a wider circulation within Portugal than the religious titles, which were usually in Latin. After 1565, the Jesuit letterbooks printed at Coimbra were often translated into Spanish to make them more readily accessible to the European educated public at large. Since exact figures are bound to be imprecise in matters of this sort, a conservative estimate shows that about 10 per cent of the total number of Portuguese publications between 1540 and

[149] This count based on Manuel II, *op. cit.* (n. 33), Vol. I and the supplement in Vol. III, pp. 274–81. Fernandes printed at Lisbon from 1495 to 1518 (*ibid.*, I, 57). On Fernandes' book see above, pp. 158–59.

[150] See the letter of the officials of the Casa da India (October 3, 1514) to Fernandes, which refers to the fact that the printer has published one thousand copies of the popular *Ordenacões* or laws of King Manuel. Included in Venancio Deslandes, *Documentos para a história da typographia portugueza nos séculos XVI e XVII* (Lisbon, 1888), pp. 6–7. Also cf. below, pp. 183–84 on numbers of books published in Spain. For further printing statistics on the early years see Konrad Burger, *Die Drucker und Verleger in Spanien und Portugal von 1501 bis 1536* . . . (Leipzig, 1913).

[151] This count based on Manuel II, *op. cit.* (n. 33), Vols. II and III.

[152] *Ibid.*

1600 deal with the East. Such a raw figure is misleading, particularly when it is considered that the chronicles, Jesuit letterbooks, and other titles dealing with Eastern matters were often lengthy, multivolumed affairs in contrast to many of the numerous titles classified under religious or governmental decrees which were often little more than pamphlets of limited and temporary interest. It is perhaps more revealing to observe that the number of titles of this period (1540–1600) dealing directly with the East (including a few of the chronicles in this number) outstrips significantly all other categories except for religious works and governmental decrees, and probably exceeds by far the number of printed pages in all categories except religion.[153]

But in the history of the printed book in Spain, as might be expected, Eastern affairs receive less direct attention. The first press was set up at Valencia in 1474, and before 1500, presses were established in twenty-four other Spanish cities.[154] In the sixteenth century, Seville became the greatest single center of printing, but the presses of Alcalá, Barcelona, and Saragossa were not far behind in the number of titles which they issued.[155] At the end of the century, Madrid began to rival Seville as a printing center; its presses turned out at least 769 titles between 1566 and 1600—many of them governmental decrees.[156] While it is difficult to obtain figures for the separate printings, it seems that Spanish presses rarely issued more than one thousand copies at a time.[157] Spanish printers, like those in Portugal, never were able to match the large editions of best-sellers produced in France, Germany, and Italy.[158] The press operated by the Kromberger family at Seville from 1503 to 1557 issued at least 239 books,

153 These conclusions based on study of the three volumes of *ibid.* A reservation must be added, however, because the four hundred-odd items listed in the collection of King Manuel represent just about one-third of the 1,312 items listed in Anselmo, *op. cit.* (n. 33). It is not feasible, however, to use Anselmo for this kind of analysis because he gives little beyond the title, publication data, and location of extant copies. Even so, a quick rundown of his titles shows that at least sixty of them (or about 5 per cent) deal with the East, excluding from this count all those which are not clearly on Eastern subjects by title. Moreover these figures from Anselmo are for the century as a whole, and it should be recalled that only one book (the compilation of Valentim Fernandes) on the East was published in Portugal before mid-century.

154 Konrad Haebler, *The Early Printers of Spain and Portugal* (London, 1897), p. 84.

155 At least 862 titles are known to have been published in Seville between 1476 and 1600. See Francisco Escudero y Perosso, *Tipografía Hispalense: Anales bibliográficos de la ciudad de Sevilla desde el establecimiento de la imprenta hasta fines del siglo XVIII* (Madrid, 1894). The Complutense press at Alcalá published 759 known works of all kinds between 1502 and 1600. See Juan Catalina García López, *Ensayo de una tipografía Complutense* (Madrid, 1899). From the several printing centers of Aragon at least 905 titles were published during the sixteenth century. See Juan M. Sanchez, *Bibliografía Aragonesa del siglo XVI* (2 vols.; Madrid, 1913–14).

156 Count based upon Pérez Pastor, *Bibliografía Madrileña* (3 vols.; Madrid, 1891–1907).

157 At Barcelona, for example, books were issued between 1483 and 1489 in average editions of 483 copies, between 1500 and 1524 in 564 copies, and between 1534 and 1550 in 802 copies. Computations based on an analysis of the manuscripts printed in José Maria Madurell Marimon and Jorgé Rubio y Balaguer (compilers and eds.), *Documentos para la historia de la imprenta en Barcelona (1474–1553)* (Barcelona, 1955). Most of the books which appeared in editions of 1,000 or over were devotional works and grammars.

158 The works of Erasmus were printed and sold in especially large numbers in northern Europe, but such large issues were uncommon everywhere in Europe throughout the sixteenth century.

including the first editions of the various parts of the *Historia general de las Indias* of Oviedo, and the works of Peter Martyr on America.[159] Of 134 titles printed at Alcalá during the decade 1560–69 not one, strictly speaking, was about the East.[160] From 1575 to 1599, the same press published 240 titles, of which just three are unmistakably about the East and are translations of works published earlier in Portugal.[161] For the same period, 160 items were printed at Seville, of which only three relate to Eastern affairs.[162] Of 203 titles published in Aragon during the decade 1590–99, one is unmistakably about the East—Buxeda de Levya's work on Japan published at Saragossa in 1591.[163] The most important book on China, the work of Mendoza, was issued in Spain in its original Castilian version on seven different occasions between 1585 and 1595.[164] From what can be gathered from this sort of quantitative study it appears that a few retrospective works were issued at Seville before 1520, and that thereafter practically nothing was published in Spain on the East until shortly before mid-century. A number of the Spanish works of the latter half of the century, particularly the Jesuit letters, were translations of Portuguese originals, probably for the purpose of giving them wider diffusion in one of the great international languages.

Among the earliest of the chroniclers to bring Asia into his discussion of overseas exploits was a Spaniard, Gonzalo Fernandez de Oviedo y Valdés, named "chronicler of the Indies" by the king of Spain in 1532.[165] While in this post Oviedo completed Part I of his monumental *Historia general y natural de las Indias, islas y tierra-firme del mar océano* and published it at Seville in 1535.[166] The first book of Part II (Book XX of the entire work), which summarizes what was known in Spain on the insular world of Asia, was originally published in 1548[167] and then reissued in 1557. Incidental to his account of the Spanish expeditions of 1519 to 1529, Oviedo incorporates materials into his book based upon information received from participants in the post-Magellan voyages, such as Andrés de Urdaneta. From oral testimony, as well as from the published accounts of Maximilian and Pigafetta, he is able to provide a discussion of early

[159] Haebler, *op. cit.* (n. 154), p. 59. For further discussion see Francis M. Rogers, *The Travels of the Infante Dom Pedro of Portugal* (Cambridge, Mass., 1961), pp. 121–22.

[160] Count based on García López, *op. cit.* (n. 155).

[161] *Ibid.* The three are: a compendium of Jesuit letters (1575), Camoëns *Lusiads* (1580), and Jerónimo Côrte Real's description of a siege of Diu (1597).

[162] Count based on Escudero y Perosso, *op. cit.* (n. 155). The three are: Escalante's book on China (1577), a collection of materials on the Japanese emissaries to Europe (1586), and Acosta's famous *Historia natural* (1590).

[163] Based on Sanchez, *op. cit.* (n. 155).

[164] For a complete review of its publication history see Carlos Sanz, *Primitivas relaçiones de España con Asia y Oceanía* (Madrid, 1958), pp. 386–97.

[165] Swecker, *op. cit.* (n. 148), p. 189.

[166] The only complete edition is that edited in four volumes by José Amador de los Rios for the Royal Academy of History of Madrid between 1851 and 1855.

[167] A copy of this rare book is in the Newberry Library of Chicago. For the dating of it see Agapito Rey, "Book XX of Oviedo's *Historia general y natural de las Indias*," *Romanic Review*, XVII (1927), 52–57.

Spanish activities in the Philippines, of the kingdom of Brunei in Borneo, the terms of trade in the Spice Islands, the people and products of the Ladrones (Marianas), as well as to give one of the fullest accounts of Java produced in the sixteenth century.[168] The *Historia general de las Indias* of Francisco Lopez de Gómara was even more popular than Oviedo's distinguished chronicle. First published at Saragossa in 1552, it was quickly reprinted by other Spanish presses and soon after translated into other European languages.[169] Like Oviedo, Gómara includes a substantial section on the "discovery of the South Seas" in which he discusses in brief compass the insular world of the Spiceries and the Philippines.[170] But, unlike Oviedo, he discourses upon the growth of the Portuguese empire, the Atlantic spice trade, and the effort of the two powers to resolve their differences over the Moluccas at Badajoz-Elvas. In both these chronicles the Moluccas are at the center of the stage, while the great continental states and peoples of Asia cut almost no figure at all. The view of the East that readers of these two renowned Spanish chroniclers were given was clearly limited to generalities about everything but the Spiceries, the Philippines, and Borneo.

Long before 1550 the Portuguese had available in Lisbon an extensive documentation on all parts of Asia. Aside from the incidental data to be gleaned from the reports of merchants, officials, and missionaries,[171] the geography of Asia and the social practices of its inhabitants were the subjects of several substantial narratives. But these earliest writings were not published in Portugal during the sixteenth century. The first of these pioneering books still extant is the *Suma oriental* of Tomé Pires, written between 1512 and 1515, and presumably dispatched shortly thereafter to the Casa da India, where it was kept as a secret document.[172] Addressed to King Manuel, Pires' work, while mainly devoted to matters of trade, is especially notable for its discussions of places east of Bengal. In writing about India itself, Pires describes at some length the ports of the west coast and their connections with the hinterland, the political and economic situation in Gujarat, Ceylon, and Bengal, and a good deal about the social practices of the peoples of various coastal areas of the

[168] See the summary in Swecker, *op. cit.* (n. 148), pp. 191–99.

[169] For a list of the editions in all languages see Henry R. Wagner, *The Spanish Southwest, 1542–1794* (Berkeley, 1924), pp. 50–81. For further detail on the sources of this chronicle see the same author's "Francisco Lopez de Gomara and His Works," *Proceedings of the American Antiquarian Society*, LVIII (1949), 263–68.

[170] See *Historia general de las Indias* (Madrid, 1932), Pt. I, pp. 142–45.

[171] A compilation of such documents, organized chronologically for the period before 1550, may be found in António da Silva Rêgo, *Documentacão para a história das missões do padroado português do Oriente* (Lisbon, 1947–50), Vols. I–IV. Documents for the critical years 1538–52 were assembled after 1545 under the auspices of D. João de Castro. These reports, numbering around six thousand, have been preserved almost totally. Very few periods of Indian history can boast such excellent documentation. A calendar of these materials written by native kings and Portuguese officials, merchants, and sailors may be found in Georg Schurhammer, S.J., *Die zeitgenössischen Quellen zur Geschichte Portugiesisch-Asiens und seiner Nachbarländer zur Zeit des Hl. Franz Xaver (1538–1552)* (Leipzig, 1932).

[172] Armando Cortesão (ed.), *op. cit.* (n. 84), I, lxv and lxxiii.

subcontinent. The materials on Ceylon, India, continental southwest Asia, China, Japan, Borneo, and the Philippines were published by Ramusio in 1550 with occasional phrases or sentences omitted.[173] Information on Malacca, Sumatra, Java, and the Spiceries was apparently so closely watched in Lisbon that Ramusio's agents were unable to acquire copies of Pires' descriptions of them for publication. They therefore remained unpublished until 1944.

The *Book* of Duarte Barbosa,[174] written around 1518, is focused much more on India than is Pires' earlier account. Its author arrived in India with the fleet of Cabral in 1501. Except for two brief trips back to Portugal, Barbosa lived and worked on the Malabar Coast during the entire period before he wrote his report. As a royal factor, he was in a position to study commerce closely. He also possessed the decided advantage of knowing the Malayālam language. Barbosa is particularly informative, as might be expected, on the country, the people, and products of South India and the Malabar region. His knowledge of other places is far less detailed and profound. Like Pires', Barbosa's manuscript was probably kept in Lisbon under lock and key, even though it may be assumed that copies of it were permitted to circulate to selected persons.[175] The Italian version, incorporated in Ramusio's first volume of 1550, was first translated at Vittoria around 1524 from a Portuguese original by the Genoese emissary Martin Centurion, with the aid of Diogo Ribeiro, a Portuguese cartographer in the service of King Charles I.[176] Until the nineteenth century this was the only version of Barbosa's *Book* known to scholars. In 1812, a Portuguese version was discovered and published;[177] not in Barbosa's hand, it is presumed to be a copy of some unlocated original. The differences between the Ramusio and the other versions are slight and relatively unimportant from our viewpoint. What is significant for us is that Ramusio, not the Portuguese, made available as early as 1550 two of the best firsthand accounts of India and points farther east that would appear in the sixteenth century.

Other manuscript materials of various sorts were collected in Lisbon, perhaps at Barros' instigation. Although some of the most important descriptions were not printed, they were used as sources by the chroniclers. Of this class of unpublished source material there are many examples, but two of them are particularly worthy of comment. The letters of the two captives, Cristavão

---

[173] Ramusio, *op. cit.* (n. 117), Vol. I, fols. 349–63.

[174] On the much debated question of his identity see Eduardo Reis, *Duarte Barbosa, pioneiro revelador dos costumes das Índias; relação biográfica* (Macao, 1948), pp. 86–92; for further details see Swecker, *op. cit.* (n. 148), pp. 20–30. Both authors conclude that he was *not* the same Duarte Barbosa who sailed with Magellan. In fact, it is not possible to be absolutely certain of his identity.

[175] Dames (ed.), *op. cit.* (n. 85), I, lix–lx.

[176] See the preface to the English translation of Henry E. J. Stanley, *A Description of the Coasts of East Africa and Malabar* ("Hakluyt Society Publications," Old Ser. Vol. XXXV [London, 1866]), p. i.

[177] Academia dos Sciencias de Lisboa, *Collecção de noticias para a história e geografia das nações ultramarinas* ... (Lisbon, 1812), II, 231–394. Translated into English and annotated by Dames (ed.), *op. cit.* (n. 85).

Vieira and Vasco Calvo, evidently prepared in 1524 in a Cantonese prison, are probably the first comprehensive eyewitness accounts of life in China to reach Portugal.[178] The letters possibly arrived in Lisbon as early as 1527, and are of utmost importance because they describe the first Portuguese mission to Peking of 1520–21 and relate the terms set by the Chinese for international relations. Two manuscript narratives on India were also available in Lisbon before 1540. One was written by Domingo Paes, around 1520, and the other by Fernão Nuniz, about fifteen years later.[179] Both these documents were apparently sent from Goa around 1537 to Barros in response to his request for more detailed information in India.[180] The Paes account is particularly valuable for its description of Vijayanagar at the peak of its glory as the Hindu capital of south India. Nuniz, a Portuguese horse-trader who spent three years in Vijayanagar, was fascinated with the great city, inquired into its traditional history, and recorded his findings. Both accounts are well supplied with personal observations of the contemporary scene, and together they still constitute two of the most important foreign sources for historians of Vijayanagar.

While these firsthand reports were being channeled back to Lisbon, a history of the Portuguese in the East was being systematically prepared by Fernão Lopes de Castanheda (1500–1559).[181] A native of Santarem and the son of a judge, Castanheda had received a classical education in his youth and, according to his own testimony, read avidly in the histories of antiquity. For a short while he was a member of the Dominican order, but left the friars before setting out in 1528 for India in the company of his father. The next ten years he spent in Asia apparently traveling extensively, and may at one time have reached the Moluccas.[182] It was in this decade also that he began to compile materials for his history and to acquaint himself with great numbers of documents and with people who had taken part in salient events. Around 1538 he returned to Portugal in frail health and straitened financial circumstances. He settled at Coimbra where he became associated with the Faculty of Arts as archivist and librarian. While fulfilling his duties in these modest posts, Castanheda continued to interview persons who had been in the East and to use the resources of the library to augment and check his information as he began to write his narrative. Finally, after twenty years of painstaking research, interviewing, and writing, he published in 1551 the first book of his *História do descobrimento e conquista da India pelos Portuguezes*.

Originals of the first edition of his first book are now extremely rare, though copies of it are to be found in the Ajuda Library (Lisbon), the British Museum,

---

[178] The Portuguese texts and English translations of these letters are given in D. Ferguson, "Letters from Portuguese Captives in Canton, Written in 1534 and 1536 [both actually written in 1524, see below, p. 734n]," *Indian Antiquary*, XXX (1901) 467–91; XXXI (1902), 53–65.

[179] First published in David Lopes (ed.), *Chronica dos Reis de Bisnaga* (Lisbon, 1890); translated into English in Robert Sewell, *A Forgotten Empire* (*Vijayanagar*) (London, 1900), pp. 235–398.

[180] Sewell, *op. cit.* (n. 179), pp. v–vii.

[181] On his scholarly activities see Manuel II, *op. cit.* (n. 33), II, 277.

[182] Diogo do Couto, *Da Asia* (Lisbon, 1778), Vol. IV, Bk. v, chap. i.

and the collection of the kings of Portugal.[183] So few copies have survived, it seems, because Castanheda was forced, shortly after publication, to withdraw his book from circulation as it wounded the sensibilities of some people in high positions.[184] While revising the offending first book, Castanheda published the second and third books in 1552, and two years later the fourth, fifth, sixth, and seventh books came off the press at Coimbra. The revised version of the first book, which gives greater credit in its earlier chapters to Dom Manuel than did the previous version, was also issued in 1554. Two years after Castanheda's death in 1559, his sons published the eighth book at Coimbra. No part of the ninth book was known until 1929,[185] and the tenth book has not yet come to light.

Aside from his personal experiences in Asia and his interviews with participants, Castanheda's *História* was dependent upon a number of reports which he apparently saw either in Goa or Lisbon. His account of the first voyage of Vasco da Gama derives in large measure from the anonymous *Roteiro* prepared by a participant.[186] He also refers at several points to the *Suma oriental* of Tomé Pires,[187] and mentions the pilot and cartographer, Francisco Rodrigues, who prepared data and maps of the Portuguese enterprise in the East.[188] He depends heavily upon Barbosa at particular points in his narrative, but without always acknowledging his indebtedness. The rest of Castanheda's information seems to have been taken from other official reports, the testimony of participants, and from personal observation. The care with which he used his farrago of sources contributes greatly to the accuracy of the *História*. For it is remarkable, when we recollect that no previous writer had prepared a comprehensive narrative of the genesis of the Portuguese empire, that Castanheda was able, largely through his personal enterprise, to provide his own generation and posterity with a factual record, if not a brilliant narrative,[189] of the Asiatic activities of the Portuguese from the voyage of Vasco da Gama up to 1542, the end of Dom Garcia de Noronha's tenure as viceroy of India. And more than this, he was able through his personal observations to give greater substance to his account by describing in some detail the peculiar customs and techniques

---

[183] Manuel II, *op. cit.* (n. 33), II, 274.

[184] *Ibid.*, pp. 274–76.

[185] Couto claims that the last two books of Castanheda's history had been suppressed by royal command and that their author was charged with being excessively fond of the truth. Whatever the merits of Couto's charge may be, it is certainly true that Castanheda's last two books were not published in the sixteenth century. Thirty-one chapters of the ninth book (dealing with events of 1539–42) were found in the papers of Maffei (cf. below, pp. 325–26) preserved in the archives of the Society of Jesus in Rome. Edited by C. Wessels, S.J., in *Lopes de Castanheda, Historia do descobrimento e conquista da India pelos Portugueses (1552–1561). Thirty-one Chapters of the Lost "Livro IX" Re-discovered and Now Published for the First Time* (The Hague, 1929).

[186] Ravenstein (ed.), *op. cit.* (n. 23), pp. xx and xxiv.

[187] Armando Cortesão (ed.), *op. cit.* (n. 84), I, xx.

[188] *Ibid.*, p. lxxviii.

[189] For a collection of the evaluations of the work of Castanheda see the introduction to the standard edition of Pedro de Azevedo (ed.), *História do descobrimento & conquista da India pelos Portugueses por Fernão Lopes de Castanheda* (Coimbra, 1924), I, xvi–xxi.

followed in India and thereby to make more explicit the cultural problems of Europeans in the East.

Castanheda was more widely translated into other European languages than were his contemporaries who wrote about the Portuguese in the East. Nicolas de Grouchy, originally from Bordeaux and a professor in the Faculty of Arts at Coimbra from about 1548 to 1550, translated Castanheda's original version of his first book into French and had it printed in Paris in 1553.[190] The following year Grouchy's translation was republished under a somewhat different title at Antwerp.[191] It was also in 1554 that a Spanish version was printed at Antwerp.[192] Not long thereafter a copy of the Spanish translation found its way into the Fugger library at Augsburg.[193] In Rome meanwhile an Italian translation appeared in 1556, evidently prepared by A. de Cravaliz from Grouchy's French version.[194] An English translation of Castanheda's first book, one of the very few Portuguese works rendered into English during the sixteenth century, appeared at London in 1582.[195] It was the work of Nicholas Lichefield, probably a pseudonym for Thomas Nicholas, a Tudor translator of several Iberian works.[196] It was rare at this period for translations to be made directly from Portuguese, and it is possible that Lichefield derived his text from the anonymous Spanish version of 1554.[197] While Castanheda's first book appeared in a number of languages, it was not until 1577–78 that some of his other books were translated out of Portuguese. In those years Alfonso Ulloa, who was also a translator of Barros, issued an Italian version of the first seven books at Venice.[198] John Dee, the sixteenth-century mathematician and geographer, owned Ulloa's Italian translation and the Spanish version of Castanheda, and he classified

---

[190] Bibliographical data in G. Atkinson, *La littérature géographique française de la Renaissance* (Paris, 1927), p. 83. As an illustration of the low regard in which Grouchy held Portuguese learning and language, see the introduction to his translation in which he caustically remarks that the Portuguese writers, presumably meaning Castanheda, "have had much more experience than learning." As quoted in the introduction of Azevedo to his edition of the *História, op. cit.* (n. 189), pp. xv–xvi. Also consult Georges le Gentil, "Nicolas de Grouchy, traducteur de Castanheda," *Bulletin des études portugaises et de l'Institut français au Portugal*, New Ser., Vol. IV (1937), fasc. 1, p. 32. The author points out that Grouchy was subsequently the teacher of Montaigne at the Collège de Guyenne.

[191] This edition reissued in 1576. See Atkinson, *op. cit.* (n. 190), pp. 87–88.

[192] Bibliographical data in J. Peiters-Fontaines, *Bibliographie des impressions espagnols des Pays-Bas* (Louvain and Antwerp, 1933), p. 82.

[193] Listed as No. 171 in the Fugger shelf catalogue and presumably still in the State Library at Munich. K. L. Selig, "A German Collection of Spanish Books," *Bibliothèque d'Humanisme et Renaissance. Travaux et documents*, XIX (1957), 66.

[194] A. Palau y Dulcet, *Manuel del librero hispano-americano* (Barcelona, 1923–27), IV, 262.

[195] *The First Booke of the Historie of the Discoveries and Conquest of the East Indies by the Portingals, in the Time of King Don John, the Second of That Name.* Reprinted with notes in Robert Kerr (ed.). *A General History and Collection of Voyages and Travels* (London, 1824), II, 292–505.

[196] E. G. R. Taylor, *Tudor Geography, 1485–1583* (London, 1930), p. 190.

[197] Henry Thomas, "English Translations of Portuguese Books before 1640." in *Miscelânea de estudos em honora de D. Carolina Michaëlis de Vasconcellos* (Vol. XI of *Revista da Universidade de Coimbra* [Coimbra, 1933]), pp. 691–92. It should be noted, however, that Lichefield in the dedication to his translation which he addressed to Sir Francis Drake says that he made "this simple translation out of the Portingale tongue."

[198] *Historia dell'Indie Orientale, scoperte, & conquistate da Portoghesi . . .* (2 vols.; Venice, 1577–78).

it as one of those books which he considered to be a most important manual for Eastern navigation.[199]

While Castanheda's books were being published at Coimbra, the great João de Barros (*ca.* 1496–1570) began printing at Lisbon in 1552 his *Décadas da Ásia*. The Livy of Portuguese historiography was probably born at Vizeu, a small village north and east of Coimbra.[200] The bastard son of a *fidalgo*, young Barros was educated in the palace of the heir apparent to the Portuguese throne. Here he received excellent training in the classics. Around 1520 he caught the eye of King Manuel by publishing a vivacious novel. Realizing that Barros was a man of talent and training, Manuel encouraged him to go ahead with his idea of writing the history of Portuguese enterprise in Asia. Under King John III, his enthusiastic patron, Barros was sent to Guinea for a short while, his only visit to the overseas world. From 1525 to 1528 he acted as treasurer of the Casa da India. In 1530, to escape the plague, Barros left Lisbon for his country home near Pombal. It was apparently in 1531, during his sojourn away from the capital, that he began writing his history. Two years later he returned to Lisbon and assumed the post of Factor, a position which made him managing executive of the African and Asian colonies and the spice trade. For the remainder of his life, and while performing the duties of his exacting office, Barros spent his free time compiling and writing his great chronicle. Modeled on the history of Livy, the first draft of the *Ásia* was completed in 1539. Thereafter Barros continually revised and expanded it as new information became available.

The first volume described by the subtitle as *Deeds Done by the Portuguese in Their Discovery and Conquest of the Seas and Lands of the East* was published at Lisbon in 1552. The *Décadas da Ásia*, as the four decades are called collectively, might be categorized as a chronicle-narrative organized on geographical lines. The first decade covers the background from Prince Henry to 1505, the end of the first decade of King Manuel I's reign. The second decade, first published in 1553, deals with Portuguese activities in the East from 1505 to 1515. The third decade, first published in 1563, carries the story down to 1525 and includes much information on southern and eastern Asia, and the fourth, covering the period from 1526 to 1538 (through the first siege of Diu), was not published until long after Barros' death. The original draft of the fifth and last decade was edited and revised for publication by Philip III's cosmographer, João Baptista Lavanha, and it was printed in Madrid in 1615. Hence, since we are surveying only what was actually published and circulated during the sixteenth century, we shall omit this last decade from our considerations as well as the *Décadas* of Diogo do Couto (1542–1616), which continued Barros' *Ásia* but were not published until later dates.

[199] Taylor, *op. cit.* (n. 196), pp. 219–20.
[200] On Barros' career see C. R. Boxer, "Three Historians of Asia (Barros, Couto, and Bocarro)," *Instituto Português de Hongkong, Boletim*, No. 1 (July, 1948), pp. 18–24; and Manuel II, *op. cit.* (n. 33), II, 286–301.

Because of his official position, Barros had at his disposal the full facilities, documents, and reports of the Casa da India. All the Portuguese manuscript sources now extant—such as the accounts of Tomé Pires, Domingo Paes, and Fernão Nuniz—were used in the preparation of the *Décadas*. For geographical locations he depended implicitly upon the written and oral accounts of the pilots and navigators who had sailed in Eastern waters and, on their testimony, did not hesitate to point out the mistakes of the Ptolemaic geographers. Nor was he satisfied to use the evidence of European observers exclusively. He was constantly trying to procure native accounts of the Eastern regions. For his remarks on India, he assembled Persian, Arabic, and Indian manuscripts and bought educated slaves to translate them for him. He also had Chinese books and a Chinese slave as a translator. He likewise sought to assemble information from the oral tradition of places which had no written histories. But, whether his sources were of European or Asian provenance, he tried, according to his own statement, to use them judiciously in order to produce a balanced narrative without "too much of any one thing."[201] The result of his labors was a history that stands as one of the classics of Portuguese literature and of European historiography.

The rest of Europe was not long left in the dark about Barros' great work. In the 1554 edition of Volume I (fols. 426–36) of Ramusio's *Navigationi*, the great collector published in Italian six chapters about West Africa and India extracted from the first *Década*. The first two *Décadas* in their entirety were rendered into Italian before the third was even published in its original Portuguese.[202] In 1562, Alfonso Ulloa, who later translated Castanheda, brought them out at Venice and dedicated his version to Guglielmo Gonzaga, the Duke of Mantua. Other Italians were also aware of Barros' work, and eventually his portrait was placed in Venice among those of the literary great, even though contemporaries were not unanimous in praising his book.[203] Pope Pius IV is said to have placed his portrait next to the statue of Ptolemy in the Vatican.[204] The first two of his *Décadas* in their original Portuguese versions found their way into the Fugger collection.[205] The catalogue of John Dee's library dated 1583 includes the Italian translation of Barros.[206] But for all Barros' immediate fame, the *Décadas* were not republished in Portugal during the sixteenth century and were not translated as widely as the work of Castanheda. In a letter of 1597 addressed to King Philip II of Spain, Diogo do Couto refers ironically to the treatment accorded the greatest of Portugal's histories:

---

[201] As quoted from Barros' prologue to his second decade in Manuel II, *op. cit.* (n. 33), II, 300.

[202] Bibliographical data in N. F. Haym, *Notizia de libri raro nella lingua italiana* (London, 1726), p. 87.

[203] For a highly critical evaluation by a contemporary see the comments of the Florentine Humanist, Filippo Sassetti, in E. Marcucci (ed), *Lettere edite e inedite di Filippo Sassetti* (Florence, 1855), pp. 417–19.

[204] Cf. Manuel II, *op. cit.* (n. 33), II, 295–96.

[205] Selig, *op. cit.* (n. 193), p. 53.

[206] Taylor, *op. cit.* (n. 196), p. 199.

The *Décadas* of João de Barros, our fellow countryman . . . were so esteemed by us, that there was no edition after the first, which has been so consumed by time, that I do not know if there are ten copies left in Portugal and even one in India.[207]

In addition to the great historians' extended general accounts of the discoveries, there appeared in Lisbon during 1557 a book called *Commentarios de Afonso Dalboquerque*.[208] Actually this was a narrative compiled by Braz de Albuquerque, the son of the great Portuguese conqueror and governor. To prepare his work the son collected, extracted, edited and commented upon the letters written by his father to King Manuel in the period before death overtook Albuquerque in 1515. The resulting work evidently excited some interest, for the author republished it in a "corrected and augmented" version in 1576 at Lisbon.[209] The younger Albuquerque wrote his book to celebrate the deeds of his famous father which were, as he complains, touched upon only briefly in the general histories of the Portuguese conquest.[210] For our purposes the *Commentarios* is of value mainly because it provides additional details on India and southeast Asia from a firsthand observer and corroborates statements which appear in the more general works.

Of similar collateral value, but far greater general importance, is the work of Garcia da Orta, Portuguese physician and Humanist, who lived in India for almost thirty-five years (*ca.* 1535–*ca.* 1570).[211] Born probably at Elvas near the Spanish frontier, Orta received his education at the universities of Salamanca and Alcalá de Henares in Spain. On his return to Portugal in either 1525 or 1526, he practiced medicine for a year or so and then began to lecture on natural philosophy at the University of Lisbon. In 1534 he shipped out to India in the armada commanded by his patron, Martim Affonso de Sousa (governor of Portuguese India from 1542 to 1545). A man of erudition and curiosity, Orta

[207] As quoted in Manuel II, *op. cit.* (n. 33), II, 288–89. Since the sixteenth century, Barros has been translated into French (1696), Dutch (1706–7), and German (1821). Except for excerpts, the *Décadas* have not yet been translated into English. What is very puzzling is the question of what happened to Barros' other works on Asia, especially the *Geographia* to which he refers repeatedly in the *Décadas*. It is generally assumed that both the geography and a commercial handbook of the oriental trade were completed in large part before his death in 1570. So far, however, the manuscripts, if they exist, have not come to light. See Boxer, *op. cit.* (n. 200), pp. 19–21. Faria e Sousa declared in the seventeenth century that neither Castanheda nor Barros was widely read, one of the reasons being the inordinate length of their chronicles. See Bell, *op. cit.* (n. 135), p. 193, n. 2.

[208] Five copies of this rare first edition are known to be extant. For additional data see Manuel II, *op. cit.* (n. 33), II, 496–506.

[209] This work is more readily available today than the first edition. See *ibid.*, III, 98–99. A third edition appeared in 1774 and was translated into English and edited by Walter De Gray Birch as *The Commentaries of the Great Afonso Dalboquerque, Second Viceroy of India* (4 vols.; "Hakluyt Society Publications," Old Ser., Vols. LIII, LV, LXII, LXIX [London, 1875–84]). A more complete edition of Albuquerque's correspondence on which these early works were based is to be found in the collection published by the Portuguese Academy of Sciences under the title *Cartas de Afonso de Albuquerque* (7 vols.; Lisbon, 1884–1935).

[210] Cf. Braz de Albuquerque's preface as translated in Manuel II, *op. cit.* (n. 33), II, 501.

[211] See for details the excellent biography by Francisco Manuel Carlos de Melho, Conde de Ficalho (by which title he is usually known), called *Garcia da Orta e o seu tempo* (Lisbon, 1886; rev. ed., 1898). For shorter accounts see Silva Carvalho, *Garcia da Orta* (Lisbon, 1934) and Manuel II, *op. cit.* (n. 33), II, 652–53.

acquired from his practice of medicine and his daily experiences a vast knowledge of the botany, medicinals, and spices of western India. Aside from his lengthy sojourn in the Goa and Bombay regions, he visited Diu, Cambay, Cochin, and Ceylon. And, because he was curious about everything, he also learned by report about affairs in Vijayanagar, Delhi, Berar, and Bengal, as well as those farther east.

This information he published at Goa in 1563 in his *Coloquios dos simples, e drogas he cousas mediçinais da India. . . .*[212] The seventh book to be published in Portuguese India, this work was badly marred by the poor work of the German printer, Johannes de Endem.[213] Orta was possibly the most learned Portuguese to reside in India permanently during the sixteenth century. The dialogue form in which he casts his *Coloquios* shows something of the intellectual conflict that went on within him between the European Humanist and the practical observer. The two leading conversationalists are a fictitious Dr. Ruano (Portuguese for "the man in the street"), a devotee of the schools, and Dr. Orta, the pragmatic physician. In constructing their imaginary conversations, Orta quotes the opinions of over fifty ancient and contemporary writers on medical and scientific subjects. In most cases the learned of Europe come off second best, as he delights in twitting the ancients. "Do not try to frighten me," says Orta, "with Dioscorides or Galen, because I merely speak the truth and say what I know."[214] He asserts in another place: "For me the testimony of an eyewitness is worth more than that of all the physicians, and all the fathers of medicine who wrote on false information."[215] Or in commenting about cinnamon: "I say that you can get more knowledge now from the Portuguese in one day than was known to the Romans after a hundred years."[216]

Of the Indian literature on medicine Orta seems to have had no knowledge, probably because he did not know Sanskrit. It was largely through informants and personal observations that he acquired his encyclopedic information of the botanicals of India. But the *Coloquios* contain much more than simple descriptions of plants and their therapeutic properties. In connection with his visit to the court of Nizam Shah of Ahmednagar, Orta discusses episodes in the history

[212] At least fourteen copies of this work are still extant. See Manuel II, *op. cit.* (n. 33), II, 647. On the various editions and translations of the *Coloquios* see Ficalho, *op. cit.* (n. 211), pp. 367–92. Ficalho also published the most authoritative edition in two volumes of the *Coloquios* (Lisbon, 1891–95). An English translation of Ficalho's edition by Sir Clements Markham (ed. and trans.) entitled *Colloquies on the Simples and Drugs of India* (London, 1913) was published under the auspices of the Hakluyt Society. Unfortunately, Markham's work as a translator and editor leaves much to be desired. See Harry Bernstein and Bailey W. Diffie, "Sir Clements Markham as a Translator," *Hispanic American Historical Review*, XVII (1937), 546–57; also consult Swecker, *op. cit.* (n. 148), pp. 244–45. Although I have cited Markham's translation, I have checked the references which I have used from his work against Ficalho's edition.

[213] On Johannes de Endem see Anselmo, *op. cit.* (n. 33), p. 151; for a list of the books printed at Goa see A. K. Priolkar, *The Printing Press in India* (Bombay, 1958), pp. 14–17.

[214] As translated in Markham (ed.), *op. cit.* (n. 212), p. 60.

[215] *Ibid.*, p. 125.

[216] *Ibid.*, pp. 127–28.

of the Deccan. The caves of Elephanta and the mines of Golconda are described for the first time in a European language. Aside from a number of such excursions into contemporary events and descriptions of natural and constructed marvels, Orta's book is noted in scientific circles even yet for its precise information on *materia medica*.[217] For contemporary discussions of the use of spices, both in Europe and India, as condiments, drugs, and incense no other sixteenth-century source rivals it.

Four years after its appearance in India, the Flemish physician Charles de L'écluse (often called Clusius),[218] published at the Plantin press in Antwerp during 1567 an abbreviated Latin translation of Orta's work. L'écluse, who had been the tutor of Anton Fugger's sons, escorted Jakob Fugger on an Iberian visit during 1564–65. It was evidently while on this tour that he acquired a copy of Orta's book, which he began to translate into Latin immediately after his return to the Netherlands in 1565.[219] Dedicated to Jakob Fugger, L'écluse's Latin version[220] of Orta was revised repeatedly and republished by Plantin four times before the end of the sixteenth century.[221] In 1576 Annibal Briganti brought out at Venice an Italian translation of L'écluse's version of Orta.

In 1578, two years after L'écluse's adaptation was published in Antwerp, another version of Orta's work appeared at Burgos in Spain. The work of Cristobal de Acosta,[222] this narrative, based on Orta's *Coloquios*, was entitled *Tractado de las drogas, y medicinas de las Indias Orientales, con sus plantas debuxadas al biuo*. A native of Portuguese Africa, Acosta had traveled extensively in Persia, India, and China as he followed eastward the course of empire. While in India, he became acquainted with Orta and his book. Because the original was so poorly printed and lacked illustrations, Acosta decided to prepare a more accurate version of Orta's work and to amplify it with illustrations of plants and animals which he drew while observing them in their natural state. On his return to Europe he settled in Burgos where he accepted a post as surgeon in 1576. Two years later the *Tractado*, his most famous book,[223] made its appearance.

The *Tractado*, while based on the *Coloquios*, contained many independent observations. Acosta is in no way indebted to L'écluse, since he worked exclusively from Orta's Portuguese original. In form, Acosta's book is quite different from Orta's, inasmuch as he abandons the dialogue style of the

[217] See F. A. Flückiger, "Indische Pharmakognosie," *Archiv der Pharmacie*, XXII (1884), 253; also see references at various places in F. A. Flückiger and G. Hanbury, *Pharmacographia* (London, 1874).

[218] For his intellectual biography see Johannes Theunisz, *Carolus Clusius, het markwaardige leven van een pionier der wetenschap* (Amsterdam, 1939).

[219] *Ibid.*, pp. 30–32; also Ficalho (ed.), *op. cit.* (n. 211), p. 372.

[220] Entitled *Aromatum et Simplicium aliquot medicamentorum apud Indos nascentium historia. Nunc vero primum Latina facta, et in Epitomen contracta a Carlo Clusio Atrebate.*

[221] Theunisz, *op. cit.* (n. 218), p. 107.

[222] Details in Joaquin Olemedilla y Puig, *Estudio histórico de la vida y escritos del sabio médico, botánico, y escritor del siglo XVI, Cristobal de Acosta* (Madrid, 1899); also see Swecker, *op. cit.* (n. 148), pp. 240–43.

[223] On his other works see Swecker, *op. cit.* (n. 148), pp. 246–48.

Coloquios in favor of straight narrative, and necessarily rearranges the order in which he discusses particular items. Although each work contains descriptions and observations not to be found in the other, the two are substantially the same. The most striking contribution of Acosta was his inclusion of thirty-seven woodcuts which depict faithfully, if not artistically, some of the most unusual and hence exotic plants and animals discussed in Orta's and his own work. In 1582, Plantin published L'écluse's abbreviated translation[224] of Acosta's *Tractado* and reissued it in the collected works of L'écluse published in 1593.[225] Acosta's work also had two further Spanish editions of 1582 and 1592.[226] In 1585 it was published at Venice in an Italian translation.[227]

Like Orta, António Galvão (d. 1557) spent a number of years in the East, where he served as a soldier and as an administrator for the crown. In 1536 he was appointed governor of the Moluccas for a three-year term, with his head-quarters on the island of Ternate. The period of Galvão's tenure was devoted to the establishment of the rule of law over both the natives and the Portuguese. He took a genuine interest in the problems of the islanders, sought to introduce European techniques in agriculture and construction, and encouraged the intro-duction of Christianity as a civilizing and stabilizing force. Galvão was so popular on Ternate that he was proffered the kingship by the natives to keep him from departing. He nevertheless left the Moluccas to his duly appointed successor and returned to Portugal around 1540. In the seventeen years preceding his death in 1557, the retired administrator and soldier occupied himself with writing a history of the Moluccas and putting together a narrative of the discoveries.

At Galvão's death his unpublished manuscripts were entrusted to his friend, Francisco de Sousa Tavares. Shortly thereafter, Tavares, possibly in the interests of security was instructed to turn the history of the Moluccas over to Damião de Góis,[228] head of the royal archives and official historian in charge of preparing the chronicle of King Manuel's reign. In Galvão's *Tratado . . . dos descobrimentos* (1563),[229] which was prepared for the press by Tavares, there is to be found no systematic treatment of southeast Asia or the Moluccas. Nevertheless, the incidental and scattered references to such matters, as, for example, the Spanish expeditions to the Moluccas, provide the patient scholar with references for which no other contemporary source exists. In general, it is clear from the fate suffered by Galvão's papers, including the disappearance of his history of the

---

[224] Dedicated to Duke William IV of Hesse, this book was entitled *Aromatium et medicamentorum in orientali India nascentium liber.*
[225] See Theunisz, *op. cit.* (n. 218), p. 107.
[226] Swecker, *op. cit.* (n. 148), p. 246.
[227] *Trattato di Christoforo Acosta* in the Bibliothèque Nationale, Paris.
[228] Swecker, *op. cit.* (n. 148), p. 113, n. 3.
[229] The standard critical edition is by the Visconde de Lagoa and Elaine Sanceau (eds.), *António Galvão. Tratado dos descobrimentos. Terceira edição* (Porto, 1944). Vice-Admiral Bethune edited and republished the Hakluyt translation of 1601 under the title *The Discoveries of the World from Their First Original unto the Year of Our Lord 1555* ("Hakluyt Society Publications," Old Ser., Vol. XXX [London, 1872]).

Moluccas, that information on the Spiceries was still classified as a state secret until about 1565.[230]

The historians of the reign of King Manuel, Góis and Jerónimo Osório, show surprisingly little interest in Asian affairs and derive most of their materials on the East from books published earlier. The *Crónica do felicíssimo Rei Dom Manuel* (1566–67)[231] of Góis has only the most general observations to make about trade, products, and peoples of the East. Strangely, in view of the vast amount of published material on continental Asia, Góis has almost nothing to say about Portuguese activities in Pegu and Siam. The only places which receive more than incidental mention are India, Ceylon, Malacca, Java, and China. Although he had Galvão's history of the Moluccas in his charge, he evidently made no use of it except perhaps for materials on Java. His main contribution is his account of Java, which far surpasses in detail anything contained in the earlier chroniclers. While China receives a more detailed treatment than many other places, Góis seems to rely heavily on Castanheda for his other materials.[232] Osório's Latin history of Manuel's reign,[233] which was designed for consumption in Europe at large, relies heavily on Góis for its references to Asia.[234] Published at Lisbon in 1571, it was soon translated into other languages and won the praises of such luminaries as Montaigne and Lopé de Vega. The only departure from Góis on Eastern matters comes in his treatment of China, for which he seems to have used Barros and possibly the work of Gaspar da Cruz.[235]

The poetic hymn of praise to the pioneering Portuguese, the *Lusiads* of Luis de Camoëns (1542–80), was first published in 1572, the year after the publication of Osório's history. Following a hectic career in Portugal itself, Camoëns was exiled to India in 1553. For the next fourteen years he led a swashbuckling life at Goa, Macao, and elsewhere, serving his nation as soldier and administrator, and writing extraordinary lyrical poetry. It was during his years in the East that he came to appreciate the epic proportions of the Portuguese enterprise and to prepare his own poetic version of it. Near the end of his days in India, he settled down in Goa and made warm friends of Diogo do Couto, the historian,[236] and Garcia da Orta, herbalist supreme. Orta, a great collector of books,

---

[230] Gabriel Rebello, who spent thirteen years in the Moluccas, had prepared by 1569 his *Informação das cousas de Maluco*. Though it was later used by Couto extensively, it was not published until 1856.

[231] The modern edition was published in four volumes at Coimbra in 1926.

[232] Swecker, *op. cit.* (n. 148), pp. 117–18. His addition to Castanheda's account is to be found in Góis' remark that Fernão Peres d'Andrade brought back from China, subsequent to his visit there in 1517–18, three religious figurines and other things for King Manuel.

[233] *De rebus Emmanuelis regis Lusitaniae invictissimi virtute et auspicio gestis libri duodecim.*

[234] Swecker, *op. cit.* (n. 148), pp. 118–20.

[235] For details on Cruz, see below, pp. 742, 748.

[236] Couto spent the best part of half a century in India, where he was an administrator of trade and keeper of the Goa archives. His *Décadas* were not published until the seventeenth century, perhaps because they dealt with matters too contemporary. See Bell, *op. cit.* (n. 135), pp. 195–98. The same can probably be said about Gaspar Corrêa's (*ca.* 1495–*ca.* 1565) *Lendas da India* which was not published until the nineteenth century.

probably opened his library to the poet. Though it is next to impossible to trace the literary sources of the *Lusiads*, it is likely that Camoëns had available both in Goa and Lisbon, after his return to the capital in 1570, a substantial number of chronicles, accounts of sieges and shipwrecks, and Jesuit letters.[237] From these literary materials as well as his own experiences, the poet constructed the epic of the Portuguese nation. By the time of his death the *Lusiads* had been published twice in Lisbon and had been translated into Spanish (1580). Throughout the last generation of the sixteenth century, the *Lusiads* was widely read in Iberia as it quickly became the symbol of national pride about past achievements in an era of Portuguese subjection. In poetic circles the stanzas of Camoëns were both extolled and reviled by contemporaries. Even its factual detail became a source for more prosaic writers on the East; Linschoten evidently knew it well and borrowed from it in the preparation of his book.[238]

A number of the Portuguese works published after mid-century deal with the dramatic sieges of Diu and Malacca or the horrors of piracy and shipwreck on the high seas.[239] Other books by Iberian secular writers, such as that of Bernardino de Escalante, deal with individual countries; these works will be taken up in the later chapters which focus on the separate countries. One of the few Portuguese works to get into print which recounts the march of events in Asia after 1560 was from the pen of Jorgé de Lemos (d. after 1593). He was born in Goa, probably of Luso-Indian parents, and spent most of his life in Portuguese service in the East. His *Historia dos cercos* . . . [240] (Lisbon, 1585) describes the sieges of Malacca of 1574 and 1575, and provides information on the conflicts in northern Sumatra following the death of the Sultan of Acheh (Achin) in 1579. His book, like other Portuguese works on the sieges of Diu and Malacca, has a propaganda purpose. Lemos urges the Portuguese to take advantage of the disruption in Sumatra to attack Acheh. It incidentally also describes conditions in Sumatra more generally, and makes mention of affairs in Johore and Java. Only three printed copies and two manuscripts of Lemos' work are extant.[241]

---

[237] For a listing of books on the Orient published in Portugal, which Camoëns could have read, see the compendium prepared by Francis M. Rogers and included as Appendix III in Henry H. Hart, *Luis de Camoëns and the Epic of the Lusiads* (Norman, Okla., 1962). It should be observed that Camoëns also probably had available a sizable body of Latin and Spanish literature on the East.

[238] See below, p. 201. One of the best of the English translations of Camoëns is that of Richard Fanshawe made in the eighteenth century. It was edited and reissued in 1940 by Jeremiah D. M. Ford (Cambridge, Mass.).

[239] For example, see Lopo de Sousa Coutinho, *Livro primeyro de cerco de Diu, que os Turcos poseram a fortaleza de Diu* (Lisbon, 1556). On maritime disaster in Portugal's literary history see James Duffy, *Shipwreck and Empire* (Cambridge, 1955).

[240] The full title is *Historia dos cercos que em tempo de Antonio Monis Barreto Governador que foi dos estados da India, os Achens, & Iaos puserão û fortaleza de Malaca, sendo Tristaõ Vaz da Veiga capitão della.*

[241] I. A. Macgregor, "Some Aspects of Portuguese Historical Writing of the Sixteenth and Seventeenth Centuries on South East Asia," in D. G. E. Hall (ed.), *Historians of South East Asia* (London, 1961), p. 196.

The Iberian secular writers provide no more general sources of significance during the remainder of the eighteenth century. The only works not from the pens of churchmen which appear after 1585 are written by outsiders, particularly Italian, Dutch, and English commentators. The most important of the firsthand accounts published independently of the great travel collections came from the pen of Jan Huygen van Linschoten (*ca.* 1563–1611). He left his home in Enkhuizen, a small seaport in northern Holland, when he was but thirteen years of age. He took passage to Spain to join his two older brothers who were already in business at Seville. Although Spain was officially at war with the Dutch, neither side could afford the luxury of suspending trade. Consequently, Dutchmen (particularly Catholics like the Linschotens) continued to do business in Spain and Portugal until they, along with the English, were finally forbidden in 1594 to participate in the spice trade at Lisbon. The Dutch, according to Linschoten's testimony,[242] were also permitted in his day to engage in the spice trade in India itself while the nationals of England, France, and Spain continued to be excluded.

Disorders swept the Iberian Peninsula shortly after 1581 as Philip II took over the Portuguese crown in spite of the resistance mounted by the protagonists of Dom António, one of the rival claimants. These disruptions seem to have affected the business activities of the Linschotens and led them to make their way to Lisbon, where Jan had an opportunity to observe at first hand the struggle which accompanied the change in dynasty. Civil disturbances being bad for business, Jan and one of his brothers volunteered for service in India. The younger Linschoten, through the connections which his brother had in the court of Philip II, soon became attached to the retinue of the new archbishop, Vicente de Fonseca, who was being sent to Goa by the new ruler. The two brothers (Jan then being about twenty years old) went aboard the archbishop's vessel just before it started down the Tagus on April 8, 1583.

For five years after his arrival at Goa on September 21, 1583, Linschoten lived mainly in the metropolis of the East—precisely the period (1583–88) when Filippo Sassetti was active in Cochin and Goa, but there is no evidence that their paths crossed.[243] Although Linschoten seems not to have traveled much beyond the west coast settlements of the Portuguese, he reports that he made a few visits to the mainland of India behind Goa. It was probably the responsibilities of his position in the office of the archbishop which kept the adventurous young Dutchman confined to the capital; it may also have been that as a for-

---

[242] A. C. Burnell and P. A. Tiele (eds.), *The Voyage of John Huyghen van Linschoten to the East Indies from the Old English Translation of 1598* ("Hakluyt Society Publications," Old Ser., Vols. LXX, LXXXI [London, 1885]), II, 222. On the Spanish official policy toward the Dutch before 1594 see G. F. Preuss, "Philipp II, die Niederländer und ihre erste Indienfahrt," *Mitteilungen der schlesischen Gesellschaft für Volkskunde*, XIII–XIV (1911–12), 281–97.

[243] Their independent observations, however, may be used by historians as checks one upon the other and upon the events which they report. For they are both, so far as I can determine, truly independent witnesses and excellent observers. For Sassetti see Marcucci (ed.), *op. cit.* (n. 203), and below, pp. 475–77.

eigner he was not permitted much freedom of travel. To a degree, however, he was able to compensate for his dearth of personal experiences by taking advantage of his stragetic location to interview at length other Westerners who came to Goa. From the Italian and English interlopers who arrived in Portuguese India, he learned in detail about the land route. From Dutch sailors, gunners, and merchants in the service of the Portuguese, he gathered information about the places farther to the east. From his own experience on the return voyage, when he was hired as a pepper factor by the Fugger and Welser interests, he learned at first hand about the organization and administration of the spice trade under the contract system. Though Linschoten left India in 1589, he did not actually make his way back to Holland until September, 1592, primarily because he made a two-year stay on the island of Tercera in the Azores.

In the sixteen years of Linschoten's absence, events had been moving swiftly in his homeland, and in Europe generally, which were of momentous importance to the rising interest of the Dutch in overseas enterprises. In 1576, the year when Linschoten had left home, the Spanish sacked Antwerp and the cause of Dutch independence appeared to be in grave danger. By the time of his return voyage from India, Philip II's sea power was at such a low ebb that his ship narrowly escaped being captured by marauding English vessels. In 1592, the year of his return to Enkhuizen, Maurice of Nassau was firmly in control of the northern Netherlands, and the ports of Holland and Zeeland were buzzing with prosperous activity as the seagoing Dutchmen, reinforced by merchants and capital that had fled from Antwerp, were swiftly making Amsterdam into a trading and financial center of northern Europe.

The enterprising Dutch were not content to confine their commercial activities and economic ventures to the marts of the Baltic, the Mediterranean, and the Atlantic. Like the English, the merchants of Holland had long been trying to make themselves independent of the Portuguese-Spanish monopoly of eastern trade. Both the northern maritime powers had been seeking to circumvent Iberian control of the southern routes by efforts to find northwestern or northeastern passages to Asia. The southwestern passage through the Strait of Magellan was still deemed, even after the successful voyages of Drake and Cavendish, to be too long, expensive, and dangerous for a regular trading route. While hope for a northwestern passage was waning by the last decade of the sixteenth century, the prospects for a northeastern passage still appeared promising to the Dutch. Then the return to Holland in 1590 of Dirck Gerritsz, a merchant who had been in the East for twenty-four years and had befriended Linschoten in Goa, and the return of Linschoten himself two years later, served to stimulate hope that Dutch ships could sail directly to the Spice Islands around the Cape of Good Hope. From Gerritsz and Linschoten the Dutch merchants learned that they might sail directly to Java and would probably be safe from Portuguese interference so long as their ships avoided Goa and Malacca. Even the Duke of Lauenburg, a petty German ruler whose principality lay on the Elbe, was planning an expedition to Asia in 1592.[244] The final stimulus to this movement was given by Philip II himself when in 1594 he barred Dutch and English vessels from calling at Lisbon.[245]

The Dutch, like the English, had long been collecting information on the problems of navigating in the Indian Ocean from returning sailors of all nationalities who had shipped out with the Portuguese. The cartographers of the Netherlands had likewise been systematically collecting Portuguese *roteiros* and maps of the East, and by the time of Linschoten's return Cornelis Claesz (who was to become his publisher) and others had already printed accurate maps of Eastern oceans and lands. The notes on navigation which Dirck Gerritsz (nicknamed "China")[246] brought back were used almost at once by L. J. Waghenaer in the preparation of his *Tresoor der zeevaert* (Leyden, 1592). In addition, the Netherlanders, with their Spanish background and their established strategic position as European intermediaries in the spice trade, had at hand the resources, literary and commercial, for understanding the spice business. From his residence of 1592–94 in Lisbon as an agent of an Amsterdam commercial group, Cornelis de Houtman brought back to the north the latest data on the spice trade.[247] Meanwhile, the search for a northeastern route was still being promoted by Balthasar de Moucheron, a merchant of Middelburg in Zeeland who was discouraged neither by the failure of earlier projects nor by the new interest in the direct southern route. From these indications it is clear that the Holland to which Linschoten returned was eager to learn about his experiences in the East and prepared to profit from them.[248]

Immediately upon returning to Enkhuizen, Linschoten began the preparation of his *Itinerary*. It would seem from reading this work that he brought back with him a fairly comprehensive set of notes on conversations with informants and perhaps a diary or a record of the main events that had occurred in Goa while he was there. But Linschoten's book is far more than a series of reminiscences. It combines firsthand information with materials derived from the publications of the writers of classical antiquity and of the other observers of the

[244] See J. E. Heeres, "Duitschers en Nederlanders op de zeewegen naar Oost-Indië voor 1595," in *Gedenkboed van het Kon. Institut voor Taal-, Land- en Volkenkunde van Nederlandsche Indië* (The Hague, 1926), p. 171.

[245] General studies of expansion too frequently credit Philip II's decree with causing, instead of merely hastening, the northern European powers, especially the Dutch, to sail directly to the East. For a discussion of this question see Preuss, *loc. cit.* (n. 242), 279–81. Also see the letter from Lisbon dated at the end of 1594 which alleges that Philip II believed that the Dutch had found a shorter route to the East Indies and was uncertain about how to prevent them from using it. Among the suggestions made was one which included detaining all Dutch ships calling at Spanish-controlled ports, an indication that the Dutch were still coming into the seaports of Spain. Reproduced in W. Noel Sainsbury (ed.), *Calendar of State Papers, Colonial Series: East Indies, China and Japan* (London, 1862), p. 97, item 246.

[246] For his biography see Arthur Wichmann, *Dirck Gerritsz. Ein Beitrag zur Entdeckungsgeschichte des 16ten und 17ten Jahrhunderts* (Groningen, 1899). He was called "China" because he had made at least two visits to China and Japan.

[247] F. Stapel, "Het verblijf van Cornelis de Houtman te Lissabon," *Tijdschrift voor Geschiedenis,* LI (1936), 372.

[248] See the introduction by P. A. Tiele in Burnell and Tiele, *op. cit.* (n. 242).

sixteenth century. He mentions in the first sentence of the *Itinerary* that even before leaving Holland on his travels he delighted in reading about strange lands. Being of a studious nature, he apparently learned Spanish and Portuguese quite readily during his residences in Iberia and India and so made many more of the contemporary accounts available to himself. He refers to the "chronicles" of the Portuguese,[249] but does not appear to have used either Castanheda or Barros extensively in the preparation of his account.[250] He does, however, use the *roteiros* of the Portuguese and Spanish as sources for his discussions of routes. For the place names of Asia, as they were used by the historians of antiquity, he appears to derive his information from "old histories" and especially from the *Lusiads* of Camoëns.[251] The only contemporary author actually cited in his text is the Spanish Augustinian, Juan González de Mendoza. Linschoten appears to have used the Latin translation of Mendoza's original Spanish work which was published at Frankfurt in 1589.[252] His account of China is taken almost word for word (including spellings of proper names) from Mendoza, and he also extracts items from the Spaniard's work about other matters without crediting him. Linschoten's detailed description of the plants and animals of the Eastern countries, especially India, is clearly derived in part from Cristobal de Acosta's *Tractado de las drogas* which, as we have previously noted,[253] was itself based on Orta's *Coloquios*. His dependence on Acosta and Orta is indicated by textual comparison and by the notes inserted into Linschoten's text by Dr. Paludanus. This learned physician of Enkhuizen, whose Dutch name was Bernard ten Broecke, almost certainly put the works of Acosta and Clusius into Linschoten's hands, for in his interpolations Paludanus repeatedly cites both authors as well as a large number of classical writers. Paludanus may also have introduced him to the work of Maffei, for there are many references in Linschoten's text which remind the reader of the Jesuit's study.[254] On certain points, there is also a striking resemblance to the narrative of Fedrici, though he makes no mention of the Venetian's travel account.[255] And it appears that he used the official Jesuit account of the Japanese mission to Europe.[256]

In 1594 the States-General granted Linschoten a license to publish his work. His *Reysgheschrift*,[257] the second part of what finally became the total work, was put into print before the rest of the *Itinerary* and appeared in 1595. It discusses

[249] *Ibid.*, I, 58.

[250] See H. Kern (ed.), *Itinerario. Voyage ofte Schifvaert van Jan Huygen van Linschoten naar Oost ofte Portugaels Indien, 1579–1592* (The Hague, 1910), I, xxviii–xxix, where it is asserted that if he had used Barros his account of the Moluccas would not have been so inaccurate and incomplete. Also see W. J. van Balen, *Naar de indische Wonderwereld* (Amsterdam, 1946), pp. 11–12. The second edition issued by the Linschoten Vereeniging appeared in 3 vols., 1955–57, under the supervision of H. Terpstra.

[251] Burnell and Tiele (eds.), *op. cit.* (n. 242), I, 36.

[252] On Mendoza and his description of China see below, pp. 743–45.

[253] See above, pp. 194–95.

[254] See Kern (ed.), *op. cit.* (n. 250), I, xxviii. On Maffei, see below, pp. 325–26.

[255] Cf. below, pp. 469–70.

[256] Cf. below, pp. 701–2.

[257] *Reysgheschrift van de Navigatien der Portugaloysers.*

the sea routes most commonly followed, along with a summary of the domains, duties, tributes, and revenues enjoyed by the king of Spain. The other two parts of his text which include his *Itinerary* proper[258] (Pt. I) and his descriptions of the coasts of Africa and America compiled with help from Paludanus and from the writings of others (Pt. III) appeared in 1596. A copy of this first edition which I have seen includes the second part in its proper place, as provided for in Linschoten's original list of maps and illustrations.[259] A feature of this work which makes it distinctive and valuable is the thirty-six plates, drawn by Linschoten himself and engraved by Joannes and Baptista à Doetechum, which depict the people, manners, and products of India, particularly of Goa and its environs. The original edition also contains a number of excellent maps, three of which are of great value for the study of Asia.[260] These maps, which are much better and more detailed than earlier printed maps, were clearly derived from the latest and best Portuguese charts of the Eastern oceans and sea coasts.[261]

The first part, or the *Itinerary* proper, was translated into English and German in 1598.[262] In the following year two Latin translations of it were published, one at Amsterdam and the other at Frankfurt. In the seventeenth century it was translated into French (1610), and several reprintings of the Dutch original and of the Latin and French translations came off the presses of northern Europe. Linschoten's contemporaries, like later scholars, were clearly much more interested in those parts of the *Itinerary* which were based upon his personal observations than in his secondhand accounts of the West Indies and other places which he had not himself visited.[263]

As noticed earlier, Linschoten's remarks on India refer to the years 1583–89, a period when the Portuguese stations were under almost constant attack by the Moors and by the native rulers of India, and when the administration of the empire was being brought more closely under the supervision of Philip II. Linschoten himself, being attached to the suite of the newly appointed archbishop, represented to the Portuguese in India the servitors of the new order. Archbiship Vicente de Fonseca, a Dominican and a trusted ally of Philip II,

[258] The entire text of three parts is generally referred to as the *Itinerario*, but this designation is somewhat misleading since only the first part bears this title in the original volume. The full title is *Itinerario, voyage ofte schipvaert van Jan Huygen van Linscoten naar Oost-ofte Portugails Indien*.

[259] Ayer collection, Newberry Library (Chicago).

[260] See below, p. 225.

[261] For a more detailed discussion see Burnell and Tiele (eds.), *op. cit.* (n. 242), I, xxxi–xxxiii.

[262] The English edition was translated from the Dutch by William Phillip and published at London by John Wolfe under the title . . . *Iohn Hvighen van Linschoten. His Discours of Voyages into ye Easte & West Indies*. A copy of this original work, which is now exceedingly rare, may be seen in the Library of Congress. The English version is loose, paraphrastic and full of the translator's interpolations. Nevertheless, in Burnell's view, the translation is sufficiently accurate and intelligible to make impractical the preparation of a modern, corrected version. It was for this reason that Burnell and Tiele reissued an edited version of the 1598 translation for the Hakluyt Society series (*op. cit.* [n. 242], I, xli). It is also for this reason, as well as for convenience in locating references, that we are depending in what follows (and in other references) upon the 1598 translation as edited by Burnell and Tiele.

[263] Linschoten himself recognized the inadequacy of his description of the West Indies and he acknowledges it in the dedication to his Dutch translation (1598) of J. de Acosta's *Historia natural y moral de las Indias* (Seville, 1590). See Burnell and Tiele (eds.), *op. cit.* (n. 242), I, xxxviii.

was apparently shocked by what he found in Goa and he was soon at odds with the viceroy, Dom Duarte de Menezes (1584–88). In 1587, when the archbishop left Cochin to return with a report to Philip II, Linschoten, as his treasurer, awaited his return to India.[264] When the Dutchman learned that his master had died at sea, he resolved to return to Europe himself even though at one time he had apparently decided to spend the rest of his days in India.[265] Through his acquaintance with the pepper farmers representing the Fuggers and Welsers in India, Linschoten obtained the post of factor on one of their ships and thereby acquired the papers which gave him permission to leave India for Portugal.[266] Linschoten's comments obviously need to be considered in terms of his own position as Dutch confidant of a Dominican archbishop who was highly critical of Portuguese and Jesuit activities in the empire and at Goa. His observations, however, are valuable precisely because he did not have a vested interest in the status quo and was in a position, once he had returned to Holland, to expose the worst aspects of Portuguese rule in India.

The *Itinerary* begins with a sketch of the places in which the Portuguese have outposts, and includes comments on the vast area stretching from Mozambique to Japan. Most of this information was derived by Linschoten from others, however, and is much less detailed and illuminating than his remarks on Goa. His vague and confused account of Goa's history he apparently derived in great part from Clusius' abridgment of Orta's *Coloquios*.[267] But his description of the administration, manners, and foreigners in the "chiefe Cittie of India" is one of the most original and reliable narratives prepared during the sixteenth century on life at the hub of Portugal's Eastern empire and still is regarded as one of the best sources for Goa's history at the peak of its glory.[268]

The great Iberian chronicles, all of which had appeared in print before Philip II took the Portuguese crown in 1581, were the richest sources for the general depiction of the East (as well as for Portuguese expansion) available in the sixteenth century. They all, however, had their limitations and nationalistic biases. For example, the greatest chroniclers (Oviedo, Gómara, Castanheda, and Barros) deal exclusively with events of the period before 1540. In geographical terms, Oviedo and Gómara limit themselves to the eastern islands of the archipelago. While the Portuguese chroniclers cover a much greater part of the East, they are weak on the insular world, especially so on Java. The more individualistic special narratives of Albuquerque, Orta, Galvão, and Lemos supplement the generalized chronicles on particular subjects or areas, and, since they are all by firsthand observers (even Albuquerque to an extent), they can be used as a check upon and as an amplification of the comprehensive histories. The epic of Camoëns stands by itself, but there were other Portuguese poets who likewise

---

[264] Burnell and Tiele (eds.), *op. cit.* (n. 242), II, 190.

[265] *Ibid.*, pp. 216–17.

[266] *Ibid.*, p. 219.

[267] See *ibid.*, I, 165, n. 4, and above, p. 194.

[268] See José Nicolai da Fonseca, *An Historical and Archaeological Sketch of the City of Goa* (Bombay, 1878), pp. 151–52.

celebrated the victories of their countrymen on the seas, in India, and at the great sieges. It is particularly striking that no Portuguese prose travelogues were printed in the sixteenth century. Portugal produced no Marco Polo or even a Ralph Fitch.[269] Linschoten's book, a mélange of firsthand observations and data acquired through informants, printed books, and maps, is particularly valuable on the situation in Goa. It can also be used to extend the available information chronologically and to offset the adulatory bias of the Iberian writers. While the printed works of the sixteenth century are by no means the only European works available today for the study of Asian history in the sixteenth century, it is a sad fact to record that even they have never been fully exploited by the specialists who write in this field.

5

THE GREAT COLLECTIONS OF TRAVEL LITERATURE

Once the floodgates opened after 1550, Europe was deluged with materials on the overseas world. Among the most dramatic of the new productions were the travel collections, an independent literary genre with antecedents going back to Long John of Ypres in the mid-fourteenth century and to the compilers of the *Paesi* and the *Novus orbis* of the early sixteenth century. But it was only in the latter half of the sixteenth century that the great published collections of travel narratives began to appear in Venice, London, and Frankfurt. Before this the only great collections of published historical documents had been compilations of laws and decretals. While the travel collections were being produced, the historians of the Protestants and Catholics were compiling vast numbers of sources to support their polemical attacks upon each other. The interest in the new lands, however, was not yet vitally affected by Christian differences, and throughout Europe travel accounts seem to have been read by men of all persuasions for instruction and pleasure.

The earliest of the great travel compendia was that of Giovanni Battista Ramusio (1485–1557), a Venetian Humanist and civil servant. The first huge tome of his three-volume *Delle navigationi et viaggi* appeared in 1550. The next two volumes were completed by 1553,[270] four years before Ramusio's death. The printer Tomasso Giunti published the third volume in 1556, and the second volume appeared in print three years later. The first volume, the one which mainly included new information on Asia, was republished with emendations in 1554, 1563, 1588, 1606, and 1613. No new edition of this standard travel

---

[269] The *Itinerário* of António Tenreiro, first published in 1560, was issued twice in the sixteenth century. But Tenreiro, who followed the land route across from Ormuz to Europe, has very little to say about Asia beyond the Indies. For an edited version of his travels see António Baião (ed.), *Itinerários da India a Portugal por terra* (Coimbra, 1923), pp. 3–127.

[270] George B. Parks, "Ramusio's Literary History," *Studies in Philology*, LII (1955), 127.

collection has appeared since 1613 and no Ramusio society has kept his name alive. But in recent years a group in Italy has begun to issue another collection called *Il nuovo Ramusio.*[271]

Very little has so far been published about the history of Ramusio's work, even though it heads practically every list of travel literature ever compiled.[272] About the compiler's life the details are likewise not numerous. Although he was a man with but one big book to his credit, he had many intellectual interests besides his concern with the travel literature of antiquity and of his own day. A public servant of the Venetian state for over fifty years, he traveled to France on official business but appears to have had no professional or business interest in travel itself. Nor is there any evidence to show that his government posts gave him extraordinary access to the narratives of travel that it may be presumed were of vital concern to Venice. The contrary, if anything, is true, for he refrained from including in his *Navigationi* the reports of Venetians who, as we have seen, extended themselves greatly at times to obtain information on the spice trade and overseas developments. The possibility is that he worked with some of the Venetian printers who were constantly publishing and republishing narratives of travel. Such a supposition is strengthened by Giunti's failure to put Ramusio's name on the title page or table of contents until Volume I was reissued in 1563.[273]

Ramusio appears to have collected his travel narratives with the help of the Venetian printers and his circle of Humanist friends. Shortly after leaving the University of Padua, the young Ramusio had become associated with a group of Venetian literati who included within their circle such luminaries as Pietro Bembo, Andrea Navagero, Paulus Manutius Aldus (manager of the Aldine Press), and Girolamo Fracastoro. His correspondence with these Humanist friends reveals the breadth and diversity of his interests, and his gradual dedication to the compilation and editing of travel narratives. It is not until around 1534, however, that he appears to have plunged into the business systematically, even though Navagero was gathering material for him in Spain as early as 1525. Ramusio did not begin seriously putting his materials into shape for publication until 1548.

The first volume of the *Navigationi* brings together materials on Africa, the country of Prester John, and the region from the Red Sea to the Moluccas. In the introduction, after thanking Fracastoro for his encouragement, Ramusio states that the purpose in compiling the work is to collect materials and charts to aid in correcting Ptolemy's maps of Africa and the East, and presumably many of the other notions about these regions inherited from the writers of

---

[271] This started publication in 1950, the four-hundredth anniversary of the original Ramusio. It is being published by the *Istituto italiano per il medio ed estremo oriente* under the direction of Giuseppe Tucci.

[272] Most complete is the study of Antonio de Piero, "Della vita e delgi studi di Gio. Battista Ramusio," *Nuovo archivio veneto*, N.S., IV (1902), 5–112.

[273] See Parks, *loc. cit.* (n. 270), p. 129; and Parks, *op. cit.* (n. 133), pp. 7–8.

antiquity and the Middle Ages.[274] The initial materials on the Portuguese voyages to India include a series of letters and reports written between 1499 and 1510 by actual participants or by observers at Lisbon. He republished the letters of Sernigi and Vespucci and the narrative of the anonymous Portuguese pilot from the *Paesi.* And in his introductory discourse to them, Ramusio remarks on how few records were readily available in his day relating to the great Portuguese discoveries in the East. Of the unique items not previously published, Ramusio brought to light the accounts of Tomé Lopez of 1502 and that of Giovanni da Empoli of 1503.[275] These are followed by a translation into Italian of the Spanish text (1520) of Varthema's itinerary. Then, as if to show his interest in using the new materials to check the older accounts, Ramusio inserts an Italian translation of the imaginary travels of Iambolus from the book of Diodorus Siculus, and follows it with a commentary on its veracity by an unidentified Portuguese nobleman. The letters of Andrea Corsali to Giuliano de'Medici he publishes from the original manuscripts even though previously they had been printed separately.[276]

After a series on Ethiopia and Egypt, Ramusio returns to accounts dealing with India and the East Indies. The first one in this group of selections is taken from the *Viaggi fatti alla Tana,* and it recounts, as earlier mentioned, the Turkish siege of Diu and other activities on the Indian coast in 1537–38. This is followed by a translation into Italian of the *Periplus of the Indian Ocean* ascribed to Arrian by sixteenth-century scholars. As an introduction to his translation of this Greek text, Ramusio wrote an essay in which he sought to reconcile ancient and recent knowledge of the shores of the Indian Ocean. Presumably as the most authoritative example of the sixteenth-century accounts of the Indian Ocean, he next includes a discourse on and the text of the *Book* of Duarte Barbosa. The manuscript of this excellent account, which had been seen by the Spanish at the negotiations at Badajoz-Elvas in 1524, may have been relayed to Ramusio around 1525 by Andrea Navagero.[277] The other document which Navagero may also have obtained for him is the partial version of the *Suma oriental* of Tomé Pires which appeared in Italian translation in Ramusio as *Sommario di tutti li Regni, Citta & Popoli orientali.* . . . In his introductory discourse, Ramusio observes that publication of the accounts of Barbosa and Pires was not allowed in Portugal. So these two important accounts remained unique in Ramusio until Barbosa's *Book* was issued in Portuguese in 1812; Pires' *Suma oriental* was published by Armando Cortesão in 1944.[278] As appendixes to these detailed accounts of Asia, Ramusio gives a one-page (fol. 363 v.) drawing of the betel leaf with a brief explanation of the custom of chewing betel and follows this with quotations from Propertius and Strabo on the practice of *sati* (fol. 364 r.).

---

[274] Parks, *loc. cit.* (n. 270), pp. 133–35.
[275] See first edition of Vol. I of the *Navigationi:* for Lopez (fol. 143 v.–156 r.) and Empoli (fol. 156 r.–158 r.).
[276] For further details see Parks, *op. cit.* (n. 133), pp. 12–15.
[277] *Ibid.,* p. 17. See above, p. 116.
[278] In the publications of the Hakluyt Society. See above, pp. 185–86.

Ramusio included the next group of books as background to the accounts of Magellan's voyage around the world. In the discourse preceding the fifteenth-century narratives of Nicolò de' Conti and Girolamo da Santo Stefano, he expresses his wonder as to why the Portuguese have not retraced Polo's and Conti's routes by sea from China to Europe. The first voyage around the world apparently caught his imagination, for he hails it as the achievement, in an age filled with colossal discoveries, which most strikingly surpasses anything done by the ancients. Ramusio regrets not being able to present the report of Magellan's expedition written by Peter Martyr, and explains that it was lost in the Sack of Rome in 1527. So he does his best by including Italian versions of the accounts of Maximilian of Transylvania and Pigafetta.[279] This is followed by the most impressive of Ramusio's discourses, an attempt to provide a historical discussion of the spice trade. The first volume then concludes with a report addressed to the Emperor by Juan Gaetano, a navigator who accompanied Ruy Lopez de Villalobos from Mexico across the Pacific in 1542 and who returned to let Europe know of this most recent failure of the Spanish to establish maritime connections between Mexico and the Philippines.

In the 1554 edition of Volume I, several significant additions were made to Ramusio's original compilation. A brief narration by a Portuguese who had sailed with Magellan was added, but it is "so short as to be of small value."[280] Of greater significance are five Jesuit letters on Japan written in 1549 and 1550 which he inserted, for this is the first time that Japan makes a significant appearance in travel literature. He incorporates six chapters translated into Italian from the *Décadas da Ásia* of João de Barros, the first decade having been published in Portugal in 1552. Finally, he adds three double-paged maps of Africa, the East Indies, and India. The later editions of Volume I, which appeared after Ramusio's death, received no significant additions though the materials were slightly rearranged from time to time.

The second volume of the *Navigationi* concentrates mainly on the literature dealing with northern and eastern travel. It was originally designed as the counterpart to the first volume, which covered southern and eastern travel. Here Marco Polo occupies the place of honor at the beginning of the volume. In his preface to Polo's travels, Ramusio remarks that, though many people had once been dubious about the veracity of Polo's stories, he certainly did not report marvels any more incredible than the tales of the New World that were circulating in the sixteenth century. Ramusio clearly is inclined to accept Polo at face value. He even prepared a table of latitudes and longitudes from the geography of Abulfada Ismael to identify as closely as possible the places in Asia mentioned by Polo. The original of the text printed in Ramusio has never been located and so his is still considered one of the several basic extant versions of Marco Polo. Ramusio buttresses Polo's account by

---

[279] Taken from the book, perhaps edited originally by Ramusio, called *Il viaggio fatto da gli Spagnivoli a'l mondo* (Venice, 1536).

[280] The opinion of Angela de Poli in *Nuovo archivio veneto*, XXXVIII (1920), 127.

following it with the narrative of King Hayton of Armenia.[281] At the end of Volume II he reprinted the accounts of John of Plano Carpini and Odoric of Pordenone, recording their journeys across the land routes to the East. The third of Ramusio's volumes is primarily concerned with descriptions of the New World, though it includes also the voyage of the Parmentiers to Sumatra.[282]

Ramusio, when necessary, translated the travel accounts into the Tuscan dialect from Greek, Latin, Spanish, Portuguese, and French. They were also prefaced by the learned, if sometimes faulty, discourses of the compiler. In terms of wealth of material no previous compilation of travels could match Ramusio's achievement. For the first time the travels to the Eastern regions were separated from other travel accounts and collected, with the exception of the overland travelers like Marco Polo, into a single volume. And for the first time the overland and sea voyages were put into juxtaposition so that each group could be seen in relation to the other. The illustrative materials, such as maps and pictures, were more numerous than in any previous compilation. It was thus possible for a person with a knowledge of Italian, not a rare accomplishment among educated Europeans, to read in the first two volumes most of the major travel accounts of Asia written before 1550. And this included, of course, some narratives which had previously not been published.

Of the three Ramusio volumes, the first, which is devoted to southern Asia and Africa, was printed twice before the editor's death in 1557, and three times thereafter. Neither of the other volumes matched this record. In 1556, a French translation of part of the first volume was prepared by Jean Temporal and published at Lyons in two volumes. The materials on Asia, despite the title, dominate this work, which is called *Tome seconde de l'Afrique....*[283] Apparently no other direct translations were made in the sixteenth century, but Ramusio's volumes were used as models for the collections of Hakluyt and De Bry. To practically all the cosmographers, cartographers, and historians of the discoveries who wrote in the sixteenth century, the collection of Ramusio was either the logical starting-point for their work or one of their most reliable reference books. For the cultivated public the Ramusio must have aroused both interest and pride in the spectacular contributions of Italians from Marco Polo onward to the great age of discovery.[284] In the seventeenth century the English philosopher John Locke wrote of Ramusio's collection that it is free from that "great mass of useless matter which swells our English Hakluyt and Purchas, much more complete and full than the Latin De Bry, and in fine is the noblest work of nature."[285]

---

[281] See above, p. 42.

[282] See above, pp. 178–79.

[283] *Tome second de l'Afrique, contenant les navigations des capitaines Portugalois, autres, faites aux Indes tant Orientales, qu'Occidentales* is the complete title of this work which is now quite rare. For a summary of its contents see Le Président Baudrier, *Bibliographie lyonnaise . . . quatrième série* (Lyons, 1899), pp. 385–87.

[284] Cf. Böhme, *op. cit.* (n. 33), p. 90.

[285] As quoted in E. G. Cox, *A Reference Guide to the Literature of Travel* (Seattle, 1935), I, 28.

The two great British collectors—Richard Eden and Richard Hakluyt—did not have Ramusio's native heritage of exploration and discovery to celebrate. The British collections, unlike those compiled elsewhere, were not written after great national achievements in overseas expansion. If anything, they were designed to stimulate interest in expansion by showing how, by overseas enterprises, other people had enriched themselves and made their nations great.

The pioneer collector in England was Richard Eden, a graduate of Cambridge. In 1527 when Eden was a boy, Robert Thorne had written to King Henry VIII advocating the exploration of the northern passages to Cathay and the Moluccas. There was little immediate reaction to this suggestion, and so long as England remained the ally of Charles V the court was not in a position, even if it had been so inspired, to send ships to the marts of Asia.[286] Certain individuals, however, continued to press for action, and, shortly after the death of Henry VIII, Sebastian Cabot once again appeared in England after deserting his post as Pilot Major of Spain. He was probably brought to England by the wealthy combination of courtiers and merchants who made up the Society of Merchant-Adventurers which sent out Willoughby's fleet in 1553 to hunt for a strait giving a northeastern passage to Cathay. Young Eden, who was then secretary to Sir William Cecil,[287] a leading figure in the Cathay enterprise, began to translate and compile travel materials to awaken his countrymen to the exploits of the Continental nations in the overseas world and indirectly to England's own prospects for sharing its wealth.

Eden's first publication, which includes a translation of parts of Sebastian Münster's *Cosmographia* (1540), appeared in 1553 and was called *A treatyse of the newe India*. . . . Although this book was experimental and tentative, it brought before the English public for the first time the systematic story of the great discoveries. In his preface to the reader, Eden makes clear his feeling that the knowledge of the discoveries contained therein would have a profound impact upon the intellectual insularity of his countrymen. He commences his preface in this manner:

Whereas in this Booke (welbeloved Reader) thou mayest reade many straunge thinges, and in maner incredible, except the same were proued most certayn by dayly experience and approued auctoritie (as shall hereafter appeare) I thought it good for thy better instruction to make this Preface, wherby thou mightest more playnly and sensibly comprehend the reasons and causes, yf not of al, yet some of the chiefest things, which are conteyned in the same. Therefore whereas thou shalt reade of the great abundaunce of gold, precious stones and spices, which the Spaniardes and Portugales have brought from the South as opposed to North partes of the worlde, as from the newe founde landes and Ilandes, the *sodeyn straungenes or greatnes of the thing shall not so much amaze thy wittes, and gender in them incrudelitie*, yf thou consider the saying of Wyse Salomon who affyrmeth yat there is no new thing under the Sunne. . . .[288]

---

[286] Cf. J. A. Williamson, *Maritime Enterprise* (Oxford, 1913), p. 240.
[287] Details on Eden's career in Arber, *op. cit.* (n. 59), pp. xxvii–xlvii.
[288] As reproduced in *ibid.*, p. 7. Italics mine.

Events in England had meanwhile been changing rapidly after the death of King Edward VI in 1553. The inauguration of the Marian religious reforms, the queen's marriage in 1554 to Philip II of Spain, and the hostility of the Protestants to Mary's program all figure in Richard Eden's preface to *The Decades of the newe worlde or west India* ... (1555), a new collection derived in large part from the Spanish writers. Eden greeted the Spanish marriage as an event which seemed to promise that England might become a party to and one of the heirs of Spain's great overseas empire. In company with a group of printers Eden prepared his collection in the year following the queen's marriage and wrote the preface which still stands as a masterpiece of political propaganda in the Marian cause and of sophisticated argument setting forth the benefits that Spanish colonialism had conferred upon the conquered peoples of the overseas world. And he admonished his reader, should he be a political recalcitrant, to "consider what benifites thou mayst receaue at theyr hands [Philip's and Mary's] if thou doo thy dewtie towarde them." [289]

The first section of Eden's collection is devoted to his translation of the first three *Decades* of Peter Martyr and to the Latin text and English translation of the famous demarcation bull published by Pope Alexander VI in 1493. Eden's second section is comprised entirely of his abridged translation of Oviedo's history of the West Indies first printed in 1526. In this work Oviedo talks about the prospects for circumventing Portugal's spice monopoly by developing the Pacific trade via Spain's American empire, but the remainder of Oviedo here translated is devoted entirely to America. Eden's third section is devoted to the standard accounts of the first circumnavigation of the globe and to the Molucca controversy. Here appear telescoped versions of the accounts of Maximilian of Transylvania and of Pigafetta, probably translated from the separate Italian work published at Venice in 1536.[290] These are followed by short accounts of the places of origin of the precious stones and spices, a few price lists, and a discussion of the weights of Portugal and India, so that "we may not vtterly bee ignorant of the thinges which we so grately esteem and bye so dear." [291] And then Eden, without any attempt to state the Portuguese position in the Molucca controversy, includes a partial translation of the partisan account written originally in Spanish by Gómara, the noted Spanish chronicler and apologist. This section is then concluded with extracts from the letters of Amerigo Vespucci and Andrea de Corsali concerning the "Pole Antarctica," materials possibly derived from Ramusio's first volume. Section IV, entitled "Of Moscovy, Cathay, and the North Regions," was unquestionably inspired by the voyages of Willoughby and Richard Chancellor in search of a northeastern passage to Cathay. For this section he gathered material from Münster's *Cosmographia*, from the *Novus orbis*, and from discussions with Richard Chancellor, who was just then preparing to embark on his second voyage, from which

---

[289] *Ibid.*, p. 53.

[290] See above, n. 279.

[291] Arber (ed.), *op. cit.* (n. 59), p. 263.

he did not return.[292] But Eden fails abysmally in this section to provide any substantial information on Cathay; most striking is the fact that he does not use Marco Polo or other late medieval travelers to Cathay. Section V related "other notable things as touching the Indies out of the writings and maps of Francisco Lopez de Gomara and Sebastian Cabot" for the years from 1552 to 1555.

Eden, though he clearly hoped to do so, was not to have an opportunity to revise or add to his travel collection. In the years immediately before his death in 1576, he began again to gather accounts of the English voyages to Muscovy and Persia and prepared a translation of Varthema from the Latin version of 1511 by Madrignanus.[293] The revised work was ultimately issued by his literary executor, Richard Willes, in 1577 as *The History of Trauayle in the West and East Indies.* . . . Willes, who had been a professor at Perugia, enjoyed having a wide circle of scholarly friends on the Continent, including the Jesuit Giovanni Maffei.[294] Willes was himself a renegade Jesuit and had long been interested in cosmography before his return to England in 1572 and before the beginning of his association with Eden. In the work printed at London by Richard Iugge five years later, Willes rearranged Eden's *Decades of the newe worlde*, omitted some parts of it, and added a number of new translations, including Eden's own unpublished translation of Varthema. Willes excised Eden's original preface and other notes and comments which Elizabethan Protestants might consider to be offensive. He divided the volume into four parts, and rearranged Eden's material to fit into his new organizational framework. Like Ramusio, Willes divided the voyages according to geographical areas.

It is in the second part, which is entirely new and may have originally been planned for separate publication,[295] that Willes brings together and publishes significant, fresh material on Asia. He translates into English a portion of the account of conditions in China prepared by the Portuguese merchant Galeote Pereira, who had been held captive by the Chinese from 1549 to 1553 for illegal trading. In 1561 Pereira's report had been sent from the Jesuit college in Goa to the headquarters of the Society in Rome. Four years later it was published in an abridged Italian version at Venice.[296] It was from this abridged account that Willes made his translation. He followed it with an account of Japan "and other little Isles in the East Ocean" translated from the 1571 compilation of Jesuit letters published by Maffei[297] and from a letter of Father Luis Fróis. Willes here refers to Maffei as "my old acquaynted friend," an indication

---

[292] For further discussion on Eden's sources for this section see Taylor, *op. cit.* (n. 196), p. 21.

[293] For a critical commentary on both Madrignanus and Eden as translators see Sir Richard Temple in Jones and Temple (eds.), *op. cit.* (n. 61), p. xxi. Also see above, p. 164.

[294] See below, p. 324.

[295] Taylor, *op. cit.* (n. 196), p. 38.

[296] *Nuovi avisi delle Indie di Portogallo, venuti nuovamente dalli R. padri della compagnia di Giesu & tradotti dalla lingua Spagnola nella Italiana, Quarte parte* (Venice, 1565), pp. 63–87. Also see below, pp. 748–49.

[297] See below, p. 324.

that Willes had probably heard a great deal about Asia through the Jesuit.

Certainly it can be said that Willes gave better proportion to Eden's collection by including materials on Asia from Portuguese and Jesuit sources. It may be that Eden himself was aware of the imbalance in his collection, caused in part by his desire to extol the achievements of Spain. This conjecture is supported by the fact that shortly before his death he translated the travels of Varthema, the Italian. *The History of Trauayle*, the work of both Eden and Willes, now provided the English reader for the first time with recent accounts of Asia and the various roads for getting there that Europeans had used or were hoping to find. In fact, Willes' book was part of the publicity for Martin Frobisher's third effort to find a northwest passage through America to the Pacific Ocean. Indicative of Willes' hopes that Frobisher might reach the Moluccas is the little section of his work derived from Maffei and entitled "Of the Isles beyond Giapan, in that way from China to the Moluccas." If anything further is required to support the assertion that both Eden and Willes were essentially interested in the voyages as promotional literature for maritime enterprise, it need only be repeated that the second English compilation, like the first, included none of the travel accounts of the period before the great discoveries, though of course there are passing references to them in some of the translated accounts.

Substantial additions were made to the travel literature available in English by Willes' two contemporaries, Thomas Nicholas and John Frampton. Both men had been active in business at Seville, and so most of their translations are of Spanish accounts. In 1577, Nicholas translated "out of the Castylin tongue" a book which was published in English under the title *News lately come from the great Kingdom of China*. In the following year he wrote Sir Francis Walsingham that he intended to translate a work "of the East India which is now enjoyed by the King of Portingal." [298] But he may have been frustrated in this intention by the appearance in 1579 of Frampton's translation from Spanish of the *Discorso* of Bernardino de Escalante, called in English *A Discourse of the Navigations which the Portingales do make*. In the same year Frampton also published a version of Marco Polo translated into English from the Castilian version of Santaella (1503). [299] And in 1580, probably in conjunction with the renewed search then being made for the northeast passage to Cathay, he published the collection of Francisco Thamara of Cadiz entitled in English *A Discovery of the Countries of Tartaria, Scythia, and Cataia by the North-east*. In 1582, two years after Drake's return from his circumnavigation of the world, a translation was dedicated to him, perhaps by Thomas Nicholas, that had been made from a Spanish version of Castanheda's authoritative history of Portuguese enterprise in the East. [300]

The greatest collector in English history, Richard Hakluyt, began his serious collecting and publishing activities in an England that was seething with

[298] As quoted in Taylor, *op. cit.* (n. 196), p. 186.
[299] See above, p. 159.
[300] See above, p. 189.

excitement over the exploits of Drake.[301] The second son of a leather merchant, Hakluyt was elected into a scholarship at Christchurch, Oxford, in 1570 and received his bachelor's degree four years later. After taking a master's degree in 1577, Hakluyt was shortly ordained as priest in the Anglican church. Through the influence of his lawyer uncle of the same name, Hakluyt very early in his university career began to take a serious interest in the new geographical learning. He met Ortelius in 1577 and shortly thereafter began corresponding with Mercator. But the mainstay of his study in these early years was the works of Ramusio, the separate books of which were to serve in a number of ways as a model for his own great collection.

Yet Hakluyt's methods and objectives were notably different from those of his Italian predecessor. He began quite early in his career to interview as many people as possible in his search for information, books, and manuscripts. While his great interest was initially in the American voyages, he took advantage of every possible opportunity to learn about the Portuguese activities in the East. In 1581 he talked with the Portuguese émigrés in London. In his *Divers Voyages touching the Discovery of America* (1582), Hakluyt included the two letters by Robert Thorne sent to England from Seville in 1529 regarding the Portuguese empire, the Moluccas, and England's need to seek a northern passage to the East. In 1583, when he went to France as chaplain to the British embassy, he repeatedly interviewed the Portuguese who were in exile there as refugees from the government of Philip II. He apparently watched closely England's efforts to follow up Drake's success which culminated in 1586 in Thomas Cavendish's successful expedition to the Moluccas through the Strait of Magellan.[302] He received a copy of the letter from Goa written by the English Jesuit, Thomas Stevens, and consulted with John Newbery in 1583 before his departure for India over the Levant route. In 1588, the year of the Armada, Hakluyt returned to England from his post in France, and immediately plunged into the work of preparing for the press the first edition of *The principall Navigations, Voiages and Discoveries of the English nation, made by Sea or over Land . . . at any time within the compasse of these 1500 yeeres (1589–90)*.

The materials on Asia in Hakluyt's first edition were slight. His main objective, as stated in his title, was to record the achievements of the English nation. To his day the connections of Englishmen with India and points farther to the east had been few and sporadic. The search for the northern routes to Cathay since mid-century had not revealed the passage that its sponsors had hoped for. Nor had British enterprises in the Levant been crowned with success, for their vessels found it difficult, because of Spanish hostility, to pass safely through the

---

[301] For details of his biography see G. B. Parks, *Richard Hakluyt and the English Voyages* (New York, 1928), Appendix II, pp. 242–59.

[302] Cavendish returned with a great map of China that he turned over to Hakluyt. Apparently, Cavendish also brought back two Japanese and one Filipino, whom Hakluyt "interviewed" but without making notes. See E. G. R. Taylor, *The Original Writings and Correspondence of the Two Richard Hakluyts* (London, 1935), I, 48.

Straits of Gibraltar. Drake's voyage, profitable though it had been, had not been easy to follow up and, like the Spanish before them, the English reluctantly had to admit that the southwestern route to the Moluccas was too precarious for regular trade. It was the defeat of the Armada which permitted the British in the last decade of the sixteenth century to plan seriously the establishment of direct trade connections with India, following the same route that Vasco da Gama had marked out almost a century earlier.[303]

One of the most avid planners and assiduous collectors of information on Asia after 1590 was Richard Hakluyt. As British men-of-war brought Spanish and Portuguese prize ships into port, Hakluyt acquired their logs, price records, and any other materials that might yield further information on the India trade. Like many of his contemporaries, Hakluyt's objective was to provide the first tiny fleets destined for India with as much authoritative navigational and trading data as possible. Hakluyt was no cloistered scholar; in these years he was rapidly becoming one of the leaders in the organization of Eastern trade, as is proved by the active part he took in the founding of the East India Company. A memorial written in 1600, probably by Hakluyt, confirms his importance in the establishment of English trade on a regular basis; it was called "Certain Reasons why the English Merchants may trade into the East Indies. . . .[304]

The first edition of Hakluyt's *Voyages* included only the report of Cavendish and a few Newbery letters on India. No mention was made of Cesare Fedrici's book on India or of Mendoza's *China*, both of which had just previously been translated into English. The materials on Asia from the first edition were reprinted in the final edition of 1598–1600. But the last edition of the *Voyages* was greatly amplified, especially with regard to materials bearing on the East and on England's quickening interest in the India trade. Hakluyt also provided a better background for the voyages of the sixteenth century by including some of the medieval narratives, though not Marco Polo's.

To the modern sections he added new materials derived from foreign sources. Perhaps most striking was the translation of Cesare Fedrici's account of his peregrinations in India and the East Indies, certainly the fullest and most authoritative account of these regions known at the time.[305] Mendoza's *China*,[306] which was published separately in English translation in 1589–90, was never reissued by Hakluyt, though he had helped to inspire its translation and publication in the first place. But Hakluyt's second edition carried a most interesting dialogue on China written by Duarte Sande and printed at Macao in Latin in 1590. This "excellent treatise,"[307] as Hakluyt calls it, was one of the prizes found aboard

303 For a convenient summary see Sir William Foster, *England's Quest of Eastern Trade* (London, 1933), chaps. v–xiii.

304 For a detailed discussion of Hakluyt's authorship see *ibid.*, pp. 153–56. For the text of the memorandum, see Taylor, *op. cit.* (n. 302), II, 465–68.

305 See below, p. 469.

306 See below, p. 744.

307 This is but one part of a treatise prepared by the Jesuits in connection with the Japanese embassy to Europe of 1584–86. See below pp. 809–10.

the Portuguese carrack, "Madre de Dios," captured in 1592. The three-cornered conversation about China is based upon information that the Jesuits had been accumulating at Macao. Hakluyt also included the translations that Willes had earlier published of Pereira's account of China and of the letters of Maffei and Fróis on Japan. A short letter on Pegu by Friar Peter of Lisbon, Linschoten's brief report on Newbery, and Ralph Fitch's imprisonment and escape at Goa conclude the materials on Asia.

All of the English accounts, in contrast to the foreign narratives, deal with navigational, travel, or commercial problems rather than with the Eastern countries. This is even true of the letter of Thomas Stevens, the English Jesuit, who wrote a letter from Goa in 1579 which Hakluyt included. Of course the narratives relating to the circumnavigations of Drake and Cavendish are featured prominently, but perhaps of even greater interest is the story of the voyage of James Lancaster to the East Indies in 1591 as told in three separate accounts by participants. Fitch's narrative of his travels in Pegu and India relies heavily on Fedrici, for Fitch, under persuasion from Hakluyt, recorded his story apparently from memory and from available published materials after returning to England.[308]

By the year 1600 the final volume of Hakluyt's three immense folios had come off the press. With its appearance, the English nation, in the words of Froude, had its epic. The English reader, who at mid-century had almost nothing available in his own language on the overseas world, now had at his disposal one of the finest collections of original sources to appear in the sixteenth century. Hakluyt, even more than Ramusio, was painstaking in his efforts to obtain and reproduce the whole text of his narratives, charts, and letters. He rarely summarized. And he, perhaps more than Ramusio, enlisted the help of others in tracking down travel expositions. By putting the voyages into readable English, Hakluyt aided greatly the growth of sentiment in England favoring overseas ventures. But while he was a popularizer, he was not a synthesizer. He was a collector of primary materials and did not interpret their relevance to trade or geography. His interpretations appeared elsewhere, as in the memorial prepared for the East India Company in 1600.

The German collections of the sixteenth century differed in their objectives from the English and the Ramusio collections. Prepared mainly by printers and engravers, the German collections which appeared after mid-century at Frankfurt were primarily designed as entertaining and eye-catching examples of literature. They were produced in attractive formats, in various languages, and with a profusion of engraved illustrations. The texts were frequently garbled, mistranslated, or severely excised; travel literature, in becoming a marketable product, lost much of the scholarly point that Ramusio had striven for and much of the nationalist fervor with which Hakluyt endowed his *Voyages*. But the German collections, as popular literature, probably contributed significantly

---

[308] See below, pp. 478–79.

to the diffusion of information on the overseas world, particularly in northern Europe.

The earliest of these collections designed to sell at the German fairs was the work of Sigmund Feyerabend, a leading Frankfurt publisher.[309] In 1567, his agents began selling a two-volume collection called *Warhafftige Beschreibunge aller theil der Welt.* The first volume of this compendium was derived mainly from Sebastian Franck's *Weltbuch* which had first been published in 1533, and to a lesser extent from the *Novus orbis.* Among the works extracted here were the accounts of the first five Portuguese voyages to the East, the fullest narrative of those heroic events so far to appear in the German language. While Feyerabend's apparent main purpose was to produce a marketable book, he asserted in his preface that he hoped through its publication to honor the fatherland and to inspire in its youth the desire for foreign adventure.

At the very end of the century the publication of a lavish travel collection was started by Theodor de Bry and his family.[310] A native of Liége and a Protestant, De Bry left his homeland to escape the "Spanish Fury" and settled in Frankfurt around 1570. An engraver by training, De Bry and his sons established in Frankfurt a publishing house specializing in profusely illustrated books. In 1587 De Bry visited England, where he consulted with Hakluyt and received encouragement in his work of collecting. His main undertaking was the *Collectiones peregrinationum in Indiam orientalem et occidentalem . . .,* which began appearing in 1590 and was not concluded until 1634. These stately folios, issued in twenty-five parts, were divided into two series: *Grands voyages* and *Petits voyages*—so-named because of a slight difference in the format of the volumes. The section on *India orientalis* belongs under the *Petits voyages* which were issued in Latin and German between 1598 and 1628.[311] In those volumes, issued before the end of the sixteenth century, the most notable additions to the travel literature then available were the narratives of the Dutch voyagers Linschoten and Houtman. Most impressive were the engravings of peoples, scenes, and maps, many of them highly imaginative.

A similar gigantic enterprise was undertaken in the last years of the sixteenth century by Levinus Hulsius. A native of Ghent,[312] Hulsius, like De Bry, fled his homeland because of religious persecution, and took up residence in Frankfurt. Here he too established a publishing house, and quickly became famous as a compiler of German and foreign language dictionaries. In 1598, he began to publish his famous collection of "26 voyages." These were issued in the convenient quarto size, existed only in German, were more lavishly produced than

[309] See Böhme, *op. cit.* (n. 33), pp. 96–105.

[310] *Ibid.,* pp. 120–25. For further biographical details see A. C. Camus, *Mémoire sur la collection des Grands et Petits Voyages . . .* (Paris, 1802), pp. 13–15. Also see T. Weigel, *Bibliographische Mittheilungen über die deutschen Ausgaben von de Bry's Sammlungen* (Leipzig, 1845).

[311] For a full analysis of the *Petits voyages,* now difficult to find except for isolated volumes or parts of the set, see Camus, *op. cit.* (n. 310), pp. 182–278; consult also Pieter Tiele, *Mémoire bibliographique sur les journaux des navigateurs néerlandais réimprimés dans les collections de De Bry et Hulsius* (Amsterdam, 1867).

[312] Böhme, *op. cit.* (n. 33), pp. 125–28.

the De Bry folios, and presumably were designed to attract readers with less money to spend. The project was apparently successful for it was continued by Hulsius' successors until 1663, a total of sixty-nine volumes appearing in the span of sixty-five years. Like De Bry, Hulsius brought the Dutch narratives of the East into the earliest volumes issued, and the series throughout centers on Dutch and English exploits. Hulsius' collection, perhaps even more than De Bry's, seems to have been intended to appeal to the general reader, for the narratives are presented without even the rudiments of a critical apparatus. The Hulsius collection reveals no over-all organizational or conceptual framework. It appears that the travel narratives were published just as they became available.

The great collections of travel literature from Ramusio to Hulsius were compiled for differing reasons. The Ramusio volumes had a more clearly expressed scientific and intellectual purpose than the others, and in general, though the pioneer collection, it benefited from the critical sense of its Humanist compiler. Ramusio's work was also the model for the others, even though each of the great compilers followed directions and general plans of his own devising. Still these were modifications rather than complete departures from the Ramusio prototype. Eden and Hakluyt (in his *Voyages*) were intent upon promoting English overseas enterprise, and were content to leave problems of interpretation and criticism to others. The German compilers were mainly concerned with the publication of travel accounts which would appeal to the popular taste for the remote and exotic. But irrespective of the purposes of the compilers, the publication and diffusion of the great collections made available a vast new body of literature which others would readily consult and easily use for a host of widely differing purposes. To put it simply, by 1600 the archives of travel, while not complete, stood ready and waiting in various languages for the study of the learned and the enjoyment of the literate public.

6

THE EVIDENCE OF MAPS

No survey of literary sources could possibly be complete without reference to the evidence of cartography—particularly when it is recalled that a veritable revolution took place in map design and projection during the sixteenth century, owing in large part to the influence of the discoveries. The contributions of Waldseemüller, the Reinels, the Homems, Ortelius, and Mercator, as well as many anonymous cartographers of their day, had the effect of gradually eliminating the Ptolemaic and Poloan conventional pictures of Asia and replacing them with maps based on empirical data. By 1600 the major outlines of Asia and the Pacific assumed the general configurations in European cartography that they would retain with but minor modifications until the eighteenth century. Such additions as were introduced in the seventeenth century generally were designed to fill in the interiors of the great Asian countries, like India and China, about which the cartographers of the sixteenth century had little specific information.

A few, faltering steps had been taken before 1500 to provide a clearer and more accurate depiction of Asia. The contributions of Marco Polo and Nicolò de' Conti to the development of a more concrete cartography have already been noted. The return to the *Geography* of Ptolemy as part of the humanistic revival of the classical past had the opposing effects of both stimulating an interest in a realistic cartography of Asia and making it difficult for humanistic geographers to accept new information when the data failed to conform to the Ptolemaic traditions. This conflict, which continued to dominate cartography until about 1570, was particularly noticeable in the printed or "literary" maps. The portulan charts, or mariners' maps, usually preserved in manuscript, were more practically oriented, very meticulously drawn, less likely to preserve fallacious elements from earlier maps, and more easily and frequently modified as new information became available. Made by seamen for the everyday use of seamen, the portulans are among the best records available for charting the progress of discovery. The printed maps, which appeared in books and atlases, were usually based on the available portulans and the world maps of the past. It was these literary maps, available to the general public, from which Europeans derived their visual image of Asia's configuration. We shall therefore emphasize in what follows the evolution of the printed map rather than the portulans and manuscript maps which were accessible only to persons involved in the discoveries and to a select group of collectors and cartographers.

The greatest makers of the portulan charts in the sixteenth century were the Portuguese.[313] They had begun to manufacture profile charts of Africa's coast even before the death of Prince Henry in 1460. As the Portuguese progressed eastward after the first voyage of Vasco da Gama, representations of the sea routes and coastal areas were faithfully prepared by the navigators and chart-makers who accompanied the fleets. On their return the portulans were deposited in Lisbon to be used as guides by the commanders of subsequent voyages. The more detailed of the portulans were also used every so often in the preparation of more generalized maps designed to show the progress of Portuguese enterprise in the East. A standard map of the world, referred to as the official *padrão*, was kept in the *Armazens da Guiné e India*; on this all the new discoveries were

313 The basic sources on Portuguese cartography are: Armando Cortesão, *Cartografia e cartógrafos portugueses dos seculos XV e XVI* (2 vols.; Lisbon, 1935); and A. Cortesão and A. Teixeira da Mota, *Portugaliae monumenta cartographica* (5 vols.; Lisbon, 1960-2). The monumental tomes of Cortesão and Teixeira da Mota with their magnificent colored reproductions of maps and other illustrative materials were published to commemorate the five-hundredth anniversary of the death of Prince Henry the Navigator, and their appearance coincided with the Congress on the History of the Discoveries, held in Lisbon during September, 1960. Also see Roberto Almagià, *Monumenta carto-graphica Vaticana* (2 vols.; Rome, 1944). For a brief summary of cartography see Penrose, *op. cit.* (n. 62), chap. xvi.

recorded as soon as information reached Lisbon. The charts supplied to the Portuguese fleets were meticulously drawn according to the latest data on the *padrão*.[314] Like other data on Africa and Asia, the routiers, charts, and maps were classified as state secrets in an effort to prevent others from taking advantage of the Portuguese experience.[315] But, as with the other classified information, copies of the portulans and the general maps were smuggled out of Portugal and were increasingly used by cartographers in Italy, Germany, and the Low Countries as sources for their own routiers and for the engraved and woodcut maps prepared for their atlases.[316]

Da Gama's first voyage was initially recorded on the manuscript world map prepared in 1500 by Juan de la Cosa, formerly Columbus' pilot. It retains the truncated India, the two overextended peninsulas of southeastern Asia, and the Sinus Magnus of the Ptolemaic tradition. A simple legend inserted on India is all that indicates that this was the land discovered by the Portuguese. A few additional steps toward more accurate depiction occur in the anonymous world map of *ca.* 1502 called the King-Hamy-Huntington chart. Calicut is located on the shore of western India and the peninsula is elongated on its western side. Southeastern Asia, however, retains its Ptolemaic shape and vagueness. The greatest advance of these early years appears on the Cantino planisphere of 1502. Probably prepared in Lisbon,[317] this anonymous manuscript was sent as a gift to Hercules d'Este, Duke of Ferrara, by his agent, Alberto Cantino. Today it reposes in the Bibliotheca Estense in Modena. The Cantino depiction of Asia was probably derived from Arab maps and informants. On it India is given a shape very close to its true configuration, though somewhat too pointed at the tip. The Malay Peninsula, though still too broad and long, is portrayed as a single arm reaching out from southern Asia and the Sinus Magnus has completely disappeared. Ceylon and Sumatra, though slightly misplaced, are outlined with some accuracy. Finally, the world map prepared some time between 1502 and 1504 by Nicolò de Canério, a Genoese who presumably lived in Lisbon, shows a more precise and blunter India than any of the earlier charts.[318]

The first of the printed maps to incorporate bits of the new geographical information was the Contarini engraving prepared in 1506, probably in Florence. It elongates the western side of India, but the rest of Asia follows the Ptolemaic

---

[314] Cortesão and Teixeira da Mota, *op. cit.* (n. 313), I, 21, n. 7.

[315] On November 13, 1504, King Manuel's decree prohibited the graphic reproduction of the routes followed by ships in the waters of Africa to those of the Rio Manicongo, and forbade the construction of all terrestrial spheres without distinction. See Jean Denucé, *Les origines de la cartographie portugaise et les cartes des Reinels* (Ghent, 1908), pp. 1–4.

[316] On the collecting of maps in Germany by Peutinger and others see Cortesão and Teixeira da Mota, *op. cit.* (n. 313), I, 15.

[317] For a summary of the controversy about whether it was drawn by a Portuguese or an Italian cartographer see *ibid.*, I, 8–9.

[318] Like the other portulan designers of his day Canério gives only the traditional names (Tartaria, India Exgangem, India Superior, and Cataio) for interior regions. See E. L. S. Levenson, *Marine World Chart of Nicolò de Canério Januensis (1502)* (New York, 1908), p. 20.

tradition. The huge world map designed by Martin Waldseemüller in 1507, though it depended for its representation of the Americas upon the Canério chart, ignores or rejects the new information on Asia and perpetuates unmodified the Ptolemaic and Poloan conventions. The map of Johann Ruysch, which was bound into the *Geography* (Rome, 1508) of Ptolemy, probably owes its relatively advanced picture of Asia to the cartographer's willingness to follow the Cantino map—which he might have seen in Italy. But the greatest effect of the manuscript charts and the printed material circulating in Europe in the first decade of the sixteenth century is to be observed in the 1513 edition of Ptolemy printed at Strassburg. Among the additions to this monumental atlas undertaken by Waldseemüller and his colleagues at St. Dié was a map of southern Asia based on the Canério chart.[319] This new Ptolemy, which became the standard atlas until the publication in 1570 of Ortelius' *Theatrum*, was enriched in 1522 by the addition of a new, albeit faulty and fanciful, map of the East Indies[320] and another of China and "Zipangu" (Japan).

It was possible to bring most of Asia into the Ptolemaic atlas by 1522 because of the rapid progress made during the previous decade in the exploring and charting of Asia east of India. In the manuscript charts of 1508–9 (Egerton and Wolfenbüttel), India is depicted with greater accuracy than it previously had been and so is the Indian Ocean.[321] But it was in conjunction with Abreu's voyage to Malacca in 1512 that Francisco Rodrigues collected a mass of cartographic intelligence on the East Indies, southern Asia, and China which inaugurated the scientific charting of those regions in the West.[322] In his *Book*, written about 1514, Rodrigues included several charts of the Spice Islands founded on direct observation as well as charts of China, probably based upon information gathered from sailors on the wharves of Malacca. These detailed charts evidently were used by Pedro and Jorgé Reinel in their unsigned charts of 1517–19 on which the East Indies are shown in some detail, the bulge of Indochina begins to appear, and the coastline is run northeastward to the vicinity of Canton.[323] The atlas (1519) of Lopo Homem, master of the navigation charts of Portugal,

[319] On the geographical Renaissance in Germany and the growth of the Alsatian school of which Wäldseemüller was a member, see Gallois, *op. cit.* (n. 47), pp. 40–45.

[320] Waldseemüller first depicted Java and the East Indies in his woodcut planisphere of 1516. Evidently he copied this data from the Canério map. For details see J. Fischer and F. von Weiser, *The Oldest Map with the Name America of the Year 1507 and the Carta Marina of the Year 1516 by M. Waldseemüller* (Innsbruck, 1903).

[321] Cf. R. Uhden, "The Oldest Portuguese Original Chart of the Indian Ocean, A.D. 1509," *Imago mundi*, III (1939), 8–11. See also for a similar representation the anonymous Wolfenbüttel chart of 1510 as discussed in Cortesão and Teixeira da Mota, *op. cit.* (n. 313), I, 29–31.

[322] For a detailed analysis of Rodrigues' charts of the Gulf of Tongking and the China coast see Albert Kammerer, *La découverte de la Chine par les Portugais au XVIème siècle et la cartographie des portolans* (Leyden, 1944), pp. 197–202. It is possible that Rodrigues used a Javanese chart for his depiction of the archipelago and the coastal areas of southern Asia. See Cortesão and Teixeira da Moto, *op. cit.* (n. 313), I, 80.

[323] Jorgé Reinel, who defected to Seville while the Magellan expedition was being prepared, may have provided the Spanish expeditions with materials to which he had previously had access in Portugal. See Cortesão and Teixeira da Mota, *op. cit.* (n. 313), I, 19–20.

gives a representation of the world in terms of prevailing notions of cosmography and provides excellent detail on India and the East Indies.[324] In 1522 the chart by the Spaniard Garcia de Torreno locates and outlines the Philippine Islands for the first time, thus completing the mapping of insular Asia.

Torreno's information on the Philippines almost certainly was acquired from the survivors of the Magellan voyage. It was also in the years immediately after the first circumnavigation that the Pacific Ocean became a reality on European maps.[325] The hypothetical Pacific, which earlier cartographers had deduced, became increasingly real after reports reached Europe of Balboa's sighting in 1513 what he called the "South Sea." Peter Martyr suggested in 1516 that the Spice Islands lay in the sea between America and Asia. Spain, as we have seen, began to look westward hereafter in the hope of being able to invade the East Indies from their Pacific side. And, as an aftermath of Magellan's great voyage, argument began to rage between Spain and Portugal over the demarcation line in the East. To win cartographic support for their position, the Spanish evidently tried to hire Lopo Homem, the Reinels, and others to support their delegation at the meeting of 1524 held at Badajoz-Elvas. The Portuguese experts apparently remained loyal and continued to insist in 1524 and thereafter that the Spiceries should be placed within the Portuguese demarcation.[326] In the discussions which culminated in the Treaty of Saragossa (1529), the new geography, both by virtue of what was known and what still remained in dispute, was invited to play a significant role. Finally, from the point of view of the cartographers, if not of the diplomats, the Pacific was given boundaries on the east and west. Its northern and southern boundaries were not be be known until the eighteenth century.

It was the cartographer, Diogo Ribeiro, a Portuguese in the employ of Spain, whose esteemed world maps (1527, 1529) were used in their basic outlines for most of the subsequent depictions of the Eastern hemisphere and the Pacific region. The first cosmographer of Spain, Ribeiro had acted as one of the experts at the Junta of 1524 at Badajoz-Elvas. He helped Martin Centurion to translate Barbosa's book at this time.[327] After the meeting he moved his workshop to the Casa of the Spiceries at La Coruña, where he stayed until 1528. Although the Portuguese arrived in China in 1514, maps did not immediately

---

[324] *Ibid.*, I, 56–57. This compendium of information, prepared possibly with the help of the Reinels (*ibid.*, pp. 59–61), was commissioned by King Manuel. It may have been designed as a gift for King Francis I of France. This group of charts, which were probably once put together as an atlas, are now in the Bibliothèque nationale at Paris.

[325] See L. C. Wroth, "The Early Cartography of the Pacific," *The Papers of the Bibliographical Society of America*, XXXVIII (1944), 137–51.

[326] Cortesão and Teixeira da Mota, *op. cit.* (n. 313), I, 50–51.

[327] *Ibid.*, pp. 87–89. Tradition has it (*ibid.*, pp. 95–96) that the anonymous planisphere of 1525 attributed to Ribeiro and usually known as the "Castiglione planisphere" was given as a gift by Charles V to Baldassarre Castiglione when he was papal nuncio to Spain. This map locates the Moluccas in the Spanish demarcation, as do Ribeiro's other maps, on the basis of information given to the cartographer by "El Cano."

register this triumph.[328] But the coasts of southern Asia from Ceylon to north of Canton are drawn in the Ribeiro maps with considerable detail and accuracy. The East Indies and the Philippines are placed within the Spanish demarcation, and much more detail is indicated on the western side of the Malay Peninsula. Japan had still to be uncovered and to assume its correct identification and position.

While the Portuguese continued to produce excellent charts, the cartographers of other European countries began after 1530 to prepare maps of their own. Portuguese students and professors at the College of Sainte-Barbe in Paris relayed information on the discoveries of their compatriots to interested French geographers and cosmographers.[329] To Dieppe, as that Norman town began to participate prominently in overseas activities, Portuguese captains carried information on geography and navigation and other well-guarded secrets of the Portuguese admiralty.[330] João Afonso emigrated from Portugal to France around 1528 and probably settled at La Rochelle, where he prepared charts and cartographic sketches for the French expeditions.[331] Originally the maps prepared in France were based almost entirely upon the Portuguese portulans. But, around 1540, the Dieppe school, led by Pierre Desceliers, began to produce maps and atlases on which new information from their own voyages was incorporated. In 1544, a world map attributed to Sebastian Cabot and probably engraved in Antwerp retains Japan as the only conventionalized part of Asia. The rest of the Eastern Hemisphere is depicted accurately and, for the period, good detail is given on China. These developments in northern Europe were harbingers of the predominant role that the Netherlanders would soon play in the cartographic revolution of the sixteenth century.

The middle years of the century were dominated by a considerable effort to revive and revise the atlas of Ptolemy. In Basel, Sebastian Münster, who was mainly interested in descriptive geography, published four undistinguished revisions of Ptolemy between 1540 and 1552. A series of refined and elegant Italian editions of Ptolemy, mainly the work of Giacomo Gastaldi, a skilled cartographer, appeared in Venice between 1548 and 1574. A substantial number of individual and regional maps were also prepared in Venice and Rome during these years, as Italy temporarily became prominent in map-making and the publishing of maps. It is on a Gastaldi map of 1550 that the word "Giapam" (Japan) appears in place of "Zipangu" for the first time.[332] It was certainly from the Gastaldi map that Ramusio learned a few years later to identify Japan as

[328] Kammerer, *op. cit.* (n. 322), p. 191.

[329] F. Dainville, S.J., *La géographie des humanistes* (Paris, 1940), pp. 14–15.

[330] Kammerer, *op. cit.* (n. 322), p. 205.

[331] He also wrote treatises on navigation and cosmography in French and was celebrated in Rabelais' *Pantagruel* as the great sailor, "Xenomanes." See Cortesão and Teixeira da Mota, *op. cit.* (n. 313), I, 149.

[332] E. W. Dahlgren, "Les débuts de la cartographie du Japon," in *Archives d'études orientales*, IV (1911), 15. However, contrary to what Dahlgren contends, this is not the first time that the word "Giapam" or a variant of it is noted on a European document (see below, pp. 652–53).

the "Zipangu" of Marco Polo.[333] It may have been from him that Ramusio obtained the maps of India and the East Indies which he published in the 1554 edition of Volume I of his collection. On the basis of the Jesuit letters and the Portuguese portulans, Japan soon came after mid-century to be more realistically depicted and the tradition of its being one island, though it never disappeared in the sixteenth century, was gradually challenged as Portuguese cartographers and others began to distinguish three islands.[334]

From the generation following the Ribeiro planisphere of 1529, very few Iberian charts or maps are extant which show much progress in depicting the Eastern hemisphere. One of the great exceptions to this generalization is the anonymous chart of about 1535 (owned by Boies Penrose of Philadelphia since 1928) which shows great advance in the details given on the Philippines and Borneo.[335] From 1529 to 1548 new literary materials were also relatively few. In other words, once the great discoveries had all been made, with the exception of Japan, the news which came into Europe was no longer startling and no longer the subject of widely diffused newsletters. It was only when the Jesuits began to operate in the Asiatic mission field that newer materials poured into Europe and were used for cartographic documentation. Around mid-century the Jesuit letters were increasingly employed to supplement data gathered from the portulans. And it was not long thereafter that information from maps made by the Japanese arrived in Europe[336] and was used by the cartographers as they sought, in the last years of the century, to reconcile on maps their diverse and sometimes conflicting sources of information.

The portulans of the latter half of the century are extremely numerous; in Lisbon alone there were six offices which employed eighteen people in all to make sea charts.[337] The anonymous portulan of 1546, attributed to Lopo Homem[338] and drawn exclusively from navigational data, shows the Chinese coast in some detail as far north as the delta of the Yangtze, which was known to the Portuguese as the Gulf of Nanking. A series of islands located to the north and east resembles the shape of Korea. The outlines of the coasts of Indochina and Malaya, though still somewhat crude, begin to approach their true configuration. The Philippines, the Liu-ch'ius, the Spice Islands, and Sumatra, as well as many smaller islands and archipelagoes, show up clearly. The shores of Ceylon and India are almost solidly lined with names. No interior places are designated except in south India; Japan, which had been discovered three years

[333] See below, p. 653.

[334] See below, pp. 709–10.

[335] Dating of this chart following Cortesão and Teixeira da Mota, *op. cit.* (n. 313), I, 123–24.

[336] See below, pp. 709–10. For discussion of sources of the chart of 1581 in Florence, see Cortesão and Teixeira da Mota, *op. cit.* (n. 313), II, 127–28.

[337] *Ibid.*, I, 120.

[338] For a reproduction and a discussion of this attribution see Kammerer, *op. cit.* (n. 322), pp. 208–9; Cortesão and Teixiera da Mota, *op. cit.* (n. 313), I, 147–48 describe it as an anonymous chart of *ca.* 1540.

before, is not located on this planisphere or even on the coastal map of the Far East in Diogo Homem's atlas of 1558.[339]

The first realistic representation of the Japanese archipelago which we know about came in 1561 in the Asian chart of Bartolomeu Velho, his depiction including the island of Yezo.[340] Velho also places the wall between China and Tartary, and in India he gives the names of most of the important states correctly.[341] In the atlas of 1568, prepared by Fernão Vaz Dourado, separate charts of Japan and Korea appear for the first time.[342] A special chart of Ceylon which contains very full nomenclature also helps to make this one of the most distinctive atlases. In the Vaz Dourado collection of 1580 the names of Hangchow, Macao, and New Guinea appear for the first time. In 1573, on the planisphere of Domingos Teixeira, the Gulf of Pohai makes it first appearance on European maps.[343] And finally on the anonymous planisphere of 1590, attributed usually to Pedro de Limos, the Portuguese sea routes followed throughout the Far East from Calicut to Nagasaki are sketched in considerable detail.

While the coastlines of practically all of southern Asia and the Far East were known by 1590, the mapping of interior regions showed only slight progress. The Jesuits, who penetrated deeper into Japan, China, and India than any other group, provided some data in their letters on inland topographical features and cities. They and the Franciscans in the Philippines were responsible toward the end of the century for bringing copies of Chinese and Japanese maps to Europe, and these were probably used by some cartographers to help rectify their own designs.[344] The Jesuits also brought in some data on the physical geography of the Mughul empire, the Hokkaido, and Korea before 1600.

The great atlas of Abraham Ortelius, *Theatrum orbis terrarum*, first published in Antwerp in 1570, gives a fine general impression, through its successive editions, of how Asia became a part of the European cartographical image in the last generation of the sixteenth century. The first edition contained a separate map of Asia which had originally been issued independently by Ortelius in 1567, as *Asia orbis partium maximae nova descripto*.[345] This and the map incorporated in the atlas depended heavily upon the earlier maps of Asia prepared by the Piedmontese geographer Giacomo Gastaldi.[346] The first edition also contained

---

[339] See Cortesão and Teixeira da Mota, *op. cit.* (n. 313), II, 13–15.

[340] See *ibid.*, II, p. 96 and Plate 235.

[341] For discussion of his treatment of India see F. L. Pullé, "Il planisfero portoghese di Bartolomeo Velho," *Revista geografica italiana*, V (1898), 50–52.

[342] For his presumed career in India see Cortesão and Teixeira da Mota, *op. cit.* (n. 313), III, 4–6. These authors believe that his atlases of 1568 and 1580 were made in Goa. For the evolution of his cartography in general see *ibid.*, p. 7. The atlas of 1568 is now in possession of the Dukes of Alba and is preserved in the Palácio de Liria in Madrid.

[343] Kammerer, *op. cit.* (n. 322), pp. 210–11.

[344] See below, pp. 705, 710.

[345] Leo Bagrow, "A. Ortelii catalogus cartographorum," in *Petermanns Mitteilungen*, Vol. XLIII 1928), No. 199, p. 13.

[346] On Gastaldi's maps of Asia which began to appear in 1548, see *ibid.*, pp. 79–96.

regional maps of Tartary and the East Indies, the former apparently based on the Poloan tradition and the latter on the Portuguese portulans. In 1575, Ortelius, despite some doubts about his Catholic orthodoxy, was designated geographer to the king of Spain. Once Philip II became king of Portugal in 1580, it was not long before Ortelius developed close connections with Portuguese map-makers. In Ortelius' edition of 1584 a separate map of China was added to the atlas which had been drawn by Ludovicus Georgius (Luis Jorgé de Barbuda), a Portuguese cartographer.[347] The additions to the atlas made in 1590 include as the first item a map of the Pacific Ocean.[348] Five years later a separate map of Japan which first correctly located the islands between 30° and 40° north latitude was included in Ortelius. It had been prepared originally by Luis Teixeira, a Portuguese cartographer.[349] The maps of both China and Japan include signifi-cant new materials on the internal regions. Korea was shown as a peninsula on the Lopo Homem planisphere of 1554, but some maps of the later 1500's still incorrectly depict it as an island.[350]

The maps included in the works of Jan Huygen van Linschoten (1563–1611) are the last important depiction of Asia to be produced for general distribution in the sixteenth century.[351] While in India, where he spent six years (1583–89), Linschoten collected at Goa all of the detailed information he could acquire about India, the Spice Islands, China, and Japan, and assembled detailed direc-tions on the sea routes of the East. In addition to the travelogue, charts and mariners' guides which he provided in his *Itinerario*, Linschoten made public to northern Europe the best Portuguese cartography on the East then available. He also made use of the maps of Pieter Plancius, who prepared the nautical charts of the East used by the Dutch seamen for their earliest voyage.[352] Three maps of importance for the study of the East are included in the *Itinerario*: a folding map of the world in two spheres, a folding map of the Indian Ocean and the Gulf of Bengal; and a large-scale map of Goa and its surroundings with a superscript in Portuguese. Linschoten's map of the world east of India, based in part on the portulans of Fernão Vaz Dourado and Bartolomeu Lasso, are certainly superior in detail to those produced in Ortelius.[353] Both Japan and a fantastic

---

[347] This man's identity has been a matter of some controversy among cartographers. At one time he was tentatively identified as Giovanni Giorgio Settala of Milan. See Bagrow, *loc. cit.* (n. 345), Vol. XLV (1930), No. 210, p. 58. Most cartographers now believe (following A. Cortesão, *op. cit.* [n. 313], II, 276–78) that he is correctly identified as Luis Jorgé de Barbuda. For more detail on Barbuda see Cortesão and Teixeira da Mota, *op. cit.* (n. 313), II, 123–25.

[348] Bagrow, *loc. cit.* (n. 345), Vol. XLIII (1928), No. 199, p. 19.

[349] For his work on Japan see A. Cortesão, *op. cit.* (n. 313), II, 265–67. For Teixeira's letter of 1592 to Ortelius see Cortesão and Teixeira da Mota, *op. cit.* (n. 313), III, 43. For more details on the evolution of Japan in European cartography see below, pp. 709–10.

[350] See below, p. 710.

[351] Gerhard Mercator's work on Asia was very limited during his own lifetime (1512–94). The depiction included in his world maps of 1569 retains many of the Ptolemaic conventions and is undetailed. In the Mercator atlas of 1595 this earlier general map of Asia, amplified and revised by his grandson, is the only depiction of Asia included. See J. Keuning, "The History of an Atlas. Mercator-Hondius," *Imago mundi*, IV (1947), 37–62.

[352] F. C. Wieder, *Monumenta cartographica* (The Hague, 1932), II, 36–38.

[353] For a reproduction of the Eastern hemisphere map from his book see illustrations.

"Island of Korea" figure prominently on this new map, and the East Indies (especially Java) and Malaya are given more accurately and in greater detail than on any earlier printed map.

Maps, like other literary sources, reveal that news of Asia came mainly through the printed word by way of Iberia to the rest of Europe. It is clear that, in spite of the policy of control maintained by Portugal in the first half of the sixteenth century, details about Asia and the sea lanes gradually became known in Italy, France, and northern Europe. The valuable spice trade and Portugal's control of it made the merchants of Italy, southern Germany, the Netherlands, and England eager for reliable information. Some obviously wanted news to help them decide whether or how much to invest in the Portuguese spice traffic. Others, particularly after Magellan's successful circumnavigation and the running of the Portuguese blockade by his survivors, hoped to learn how to navigate directly to the East to send out ships of their own. Still others, like the Humanists, had a purely intellectual interest in learning about the East. The Catholic missionaries, who hoped to counterbalance their losses to Protestantism and the Turks in Europe by converting the heathen and setting up new ecclesiastical establishments in distant lands, were assiduous in studying the secular sources on the East. All of these groups, with their various independent and intermingled aspirations, gradually learned enough about Asia during the sixteenth century to make such knowledge the common property of educated Europeans.

That the control of information was partially effective can be substantiated in a number of ways. One of the most striking is the fact that two major Portuguese treatises on the East (Pires and Barbosa) were not published in whole or in part until after mid-century and then by a Venetian collector of travel literature. It was only after the monopoly on the spices was no longer effective (post-1549) and after the Jesuit letterbooks began to be published in France and Italy that the control on information was relaxed and the chronicles of Castanheda and Barros were published. Detailed data on the Moluccas remained a state secret for a long time thereafter, and practically nothing new was published on the Spiceries in the generation (1550–80) when books on the East were coming off the presses of Portugal at a rapid rate. News was disseminated officially throughout the century by the king's letters, ambassadors' reports, and royal embassies. Such information was usually factual, but fragmentary and undetailed. Intelligence about the sea routes, the spices, and conditions in Asia was diffused unofficially by spies and commercial agents, itinerant navigators, merchants, and students, and by the journals and routiers of foreign seamen and merchants who had hired out to the Portuguese for one or more voyages. Both official and unofficial accounts were eagerly assembled, and pamphlets, often called chapbooks or newsletters, were published in many European centers to bring the news of the discoveries to public attention. But *not a single book* dealing with the new discoveries came off the presses of Portugal before mid-century. In fact, for the generation between 1520 and 1550, practically all of the literature published on Asia was the work of non-Iberians, Italians and Germans especially. As for printed maps, during most of the sixteenth century they were generally the work of Italian, German, French, and Netherlander adapters of the unpublished Portuguese portulans.

In the first half of the sixteenth century India, the East Indies, and the Philippines primarily occupied the compilers of newsletters and the engravers of maps. Even before the capture of Malacca in 1511, Europe was able to read about India and the Spice Islands in Varthema's account. The Portuguese embassy to Rome of 1514 brought news of Albuquerque's conquest of Malacca and let Europe know that the East with all its wealth had fallen to Portugal. The voyage of Magellan shattered the illusion of Portugal's absolute supremacy on the Eastern seas, and hence over the spice trade, and stimulated the hope in Spain and elsewhere that the wealth of the Spiceries might be available to all comers. Efforts to capitalize on Magellan's experience through negotiation and blockade-running were made, but the Portuguese managed until mid-century to retain their virtual monopoly on spices and information.

In the latter half of the century the attention of the Europeans gradually became focused on Japan and China rather than on India and southeast Asia. This shift of interest to eastern Asia was brought about in part by the setbacks experienced in India, by the missionary successes in the Philippines and Japan, and by the growing hope that the Asiatic continent might be forced to open its doors, either through Indochina or southern China, to the representatives of Philip II, the personal ruler of all European outposts in Asia.[354] Even though it might seem obvious that France would be more interested in the Levant and America than in Asia, examination of the new titles printed in France for the period from 1480 to 1609 shows that there were one hundred books about Asia to eighty about the Turks, and to forty on the New World.[355] A substantial portion of those issued in the last generation of the sixteenth century were titles dealing with China and Japan as independent countries.

The great travel collections and printed atlases of the latter half of the century were designed to appeal to an international audience. The atlases, in particular, were comprehensible to and could be studied by all language groups. The atlas of Ortelius, which replaced Ptolemy, was in great demand and went through many editions and translations in the last generation of the century—mostly in northern Europe. The travel collections were likewise translated, printed, and circulated, not from Madrid or Lisbon, but from Italy and northern Europe. The works bearing the names of Ramusio, Hakluyt, and De Bry were well illustrated with engravings and maps. The atlases often included, on their side, interesting textual data. Linschoten, whose fame rests mainly on his narrative, also provided the reading public with some of the best maps of Asia printed in the sixteenth century. Of the secular sources which appeared in printed form,

[354] See below, pp. 296-301.
[355] G. Atkinson, *Les nouveaux horizons de la renaissance française* (Paris, 1935), pp. 10-11.

the atlases and comprehensive travel books with their rich illustrative materials summarized within themselves the European state of knowledge about Asia. Ortelius and Mercator, it is often forgotten, were themselves collectors and adapters. In preparing their maps they borrowed freely from the existing cartographic, narrative, and pictorial materials. The collectors of travel accounts were likewise heavily dependent upon works already in print. The printed word, whatever form it assumed, was undoubtedly the main channel through which Europeans received the information on which to base their evolving conception of the countries of the East.

The Christian Mission

The sixteenth-century Portuguese were by no means novices in questions pertaining to the propagation of the faith, the battling of infidels, and the conversion of heathens. In the past their country had played an active part in the Crusades and as early as 1319 had a national crusading militia called the Order of Christ which was the Portuguese counterpart of the Knights Templar. A century after its establishment, Prince Henry the Navigator became the apostolic administrator of the Order of Christ, and with his death in 1460 this office was assumed by the crown. In connection with Portugal's explorations and conquests in Africa during the fifteenth century, the crown used the Order of Christ to bring Christian teachings to its new subjects. In assuming the role of protector and propagator of Christianity in the overseas world, the Portuguese kings acted with Rome's approval and encouragement. The progress of the Christian mission in the East was consequently related to the successes and failures of the empire-builders.

Missionaries and secular priests were aboard the first vessels to round the tip of Africa bound for the ports of Malabar. Men of religion triumphed and died beside the swashbuckling *fidalgos* who relentlessly fought the Muslims as holy enemies and sincerely believed that they were helping to bring Christian light to peoples living in pagan darkness. Goa became the administrative center of the empire in 1530 and shortly thereafter it was made an episcopal see. Other Portuguese centers of trade and colonial endeavor—such as Malacca and Macao—likewise became great ecclesiastical centers. Although some of the missionaries ventured to carry the gospel to places where the Portuguese were not firmly entrenched, they were few in number and their successes came only at the end of the century. That the propagators of the gospel initially depended upon the secular arm is neither unusual nor unseemly. While numerous books on Portuguese expansion recount the details of the administrative structure of the empire, no monographic study has yet been made of the politico-religious developments within the *padroado* (patronage) during the sixteenth century. What follows will not remedy this deficiency. But, considering the lack of a general survey of this kind, we have here provided a quick summary, based on secular and religious scholarship, of the relationship between religion and the state in Asia, of the central role played by the Jesuits therein, of the evolution of the Jesuit system of communication, and of the publication in Europe of the Jesuit letterbooks and histories. What appears in this chapter is offered as background so that the Jesuit letters and missionary histories may be effectively used as sources for Asian history and for Europe's awakening to the Asia of reality.

I

THE PORTUGUESE "PADROADO" (PATRONAGE) OF THE EAST

By a series of papal bulls issued in the fifteenth and sixteenth centuries the Portuguese crown was entrusted with what came to be called the *padroado*. This meant that the crown was granted the use of certain ecclesiastical revenues within Portugal and the right to propose candidates to the papacy for the sees and ecclesiastical benefices in Africa and the Indies. Such a concession hinged on the condition that the crown would assume responsibility for providing good missionaries and the appropriate financial support for the religious establishments and activities in the territories acquired by conquest.[1] Questions soon arose between Portugal and Rome, and Portugal and the other secular powers, as to the correct interpretation and application of the papal grants. Once the demarcation line had been established in 1494, the Portuguese claimed a religious monopoly, similar to their economic and information monopolies, of Asia, India, the East Indies, China, and Japan. The papacy, for its part, insisted that the grant applied only to those territories actually acquired and held by the Portuguese crown and not to the greater part of the continent of Africa and the countries of the East. A long time was to pass before the limits upon the Portuguese patronage were agreed to by all the parties concerned, and during the entire sixteenth century many unresolved differences over ecclesiastical

---

[1] For a general discussion of the *padroado* and its early historical development see Father António da Silva Rego, *História das missões do padroado português do Oriente. India (1500–42)* (Lisbon, 1949), I, 91–102; P. A. Jann, *Die katholischen Missionen in Indien, China und Japan. Ihre Organisation und das portugiesische Patronat vom 15. bis ins 18. Jahrhundert* (Paderborn, 1915), pp. 55–63; C. R. Boxer, "The Portuguese *Padroado* in East Asia and the Problem of the Chinese Rites, 1576–1773," *Instituto Português de Hongkong, Boletim*, No. 1 (July 1948), 199–226. For a vast collection of pertinent material see Silva Rego (comp. and ed.), *Documentação para a história das missões do padroado português do Oriente* (12 vols.; Lisbon, 1947–60). For detail on the functioning of the system see Fortunato Coutinho, *Le régime paroissial des diocèses de rite latin de l'Inde des origines (XVI siècle) à nos jours* (Louvain, 1958). For Rome's official position see the article by Joseph Brucker on "Protectorate of Missions" in *Catholic Encyclopedia* (New York, 1911), XII, 488–92.

jurisdiction complicated the work of the missionaries. The most recent definition of the *padroado* is contained in the Portuguese Concordat of 1940.[2]

When Vasco da Gama landed near Calicut in 1498, a Trinitarian, Pedro de Covilham, disembarked with him. Though next to nothing is known about his work or how he died, Covilham inaugurated the modern phase of Christian missionary activity in India.[3] Cabral's fleet of 1500 carried a vicar, eight secular priests, and eight Franciscans to the East. Even before arriving at Calicut, the Franciscans had baptized twenty-two inhabitants of the island of Anjediva. The eager friars, shortly after their arrival in Calicut, reputedly converted a Brahman and some leading Nāyars. These successes alarmed the Moors of Calicut, and in their turn they reportedly convinced the Zamorin that the Portuguese were advance agents of a conquering army.[4] In the course of the clash which then ensued between Cabral and the Zamorin, three of the Franciscans were killed and their superior, Father Henrique Alvaro of Coimbra, was sorely wounded.[5] The Portuguese, after their break with the Zamorin, sailed to Cochin where they met with a friendlier reception. Thus in Cochin and southern Malabar generally, the Franciscans were permitted to carry on the work of John Marignolli, a Franciscan who had tried to begin Christianizing there in 1346–47.

Like their Italian forerunner, the Portuguese Franciscans immediately took a great interest in the Christians of St. Thomas. About thirty thousand families of St. Thomas Christians then lived in twenty towns and a great number of villages in the interior hills of Malabar, Quilon, and Travancore. Shortly before the arrival of the Portuguese, the Christians of south India had received a Metropolitan and three suffragan bishops from Mesopotamia. These Chaldean prelates had just reorganized the Syro-Malabar church before the arrival of the Latin Christians. Aside from their devotion to Christianity, the adherents of St. Thomas were of interest to the Portuguese because of their economic and social position. Traditionally, the Malabar Christians of Quilon were charged with supervising the weights and keeping the seal of the city (i.e., administering customs). Although they had lost some of these privileges by 1504, they were still respected and influential members of the trading community. Moreover, they were valued by the Portuguese as excellent soldiers. Consequently, the Portuguese recognized from the outset that their co-operation in the spice trade and in negotiating with local rulers could be very valuable.[6] But, even

[2] For appropriate articles of the mission agreement see B. J. Wenzel, *Portugal und der Heilige Stuhl* (Lisbon, 1958), pp. 301–19.

[3] See M. Müllbauer, *Geschichte der katholischen Missionen in Ostindien* (Freiburg i. B., 1852), p. 42. While this is an indispensable survey of the Indian mission, it is far from trustworthy on detail—especially statistics.

[4] L. Lemmens, *Geschichte der Franziskanermissionen* (Münster, 1929), pp. 95–96.

[5] For confirmation from Malabar sources see G. Schurhammer, S.J., "Three Letters of Mar Iacob, Bishop of Malabar, 1503–50," *Gregorianum*, XIV (1933), 66.

[6] On the religious reorganization of the Syro-Malabar Church see Cardinal Eugene Tisserant, *Eastern Christianity in India* (Calcutta, 1957), pp. 30–31; on its social and economic role see Leslie W. Brown, Bishop of Uganda, *The Indian Christians of St. Thomas* (Cambridge, 1956), p. 75.

though the Indian Christians had preserved their faith while living in the midst of non-Christians, their social assimilation into the Hindu caste system soon made them seem strange and heathen to some of the Portuguese.

Many of the St. Thomas Christians, on their side, apparently felt from the beginning that they were brothers in the faith with the Portuguese and that they might view the Portuguese king as a Christian ally.[7] Though the Indian Christians were generally considered by the Europeans to belong under the patronage of Portugal, factions developed very early among the Indian Christians themselves to resist the Latin assumption of supremacy and to retain the older relationship of the St. Thomas church with the Chaldean rite.[8] Throughout the first half of the sixteenth century, the Franciscans, with the tacit cooperation of the Malabar bishop, Mar Jacob, quietly sought to win the St. Thomas Christians over to the Roman rite through missionary work and the education of a native Latin clergy in both Europe and Cranganore. In 1539, four Malabar students were sent to Lisbon to study for the priesthood, and it was from one of these young seminarians that Barros obtained some of his information on the St. Thomas Christians.[9] Apparently the training that the Malabar Christians received in Europe and in the seminaries which shortly thereafter were set up in India was insufficient to turn them away from their non-Latin rites, ceremonies, practices, and customs.

When Cabral sailed back to Portugal in 1501, he had aboard Father Henrique, the Franciscan superior. The friar was carrying news to Lisbon of the prospects for Christianity in south India and had in his charge two Malabar priests destined for Europe.[10] He left behind in India three Franciscan missionaries: Francisco da Cruz, Simão de Guimaraes, and Luís do Salvador. By 1502, when thirteen more Franciscans disembarked in Malabar, two of these pioneering missionaries were dead. The fleet of the following year brought five Dominicans under the leadership of Domingo de Sousa, who had been sent to work in India at the invitation of King Manuel. Shortly thereafter the Portuguese built at Cochin a wooden church, the first in India, over which the Dominicans assumed pastoral care.[11] The Franciscans concentrated on winning the St. Thomas Christians over to the Latin rite, on preaching to the heathens, and on studying local customs and religious practices.[12] At the outset they generally worked at the ports where the Portuguese exercised control or had significant

[7] Brown, *op. cit.* (n. 6), p. 15, and Schurhammer, *loc. cit.* (n. 5), pp. 69–70.

[8] For a genealogy which graphically simplifies the complex ecclesiastical organization of the various branches of the Christian church and which shows the precise placement therein of the Syro-Malabar Catholics see Francis M. Rogers, *The Quest for Eastern Christians: Travel and Rumor in the Age of Discovery* (Minneapolis, 1962), pp. 16–17.

[9] See Schurhammer, *loc. cit.* (n. 5), pp. 81–82. As early as 1518, Pope Leo X published a bull which empowered the chaplain of the king of Portugal to admit Indians staying in Portugal to all Holy Orders. In 1552, the two Malabar youths were reported as living in Cranganore. M. D'Sa, *History of the Catholic Church in India* (Bombay, 1910), I, 121.

[10] On Priest Joseph in Europe see above, p. 157.

[11] Müllbauer, *op. cit.* (n. 3), p. 45.

[12] Silva Rego, *op. cit.* (n. 1, *História das missões*), p. 157.

influence. When Friar Luís do Salvador in 1512 went inland to Vijayanagar, beyond the confines of Portuguese power, he was murdered by a Moor. But it may have been that Salvador was killed because he had been sent to propose an alliance with Vijayanagar against Calicut. Somewhat later, other Franciscans, through their association with the St. Thomas Christians, safely crossed south India to the tomb of St. Thomas at Mylapore and to Negapatam on the Coromandel Coast.[13]

While the missionaries in south India were breaking ground, events were transpiring elsewhere which were to affect vitally the conduct of Christian affairs in the East. The capture of Goa in 1510, the progress of the Portuguese northward to Cambay, and the seizure of Malacca in 1511 had religious as well as political repercussions. King Manuel, who expressed his elation at the swift progress of the eastward conquest by dispatching an embassy to Rome in 1514, determined in the same year to regularize the religious administration of the East. By a bull of 1500, Pope Alexander VI had granted to the Portuguese crown the power to name an Apostolic Commissary for India, who should possess all the usual powers of the bishop's office. He was to be responsible directly to the church hierarchy,[14] though it was not required that he should belong to the Order of Christ or be accountable to its administrator, the Vicar of Tomar. Not until 1514 did King Manuel decide to create, with the concurrence of Rome, an independent bishopric for the overseas world. The seat of the new diocese was then established at Funchal in the Madeiras, the first incumbent being the Dominican, Bishop Duarte Nunes.[15] He was lord over all ecclesiastical activities in Brazil, India, the Indies, and China, and responsible to the Metropolitan of Lisbon. Nunes eventually went to India himself in the fleet of 1520 to visit as Apostolic Commissary the Christian establishments in Goa, Cannanore, and Cochin. From these places he reported to Europe by letter on the sad state of Christian affairs in India. He evidently returned to Portugal in 1525.[16]

After capturing Goa, Albuquerque re-enunciated what by this time had become the religious and social policies of the Portuguese crown within the *padroado*: relentless war against the Muslims, and friendship and toleration for the heathens. One of the conqueror's first acts in Goa was to build a simple Christian church dedicated to St. Catherine, on whose feast day he had occupied the city. This chapel, which still stands, was initially given over to the ministrations of the Dominicans and later to the seculars. In 1514, along with the other administrative innovations of that year, the office of vicar-general was created in the East. Its first occupant was a Dominican, Domingo de Sousa. He and Albuquerque were responsible for inaugurating the policy at Cochin

---

[13] A. Meersman, *The Friars Minor or the Franciscans in India, 1291–1941* (Karachi, 1943), p. 9.
[14] Jann, *op. cit.* (n. 1), pp. 61–62.
[15] For this identification see B. M. Biermann, O.P., "Der erste Bischof in Ost-Indien," *Neue Zeitschrift für Missionswissenschaft*, IX (1953), 81–83. Hereafter cited as *NZM*.
[16] *Ibid.*, pp. 83–89.

and Goa of encouraging and subsidizing marriages between native women and the Portuguese. Since most of the marriages contracted were between common Portuguese and low-caste natives, the *fidalgos* and the higher-caste Hindus were very critical of this policy. The marriage of Christians with low-caste women, it was contended, had the effect of lowering all Christians in the eyes of the higher castes. For his part, Bishop Nunes felt that the sacramental vow of marriage was often taken too lightly by the Portuguese and was not clearly understood by their mates. He also deplored the generally irresponsible conduct of the Portuguese which he felt showed the Europeans in their worst possible light and brought disrepute to Christianity.[17] Nevertheless, the growth of Luso-Indian families and communities in Goa and elsewhere ultimately provided a solid foundation for the extension of Christianity in India.

While the Dominicans and the seculars in the better established Portuguese communities of India devoted their time to caring for the Christian families, the Franciscans concentrated on proselytizing the natives. The first sizable contingent of Franciscans arrived in Goa in 1517 and began at once to baptize large numbers of the lower-caste natives and to establish a center there.[18] By 1521 they had refurbished some local houses and converted them into the convent and church of St. Francis.[19] In the following year another Franciscan convent was completed at Cochin.[20] The royal hospitals and schools, some of which had been established as early as 1510, were also staffed in large part by Franciscans and their converts. From such centers the friars accompanied or followed the Portuguese fleets into other Indian coastal towns.

The Portuguese Franciscans active in India belonged almost exclusively to the mendicant Observants, or Friars Minor. Stressing close observance of St. Francis' rule of poverty, the Observants had become by the sixteenth century the most influential branch of the Franciscans. In the interest of the Order's internal peace, Pope Leo X in 1517 divided the Franciscans into two distinct and independent bodies: the Conventuals, who were allowed to possess property and fixed income, and the Observants. Each of these bodies was permitted thereafter to have its own minister general, provinces, and general chapter.[21] The Observants, therefore, classified India as the Vice-Province (custody) of St. Thomas and placed it organizationally under the Observant province of Portugal. It was not until 1612 that the papacy officially raised the Franciscan establishment as a whole in India to provincial status.

By 1534 the Vice-Province of St. Thomas included thirteen Franciscan establishments on India's west coast: Diu, Damão, Bassein, Tana, Karanja, Chaul, Goa, Anjediva, Mangalor, Cannanore, Calicut, Cochin, and Quilon.

---

[17] *Ibid.*, pp. 85–86.

[18] Silva Rego, *op. cit.* (n. 1, *História das missões*), p. 109; Lemmens, *op. cit.* (n. 4), p. 97.

[19] For descriptions of those edifices which still stand see J. N. de Fonseca, *An Historical and Archaeological Sketch of the City of Goa* (Bombay, 1878), pp. 220–25.

[20] Silva Rego, *op. cit.* (n. 1, *História das missões*), p. 158.

[21] On the complete separation see R. M. Huber, O.F.M. Conv., *A Documented History of the Franciscan Order* (Milwaukee, 1944), I, chap. xxxvii.

The establishments on the Malabar Coast were generally the earliest founded, but the mission at Calicut was never developed extensively because of the political opposition of the Zamorin to the Portuguese. The west coast missions to the north of Goa were all established in 1534, when the Portuguese obtained political control over those territories, though several friars had preached in this region at earlier dates. On the east coast, where Portuguese control had not been established, the Franciscans had mission stations at Tuticorin, Negapatam, and Mylapore. The tomb of St. Thomas at Mylapore was a major object of interest to the Franciscans because of its reputation in Europe and because of the immediate concern to win over the St. Thomas Christians to the Latin rite. Groups of Portuguese made pilgrimages to the shrine of St. Thomas on several occasions. The Franciscans built a small church there, allegedly as early as 1516.[22] A delegation was sent out in 1523 by the governor at Goa to investigate the matter more thoroughly. It was this group which opened the tomb reputed to be that of the apostle and placed his remains in a coffer on the main altar of the small church. The Franciscans, who built a church at Colombo in Ceylon shortly after 1518, by 1534 were likewise becoming established there, after weathering a number of storms.

As Christian responsibilities spread in India and as Goa increasingly became Christian and Portuguese, it was necessary once again to adjust the ecclesiastical organization to meet the new conditions.[23] In 1530, Goa officially became the viceregal capital; four years later Pope Paul III formally elevated it to the status of an episcopal see, suffragan to Funchal. The Bishop of Goa in 1534 was given ecclesiastical jurisdiction over the vast territory lying between the Cape of Good Hope in the west and the "islands of China" in the east. Thus within his episcopacy he counted the various states of East Africa, Arabia, Persia, India, the East Indies, and China. The Portuguese interpreted the bull of Goa's elevation to mean that all these lands, whether under Portuguese or native control, were subject to Goa's ecclesiastical jurisdiction and within the *padroado*. Rome contended that Goa's authority, like that of Funchal, was limited to areas that could reasonably be considered parts of Portugal's colonial empire.[24] At this time, however, differences in interpretation remained academic since the missionaries ordinarily worked in territories where Portuguese factories already existed. The new Bishop of Goa and his chapter at the Cathedral of St. Catherine were paid their annual salaries by the Archbishop of Funchal and the Portuguese crown jointly.

A good example of the way in which church and state worked together in India during these early years is to be found in the story of the Christian

---

[22] Lemmens, *op. cit.* (n. 4), p. 94, gives 1518 as its founding date; Meersman, *op. cit.* (n. 13), p. 100, traces its founding back to 1511. Meersman, p. 96, assails other scholars, Jesuits included, who refuse to believe the inscription on an "ancient-looking" stone which credits Brother Pedro da Stongia with building this church in 1516. The others refuse to accept the legend of the stone because it is not confirmed by any contemporary source.

[23] See above, p. 233.

[24] Jann, *op. cit.* (n. 1), pp. 87–90.

conversion of the Paravans of the Fishery Coast.[25] On this narrow and barren coastal strip, which runs eastward from the southern tip of the peninsula to Adam's Bridge, the Tamil-speaking Paravans had fished for pearls throughout historical times. Under the Pândyan kings, the Paravans enjoyed a monopoly of the pearl-fishing rights.[26] At the beginning of the sixteenth century, as the power of Pândya waned, the neighboring kings turned covetous eyes toward the revenue-producing fisheries, and a series of wars ensued. To carry on their campaigns for this rich prize, the kings of the south needed horses from Arabia. These were supplied to them mainly through the *Mophla* and *Labbai* traders based in the Indian-Muslim colonies of the ports of Malabar and Coromandel. By combining efforts with certain of the local rulers, these Muslims were gradually able to gain control over the fisheries and to enslave the Paravans.[27] As a part of their general attack upon Muslim holdings in India, the Portuguese, from their vantage points in Malabar and Ceylon, began around 1524 to participate in the struggle for the fisheries. For the next fourteen years, in alliance with friendly groups of Paravans, the Portuguese fought the Muslims and their cohorts for control of the Fishery Coast and this struggle quickly became related to their wars with Calicut. Although Calicut was forced to bow to the Portuguese by 1530, the struggle on the Fishery Coast was prolonged by the entrance of Vijayanagar into the fray. Four more years of war plagued the Paravans until finally, in 1534, they and their Portuguese allies emerged triumphant. As peace became a reality, the Paravans, at the urging of D. João da Cruz, a Christian *chetty* (merchant) from Calicut, agreed to accept Christianity as part of the price of Portuguese protection. Three Franciscans, possibly from the convent at Cochin, then journeyed to the Paravans to instruct them in Christian teachings. Although the friars claimed to have baptized as many as 140,000 Paravans by 1537, it is evident from later reports that most of these were conversions in name only. Letters were sent back to Portugal in 1536–37 and news was relayed to Rome telling of the great progress being made in Christianizing this desolate bit of coast. This hopeful news and urging by some of the Portuguese officials prompted Francis Xavier, shortly after his arrival in India in 1542, to visit the Fishery Coast.[28]

Christian successes in the south were more than matched in the north by the Franciscan activities undertaken after 1534 in the territories which the Portuguese had acquired from the Sultan of Gujarat. At Bassein, Chaul, and Damão, as well as on the islands of Salsette and Diu, the Franciscans made large numbers of converts and, with financial aid from the crown, founded a number of convents, churches, hospitals, orphanages, schools, and seminaries. At Goa, meanwhile,

---

[25] Georg Schurhammer, S.J., "Die Bekehrung der Paraver (1535–37)," *Archivum historicum Societatis Iesu*, IV (1935), 201–33. Hereafter cited as *AHSI*.

[26] K. A. Nilakanta Sastri, *The Pândyan Kingdom from the Earliest Times to the Sixteenth Century* (London, 1929), pp. 194–95.

[27] Cf. comments of Duarte Barbosa as summarized below, pp. 408–9.

[28] Schurhammer, *loc. cit.* (n. 25), p. 220; Meersman, *op. cit.* (n. 13), p. 63.

the reputation of the Christians, which had suffered at the outset from its almost exclusive association with the lower castes, was enhanced through the policies inaugurated after 1538 by the Franciscan bishop, João de Albuquerque. He was more than a little concerned with the recruitment and training of native Christians, and in 1541 Master Diego de Borba founded the College of the Holy Faith in Goa as a training center.²⁹ At about this same time Friar Vicente de Lagos established a seminary at Cranganore whose student body came to include one hundred boys from the most aristocratic families of the St. Thomas Christians.³⁰

While the missionaries made converts and built schools, the Portuguese state in conjunction with the church began to lay down a harsher policy in India. To the European statesman of the sixteenth century, religious uniformity was normally deemed an essential prerequisite for political stability and unity. The presence of Muslims and heathens within the body politic of Portuguese India could only be viewed in Lisbon and Goa as a threat, actual and potential, to effective governing and internal peace. War against the Muslims was generally considered to be "holy," and was looked upon by the Portuguese as a continuation in India of the struggle in Europe and Africa against the Moors. The problem of what to do about those heathens who persisted in the error of their ways was more difficult to resolve. Albuquerque, perhaps because he was continually on the defensive, had pursued a policy of friendship and toleration toward heathens; but this mild policy had failed to produce the desired religious uniformity.

Friction between the missionaries and the secular authorities meanwhile contributed to the problems of both church and state in Portuguese India. The Orders had apparently been assured that most of the menial posts in the administration at Goa would be given to the neophytes and orphans in their charge.³¹ This was an important arrangement because conversion usually meant expulsion from the caste relationship and from former employment. But the royal officials in Goa often appointed and retained heathens in posts which the missionaries wanted to fill with converts. The Portuguese officials were also charged with refusing to pay the bequests which the king intended for the support of the church and the missionaries. The failure of the officials in Goa to meet these obligations should not be attributed entirely to stinginess or to a simple willingness to accept bribes for jobs from the highest bidder. It is important to keep in mind that the demands upon them were numerous, because the military situation was precarious: the siege of Diu was relieved only in 1546, the Adil Khan was constantly threatening Goa itself, and vast sums were consequently being paid out for defense. Nor should it be overlooked that the honest administrator probably preferred a Hindu of influence and experience to a neophyte whose only claim to a job was his Christianity. Although religious

---

²⁹ Carlos Merces de Melo, S.J., *The Recruitment and Formation of the Native Clergy in India* (Lisbon, 1955), pp. 65–109.

³⁰ For Franciscan activities at Cranganore see Meersman, *op. cit.* (n. 13), pp. 68–74.

³¹ H. Heras, S.J., *The Conversion Policy of the Jesuits in India* (Bombay, 1933), pp. 57–58.

historians often assert that the crown was contributing a mere pittance to the missionary effort in relation to the returns from trade,[32] it is essential to keep in mind, as we have discussed earlier,[33] that the returns to the royal treasury from commerce with India were often not enough at this time to pay for the expenses involved. It may be suggested that the missionaries in the field, who had to depend for their existence upon the royal donations and alms, were comparing their state to that of the merchants and officials in the colonies, many of whom were living in ostentatious style.

Conversion policy was also a divisive political and religious question. The early mass conversions performed by the Franciscans in Goa and on the Fishery Coast were supported by the political authorities. The people so converted were usually not prepared to give up native practices considered to be un-Christian by the orthodox, or sufficiently instructed in Christian doctrine to understand what they were affirming. Nor could it be said that the Portuguese in India helped the cause of Christianity by their behavior. During Xavier's decade (1542–52) of service in the East, he discouraged forced conversions and stressed in his brief visits to Goa a greater emphasis upon teaching the young and the slaves and educating a native clergy who could communicate with the laity in their own tongues.[34] The ordination of Indians as priests had begun in 1534, but their numbers were never large. Although Xavier apparently was not interested primarily in dramatic conversions of important Brahmans or Hindu officials, when the situation required it he showed no hesitancy in calling on the secular arm.[35] It was this open reliance upon secular power which made the Portuguese authorities take more than a passing interest in religious affairs. And from the secular viewpoint, the program adumbrated by Xavier,[36] like that of Albuquerque, was too slow in bringing about the desired religio-political unity.

In Europe and Africa the Portuguese had often used the power of the state in their efforts to achieve religious uniformity. Jews and Muslims had been cajoled, bribed, and forced into accepting Christianity. Those who finally proved to be truculent, insincere, or too much motivated by material interests were forcibly expelled from Portuguese territories. In India, so long as the Portuguese were on the defensive, the viceregal government made no systematic effort to enforce religious uniformity. Once a permanent secular and ecclesiastical administration based on Goa had come into existence, a more forceful policy toward dissent gradually evolved. Mosques, temples, and idols, the outward symbols of nonconformity, were attacked first. In 1541 the Hindu temples

[32] For example, Müllbauer, *op. cit.* (n. 3), p. 77; for some figures on the crown's contribution to the maintenance of religious institutions in Goa see D'Sa, *op. cit.* (n. 9), I, 204.

[33] See above, p. 140.

[34] See G. M. Moraes, "St. Francis Xavier, Apostolic Nuncio, 1542–1552," *Journal of the Bombay Branch of the Royal Asiatic Society,* New Ser., XXVII (1950), 279–313. Cf. the account of Portuguese policy in Ceylon, below, pp. 271–74.

[35] *Ibid.,* p. 298.

[36] See below, pp. 247–50.

of Goa and the neighboring territories were systematically destroyed, and the tie between church and state was formalized in 1545–46 by a series of reports and decrees which laid down general lines for the future development of the missionary enterprise within the *padroado*.[37]

Miguel Vaz, Vicar-General of Goa (1533–47), was sent to Portugal in 1545 to deliver a report to King John III on the condition of the mission. In his detailed written reply to this report, the king urged Vaz to appeal for help to the secular arm and to expect backing whenever and wherever it should be required. Specifically he urged that conversions should be carried on as swiftly and as inoffensively as possible. The king of Cochin, a Hindu ally of the Portuguese, who had customarily taken away the properties and positions of the Christian converts, would be forbidden to continue his anti-Christian practices. But, the king in Lisbon exhorted Vaz to maintain good relations with the Christians of St. Thomas so that they should have no cause to complain in their business dealings with the Portuguese pepper traders.[38] Where the missionaries experienced difficulty in constructing churches or carrying on missions, they were told to appeal to the governor for aid in getting personnel, materials, or whatever else they needed. Schools for religious instruction should be built in all the villages of the island of Goa. Twice each year, at least, preachers should be sent to the schools and non-Christians must be required to attend the services.

Three days after preparing his directive to Vaz, the king produced a series of detailed instructions for the governor, D. João de Castro, which brings out clearly how closely church and state were bound together in India. In this brief the king orders that neither public nor private "idols" be tolerated on the island of Goa and that severe punishment must be meted out to those who persist in keeping them. The houses of people suspected of keeping hidden idols are to be searched. Heathen festivals are not to be tolerated and every Brahman is to be banished from Goa, Bassein, and Diu. Public offices are to be entrusted to neophytes and not to heathens; Christians are to be freed from heavy labor at the port of Goa, such tasks in the future being reserved exclusively for heathens. Portuguese, under pain of severe punishment, are forbidden to sell heathen slaves to Muslims, since heathens are converted more easily to Christianity under Portuguese and to Islam under Muslim ownership. Revenues previously used for the support of mosques and temples should be diverted to aid in spreading the gospel. The governor should help the vicar by building churches and schools, by limiting the anti-Christian activities of the king of Cochin, and by doing nothing to induce the St. Thomas Christians to be troublesome about the weights in the pepper trade. Heathens everywhere should be prevented from painting pictures of Christ, the Virgin, and the Saints, and from peddling them

---

[37] J. Wicki, "Die ältere katholische Mission in der Begegnung mit Indien," *Saeculum*, VI (1955), 362–66.

[38] It was possibly Xavier who urged Vaz to inform the king about the fraudulent practices of the Portuguese merchants in their dealings with the native Christians. See Moraes, *loc. cit.* (n. 34), p. 288.

from door to door. Many of these directives soon acquired the force of law, and on occasion the viceregal law was more severe than the king's instructions.

In the middle of the sixteenth century, as the Christian decrees and directives of the Portuguese authorities multiplied, a special officer was delegated to see to their administration. The "Father of the Christians" (*Pai dos Cristãos*), who was a layman at first, acted as the protector and supervisor of the neophytes in the major mission stations of India, and ultimately of those in Malacca and Macao. Slightly later, when members of the religious Orders took over this office, the royal directives were compiled for their guidance and several of these manuscript volumes have been preserved.[39] From these voluminous and disorderly compilations, it is possible to see that the natives resisted most stubbornly those measures which endangered their religious, financial, and social institutions. Even in Goa, the populace fought bitterly against the diversion of tax revenues to the support of the Christian establishment, against state interference with inheritance practices, against the monopoly by Christians of state offices, against the expulsion of Brahmans, and against the decree which ordained that the minor children of deceased heathen parents were to be educated as Christians. While the directives of the Portuguese authorities look extremely severe on paper, it is evident from the fact that they are repeated again and again that they were not always effectively enforced. Perhaps part of the reason for this delinquency may be found in the conflict between church and state.[40] For, while the missionaries regularly sought state support, they sometimes opposed state interests, as in their growing determination to force the Christians of St. Thomas to abandon many traditional, social and religious practices even at the risk of endangering Portuguese commercial relations with the influential native Christians of Malabar.

Adjustments in church organization were again undertaken in Europe in response to the expansion of Christian responsibilities and interests in the East. Pope Julius III in 1551 conferred upon King John III the hereditary office of Grand Master over all three of Portugal's militant religious orders, with all of their foundations, estates, and revenues. Shortly thereafter, the archbishopric of Funchal, which was too close to Lisbon and too far from the colonies to act independently and effectively, was shorn of its powers. Bishop João de Albuquerque, shortly before his death in India in 1553, had raised the question of elevating Goa to be the Metropolitan center for the entire Portuguese East. In Lisbon, meanwhile, affairs were complicated by the demise in 1557 of King John III. So it was not until 1558 that Goa actually became an effectively working archdiocese, with control over East Africa, India, the East Indies,

---

[39] For details see Wicki, *loc. cit.* (n. 37), p. 364

[40] *Ibid.*, p. 365. Also see Xavier's letter from Cochin (January 20, 1548) to King John complaining about the failures of the governor to support the mission and reproaching the king for not being more severe with his servants. "All that is needed," writes Xavier, "for everyone in India to become Christian is for Your Majesty to punish a Governor severely." (G. Schurhammer and J. Wicki [eds.], *Epistolae S. Francisci Xaverii aliaque eius scripta* [Rome, 1945], I, 407.)

China and Japan. Portugal, by the terms of the papal bull of elevation (1558) was, as before, to retain all rights of patronage in the East. And, because of its distance from Europe, Goa was soon to achieve unrivaled independence as a Metropolitan center.[41]

Along with the creation of the archbishopric of Goa, two suffragan sees came into existence at Cochin and Malacca in 1558. The archdiocese of Goa was thus divided into three administrative units. Goa itself exercised direct authority over the East African and Persian possessions of the Portuguese as well as the entire west coast of India as far south as Kanara. Cochin was given episcopal powers over the southwest and the east coasts of India as well as over Ceylon and Pegu (Burma). The diocese of Malacca comprised all of Asia east of Pegu, including China and Japan.[42] But in 1576 the suffragan see of Macao, with jurisdiction over China and Japan, came into existence. Twelve years later, after numerous conversions had been made in Japan, a separate diocese for the Mikado's empire was ordered for Funai in 1588. Throughout the sixteenth century, as an independent archbishopric, Goa continued to hold the reins of ecclesiastical power through its suffragans, and the crown of Portugal retained its patronage rights throughout its Eastern empire. In matters where crown and pope came into conflict, the archbishops of Goa often sided with the secular power. On its side, the secular power often used missionaries as its accredited envoys to places like Japan and China. Little wonder that the archbishops of Goa were sometimes compared to the Patriarchs of Byzantium as wielders of political and religious power over a vast area and over many people of diverse backgrounds.[43]

Firm hands were at the helms of both church and state in Goa in 1560 with the appointments of the new archbishop, Dom Gaspar de Leão Pereira (in office 1560–67; 1571–74) and the viceroy, Dom Constantino de Braganza (1558–61). Pereira, previously Canon of Evora and tutor of Cardinal Henrique, arrived in Goa accompanied by two lay inquisitors from Portugal. These three men founded the Inquisition of Goa shortly after their arrival, and the new archbishop at once assumed the presidency of its tribunal.[44] The Holy Office henceforward sought to keep strict control of the proselytes lest they should relapse into paganism or succumb to heresy. It also sought to isolate them from the New Christians, who were often thought to be unreliable, to improve the morals of all Christians, to punish those who continued to observe forbidden

---

[41] Jann, *op. cit.* (n. 1), pp. 111–12.

[42] *Ibid.*, p. 118.

[43] *Ibid.*, p. 112.

[44] António Baião, *A Inquisição de Goa* (2 vols.; Lisbon, 1930–45), I, 35. Both Miguel Vaz and Xavier had requested the king to set up the Inquisition. Xavier wrote to John III from Amboina on May 16, 1546: "... in order to make the people who live in India into good Christians, [it is necessary] for Your Majesty to send out the Holy Inquisition for there are many here who live according to Mosaic Law or who are of the Moorish sect.... And as they are many and spread out among all the fortresses, many preachers as well as the Holy Inquisition are required...." (Schurhammer and Wicki [eds.], *op. cit.* [n. 40], I, 346–47.) A fruitless attempt had previously been made at Goa in 1554 to establish a branch of the Holy Office. See Wicki, *loc. cit.* (n. 37), p. 366.

customs, and to censor books. Shortly thereafter, it expanded its efforts to the entire Portuguese East and continued to operate therein until 1814, except for a brief interruption in 1774–78.

Bartolemeu da Fonseca,[45] who had taken over the archbishop's function as head of the inquisition at Goa, collaborated with the viceroy in establishing in 1571 the Mesa da Consciéncia, a board modeled on the institution of the same name earlier founded in Lisbon by King John III to help him in dealing with matters laid to the charge of the king's conscience.[46] Put less abstractly, the Mesa in Lisbon was designed to look after the king's religious institutions such as the royal chapels, chantries, and hospitals, persons and groups receiving royal endowments for religious work, and the military orders. The Mesa in Lisbon also advised on spiritual affairs in the *padroado* and examined, visited, and supervised the clerics sent to India. The Mesa in Goa, acting in collaboration with the viceroy, apparently carried on in India and the colonies the same or similar functions, concerning itself particularly with problems of a religious nature which arose between the Christian and non-Christian subjects of the king. The Jesuits at first worked closely with these royal agencies, but in 1575 the Jesuit Visitor, Alessandro Valignano, sought to reduce such relationships to a minimum.[47]

With the help of the state, the missionaries in the year 1560 converted almost thirteen thousand persons on the islands of Goa, Chorão, and Divar alone. The new archbishop, who was not entirely friendly to mass conversions, quickly forbade the pomp and circumstance attending general baptisms. The viceroy disagreed with him and supported the Jesuits, but the archbishop temporarily prevailed and the number of conversions in 1561 fell sharply to 3,437.[48] The Jesuits meanwhile appealed to Lisbon, and in 1563 King Sebastian and Cardinal Henry sent orders to the new viceroy, Dom Francisco Coutinho, that the baptisms should be celebrated as they had been earlier and that all stubborn heathens should be expelled from Portuguese territories.[49] Internecine conflicts such as these ultimately led to the convocation of a series of provincial councils designed to work out differences, lay down lines of jurisdiction, and establish ecclesiastical discipline.

Between 1567 and 1606 five synods of the archiepiscopal province of Goa were attended by the suffragan bishops, the superiors of the religious orders, a number of theologians, and representatives of the viceroy. The synod of 1567 was formally called to conform to the decree of the Council of Trent requiring

[45] For his career see Baião, *op. cit.* (n. 44), I, 185–87.

[46] Founded in 1532, the Mesa was not officially dissolved until 1833. For the clearest available definition of its functions see Charles-Martial de Witte, O.S.B., "Le 'Regimento' de la 'Mesa de Consciéncia' du 24 novembre 1558," *Revista portuguesa de história*, IX (1960), 277–84. For additional detail see Pedro Augusto de S. Bartolomeu de Azevedo and António Baião, *O Archivo da Torre do Tombo; sua história, corpos que o compõem e organisação* (Lisbon, 1905), pp. 152–56.

[47] Josef Franz Schütte, S.J., *Valignanos Missionsgrundsätze für Japan* (2 vols.; Rome, 1951–58), Vol. I, Pt. I, p. 148.

[48] D'Sa, *op. cit.* (n. 9), I, 104.

[49] Müllbauer, *op. cit.* (n. 3), p. 83.

the various provinces of the church to realign themselves in the light of the reforms agreed upon in the great ecumenical meeting. The decrees of the Goa Councils, while being excellent sources on the problems of the church, do not provide a comprehensive statement of the condition of Christianity in the East. It is the nature of such official church assemblies that they concern themselves primarily with remedies for matters which are out of joint. From the decrees of the Councils, it seems certain that the churchmen were much more concerned about the resistance put up by the Hindus than with the hostility of the Jews and Muslims.[50] Long experience with the latter two groups had convinced most churchmen that no quarter could be expected or given in the struggle of the monotheistic faiths. In India, where the gods were many, the churchmen expected that compromise might more easily be worked out, but in this they underestimated the strength of the Brahmans and their control over the deeply rooted Hindu ways of life. Although temples were destroyed, baptisms forced, and religious leaders exiled, the church found that conversion to the ideas, values, and practices of Christianity was impossible to effect quickly. Clearly it took more than baptism, a European suit of clothes, and a new job to make a Hindu desert the customs of his fathers and take up the foreign practices of the Christians. It need only be recalled that heathen practices persisted for centuries in ancient Rome where the church had, as it did not have in India, the support of the local rulers and an elaborate hierarchy with its center in the Eternal City.

Aside from ecclesiastical matters, the decrees of the Goa Councils dealt primarily with problems relating to conversion and the elimination of heathen practices. Time after time the decrees called upon the secular authorities to expel from the Portuguese territories all Muslim teachers, Hindu priests, yogis, gurus, and sorcerers. The Councils inveighed against mass conversions and ordained that the number baptized on any given occasion should not exceed one hundred.[51] The training of orphans in Christian schools, as required by secular law after 1559, was a source of continuous conflict between the natives and the missionaries, and the decrees of the Councils tended to become stiffer in defining the word "orphans" and in advocating punishment for relatives who hid children or fled with them from Portuguese territories.

The social customs most affected by the decrees of both church and state had to do with marriage and the family. The church, in its administration of the marriage sacrament to natives, had to abide by the Portuguese definitions of legal age and the degree of relationships between the parties—laws which often ran counter to native practices. Marriages between heathens and converts were outlawed, while the church upheld the right of slaves to marry. *Sati* was repeatedly condemned and widows were forbidden to cut their hair or wear the clothes of penitents, and were expressly authorized to remarry. Several common forms of wedding celebration were outlawed, particularly one which required

---

[50] Wicki, *loc. cit.* (n. 37), pp. 355–56.
[51] *Ibid.*, pp. 356–57.

that the bride's father wash the feet of his daughter and son-in-law at the nuptial feast. The "superstitious" rites normally performed at the birth of a child were also condemned by the councils.[52]

"Heathenism" in many of its other forms also came under close scrutiny and many practices were expressly forbidden, particularly if they seemed to violate the "natural law." Soothsaying, medical wizardry, and religious bathing were condemned with special zeal. Pilgrimages to Hindu or Muslim holy places, celebration of heathen festivals and holidays, lascivious dances, gambling, and traveling about in enclosed palanquins were all forbidden to converts living in the Portuguese territories. Religious processions, for which the Indian Christians seemed to have had an unusual predilection, were not permitted at night; they were required to follow prescribed forms, and the statues and pictures carried in them had to be worthy and respectable. Repeatedly, though apparently without much success, the Councils called for elimination of all caste lines among the neophytes. Aside from prohibitions of specific native practices, the decrees of the Councils exhorted the converts to observe Sunday and other Christian holidays, to abide by Christian moral standards, and to be simpler and more austere in their religious celebrations.[53] From the constant repetition of these decrees and from the evidence of travelers, both Catholic and non-Catholic, it can clearly be seen that the Portuguese were never completely successful in the sixteenth century in expelling the non-Christians and were therefore unable to impose religious uniformity within their own territories. In practice, it seems clear that Hindus, Muslims, and Jews[54] were permitted even in Goa to practice their religions in private and to bury their dead according to their own traditions.[55] Still, the fact that the Christians, whether secular or religious, sought to impose their beliefs on everyone and to place non-Christians under severe religious and temporal disabilities induced in the non-Christians a profound hostility toward their overlords in Portuguese India. The close ties between church and state, strained though they sometimes were, gave the natives the impression that they were but two ends of the same stick that could be administered at the will of either power. The animosity of the natives was exhibited through their flights into the interior, through cutting into Portuguese revenues by flooding their rice paddies with salt water and shutting down their silk and food stores, and through mass protest meetings, petitions, and other means of passive resistance.[56] Such actions often brought reprisals from the Portuguese in the form of destroying temples, killing cows, and polluting watering places.[57] Open revolt and the killing of missionaries and converts sometimes followed, particularly in areas where the power of Portuguese arms

[52] *Ibid.*, p. 358.

[53] *Ibid.*, p. 359; also D'Sa, *op. cit.* (n. 9), I, 165–66.

[54] Forbidden officially by a viceregal degree of 1565 from sojourning in Portuguese territories, the Jews nevertheless continued to stay on. See Wicki, *loc. cit.* (n. 37), p. 365.

[55] Heras, *op. cit.* (n. 31), p. 27.

[56] *Ibid.*, pp. 37–8.

[57] Müllbauer, *op. cit.* (n. 3), pp. 99–100.

could not readily be brought to bear. While the Portuguese were clearly power-less to conquer Hinduism by arms, it is worth recalling that the Muslims, who conquered far more of India, were equally unable to exterminate the native beliefs.

2

THE JESUIT ENTERPRISE, 1542–1600

Francis Xavier (1506–52),[58] a nobleman from Navarre, left his family castle and native mountains in 1525 to study in Paris at the College of Sainte-Barbe, an important center of theological and humanistic learning. Although never a remarkable student, Xavier for the next eleven years found in the College a congenial home away from home. The student body of Sainte-Barbe then included many youths from Spain and Portugal, and the College itself was patronized by King John III. The willingness of the Portuguese government to give financial support to the College and scholarships to able students may be attributed to the crown's need for young clerics (especially Portuguese)[59] prepared to staff the posts awaiting them within the *padroado*. In Xavier's time the master of the College was Diogo de Gouvea, a Portuguese Humanist, scholar, and diplomat of considerable renown. Through the Portuguese students and faculty at Sainte-Barbe, Xavier began to learn a great deal about the achievements of Lusitania in the East.

Ignatius de Loyola, also a native of Navarre, arrived in Paris in 1528. Older than Xavier and the other students, Loyola soon attracted a group of the pious youths of Sainte-Barbe to his militant view of Christian life. In 1534, Loyola and six of his friends, including Xavier, took a vow at Montmartre to make a pilgrimage to Jerusalem, to carry the gospel to the Turk and the heathen, and to be prepared to accept the pope's orders as to future activities. Political events forced them to abandon their pilgrimage to Jerusalem, but with a few others who joined their ranks later, they made their way to Rome by 1537.

---

[58] His biography has been written many times since his death, most frequently by overly zealous Catholics or overly critical Protestants. In recent years the man has begun to emerge from the myth, thanks primarily to the arduous and objective research efforts of the Jesuit historians, Georg Schur-hammer and Josef Wicki. For his career in Europe see G. Schurhammer, *Franz Xaver* (Freiburg, 1955), Vol. I. Unhappily, Schurhammer's account of Xavier in the East has not yet been published and we are forced to rely on a multitude of articles and monographs, prepared by the Jesuits and others, on the Asian mission. The best general biography in English is James Brodrick, S.J., *St. Francis Xavier (1506–1552)* (New York, 1952). Unfortunately, Brodrick's work, which is based heavily on the writings and editions of Schurhammer and Wicki, is more tendentious and less reliable than theirs.

[59] In 1526, King John III agreed to provide funds for fifty Portuguese students to study without charge at Saint-Barbe (Schurhammer, *op. cit.* [n. 58], I, 106). Saint-Barbe, unlike many Paris colleges, was not supported by a foundation but had to survive on student fees.

Here, after considerable privation, Loyola and his band won the attention of highly placed prelates and the pope himself. Although opposition existed in Rome to the establishment of still another religious order, in 1540 Pope Paul III ultimately acceded to Loyola's pleas and officially authorized the creation of the Society of Jesus.

While the Society was being formed in Rome, Diogo de Gouvea in 1538 drew the attention of King John III to the activities of his former students. From the young men themselves, De Gouvea soon learned that they were palpitating with desire for heroic exploits in evangelizing and would be delighted to be sent to India, if the pope consented. The king in 1539 addressed a letter to his ambassador in Rome, Dom Pedro Mascerenhas, asking him to investigate these young men and to ascertain their qualifications for service in the East. Consequently, in 1540, Xavier, Simão Rodrigues, and Paul of Camerino were selected to accompany the ambassador back to Lisbon. So, even before the Society had received formal papal approval, Xavier had started out on his great adventure.

Xavier stayed in Lisbon from June, 1540, until he set sail for India with the fleet which left in April, 1541. While in the capital, Xavier improved his Portuguese by ministering and preaching to the poor and the sick. His companion, Rodrigues, showed a greater predilection for working among the upper classes and the educated. Both Jesuits ministered to prisoners of the Inquisition in Lisbon, and acted as confessors to the two men condemned to death at the first auto-da-fé held in Portugal. Despite their differing approaches, both Jesuits were highly regarded in Lisbon, and the king even tried for a short period to dissuade them from leaving for India. Ultimately, Rodrigues was retained in Portugal where he performed admirably as one of the founders of the Jesuit College at Coimbra and as the first Jesuit Provincial of Portugal. Xavier, shortly before his departure, was appointed Apostolic Nuncio, an office which endowed him with extensive and extraordinary powers in dealing with Christian problems in the East.[60] The vessel carrying Xavier to India started sailing down the Tagus on his thirty-fifth birthday, and on the following day, though Xavier was not to hear of it for more than a year, Loyola in Rome was officially elected General of the new Society.

The fleet carrying Xavier to India was under the supreme command of the newly appointed governor, Martim Affonso de Sousa. Even before the fleet left Lisbon, Sousa and others, who had served in India at an earlier date, led Xavier to believe that a rich harvest awaited him and that within a few years he would have no trouble in converting two or three Indian kingdoms. King John had exhorted Xavier to concentrate his efforts on the sons of aristocrats, and through them make wholesale conversions.[61] Sousa told him that in Ceylon "where there

[60] Actually the papal bull appointed both Rodrigues and Xavier to be Apostolic Nuncios. For its terms see *ibid.*, pp. 685–87.

[61] Xavier to Loyola, Lisbon, July 23, 1540, in Schurhammer and Wicki (eds.), *op. cit.* (n. 40), I, 42.

are no Moors or Jews but only heathens, we are sure to . . . convert without difficulty the king of the said island and all his people."[62] And, shortly after his arrival in Goa, Xavier was told about the great Christian achievements on the Fishery Coast and what remained to be done there. So, from the outset he believed, and continued to believe, that the harvest of souls would be great even though the workers were few and the support of the state not always reliable.

In May, 1542, four months after his arrival at Goa, Xavier addressed a letter to the fathers in Rome in which he calls Goa an "entirely Christian City."[63] Such a statement was more edifying than truthful and was possibly designed to attract less courageous souls to join him. The College of the Holy Faith, he informed Loyola, was being constructed and its church he declared to be "almost twice the size of the church in the College of the Sorbonne."[64] The governor was supporting the construction of the college, and it already had sufficient income for the maintenance of one hundred students. Its object was to train native students in the faith to enable them to communicate Christian principles directly to their own people. While the people received the priests kindly, Xavier stressed that the hardships for foreigners were numerous: "This land is only for men of strong constitution and not too old. . . ."[65] Then he went on to inform his companions in Rome that he was being sent by the governor to Cape Comorin "where, according to everybody, I shall convert many to Christianity."[66] On this trip, he was to be accompanied by three men, presumably students from the Goa college, and "natives of that land . . . who know Portuguese very well and also their own tongues."[67]

It was with Xavier's appearance in India that the Jesuits became the acknowledged leaders of the Christian missionary effort within the *padroado*. As Apostolic Nuncio, Xavier had both the power and the need to be an innovator. At times he played the part of the simple missionary, while on other occasions he clearly acted as the mission leader. Perhaps because of his Iberian background, he was forthrightly hostile to anything having to do with Islam. The brief catechism from which he taught, and which he had translated into Tamil (1542), Malay (1545), and Japanese (1549), was a book which had been especially prepared by João de Barros[68] for the instruction of children. While evangelizing among the common folk, Xavier sought, whenever possible, to convert kings and the leaders of society as well. In India, where he had the strength of Portugal behind him, he never hesitated to call upon the power of the state and complained bitterly and bluntly on several occasions that the secular rulers were not

[62] *Ibid.*, pp. 79–80.
[63] *Ibid.*, p. 121.
[64] *Ibid.*, p. 132.
[65] *Ibid.*, p. 135.
[66] *Ibid.*, p. 127.
[67] *Ibid.*
[68] Prepared *ca.* 1539 for young Prince Philip's instruction. For the history of how Xavier amended it and had it translated into various Eastern languages, see *ibid.*, pp. 94–100.

co-operative enough. And, while busy with politics, administration, and teaching, he wrote indefatigably to his companions in Europe and the East. Of his numerous epistles, a few of them being the size of small books, 108 are still extant. In their original language (many of them were tampered with and "improved upon" in Europe by editors, censors, and historians), his letters are simple, direct, and generally show signs of being hastily prepared. Like those of his successors, his letters directed to the "fathers in Rome" were general and edifying; those written on separate sheets to Loyola, known as *hijuelas*, are generally more critical. Xavier was conscious of the inadequacy of letters as a means of keeping Europe fully informed, and so he encouraged Miguel Vaz, the vicar-general, to go to Portugal in 1545 and make a personal report to the king on the mission in India.[69]

The various peoples living in India, Xavier realized, had in common only their ignorance of Christianity and its message. Each group, he believed, had to be approached in terms which it would understand and value. Among the Europeans he taught the adults by preaching and tending the sick.[70] Their children, in whom he saw the hope for the future, he would instruct daily by teaching them prayers, the Ten Commandments, and the catechism. On Sundays and holidays he preached in very elementary language and simple terms to the native Christians living in the Europeanized port cities, and on Wednesdays and Fridays he gave special instructions to the native wives of the Portuguese. On such occasions he would speak in Portuguese, incorporating into his speech as many elements from the native languages as he could command. With those new Christians who had had little or no exposure to Portuguese or European ways, he attempted to communicate in their own languages. He would teach the native children to sing their prayers, the Ten Commandments, or the catechism to popular tunes. Through the children, their parents and relatives were to learn about the Christian teachings. On the Fishery Coast he had the catechism and prayers translated into Tamil; he then committed them to memory and repeated them before assemblages of villagers. Outside the Portuguese centers, he often performed baptisms after exceedingly cursory instruction, usually without a period of trial, and also without the customary rites. Theologically, he justified these hasty baptisms by the scriptural quotation: "He who believes and is baptized will be saved."[71]

Xavier spent most of two years (1542–44) on the Fishery Coast and in Travancore. Late in 1544 he left Quilon for short visits to Cochin and Goa. After his departure for Malacca and the Spiceries in 1545, Xavier had personally very little to do with evangelizing in India. When he returned from farther east on his subsequent visits to Goa, he generally acted as an administrator. The work of maintaining the enterprise in India was thus left in the hands of his colleagues,

---

[69] J. Wicki, "Die ersten offizielen mündlichen Berichterstattungen in Europa aus den überseeischen Missionsgebieten der Gesellschaft Jesu (*ca.* 1553–1577)," *NZM*, XIV (1958), 253.

[70] J. Wicki, "Zur Missionsmethodes des hl. Franz Xaver," *NZM*, II (1946), 87–88.

[71] *Ibid.*, p. 103.

most of whom were new arrivals from Europe. In 1545, the first contingent of reinforcements arrived in Goa: they included three Jesuits, one of whom was Nicolo Lancillotto,[72] the superior of the college until 1548. Five more priests and five additional lay brothers arrived in Goa in 1546 under the leadership of Henrique Henriques.[73] Almost immediately Henriques was dispatched to the Fishery Coast, where he spent his entire career. Two years later, an even larger delegation arrived in the East, one of whom was Luis Fróis, probably the greatest of the mission's letterwriters. The first catalogue of the Jesuit mission in the East, compiled in Portugal in 1554, indicates that in 1553 there were seventy members[74] of the Society working in the *padroado*, thirty-two of whom were stationed at Goa, sixteen in the rest of India, five in southeast Asia, and five in Japan.[75] Most of the leading lights in the mission had received training at the Jesuit College in Coimbra (founded in 1546) before setting out for the East.[76]

Those who worked in Asia during Xavier's tenure there (1542–52) generally carried on the task of missionizing along the lines he had laid down. For adolescent male Portuguese-speaking Christians of both Portuguese and native origins, the fathers founded schools in which instruction in reading and writing was offered. Beside the school at Goa, instruction centers were set up at Malacca, Ormuz, Cochin, Quilon, and Bassein by 1552. Practically all of these schools had enrollments of well over one hundred youths. Once in the schools, the boys were gradually introduced by their teachers to the fundamentals of the faith. For children who could not attend the schools, as well as for adult native Christians and slaves, instruction was given daily in the church. Like the schoolboys, those instructed in the churches learned to sing their prayers and to keep on singing them at their work and in their homes. Those followers of Xavier stationed among the non-Portuguese-speaking Christians, especially on the Fishery Coast and in Travancore, worked at learning the native languages and at selecting and training native converts to carry on the teaching of Christianity in their villages after the missionaries had departed.[77] Like Xavier, his successors worked mainly from the "little catechism" originally prepared by Barros, and after 1546 from the "larger catechism" which Xavier himself had prepared on the basis of Barros' briefer instructional manual. In 1557, the "larger

[72] Biography in J. Wicki (ed.), *Documenta Indica* (Rome, 1948), I, 43*–45*.

[73] *Ibid.*, pp. 46*–47*.

[74] For a definition of the word "member" and for figures on the total membership of the Society see below, p. 251.

[75] Wicki (ed.), *op. cit.* (n. 72), II, 618–21; also Silva Rego (ed.), *op. cit.* (n. 1, *Documentacão*), VI, 154–64. For a catalogue of the Jesuits see J. P. A. da Camara Manoel, *Missões dos Jesuitas no Oriente nos seculos XVI e XVII* (Lisbon, 1894), pp. 129–57.

[76] Theophilo Braga, *História da universidade de Coimbra* (Lisbon, 1892), I, 480–82. As early as 1547, the College at Coimbra had an enrollment of 115, a large proportion coming from the best Portuguese families. See A. Huonder, *Der heilige Ignatius von Loyola und der Missionsberuf der Gesellschaft Jesu* (Aachen, 1922), pp. 23–24.

[77] J. Wicki, "Xavers Mitarbelter in der Unterweisung der Christlichen indo-portugiesischen Bevölkerung (1545–1552)," *NZM*, III (1947), 179–92.

catechism" was published at Goa by Brother Juan de Bustamente (*ca.* 1536–88), the first printer in India.[78]

The immediate followers of Xavier generally depended upon peaceful evangelizing of the heathens rather than forced mass conversions.[79] Most of their converts were made on the streets and through their pupils. To win Hindus and Muslims to Christianity they preached in the squares; they disputed publicly with Brahmans and Mullas; they sang the catechism to a popular tune in public places; they permitted heathens and Muslims to attend mass; and they had their students hold sermons in Konkani on Sundays and holidays. Through the pupils who studied in the Jesuit schools, heathen relatives and friends received knowledge of Christianity. Nevertheless with the exception of a few yogis and Brahmans who professed to acknowledge the superiority of Christian teachings, most of the early converts accepted conversion out of either political or diverse individual interests: slaves wanted freedom, parents wanted greater security and better training for their children, and others wanted the new European clothes which went to every convert. Many obstacles and disabilities also stood in the way of conversion: loss of caste and inheritances, loss of the prince's favor where Portuguese control was indirect and distant, and the requirement to tithe.

Political interest motivated a quartet of Indian and Sinhalese princes to become Christian converts before 1555.[80] In 1549 great excitement reigned among the Christians as they hoped that the conversion of the prince of Tanur, whose territories were south of Calicut, meant the beginning of a more general movement to Christianity among the native princes.[81] Once this ruler had received the desired military aid from the Portuguese, he raised a question which was to perplex and divide the missionaries in Asia for more than a century thereafter and was to be basic to the bitterly fought "Rites Controversy" in Europe itself. While formally professing Christianity, the rājā wanted permission to continue wearing his Brahman thread. In Goa, opinions were divided on whether or not it was ethically and canonically possible to accede to his request by what theologians call "accommodation" to local practices. While the Christians disputed among themselves, the rājā apparently returned to his old ways. Practically all such political conversions failed to meet the expectations of the missionaries that acceptance of Christianity by prominent persons would lead to an epidemic of baptisms among their followers. In Japan,

[78] J. Wicki, "Juan de Bustamente, el primer impresor de la India," *Siglo de las missiones*, XLIII (1956), 492–95, 499; also see G. Schurhammer, "Ein seltener Druck (der erste gedruckte tamulische Katechismus)," *Katholische Missionen*, LVIII (1930), 211–12.

[79] J. Wicki, "Die Heidenbekehrung in der Jesuiten-Niederlassungen von Portugiesisch-Indien, 1545–1552," *NZM*, III (1907), 39–48.

[80] Cf. the undated letter sent by King John III to the pope. It was published in Italian and entitled *Copia de una lettera di nuove delle Indie Orientali . . . la qual narra la conversione di quattro Re con il loro Popoli . . .*, as cited in Rogers, *op. cit.* (n. 8), p. 193.

[81] Tanur, now a fishing village a few miles from Calicut, had its own ruling house and governed a sizable area along the Malabar Coast. For the details of this conversion see D. Ferroli, *The Jesuits in Malabar* (2 vols.; Bangalore, 1939–51), I, 130–37.

however, as we shall see, a system of "accommodation" evolved slowly and helped to account for the great Jesuit successes there.[82]

Conversions of the ordinary people were not numerous enough before 1556 to please the authorities of either church or state. On the island of Goa in 1548 there were some 40,000 non-Christians and only 7,000 Christians; on the nearby island of Chorão in 1551 only 300 out of its population of 3,000 professed Christianity. The Jesuits, before 1557, rarely succeeded in converting more than a few dozen each year in the Portuguese capital of the East. Those who were converted often knew next to nothing about the faith. The missionaries would ordinarily baptize them after the most superficial instruction and would then try, after the individual had put on his European clothes, to teach him his prayers. Many of the converts, being Christians in name and costume only, were sometimes quick to lapse into "error" or were prone to observe the forms of the faith without understanding their meaning. Nor was the spiritual condition of the native converts significantly improved when forcible mass conversions began in India after 1556.

In Europe, the young Society, with its rigorous demands upon the individual, had attracted many able and leading men to its ranks after its formal recognition in 1540. It is said that by the time of Loyola's death in 1556 the new order had one thousand members and one hundred houses.[83] The term "member," as used in reference to the Society, requires explication. To the three customary vows of poverty, chastity, and obedience, Loyola added a fourth vow of special obedience to the pope. Only certain elite members of the Society were to add the special fourth vow to the other three and they belonged to the top grade of membership, the "Professed." The founders of the Society provided for other levels of membership: coadjutors spiritual and temporal, scholastics, and novices. The temporal coadjutors, often called lay brothers (*irmãos* in Portuguese), minister to the everyday needs of the other members to enable them to give their full time and attention to the apostolate. Members of all grades were intended to live a common life and be subject to the same rules, though special houses were established in Europe and Asia for the Professed. In 1556 the Constitutions of the Society, its fundamental law and its program of intentions, was promulgated and thereafter applied to the order's eleven provinces (two in Italy, four in Iberia, two in Germany, and one each in France, India, and Brazil).

In Goa, the condition of the Jesuit organization declined in the decade following 1545. While Xavier was absent, the leadership in Jesuit activities had passed into the hands of António Gomes, superior of the College at Goa (1548–52) and a favorite in Portuguese official circles. Impatient with Xavier's policy of working with children and lower castes, Gomes turned his attention to the

[82] See below, pp. 679–80.

[83] James Brodrick, S.J., *The Origin of the Jesuits* (London, 1940), p. 262; H. de la Costa, S.J., *The Jesuits in the Philippines, 1581–1768* (Cambridge, Mass., 1961), p. 4, claims a membership of "over 1,500" as of 1556.

Portuguese community and sought to transform the college into a center of higher education on the model of Coimbra. When Xavier returned from Japan for a short time in 1552, he replaced Gomes as superior of the College and nominated the Flemish priest, Gaspar Barzaeus,[84] to take charge of the Jesuit enterprise in India. Barzaeus died shortly thereafter and his successor, Melchior Nunes Barreto, suddenly left for Japan in 1554. To make matters worse, the episcopal seat was left vacant when Bishop João de Albuquerque died in 1553, and the secular church was likewise left under uncertain leadership. By the following year the Jesuit colony at Goa had been reduced to three priests leading an organization of thirty-two members, with Father Bartholomeu Dias, an ineffective and newly arrived Jesuit, as its superior.[85] It was also at this time of "interregnum" that the viceroy took it upon himself to divide the thirty districts of Goa into two mission areas: fifteen to the Dominicans and fifteen to the Jesuits.[86]

The first crisis in Jesuit leadership began to pass in 1555. Nine Jesuit priests arrived in India as replacements in that year, and they brought with them the newly formulated Constitutions of the Society. Father Anton de Quadros, who explained the Constitutions to the Jesuits in India, was elected Vice-Provincial and superior of the mission by the fathers assembled at Goa, and thereafter Christian affairs under Jesuit leadership took a turn for the better. But in September, 1556, Father Dom Gonçalo da Silveira arrived in Goa to take office as the designated Provincial of India. A sophisticated, devout, and well-educated man of noble lineage, Silveira proved to be a bitter disappointment as Provincial. He quarreled with the secular authorities, insulted the Dominicans and Franciscans, and was described by the Jesuits themselves as being headstrong, choleric, and generally disliked. In July, 1558, Diogo Lainez was chosen to be the Jesuit General in Rome. One of his first acts was to dispatch a letter to Goa, which arrived there in September, 1559, ordering Quadros immediately to replace Silveira as Provincial.[87] Lainez had evidently heard of the growing discouragement of the Jesuits in India and of the feeling of some of them that the mission should be abandoned. A good deal of the blame for this low level of Jesuit morale can probably be placed upon the shoulders of Silveira. An order from Lainez of 1560 commanded the demoralized Jesuits not to leave their posts.[88] After the elevation of Quadros, who remained Provincial in spite of

[84] For biography see Wicki (ed.), *op. cit.* (n. 72), I, 49*–50*.

[85] D'Sa, *op. cit.* (n. 9), I, 100, talks about the period from 1553 to 1560 as an "interval" in mission activity. He attributes this lag to the efforts that the Orders were making in other parts of the world and to a desire on the part of the missionaries to strengthen their converts in the faith before adding others to their responsibilities. This was also a period during which the government of the diocese was in the hands of a vicar capitular elected by the cathedral chapter while Goa awaited the first of its archbishops. Also see the introductory section in Wicki (ed.), *op. cit.* (n. 72), Vol. III.

[86] In 1550 the Franciscans had been allotted the Province of Bardez, just north of the island of Goa, of which the Portuguese had acquired control in 1543. They did not begin working there seriously until 1555 (Meersman, *op. cit.* [n. 13], p. 27).

[87] See the introductory chapters to Wicki (ed.), *op. cit.* (n. 72), Vols. III and IV.

[88] See Lainez to Quadros (1560) as reproduced in J. Wicki, "Auszüge aus den Briefen der Jesuitengeneräle an die Obern in Indien (1549–1613)," *AHSI*, XXII (1953), 117.

his personal protests until 1569, discipline was restored and the mission effort carried ahead.

The secular interregnum (1553–60) likewise came to an end in 1560 with the arrival at Goa of the first Archbishop of India, Dom Gaspar de Leão Pereira (in office 1560–67; 1571–74). The new prelate, together with Quadros and the viceroy, Dom Constantino de Braganza (in office 1558–61) formed a trium-virate which helped to instill new vigor into the joint activities of church and state in India. The Jesuits under Quadros[89] immediately began to co-operate in the policy of mass, forcible conversions being carried out in Goa and its sur-rounding territories by the viceroy. In 1559 there were one hundred and twenty-four Jesuits in the *padroado* (thirty-seven fathers and eighty-seven brothers) of whom seventy-one were in Goa, twenty-seven in the rest of India, ten in southeast Asia, eight in Japan, and eight in Ormuz and Abyssinia.[90] The heavy concentration of Jesuits at Goa is reflected in the conversion effort which they subsequently made there. On the island alone in 1560, the Jesuits held twenty-seven mass conversions in which they baptized 12,967 persons.[91]

The decade of the sixties was full of the kind of action that King John's instructions of 1545, outlined above, had anticipated and directed. Through a learned Hindu interpreter who had become a convert, the Jesuits now engaged in disputations with some of the leading Brahmans—disputations which ended in the exile of forty of the obstinate Hindu teachers. Baptisms of even the lowliest were celebrated with such pomp and circumstance that the new archbishop felt compelled to forbid them as unseemly displays. In 1560, as we have seen, the Inquisition was established in Goa. In the following year new converts were released for ten years from the obligation to tithe, and later this exemption was extended to fifteen years.[92] In 1565 Jews were prohibited from sojourning in the Portuguese settlements. Two years later, as we have seen,[93] the first of the synods of the archiepiscopacy of Goa was convened as part of the church's effort to regularize its relations with the state, to define internal lines of juris-diction, and to plan a concerted attack upon the problem of dealing with the heathens, particularly the Hindus. In 1568, when D. Luis de Ataide was ap-pointed viceroy, the king proclaimed that his chief responsibility should be advancing the conversion of the heathens within his jurisdiction.[94]

Both in India and in Rome, in these early years of the mission, the Jesuits were dissatisfied with their system of communication. Although letters were

---

[89] In this group were a number of leading figures such as João Nunes Barreto, the designated patriarch of Ethiopia, and Andreas Ornieto, the designated bishop of Hierapolis, and several others sent out to staff the mission to the "Land of Prester John." This was one of Loyola's "pet projects" which Lainez did not choose to follow up because of the greater progress being made in Asia.

[90] Figures based on Fróis' report in Wicki (ed.), *op. cit.* (n. 72), IV, 301–6.

[91] In 1560 there were 132 Jesuits in the Eastern mission; their distribution in the various settlements was roughly the same as in 1559 (*ibid.*, pp. 862–69); in 1561 the total number had increased to 147 (*ibid.*, V, 265–70). Also see Müllbauer, *op. cit.* (n. 3), pp. 81–82.

[92] Wicki, *loc. cit.* (n. 37), p. 365.

[93] Above, pp. 242–45.

[94] Wicki, *loc. cit.* (n. 37), p. 365.

exchanged annually, both sides of the mission enterprise felt a need for personal conversations. As early as 1546, Lancillotto suggested in a letter to Loyola that a "reporter," or in the language of the Society a "procurator," should be recalled from India to give full intelligence to Rome about what was happening in the field. The Jesuits in India found it next to impossible to release one of their scanty numbers, but in 1553 Brother Andreas Fernandes was dispatched to Europe, accompanied, as a living exemplar of his people, by the young Japanese convert, Bernard. Fernandes stayed in Rome for almost a year (October 14, 1554–September 8, 1555), where he made a good impression upon Loyola and other church dignitaries and stirred their interest in the mission. In the Constitutions of the Society, which were being hammered out at this time, it was ordained that regular emissaries from the field were as necessary for full intelligence as regular and exact reporting by letter. Procurators, it was stipulated, should be selected by the Provincial congregations which were scheduled to meet every four years. But in India these requirements remained only on paper, for the first Provincial congregation could not even be convened until 1575. The "living letters," which both sides so ardently desired, were never dispatched with any regularity from the huge Province of India during the sixteenth century.[95]

The Province of India, which stretched from Mozambique to Kyūshū, encompassed a greater geographical area than all of the Society's European provinces combined.[96] Originally, it had been placed within the administrative jurisdiction of the Province of Portugal, over which Simão Rodrigues had been named superior, beginning in 1546. Three years later, letters patent were sent from Rome to Xavier making him the Provincial of India. But because Xavier traveled about so much, the superior of the College in Goa was the practical governing head of the Society's activities in the East. During Xavier's absences and after his death, jurisdictional difficulties, personal rivalries, and the acute shortage of competent individuals combined to weaken the Jesuit effort. It was only after the elevation of Quadros in 1559 that this unwieldy province began to resemble the European provinces of the Society in form and discipline.[97] He appointed a superintendent of Goa to deal with general problems in the city, and the rector of the college, previously second in command in Goa, was confined in his activities to education. In 1565–66, Quadros went to Malacca on a voyage of visitation. On the basis of this experience he wrote to Rome complaining about the poor quality of the missionaries being sent to India, frankly stating his preference for trained priests of established virtue, and testily remarking that the "East is not a school for training novices."[98] Quadros continued to insist in later letters to Lainez that illiterate and untrained brothers were of little use in backward areas. Unlike Xavier, he indicated a decided

[95] For further details see Wicki, *loc. cit.* (n. 69), pp. 253–61.
[96] Schütte, *op. cit.* (n. 47), Vol. I, Pt. 1, p. 165.
[97] Wicki (ed.), *op. cit.* (n. 72), III, 5.
[98] *Ibid.*, VI, 506.

preference for fewer missionaries who had been carefully chosen, well trained, and of proven virtue. The catalogue of the Indian province for the end of 1565 records that there were one hundred and ninety-three Jesuits scattered throughout the East, of whom eighty are classified as fathers and one hundred and thirteen as brothers and novices.[99] From this decline in the relative number of fathers to brothers, when contrasted with the figures of 1559 (thirty-seven fathers and eighty-seven brothers), it is perhaps safe to conclude that Quadros' pleas were not immediately heeded in Rome. The distribution of the missionaries in various posts in the East remained very much the same as at the beginning of Quadros' tenure: ninety-five in Goa and vicinity, fifty-four in the rest of India, eighteen in southeast Asia, seventeen in the Far East, and nine in Africa and Ormuz. At the end of Quadros' term in office (1569), Gonçalo Alvares was sent to India as the first Jesuit Visitor. Alvares apparently felt satisfied with conditions in India, but he perished in 1573 on his way to Japan before completing his tour of investigation. The storm again broke on the mission around 1570–71 when the Portuguese settlements were under military siege.[100] At the time of Alvares' death, there were almost no Professed Jesuits in the entire Indian province and so the Provincial Congregation ordered for that year by General Francis Borja could not be convened.[101]

It was into this declining and dismal situation that the new Visitor, Alessandro Valignano, was sent to inspect the Jesuit Province of Goa, entrusted with powers second only to those possessed by the General himself. From his arrival in India in 1574 until his death in 1606, Valignano was the dominant figure and shaping force of the mission both "within and beyond the Ganges." The son of a Neapolitan aristocrat, Valignano was born in Chieti in 1539. As a young man he left the Kingdom of Naples to pursue collegiate studies at Padua. Before reaching his twentieth birthday, he received a doctorate in law and then returned to his native town. The young jurist, whose father was a friend of Pope Paul IV (in office 1555–59), soon went to Rome to find a post. In 1562 he was again at Padua, carrying on advanced studies. Here he got into trouble with the Venetian authorities who then had Padua within their jurisdiction. After spending almost a year in jail, he was banned from Venetian territory for four years. He then returned to Rome and in 1566 was admitted to the Society of Jesus. By 1571 he had taken Holy Orders and two years later the fourth vow of the Professed. In 1572–73, he acted as rector of the Jesuit College of Macerata until he was named Visitor to the Province of India by General Mercurian.[102]

Along with forty other members of the Society, the aristocratic Valignano sailed from Lisbon in the spring of 1574. Shortly after his arrival in Goa, he

99 *Ibid.*, pp. 623–31.

100 Müllbauer, *op. cit.* (n. 3), pp. 88–89.

101 Wicki, *loc. cit.* (n. 69), pp. 260–61.

102 Biographical summary based on Wicki (ed.), *Alessandro Valignano. Historia del principio y progreso de la Compañía de Jesús en las Indias Orientales* (1542–64) (Rome, 1944), pp. 45*–48*.

became ill and so was unable to visit the south India stations of the Society until 1575. In that same year he called into session, on the island of Chorão near Goa, the first Congregation of the Indian province. As a result of its deliberations, the decision was taken to establish training centers wherever possible for the instruction of the missionaries in the pertinent Indian languages. Father Martine da Silva was elected procurator at the assemblage and was shortly thereafter dispatched to Europe.[103] Then, Valignano, in the company of the Provincial, Ruy Vicente, visited the mission stations in north India. The following year, after making a second visit to the north, Valignano sent to Rome a summary of his observations about the mission in India.

The *Summarium* of 1577,[104] written entirely in Italian and in his own hand, outlined for the General Valignano's appraisal of and recommendations for the Goa province. He concluded that the spiritual condition of the Indian mission was not alarming, despite the fact that it suffered from a number of major shortcomings, especially from a failure on the part of the missionaries to comprehend and observe the Constitutions of the Society. The Visitor observed that difficulties arose in India primarily because of the double task before the Society: ministering to the Christians in the Portuguese settlements, and evangelizing the native populations. Although concerned about the spiritual state of the Europeans in India, Valignano felt that the primary aim of the Society should be to win the natives over to the Christian faith. Realizing that the mission field was immense and the workers few, Valignano insisted that evangelizing should not be carried on indiscriminately and without plan. And since he comprehended from the outset that not all the indigenous peoples of Asia with their diverse backgrounds would make equally good converts, he proceeded in his estimate of the situation to point out where the Jesuits should concentrate their efforts.

After dispatching his first report to Rome, Valignano left Goa in 1577 to inspect the mission establishments in Malacca, Macao, and Japan. He spent from 1579 to 1582 in Japan from where he dispatched his second *Summarium* (1580) to Rome.[105] It was both a revision of the earlier *Summarium* and an extension of it, and included his appraisal of the missions in Ethiopia, China, and Japan. A third *Summarium*, started around 1580, was completed shortly after his return to Cochin in 1583, and it deals primarily with Japan.[106] Although he hoped at this time to go back to Europe, Valignano received an order in Cochin from

---

[103] Apparently Da Silva was a bad choice. When he returned from Europe to India in 1578, the Provincial, Ruy Vicente, sent him back on the next ship. Thereafter he was dropped from the Society and in many extant manuscripts his name is stricken out. See Wicki, *op. cit.* (n. 69), p. 261.

[104] Schütte, *op. cit.* (n. 47), Vol. I, Pt. I, p. 161. Though it remained unpublished in the sixteenth century, the *Summarium* was used by several of the missionary historians in Europe for their accounts of Asia and the progress of Christianity there, and by Valignano himself in the preparation of his *Historia*. See Wicki, *op. cit.* (n. 102), pp. 85*–86*.

[105] Wicki, *op. cit.* (n. 102), p. 86*. Apparently it was dictated to several secretaries. The extant text is in Spanish.

[106] For the text and the additions to it which Valignano made in 1592 see the excellent work of José Luis Alvarez-Taladriz (ed.), *Alejandro Valignano S.I., Summario de las cosas de Japon (1583)*, No. 9 of the "Monumenta Nipponica Monographs" (Tokyo, 1954).

the General in Rome which named him Provincial of India. He then returned to Goa, where he busied himself with administrative problems until 1588 when he set out to visit the Far East again. Valignano was in Macao from 1588 to 1590 and from there he was sent to Nagasaki as the diplomatic representative of the Viceroy of Goa. He returned to Macao in 1592 where he spent an additional two years working on the problem of accommodating Christian practices to the task of penetrating China. By 1595 he was again back in Goa, where he learned that his duties had once more been redefined, and that he would thenceforward occupy himself with Jesuit affairs in China and Japan. Father Nicholas Pimenta was named Provincial Visitor for the mission in India. In 1597 Valignano finally left Goa and, after spending another year in Macao, he journeyed to Japan for the third and last time. After five years in Japan, he returned to Macao where in 1606 he died, like Xavier, before having had the opportunity to visit the Chinese mainland.

Valignano's three *Summaria*, with their corrections and alterations, formed the basis for his *Historia del principio y progresso de la Compañia de Jésus en las Indias Orientales*, and word for word excerpts from them appeared in the text of the *Historia*. The *Summaria* themselves are more valuable than the *Historia* as sources for details on Asian lands, places, and peoples. The *Historia*, while including some regional data, is primarily concerned with the progress of the Jesuit missions. The first part of the *Historia*, which deals with Xavier's period, was sent to Europe at the beginning of 1584 and was probably carried there by Diogo de Mesquita, who escorted the four Japanese youths then being sent to Rome.[107] The second part, which sketched the progress of the missions from Xavier's death to 1564, Valignano, after many delays, finally sent to Europe from Macao at the end of 1588. The third part, which was originally supposed to deal with his own times,[108] was never completed, presumably because he could not obtain from Europe the printed collections of Jesuit letters that he constantly requested. Lacking these, in 1601 he compiled a history of the foundation and evolution of the Jesuit mission in Japan.[109] None of Valignano's writings was published in the sixteenth century, but they were used extensively as sources by the historians of the Jesuit missions.

Through his own travels, Valignano had obtained a bird's-eye view of the mission and its problems. He reports that the vast distances separating the mission outposts made the connections between the administrative centers and the individual stations extremely difficult and tenuous, with supervision being ordinarily very remote. Between Rome and the Asian centers connections were even harder to establish and maintain—a problem which seemed to vex Valignano exceedingly. Fourteen to sixteen months usually elapsed before Rome received a reply

[107] See below, p. 693.
[108] Valignano initially planned to write three parts divided as follows: Xavier's period, from Xavier's death to his own advent in India, and the mission of his own day. For various reasons he found it impossible to carry through with his original plan.
[109] Wicki, *op. cit.* (n. 102), pp. 88*–89*.

to a question directed to Goa; correspondence between Japan and Goa required at least two years and often three, and an exchange of letters between Goa and the Moluccas ordinarily took twenty-two months. Missionaries in the field often had to wait two or three years before hearing anything from Europe, and so had to proceed independently in the meanwhile. And, since Goa was the center through which all communications had to pass, the workers there were usually overburdened with administrative detail. The missionaries were also plagued by tropical heat and diseases, which sapped the vitality of some and brought death to others. Many were also the victims of rebellions or wars, particularly when the Portuguese centers were under siege.[110] Within four years (1571–74), fifty-eight Jesuits died in India, some of them leading figures in the province.[111]

Valignano soon learned that very few natives or Luso-Indians were being trained for the priesthood and that the native Portuguese in the East were much more preoccupied with war and trade than with Christianity. The Jesuits had no alternative, he realized, except to depend upon Europe for recruits, and these were increasingly hard to find after the Council of Trent in 1563 made the requirements for clerical training more stringent. Although most of the missionaries came from the colleges at Coimbra and Evora in Portugal, these institutions could not possibly hope to meet the quotas required in both Brazil and India. They were certainly not prepared to supply the number of men of extraordinary learning and stature required to lead the Asian missions. As in their mercantile enterprise, the Portuguese were forced out of need to admit other Europeans into the *padroado* if the missions were to be effectively carried forward. Northern European Jesuits, however, were needed in their own countries to combat Protestantism. Their language backgrounds were also entirely different, and it was felt that they might be even less able than the southern Europeans to endure life in the tropics. Although some Spaniards and Belgians were members of the mission, the political differences between Spain and Portugal until the union of the crowns in 1581 kept the number of subjects of the Spanish crown down to a minimum. Thus, practically all non-Portuguese groups except the Italians were eliminated for one reason or another from participating in the mission. Indeed, from the very beginning, some of the mission's leading figures, like those merchants who participated in Portugal's trading activities, were of Italian origin and training.[112]

In sizing up the native peoples living within the *padroado*, Valignano divided them into two sharply defined groups: the blacks and the whites. Africa and India were inhabited by black peoples; China and Japan by the whites. Even before arriving in India, the Italian aristocrat, Humanist, and lawyer, described

[110] Schütte, *op. cit.* (n. 47), Vol. I, Pt. I, pp. 165–69.

[111] *Ibid.*, p. 178.

[112] *Ibid.*, pp. 178–87. Three Italians were in the first two delegations to arrive in India; and the first Jesuit to be martyred was the Italian father Antonio Criminale, who was murdered in India in 1549. The French Franciscan, Pierre Bonifer, was one of the few of his nation to evangelize in the *padroado* during the sixteenth century.

for Rome the Negroes of Africa as a barbarous people with almost no capacity for comprehending Christian teachings and customs who live in sloth and ignorance and who seem naturally destined to serve rather than govern.[113] While he esteems the Hindus somewhat more highly than the Africans, he still believes, after three years in India, that the Hindus, in contrast to the Moors, are a servile and lowly people. Even the Brahmans, their highest class, work for their bread by performing menial tasks usually left to the lowliest in Europe.

Valignano continued throughout his lifetime to look upon India as a poor mission field, though his later reports are somewhat less harsh. While the Indians may possess sufficient intelligence, unlike the Africans, to comprehend Christian teachings, there are vast obstacles such as caste, the political fragmentation of the subcontinent, the vast diversity in native religious groups and practices, and the opposition of the Moors, which make the problem of converting India next to impossible. Even the St. Thomas Christians persist in their adherence to caste and show little ability or desire to turn their backs on it. Valignano further declares, on the basis of his limited experience on the coast of India, that the Indians have very little interest in religion and their ideas about it are so conditioned by superstition, immorality, and caste beliefs that they possess no clear, universal understanding of their own gods or their own religious precepts.[114] By contrast with the Japanese, the Indians, as Valignano saw them, had only a limited capacity for grasping and retaining the truths of Christianity and the intellectual presuppositions of Western civilization. Obviously, the Jesuit Visitor, who knew nothing of the famous Indian schools in the interior where Hindu philosophy and theology were systematically taught, was a victim of his own limited experience in a number of his generalizations about Indian character and ability. Had he had the understanding of Indian civilization that De' Nobili acquired a generation later, Valignano might have advocated a policy of accommodation in India as he did for Japan and China.[115]

The Visitor decreed that the Jesuits in India should concentrate on working among the natives and that they should leave the pastoral care of the Europeans mainly in the hands of the seculars and the other Orders.[116] Customarily, Valignano also discouraged the Jesuits from accepting posts in the secular hierarchy, even as bishops and archbishops. To gain the interest and the confidence of the Hindus, he insisted that the Jesuits should study the native language of the area to which they were assigned. Some of the missionaries did not take easily to this prescription for they feared that by becoming proficient in an Indian language they might be condemned to work for the rest of their lives with a particular native group, and would cut themselves off from the opportunity of working in the more congenial atmosphere of the Portuguese cities or

[113] Schütte, *op. cit.* (n. 47), Vol. I, Pt. I, pp. 170–72.

[114] See L. Castets, "L'Eglise et le problème de la caste au XVIe siècle," *Revue d'histoire des missions*, 1930, pp. 547–65.

[115] Schütte, *op. cit.* (n. 47), Vol. I, Pt. I, p. 171.

[116] *Ibid.*, p. 199.

from going off to distant exotic Japan.[117] To implement his insistence on study of the native languages, Valignano proposed that seminars be organized for the training of the Jesuits in the languages of India, the Moluccas, and Japan. As early as 1577, language seminars were actually set up at Punical on the Fishery Coast, at Salsette, and at Trinidade near Bassein.[118] And, on Valignano's insistence, seminars for the training of native clergy were planned for the Paravans of the Fishery Coast and the St. Thomas Christians, the only two large concentrations of native Christians in India.[119]

The difficulty of finding leaders for the mission is emphasized by Valignano in his discussion of the functions, duties, and problems confronting the Provincial of the Province of India. In Valignano's view, this man, to put it succinctly, should be second only to the Jesuit General himself in strength of character, personality, intelligence, and physical durability; he should be granted extraordinary powers, and he should be backed up by capable and responsible subordinates to help him administer the most extensive of the Jesuit provinces. While it would be desirable for the Provincial himself to visit the scattered stations of his vast province, it was obviously impossible for a particular individual to be in two places at once. To travel throughout the entire province would require an estimated six to seven years, and the Provincial could certainly not afford to be away from the Goa headquarters for even as long as one year. Nor could the Provincial be as limited in his religious powers as were his peers in Europe. He would have to be a man to whom very full powers could be entrusted because clearly he could not refer to Rome for anything but the most general decisions, and for this reason also his term of office should last for at least five years. The Provincial, more than his confreres in Europe, should be a man of political acumen and capable of giving counsel to the other secular and religious leaders in India. For Valignano clearly felt that leaders of genuine ability were far too few in all types of European activity in India.[120]

Malacca, Valignano advised Rome, should be set up as the seat of a Vice-Provincial who would have jurisdiction over the stations east of India. Although responsible to Goa, the Vice-Provincial of Malacca should be given the right to make independent decisions and the powers comparable to those enjoyed by Provincials in Europe. The Vice-Provincial should be appointed for a five-year period, for, it is estimated, it would take him three years and four months of his tenure to visit the Far Eastern stations of the Society. Valignano also felt that it would be desirable, if not absolutely necessary, to appoint a superintendent of the missions of India lying south of Goa's immediate jurisdiction who would have powers equal to that of a Vice-Provincial in Europe. The local rectors throughout the Indian province, because of their distance from supervisory

[117] *Ibid.*, p. 200. Some of the Jesuits had actually learned Konkani, the language of Goa, before Valignano arrived in India.
[118] *Ibid.*, p. 203.
[119] *Ibid.*, pp. 204–6.
[120] *Ibid.*, pp. 208–9.

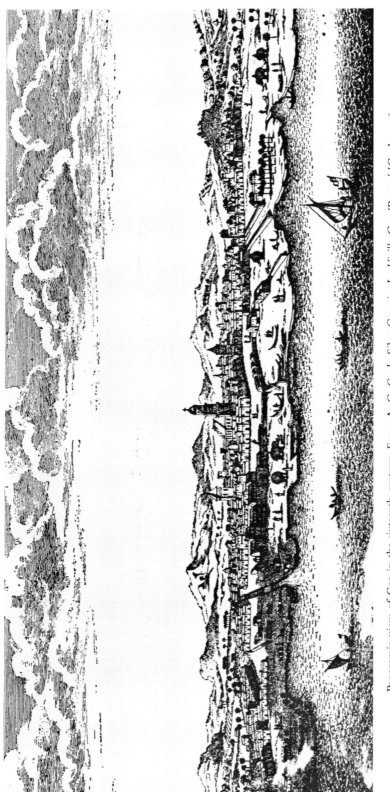

Panoramic view of Goa in the sixteenth century. From A. C. G. da Silva Correia, *La Vieille-Goa* (Bastorá [Goa], 1931).

Chapel of Saint Catherine constructed in 1510 by Albuquerque and rebuilt in 1550 by Jorge Cabral. From Silva Correia, *La Vieille-Goa*.

Cathedral of Old Goa. Construction begun in 1562, but not completed until the seventeenth century. From *Garcia da Orta* (Special Number) (Lisbon, 1956).

Dom Costantino de Braganza, viceroy of Goa from 1558 to 1561. From Jose F.
Ferreira Martins, *Os Vice-Reis da India* (Lisbon, 1935).

Alessandro Valignano, S.J. (1539–1606), from an engraving by N. Oddi. From J. F. Schütte, *Valignanos Missionsgrundsätze für Japan* (Rome, 1951).

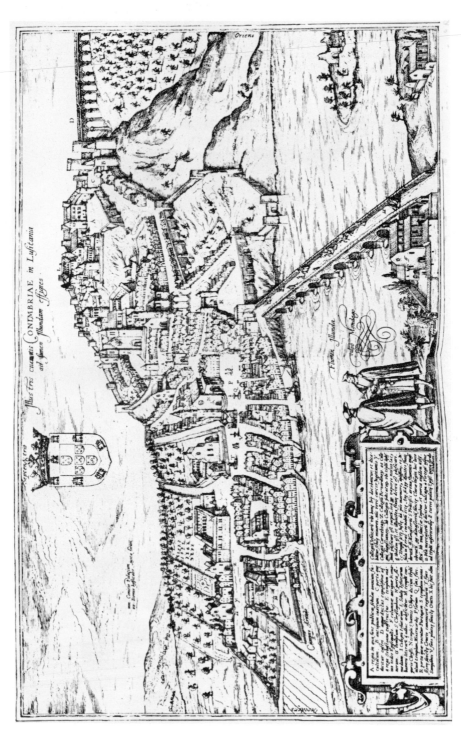

Coimbra in the sixteenth century. From G. Braun, *Civitates orbis terrarum* (Cologne, 1572).

The ruins of the façade of the Church of Saint Augustine (Goa) constructed in 1572. From Silva Correia, *La Vieille-Goa*.

P. MATTHEVS RICCIVS MACERATENSIS QVI PRIMVS E SOCIETAE
IESV EVANGELIVM IN SINAS INVEXIT OBIIT ANNO SALVTIS
·1610·ÆTATIS·60·

Matteo Ricci, S.J. (1552–1610). Painting executed at Peking immediately after the death of Ricci. From Pasquale D'Elia, *Fonti Ricciane: Documenti originali concernenti Matteo Ricci . . .* (Rome, 1942).

COPIA

DI DVE LETTERE

SCRITTE

Dal P. Organtino Bresciano della compa
gnia di Giesù dal Meaco del
Giapone.

Al molto R. In Chrifto P. N. Il P. Claudio Acqua-
uiua Prepofito Generale.

*Tradotte dal P. Gio. Battifta Peruſchi Romano
della medeſima Compagnia.*

Con licenza de' Superiori.

*In Roma, Appreffo Luigi Zanetti, Et in Milano, nel
la Stampa del quon. Pacifico Pontio.* 1597.

ſb

Title page from a typical Jesuit letterbook. Courtesy of the Newberry Library.

Akbar and Prince Salim. Original portrait in British Museum (Add. MS. 18801, No. 10). From Vincent A. Smith, *Akbar, the Great Mogul, 1542–1605* (2d rev. ed.; New Delhi, 1958).

IO PETRI
MAFFEII
BERGOMATIS
E SOCIETATE IESV
HISTORIARVM
INDICARVM LIBRI XVI.

SELECTARVM ITEM EX INDIA
Epiſtolarum eodem interprete Libri IIII.

Acceſſit Ignatij Loiolæ Vita poſtremo recognita. Et in Opera
ſingula copioſus Index.

CVM PRIVILEGIO.

VIRTVTI SIC CEDIT INVIDIA.

VENETIIS, Apud Damianum Zenarium. 1589.

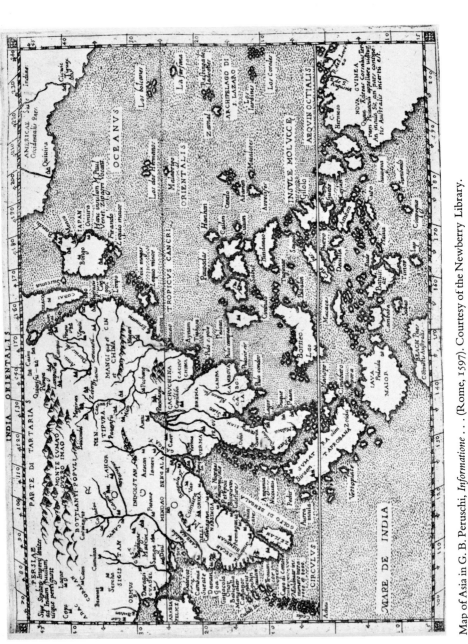

Map of Asia in G. B. Peruschi, *Informatione . . .* (Rome, 1597). Courtesy of the Newberry Library.

agencies, should be highly capable men who could be entrusted with powers greater than their counterparts in Europe.[121]

Over all the regularly constituted officers of the Society in India, Valignano advocated the appointment of an extraordinary official, called either the Visitor or the Commissary, who would perform on a permanent basis what Valignano was undertaking as a special assignment. This extraordinary official should be a person who knew the entire territory personally and who could therefore co-ordinate the activities of the various parts of the Indian province. The permanent Visitor's appointment should last long enough to enable him to inspect the entire province, and he should not be removed until his term had been completed, even if the ruling General in Rome should die and his successor should want to replace the Visitor with one of his own choice.[122] For this post, it is hard to believe that Valignano had a candidate other than himself in mind.

While acting in Goa as Provincial (1583–88), Valignano continued his efforts to introduce into the Jesuit enterprise in Asia an order similar to that prevailing in the European provinces. From this time forward, Provincial Congregations were held regularly (1583, 1588, 1594, and 1599) and "Procurators" were sent more frequently to Europe. Long dissatisfied with the letters which his co-workers were preparing for Europe, Valignano sought to impress upon the writers the need for greater accuracy in reporting and writing. He also used his influence in Rome to see to it that the official publications of "true" annual letters (*Litterae annuae*), which had begun to be issued in 1581, should be prepared with a concern for truth as well as edification. As the first Jesuit superior to work with King Philip II's regime, Valignano helped to inspire Madrid's interest in the Asian mission by sending the Japanese embassy to Europe and by his great personal gifts as a diplomat. Among the Jesuits in India, however, there were a number who did not take kindly to the obedience and discipline exacted by the mission leader and consequently a substantial group of them left the Society.[123]

Like Xavier, Valignano, during his thirty-two years in Asia, had personally very little to do with the everyday work of evangelizing. He contented himself with urging the missionaries to follow the precepts and methods inaugurated by Xavier as defined and redefined by his followers in the field. Like Quadros, he was anxious to recruit missionaries from Europe who were among the best young priests available. Though he knew no Asian language himself, Valignano was uncompromising in demanding that the missionaries learn the languages of the people to whom they were assigned. Valignano devoted his own attention to the imposition of order, to organization, and to writing reports. The material foundations of the mission also concerned him: he provided for the construction of houses, raised funds, and helped the Jesuits to participate effectively in the Japan trade, and he cultivated relations with the ruling circles. He seemed to

---

[121] *Ibid.*, pp. 210–11.
[122] *Ibid.*, pp. 211–12.
[123] Müllbauer, *op. cit.* (n. 3), pp. 90–91.

believe that the strength of Portuguese arms in India and southeast Asia would be sufficient to insure the progress of the faith and that the weak and divided cultures of these regions would gradually be forced to succumb to the superior culture of the West.[124]

Valignano clearly believed, as Xavier had earlier, that the future of the mission lay in Japan and China rather than in India. It was as a result of this belief that he advocated utmost attention to all aspects of Far Eastern culture, particularly language, as the best means of winning the confidence and respect of the elites of Japan and China. The training of a native clergy, for which he assumed the Chinese and Japanese were better fitted than the Indians, was also high on Valignano's list of priorities in the Far East. When Christian or European teachings conflicted with native ideas, institutions, or traditions, he advocated a policy of compromise or "accommodation" in Japan and China. He sent a mission of four young Japanese aristocrats to Europe and constantly hoped to be able to send a similar Chinese embassy. His desire to introduce Western and Christian literature to the peoples of East Asia led to the foundation of Jesuit printing establishments in Macao and Japan.

3

THE MISSION STATIONS OF INDIA

When Xavier arrived at Goa in 1542, the Franciscans had already established eleven friaries, three colleges, and eighty residences within the *padroado*. The Franciscans thereafter gradually relinquished to Jesuit administration a number of their established mission stations and seminaries in Goa and south India. The College of Reis Magos, on the peninsula of Bardez just north of Goa, became the center of Franciscan activity in the latter half of the century. Within this territory there lived an estimated seven thousand Christians. In 1587 the Franciscans still ministered to an estimated total of forty thousand Catholics, mostly in Bardez, the Bassein area, Cochin, Travancore, and Ceylon.[125] The Dominicans, who began coming to India in substantial numbers only in 1548, founded convents of their own and undertook missionary work, especially in the established Portuguese cities.[126] The Augustinians, who became active in the Philippines in 1565, sent their first missionaries to India in 1572. Between this date and the end of the century, around seventy Augustinians had set out from Lisbon for India, and by 1595 one of their number had become Archbishop of

---

[124] Cf. discussion in Wicki, *op. cit.* (n. 102), pp. 48*–49*.

[125] Lemmens, *op. cit.* (n. 4), p. 100.

[126] D'Sa, *op. cit.* (n. 9), I, 87, and for more detail see B. Biermann O.P., "Documenta quaedam initia missionum Ordinis Praedicatorum in India orientali illustrantia (1503–1548)," *Archivum fratrum praedicatorum*, X (1940), 132–57.

Goa.[127] The members of the four Orders worked independently and without great friction and had in common a highly critical attitude toward the secular priests for their incompetence and bigotry.

From the beginning of their enterprise, the nerve center of the Jesuit mission was the College of St. Paul in Goa. Originally, the Professed and the novices lived there together. In Xavier's day around sixty persons were housed in the College, and later on the number rose to more than one hundred. Around 1555 the Cathecumen House (instructional center for those learning the catechism) was opened and it was divided into two parts: one for men and the other for women. The cornerstone for the church of the College at Goa was laid in 1560 and the first mass was sung in it twelve years later. In 1581 a House of the Professed was built; it usually had forty occupants, who had in their charge the spiritual care of the city and the running of the royal hospital. By 1596 all the residences of Goa together housed eighty-three members of the Society: twenty priests and sixty-three novices and lay brothers.[128]

In the College the Jesuits taught everything from elementary Latin to advanced theology. The student body was a cosmopolitan lot of adolescent youths: Hindus, Sinhalese, Moluccans, Chinese, Japanese, Kaffirs, and Ethiopians. In 1546 the fifty-two boys living in the school represented eleven different nations or peoples. A decade later the picture was changed somewhat by the admission of Portuguese and mestizo youths, by a greater concentration of youths from the various parts of India itself, and by more than doubling the enrollment.[129] Besides Christianity and elementary studies, the boys (generally they could enter at fifteen) received training in Latin, Portuguese, music, and mathematics. Apparently the Japanese and Chinese were regarded as the best learners of academic subjects, while the East Indians seemed best suited for training as singers and interpreters. The Indians excelled in memorization, debating, and dramatics. Some of the boys also learned farming and crafts.

The best students in the College went on to study philosophy and theology and, if successful, were ordained and sent to their homelands as priests. But actually very few native Indians were permitted to become priests or enter the religious orders. The ones who were admitted usually received their training and investiture in Europe. Papal decrees explicitly excluded Indians trained exclusively in the colonies from taking Holy Orders, though in the early years of the mission a few colonial Portuguese and Luso-Indian youths were recruited for the Orders.[130] Valignano in 1575 specifically stated that no dark-skinned

---

[127] Figures based on data given in Silva Rego (ed.), *op. cit.* (n. 1, *Documentação*), XII, 99–141.

[128] Müllbauer, *op. cit.* (n. 3), pp. 91–93.

[129] J. Wicki, "Der einheimische Klerus in Indien (16. Jahrhundert)," in *Der einheimische Klerus in Geschichte und Gegenwart* (Schöneck–Beckenried, 1950), p. 24. Also see H. Hosten, S.J., "List of the Pupils of the College of S. Paolo de Santa Fe (1558)," *The Examiner* (Bombay), LXXI (1920), 429–30. The catalogue of December, 1557, gives an enrollment of 134, of whom 95 are listed as full-blooded natives. This group included 40 from the Goa area, 17 from other parts of India, 8 from southeast Asia, 6 from the Far East, and 13 Negroes. See Wicki (ed.), *op. cit.* (n. 72), III, 783–91.

[130] A. Meersman, "The Question of Admitting Indians to the Franciscan Order," *NZM*, XIII (1957), 30–31.

natives (as opposed to Japanese and Chinese) should be admitted to the Society. They were considered inadmissible as a group since it was said that they were naturally inclined to wrongdoing, animated by base instincts, and held in contempt by European Christians.[131] A report to Rome of 1645 indicated that there was not a single Indian member in any of the Orders.[132]

Though forcible mass conversions were undertaken after 1556 in the Goa area, their effectiveness was limited, and heathens, Muslims, and Jews continued to live in the city throughout the century. At times, when the pressure was greatest, the "unredeemed" could always flee to the interior. The ruler of Bijapur could usually be counted on to give them sanctuary and to use the unrest in the Portuguese colony for his own political or military ends. For example, the peninsula of Salsette just three miles south of the island of Goa was technically Christianized by force in 1560. But it took the Portuguese and the missionaries seven years of struggling against native resistance before Christianity was definitely established there. Even with careful nurturing by the Jesuits, the Christian community of Salsette in 1583 was estimated as numbering eight thousand out of a total population of about 80,000.[133] The difficulties experienced by the Christians in Salsette were repeated in most of the other territories in the vicinity of the archiepiscopal see.

Outside the Goa area the Indian stations of the missionary Orders faced a still wider variety of problems. The northern stations, which by 1560 included the cities of Bassein, Chaul, and Damão as well as the islands of Salsette and Diu, were gradually taken over by the Jesuits from the Franciscans. Xavier visited Bassein and the town of Tana on Salsette, where he founded a house and a church. In both these cities the progress of Christianity was swift, and Bassein soon had its own college as it became the Christian headquarters in the north. In 1576, five Jesuits were stationed at Tana to study the Kanarese language. By 1588 about 9,400 persons had been baptized in Bassein and Salsette, and less than a decade later they were being ministered to by twenty-five priests.[134] The Franciscans in 1600 still had eight churches on the peninsula of Salsette.[135]

At Damão, where the Jesuits accompanied Viceroy Braganza in his conquest of 1560, the Society was given the best mosque in the city for a church. But here they encountered strong native resistance to conversion, and eventually Damão was used mainly as a way station on the route to Ethiopia or Gujarat. The Dominicans had a cloister in Chaul, but the Jesuits did not get a permanent establishment there until 1580. As in Damão, no more than five or six Jesuits resided at Chaul permanently. Before 1600, the Jesuits occasionally visited Diu, but most of the missionizing on that rocky island was left to the Dominicans and Franciscans.[136]

[131] Wicki, *loc. cit.* (n. 129), p. 36.
[132] Meersman, *loc. cit.* (n. 130), p. 32.
[133] Müllbauer, *op. cit.* (n. 3), pp. 97–99.
[134] *Ibid.*, pp. 103–5.
[135] Meersman, *op. cit.* (n. 13), p. 108.
[136] Müllbauer, *op. cit.* (n. 3), pp. 104–6.

After Goa, Cochin was the most important Portuguese trading and mission center in India. It was from here that the missionaries were sent out to other places in Malabar, Travancore, Comorin, and Madura. Although the Franciscans were active in south India long before the Jesuits, the latter soon took over the leadership of the mission there as they had done earlier in Goa. On one of Xavier's visits to Cochin he baptized the Muslim king of the Maldives who was in exile there while trying to get Portuguese support for a return to his throne. In 1552, Francisco Peres, then at Malacca, was appointed rector of the new Jesuit College established in Cochin. Father Nunes Barreto returned from China and Japan to India in 1556 and replaced Perez as rector. One year later Cochin was elevated to a bishopric and George Themudo, a Dominican, was appointed to the episcopacy. The new bishop and the rector quickly combined forces and the College at Cochin, with their joint efforts behind it, reached its fullest flowering in the decade following. It was only around 1572, however, that Manuel Teixeira, Barreto's successor, received official permission from the Cochin king to preach freely in his territories. Although he had long been allied with the Portuguese and tolerant of the missionaries, the Cochin ruler generally deprived his officials of their jobs if they tried to or actually did become Christians. As at Goa, the College at Cochin undertook the education of Asian youths and the station was also provided with a separate house for the catechumens. In 1595 there were twenty-five Jesuits located in the city itself and a number of others in the settlements dependent on Cochin at Palluruthi, Venduruthi, Vaipikkotta, and Porakád. The Jesuits did not become active in Calicut until the Zamorin signed a treaty in 1598 with the Portuguese in which he guaranteed that his subjects had the right to become Christians.[137]

South of Cochin the Jesuits built up a missionary enterprise in Travancore based on the city of Quilon. In 1328, as we have already seen, Jordanus of Severac had become bishop of the see of Columbum (Quilon),[138] but Roman Christianity evidently died out there not long afterward. Although Xavier visited Travancore, his immediate successors were forbidden by Kerit Ram Rájá to enter his territory. In the city of Quilon itself, the Jesuits were tolerated because of the local ruler's dependence upon the Portuguese, and in 1552 Nicolo Lancilotti was sent there to establish a residence. From Quilon, Lancilotti ruled over the Jesuits of the Fishery Coast and Mylapore until his death in 1558, when Peres was transferred from Quilon to take his place. Around 1560 Viceroy Braganza sent a fleet against the ruler of Travancore and forced him to agree to give the Jesuits freedom to preach Christianity in his territories, and his subjects the right to become converts. Within a decade there were twenty-five Christian stations in Travancore and about 15,000 converts. Feuds between

---

[137] *Ibid.*, pp. 107–14. For an analysis of the report of the Bishop of Cochin written in 1597 see Placid T.O.C.D., "Portuguese Religious Conquests in Malabar under the Diocese of Cochin during the Sixteenth Century," *NZM*, XIII (1957), 287–306.
[138] Columbum (Latin) = Kolamba (Sanskrit) = Kollam (Tamil) = Coulam (Portuguese) = Quilon; see above, pp. 43–44.

the Orders, wars between the local rulers, and the periodic intervention of the Portuguese produced frequent attacks upon Christian residences and persons. Still, in spite of the uneasy situation in Travancore, more than fifty Christian settlements existed there by 1600.[139] It was in this same year that the Franciscans, by order of the viceroy in Goa, turned over to the Jesuits the administration of their churches in Travancore, the Fishery Coast, and the northern half of Ceylon.[140]

The St. Thomas Christians scattered, as we have seen, throughout the Latin bishopric of Cochin further complicated life for the missionaries. Under their own bishop, Mar Jacob, the Indian Christians had maintained generally friendly relations with the Franciscans and the Portuguese during the first half of the century. When the issue of giving up Malabar religious and social practices arose,[141] Mar Jacob reassured the questioning Latin Christians that he was gradually reforming his church to accord with Roman rite. The Malabar policy of temporizing worked satisfactorily until the bishop's death about 1550. Shortly thereafter the St. Thomas church began to suffer indirect consequences from the internal feuds which split the Chaldean church after the death of its patriarch in 1551. The Chaldean Catholicos-elect, Mar Simon Sulaga, shortly thereafter journeyed to Rome to be consecrated by the pope. While the union with Rome continued, Sulaga was killed in 1555 by his rivals for power. In an effort to gain official support for his candidacy, his successor, Mar Abdiso, went to Rome in 1555 to receive his pallium as Patriarch. Immediately thereafter he sought to consolidate his position as the lawful ruler over the St. Thomas Christians by sending two bishops, Mar Joseph and Mar Elias, to India. The arrival of the two Chaldean bishops accompanied by two Dominicans in Goa during 1556 immediately raised a fundamental jurisdictional question: Were the St. Thomas Christians to remain as the Portuguese contended they were, under the patronage of Portugal, or were they to be recognized officially as belonging under the Chaldean Patriarch?[142] To make matters even more complex the independent Chaldean church, as opposed to Abdiso's Uniat group, continued to claim jurisdiction over the Indian Christians and to send its representatives from time to time to the Serra (mountainous interior territories of the St. Thomas Christians).

Mar Joseph, after two years delay, was in 1558 finally permitted by the Portuguese to go south to Cochin. Although he apparently tried to introduce to the Indian Christians sacraments previously unknown to them, he was soon charged by Father Michael Carneiro, a Jesuit who had been working in the

---

[139] Müllbauer, *op. cit.* (n. 3), pp. 114–17.

[140] The Malabar province of the Society was officially founded in 1601 with headquarters at Cochin. It included in its jurisdiction all of south India, Bengal, Pegu, Malacca, and the Moluccas. See Ferroli, *op. cit.* (n. 81), I, 284–85.

[141] For a description of Malabar religious practices before the Synod of Diamper from the Portuguese and Jesuit sources see *ibid.*, I, 171–78.

[142] Brown, *op. cit.* (n. 6), p. 20; the Latin church generally asserts now that the Malabar Christians had always believed in the primacy of Rome, but that their priests and liturgical books held objectionable formulas derived from Nestorianism. See also Tisserant, *op. cit.* (n. 6), pp. 18–19.

Serra, of teaching Nestorian heresies.[143] After making a public confession of his errors in Cochin, Mar Joseph was sent to Lisbon. Apparently he made an excellent impression at the royal court, and so was sent back to India with the king's blessings in 1565. Two years later he was again arrested for teaching the doctrines of the Chaldean church, and the first Council of Goa in 1567 found him guilty of heresy. Again he was sent to Lisbon and again he managed to convince the prelates of Europe of his innocence. When he died in Rome in 1569, Mar Joseph was still in the good graces of the papacy and it was rumored that he was likely to become a cardinal.[144]

When Mar Joseph was first deported, the Christians of the Serra requested a new bishop from the Chaldean patriarch. Evading the Portuguese blockade, Mar Abraham arrived in Malabar, evidently in 1566. Jurisdictional conflicts immediately occurred, but Mar Abraham eventually made his obedience to Rome. Much to the consternation of the Portuguese, who insisted upon considering the Malabar Christians as subject to their patronage, Pius IV (pope from 1559 to 1565) had ordered that the administration of the Serra should be divided between the two Chaldean bishops. This order was never carried out, and the council of Goa in 1575 proclaimed that the diocese of the Serra should be governed by a bishop appointed by the king of Portugal or by the traditional Bishop of Ankamali, provided that he would first appear before the Council of Goa. Mar Abraham, the only bishop then in the Serra, refused to attend the Council and in this decision he was supported by the Jesuits. After the Jesuits had pleaded his case in Rome, Mar Abraham was permitted, despite the Council's decisions, to carry on in his own fashion for the next decade. As a reward for services rendered, he permitted the Jesuits to build a residence at Vaipikkotta in 1581, which soon developed into a seminary for the training of Malabar priests. It was here that the Catalonian Jesuit, Father Francisco Roz, later the Bishop of Serra, taught theology and perfected his own command of Syriac and Malayālam.[145]

While the religio-cultural mission of the Jesuits progressed in the Serra, the ecclesiastical and secular authorities in Portuguese India were far from happy about the anomalous position of the St. Thomas Christians.[146] At the third Council of Goa (1585), Roz opened old wounds by accusing Mar Abraham of

---

143 On the trials of Mar Joseph see Tisserant, *op. cit.* (n. 6), pp. 35–38. Ferroli, *op. cit.* (n. 81), I, 154–58, discusses the first mission (1557–60) of the Jesuits in the Serra. For a revision of Ferroli's account of Carneiro's charges see Jonas Thaliath, T.O.C.D., *The Synod of Diamper*, No. 152 of "Orientalia Christiana analecta" (Rome, 1958), p. 8, n. 16.

144 Ferroli, *op. cit.* (n. 81), p. 156.

145 Brown, *op. cit.* (n. 6), p. 39; also Placid, *loc. cit.* (n. 137), p. 295.

146 Many ecclesiastical historians, particularly in India, insist that the Indian Christians never denied the primacy of Rome. They accuse the Portuguese of being unable to understand that something could be in a language other than Latin and still be Christian. It is further contended that it was this same variety of cultural myopia which led the Portuguese and the missionaries to accuse the Malabar Christians of blindly accepting the errors of Nestorianism. See especially Joseph C. Panjikaran, "Christianity in Malabar with Special Reference to the St. Thomas Christians of the Syro-Malabar Rite," *Orientalia Christiana*, VI (1926), 103–5.

refusing to reform the worship of the Indian Christians, of perpetuating the Nestorian errors, and of being himself a heretic.[147] The old archbishop retaliated by refusing in 1590 to ordain the students trained at the Vaipikkotta seminary, and by staying at Ankamali instead of attending the fourth Provincial Council of Goa in 1592. Five years later he died at his episcopal see and the new Archbishop of Goa, Alexis de Menezes, appointed an Indian Christian, Archdeacon George, to be sole religious governor of the Serra. At the same time the zealous Augustinian archbishop prepared for a showdown with the Christians of St. Thomas by going to Malabar himself on a visitation tour in 1599.

Menezes was determined to bring the Serra directly and unquestionably under the administration of Rome and the metropolitan see of Goa. The Christians of St. Thomas and their leaders had been successful in procrastinating so long because of internecine rivalries, especially between the Jesuits and Franciscans in the Serra. The native rulers of Malabar had also supported the St. Thomas Christians in their independent stand, out of their fear that close association with Rome would further strengthen the Portuguese hold in southwestern India. The ordinary believers undoubtedly resented the allegations of the Latin Christians that their ancient faith and their revered forms of worship were heretical and that certain of their social customs were unacceptable to orthodox Christians. By the time Menezes reached Malabar in 1599, tension was acute and his life was more than once endangered as he visited Christian places inland far from the protection of the Portuguese coastal garrisons. Still it was the threat of retaliation by the Portuguese that made it possible for Menezes to work his will upon the powerless Indian Christians.

The proceedings of the Synod of Diamper (June 20–26, 1599)[148] were held in Portuguese and were designed to make public the complete defeat of the propatriarchal party. Even before the synod was convened, Archdeacon George was forced to acknowledge the complete supremacy of Rome, abjure Nestorianism, and denounce the Chaldean patriarch as a heretic. Once the recalcitrant leaders had been brought to heel, the synod busied itself with formulating the main tenets of Christian doctrine and with the reforms that should be introduced to make the St. Thomas creed conform to them. The major sources of error were identified as Nestorianism and Hinduism, and all practices or ideas which seemed to stem from them were ordered expunged from the liturgy, forms of worship, and religious books. The decrees against Hindu practices dealt mainly with reforming marriage and inheritance customs, forbidding the worship of idols, and extirpating belief in superstitions, omens,

[147] For decrees of the Council relating to the St. Thomas Christians see D'Sa, *op. cit.* (n. 143), I, 167. For a summary of the Jesuits' charges of Nestorianism, including the denial of the divinity of Christ, see Ferroli, *op. cit.* (n. 81), I, 172–76.

[148] The story of the synod, depicted as a triumph for the Latin rite, was diffused in Europe early in the seventeenth century by A. de Gouvea, *Jornado do Arcibispo de Goa Dom Frey Aleixo de Menezes . . .* (Coimbra, 1606). Soon translated into a number of European languages, Gouvea's work helped to set the stage for the bitter controversies which later developed over the "Malabar rites."

transmigration, and *d'harma*. Menezes was, however, forced to accept caste, and low-caste and high-caste churches and clergy were therefore permitted to exist in the same villages.[149] Finally, the Malabar church was also formally subjected to the pope as universal pastor, required to abide by the decrees of the Council of Trent, made subject to the Inquisition of Goa, and placed under the protection of the Portuguese crown.[150] Once Menezes appeared to have the whole package neatly tied up, the Jesuits took over the administration of the Serra. They were soon to find, however, that the submission of the Malabar church to Rome was not followed by the complete Europeanization of customs, by the eager adoption of Latin religious practices, or even by quiet acceptance of Jesuit control. In the middle of the seventeenth century a schism developed that caused trouble for both the Latins and the Syro-Malabar Christian communities.[151]

On the neighboring Fishery Coast, the Christians were meanwhile having other triumphs and setbacks. Five months after he landed in Goa in 1542, Xavier set out, as we have seen, for Cape Comorin where he expected to reap a rich harvest. But when he arrived there he found that the Paravans knew that they had earlier been baptized by the Franciscans and nothing else.[152] Although Xavier is celebrated for his great industry in evangelizing the Paravans, it is obvious that his instruction of the converts was only slightly less superficial than that earlier carried on by the Franciscans. Xavier left the Fishery Coast for Quilon in 1544 to seek help for his Paravan converts from the king of that city. They were being attacked by the *Badagás*,[153] Telegu-speaking people who were soldiers of the *nāyakas* (viceroys) of Madura and the empire of Vijayanagar, and who extracted tribute and booty from the Portuguese and the Christian communities of the Fishery Coast in periodic forays.[154] On his way to Quilon Xavier worked among the Tamil-speaking fishers of Travancore and likewise effected numerous mass conversions among these lowly people. Upon the Brahmans and the Nāyars his evangelizing seems to have made no impression, perhaps precisely because he concentrated on the lesser castes. Learning of his

[149] Wicki, *loc. cit.* (n. 37), pp. 360–61. Just as the ancient church tolerated slavery, so the Latins tolerated caste in India. Henrique Henriques on the Fishery Coast had even permitted the different castes to sit in different parts of the same church. See Ferroli, *op. cit.* (n. 81), I, 139.

[150] Brown, *op. cit.* (n. 6), pp. 32–37.

[151] In 1955 the Syro-Malabar Christians were estimated at 1,125,550, divided into seven dioceses with over 1,200 churches and chapels, and ministered to by about 2,000 priests and seminarians. For this recent appraisal see Placid, "The Syro-Malabarians, Their Life and Their Activities," *NZM*, XII (1956), 241–56.

[152] For the earlier Franciscan enterprise there see above, p. 236.

[153] Corruption of the Tamil *vadagar*, meaning "northerners." The Portuguese writers of this period also talk about the *Badagá* language by which they mean Telegu. See R. S. Dalgado, *Glóssario Luso-Asiático* (2 vols; Coimbra, 1919), I, 76, and H. Yule and A. C. Burnell, *Hobson-Jobson: A Glossary of Anglo-Indian Colloquial Words and Phrases* (London, 1886), p. 34.

[154] The *Badagás* were forces of the empire of Vijayanagar and from 1543 to 1558 were under the general command of Rama Raya Vitthala, viceroy of south India. He was actually trying to reimpose vassalage upon Travancore and the Fishery Coast. See H. Heras, "Rama Raya Vitthala, Viceroy of Southern India," *Quarterly Journal of the Mythic Society*, XV (1924), 176–90.

activities in Travancore, the *Badagás* also descended in 1544 upon these new Christian communities.[155] The king of Quilon, unable to eliminate the threat of the *Badagás*, apparently tried to enlist Xavier's aid to get help from the Portuguese. At this juncture, late in 1544, Xavier left Quilon for Malacca, but not before he had made provisions for other Jesuits to take up the mission on the Fishery Coast.

Father Antonio Criminale, who arrived at Goa from Lisbon in 1545, was immediately sent to the Fishery Coast and was soon elected superior of the mission. Three years later the mission included four European Jesuits, three native priests, and three lay brothers. This station, besides being one of the most dangerous and troublesome of the Jesuit outposts, was located in one of the hottest and most unhealthy parts of south India. Criminale was killed in 1549 in a raid of the *Badagás*, and by 1552 Father Henrique Henriques was the only European priest surviving. For the next twenty-five years Henriques acted as superior of the mission and did more than any other Jesuit to establish it on a firm footing. After retiring, he continued to live and serve on this coast until 1600, a tenure of fifty-three years.[156]

Weary of fighting or fleeing from the relentless *Badagás*, many of the Fishery Coast Christians began to emigrate southward or toward the interior. Such a movement coincided with the military plans of the Portuguese, who were preparing for an attack upon northern Ceylon. It was part of the Portuguese plan to re-establish the young prince of Trincomalle upon his throne. In 1552, while still a very young boy, the prince had fled his insular homeland for the Fishery Coast to escape from plots against his life by his politically ambitious tutors.[157] Upon his arrival on the Fishery Coast, he and his entourage accepted Christianity. The prince was given a Christian name, Dom Afonso, and sent on to Goa for education and political grooming. Civil war meanwhile swept along the Fishery Coast and the Portuguese encouraged the hard-pressed Paravans to move into Ceylon. While awaiting a Portuguese attack upon Jaffnapatam, the Paravans moved temporarily to the Island of Manaar and Henriques accompanied them. The Portuguese fleet attacked and burned Jaffnapatam in 1560 but left the incumbent in power on condition that he pay homage to Portugal and relinquish Manaar. The young prince, who had been expected to return to Trincomalle, had to go back to Goa, where he died a Christian.[158] By 1563, after an unsuccessful effort to establish a permanent

---

[155] T. Joseph, "St. Xavier [sic!] and the Badagas," *Journal of Indian History*, XXXI (1953), 185–88; also C. K. Mattorn, "The Sources of St. Francis Xavier to the Travancore State," *Journal of Indian History*, XXXI (1953), 75–79.

[156] The Provincial of India, Father Quadros, in a confidential report of 1559 to the Jesuit General, described Henriques as "very weak and sickly, has always been virtuous, firm in his vocation, of mediocre education, does not preach, is prudent, but has too many scruples, is very indecisive in everything." (Wicki, *op. cit.* [n. 72], IV, 397–98.)

[157] Leon Bourdon, *Les débuts de l'évangélisation de Ceylan vers le milieu du XVIe siècle* (Lisbon, 1936), p. 79.

[158] Müllbauer, *op. cit.* (n. 3), p. 122.

Jesuit settlement at Manaar, Henriques, who was suffering from ill health, as were almost all the Paravans, returned to the mainland.[159]

After the unpleasant experience of Manaar, Henriques began building a permanent Jesuit establishment at Punical, where the Portuguese had a fortress garrisoned by about forty to sixty men. Three miles from this Portuguese outpost, near the Straits of Ramanacor, stood the famous Hindu temple of Trichandur, to which many pilgrims annually journeyed from Vijayanagar. Since the Portuguese fortress blocked the road to the temple and cut it off from supplies, the *Badagás* sporadically attacked the intruders at Punical.[160] But after 1558, the efforts of the *Badagás* were not so concerted or as effective as during the previous twenty years. And so, except for limited forays, the Portuguese and the ruler of Travancore no longer had to fear organized expeditions from Vijayanagar.[161] Nevertheless, in 1580, the Jesuit mission was shifted away from Punical to the greater security of the neighboring town of Tuticorin. Here, in 1601, the rector of the mission resided with three Jesuit fathers, three brothers, and a secular priest. The Jesuits supervised elementary and Latin schools. The stations dependent on Tuticorin in 1601 were Punical, Bempara, Trichandur, Manaar, and Periapatam.[162]

In terms of numbers of converts and their firmness in the faith, the mission of the Fishery Coast is celebrated as one of the greatest Christian centers in India. Estimates of numbers of converts range from 90,000 to 130,000.[163] Although the Paravans are regularly praised for their constancy, the Jesuits found them difficult to instruct in the elements of the faith. Henriques learned Tamil and Malayālam so that he might speak to them in their own languages. Because the number of neophytes in this mission was always enormous and the Jesuits few, the majority of the converts were never very firmly grounded in the fundamentals of the faith. And because living conditions were primitive and dangerous, not many of the European fathers were both willing and able to serve on this coast for extended periods of time. The number of natives trained for the priesthood were few, a notable exception being Petrus Aloysius, a Brahman trained at Goa. He was one of the most diligent and able missionaries in India, but he worked under the handicap of being scorned by his compatriots for having deserted his caste. Still, when Valignano visited the Fishery Coast in 1574 he was more satisfied with its mission than with the Jesuit establishment in Travancore.[164]

The evangelizing of Ceylon was delayed for a long time after the Portuguese

---

[159] H. Henriques wrote to the Jesuit General, Lainez, from Manaar on January 8, 1561: "The Christians are unhappy at having to stay on this island . . . which seems to be unhealthy during certain months of the year. They sigh for their homes like Israelites in Egypt. . . . They are a weak people with no stomach, being more accustomed to fishing for oysters, shellfish, and fish than to fighting." (Wicki [ed.], *op. cit.* [n. 72], V, 11.)

[160] Müllbauer, *op. cit.* (n. 3), p. 119.

[161] Heras, *loc. cit.* (n. 154), p. 190.

[162] Müllbauer, *op. cit.* (n. 3), p. 123.

[163] *Ibid.*, p. 124.

[164] *Ibid.*, p. 123.

first arrived there in 1505.[165] Then, as now, Ceylon was divided into two religious and cultural spheres, the Sinhalese-Buddhist area of the south and central territories, and the Tamil-speaking Hindu areas of the north. The island was also divided among a number of kingdoms and vassal states, all of which were periodically at war with one another. These internal divisions, as well as a number of succession crises within the various states, helped to produce and perpetuate cleavages which outside powers were able to turn to their own profit. In Ceylon, the Portuguese maintained a factory after 1521 at the site of modern Colombo in the kingdom of Kotte. In the fratricidal struggles that beset this southwestern kingdom, the Portuguese participated only indirectly until 1539. Then, when Calicut threw its forces into the Sinhalese wars, the Portuguese intervened on behalf of Bhuvanaika Bahu VII, the ruler of Kotte. After ousting the Zamorin's forces, the Portuguese placed the Kotte ruler under their protection.

Martim Affonso de Sousa, the Portuguese naval commander, returned to Lisbon in 1540 with news of the great success in Ceylon. Sousa helped to stimulate hope in the Portuguese capital that the mission would reap a rich harvest on this island where the natives were reported to be pacific and malleable, where the Moors and Jews would provide no opposition, and where the missionaries had never tried any serious evangelizing before. Sousa conveyed this optimistic view to Xavier, who relayed it to Loyola in Rome.[166] Hereafter the court at Lisbon pressed its men in the field, missionaries and soldiers alike, to bring about the conversion of Ceylon.[167]

The Portuguese triumph in Ceylon coincided with a succession crisis in Kotte, and Bhuvanaika Bahu appealed to his new suzerain, King John III, for a decision in the dispute.[168] Not having received a satisfactory answer from the Portuguese by 1541, the Kotte ruler sent Sri Radaraxa Panchta, a Brahman, to Lisbon as his personal emissary. He carried with him a golden image of the young prince, Dharmapala Astana, whom Bhuvanaika wanted confirmed as his successor. The Sinhalese envoy was well received in the Portuguese capital, but no records of his negotiations are available. Rumors were circulated in Lisbon that Radaraxa had accepted Christianity and that the king of Kotte would shortly follow suit. Although the envoy was not actually converted at this time, King John III sent him back to Ceylon in 1543 in the company of six Franciscans led by Friar João de Vila de Conde who carried a pledge of Portugal's support for Dharmapala. The missionaries met with a kind reception from Bhuvanaika,

---

[165] P. E. Pieris and M. A. H. Fitzler, *Ceylon and Portugal* (Leipzig, 1927), pp. 1–3.

[166] Schurhammer, *op. cit.* (n. 58), I, 689.

[167] This was by no means the first news of Ceylon which reached Europe. In the book *Le grant voyage de hierusalem* (Paris, 1517), news was included of the Portuguese advent in Ceylon. See G. Atkinson, *La littérature géographique française de la Renaissance* (Paris, 1927), p. 37, n. 26.

[168] The documents for the period are collected in G. Schurhammer and E. A. Voretzsch (eds.), *Ceylon zur Zeit des Königs Bhuvaneka Bahu und Franz Xavers, 1539–1552* (2 vols.; Leipzig, 1928). An excellent summary of these documents and related materials is to be found in Bourdon, *op. cit.* (n. 157).

but he stoutly rejected their suggestions that he should give up the faith of his ancestors and accept Christianity. The Kotte king clearly wanted a politico-commercial alliance with Portugal, but he remained adamant throughout his lifetime (d. 1551) in his refusal to accept baptism.

As the friars disputed publicly with native scholars and persisted in their evangelizing efforts in Ceylon, tempers flared on both sides and Friar João returned to Goa in a huff. The missionaries and the Portuguese continued to advance their interests by playing off the various parties in the succession issue against one another. As a consequence of this meddling in politics, many Christian converts accused of defying their secular rulers were killed in Kotte during 1544–45. Although two of the outstanding Sinhalese princes were baptized and taken to Goa in 1546, they both died before the Portuguese were able to use them as political pawns.

The Portuguese administrators in Goa were constantly under pressure, both from the missionaries and the court of Lisbon, to act forcefully to bring Christianity to Ceylon. But shortages of men and commitments elsewhere in the East made a major military expedition extremely difficult to mount. Before 1551, a number of desultory and unco-ordinated forays were made, not only against Kotte but also against Jaffna and Kandy. The missionaries, eager for a royal conversion in Ceylon, aided and abetted the attackers. Jaffna, which controlled the pearl fisheries and commanded the Straits of Manaar, had been nominally under Portuguese vassalage since 1543. The kingdom of Kandy, situated in the mountainous center of the island, was receptive to Portuguese overtures concerning trade until it became clear that the Europeans were set upon controlling Trincomalle, its only outlet to the sea, and upon converting its king and royal family to Christianity. But until 1551, the Portuguese governors in Goa hesitated to commit the necessary forces to the enterprise in Ceylon and so very little was accomplished either religiously or politically in the decade of the forties.

In 1551 Bhuvanaika was murdered. It is not clear whether his death was engineered by the Portuguese or by the king's rivals for power,[169] but whichever the case, the viceroy, D. Afonso de Noronhas, resolved to use the opportunity provided by the king's death to move in force against Kotte. While the new king, Dharmapala, staunchly resisted conversion, the viceroy had his infant son and heir baptized and sent to Goa in the company of Radaraxa. The Brahman adviser finally became a Christian himself in 1552. Shortly thereafter, he left the Portuguese capital in the company of the Jesuit priest Manuel de Moraes. In Ceylon, Moraes converted a number of Kotte's leading men and women, but Dharmapala continued in his refusal. Churches and Franciscan residences were attacked repeatedly as the Sinhalese resisted conversion at gunpoint. But superior force eventually won the day. In 1557, Dharmapala and his entire family and court accepted Christianity, and Kotte thereafter became

[169] Bourdon, *op. cit.* (n. 157), p. 75.

a friendlier place for the missionaries. The attack of D. Constantino de Braganza on Jaffna in 1560 did not force its king to accept Christianity, but it did require him to cease persecuting Christians and it placed the island of Manaar firmly in Portugal's hands. Thereafter it was only a matter of time until the king of Kandy succumbed to Portuguese pressure; in 1565 he accepted baptism. Then, under the Christian rulers of Kotte and Kandy, the missionaries took up the task of converting and teaching Christianity to the masses. At the end of the sixteenth century there were an estimated seventy thousand converts and forty-five Christian churches in Ceylon,[170] mostly located in Kotte and Kandy and under the jurisdiction of the Franciscans. The Jesuits assumed the initiative in northern Ceylon in 1601 and set up a residence at Jaffnapatam.

It was likewise not until the last years of the sixteenth century that the Jesuits began to penetrate into the interior of Vijayanagar from the Christian settlements of the southeast coast. The Jesuit Visitor, Nicholas Pimenta, who arrived at Negapatam in 1597, in the following year pushed on into the southern provinces of Vijayanagar to arrange for missions in the territories of the *nāyakas* (viceroys) of Gingi, Tanjore, and Madura. The ruler of Gingi gave the Visitor written permission to build a church and other buildings at Chistapatam, subscribed money for support of the mission, and gave unconditional assurances that his subjects might accept Christianity. Two Jesuits were sent from Travancore to Chistapatam in 1599. They built a church there, but the mission seems to have foundered shortly thereafter. At Tanjore, Pimenta received similar assurances, but the Jesuits waited for thirty years before actually founding a Christian community there. Upon arriving in Madura, Pimenta found a Paravan Christian community already established and developing. It was not, however, until 1606 that Robert de' Nobili put the Madura mission on a solid footing.[171]

At Mylapore, where Xavier himself visited for four months, the Jesuits before 1600 as a rule maintained three or four missionaries to work with the Europeans and a small group of native converts. When Pimenta visited this outpost in 1597, he charged the rector of its College, Simon Sà, with the responsibility of penetrating inland into Vijayanagar at any cost. A Mylapore merchant, originally hailing from Chandragiri, which became the capital of Vijayanagar after 1592, acted as an intermediary for the rector with the Rājā of Chittoor. Invited to Chittoor, Sà and Father Francisco Ricci, in company with the merchant, made the journey there in 1598. After holding long conversations with the rājā about Portugal and Christianity, the Jesuits received permission to build churches at Chandragiri and at Condur. When local hostilities made impractical the construction of a church at Condur, the Jesuits were given a similar permission at Cotapatnam. In 1599 the Visitor sent a delegation of six Jesuits to the court of Vijayanagar, including Emanuel Vega, the rector of the House of the Professed in Goa. The Jesuits were cordially received, granted

[170] Lemmens, *op. cit.* (n. 4), p. 106.
[171] Müllbauer, *op. cit.* (n. 3), pp. 125–27.

living allowances, and assured that the subjects of Vijayanagar might embrace Christianity freely. But though the mission had such a bright beginning, it failed to prosper because of the interminable wars which swept the declining Vijayanagar state.[172]

While personally occupied in south India, Pimenta in 1598 sent two Jesuit fathers to minister to the Portuguese trading colonies in Bengal and in the neighboring state of Arakan.[173] Two Jesuit priests had arrived in Bengal as early as 1576, but they were unable to set up a permanent mission there.[174] Fathers Francisco Fernandes and Domingo Sousa, the two appointees of Pimenta, were instructed to establish permanent stations in the Portuguese outposts on the Bay of Bengal. After a short stay at Gullo, where they built a hospital, Fernandes and Sousa were called to Chandekan both by the native king and the Portuguese residing there. Here they were joined in 1599 by Melchior Fonseca and João André Bovesius, the former of whom built the church of Chandekan. Fernandes and Sousa made their way from one Portuguese outpost to another and ultimately came to the court of the king of Arakan. This ruler, who was also master of Chittagōng and part of Bengal, was favorably inclined toward the Portuguese because of the military aid which they had previously rendered him. Shortly after Fernandes founded a church at Chittagōng in 1601, the king of Arakan, fearful lest the Portuguese become too powerful, turned against them and, combining forces with the Mughul governor of Bengal, tried to drive them out. While the Portuguese, supported by a fleet sent by the viceroy, managed to retain the area of the Bay of Bengal, the Jesuits shortly after this time deserted it for friendlier places and left its Christianizing primarily to the Augustinians and the Dominicans.

The most dramatic and fruitful of the Jesuit enterprises in the interior were the three missions of 1580–83, 1591, and 1595–1605[175] to Akbar, the Mughul ruler (reigned 1556–1606). Akbar's first negotiations with Portuguese from Goa were held in 1573, coincident with his conquest of Gujarat. Four years later, Pedro Tavares, the commander of the Portuguese garrison at Satgāon, and Julian Pereira were sent to Akbar's court at Fatehpur Sikhri. Pereira talked to the king about Christianity and mentioned the work of the learned Jesuits at Goa. The Mughul ruler, surrounded by Muslims of various sects, Brahmans, Parsees, and Jews, apparently felt, like the European monarchs of his day, that political stability in an expanding empire was almost impossible to obtain and maintain in the face of deep religious divisions. Even at that early date he perhaps felt that Christianity might provide the basis for the eclectic religion which he

---

[172] *Ibid.*, pp. 128–30. See also H. Heras, "The Jesuit Influence in Vijayanagar," *Quarterly Journal of the Mythic Society*, XIV (1923), 131–34, for a contemporary account of the residence at Chandragiri.

[173] On Arakan see below, pp. 550–52.

[174] H. Hosten, "A List of Portuguese Jesuit Missionaries in Bengal and Burma, 1576–1742," *Journal of the Asiatic Society of Bengal*, VII (1911), 15–23; also see H. Josson, *La mission du Bengale occidentale* (Bruges, 1921), I, 49–138, and J. J. A. Campos, *History of the Portuguese in Bengal* (London, 1919), pp. 100–02.

[175] See Edward Maclagan, *The Jesuits and the Great Mogul* (London, 1932), chaps. ii–iv.

spent most of his life trying to evolve. At any rate he sent two emissaries to Goa in 1579 with a request for the dispatch to his court "of two learned priests who should bring with them the chief books of the Law and the Gospel."[176]

In November, 1579, the first mission set out from Goa under the leadership of Rudolf Aquaviva, an aristocratic Italian and nephew of Claude Aquaviva, later General of the Society. He was accompanied by the two legates sent by Akbar and by Fathers Antonio Monserrate and Francisco Henriques. The latter, who was to help with interpreting, was a Persian from Ormuz who had been a convert from Islam. Starting inland from Surat, the mission arrived at Fatehpur in February, 1580. Because Akbar was obviously seeking a solution to his religious problem, both personal and national, the fathers concentrated upon converting him to the faith. While cordial to the missionaries and sympathetically interested in their doctrines, Akbar found himself disinclined to accept certain of the Christian mysteries and social customs, particularly monogamy. Although the missionaries were free to preach and make conversions, they preferred to stay close to Akbar and spend their time teaching Portuguese to his son, learning Persian themselves, and accompanying the ruler on his military campaigns. For example, Father Monserrate, who later on wrote about Akbar's exploits, accompanied the Mughul ruler to Kabul during 1581 on a campaign against his Muslim enemies. The following year Monserrate was sent to Goa to recruit more missionaries and to send congratulations from Akbar to Philip II on his accession to the throne of Portugal. Since Henriques had returned to Goa in 1581, Aquaviva remained alone at Fatehpur until Akbar permitted his departure in February, 1583.

At Goa, nothing was heard from Akbar again until 1590, by which time his court had moved to Lahore. Leo Grimon, a Greek priest, brought tidings from Akbar and a renewed request for teachers of the Christian faith to engage in disputations with the representatives of the other religions at his court. Fathers Duarte Leitão and Christoval de Vega, accompanied by a lay brother, were sent to Lahore in 1591. Although they had been told that Akbar was even less devoted to Islam than before, they soon found that he was personally still unwilling to embrace Christianity. While they were cordially received by the king and permitted to set up a school for the training of aristocratic youths, the missionaries soon perceived that they were being violently opposed at court by a strong Muslim faction. The situation being so unfavorable to their cause, the Jesuits quickly returned to Goa without any significant achievements to their credit.

Disappointment ran high in Goa, and possibly in Madrid, at the hasty retreat of the mission of 1591; many still believed that Akbar was ready to be converted. Those who held such optimistic views foresaw that his conversion might have important political as well as religious consequences. The Jesuit Provincial at Goa, who was pessimistic about the prospects for a new mission, finally yielded

176 As quoted in *ibid.*, p. 24.

to pressure from the viceroy and from Akbar himself. Father Jerome Xavier,[177] a grandnephew of the Apostle of the Indies and superior of the House of the Professed in Goa, was ultimately selected to lead the third mission. Two other highly competent missionaries, Father Manuel Pinheiro and Brother Benedict de Goes, as well as a Portuguese painter and Domingo Pires, an interpreter, accompanied Xavier to Lahore. After a laborious journey of five months, the caravan to which they were attached entered Lahore in May, 1595.

Xavier was at Akbar's side throughout most of the last decade of the great Mughul's life. When the court moved, he went with it. He stayed with Akbar at Lahore (except for a summer visit to Kashmir in 1597) from 1596 until the Mughul ruler embarked in 1598 on his Deccan campaign. On the way to the Deccan the court stopped over in Agra, and it returned to Agra after an inconclusive campaign in May, 1601. For the remaining years of Akbar's life, Xavier remained with him at Agra. Pinheiro, who was the first of the Jesuits to turn his attention to the "Mughul populace," generally remained in Lahore with his church and congregation. Goes, who had accompanied Akbar on his Deccan campaign, was sent to Goa in 1601, where he received orders to make an overland trip from India to Cathay. This intrepid traveler turned up in Agra in 1602 with Father Antonio Machado, and in the following year set out from the Mughul seat of government on his journey to China. At Akbar's death Xavier and Machado were at Agra, and Pinheiro and Father Francisco Corsi, who had been sent to aid Pinheiro in 1600, were at Lahore.

Xavier learned Persian to communicate with Akbar and his associates, but the Mughul ruler persisted in his refusal to accept Christianity. Although Akbar openly abandoned Islam and gave written permission in 1601 for his subjects to embrace Christianity freely, he persisted doggedly in his search for an eclectic faith and refused to acknowledge the divinity of Christ. The missionaries, especially Xavier, had remarkably close and friendly relations with Akbar, even though he at times suspected them of being political agents of the Portuguese. Nor was his suspicion on this point without foundation. Philip II, the viceroy of Goa, as well as the Jesuit authorities continued to encourage the missionaries in "Mogor" to persist in their enterprise, because as the king of Spain wrote in 1598: "The fruit . . . may appear when human hopes are smallest." During the Deccan campaign, when Akbar was conducting hostilities against the political allies of the Portuguese, the Jesuits in his entourage were embarrassed at having to refuse his request to ask their coreligionists for arms and ammunition. While they managed to escape Akbar's wrath, their Muslim enemies took advantage of the king's disenchantment to stir up hostility against the missionaries and their converts at Lahore and Agra. So, despite the king's generally sympathetic attitude and his tolerance of Christian evangelizing, he died in 1605 without accepting the faith himself and without forcing his subjects to acknowledge it.

---

[177] For his life and activities see Arnulf Camps, D.F.M., *Jerome Xavier and the Muslims of the Mogul Empire*, Supplement VI (1957) of *NZM*.

Information about the missions to Akbar was generally available in Europe before 1600.[178] While at the Mughul court during the first mission, Monserrate kept a diary of his experiences which became the basis for his later writings. It was from this first mission and the data collected by Aquaviva and Monserrate that the idea of a mission to Tibet beyond the Himalayas was broached and its practicality investigated.[179] Confusion over the identification of Cathay as both Tibet and China led the Visitor Nicolas Pimenta, with the support of King Philip III of Spain, to instruct Goes to make his arduous journey of 1603–7 to China by way of central Asia. And while exploring geographically the interior of Asia, the Jesuits did not neglect to aid the process of cultural interchange. The missionaries presented Western books, Christian paintings and engravings, and prints made in Japan to the enthusiastic Mughul ruler. The non-Christian artists at Akbar's court often copied Christian paintings or incorporated European subjects, sometimes taken from the paintings and at other times from life,[180] in their own works. And, as earlier mentioned, while the Jesuits taught Portuguese to "Mogor" youths, they themselves studied Persian, the court language, and so began to have some appreciation of its great literature. Jerome Xavier, who studied Persian for nearly twenty years at the Mughul court, composed a number of Christian writings in this language and prepared a Persian grammar.[181] Father Corsi, it appears, as he tried to get closer to the populace at Lahore, learned enough of the Hindustani vernacular spoken in the area to communicate with the members of his congregation. Here, as in China and Japan at the same period, the Jesuits had seriously begun to penetrate non-Western culture because they were far removed from the Portuguese centers and so were forced to learn the ways of others.

India was the first high culture that the missionaries encountered in the sixteenth century, and they soon found that it had within it as many or more regional linguistic, religious, and social divisions as Europe itself. Because of their limited numbers, their dependence upon the Portuguese, and their reluctance to compromise with the native cultures of India, the missionaries had only limited successes in evangelizing the heathens or in understanding the people with whom they worked. The most important first step in the penetration of India, the learning of the native languages, they were very slow to undertake.[182] The Franciscans, the earliest in the field in significant numbers, appear to have been particularly reluctant to apply themselves to language study. Actually, when we consider the areas in which they worked, it was probably

---

[178] See below, pp. 452–53.

[179] Maclagan, *op. cit.* (n. 175), p. 337.

[180] See, for examples, Emmy Wellesz, *Akbar's Religious Thoughts Reflected in Mogul Painting* (London, 1952).

[181] For a list, discussion, and appraisal of Xavier's Persian writings see Camps, *op. cit.* (n. 177), pp. 13–39.

[182] For a general discussion of the problem see Joseph Dahlmann, *Missionary Pioneers and Indian Languages* (Trichinopoly, 1940); also, particularly for later language students, see Ambrogio Ballini, "Il contributo delle missioni alla conoscènza delle lingue della cultura dell'India," in C. Costantini *et al., Le missioni catholiche e la cultura dell'Oriente* (Rome, 1943), pp. 233–60.

necessary for them to study only one or more of four different Indian tongues: the Marathi-Konkani languages for the northern stations and Goa; and for the southern stations, Malayālam (Cochin and Travancore), Tamil (South Travancore and the Fishery Coast), and Sinhalese (Ceylon). Yet no evidence exists to show that the Franciscans seriously began language study until near the end of the century, after they were admonished to do so by papal brief, royal declarations, and a direct command of their Custos and Commissary-General.[183] They generally communicated through lay interpreters, though a few of them knew an Indian language by 1600. Friar Francisco di Oriente learned Tamil and Manoel de S. Mathies instituted a class in Sinhalese at Colombo which was presided over by another friar. In Bardez, the Franciscan area north of Goa, two friars knew Konkani so well by 1575 that they were able to translate Western works into that tongue[184] and to censor Konkani publications for the Inquisition.

Naturally the acquisition of Indian languages was made difficult by the lack of suitable tools such as dictionaries and grammars. The Jesuits, however, from Xavier onward showed themselves able, in several cases at least, to overcome this handicap. Perhaps this was true because the officials of the Society and its Constitutions required the Jesuits in the field to make the attempt. The superiors in India rewarded language competence by promotions. Generally, it was not the leading lights of the Society who studied language, but rather the lay brothers and younger priests who worked in remote places. In 1560 the Provincial, Quadros, encouraged a few younger members of the Order to learn Konkani systematically by releasing them from their other duties, a practice which Valignano later continued and extended. Unfortunately, most of the missionaries learned only the local dialects useful to them in their work and were therefore generally unable to understand the literary languages.[185] Nor was anyone sufficiently talented or well enough trained to translate the Holy Scriptures into any one of the native tongues.[186] Still, considering the handicaps under which they worked, it is impressive to recall that in 1578–79 a catechism in Tamil was printed in India by the Jesuit press and that at the end of the century Jerome Xavier was beginning to write Christian works in Persian. Copies of the religious books which had been translated into Asian languages were also sent back to Europe as "curiosities."

Without access to the literary languages, especially Sanskrit, the missionaries had very few opportunities to observe more than the surface trappings of Hindu

[183] Since surprisingly few Franciscan documents survive and since almost none appeared in print during the sixteenth century, the history of the Franciscans in India has had to be constructed from references to their activities in other sources, especially the Jesuit letters. See A. Meersman, "Notes on the Study of Indian Languages by the Franciscans," *NZM*, XVI (1960), 41–42.

[184] Friar Amador de S. Anna translated the *Flos Sanctorum* (*Flower of the Saints*) into Marathi. See *ibid.*, pp. 43–44.

[185] See Wicki, *loc. cit.* (n. 37), p. 348. Thomas Steven, the English Jesuit, apparently knew literary Marathi.

[186] *Ibid.*, p. 367.

culture. The classics of Sanskrit literature were kept strictly secret by the Brahmans, and it is likely that no European before De' Nobili in the seventeenth century, had learned the holy language of India. However, some help in understanding the mysteries of their learning came with the acquisition and translation of certain classical texts. In 1548 a basketful of Brahmanical books was confiscated on the island of Divar and brought to the College of Goa for translation, at which point they seem to disappear from the records. Ten years later, however, events took a more auspicious turn. A convert, learned in Brahmanical literature, stole a number of manuscripts from a former friend of his (evidently a Brahman) and brought them to Goa, where he set about rendering some of them into Portuguese. Through these translations the Jesuits learned something about the ten Avatars of Vishnu and the high literature written in Marathi. A considerable part of the thirteen books of the *Bhagavadgītā* was translated into Portuguese from the free rendition of Jnāneśvar. The translation of the *Yogarāj Tilaka*, a charming Marathi dialogue between a pupil and his teacher, dealing with eternal questions, let the Christians know something about the beliefs currently being discussed by Indian writers. The Europeans also became acquainted at this time with the Sannyāsis, Yogis, Avadhūtas, and the four life-stages of the Brahmans. Manuscript copies of these translations were sent to Europe, where they are still preserved at Evora and Rome. In India, the Jesuits used this information acquired by dubious means for equally dubious ends. Instead of valuing them for their genuine intellectual worth, the missionaries used these writings in their disputations with the Brahmans as examples of the absurdities of Hindu traditions and beliefs.[187]

Even Valignano, the humanistically trained and sophisticated Italian aristocrat, showed almost no understanding of Hinduism and, like his simpler brethren, derided it as "so much laughable and fabulous stuff repellent to every sound mind and to reason."[188] Ultimately, however, the Renaissance Italian prevails in Valignano's enthusiastic admiration for the massive size, clean lines, and fine workmanship of the Hindu temples.[189] Lest he should seem to be too much carried away by buildings dedicated to ridiculous heathen gods, he hastens to add that their interiors are melancholy and dark, and that their statuary is grotesque and reeks of the oil with which the Hindus anoint their gods. He also condemns many other externals of Hindu life without seeming to realize that he was, in this instance, a victim of his own cultural myopia. Valignano's lack of perception and his intolerance of Indian practices is particularly hard to understand when it is contrasted with his genuine admiration for much of the traditional culture of Japan.

---

[187] *Ibid.*, p. 349.

[188] See Pt. I, chap. v of his *Historia* as reproduced in Wicki, *op. cit.* (n. 102), pp. 30–40, especially p. 34.

[189] Of the temples he also remarked: "[They are] really worth seeing, and I found much pleasure in seeing them often." (*Ibid.*, p. 35.) Earlier Jesuits, like Xavier and Nunes, were also impressed by the Hindu temples.

4

THE MISSION STATIONS IN FURTHER ASIA

From the first, the missionaries used Malacca as a base and as a point of departure for the places of greater intrinsic importance east of India.[190] Intrepid Franciscans started evangelizing in Celebes as early as 1525 when the Portuguese first touched on the southwestern tip of that island. Though forced to abandon this early enterprise rather hastily, the Franciscans soon followed the spice route eastward to the Moluccas and beoynd. From 1533 to 1544 they made large numbers of converts among the backward pagans of the Moro Islands[191] to the north of the Portuguese fortress of Ternate. In 1545, at the insistence of the governor of Malacca, other missionaries were sent to Makassar (Celebes)[192] and when Xavier was first in Malacca in 1545–46, it was reported that two local kings had already become Christians and that "the land is [therefore] ready for the conversion of many people."[193] Xavier, who waited for a time in Malacca for more authoritative reports on the progress being made in Celebes finally gave up his plan of going there and sailed directly for Amboina on January 1, 1546.

A. XAVIER'S RECONNAISSANCE, 1546–52

The island of Amboina, which was the main assembly point for the Portuguese spice fleets in the East Indies, already possessed seven Christian settlements when Xavier first arrived there.[194] From mid-February to June, 1546, the Jesuit pioneer ministered to the spiritual needs of the Christians and arbitrated disputes among the Portuguese garrisoned on the island. He was also present to witness the arrival on March 10 of the fleet of Fernão de Sousa da Tavora which had aboard some of the survivors of the Spanish expedition sent out under Villalobos.[195] Among the Spanish prisoners was a secular priest, Cosmas de Torres, who was so impressed by the personality and character of Xavier that

[190] I. A. Macgregor, "Notes on the Portuguese in Malaya," *Journal of the Malayan Branch of the Royal Asiatic Society*, Vol. XXVIII, Pt. II (1955), p. 39.

[191] Lorenzo Pérez, "Historia de las misiones de los Franciscanos en las islas Malucas y Celebes," *Archivum franciscanum historicum*, VI (1913), 49–50.

[192] Schurhammer and Wicki (eds.), *op. cit.* (n. 40), I, 325.

[193] *Ibid.*, p. 298. Father Vicente Viegas, a secular priest, accompanied by Manuel Pinto was in Makassar from 1545 to 1548. In a letter of 1548 sent by Pinto to the bishop of Goa from Malacca, he speaks of converting the two kings known to the Portuguese as Dom Luis, ruler of "Supa" (or Soeppa) and Dom João, ruler of Siam (or Sião) Island in Lower Makassar. See Wicki (ed.), *op. cit.* (n. 72), II, 419–23.

[194] Schurhammer and Wicki (eds.), *op. cit.* (n. 40), I, 323. On Xavier in Amboina see C. Wessels, S.J., *Histoire de la mission d'Amboine, 1546–1605* (Louvain, 1934), chap. ii.

[195] See below, p. 602.

he decided to go to Goa and join the Society of Jesus.[196] While meeting new peoples and situations, Xavier continued his habit of correspondence. In his letters from Amboina, Xavier observed that Islam was known to the islanders, but concluded that the local Muslims "know nothing about their own perverse sect."[197] The primitive peoples of these numerous islands "are not Christians only because there is no one to convert them."[198] A college ought to be founded in the Spice Islands, and a dozen or more missionaries (even though not endowed with a surplus of learning or ability) should be sent to the islands annually to live and die with these people and to bring them to the true faith. As an immediate first step, Xavier ordered Francisco de Mansilhas and João de Beira to leave Goa for the Spiceries as soon as they received his letter.[199]

Upon his arrival at Ternate in the Moluccas in July, 1546, Xavier learned that ten thousand Christians were living in the Moro Islands and that they had been left without spiritual guidance for over two years.[200] In the autumn of 1546, he spent three months in this wild country visiting its scattered Christian communities. Quadros reported in 1555 that Xavier had concluded after his experiences there that these barren and savage places should be called "the islands waiting for God" rather than the Moro Islands.[201] The next three months Xavier spent at Ternate ministering to the Portuguese and working for the conversion of Sultan Hairun and his family. Though Hairun himself refused to abjure Islam, Xavier succeeded in converting a number of the royal ladies including Doña Isabel, the sultan's stepmother.[202] Xavier returned to Malacca in June, 1547, full of hope that an auspicious beginning had been made in the Spiceries and that Hairun himself might eventually accept the faith.[203]

Even while optimistic about prospects in the Spiceries, Xavier became increasingly eager to survey the mission field in the Far East. Writing from Amboina in 1546, he recalls having met a Portuguese merchant on his first visit to Malacca who told him many things about "a great trading land called China."[204] Among other matters he reported hearing that there were people in the interior of China who would not eat pork. Since most informants were certain that the Chinese were not Muslims, Xavier's curiosity caused him to

---

[196] He became a Jesuit in 1548 and three years later Xavier appointed him to be superior of the Japan mission. See Wicki (ed.), *op. cit.* (n. 72), I, 475, n. 26.

[197] Schurhammer and Wicki (eds.), *op. cit.* (n. 40), I, 329.

[198] *Ibid.*, p. 328.

[199] *Ibid.*, pp. 339–40. Xavier's letters from Amboina were taken to Malacca by Sousa da Tavora's fleet. Mansilhas proved to be unwilling and disobedient, and was shortly thereafter dismissed from the Society. Beira arrived at Ternate in 1547 and worked there and on Halmahera until 1552. He then went back to India to get reinforcements. Nunius Ribero meanwhile worked at Amboina from 1546 until his death in 1549. Beira died at Goa in 1564. See Wessels, *op. cit.* (n. 194), pp. 206–7.

[200] Schurhammer and Wicki (eds.), *op. cit.* (n. 40), I, 325.

[201] Quadros to Diego Mirón, provincial of Portugal (Goa, Dec. 6, 1555) in Wicki (ed.), *op. cit.* (n. 72), III, 344.

[202] Also known as Elizabeth Niachile Pocarago. See Schurhammer and Wicki (eds.), *op. cit.* (n. 40), II, 126, n. 15.

[203] Wessels, *op. cit.* (n. 194), p. 42.

[204] Schurhammer and Wicki (eds.), *op. cit.* (n. 40), I, 334–35.

speculate upon the real identity of a non-Muslim people averse to eating pork. Were these people possibly Christians of the old and new law like those of Abyssinia, or remnants of the lost tribes of Judah, or followers of St. Thomas, whose career was supposed by many to have ended in China? To find answers to these and various other questions, he asked the Portuguese who annually voyaged from Malacca to China to learn what they could about this peculiar sect. Whether or not he ever received a clear answer is not known, but he continued to inquire ceaselessly about the Far East. On his return to Malacca in 1547 Xavier heard about the discovery of the islands of Japan where, according to his Portuguese informants, "much could be done to increase the faith, more so than in India, for they are a people who greatly desire to learn, which is not true of the gentiles of India." [205] The truth of this opinion was brought home to Xavier by his meeting with a Japanese gentleman, Yajirō, who showed himself eager to learn the Portuguese language and Christian doctrine. It was also on this occasion that Xavier asked the Portuguese merchant, Jorge Alvarez, to commit to writing the account of his experiences in Japan. [206]

Xavier returned to India early in 1548 to reassess Jesuit activities there, to recruit more missionaries for the Spiceries, and to make preparations for his intended journey to Japan. Upon his arrival at Cochin, he learned of the disasters which had befallen the Franciscans in Ceylon, and of the sudden and unexpected death in 1547 of Miguel Vaz, the vicar-general, whom many believed had been the victim of foul play. Immediately, Xavier penned a letter to King John III of Portugal, complaining in bitter terms about the failure of the secular arm, especially the governors, to support and protect Christian enterprise. In this reproachful letter he remarks:

I, Sire, am not wholly decided on going to Japan, but it begins to seem to me likely, since I suspect very much that I shall not meet real favor in India in the increasing of our holy faith or in the preserving of the Christians already converted. [207]

This sentiment, like so many others expressed by Xavier, was to color Jesuit thinking about the dismal prospects for the future in India, and it evidently helped to promote the feeling among members of the mission that the real harvest would finally be reaped in Japan. [208] After fifteen months in India, Xavier set out in April 25, 1549, from Cochin on the first leg of the lengthy and dangerous voyage to Japan.

He stayed for less than one month in Malacca and by mid-August, 1549, had landed in Kagoshima on the southern Japanese island of Kyūshū. Still convinced that Japan was the promised land, Xavier wrote exuberantly to Goa

---

[205] *Ibid.*, p. 389

[206] For details on Yajirō and Alvarez, see below, pp. 657–61.

.[207] Schurhammer and Wicki (eds.), *op. cit.* (n. 40), I, 408. For a similar expression of his disgust with the inadequacies of John III's support see his letter to Simão Rodrigues of the same date (*ibid.*, 417–22).

[208] For a weak and somewhat pointless apology for Xavier's hostility toward and harsh judgment of the Indians see Brodrick, *op. cit.* (n. 58), pp. 326–31.

on November 5, 1549, that the Japanese "are the best [people] who have yet been discovered." [209] After hearing from others that Miyako (Kyōto) was the great religious, educational, and administrative center of Japan, Xavier finally saw the imperial city for himself in November, 1551. From his experiences there he received the impression that anarchy reigned, that the emperor was powerless to control his subjects, and that he was therefore not able to give a satisfactory guarantee to the Christians that they might propagate the gospel and live freely in his realm. Once Xavier learned that the *daimyo* (feudal lords) were the real rulers of their own territories, he realized that the Christianizing of Japan would not be easy. Clearly he had hoped to find in the emperor of Japan an absolute ruler who could, if he so desired, bring the entire realm into the Christian fold. The disturbed political condition of the country and the localism of political control presented the Jesuits with a situation which was disturbingly similar to that which they had left behind in India. Xavier was further distressed to find how firmly entrenched were Buddhism and its teachers in the religious and educational life of Japan. By January, 1552, he was again back in India, still writing enthusiastic letters from Cochin on his Japanese experience and explaining to the brothers in Europe that he would next reconnoiter China, the greatest country of the Far East. In the following month he was in Goa to study the general state of the Indian mission, to recruit reinforcements for the missionaries left in Japan, and to prepare his own enterprise for entering China.

Now determined that China was the key to the missionary conquest of east Asia, the indefatigable Xavier, accompanied by three missionaries destined for the Japan mission, left Goa in April, 1552, on his last great adventure and landed in Malacca one month later. Here he was supposed to join Diogo Pereira, a Portuguese merchant, who had been appointed by the viceroy in Goa as the Portuguese ambassador to the court of China. Personal animosities and jurisdictional difficulties in Malacca combined to prevent the dispatch of Pereira's mission. The failure of the ambassadorial mission deprived Xavier of his only chance to enter China lawfully. So he finally decided to proceed to the China coast on his own in the hope of being able to land secretly on the mainland with the aid of some gentile or Moor. His immediate object was to bring solace to those Portuguese rotting in the prisons of Canton for having tried to trade in China without permission; but his ultimate aim was to see conditions in China for himself and to determine, as best he could, what prospects a mission might have for developing there. In the early fall of 1552 he arrived on the island of Shang-ch'uan (St. John's Island) which was then a rendezvous for the Portuguese and Chinese engaged in clandestine trade. Lying just six miles off the mainland (and one hundred miles southwest of Canton), the island was far enough from Canton to escape the surveillance of Chinese officials and close enough to the mainland to facilitate smuggling. Here Xavier spent his last days

---

[209] As translated in C. R. Boxer, *The Christian Century in Japan, 1549–1650* (Berkeley, 1951), Appendix I. Also see below, pp. 663–65.

in a tiny wooden hut while trying to persuade or bribe the reluctant Chinese traders to smuggle him into Canton.[210]

Xavier's glorification as patron saint of India and all the East depends not so much upon his intrepidity as a traveler as upon his innovations in missionary methods. Personally kind, simple, energetic, and practical, Xavier pragmatically evolved a way of working with both Christians and natives which became a model for later missionaries to follow, modify, and extend. Within the *padroado* he ministered to Portuguese colonials and mestizos who were often Christian in name only. He evangelized among peoples who were intellectually backward but politically advanced enough to become Christians in order to enjoy the protection of Portugal. He preached to the indigenous people of Amboina and neighboring islands where conditions for Christianity were even less favorable than in India. He visited the various islands of the East Indies and Malacca; although these visits were short and hectic, he was at least able to indicate the places where his successors should work and the procedures which they should follow. In Japan, he contended with a people of high culture who could not always be easily persuaded that the religion of Jesus was superior to the teachings of Buddha. Nor was it possible to call upon the secular arm of Europe to aid the mission effort in Japan; but here, interestingly enough, Christianity had its greatest impact. Beatified in 1619, Xavier was canonized in 1622 by Pope Gregory XV and so rejoined Loyola in the company of saints.

In Xavier's sketchy outline of the field for future Jesuit endeavor in the East, he completely omitted continental southeast Asia. His followers in the Society likewise paid almost no attention to Burma, Siam, and Indochina in the sixteenth century. A few tentative efforts to establish missions in these regions were nevertheless undertaken by members of the other Orders. Two Franciscans, Pierre Bonifer and Pedro Paschasius, arrived in Pegu (Burma), probably during the autumn of 1555.[211] Unfortunately for their evangelizing hopes, the Franciscans reached Pegu when King Bayin Naung was encouraging a fervent Buddhist revival. Finally, after a few years in Pegu, Paschasius died and Bonifer left in fear of his life.[212] The Dominicans meanwhile were also pushing east of India after the arrival of twelve of their members at Goa in 1548. Friar Gaspar da Cruz arrived in Malacca in 1554 and founded there a convent of his Order. From here he struck out, as we shall see, on a reconnaissance mission to

[210] Brodrick, *op. cit.* (n. 58), chap. xvii. On the origins of Xavier's China plans see G. Schurhammer, "Der Ursprung des Chinaplans des Heiligen Franz Xaver," *AHSI*, XXII (1953), 38–56. Also see below, p. 794.

[211] For a brief account see A. Meersman, O.F.M., "The Franciscans in the Ancient Burmese Kingdoms of Ava and Pegu, 1557–1818," *Archivum franciscanum historicum*, XXXI (1938), 358. While Meersman, on the authority of earlier commentators, places him in Pegu beginning in 1557, the basic letter extant is from "Cosmi" (Bassein) and is dated February 18, 1556. He must have been there for a period before writing this letter, because it shows a degree of familiarity with Buddhism and the Mon language which would have been hard to acquire in India. Moreover, Luis Frois wrote from Malacca on December 15, 1555, that Bonifer left "just now from Santo Thome." (Wicki [ed.], *op. cit.* [n. 72], III, 364.) For the text of Bonifer's letter see *ibid.*, pp. 817–20.

[212] On Bonifer's studies of Buddhism see below, pp. 557–59.

Cambodia in 1555–56. Discouraged by what he found there, Cruz pushed on to China in 1556 and spent a few months on its south coast, also without advancing the cause of Christianity.[213] In 1567 two Dominicans were sent from Malacca to Ayut'ia, the capital of Siam, where they were soon joined by a few other preaching friars. This mission was brought to an abrupt end when the friars were killed in 1569 during the siege and conquest of Ayut'ia by the Burmese.[214] Subsequently, other Dominicans and Franciscans were sent to Siam, and a Franciscan convent was founded at Ayut'ia in 1585.[215] But these new arrivals were likewise caught up in the whirlwind of continental wars and were fortunate to escape with their lives. Spanish Franciscans and Dominicans from the Philippines had similar experiences in Siam during the last several decades of the sixteenth century.[216]

B. MALACCA AND THE SPICERIES

In the half-century after the death of Xavier, permanent Christian establishments were set up *only* in Malacca, the Spiceries, Japan, China, the Philippines, and Cambodia. And they did not all have the same dimensions, purposes, or degrees of stability. As the Portuguese gateway to the East, Malacca played host at various times to most of the missionaries as they passed through on their way to and from their posts. From the time of the conquest of Malacca in 1511, the crown supported the building of a Christian community for the administrators, soldiers, and merchants stationed there.[217] The center of this endeavor was the Church of Our Lady of the Annunciation, which was built shortly after 1511 on the river bank where the Hong Kong and Shanghai Bank was later erected. A royal hospital was also built shortly after the conquest, and by 1532 the House of Mercy, a private charitable organization, was founded by the Christians of the city to administer poor and sick relief.[218] Xavier in 1545 held mass, taught the children their prayers, visited the sick, and listened to confessions. He also tried to encourage the evangelizing of the city, a process which had been started by the secular priests and friars before he arrived there. It was soon seen, however, that Malaya, apart from Malacca and its surroundings,

---

[213] For his career in the Far East see C. R. Boxer, *South China in the Sixteenth Century* (London, 1953), pp. lviii–lix.

[214] Benno Biermann, O.P., "Die Missionen der portugiesischen Dominikaner im Hinterindien," *Zeitschrift für Missionswissenschaft und Religionswissenschaft*, XXI (1931), 306–7.

[215] Further details in B. P. Groslier, *Angkor et le Cambodge d'après les sources portugaises et espanoles* (Paris, 1958), p. 32.

[216] Lemmens, *op. cit.* (n. 4), p. 109.

[217] The permanent Portuguese residents of Malacca rarely exceeded six hundred at any one time during the sixteenth century. Most of them were servants of the crown who married or lived with local women. See Macgregor, *loc. cit.* (n. 190), pp. 6–11.

[218] *Ibid.*, p. 15.

was not likely to provide favorable conditions for missionary work. Consequently, Malacca, being a place of transit, became an administrative center for
the church but not a great mission.

The Jesuits founded a college in Malacca in 1549 for the training of Portuguese
youths for the priesthood. In 1558 the city became a bishopric and the first
occupant of the episcopal office was the Dominican, Jorgé de S. Luzia (in office,
1558–79). The Dominicans (1554), the Franciscans (1581), and the Augustinians
(after 1591) had convents in the city. In 1585 Malacca became a Custody of the
Franciscan Order with a superior who was in charge of all the Order's activities
in the Portuguese Far East. While many of the Jesuit writers deplored the religious
and moral conditions existing in sixteenth-century Malacca, no concrete
efforts were made to Christianize the entire city. Malacca, unlike Goa, never
experienced either mass or forced conversions as the Christian community
there quietly accepted its minority status—a reflection perhaps of the always
precarious hold which the Portuguese had upon the city itself.

Xavier's optimistic hopes about the development of a mission in the Spiceries
were never fully realized by his successors. Immediately after his death all
Jesuit activities in "further India" were stunted in their early growth by the
serious lack of personnel and leadership in Goa and by a temporary breakdown
in communications with the superiors in Europe. Rome, for example, was unable
to get official comfirmation of Xavier's death until 1555. In these turbulent and
uncertain years, two priests and two lay brothers tried to maintain the mission
in the Spiceries. At Goa in 1556 there was no certainty about their safety or their
progress. "We have heard news about them," writes one of the Jesuits in India,
"and that they have converted a large number—but we are waiting for their
letters as otherwise we cannot be sure of the information. . . ."[219] The letters
from the Spiceries were held up by the Portuguese involvement with wars in
the Moluccas and at a number of other strategic points within the Eastern
empire.

Father João de Beira and Brother Nicolao Nunes returned from the Spiceries
to Malacca in 1557 and then went on to Goa to recruit more workers for their
mission. At the end of the year they returned to Ternate with a company of
nine (four fathers and five brothers), including themselves. Father Francisco
Vieira was delegated to be superior of the mission with his headquarters at
Ternate—from which post he was to "furnish the others with sago to eat."[220]
Nunes, who was accomplished in the languages of Moro, was dispatched to
those savage islands with two lay brothers. The others were sent to Amboina,
the second of the two largest Christian centers in the Spiceries and the place
which seemed to offer the best hope of the future. When it is recalled how
precarious was the Jesuit position in India before 1559, and that more than one-
fifth (nine out of forty-four) of all the members of the Society in the Province of

---

[219] Wicki (ed.), *op. cit.* (n. 72), III, 186. On their activities during these years see Fróis' letter of 1556
as discussed below, p. 612.
[220] Fróis to fathers in Coimbra (Goa, Nov. 30, 1557) in *ibid.*, p. 716.

India outside Goa were in the Spiceries in 1557, the importance of the Spiceries to the Jesuits is plain. After a slow start, the mission of the islands seemed to be on the verge of prospering.

The first victory celebrated by the reinforced mission was the conversion from Islam in 1557 of the Sultan of Bachan and his subjects.[221] The ruler of this island group located between Ternate and Amboina was the nephew and son-in-law of the stiff-necked Sultan Hairun of Ternate. Bachan was at war with Ternate, and its young ruler was obliged to look to the Portuguese and the Jesuits for help against his father-in-law. Hairun himself was taken prisoner in these wars and in 1559 pledged himself not to interfere with the Portuguese and the missionaries.

Both the Jesuits and the Muslims suffered losses in these wars. The Jesuits therefore began writing again to Malacca and Goa for more missionaries. In the Moluccas the Jesuits continued to fear reprisals from Hairun and to complain about the unenthusiastic support which they received from the Portuguese administrators and ships in the Spiceries. Their annoyance was exacerbated in particular by the unwillingness of the Portuguese to support projects which might endanger trade. A case in point which they cite is the half-hearted support which the Portuguese begrudgingly gave in 1563–64 to the Jesuit project of expanding missionary operations to Menado on the northern promontory of Celebes.[222] Since Hairun claimed jurisdiction over this region, the Portuguese hesitated to support an action which was almost certain to produce reprisals against trade. The Jesuits on this, and on many other similar occasions, berated the Portuguese governors for naïvely trusting the word of a Moor, for depending upon his good will for trade, and for not committing themselves wholeheartedly to the propagation of the faith. The Jesuit policy was built on the establishment of alliances through conversion and trading agreements with the political and hereditary enemies of the hated Moor, and they stubbornly fought all Portuguese efforts to appease him in the interests of peace and trade. Even when Hairun agreed in November, 1564, to give the Jesuits freedom to preach in his territories, the missionaries suspected that his concession was made for political expediency and was not to be viewed as a genuine change of heart.

This realistic appraisal of the situation was justified by the events of the following year. Early in 1565 a combined force of Muslims from Java and Ternate pillaged and burned the Christian communities of Amboina and killed or scattered their inhabitants.[223] The Portuguese commandant at Ternate, much

---

[221] C. Wessels, "De Katholieke Missie in het Sultanaat Batjan (Molukken), 1557–1609," *Historisch Tijdschrift*, VIII (1929), 115–48; 221–45. Also see below, pp. 617–18.

[222] See letter of Father Pero Mascarenhas (Ternate, November 12, 1564) as translated in Anton Eglauer, *Die Missionsgeschichte späterer Zeiten; oder, gesammelte Briefe der katholischen Missionäre aus allen Theilen der Welt . . . Der Briefe aus Ostindien . . .* (3 vols.; Augsburg, 1794–95), II, 279–90.

[223] In an official report (Goa, November 25, 1565) of Quadros to Lainez, the Provincial of India observed: "The fathers have been expelled from Amboina by the Moors who have taken over the islands and 70,000 Christians in them." See Wicki (ed.), *op. cit.* (n. 72), VI, 493. Also see Wessels, *op. cit.* (n. 194), pp. 64–67.

to the indignation of the Jesuits, refrained from military interference at Amboina. The Jesuits expelled from Amboina were forced to seek refuge in the fortress of Ternate and at other Portuguese strongholds. In Europe, Jesuit agents soon began protesting vehemently to Lisbon about the failure of the secular arm to protect the Christians of the Spiceries. Before 1565 had drawn to a close, King Sebastian sent a sharp letter to the viceroy in Goa, charging that the royal officials in the Moluccas had long been ignoring orders, avoiding actions that might endanger their personal profits, and standing by without helping fellow Christians under infidel attack.

In response to the royal charges and to the news of Legaspi's arrival in the Philippines, a large fleet was immediately outfitted in Goa. It left Malacca for the Spiceries in August, 1567, under the command of Gonçales Pereira Marramque. Marramque followed the route north of Borneo, probably in the hope of running into the Spanish who were thought to be violating the Portuguese demarcation. The fleet did not arrive in the Moluccas until 1568, and Marramque even then continued to be more interested in hunting down Spanish interlopers than in settling the conflicts within the Spiceries. Finally, in 1569, he led an expedition against the Muslims in Amboina aided by levies furnished him by the rulers of Bachan and Tidore. After driving the Javans and local Muslims into the interior, he built a strong, palisaded fortress on Amboina to protect trade and the Christian communities.

Diogo Lopez de Mesquita had meanwhile (during 1568) arrived in the Moluccas to take over as the Captain of Ternate. He, like Marramque, was under orders to support the Jesuits in their efforts to annihilate Islam in the Spiceries and to provide protection and encouragement for the missionary effort. Father Mascarenhas, who had traveled back to the Spiceries with Mesquita, immediately set to work in an effort to repair the damage which the uprisings in 1565 and after had done to the Christian rulers and communities in Celebes. While the Jesuits helped to restore a refugee Christian king to his throne, Mesquita quickly ran into trouble at Ternate with Hairun and the Muslim alliance, which supported him in his resistance to the Portuguese. Tormented by the political wariness of Hairun and by internal questionings of his own policies, Mesquita instigated the murder of the sultan in 1570. This brutal stabbing brought Bāb-Ullāh to power in Ternate, and he at once took an oath to avenge his father's death.

War broke out in various places after this between the Portuguese and the confederation of Muslim rulers. The Portuguese fortress of Ternate was besieged and for nearly five years it held out against great odds. Finally it fell in 1574. The Christian communities, a number of which were located in areas subject to Ternate or other Muslim states, were doomed by the fall of the Portuguese fortress. Amboina was the only place to hold out against Bāb-Ullāh and his allies, and refugees from other places in the Spiceries poured into this last Portuguese stronghold. Although by 1578 the Portuguese had regained enough strength to build a new fortress on Tidore, the Jesuit enterprise in the Spiceries seems never to have regained its old vigor. For the crisis period of 1571 to 1578, there is no evidence of a single extant missionary letter from the islands, a reflection perhaps of the almost complete annihilation of the mission in the Spiceries.[224] Except for some reprints of earlier materials,[225] the Jesuits in Europe, throughout the remainder of the sixteenth century, published nothing at all on their activities in the Spiceries.

C. MASS CONVERSIONS AND REFORM IN JAPAN, 1552–82

Dispatched by Xavier from India as reinforcements for the Japan mission, three Portuguese Jesuits, Father Balthasar Gago and Brothers Duarte da Silva and Pedro de Alcaçova, arrived in Kagoshima in the summer of 1552.[226] Like Xavier before them, they were given a cordial welcome by the *daimyo* (feudal lord) of Satsuma. After a short stay at Kagoshima, the new arrivals hurried on to Funai in Bungo where they were met by an interpreter. In September, 1552, they had a series of interviews with Ōtomo Yoshishige, *daimyo* of Bungo, and presented him with a letter and presents from the viceroy of India. In the following month the little party went on to Yamaguchi, whose Christian community had been growing since Xavier was there. Here it was decided that Alcaçova should return to Goa to plead for more help, and that Gago and Silva should work in Bungo. Cosmas de Torres, who had originally come with Xavier, remained at Yamaguchi and continued to supervise all Christian activities in Japan.

Gago and his interpreter-companion reached Bungo early in 1553, only to find that Ōtomo, whom they had seriously hoped to convert, was engaged in putting down a revolt of three of his greatest vassals. Though Ōtomo protected the Christian missionaries, he would not relinquish his traditional beliefs. Still the Jesuits, after a slow start and continuous trouble with the bonzes (Buddhist priests), erected a church at Funai and before the end of the first year had baptized over three hundred persons. Soon famine menaced the community at Yamaguchi. This trying time was followed by a series of wars which destroyed the city in 1556 and forced the Jesuits of Yamaguchi to join their fellows at Funai. Setbacks there were balanced somewhat by the arrival at Funai early in 1556 of Fathers Melchior Nuñes Barreto and Gaspar Vilela, and by the admission into the Order of a former Portuguese merchant, Luis d'Almeida, who had been in Japan since 1554. The wealth of Almeida was employed to build two hospitals at Funai, and was invested in the trade being carried on by the Portuguese

[224] Wessels, *op. cit.* (n. 194), p. 90.

[225] *Ibid.*, p. 9.

[226] For details on Japanese places and personal names see below, chap. viii. For a summary of the mission in Japan see H. Haas, *Geschichte des Christentums in Japan* (2 vols.; Tokyo, 1902). Also see for more detail the manuscript history prepared by Luis Fróis as translated in German and edited by G. Schurhammer and E. Z. Voretzsch as *Die Geschichte Japans, 1549–1578* (Leipzig, 1926).

between Japan, Macao, and Malacca to help guarantee a permanent income for the mission.[227]

For the next several years, the eight Jesuits in Japan concentrated their efforts at Funai. They were particularly successful in making converts of the indigents, children, and others who were treated in Almeida's hospitals. Their activities after 1556 were extended to Hirado, Ōmura, and Hakata (modern Fukuoka), but efforts to renew their work at Yamaguchi met with failure. In 1560 Vilela was sent with some Japanese companions to Miyako, where he carried on disputations with the bonzes and made a number of converts from the upper classes. But in 1562 Vilela was driven out of Miyako by the warrior monks of Buddhism and forced to take refuge at Sakai. Gago, in poor health, left Japan earlier, before reinforcements from India could be brought to the aid of the little Jesuit group.

Three additions to the mission arrived in Japan during the summer of 1563: the Portuguese Father Luis Fróis, the historian of the mission; the Italian Father Giovanni Battista di Monte; and a Portuguese lay brother, Miguel Vaz, who had been born in India and who was to learn Japanese from Vilela. They joined Torres, then at Yokoseura, twenty-five miles south of Hirado, where the Jesuits were thriving under the protection of the *daimyo* of Ōmura, their recent convert.[228] Upon the arrival in 1564 of two more missionaries, the Jesuits tried again to establish themselves at Miyako. In 1565 Fróis and Vilela had an audience in the capital with the *Shōgun* (generalissimo), Ashikaga Yoshiteru. But the capital was still torn by the civil wars accompanying the downfall of the Ashikaga and the rise of Oda Nobunaga, and so the Jesuits were banned from residing there. They still had friends and converts on the main island, however, with whom they were able to seek sanctuary for the next four years.

While Vilela and Fróis worked on the war-torn island of Honshū, their confreres continued to propagate the faith at various more favorable locales in the western provinces. Finally, in 1569, they were able to locate a headquarters from which to control their far-flung enterprises in Japan. Their convert, Ōmura Sumitada, ceded them the right to develop and use the isolated fishing village of Nagasaki, with its splendid harbor, as the center for their operations and as the port to which Portuguese vessels could freely come. The Jesuits were able to convert this natural stronghold into a fortified city which would protect them from being pushed hither and yon by the fortunes of war and the whims of rulers. Here also the Portuguese could trade without worrying constantly about their lives and property. The entire administration of the town, even its silk trade and port revenues, was managed by the eminently practical fathers.[229] By 1571 they had opened twenty other mission centers in Japan, though in the

[227] For a discussion of the Jesuits in Japan as investors, traders, and brokers see Boxer, *op. cit.* (n. 209), chap. iii. Also see J. Murdoch and I. Yamagata, *A History of Japan* (Kobe, 1903), II, 75.

[228] Ōmura Sumitada was given the Christian title and name of Dom Bartholomeo (Fróis in Schurhammer and Voretzsch, *op. cit.* [n. 226], p. 159).

[229] Boxer, *op. cit.* (n. 209), pp. 100–102.

interim they suffered by the deaths of Andreas Fernandes (1568) and Torres (1570) and by the recall of Vilela (1571) to India.

At the death of Torres, Francisco Cabral became head of the mission.[230] There were then no more than thirty thousand converts in Japan and among them only a few who were not commoners. Cabral, a Portuguese *fidalgo* by birth and training who had previously worked only in India, set to work immediately to reform the mission and expand its enterprise. He ordered the Jesuits to doff their colored silken garments, which made them look like bonzes and don common black cotton. They were ordered to put aside all luxuries in favor of a life of stark simplicity and poverty. Cabral also stressed the importance of making converts among the ruling classes, and shortly after assuming his post he made a trip to Miyako in a fruitless effort to stimulate activities there. He also emphasized the need to open as many new centers as possible in all parts of the islands. And in 1574 he inaugurated a policy of mass conversions which rapidly swelled Christian ranks with many nominal converts.

On the main island, meanwhile, Oda Nobunaga, a military chieftain, was gradually consolidating control over Miyako and its environs. The intrepid Fróis was received in audience by Nobunaga in 1569 and as a result of this interview received permission to stay free and unmolested in Miyako.[231] Such a concession was so readily obtained because Nobunaga and Fróis had in common their hostility to the Buddhist monks; it is also possible that a Westerner of undeniable character and attainments fascinated the Japanese warlord.[232] In a short time Fróis was visited by Cabral in Miyako. The superior was also granted an audience by Nobunaga, who was then preparing for the final reduction of the Buddhist monasteries on the slopes of Hiei-zan. With the razing of the monasteries and the massacre of their monks in 1571, Nobunaga was enabled to pacify Miyako and proceed to the establishment of his personal control over its neighboring provinces. In 1572, Fróis was joined in the Home Province (environs of Kyoto) by Father Organtino Gnecchi, who was to become one of the greatest foes of the Buddhists and one of the most respected missionaries in Japan. While Jesuit fortunes were improving with each of Nobunaga's victories, hopes for future growth were also stimulated by the arrival in Japan of two more Portuguese fathers, Sebastião Gonçalves and Gaspar Coelho.

Hereafter the Jesuit enterprise progressed rapidly, both on the main island and in Kyūshū. At Miyako the Church of Our Lady of the Assumption was completed in 1575 and dedicated in the following year. In 1577 another church was erected on the outskirts of Mikayo as converts flocked to the Cross. In the western provinces the whole domain of Ōmura became Christian as Cabral encouraged in Japan the application of the European principle of religious uniformity enshrined in the dictum of *cuius regio, eius religio*. The Jesuits also

---

[230] For a thorough discussion of his personality, work, and methods see Schütte, *op. cit.* (n. 47), Vol. I, Pt. I, chap. iii. For a shorter account see Jean Monsterleet, *L'Église du Japon des temps féodaux à nos jours* (Toulouse, 1958), pp. 50–54.

[231] For details see J. Laures, *Nobunga und das Christentum* (Tokyo, 1950), pp. 3–6.

[232] Cf. Boxer, *op. cit.* (n. 209), p. 64.

stepped up their activities in Bungo after baptizing kinsmen and members of the ruling Ōtomo family in 1575. Two years later Fróis and two of his colleagues visited Bungo, and Ōtomo himself was baptized in 1578. This was followed by the conversion in 1579 of the Arima family of Takaku. In the meantime, Nagasaki was growing rapidly as both the Japanese and Portuguese began to appreciate its value as a center of trade. In 1578, forty-four missionaries were working in Japan, or three times the number that were there in 1575. All seemed to be going exceedingly well in 1579, when a young Jesuit Visitor, Valignano, arrived in the Land of the Rising Sun.

The appearance of Valignano in Japan inaugurated a three-year period of thorough review of the mission's accomplishments in which the deficiencies of the Jesuit effort came to light. Before his arrival in Japan, Valignano had read carefully the mission reports and as a result was beginning to ask questions about the language preparation of the new missionaries and about the wisdom of the Society's participation in the silk trade.[233] After his arrival his questions became even more numerous and pointed as he realized that the letters had given him an exaggerated picture of the successes scored by the mission in Japan. Very impressed personally by how totally foreign he found everything in Japan, the astute Visitor began to question the missionary methods of Cabral as well as his optimistic appraisal of the Jesuit successes in Japan.

Valignano's initial reaction of disappointment was deepened by the failure, as he saw it, of the mission to heed the instructions sent from India ordaining that new missionaries should be instructed in the Japanese language upon their arrival. Even worse than the neglect of language study in his view was the hostile relationship which he found to be existing between the Westerners and the Japanese, between the Jesuits and their converts. The basic reason for this antipathy he attributed to Cabral's attitude toward and treatment of the Japanese. Even the Japanese brothers were treated as inferiors, spoken to harshly, and generally looked down upon as second-class Christians. Toward the Japanese population, Cabral's attitude was scornful and overbearing. He thought them to be the most arrogant, avaricious, inconstant, and insincere people he had ever seen.[234] Their customs he considered to be beneath contempt, and so he required the converts to observe Western practices when in the presence of Christians. To Valignano such a policy seemed destined to bring reprisals from the Japanese and disaster to the mission.

Cabral's leadership was also attacked by the Visitor for failing to provide adequate and sufficient instruction for the Japanese converts and friars. Cabral's program of mass conversions was a classic case of Christian truths being heaped upon unprepared souls. The peak had come in the summer of 1576, when more then 15,000 persons were baptized.[235] It is small wonder that Cabral, flushed with success, dismissed somewhat cursorily Valignano's questions (which arrived in

[233] Schütte, *op. cit.* (n. 47), p. 230.
[234] *Ibid.*, p. 309.
[235] *Ibid.*, p. 292.

June, 1576) about organizational problems relating to the projected Jesuit college, and ignored the instructions calling for careful preparation of novices along lines common in European houses. Yet, even though the number of missionaries in Japan mounted sharply after 1576, Cabral continued the program of mass conversions and paid but slight attention to the thorough grounding of either the new missionaries or the new converts.

After a year of residence and observation in western Japan, Valignano instituted a series of reforms which involved changes so fundamental that Cabral's position became untenable, particularly since he disagreed with the Visitor on several basic issues. Valignano ordained that the mission should no longer be under the rigid, personal guidance of a single superior, but that it should be governed by a collective leadership bound to apply the Constitutions of the Society, to encourage the policy of accommodation, and to work from the top down. The leadership was also required to recognize the dangers inherent in the program of mass conversion, to slow down the process in the hope of placing the mission upon more solid foundations, and to eliminate the deep gulf separating the Japanese and Western Christians. A sympathetic attitude toward the Japanese and their culture was to be adopted. In the letters sent to Europe events were to be placed in context by relating them to the more general developments in the country as a whole. In this way the letters would not be misleading, and so would be suitable for publication and the eyes of the profane. Letters specifically dealing with the mission's problems would be directed to the appropriate church authorities and presumably would not normally be released for publication or circulation outside a narrow circle in Europe. Valignano apparently hoped by this method to eliminate the need for censorship in Rome, a practice which had resulted in the publication of misleading and truncated materials in Europe during the first generation of the Japan mission's existence.

The papacy had taken official cognizance of the reports of Jesuit progress in Japan as early as 1566. A letter of Pope Pius V ordered the Patriarch of Ethiopia to abandon what was almost a hopeless enterprise in Africa and to take up missionary work in the more fruitful field of Japan.[236] In 1573, Pope Gregory XIII sent letters of congratulation to the newly converted "princes" of Ōmura and Hirado.[237] Four years later Gregory issued a declaration making it clear that the Church considered both China and Japan, Spain's claims to the contrary notwithstanding, as belonging to the Portuguese conquest.[238] Gregory's special concern over the Japan mission was by now clearly apparent and he even sent a letter to the *daimyo* of Bungo, Ōtomo Yoshishige, in 1578 urging him to accept the Christian faith.[239] And on June 13, 1583, he published the

---

[236] Text in Leo Magnino, Pontificia Nipponica, *Le relazioni tra la Santa Sede e il Giappone attraverso i documenti pontifici* (Rome, 1947), pp. 5–7.

[237] *Ibid.*, pp. 14–16.

[238] *Ibid.*, pp. 21–22.

[239] *Ibid.*, pp. 22–23.

bull *Mirabilia Dei*,[240] congratulating the Jesuits on thirty years of activity in Japan, and awarding them an annual stipend to help carry on their work in the future. With this new support from Rome and with the reforms inaugurated by Valignano in Japan, it looked as if the future growth of the mission was assured —provided only that the Jesuits could retain the official tolerance of Miyako and prevent the other Europeans (especially the Spanish) from interfering with their Far Eastern monopoly.

D. MACAO AND MANILA

Xavier's project for entering China was followed up after his death by Melchior Nunes Barreto, a Portuguese Jesuit. The revival of Portuguese trading activity from the island of Lampaçāo off Kwangtung in 1554 evidently made it possible for Barreto to visit Canton for a few months in 1555.[241] He was sent there primarily for the purpose of negotiating the ransom of two Portuguese prisoners. Two letters by Barreto which include China materials were printed in Europe shortly after they were received.[242] The first of these, written at Malacca in December, 1554, to Loyola, dealt with some of the customs and laws of the Chinese; the other, prepared at Canton in November, 1555, presents a description of Canton and gives additional remarks on Chinese beliefs, customs, and trade, along with comments on the difficulties facing missionary efforts in China.[243] Barreto was not permitted to stay in China, and so he left in 1555 for the mission in Japan. The next missionary to visit Canton was the Dominican, Gaspar da Cruz, whose account of China will be surveyed later.[244]

Macao was the door through which the Jesuits sought to enter China after the Portuguese established themselves there in 1557. In July, 1563, three Jesuits accompanying a Portuguese embassy from Goa to the court of Peking, arrived in Macao. By order of Peking the Portuguese embassy was refused permission to enter the country.[245] For the following two years, Fathers Francisco Peres and Emmanuel Teixeira, who had accompanied the mission, sought to allay the suspicions of the Chinese about their motives and to win permission from the

---

[240] *Ibid.*, p. 24.

[241] J. M. Braga, "The Western Pioneers and Their Discovery of Macao," *Instituto Português de Hongkong, Boletim*, No. 2 (September, 1949), pp. 75, 85–86.

[242] In *Avisi particolari* ... published at Rome in 1558. For further information see Robert Streit, *Bibliotheca missionum* (Aachen, 1928), IV, 516.

[243] Summarized in *Le Istorie delle Indie Orientali del Rev. P. Giovan Pietro Maffei della Compagnia di Giesu* (Florence, 1589), pp. 608–18. Another letter of Barreto's written from Cochin (January 8, 1558) describes the island of Lampaçāo and a devastating flood in south China. For other descriptions of Lampaçāo from the same period see Braga, *loc. cit.* (n. 241), pp. 82–83, 98. Cf. also L. Pfister, *Notices biographiques et bibliographiques sur les Jésuites de l'ancienne mission de Chine, 1552–1773* (Shanghai, 1932), I, 8–9.

[244] See below, pp. 747–48.

[245] See A. S. Rosso, O. F. M., *Apostolic Legations to China of the Eighteenth Century* (South Pasadena, Calif., 1948), p. 46, n. 12.

officials of Kwangtung to reside and work in Canton. Finally, in November, 1565, Peres succeeded in getting into Canton in company with a Portuguese commercial group. He took advantage of this opportunity to present to the local officials copies of two memorials, written in Chinese and Portuguese, which set forth who he was, the reasons for his visit, and his desire to remain in China.[246] His request being rejected in Canton, Peres returned to Macao and busied himself with the establishment of the Jesuit house there.

The Portuguese hold on Macao, like their position in Malacca, had always been tenuous and depended upon the ability of the traders and missionaries to retain the favor of the Chinese. No mass conversions like those carried on at Goa were attempted at this outpost, where the Jesuits were thankful to have a foothold. The Portuguese authorities were extremely anxious not to anger the Chinese and were particularly fearful that illegal entries of the mainland would endanger commerce. Consequently, the Jesuits at Macao officially centered their apostolic efforts upon the Portuguese and Chinese living at the entrepôt and temporarily abandoned the penetration of China proper. The missionaries, with their heavy investments in the silk trade, were as fearful as the Portuguese about condoning or encouraging actions to which the Chinese might respond unfavorably. The determined policy of Xavier was revived only when Alessandro Valignano, the Jesuit Visitor, settled down in Macao from October, 1577, to July, 1578, to reappraise the prospects of the Jesuit mission. Not satisfied with a limited program of local missionizing, the Visitor called for additional recruits to push forward the enterprise of mainland penetration by methods "utterly different from those which have been adopted up to now in all the other missions in these countries."[247] The first of the new recruits, Michele Ruggiero, arrived at Macao in July, 1579, just two weeks after Valignano left for Japan. Valignano left a note for Ruggiero ordering him to begin learning to read, write, and speak the Chinese language as a step to cultural penetration. In November, 1580, Ruggiero made his first trip to Canton, and two years later he received permission to reside at Chao-Ch'ing, the viceregal capital of Kwangtung and Kwangsi provinces. By this act, the Jesuits had finally broken the barrier before which Xavier had lost his life.[248]

A new element was meanwhile gradually entering the Far Eastern picture which complicated life for the Jesuits in Macao and almost upset the Christian enterprise there completely. The first Spanish mission of significance was established in the Philippines beginning in 1565, in connection with the pioneering expedition of Miguel Lopez de Legaspi. A group of Augustinians, including

---

[246] Biography summarized in Pfister, *op. cit.* (n. 243), I, 9–10.

[247] Quoted in George Dunne, S.J., "The Jesuits in China in the Last Days of the Ming" (Ph.D., dissertation, University of Chicago, 1944), p. 69. A condensed version of this dissertation was published as *Generation of Giants: The Story of the Jesuits in China in the Last Decades of the Ming Dynasty* (Notre Dame, Ind., 1962).

[248] On Ruggiero and his activities in establishing himself with the Chinese see H. Bernard, S.J., *Aux portes de la Chine* (Tientsin, 1933), Pt. II, chaps. i and ii; for a summary of more recent scholarship see P. M. D'Elia, "La reprise des missions catholiques en Chine à la fin du Ming (1579–1644)," *Journal of World History*, V (1959–60), 679–91.

in their number the aged Andrés de Urdaneta who had been an officer in Loaisa's fleet twenty-two years before, disembarked on the island of Cebu along with the Spanish forces. While the soldiers and sailors built a base of operations, the Augustinians began to lay the foundations for Christian enterprise in the Philippines. Six years later the seat of Spanish authority was transferred to the shores of Manila Bay. A delegation of Spanish Franciscans arrived at Manila in 1577. Two years later, as Spanish strength mounted in both Asia and Europe, Manila was elevated to be an episcopal see. Domingo de Salazar, a Dominican missionary with Mexican experience, was appointed as its first bishop, and he led a delegation of Dominicans and Jesuits to the Philippines in 1581. While the Christians increased in numbers at Manila, the sentiment gained strength among both the secular and religious authorities that the Philippines were not an end in themselves but only a stepping stone to the richer kingdoms of eastern Asia. Guido de Lavezaris, who succeeded Legaspi as head of the Spanish enterprise in 1572, wrote to Philip II: "We are stationed here at the gateway of great kingdoms. Will your majesty aid us with the wherewithal so that trade may be introduced and maintained among many of these nations."[249]

The Jesuits at Macao, probably fearful that the Spanish might take the lead, began, like the Spanish themselves, to talk about conquest. Barreto wrote to Europe from Macao in 1569:

If the princes of Europe, instead of quarreling among themselves, would undertake to extend the Kingdom of Christ and force the sovereign of China to grant to the missionaries the right to preach and to the natives the right to hear the truth, the Chinese people would easily be converted, because our morals and religion find favor with them.[250]

The failure and frustration experienced in China was accentuated for the Jesuits by reports of the sparkling successes of their mission in Japan. The Spanish Jesuit, Juan Bautista Ribera, who attempted an entrance in 1568, wrote to the General of the Society in 1575 that "there is no hope of converting them except by force."[251]

The Portuguese, in an attempt to limit the activities of the Spanish to Manila, managed to persuade Pope Gregory XIII to create in 1576 the diocese of Macao with jurisdiction over China, Japan, and the adjacent islands.[252] In Madrid, meanwhile, there was little interest or sympathy for the proposals from the Philippines to send a military expedition against China. In 1577, Philip II rebuked the memorialists in Manila, told them to forget about such projects, and to seek the friendship of the Chinese.[253] The Franciscan Pedro de Alfaro dispiritedly wrote in 1580 that "with or without soldiers, to hope to enter China is like trying to touch the sky with the outstretched hand."[254] In 1579,

---

[249] As quoted in W. L. Schurz, *The Manila Galleon* (New York, 1939), p. 26.
[250] As translated in the dissertation by Dunne, *op. cit.* (n. 247), p. 58.
[251] *Ibid.*
[252] Rosso, *op. cit.* (n. 245), p. 49.
[253] As quoted in Boxer, *op. cit.* (n. 213), p. 1.
[254] A. van den Wyngaert, O.F.M., *Sinica Franciscana* (Florence, 1933), II, 180.

shortly before Philip II took over Portugal, the pope agreed to create a diocese at Manila as suffragan to Mexico City. There was implied in this departure the papacy's recognition of Spain's claim that the Philippines lay within her demarcation. This action also presaged the more prominent role that Philip would take in Asiatic affairs once he gained control in Portugal.

Thereafter letters from Manila to Spain regularly conjured up dreams of a rich oriental empire.[255] Since nobody knew whether eastern Asia was legally within the Portuguese or Spanish demarcation, the Spanish were eager to show that it lay within their area and that the Portuguese were actually trespassing. According to the measurements of the Spanish Augustinian Martin de Rada, everything east of Malacca was rightfully supposed to fall within the Spanish jurisdiction.[256] Once they became convinced of this, the Spanish administrators in the Philippines, both secular and ecclesiastical, sought permission from Madrid to trade and evangelize in China, Japan, and Indochina. Some eager individuals were so persuaded of the justice of their cause and of the prospects for a rich trade that they proceeded without official approval to journey to Macao and Kyūshū. After 1580, Spanish war vessels were sent out for the specific purpose of tracking back to their lands of origin those Chinese and Japanese corsairs who preyed upon the Philippines. Once it became known in the East that the crown of Portugal rested on Philip II, demands to Madrid for permission to advance to the Asiatic mainland and Japan became even more pressing.

Although both nations were subject to the same king after 1581, the Spanish colonial policy, based on the experience of Mexico, was more inclined to follow the belligerent style adopted by the *conquistadores* in America. The Lusitanians were more interested in trade than in territorial conquest, and their religious policy was based on their close working relationship with the Society of Jesus. The Spanish, while not limiting missionary enterprise in the Far East to a single Order, refused to permit persons of non-Spanish origin to work in their overseas areas. For example, the missionaries in the Philippines were mixed groups of Augustinians, Franciscans, Dominicans, and Jesuits, but all were of Spanish or Spanish-Neapolitan background. This gave a thoroughly Spanish complexion to all sides of the Philippine enterprise, and conditioned both the missionaries and traders to think of themselves as *conquistadores* dedicated to the service of the king of Spain in foreign parts.[257] Philip did nothing to disabuse them of this belief when, shortly after becoming king of Portugal, he ordered the superior of the Spanish Augustinians in the Philippines to explore the neighboring countries. Still the king refused to authorize the sending of an expedition to

[255] See Gregorio F. Zaide, *The Philippines since Pre-Spanish Times* (Manila, 1949), chap. xv.

[256] H. Bernard, "Les débuts des relations diplomatiques entre le Japon et les Espagnols des Iles Philippines (1571–1594)," *Monumenta Nipponica*, I (1938), 107.

[257] *Ibid.*, p. 103. Naples in this period was under Philip's control. For the Franciscan viewpoint, which has too infrequently been reflected in the histories of this period, see the convenient summary in Lemmens, *op. cit.* (n. 4), pp. 155–66. The scholar who published and edited most of the Franciscan records was Lorenzo Perez, O.F.M. (1867–1935). For his bibliography see J. Laures, *Kirishitan Bunko* (3d ed.; Tokyo, 1957), No. 973a.

Japan, and in 1585 he emphatically confirmed the privilege of exclusive right in Japan which had been given to the Jesuits by papal decree in 1583.

The Valignano program of slow penetration through "accommodation" failed to satisfy the conquistadorial ambitions of the missionaries stationed in the Philippines. A renewed effort at direct action was made under the leadership of the Spanish Jesuit Alonzo Sanchez, who had arrived in Manila in 1581 along with three other members of the Society. Sanchez had been sent to Mexico in 1579 and soon surpassed his fellow missionaries in talent and aggressiveness.[258] Upon his arrival in the Philippines, he quickly impressed Bishop Domingo de Salazar and Governor Gonzalo Ronquillo with his dynamism. In 1582 he was sent to Macao to obtain its formal submission to the authority of Philip II. He was also accredited by Ronquillo to carry a letter written in Chinese to the viceroy of Kwangtung province which empowered Sanchez to negotiate a treaty of friendship and commerce. With this letter in hand he and his party first landed at Liampo (Ningpo) and were then taken by river boat to Foochow, the capital of Fukien province. They were permitted to proceed overland to Canton and on their way there they presented Ronquillo's letter to the viceroy. In Canton, Sanchez met a group of Portuguese merchants and the Italian Jesuits Francesco Pasio and Michele Ruggiero. The latter, who had been officially selected to pioneer Valignano's policy of accommodation and who already had an unusual degree of influence among the Chinese, explained to Sanchez the policy which was being followed by the Jesuits of Macao. The Spanish Jesuit was clearly unimpressed and apparently went out of his way to let his feelings be known. After a series of difficulties with the Chinese authorities, Sanchez was finally permitted to travel on to Macao. Here, aided by the good offices of Valignano, he performed the thankless task of obtaining from the bitter Portuguese their oath of allegiance to the terms of the Union of Tomar.[259] In the Far East great emphasis was placed upon Philip's promise, expressed in the Union of Tomar, to keep the two empires entirely separate in terms of administrative structure, and upon the fruits which might be expected in the colonial world from the two Iberian powers presenting a common front.

Although the Portuguese accepted Sanchez' assurances about the separation of the empires, the uneasy suspicion remained that the Spanish were determined to participate in the lucrative trade between Macao and Nagasaki which the Portuguese controlled. The Chinese were likewise uneasy about the meaning of the new connection developing between Manila and Macao, and about the effect it might have on the profits which influential Cantonese merchants and officials had been indirectly enjoying. The Portuguese Jesuits, officials and merchants, along with their Chinese friends, let Sanchez know in no uncertain terms that Spanish efforts to break into the trade or any attempts to enter China illegally would disrupt the trade and probably lead to its suspension. The halting of commerce would then presumably bring about the demise of Macao itself,

---

[258] De la Costa, *op. cit.* (n. 83), p. 6.
[259] *Ibid.*, pp. 45–47.

the outlawing of missionary work in China, and a great financial loss to the Japan mission. But, even while Sanchez himself was in China, a group of Franciscans set sail for Macao, landed on Chinese soil, were thrown in jail, and finally released to the custody of the Portuguese in Macao. Both Sanchez and the disappointed Franciscans were sent back to Manila in 1583 with a warning from the Chinese that, in the future, Spaniards who came from the Philippines without authorization would be put to death upon touching Chinese soil.[260] The Portuguese in Macao apparently registered no protest against this resolution of the Chinese authorities.

Upon Sanchez' arrival in Manila, he found that the governor was dead and that the city had been destroyed by a large fire. He soon sat down, however, to discuss his experiences in China with the new governor, Diego Ronquillo. It was evidently in these conversations that agreement was reached to the effect that the Spaniards should plan the military conquest of China. An armed expedition was to be outfitted in Manila to escort the missionaries to China, and to force the Chinese government to permit them to enter and to preach the gospel. Should the Chinese resist in the face of this show of force, the Spanish were to declare war and the Chinese territory, once conquered, would be placed under the sovereignty of Spain. Initially, both the bishop and the governor warmly endorsed this fantastic project and both of them wrote to Spain for the necessary authority, ships, and men. Ronquillo, like his contemporaries, naïvely believed that the conquest could be carried out with a force of eight thousand men and ten or twelve galleons.[261] Although Sanchez claimed that the Jesuits in Macao agreed with his ideas, it is evident that Valignano and his colleagues were opposed to military conquest and determined to follow the policy of accommodation.[262]

Sanchez persisted in trying to win support for his invasion project among the missionaries in the Philippines (many of whom opposed him) and among his fellow Jesuits in America and Europe. He sent detailed accounts at his ideas to his superiors in the New World and in Rome. Almost unanimously they reacted unfavorably. Even though counsels were divided in Manila as to the project, the leadership then decided in 1584 to send Sanchez to Macao again in the company of Juan Bautista Roman, the royal factor. Aside from making complaints about the loss of a galleon off the China coast, the emissaries were instructed to set up a trading station on the Fukien coast. Should the Chinese turn down this eminently reasonable request, then, wrote Bishop Salazar to King Philip: "I say again that not only can your Majesty enter China sword in hand and by force of arms open a gate for the gospel, but . . . your Majesty is bound to do so."[263] In Macao, meanwhile, Sanchez, awaiting an answer to his request to see the Chinese authorities, took the opportunity to write to General Acquaviva in

[260] *Ibid.*, pp. 48–49.
[261] For background see below, pp. 801–2, 808.
[262] See De la Costa, *op. cit.* (n. 83), pp. 50–51.
[263] As quoted in *ibid.*, p. 53.

Rome about the worldly life of the Jesuits in the College at Macao and their unseemly preoccupation with and concern for their investments in the Japan trade. Sanchez failed to obtain a favorable reply from the Chinese to his request for a Spanish trading station, and so he and Roman, after a terribly long and difficult voyage which took them all the way to Malacca, finally got back to Manila in June, 1585.[264]

In Rome, where spirits were high about missionary prospects in Japan with the reception there of the four young missionaries from Kyūshū, General Acquaviva was in no mood to listen sympathetically to Sanchez' pleas for an invasion of China or to his criticisms of the Jesuits at Macao. He responded by ordering the Provincial in Mexico to recall Sanchez.[265] Before these instructions were received, Sanchez was appointed by the entire Spanish colony in Manila to go to Madrid himself and to memorialize the throne on behalf of the China project. Acquaviva, hearing news of these plans, instructed the Jesuits in Spain to present to Philip II his view of "how improper it is for a religious to become involved in temporal affairs, as that Padre [Sanchez] has done, and even more so in the Chinese enterprise. . . ."[266]

When Sanchez arrived in Mexico in 1587, he met with the eminent Jesuit, José de Acosta, to whom he talked about China and unfolded his plan of invasion. Acosta immediately informed Rome and Madrid of Sanchez' ideas, and gave it as his opinion that the project was unjustified and unwise.[267] Once in Spain, Sanchez was required to put himself under the orders and supervision of Acosta. On December 15, 1587, he presented himself to Philip II for the first time. While the king listened to his proposals in the spring of 1588, the Armada was being readied for the attack upon England. The failure of the undertaking against England and the hostility of the Society's leadership in Rome to Sanchez' ideas brought his overly ambitious project to an abrupt end. The invasion was undoubtedly a dream of the small Spanish colony in the Philippines who preferred to think of distant, rich conquests rather than to work laboriously to exploit the islands which they already possessed.[268]

While hotbloods were demanding action, the work of peaceful penetration was quietly going on within China. The story of the final Jesuit success in China centers on the cultural mission carried out there by Matteo Ricci from 1582 until his death in 1610.[269] The ship which brought Ricci to Macao also carried news of Philip II's accession to the Portuguese throne. Ricci was in Macao

---

[264] *Ibid.*, pp. 55–57. On his visit to Malacca see below, p. 808.

[265] See León Lopétegui, *El Padre José de Acosta y las misiones* (Madrid, 1942), p. 463.

[266] As quoted in *ibid.*, p. 476.

[267] The memorials of Sanchez and Acosta of 1587 are reprinted in full in Francisco Mateos (ed.), *José de Acosta, Obras* ("Biblioteca de autores españoles," Vol. LXXIII [Madrid, 1954]), pp. 331–45.

[268] Opinion of Lopétegui, *op. cit.* (n. 265), p. 462.

[269] The fullest and most authoritative account of Ricci's life and activities is H. Bernard, *Le Père Matthieu Ricci et la société chinoise de son temps (1552–1610)* (2 vols.; Tientsin, 1937). His works have been published in two excellent editions: Pietro Tacchi-Venturi, S.J., *Opere storiche del P. Matteo Ricci* (Macerata, 1911); and the splendid volumes edited by P. M. D'Elia, *Fonti Ricciane* (3 vols.; Rome, 1942).

when Sanchez persuaded the leaders of the city to give their allegiance to Philip II. Uncertain about what Macao's political and economic future might be under the new dispensation, Ricci nevertheless went ahead with his preparations for joining Ruggiero in Chao-Ch'ing. In September, 1583, the two Jesuits settled down on land of their own in the viceregal capital. There Ricci began to prepare for his penetration of China, seventeen years of mixed frustration and progress which finally ended with his being able in 1601 to carry the apostolic effort to Peking itself.

In 1585 the Portuguese Jesuit Duarte de Sande and his companion, Antonio d'Almeida, joined Ricci and Ruggiero at Chao-Ch'ing. Sande, who was then fifty-four years old, evidently felt that the mission in the interior of China was not likely to prove viable.[270] He was much more interested in Sanchez' project for the invasion of China, or for direct action of some sort. So he returned to Macao in 1588 along with Ruggiero, and Ricci was left alone with D'Almeida at the viceregal capital.[271] Ruggiero was then sent to Rome by Valignano to obtain a papal embassy to the emperor of China which would request imperial sanction for preaching the gospel.[272] Sande, on September 28, 1589, wrote a report to the Jesuit General on the difficulties confronting the China mission. This was published two years later in a collection of Jesuit letters.[273] But the deaths of four successive popes in Rome in 1590–91, and the great shock given to Catholic Europe and the Iberian states by the defeat of the Armada, prevented both the papacy and Philip II from responding positively in support of the request for an embassy to China.

Both Valignano and Ricci realized that in China Christianity faced one of the greatest challenges ever confronted by its dynamic message. In India and Japan, the Catholic missionaries had encountered, for the first time since the conversion of Rome, complex cultures with highly developed religious traditions of their own. In China they found a cultivated and integrated society which prided itself upon being the supreme civilization of the world and disdained the learning of others. To break through this wall of Chinese isolation and ethnocentrism, it was clear to both Valignano and Ricci, though not to all of their colleagues, that Jesuit influence in China would be directly proportional to their ability to "win friends and influence people" in high political office. So their object was not to work for conversions at once, but to prepare the ground slowly and thoroughly, and through cultural intercourse to win gradual acceptance of themselves and their faith by strategically placed members of Chinese society. Although such a program required lengthy preparation, they thought that once they had made converts in the higher echelons of government and the most influential circles of society, the conversion of the common people would be

---

[270] See biography of Sande in Pfister, *op. cit.* (n. 243), I, 44–45.

[271] Dissertation by Dunne, *op. cit.* (n. 247), pp. 114–15, 118.

[272] Cf. Bernard, *op. cit.* (n. 269), I, 127.

[273] *Lettere del Giapone et della Cina de gl'anno M.D. LXXXIX & M.D.XC scritte al R.P. Generale della Compagnie di Giesu* (Rome, 1591), pp. 200–214.

much simpler. So Ricci deliberately set out in 1582 to win the respect and admiration of the Chinese literati by conversing with them and arousing their curiosity as best he could about Western science, thought, and religion. But before such a program could win lasting successes, it increasingly became clear that Ricci and his co-workers would have to take on the native customs, acquire effective command of the language, and tutor themselves in the classics, history, and arts of China. The harvest of this temperate, wise, and necessarily slow policy would be reaped only in the seventeenth century.

E. TROUBLES IN JAPAN, 1582–1600

After the departure of Valignano in 1582, changes took place in Japan which did not augur well for the future of Christianity there. Toyotomi Hideyoshi, who had just succeeded Nobunaga, continued for a time to treat the Jesuits cordially. Like his predecessor, Hideyoshi hated the militant Buddhists and sought to encourage their rivals. He was also cautious about doing anything that might disturb the trade being conducted by the Portuguese in collaboration with the Jesuits. But, as the Jesuits continued to grow in numbers and to make converts who were militarily and politically powerful, Hideyoshi evidently began to view them as a potential threat to his supreme authority. Once he had been elevated to regent (*kampaku*) in 1584, Hideyoshi began to deal vigorously with all elements which potentially had power to resist his military domination of Japan. The lords of Kyūshū, whose relations with the Jesuits were so close, proved to be particularly difficult for him to bring to heel. It was probably therefore political considerations which caused Hideyoshi in 1587 to issue an edict banishing the Jesuits from Japan.[274] The Portuguese merchants, however, were carefully excluded from the ban. Actually, Hideyoshi did not immediately harry the Jesuits out of the land. For the next decade, he refrained from enforcing his decree. The Jesuits, who tried walking gingerly and discreetly after 1587, were tolerated but not encouraged. To make the situation even more strained, new problems appeared for the Jesuits around 1590 from the direction of the Philippines. This fresh set of difficulties produced by the Christians themselves convinced Hideyoshi that his suspicions of their motives and objectives were not unfounded.

This highly tense situation between Hideyoshi and the Jesuits was closely related to events connected with the war being fought for control of Kyūshū. Fearful for the future of Christianity in Kyūshū after the victory of the non-Christian Satsuma clan in 1584 and their subsequent occupation of Nagasaki,

---

[274] G. B. Sansom, *Japan: A Short Cultural History* (New York, 1936); for more recent research supporting this conclusion see Arimichi Ebisawa, "The Jesuits and Their Cultural Activities in the Far East," *Journal of World History*, V (1959–60), 360–61.

Father Gaspar Coelho, a Portuguese and Vice-Provincial of Japan, encouraged the Christian *daimyo* of the western islands to request help from Manila. The *daimyo* of Hirado offered to pay homage to the Spanish in return for aid, and he and Ōmura sought to entice the Spanish with offers of commercial advantages.[275] In 1586 eleven Japanese Christians journeyed to Manila from Nagasaki with a letter from Coelho himself which asked for both military and missionary help. The governor responded by sending a few vessels, presents, and two Spanish Jesuits, but he refrained from sending members of the mendicant Orders for fear of outraging the Portuguese and their Jesuit allies.

In the meantime Hideyoshi, while preparing for the conquest of Kyūshū and the subjugation of the temporarily victorious Satsumas, continued to harass the Buddhists and to favor the Christians. In May, 1586, he received Coelho at Osaka castle, his newly constructed residence. Fróis acted as interpreter for these conversations, and reported to Europe in a lengthy letter of October 17, 1586, the plans which Hideyoshi revealed to Coelho.[276] The *kampaku* let the Jesuit leader know that he intended to break the power of Satsuma in Kyūshū, and that he would leave the Jesuits in charge of Nagasaki. Hideyoshi described his intention, once order and stability had been achieved throughout Japan, of building a great fleet and recruiting a large expeditionary force to undertake the conquest of Korea and China. He asked that Coelho help him to acquire two large Portuguese carracks fully equipped with personnel. Should the Jesuits co-operate and should he be successful in reducing China to vassalage, Hideyoshi promised that he would build Christian churches in China and command its entire populace to accept Christianity. Coelho, whose predisposition for interfering in secular affairs we have already seen, readily agreed to do what Hideyoshi asked and volunteered to bring the Christian *daimyo* of Kyūshū over to Hideyoshi's side. Both the Christian *daimyo* and the Jesuits were appalled at Coelho's brashness.[277] While Hideyoshi professed to be delighted with the Jesuit co-operation, Coelho, by overplaying his hand, probably contributed his share in causing Hideyoshi's sudden change of attitude toward the Christians in 1587.[278]

Hideyoshi's reversal of policy has been the subject of much research and speculation, both in the sixteenth century and since. Now that a good deal of the evidence has been collected, it seems fairly clear that the Japanese ruler had been harboring doubts about the Jesuits for some time before he actually issued his edict of expulsion. It is probable, however, that the actual expulsion when it

---

[275] See J. O. Ronall, "Spain and Japan—Early Diplomatic Relations," *Eastern World*, Vol. XI (1957), No. 12, p. 39.

[276] For an English translation of the essential portions of this letter see Otis Cary, *A History of Christianity in Japan* (New York, 1909), I, 100–101. For a thorough discussion of Hideyoshi's plans see G. Stramigioli, "Hideyoshi's Expansionist Policy on the Asiatic Mainland," *Transactions of the Asiatic Society of Japan*, 3d ser., III (1954), 74–94.

[277] For Father Organtino's reaction to Coelho's optimistic assurances see J. Laures, *Tâkayama Ukon und die Anfänge der Kirche in Japan* (Münster, 1954), pp. 190–91.

[278] See Boxer, *op. cit.* (n. 209), p. 141.

came was not premeditated. In the midst of a drinking party, on the night of July 24, 1587, he seems to have decided to act.[279] The edict of banishment[280] was handed to Coelho the next day, and it was followed shortly by a series of decrees relating to Jesuit properties, Japanese Christians, and Nagasaki. According to Jesuit sources, Hideyoshi's decree affected Christians to the number of 200,000. Completely dismayed by this abrupt turn in events, Coelho sought to strengthen the fortifications at Nagasaki and to induce the Christian *daimyo* to resist the expulsion order by arms. However, two of the staunchest Christians, Ōmura Sumitada and Ōtomo Yoshishige, had died just previously and the other *daimyo*, even had they dared, were in no position to defy Hideyoshi. Coelho began calling for help to Manila, Macao, and Goa. These appeals having failed, Coelho and his fellow Jesuits were forced to follow a policy of withdrawal and temporizing. For reasons probably known only to himself,[281] Hideyoshi failed to execute his decrees and permitted the Jesuits to stay on and to go about their work so long as they ceased their attacks upon Shintoism and Buddhism and kept their fingers out of politics. Once it had become clear that Hideyoshi was willing to tolerate the Jesuits, their position was further strengthened by the representations made on their behalf by the *daimyo* of Arima and Ōmura and by the protection which they continued to afford the Christians within their domains. Hideyoshi, the great unifier, was often willing to disregard slight failures to observe the letter of his law so long as his authority was duly acknowledged in fundamental matters.[282] Once he had reduced the Kanto (central plain of Honshu) to his authority in 1590, the Japanese leader was ready to go ahead with his long-planned attack upon China.

As Hideyoshi began after 1587 to prepare for his continental conquest, fear spread in Manila that he was actually assembling his forces for a descent upon the Philippines.[283] Japanese commercial missions and freebooters who turned up in the Philippines were thought to be on reconnaissance assignments. Realizing that the small Spanish force available would not be able to defend the islands against an invasion fleet, the Governor of the Philippines in 1589 asked for and received permission to authorize voyages to Japan. In the following year the Bishop of Manila, thinking that all the Jesuits had left Japan in obedience to the expulsion edict, permitted three or four Franciscans to sail for Kyūshū. They arrived in Japan at about the time that Valignano returned there with the four Japanese emissaries who had been to Europe. The Jesuit Visitor, in his

[279] See *ibid.*, pp. 145–47.

[280] Text in *ibid.*, p. 148.

[281] Practically every writer on Japanese history has speculated on this question. I see no point in adding to the confusion by making guesses of my own.

[282] Cf. Murdoch and Yamagata, *op. cit.* (n. 227), II, 247–48.

[283] There were real grounds for this fear, for Hideyoshi envisaged himself as a world conqueror and was insanely outraged in 1591 when the Philippines refused to acknowledge the suzerainty of Japan. See Y. S. Kuno, *Japanese Expansion on the Asiatic Continent* (Berkeley, 1937), I, 143–44, 314–18; and Stramigioli, *loc. cit.* (n. 276), p. 96.

capacity as the diplomatic representative of the Viceroy of Goa, was received in audience by Hideyoshi at Miyako on March 3, 1591.[284] The Franciscans and Spanish merchants who had by this time made their way to Japan quickly learned that the Jesuits and Portuguese were still very much in evidence, even though the Jesuits were being forced to carry on their work quietly and often secretly.

The last decade of the sixteenth century saw the Christian position in Japan being further endangered by open conflict among the Europeans; the Portuguese and the Jesuits on one side, the Spanish and the mendicant Orders openly opposing them. Valignano in his letters and especially in his *Summarium* of 1583 had emphatically insisted that the Spanish merchants and friars should not be allowed to violate the Portuguese *padroado* by coming to Japan. He anticipated that rivalry would produce controversy which would in turn weaken the economic and religious position of the Christians in Japan. This was one of the reasons why the Jesuits had worked so hard while the Japanese mission was in Europe to obtain papal guarantees of their exclusive right to work in Japan. Valignano's worst fears were realized while he was still in Japan in 1590–91. Spanish merchants, who had entered Japan to help Hideyoshi build his invasion fleet, were angered by the refusal of both the Portuguese merchants and Valignano to help them win a financial wrangle with the Japanese. In reprisal the Spanish merchants sent complaints to Rome. Among other matters they alleged that the four Japanese envoys were not at all what Valignano had portrayed them to be. They were not princes and not even of noble blood; in fact, they were really four waifs, poor as rats, whom Valignano had picked off the streets of Nagasaki. Valignano later sent a rebuttal to Rome.[285]

In Manila, meanwhile, the Spanish were disturbed by a peremptory demand delivered to them in 1591 to acknowledge the suzerainty of Japan over the Philippines. Action seemed to be essential if peace were to be preserved. Without awaiting specific instructions from Madrid, the governor sent the Dominican Juan Cobo to Japan in an effort to obtain an explanation of Hideyoshi's letter. Cobo was received at Nagoya, but he perished on the return voyage and so Hideyoshi's reply never reached Manila. In 1593 a second mission, led by Father Pedro Bautista, a Franciscan, was dispatched to Japan to obtain a treaty of peace and friendship with Hideyoshi and to work out a system of control for what the Spanish hoped would be their growing trade with Japan.[286] Bautista and the three other Franciscans who accompanied him were received cordially and granted permission to stay on in Miyako, even though they had gained entrance, like Valignano, by acting as diplomatic agents. The Franciscans justified their continued presence in Japan to the Jesuits by arguing that in 1586 Pope Sixtus V

[284] See Alfonso Kleiser, S.J., "P. Alexandre Valignano's Gesandtschaftsreise nach Japan zum Quambacudono Toyotomi Hideyoshi 1588–1591," *Monumenta Nipponica*, I (1938), 70–98.

[285] Bernard, *loc. cit.* (n. 256), p. 121.

[286] Marcelo de Ribadeneira, O.F.M. (see below, p. 718), explained a decade later how and why the governor of the Philippines decided to send Bautista as his emissary to Japan.

had granted their Order the right to carry on apostolic works in the lands of the East and that they were therefore no longer required to respect the ban that Pope Gregory XIII had placed upon the entrance of other Orders into Japan.[287] In 1594 the Franciscans sent Hideyoshi's reply back to Manila by a Portuguese merchant. Although Hideyoshi prefaced his remarks with a command for obedience or punishment by the sword, he conciliated the Spanish with a promise of eternal friendship and of free intercourse between the Philippines and Japan. Clearly Hideyoshi, like the Spaniards, was anxious to break the Portuguese monopoly on the trade with China. He evidently hoped that competition from the Spaniards would bring down the price of the materials which he was importing to prepare for his costly continental war.[288]

The *Taiko* (a title meaning "prince" or "regent," which Hideyoshi assumed in 1591) showed his favor to the Franciscans tangibly by giving them land in Miyako on which to build a cloister. Soon the friars, despite the warnings of the Jesuits that they were endangering the entire Christian position in Japan, began to preach and to make converts openly. The Franciscans held that Hideyoshi had agreed that they might work exactly as they had in Spain and that they therefore had no need to hide their activities. Whether such a conclusion from their talks with Hideyoshi was justified or not, it is certain that the Franciscans did not possess a written patent permitting them to propagate Christianity publicly.[289] Nevertheless, they confidently went ahead with their work in Miyako and its environs, and soon founded cloisters in Nagasaki and Ōsaka as well. Father Bautista explained their success and the lack of opposition from the government by pointing out that the Franciscans, unlike the Jesuits, were not dedicated to the proselytizing of rich and influential people but were content to work with the poor.[290]

Unfortunately for the Christians, their fratricidal differences were most apparent in the capital city, where they could most easily be observed by Japanese officialdom. And in 1596, when Bishop Don Pedro de Martinez arrived in Japan, the conflict waxed hotter and came even more into the open.[291] For this Jesuit bishop denied that the Franciscans had the right to work in Japan, prohibited the bringing of more missionaries from Manila, and forbade the Christians of Japan to attend Franciscan services or to receive the sacraments from

---

[287] For details on this and on the theological arguments advanced by the Franciscans see the summary in Laures, *op. cit.* (n. 277), p. 262, and Lemmens, *op. cit.* (n. 4), p. 156. Until recently, the history of this controversy has been written almost exclusively from Jesuit sources. The Franciscan scholar Lorenzo Pérez has been mainly responsible for making the Franciscan sources available through his editions of letters and his articles in the *Archivum franciscanum historicum* and the *Archivo ibero-americano*. It is only fair to point out that Ribadeneira, one of the few Franciscans who had actually been in Japan and who wrote at length on the martyrdoms, is silent as to why Bautista decided to remain in Japan.

[288] Cf. the discussion in Boxer, *op. cit.* (n. 209), pp. 161–62.

[289] Laures, *op. cit.* (n. 277), p. 215; cf. Lemmens, *op. cit.* (n. 4), pp. 157–58.

[290] Laures, *op. cit.* (n. 277), p. 266, n. 31; and cf. Lemmens, *op. cit.* (n. 4), pp. 158–59.

[291] Sebastian de Moraes, the first bishop appointed to Funai, died en route to his see. See Joseph de Moidrey, S.J., "La hiérarchie catholique en Chine, en Corée et au Japon (1307–1914)," *Variétés sinologiques*, No. 38 (Zi-ka-wei, 1914), p. 16.

their hands.[292] After seven months in Japan, Martinez left the country at the invitation of the Japanese governor of Nagasaki.

While the Christian Orders were thus wrangling among themselves, Hideyoshi concentrated on his continental campaign. In the spring of 1592, the *Taiko*'s vast army had landed at Fusan in Korea, and a little later invested Seoul. But harassment by guerrilla forces in Korea and breakdowns in communications forced the Japanese to postpone their invasion of China until they could pacify Korea completely. Numerous losses to the Japanese navy seriously affected Hideyoshi's ability to maintain his forces in Korea and limited his chances for preparing a big push against China. The gradual arousal of China to the danger threatening her Yalu border further complicated Hideyoshi's plans. As a result of Korean harassment, logistical problems, and China's military action, the Japanese were forced to retreat from northern Korea at the beginning of 1593.

The withdrawal of the Japanese to the south produced a stalemate, and consequently negotiations began. Weary of war, particularly after it began to turn against him, Hideyoshi consented in 1593 to receive an embassy from China at Nagoya. Then, for more than three years, peace negotiations followed a tortuous course as the troops in the field became constantly more restless. Finally, the negotiations were broken off in 1596 when the Ming emperor addressed Hideyoshi as his vassal, "the King of Japan," and instructed him on how to rule his kingdom. Outraged by what he considered to be China's overbearing attitude, Hideyoshi undertook a new invasion of Korea in 1597. This second effort was much better organized than the first, and it brought to Japan a number of victories on both land and sea. Hideyoshi died on August 18, 1598, and shortly thereafter his troops were withdrawn from Korea.[293]

It was during the course of his second Korean invasion that Hideyoshi again clamped down on the Christians. He had granted the Franciscans extraordinary freedom for a few years after their arrival at Miyako. And as of 1597, there were still 137 Jesuits in Japan and an estimated 300,000 Christians, with more being converted all the time. Among the converts made in the decade during which Christian work was legally outlawed, there were many more lords and people of quality than had previously subscribed to the faith.[294] And in 1594, Father de Cespedes had even been permitted to go to Korea to minister to the needs of the Christians in the Japanese armed forces. The Jesuits had also established in these trying years their famous printing press at Amakusa and likewise expanded their educational activities through the establishment of new seminaries as they followed out their program of cultural penetration which Valignano insisted upon. But the Christians were soon forcefully reminded of their precarious hold in Japan by the resumption of persecution in 1597.

The affair of the "San Felipe" is usually credited with precipitating the second big attack on Christianity in Japan. But this is not the complete story. The

[292] Laures, *op. cit.* (n. 277), p. 267.
[293] For a detailed discussion of this "Seven Years' War" see Kuno, *op. cit.* (n. 283), I, 145–73.
[294] Murdoch and Yamagata, *op. cit.* (n. 227), II, 274–75.

attack upon Christianity must also be seen in the light of Japan's setbacks in Korea, the great economic needs of the Korean war, and Hideyoshi's growing concern over internal subversion. The "San Felipe," a galleon on the run from Manila to Acapulco, carrying a rich cargo and an unusually long passenger list was forced to seek refuge from a typhoon off the coast of Tosa on October 19, 1596. The local lord confiscated its cargo and imprisoned the passengers and crew. Urged on by the Franciscans, the hapless Spaniards sent a delegation to Hideyoshi to appeal their case. After hesitating, the hard-pressed *Taiko* refused the Spaniards' claims to their cargo and their freedom. His decision, it has been contended, was taken after it came to his ears that the Pilot-Major of the "San Felipe" had admitted that the Christian missionaries often acted as advance agents of the *conquistadores*.[295] Such a confirmation of his own suspicions and fears was enough to convince Hideyoshi that his decree of 1587 should be enforced vigorously and immediately. In February, 1597, the first of the great Christian martyrdoms in Japan took place. Twenty-six Christians (six Franciscans and twenty Japanese converts) were crucified at Nagasaki.[296] The European Jesuits, probably because of their connection with the silk trade, escaped Hideyoshi's wrath. After the *Taiko*'s death in 1598, the Jesuits, despite the executions in Japan, and the Franciscans, despite the prohibitions of Rome, continued to appear in Japan. So the Christian mission in Japan for the nonce survived the controversies and crucifixions of the late sixteenth century and was able to enter the seventeenth century still hoping that the time was not too distant when Japan would become a totally Christian state.

F. FRIARS AND ADVENTURERS IN CAMBODIA

In Indochina, where the Jesuits were not active, the Dominicans and Franciscans enjoyed a measure of success during the last two decades of the sixteenth century. There are no records of European activities in Cambodia from the failure of Cruz's mission until after the merging of the Spanish and Portuguese crowns.[297] The next recorded person to turn up in Cambodia was Diogo Veloso, a swashbuckling Portuguese adventurer who was intimately involved in the politics and wars of the peninsula until his death in 1599. It is likely that he first arrived in Lovek around 1582–85, a time when the Cambodian ruler

[295] This is the Jesuit and Portuguese version of the affair. The Spanish and Franciscans asserted that the Portuguese, fearing Spanish competition, had instigated the confiscation of the "San Felipe's" cargo and had informed the Japanese that the Spanish were a potential political and military threat. See Boxer, *op. cit.* (n. 209), p. 166.

[296] For a translation into English of Frôis' account reproduced in the *Acta Sanctorum* of the Bollandists see "The Crucifixion of the Twenty-Six in 1597," *Transactions of the Asiatic Society of Japan*, XLIV (1916), 20–45.

[297] Traditionally, it is said by modern authors that the Dominicans Lopo Cardoso and João Madeira arrived in Lovek in 1570. Boxer and Groslier have combined forces to show that this rests on a mistaken interpretation of the evidence. See Groslier, *op. cit.* (n. 215), pp. 28–29.

Sâtha (reigned 1576–96) was beginning to have trouble with Siam.[298] Veloso was accompanied and followed into Cambodia by other Portuguese adventurers looking for quick riches. As the threat from Siam became more acute, Sâtha was inclined to look favorably upon the European *condottieri* as he hoped through them to obtain a military alliance with the Portuguese at Malacca. Two Dominican missionaries from Malacca, Lopo Cardoso and João Madeira, were not slow to take advantage of this opening. They arrived in Lovek probably in 1584 or 1585. King Sâtha's initial reaction to the appearance of the missionaries and to their teachings was no friendlier than the reception accorded Cruz by his predecessor, Ang Chan. Nonetheless he tolerated them, probably because he hoped that they might also act as political intermediaries with Malacca. Madeira was replaced, possibly already in 1584, by Friar Sylvestre d'Azevedo, who was long to work in harmony with Veloso for the extension of Portuguese influence in Cambodia.

Veloso and Azevedo quickly learned the Cambodian language as they sought to establish better relations between Sâtha and Malacca. The Dominican friar was close to the commercial community, for he headed a small Christian group of Portuguese merchants and foreign (Japanese, Chinese, and Malay) converts who lived in the vicinity of Phnom Pénh. Under pressure of the increasing danger from Ayut'ia, Sâtha relaxed his attitude toward the Europeans and their priests. Veloso married a "cousin" of the king and the Cambodian chronicles refer to him as the sovereign's "adopted son."[299] Azevedo meanwhile was petitioning his superiors in Malacca for more missionaries to take advantage of the changed climate and to begin the work of converting the Cambodians. By 1585 a new delegation of Dominicans arrived from Malacca accompanied by four or five Franciscans.[300] News of the closer relations with Cambodia was quickly relayed to Europe, inasmuch as Sâtha through his European associates was constantly asking Malacca for aid in his wars against the Siamese.

The first appeals to Malacca by Sâtha and his European advisers elicited no response. Probably at the suggestion of the Europeans. Sâtha then turned to Manila, the Spanish center of power, for help in warding off the onslaughts of the Siamese. The orientation toward Manila was helped along by contemporary events. Early in 1593, two Spanish soldiers of fortune arrived in Cambodia after an arduous overland trip from Champa. Blaz Ruiz de Hernán González and Gregorio Vargas Machuca had been captured along with their ship and held as slaves in Champa, from whence they escaped to Cambodia. They were both given a warm reception in Lovek, and the Cambodian chronicles record that these "two brothers" soon became "adopted sons" of the king.[301] Ruiz

[298] L. P. Briggs, "Spanish Intervention in Cambodia," *T'oung pao*, XXXIX (1950), 148, asserts Veloso arrived there in 1585. Groslier (*op. cit.* [n. 215], pp. 35–36), who thinks that Briggs forced his evidence somewhat, is inclined to favor 1582 or 1583.

[299] Groslier, *op. cit.* (n. 215), p. 36.

[300] See E. Aymonier, "The History of Tchampa (the Cyamba of Marco Polo, Now Annam or Cochin China)," *Imperial and Asiatic Quarterly Review*, New Ser., VI (1893), 375.

[301] Groslier, *op. cit.* (n. 215), p. 37.

was retained at the court as head of the royal bodyguard when the king finally decided in the summer of 1593 to dispatch an embassy to Manila. Veloso and Vargas carried the royal letter, written on a leaf of gold, which requested military aid. In return for help against Siam, Sâtha promised to allow the missionaries freedom to evangelize and convert and guaranteed the Spanish a preferential position in trading with Cambodia.[302]

Even before the embassy arrived in Manila, the Siamese had launched their attack against the Cambodian capital. The Spanish in the Philippines, who were preoccupied with Japan and their other problems, were no more inclined than the Portuguese at Malacca to send succor to Sâtha. When Veloso and his companion returned to Cambodia early in 1594, they found that Lovek had been taken. Soon they were themselves captured by the Siamese, along with a number of the Christian missionaries. Sâtha still held out in the hinterland while Veloso and the missionaries were sent overland as prisoners to Ayut'ia. Ruiz and several others managed to escape from the Siamese and to steal off to Manila in a captured junk. Veloso meanwhile gained favor in Siam and was sent as an interpreter on a Siamese trading mission to Manila. During 1595, Veloso, Ruiz, and Vargas were all in Manila and actively engaged in trying to divert the interest of its governor from other projects to the rescue of Sâtha and the establishment of a Spanish protectorate over Cambodia. They found support especially among the missionaries, who saw this as a God-given opportunity to win a base on the mainland for further Spanish religious and political expansion.

Luis Pérez Dasmariñas, the Spanish governor of Manila, swayed by pressure from this group of adventurers and by the pleading letters of the Bishop of Malacca, decided to dispatch early in 1596 a small expedition under General Juan Xuarès Gallinato to help Sâtha regain his throne. Upon their arrival at Phnom Pénh, the Spanish found a usurper on the throne. After interfering indecisively in this chaotic situation, Gallinato decided to give it up and return to Manila. On the voyage back he sailed to Cochin-China to try to locate a ship which had previously been lost off the coast near Hanoi. Veloso and Ruiz took this opportunity to disengage themselves from the Gallinato expedition and to proceed overland in the hope of finding Sâtha in Laos. Arriving in Vientiane, they learned that both Sâtha and his oldest son had been dead for over a year.

Undaunted by this sad news, the two Spanish soldiers induced Sâtha's second son and his queens to make an effort to overturn the usurper of the Cambodian throne. In the following year, they regained the capital city of Srei Santhor and Sâtha's son took the reign title of Barom Reachea II. A weakling and a victim of the internal chaos prevailing in his country, the new king became prey to all those who were ambitious to rule from behind the throne, including the two Spaniards responsible for his being on it. Veloso and Ruiz were opposed

---

[302] On the precise nature of the king's promises the available sources are not entirely clear. Briggs (*loc. cit.* [n. 298], p. 148), for example, declared on the basis of the Spanish sources that "the King promised to become a Christian and to accept a sort of Spanish protectorate." The above is based on Groslier, *op. cit.* (n. 215), p. 37.

in particular by a strong Muslim faction at court headed by a Malay called Laksamana. In the hope of retaining what had been won, the puppet king wrote to Malacca and Manila for aid.[303] His letters apparently arrived in the Philippines at a time when the Dominicans were also urging action in Cambodia. Officially the Spanish government would have nothing to do with such an adventure. But, in 1599, Don Luiz Peréz Dasmariñas, the former governor of the Philippines, offered to finance an expedition if he would be guaranteed the governorship of Cambodia. Most of the members of this expedition were shipwrecked even before arriving at their destination. Dasmariñas was unable in any case to help Veloso and Ruiz escape from the tight situation in which they found themselves. In the middle of 1599, the two Spanish adventurers along with several Christian missionaries were killed by their Muslim enemies. This massacre at Phnom Pénh brought an end to the period of Spanish influence in Cambodia.[304]

Guzman, the Spanish Jesuit, is one of the few among the early European historians to comment accurately on aspects of this distant enterprise of missionaries and military adventurers.[305] This is not surprising when one considers that Madrid, the first European capital to be aware of Cambodia, was only beginning to take an interest in these affairs at about the time when Ruiz and Veloso were killed. While practically nothing was known of their exploits in sixteenth-century Europe, Ruiz and Veloso quickly became synonymous with courage and valor among the fighting men of the Spanish Empire.[306] Stories of their deeds were embellished as they were relayed by word of mouth throughout the entire empire. These *conquistadores* of Cambodia soon became the heros of "interventionist" factions in both Manila and Madrid. Dramas, cloak-and-dagger novels, and serious histories of the early seventeenth century celebrated their exploits. Even in foreign works their adventures soon began to figure, usually in one or another of the embroidered forms with which the Spanish soldiers regaled each other on campaigns in Peru or in the dock-front taverns of Seville.[307] In Cambodia itself, Veloso's heroic deeds were kept alive by oral tradition; as late as the mid-nineteenth century a French priest records hearing that certain of the *bakus*, hereditary guardians of the Sacred Sword, were descended from Veloso and a Cambodian princess.[308]

In further Asia there were three nerve centers of ecclesiastical administration from which the missions were superintended. Malacca and Macao, the Portu-

---

[303] Texts of these letters of 1597–98 in Groslier, *op. cit.* (n. 215), pp. 46–49.

[304] *Ibid.*

[305] *Historia de las missiones* (Alcalá, 1601), I, 173–75; also see report of the Jesuit superior, Nicolas Pimenta, from Goa of 1599 in *Newe historische Relation* (Dillingen, 1601), pp. 71–186. Pimenta's letter is also available in Eglauer, *op. cit.* (n. 222), III, 326–488.

[306] For a modern Spanish effort to lionize them see the thesis of Xavier Dusmet de Arizcun, *Una expedicion española a Cambodja en el siglo XVI* (Madrid, 1932).

[307] A. Cabaton, "L'Espagne en Indochine à la fin du XVIe siècle," *Revue de l'histoire des colonies françaises*, I (1913), 104.

[308] Briggs, *loc. cit.* (n. 298), p. 158.

guese trading bases, were dominated by the Jesuits. Manila, the Spanish outpost in the Far East, was less clearly under the influence of a single religious Order. The Jesuits within the Portuguese *padroado* followed the lines roughly sketched out for them by Xavier. They associated themselves with the trading empire of the Portuguese, and their evangelizing activities followed the routes taken by the merchants. They even went into commerce themselves in the Far East to maintain the mission in Japan. While the successors of Xavier received support from the secular arm, they were not completely dependent upon it. In the Spiceries and Japan the missionaries left the trading centers to evangelize on their own. At the end of the century they were also far ahead of the Portuguese traders in their penetration of China. It is striking, however, that the Jesuits from Xavier onward unhesitatingly bypassed the states of continental southeast Asia in their eagerness to penetrate lands of greater size, wealth, and culture in the Far East.

The attractions of China, Japan, and even Indochina for the small colony of merchants, missionaries, and traders at Manila were equally potent. With the failure of the Spanish to penetrate China, the Manila colony turned its attention to Japan and Indochina. The story of the clash which this precipitated in Japan has been recounted, but it is well to remark that when news of the danger to the Japan mission reached Europe the controversy was continued there. The Spanish missionaries, fewer in numbers and from at least four different Orders, lacked the independence and sense of direction of the more experienced and more rigorously disciplined Jesuits of the *padroado*. Although the other Orders worked within the Portuguese empire and had their own superiors and convents, they never seem to have had the close association with the secular arm which the Orders had in Manila.

All of the Christian missionaries, whether under the direction of Goa or Mexico City, had the Muslims as a common enemy. It was in their approach to the problem of converting the heathen that internal divisions and hostilities appeared. The mendicant friars, both in India and further Asia, were inclined to concentrate upon converting the lowly, to lead the way into hitherto untouched regions, and to pass their conquests on to the Jesuits for administration and development. The Jesuits themselves followed Xavier's precept of ministering to all but concentrating upon the conversion of rulers and other persons of high station. They were not always satisfied that the secular arm with its primary interest in stability and trade was giving its unqualified support to the mission. The difference in viewpoint between the trader and the missionary comes out most strikingly in the Jesuit condemnation of the collaboration between the Portuguese administrators and Sultan Hairun, the Muslim ruler of Ternate. In the Far East, the Jesuits had an opportunity to evangelize without significant help or hindrance from Portuguese arms. It was in this new situation, far from the support of gunboats and in the presence of superior native strength, that the policy was gradually adopted by which the missionaries first accommodated themselves to local practices and then attempted by argument and explanation to win the people to the faith. First experimented with in Japan, the policy of accommodation was later applied in India and China. In Japan, political and personal problems restricted its free development. In India, the missions to Akbar had to accommodate to survive, but dramatic conversions were still not made. In China, however, perhaps largely because of the unique abilities of Ricci, the policy of cultural penetration finally came to full flower. By the very end of the century real achievements were in the making in the two greatest of the Asian states, India and China.

5

THE JESUIT LETTERS, LETTERBOOKS, AND GENERAL HISTORIES

The missionaries of the Society of Jesus were the first to provide Europe with regular information on the progress of the Eastern missions, and they did so with an abundance of collateral data on the region, peoples, and cultures of India, the East Indies, Japan, and China. In the earlier half of the sixteenth century the friars of the mendicant Orders had dispatched informative letters and memoranda to Europe.[309] But it was not until the Jesuits became active in overseas missions that a comprehensive system for correspondence was developed and a plan inaugurated for routine dissemination and publication of the letters in Europe.[310] Loyola had required the members of the new Society from its beginning to keep in touch with him and with each other by regular epistolary communication. Accordingly, in 1541 Loyola explicitly enjoined certain Jesuits who went to Ireland on missionary labors to report their progress by a principal letter addressed directly to him in Rome. Lesser or more private matters were to be sent on a separate sheet (*hijuela*). All such letters, and this practice was also followed later, were to be prepared in triplicate and sent to Rome by three different routes. These reports were to be prepared with great thought and care, for they were to be used for the edification and guidance of the Society and for the inspiration of public interest in its far-flung enterprises. That Loyola was well aware of the potential value of the letters as propaganda for the Society is brought out in this passage from a letter which he wrote in 1542:

Many of our friends, when they know that we have received letters from some one of the Society, wish to see them and enjoy them. If we refuse to let them see these we shall estrange them; but if we show them letters in which the news is all thrown together in confusion, they are disedified.[311]

[309] For example see the great collection of missionary letters compiled by Silva Rego, *op. cit.* (n. 1, *Documentação*).

[310] The best available general discussions of the history of Jesuit letter-writing are in the introduction to Wicki (ed.), *op. cit.* (n. 102), pp. 19*–31*; John Correia-Afonso, S.J., *Jesuit Letters and Indian History* (Bombay, 1955); and in the introductory materials to Wicki (ed.), *op. cit.* (n. 72), at the beginning of the various volumes.

[311] As quoted in Correia-Afonso, *op. cit.* (n. 310), p. 3.

Such a system of regular reporting to headquarters required the establishment of an office in Rome charged with the responsibility of communicating with the missionaries in distant places, with sifting the incoming letters, and with selecting, editing, and translating those to be circularized in Europe. From the earliest years down to the end of the century the letters from foreign fields were circularized in manuscript, if not in printed form, to the Jesuit houses all over Europe. Communication was far from perfect at the beginning, but it was not long before the Jesuits had worked out an intelligence system unequaled by any state in Europe at the time, with the possible exception of Venice.

Once Juan de Polanco of Burgos was appointed permanent secretary of the Society in 1547, the system of letter-writing and distribution became more regularized and institutionalized. The indefatigable Polanco, until his death in 1573, acted as co-ordinator and director of the Society's information center. The instructions on correspondence issued by both Loyola and Polanco were incorporated into the Constitutions of the Order and approved in 1558 by the Society's first General Congregation in the following digested recommendation:

It will be of great help [to foster the spirit of union among the members of the Society] that letters should be exchanged between subjects and superiors; this practice will bring about a thorough knowledge of each other, and of the news and information related in those letters that come from different parts. And about this letter-writing the superiors, and in particular the General and the Provincials will take a special care. They will order things in such a way as to obtain that in every place they should know about the things that are being done in other places, which knowledge is a source of mutual consolation and edification in our Lord.[312]

This intelligence system was naturally carried on by the Jesuits who went to the East and they modified aspects of it to meet their particular needs. Xavier, whose early experience as secretary stood him in good stead, was the first Jesuit to report from India and farther East. Only annual letters, rather than the more frequent reports prepared in Europe, were required from the missionaries in Asia, because the fleets from India ordinarily arrived in Europe but once each year. Xavier inaugurated the system whereby annual letters in multiple copies were dispatched to Europe from the Jesuit outposts in the East; this system was continued until the dissolution of the Society in 1773. Both the Jesuits and their friends in Europe soon learned to request background information from the missionaries in Asia on questions of geography, climate, peoples, customs, competing religious groups, and miscellaneous information.[313] The need for background data naturally made the letters from Asia much more "curious" than those prepared in Europe.

Xavier's first letters from India, where he arrived in 1542, were promptly circularized in Europe after their reception in Rome. His maiden letter from Goa to the Society at Rome told about the voyage to India and his first impressions

[312] As quoted in *ibid.*, p. 5.
[313] Wicki, *op. cit.* (n. 102), pp. 23★–25.★

of the subcontinent. It was evidently circulated widely in manuscript, an autographed copy of it being found as far off as Vilna in 1664.[314] In 1543 Xavier addressed two letters to Loyola and a lengthy document, known as his principal letter on Japan, to the Society in Rome. These three early communications have the distinction of being the first letters from the East to be published in Europe. In 1545 a compilation of them appeared at Paris in French, to be quickly followed by a German translation printed in Augsburg during the same year.[315] Both the French and German publishers indicate in the titles which they give to Xavier's letters that they were directed not only to Loyola and the Society in Rome, but also to his aspirant brothers in Rome, Padua, Portugal, Valencia, Cologne, and Paris, In 1546 a four-page pamphlet was published in Rome bearing the Portuguese arms and carrying the title *Copia de una Littera di Nove delle Indie Orientali*.[316] Four years later, a sheaf of letters from India was sent to Father Jeronimo Nadal at Messina for publication there. It is questionable whether or not they ever went to press. In 1551 and 1552 other Xavier letters were published at Coimbra and Venice.[317] From such evidence it is clear that the young Society had learned by mid-century that the demand for news of Asia might be best met by printing certain of the letters for more general distribution.

With the expansion of Jesuit activities east of India, letters from all over the area were naturally relayed to Goa, the religious and administrative center of the region. Thus materials concerning China, Japan, the Indies, and India were all vaguely subsumed at first under the rubric "Indian letters," because all of them were relayed through India and were sent with the annual fleet to Portugal. When, around mid-century, the Jesuit college was established at Coimbra as a training center for missionaries destined for the East, the old university town also became a repository and clearinghouse for the Jesuit letters directed to Europe. Letters from the field were ever more frequently addressed to the brothers at Coimbra, and these were then copied and sent to the other Jesuit colleges in Europe and to Rome. Polanco soon had occasion to complain that the letters were not being forwarded from Coimbra to Rome with sufficient dispatch. Still, Coimbra continued to grow in importance as the first European clearinghouse for the Jesuit corrrespondence from Asia.

Like Goa, Coimbra was both a copying and a printing center. Already in 1554, the burden of copying the letters from the missionaries in Africa, Brazil, and India was becoming a task of monumental proportions. F. Diego Mirón, Provincial of Portugal, wrote to Loyola:

---

314 Schurhammer and Wicki (eds.), *op. cit.* (n. 40), I, 129.

315 For complete titles see Correia-Afonso, *op. cit.* (n. 310), p. 76; for a critical discussion of the German edition see J. Wicki, "Der älteste deutsche Druck eines Xaverius-briefes aus dem Jahre 1545, ehemals in Besitz des Basler Humanisten Lepusculus," *Neue Zeitschrift für Missionswissenschaft*, IV (1948), 105–9. Especially interesting are the glosses of the Protestant divine, Lepusculus (1501–76) in reaction to Xavier's comments on the Brahmans.

316 Wicki, *op. cit.* (n. 102), p. 28★.

317 See Correia-Afonso, *op. cit.* (n. 310), p. 176, for their titles.

We here are gathering the letters from India to be printed on your command, but we do not know if you want to look them over in Rome before their publication. We here would like to print the letters from India on their arrival, to spare ourselves the labor, which is indeed great, of copying them out for the many places. We want to know if Yr. Rev. will give us the permission to print them. . . .[318]

Permission must have been granted, for in the following year (1555) a general collection of overseas letters came off the press as Coimbra.[319] The Provincial in Portugal also complained, in 1560, that the fathers in India were imprudently sending copies of the newsletters to persons outside the Society, and he requested the General to admonish them.[320] Matters were regularized somewhat by the appointment in 1561 of Francisco Henriques to the post of Procurator-General for Portugal and its overseas provinces, and by placing him in general charge of copying and distributing the correspondence passing through Portugal.[321]

Four or five copies of the quadrimestrial letters prepared in Europe were supposed to be sent to India. It sometimes happened that none of the letters got to their destination, and if one did, it was usually worn to shreds after circulating from Goa to the other Jesuits posts in the East.[322] In Europe, the newsletters from India ordinarily went through Portugal to Rome and then to the other Jesuit stations on the Continent. The fathers in Germany were especially eager to have the edifying letters translated into Latin and printed in books. Jeronimo Nadal, for example, made such a request because he asserted, ". . . when going into Germany I could do great things with these letters."[323] The letters from India, or extracts therefrom, were sent to Brazil and some of those from America were also relayed to Goa, Malacca, and Japan.[324]

The letters from the East fall readily into five categories. Those separate sheets (*hijuelas*) intended for the superiors were more detailed and reliable than the other types, even though the writers at times were inclined to prepare them as apologies designed to justify their policies and actions. Letters directed to the Society in general tended to be hortatory in tone, in order to stimulate greater concern among the brothers in Europe for the enterprise in Asia. Accounts prepared for public distribution were ordinarily couched in restrained language and were carefully checked and censored before being released for circulation or publication. Besides these, many letters were addressed by the missionaries to personal friends, both within the Society and outside it. These personal

---

[318] Lisbon, March 17, 1554, in *Epistolae mixtae ex variis Europae locis ab anno 1537 ad 1556 scriptae* (5 vols.; Rome, 1898–1910), IV, 110.

[319] Coimbra collections, including the first one of 1552 and this more extensive one of 1555, were translated into Spanish to make them more generally readable. This book, which contains two letters from Goa and two from Malacca, as well as a short piece synthesizing the available information on China, was called *Copia de unas cartas de algunos padres y hermanos de la Compania.* . . .

[320] Wicki (ed.), *op. cit.* (n. 72), IV, 25*, n. 8.

[321] F. Serafim Leite (ed.), *Monumenta Brasiliae* (4 vols.; Rome, 1956–60), I, 57–58.

[322] L. Henriques to Francisco de Borja, Lisbon, July 30, 1561, text in *ibid.*; also see *ibid.*, IV, 348. Also see Wicki (ed.), *op. cit.* (n. 72), II, 488.

[323] Leite (ed.), *op. cit.* (n. 321), I, 59.

[324] See *ibid.*, IV, 69; and Wicki (ed.), *op. cit.* (n. 72), II, 488.

epistles deal much more than the others with the individual reactions of the writers to the new environment. Finally, the Jesuit missionaries sometimes prepared "allied documents," such as detailed reports on particular tribes, the history of a Jesuit establishment in Asia, and highly informative chronicles relating the story of Jesuit enterprise as seen by men in the field.[325]

During the first generation of the mission's activity in Asia, letters of all of the above types were prepared by a number of different people in each station. As a result, the letters, even those intended for superiors, were often contradictory, unrelated to each other, and misleading. Once the early letters accumulated and circulated in Europe, attacks on their reliability came from both inside and outside the Society.[326] In a letter of 1566 to the General from Lisbon, Father Leão Henriques remarked:

The letters from India, or some of them, were printed in Portugal, in Spain, and in Italy, and, in each place, different things were left out and different corrections made, so some people, especially those from outside the Company, who noticed this, became disenchanted and acquired a poor opinion of the letters, considering them to be impostures.[327]

Valignano, after his own disillusioning experience with the letters, determined to establish the practice of having a responsible member prepare a co-ordinated and coherent annual report of activities at his station. After 1581 these "true" annual letters, in contrast to the discrete letters sent annually with the fleet to Portugal, were published in Europe separately as the official statement of the mission's progress. Hardly a year passed thereafter when the presses in Europe were not busily turning out copies of these official reports. Once publication of the *Litterae annuae* became an established practice, they generally appeared first in Latin versions, and then in numerous European vernaculars.

The first collection in book form (to be distinguished from the broadsides previously published) of "Indian letters" appeared in Italian at Rome in 1552.[328] The following year a similar collection was issued in the Eternal City in which notice of Japan was taken for the first time. Although both these publications stressed in their titles the *cose mirabili* of foreign lands, the curiosity of their readers for a detailed knowledge of Asia, it appears, was not satisfied. Loyola in a letter of February 24, 1554, instructed Father Gaspar Barzaeus in Goa as follows:

Some leading figures who in this city [Rome] read with much edification to themselves the letters from India are wont to desire, and they request me repeatedly, that something should be written regarding the cosmography of these regions where ours [members of the Society of Jesus] live. They want to know, for instant, how long are the days of summer and of winter; when summer begins; whether the shadows move towards the left

---

[325] See below, p. 327 and above, pp. 256–61.

[326] See the quotation in Correia-Afonso, *op. cit.* (n. 310), p. 15, n. 18.

[327] Leite (ed.), *op. cit.* (n. 321), I, 58.

[328] *Avisi particolari delle Indie di Portugallo Riceuuti in Questi doi anni del 1551 & 1552 da li Reuerendi Padri de la cõpagnia de Iesu doue fra molto cose mirabili si uede delli Paesi, delle genti, e costumi loro & la grande cõuersione di molti populi, che cominciano a ricevere il lume della sãta fede & Relligione Christiana.*

or towards the right. Finally, if there are other things that may seem extraordinary, let them be noted, for instance, details about animals and plants that either are not known at all, or not of such a size, etc. And this news—sauce for the taste of a certain curiosity that is not evil and is wont to be found among men—may come in the same letters or in other letters separately.[329]

The series of letterbooks in Italian translation (the letters usually were written in Portuguese or Spanish) was continued in 1556, 1557, and 1558 with the additional volumes issuing from the press of the Jesuit House of the Professed in Rome. Similar collections were published from 1559 to 1568 by the Tramezzino press at Venice. Such Italian translations, obviously intended for propaganda purposes, were apparently sold at nominal prices. Some were circulated free of charge, in order to obtain the widest publicity possible. These compendiums were as a rule quickly republished by other printers in Italy. And it was not long before some of them were translated into the various European languages and published in the northern cities of Europe. Each succeeding miscellany of the Italian series was larger than its predecessors, inasmuch as the most important letters were reprinted each time as background to the letters most recently received. Unfortunately for their readers, the collections issued originally in Italy suffered grievously from poor translating, censorship, and an excess of zeal in reporting the initial success of the mission. The Jesuits apparently never lost the belief, expressed originally in the introduction to the first of the Italian series, that the church might offset its losses to the Reformation in Europe by converting large numbers of heathens in the overseas world. Apparently they also hoped to impress upon Catholics and Protestants alike in the regions north of the Alps that Catholicism was still a dynamic and expanding faith.

In 1555 Fathers Peter Canisius and Jeronimo Nadal began to call for carefully translated Latin editions that could readily be circulated in northern Europe without undergoing further translation.[330] It was not, however, until 1563 that a Latin compilation first appeared, the *Epistolae indicae . . .*, numbering just ninety-six pages, which was issued with imperial privilege by Sebald Meyer, a printer of the Jesuit press at Dillingen. Three years later, Johannes Rutilius, a non-Jesuit of Brabant, published a similar but unofficial collection at Louvain.[331] This unauthorized book, particularly since it was widely circulated, exasperated the Jesuits by its arbitrary excisions and fictitious additions to the reports of the missionaries. Private publishers like Rutilius were increasingly to find that printing the Jesuit letters could be a rewarding trade. Some of the editions were advertised as "very profitable and entertaining reading," and certain circumspect publishers even copyrighted some of the collections. In 1590 the Plantin press in Antwerp published a collection of letters in 856 copies.[332] Similar

---

[329] As quoted in Correia-Afonso, *op. cit.* (n. 310), p. 14.

[330] Wicki, *op. cit.* (n. 102), p. 30*, n. 1. Latin was used increasingly in the sixteenth century by the letter-writers in India. See Correia-Afonso, *op. cit.* (n. 310), p. 17.

[331] Entitled *Epistolae Indicae de stupendis et praeclaris rebus. . . .* For further details and contents see Maggs Bros., *Bibliotheca Asiatica*, No. 452 (1924), Pt. I, p. 22; also Laures, *op. cit.* (n. 257), p. 170.

[332] G. Atkinson, *op. cit.* (n. 167), pp. 282–83.

collections, presumably in similar numbers, regularly poured off other leading presses in Venice, Cologne, Paris, Rome, Seville, Dillingen, Ingolstadt, Brescia, Munich, Evora, Lisbon, Naples, Florence, and Madrid. One collection was even translated into Czech in 1583.[333]

The authorized collections of Jesuit letters published in the Iberian states, especially those emanating from Coimbra, often paralleled in date of publication and duplicated in contents the compendia issued in Italy and elsewhere in Europe. For example, a small assortment of "Indian letters" was published in Spanish at Coimbra in 1552, the date of the first collection issued in Rome. Subsequent Iberian publications and reprintings coincided similarly with those being issued elsewhere. On the whole, the Iberian collections, perhaps because most of the letters were written in Spanish and Portuguese, give more accurate renditions of the originals than do the Italian translations. And, in general, they seem not to be so heavily censored as those which came through Rome. But the Portuguese and Spanish collections were not nearly so well known in Europe generally and were apparently translated only rarely. Most of the translations made in northern Europe were from the books issued in Italy.

The size of the individual volumes was generally maintained over the latter half of the century, all but the earliest ones being every bit as lengthy, though not as numerous, as those appearing toward its end. An exception came in the decade after 1575, when translations in handy sizes were made up to supply the demand for news. An impressive German collection of 1593 anticipated by six years the monumental *Cartas* (Letters) of Evora published in 1598. Meanwhile the Imperial Printer, Johannes Albin, entered the field with an extraordinary series of publications translated from Italian into Latin.[334] The foremost among the editors and translators of these commercially published works was Gasparo Spitelli, the Society's archivist and secretary to the Father General. Private individuals also lent their support to the proliferation of Jesuit literature on Asia by defraying the publication costs from time to time. Even though the annual letters were published far and wide, enterprising printers continued throughout the latter half of the century to publish the letters of individual missionaries to their friends in Europe.

The earliest collectors made no effort to publish separately the letters from the various mission stations. It was not long, however, before the letters from Japan began to win a special place for themselves in the series of letterbooks emanating from Italy and Iberia. The appearance of the "Japan letters" in separate collections probably is related to the striking decline in letters from India which began in the early 1560's.[335] The first collection devoted exclusively to letters from Japan appeared at Coimbra in 1565, and it became the model for the series of *Cartas* which was published at irregular intervals until the appearance at Evora

333 Streit, *op. cit.* (n. 242), IV, 436.
334 For a list see Josef Benzirg, "Johann Albin zu Mainz als Reichsdrucker, 1598–1620," *Gutenberg Jahrbuch 1950* (Mainz, 1950), pp. 211–12.
335 See below, p. 446.

in 1598 of the monumental two-volume set.[336] Italian collections devoted exclusively to letters from Japan began to be published by Zanetti in Rome in 1578.[337] When the "true" annual letters began to be published in 1581, the letters originating in Japan increasingly came to be looked upon as model reports.[338]

The superior quality of the letters from Japan can probably be attributed to the fact that most of them were written by Luis Fróis, one of the ablest observers and chroniclers ever to be associated with the Society. As a rule the runs of letters are continuous from particular stations in the East for periods when the missions there enjoyed success. When trouble occurred, as in India after 1560 or in the Moluccas after 1570, the letters decrease sharply in number and shrink in size. It is owing to the prominence of the letters from Japan that many later writers refer to the Jesuit letters as "Japan letters" rather than "Indian letters." The East Indies and southeastern Asia also came into the letters regularly, even though they are not commonly called "East Indian letters." But neither China, where admission to the mainland on a permanent basis was achieved only in 1583, nor the Philippine Islands, where the other Orders dominated missionary endeavors, are treated by the Jesuit correspondents in anything like the detail given to the other areas.

The letters, because they appeared in hundreds of compilations of various kinds, were never completely satisfying to Europeans who desired information on the East in a more compact form and in a more coherent presentation. As an example of how complicated it was (and is) to obtain a clear view of Asia from the Jesuit letters alone, examine the publication history of Xavier's letters from India during the sixteenth century. Thirty-two of his letters dated from India are still extant. Eleven of these were first published at intervals between 1545 and 1570. Just four of these were printed more than once: his two missives of 1542 (printed in 1545 in two editions) and two others of 1549 (first printed in 1569 and 1570). The rest of his letters[339] were published for the first time in the collection of H. Tursellinus, *Francisci Xaverii epistolarum libri quatuour* (Rome, 1596).[340] It can readily be observed that Europe learned through print but little about India from Xavier before 1570 and nothing thereafter until 1596. To make matters even worse, the letters published before 1596 were often truncated by censors or rewritten by stylists. Tursellinus himself had no hesitation in transforming Xavier's reportorial, hurried sentences into polished Latin periods. The Xavier letters, like those of his successors, obviously cannot be relied upon to give a comprehensive picture of affairs in the various parts of Asia. They are most effectively used as sources for discrete data and as checks upon the writers of chronicles and narratives both in Europe and the East.

---

[336] For further details see below, p. 676.
[337] See below, p. 675.
[338] Correia-Afonso, *op. cit.* (n. 310), p. 17.
[339] See table in Schurhammer and Wicki (eds.), *op. cit.* (n. 40), I, 224.
[340] On Tursellinus, see below, p. 327.

The Christian Mission

How can the printed newsletters be used by interested scholars as sources for Asian history and for Europe's awakening to the East? To find this out, several roads lie open. The most obvious one is to study the letterbooks themselves; however, this is not easy since they are rare and, when available, are likely to be found in widely separated repositories. A listing of the letters contained in all the major collections except one[341] can be found in R. Streit, *Bibliotheca Missionum* (Aachen, 1928), Volume IV. A definitive collection of the Xavier letters has been published by Georg Schurhammer and Josef Wicki, two devoted scholars of the Society. Because of the inaccessibility of the original letters and compilations, Anton Eglauer at the end of the eighteenth century issued a series of volumes in which many of the sixteenth-century letters were extracted from several of the early compendiums in Italian, Latin, and German. Eglauer arranged them in chronological order by region (East Indies and Japan) and translated them, without critical examination, into German.[342] The German compiler made no use whatsoever of the Spanish or Portuguese collections, though he knew of the works of Barros and Osorius. In recent years excellent annotated editions of the extant letters (published and unpublished) by the successors of Xavier have been issued by the Society. Josef Wicki, for example, has compiled and published with splendid documentation in seven large volumes all the available letters written between 1540 and 1569 in his *Documenta Indica* (Rome, 1948–62). In Lisbon, meanwhile, Father A. da Silva Rego has so far issued twelve volumes of his massive *Documentação para história das missões do padroado português do Oriente* (1947–60), which now covers the years to 1573 and includes in its pages a number of Jesuit letters and valuable ancillary documents. It is from these published collections, rather than from the letterbooks themselves, that the modern scholar can most effectively make use of the Jesuit correspondence.

The extant corpus of Jesuit letters is not of equal value for the various parts of Asia. It is likewise much better for some epochs than for others. While printed collections of letters appeared in Europe almost annually from 1552 to 1571, a noticeable decline in the number of individual letters from India set in after 1560.[343] This decline perhaps reflects the readjustments in the missionizing of India as forcible mass conversions become more common, the serious military challenge posed by the Moors as they revived their attack on Portuguese India, and the greater attention being directed to the Far East. In Europe a sharp

341 The sole exception, so far as I know, is the Spanish edition published at Coimbra in 1565 under the title *Copia de las cartas.* . . . A listing of its contents taken from the copy in the National Library at Madrid is to be found in Zoe Swecker, "The Early Iberian Accounts of the Far East, 1550–1600" (Ph.D. dissertation, University of Chicago, 1960), pp. 289–90. I have seen this same volume in the National Library at Lisbon, but it is somewhat mutilated. While Streit apparently had not seen this volume, he lists most of the letters included in it under the year in which they were written.

342 The general title is *Die Missionsgeschichte späterer Zeiten; oder, Gesammelte Briefe der katholischen Missionäre aus allen Theilen der Welt*. His compilation of "Indian" and "Japan" letters have particular value for us because Eglauer often reproduced the letters verbatim from the printed letterbooks.

343 Observe that in Vols. V (letters of 1561–63) and VI (letters of 1563–66) of Wicki (ed.), *op. cit.* (n. 72), most of the letters were not published in the sixteenth century.

break likewise occurs in the total number of letterbooks published in the decade after 1571. This decrease may be a reflection of the dissatisfaction felt in the Society and among its friends with the earlier publications. Or it might be related to the contemporary effort that General Mercurian was making to consolidate the Jesuit position in Europe itself, after the momentous ecclesiastical decisions of the Council of Trent. The decline in both individual letters written from the field and in letterbooks published in Europe can possibly be attributed also to the preoccupation of the Portuguese crown with the shaky financial structure of the spice monopoly, with wars in Africa, and with the growing seriousness of the succession issue in Iberia.

Political events in Europe and reform of the Jesuit system of publishing the letters show a remarkable coincidence in terms of dates. Philip II came to the Portuguese throne in 1581, the very year in which the first of the official annual letter collections appeared in Rome. Since the official publications were carefully compiled, edited, and censored, they are less informative than both the earlier authorized collections and the unofficial compilations which continued to come off the presses in other printing centers of Europe. The affairs of India receive progressively less attention after 1570, in both the official and the unofficial collections, as the more spectacular triumphs in Japan, China, and the Philippines are constantly given greater space. The sole exception to this trend comes during the last two decades when the story of the penetration of the Mughul empire by the three Jesuit missions to Akbar is broadcast far and wide as a great Jesuit triumph.

From what has been observed about the publication history of the letterbooks, it seems clear that the interested reader in Europe could draw from them at best an episodic view of what Asia was like and how the Europeans were faring there. Only occasionally were separate collections of "Indian letters" published comparable to the weighty and comprehensive tones of "Japan letters" which appeared in the last generation of the century. Nor did India ever have a single spokesman of the stature of Fróis, the great interpreter of Japan to Europe.[344] Among the immediate successors of Xavier, the most popular writers of letters about India were Barzaeus, Henrique Henriques, and Fróis himself before his departure for Japan. Though Valignano was extremely well informed about all the mission stations in the various parts of Asia, only a few of his letters appeared in print. What was requested increasingly as time went on was a continuous narrative which would put the activities of the missionaries into a total perspective and give both the Society and its friends in Europe a summary history of the mission in Asia.

Influential Jesuits began to write to Rome as early as the 1550's and 1560's asking that an official synthesis of the letters be prepared by a qualified member

---

[344] Of Fróis, while in India, Quadros wrote in a confidential report of 1559 to General Lainez (Wicki [ed.], *op. cit.* [n. 72], IV, 403): "physically fit and healthy, a good man but not religious, makes too many jokes, attends his classes and understands them well, he may make a graceful preacher, he is very capable at every kind of secular task, seems to be firm in his vocation."

of the Society.[345] In part the Jesuits were motivated by the fear that if they failed to provide such a history themselves, others would do it for them. Ultimately they selected a young novice and skilled Latinist and Humanist, G. P. Maffei, to prepare an official history of the mission in Asia based on the letters from the East and whatever other sources might be available to him. Maffei's first publication in 1571, a date which coincides with the decline in the publication of the letterbooks, was not up to expectations. It was a translation into Latin of a previously unpublished Portuguese manuscript, Manuel da Costa's *Historia dos missiones do Oriente até o anno de 1568*, that had been sent to Maffei in Rome. A Jesuit missiologist and bibliographer, Da Costa taught at Coimbra where most of the Jesuit letters were available in uncensored form. Maffei, in the introduction to his Latin version, *Rerum a Societate Jesu in Oriente gestarum commentarius* (Dillingen, 1571), congratulates Da Costa on his effort in bringing the substance of these letters together into a short commentary. Maffei also added, as an appendix to his translation of Da Costa, letters from Japan in Latin translation and in abridged form. This appendix is entitled *De Japonicis rebus epistolarum libri IV*.

Maffei's Latin version of Da Costa's work was immediately denounced on all sides as highly unreliable. Da Costa himself, while not blaming Maffei directly, commented bitterly: "So many lies put together would distress even a man who prided himself on them. . . ."[346] Da Costa alleged that in Rome "strange dissections" had been made and unwarranted inferences written into his book. The Latin version of his work, he asserted, is full of "errors and lies." In 1575, Da Costa's book, as issued by Maffei, was sent to India for criticism. Although a detailed reply was not immediately forthcoming from the East, Matteo Ricci wrote from India in 1580: "Know that the commentary and the Indian and Japanese letters are full of very evident errors."[347] The blame for the distortions, it was alleged, had to be placed mainly upon the Roman censors who introduced major blunders into the work through their clumsy editing and rewriting efforts.[348] Nevertheless, Maffei's first work appeared in several more Latin editions.[349] In 1571, the year of its original publication, it was translated into French by E. Auger and published at Lyons.[350] And it was known to Richard Willes, the editor of the *History of Travayle* (1577), who used it in the preparation of his discussion "Of the Island Giapan."[351] In 1586, Maffei's book was translated into German by J. C. Götzen.

---

345 Wicki (ed.), *op. cit.* (n. 102), pp. 31*–32*.

346 Letter of Da Costa reproduced in *ibid.*, pp. 486–89.

347 As quoted in G. Schurhammer, "Xaveriusforschung im 16. Jahrhundert . . .," *Zeitschrift für Missionswissenschaft*, XII (1922), 148.

348 See Correia-Afonso, *op. cit.* (n. 310), pp. 486–89.

349 C. Sommervogel, *Bibliothèque de la Compagnie de Jésus* (Paris, 1894), Vol. V, col. 295, notes that a Czech translation presumably appeared in 1573. I have found no other record of this work.

350 Entitled *Histoire des choses memorables sur le faict de la religion Chrestienne dictées et executées aux pays et royaumes des Indes Orientales*.

351 For a modern version of this material see M. Parke-Smith (ed.), *England and Japan* (Kobe, 1928).

While Maffei's first undertaking was being distributed, republished, translated, and criticized, the young Humanist was sent in 1578 to the Iberian Peninsula to gather materials for a general Latin history of Jesuit activities in the East.[352] Here he received the fullest co-operation of the authorities and obtained permission to use the state archives in Lisbon. Long extracts were made for him in Lisbon of the reports of the viceroys and of others who had worked for the Portuguese crown. He consulted the Jesuit collections at Coimbra and Evora. He used the published works of A. Galvão, F. Lopes de Castanheda, J. de Barros, and Damião de Góis. He interviewed H. Osorius, Braz de Albuquerque (who edited his father's *Cartas*), and Antonio Pinheiro (archivist and chronicler). And in company with Father Gaspard Gonçalves he interviewed Fernão Mendes Pinto in October, 1582, just nine months before the great adventurer's death.[353] Meanwhile, extracts were being made for him in Rome of materials housed there in the Jesuit archives. He also had at his disposal the *Chronicon* of Polanco, a yearly record of the state of Jesuit missions which the great secretary compiled until his death. At Maffei's request Fróis in Japan was assigned the task in 1579 of compiling a history of the Christian church in Japan.[354] Valignano himself was greatly interested in Maffei's project and sought to obtain as much digested material for him as possible. In 1584 Maffei returned to Rome and was there when the Japanese mission visited the Eternal City in 1585.[355] He was in the company of the Japanese legates and probably had an opportunity to interview them and their knowledgeable interpreter, Father Mesquita. The first part of Valignano's *Historia del principio y progresso de la Compania de Jesus en las Indias Orientales* (1542–64) arrived in Europe with the mission from Japan, and Maffei freely drew upon it for many of his descriptions.[356]

Maffei's principal work was published at Florence in 1588 under the title *Historiarum Indicarum libri XVI*. Based on primary materials and written in elegant Latin, it received an enthusiastic reception all over Europe. The way had been prepared for its appearance by the enthusiasm aroused by the Japanese embassy. Like Mendoza's book on China,[357] it hit the market when curiosity about the Far East was at its height. Before the end of the sixteenth century, it was reissued in Latin at Venice (1588), Lyons (1589), Bergamo (1590),[358] and Cologne (1589, 1590, and 1593).[359] Translations in Italian were published

---

[352] Filippo Sassetti, the Florentine Humanist, reports that Maffei was active in Lisbon during 1583, the year when Sassetti embarked for the East. Sassetti also informed his Florentine friends that they need only wait for Maffei's book to have available a more satisfactory account of the East than Barros had produced. Of his Latin, Sassetti comments that Maffei has a *bellissimo stile*. See E. Marcucci (ed.), *Lettere edite e inedite di Filippo Sassetti* (Florence, 1855), pp. 418–19.

[353] See Schurhammer, *loc. cit.* (n. 347), p. 140. The Gonsalves mentioned here is the same person who in 1585 gave the oration at the public consistory held in Rome in honor of the Japanese legates. See below, p. 696.

[354] See below, p. 686.

[355] See below, p. 696.

[356] See Wicki, *op. cit.* (n. 102), p. 101.

[357] See below, pp. 743–44.

[358] This was Maffei's home town and so his portrait was added to the work.

[359] A map was added to this edition. See *Alt-Japan-Katalog*, p. 214.

in 1589 at both Florence and Venice. So far as is known, it did not appear in French until 1604 and no translations in either German or English have ever been printed. To date the *Historiarum* has been reissued at least twenty-six times.[360] Unlike many of the letters from the East, Maffei's work is couched in careful language and rhetorical flourishes are notably few. Even Valignano, who had warned that Maffei's work should not be published until it had been seen in the East, appeared to be happy with his discussion of Japan. In 1603, the Jesuit Visitor wrote from Macao: "Of all those who have so far written about Japan, none has done it with greater precision or in better order than Father G. P. Maffei."[361]

Most of Maffei's work is concerned with the Portuguese conquests and the Jesuit stations in India, the East Indies, and the region of the Arabian Sea to about 1557. The first five books appear to follow rather closely the model of Barros. Book VI, dealing with China, like Book XII, which is mainly concerned with Japan, is heavily indebted to Valignano's account of those countries. The appendixes of letters which take up about one-third of the book's nine hundred pages were almost all written either about or from Japan in the years between 1549 and 1574. While reproducing here many of the same letters which he had earlier appended to his translation of Da Costa's book, Maffei appears to have exercised greater care in the selections which he made for this second compendium. Furthermore, this second effort did not suffer from the excisions and revisions of the Roman censors. In fact, it is worth observing that it originally appeared in Florence, and that none of the subsequent editions was produced in Rome.

Maffei's work is written with probity as well as elegance, for the Jesuit Humanist was writing at a time when the "Indian letters" were being attacked for their falsities and exaggerations by leading figures in the Society both in Europe and India. It was prepared in the midst of a flurry of Jesuit activity which revolved about the related efforts of the young Society to prepare a history of its activities and the biographies of its great founders: Loyola and Xavier. Polanco's manuscript *Chronicon*, which gave year-by-year summaries of the activities of all the houses and missions of the Society formed the working base for the researchers. After Polanco's death in 1576, Maffei and others began to work on separate aspects of the Society's historical and biographical projects.[362] The biographies were given meticulous attention because they were to be the foundation of the Society's case for the canonizations of Loyola and Xavier. Pedro de Ribadeneira's life of Loyola first appeared in print in 1583 and the founder of the Society was canonized in 1622. The preparation of a Xavier biography as a prelude to his elevation to sainthood is a parallel story, but with the difference that it naturally relates much more to affairs in India and farther East.

---

[360] Based upon an independent account of editions cited in *ibid.*, pp. 214–19. Schurhammer, *loc. cit.* (n. 347), p. 158, mentions twenty-three separate issues.

[361] As quoted in Schurhammer, *loc. cit.* (n. 347), p. 163.

[362] *Ibid.*, pp. 142–43.

The first solid confirmation of Xavier's death reached Europe in 1555, and the fleet of the following year carried instructions from King John III to his viceroy to collect immediately all eyewitness accounts of the life, works, deeds, and miracles performed by Xavier in the East and to forward sworn statements about them to Lisbon by three different routes.[363] Testimonials from sixty-three Portuguese witnesses who had known Xavier over a long period were compiled by the secular authorities in India during 1556–57 and dispatched to Europe. Upon receipt of the first batch of eyewitness accounts, King John began to urge Xavier's canonization on the papacy and requested permission even at this early date to celebrate Xavier's Feast Day. With the king's death in 1558, the pressure from Lisbon ceased but not before a substantial amount of worthwhile material on Xavier's activities in the East had been assembled and made potentially available both for his personal biography and for the history of the Society. In the meantime the canonization proposal was kept alive by repeated appeals to the papacy, one of the most dramatic being the petition of the Japanese ambassadors in 1585.[364]

Work on the biography of Xavier was temporarily postponed by the attention which the Jesuits focused from 1567 to 1583 on readying De Ribadeneira's *Loyola* for publication and general distribution. Maffei, however, devoted a measure of his attention to Xavier while collecting information for his Latin history. During his researches a number of the Jesuits in the East began to verify the data on Xavier's life already assembled. As a result of their work, many miraculous acts attributed to Xavier were either completely discounted or put into a more reasonable perspective. Manuel Teixeira, a pioneer member of the Indian mission, was meanwhile delegated to collect Xavier's letters and to write his biography from India. Completed in manuscript in 1580, Teixeira's biography was thereafter circulated and corrected within the Society in Europe and became, along with the first part of Valignano's history, the basis for the published biographies which began to appear near the end of the century.[365]

The first full-scale biography of Xavier was prepared by Horatio Tursellinus and was printed in Latin at Rome in 1594. The first edition was full of misprints, but was corrected, revised, and reissued in 1596, with a comprehensive collection of Xavier letters added to it. Although Tursellinus accepted uncritically his eyewitness sources and the romanticized "history" of Fernão Mendes Pinto, his clear and concise biography of Xavier is a masterpiece which compares favorably with Ribadeneira's *Loyola*. Many later biographies of Xavier were steps backward in objectivity.[366] Shortly after Tursellinus' death in 1599, the Portuguese biography by João de Lucena appeared at Lisbon (1600)[367] and this attempted more than its predecessor to place Xavier in the historical setting

---

[363] *Ibid.*, p. 133.
[364] See below, p. 695.
[365] Schurhammer, *loc. cit.* (n. 347), pp. 150–59.
[366] Cf. *ibid.*, p. 160.
[367] *Historia da vida do padre Francisco de Xavier.*

in which he lived and worked. A third biography by Pedro de Ribadeneira, Loyola's biographer, appeared in Spanish at Madrid (1601), and it preserved many of the holy legends which the earlier biographers had omitted and so contributed to the persistent growth of reputedly miraculous deeds which were to remain a part of the Xavier legend for a long time to come. Like Loyola, Xavier was canonized in 1622 by Pope Gregory XV and was later designated patron saint of India and the East by Pope Benedict XIV.[368]

The last general work of Jesuit historiography to concern us is Luis de Guzman's two-volume *Historia de las missiones que han hecho los religiosos de la Compañia de Iesus, para predicar el Sancto Euangelio en la India Oriental, y en los Reynos de la China y Iapon* (Alcalá, 1601).[369] Little is known of Guzman's life and career. He seems to have spent most of his life (1544–1605) in Spain acting as rector in several Jesuit colleges and as provincial in Andalusia and Toledo. In his official capacity he obviously had access to the Jesuit letters which poured into Spain throughout the latter half of the century. He seems also to have used the *Cartas* of 1575 and 1598,[370] and Valignano's manuscript *Historia*[371] as well as other materials. Since the Spanish archives of the Jesuits have been lost, Guzman's work is also important for the primary materials it contains, particularly on the last decade of the century.

Guzman traces the history of Jesuit activities in the East from Xavier's day down almost to the date of his own publication. The Spanish Jesuit gives very little space to India and the East Indies. A sizable section on China (Book IV) is followed by a lengthy account of affairs in Japan that extends over more than half of the total number of pages in both volumes. Unlike Maffei, Guzman does not present the Jesuit enterprise in strictly chronological order. His chapters deal with the particular regions first and then with the activities of the Jesuits in them. He also makes an effort to relate the regions to each other and is much more conscious than Maffei of their independent traditions. Unlike both Valignano and Maffei, he is not so interested in comparing and contrasting Asia with Europe for the edification of the latter. His narrative is simple, straightforward, and relatively free from verbosity and sermonizing.

The Christian mission, whatever else it was, must certainly be considered one of the three main channels by which Europe received its lasting impressions of Asia. Ecclesiastics from the Iberian states and Italy dominated Christian affairs in the East, and even a few northern European churchmen worked within the *padroado*. The missionaries, while closely associated with secular affairs, added a dimension of their own to the European adventure in the East. While some of the missionaries were as bigoted as any of the administrators, the tendency of the Jesuits under the guidance of Valignano was to avoid cultural antagonism

---

[368] For the apotheosis of Xavier see Brodrick, *op. cit.* (n. 58) pp. 527–38.
[369] There is also a one-volume reprint published at Bilbao in 1891.
[370] See below, pp. 675–76.
[371] Wicki, *op. cit.* (n. 102), p. 103; and see also José Luiz Alvarez-Taladriz (ed.), *op. cit.* (n. 119).

and religious hostility and finally to move toward a policy of accommodation with the great cultures of Japan, China, and India. The evolution of the Valignano program was challenged in the Far East by the doctrine of direct action advocated by the missionaries and the Spanish in the Philippines. This movement based on force was abruptly checked when it was rejected by the policy-makers of church and state in Europe. The program of accommodation, which had the sanction of the governors of church and state in Europe, finally won the day in China and northern India. In Japan the fight between the proponents of force and those who believed in peaceful penetration continued to 1600.

News of the victories, defeats, and conflicts of the missionaries in the field was relayed to Europe through the official reports of both the secular and ecclesiastical administrators. The return of missionaries to Europe from Asia was not a particularly significant channel of communication unless they were officially dispatched from the field to report to their superiors in Europe. The greatest missionaries in Asia (Xavier, Fróis, Valignano, and Ricci) as well as many lesser lights died in the field without ever having returned to Europe. Consequently their experiences and their knowledge of the East had to be relayed to Europe through their own writings and the reports of others. Fortunately for the modern scholar, the Society of Jesus has preserved in its archives and publications an extensive documentation of the heroic missionary enterprise which the Catholic church undertook in the East.

The writings of the missionaries in the field, in contrast to those of the European secular authors, are generally very little concerned with matters relating to trade. They do recount the military activities of the secular arm, since conquest was often of either immediate or potential importance to the spread of the gospel. The missionaries are naturally more interested in native religious beliefs and writings than the merchants and administrators. On several occasions when the missionaries penetrated to places inaccessible to the secular writers, their comments are far more profound and authoritative than those to be found in other European sources. The authoritative writings of Henrique Henriques for the Fishery Coast, Fróis on Japan, Valignano on China, and Jerome Xavier on the realm of Akbar are not matched by any secular authors. Because a number of the missions were located in territories far removed from the Portuguese footholds, the missionaries were required to learn the languages and live according to the customs of the region in which they worked. It was these people especially who first began to enter into Asian life. Many of the missionaries (especially Valignano) who were confined to the ports under Portuguese control were likewise convinced of the need to penetrate the native cultures, even though they themselves were not in a position to do so. The fact is that the Jesuits had become certain by the end of the sixteenth century that cultural affiliation was an indispensable first step if the Christians were to win acceptance among Asian peoples of high culture. The Jesuits, as revealed in their writings, nonetheless retained conversion as their ultimate goal, and this objective should never be lost sight of in using their writings as historical sources.

The Jesuit letters and general histories were not the only missionary works of significance to appear during the sixteenth century. The other Orders, as we have seen, were active in both the Portuguese and Spanish empires of the East. It is, however, mainly from the Jesuit writings that we learn about Christian activities, for none of the other Orders had a system of regular reporting and publishing to compare with the Jesuit system. This is not to say that the other Orders were completely inarticulate about the opening of Asia, or that they contributed nothing to Europe's understanding of it. Particularly notable were the contributions that writers of the other Orders made to the accumulation and dissemination of knowledge about China. The Portuguese Dominican Gaspar da Cruz published in 1569 the first European book devoted exclusively to China. The Spanish Augustinian Juan González de Mendoza published in 1585 the most comprehensive and popular book on Ming China to appear in Europe. While the Jesuits ordinarily did not publish accounts restricted to one nation or one mission, the Italian Jesuit Giovanni Battista Peruschi had a book printed in 1597 which summarized what was known about Akbar's realm.[372] The books on particular nations, as distinct from the general histories of missionary activity in the East, will be discussed in the chapters which follow as we take up the individual countries. We will likewise leave for discussion in the following chapters those books which are centered on other regions but which contain relevant and important materials on Asia.

For certain segments of Asian history in the sixteenth century, the Jesuit letters are indispensable as sources. They are especially valuable as aides in the reconstruction of Japanese history for the vital period of its unification under Nobunaga and Hideyoshi. For the other areas of the East they are far less comprehensive, accurate, and detailed. On India, Ceylon, and the Moluccas they provide precise data, statistics,[373] and dates on places and periods for which other sources are either non-existent or maddeningly unconcerned with exact chronology. If used along with Muslim (especially Persian and Arabic) sources, the Jesuit materials on south Asia and the Spiceries provide checks as well as additional material. For China the published Jesuit materials, in contrast to the unpublished Jesuit writings and the books of Cruz and Mendoza, are disappointingly fragmentary and unenlightening. Except for a few isolated exceptions, the Jesuit materials have almost no value for students of the countries of continental southeast Asia. In the case of countries for which they are the most valuable (Japan, India, Ceylon, and the Spiceries), their contributions are mainly limited to the events of the latter half of the sixteenth century. Even for this fifty-year period they are far from continuous, except perhaps in the instance of Japan. On India, they are particularly valuable for the periods from

---

[372] For details see below, pp. 452–53.

[373] As a general rule, one must be careful in using the statistics from the Jesuit reports. Round numbers are usually considered to be satisfactory and often, especially when referring to converts, the Jesuits inflate the numbers substantially. See A. Brou, S.J., "Les statistiques dans les anciennes missions," *Revue d'histoire des missions*, September, 1929, pp. 361–84.

1542 to 1560 and from 1582 to 1600. For the Spiceries they are of uneven and fluctuating worth for the entire period from 1545 to 1574.

The contribution of the published missionary writings to Europe's awakening consciousness of the East is likewise uneven though somewhat less episodic. The general histories (by Maffei and Guzman), as distinct from the letterbooks, give a comprehensive account of the Jesuit mission in the East from the beginnings through most of the sixteenth century. The published compilations of letters from the field divide roughly into three periods: the first impressions of 1545 to 1570; the sporadic publication mainly of reprints and "Japan letters" of the 1570's; and the period of more careful supervision of the latter years of the century, beginning with the issuance in 1581 of the "true" annual letters as official compilations. It should be recalled, however, that the diffusion of the *unpublished* letters and reports from the field, systematically carried out as it was by the Jesuits, likewise contributed materially to Europe's growing stock of information. But it is practically impossible to determine just how much impact the circulation of these unpublished writings had upon the European public. It is clear, however, that parts of Valignano's unpublished *Historia* were incorporated into a number of the published histories. The same assertion would likewise hold good, it seems certain, for a number of the other documents prepared in the field which went unprinted themselves in the sixteenth century. In what follows we confine our conclusions to the materials *actually published* in the sixteenth century. Even from this arbitrarily limited base, we can see clearly that during the latter half of the sixteenth century the missionary materials added significantly to the broadening and deepening of Europe's understanding of Asia.

*Four Images
and
a Composite Picture*

Introduction

Asia's image, as it gradually evolved in Europe during the sixteenth century, retained shadings from the past but became sharper and more definite in its outlines and divisions. The vague geographical terms inherited from the Ptolemaic and medieval traditions (India before and beyond the Ganges, Further India, and Cathay) were gradually replaced in Europe by names similar to those then in use in Asia itself. India, Southeast Asia, Japan, and China were recognized for the first time as being distinct and different parts of Asia, and Europeans came to think of them along roughly the same lines that we do today. And, as Europeans of the sixteenth century came to understand that Asia was not simply of one piece, they also learned that its parts and peoples were as numerous and different from one another as were the various parts and peoples of Europe itself.

By 1600 a literate European might easily have known a good deal about the East from the published writings of merchants, travelers, and missionaries, and from the printed maps of the cartographers. Dimensions of depth and increased realism were added to the European impressions by the regular appearance of Asian merchants, emissaries, and goods in the commercial, administrative, religious, and intellectual centers of Europe. During the course of the century, images of the four parts of Asia and a new and composite picture of Asia as a whole emerged from Europe's great experience in the East, and this new conception became and remained a permanent part of Europe's view of the world.

CHAPTER VI

India

Most of what Europe in general learned about the East during the first half of the sixteenth century related to the spice trade. In connection with it a number of Indians were taken to Portugal and Priest Joseph of the Malabar church even visited the papacy. While the Portuguese titillated the curious of Europe by sending rich embassies to Rome to announce their successes, the concrete information on India which leaked out was not much more specific or extensive than that which Varthema provided in 1510. The circumnavigation of the world by Elcano, Pigafetta, and their companions awakened Europe to the great breadth of the Pacific Ocean and provided additional details on the East Indies. But of India only very little was added to the store of Europe's information from 1520 to 1550. Even the accounts of the voyages to India, which the Aldine Press of Venice published in 1543 as *Viaggi fatti alla Tana*, were confined to discussions of the conditions of trade on the Malabar Coast.

Before 1550 the European image of India was formed by the traditions inherited from the prediscovery period as modified by the short accounts of the coastal areas and Vijayanagar provided by Varthema and others. Still, certain notions inherited from the past were rectified even on the basis of the scanty information which the Portuguese let escape. It had been learned, though the tradition died slowly, that the Indians, except for the Malabar Christians and the Moors, were not Christians but "heathens." Calicut was reported to be larger than Lisbon, and the people of India, even though "heathen," were recognized to possess a complex civilization. Through the spice trade, it had become general knowledge in Europe that the Moors were powerful in India, especially in the north. By similar means it was learned that the rest of India was divided among a number of rulers who persistently fought among themselves. The early Christian missionaries who settled at Goa and other Portuguese merchant communities had soon let it be known in Europe that extensive religious conquests were about as unlikely as great territorial acquisitions. Europe learned that the Moors, who were waging successful religious war in Africa and Europe, were also making many more conquests, both political and religious, in India than the Portuguese and Franciscans could possibly hope to match. India, it was generally realized, was going to be a hard nut to crack.

The European literature on India actually published during the latter half of the sixteenth century divides into three major categories: the Portuguese commercial reports and the great chronicles of conquest, the Jesuit newsletters and histories, and the *fin de siècle* reports of Italian, English, and Dutch commentators who managed in one way or another to travel and reside in India. The Portuguese materials deal with India down to 1540. The Jesuit newsletters, while recording details on events as they unfold, provide a helpful documentation, which is unfortunately not always continuous, for the period after the Portuguese secular histories break off their narratives. The Jesuit histories combine information from the secular sources with systematic accounts of the mission's progress to give more general coverage for the entire century. The travelogues of the non–Iberian writers which were published at the end of the century deal with India during the period from 1564 to 1591. Since they are unofficial reports which were issued outside of Portuguese and ecclesiastical jurisdiction, they act as something of a check upon the semiofficial Portuguese and Jesuit materials and are much more critical of the Portuguese rule and the Catholic mission.

I

THE PORTUGUESE PROFILE

Practically all the Portuguese works dealing with the discoveries contain information on India.[1] Before 1600, many of them were in print and all of those originally published in Portuguese were translated, in whole or in large part, into other European languages.[2] On the basis of four works (by Pires, Barbosa,

---

[1] For a survey of them see above, pp. 181–200.

[2] A contemporary work of great value by Gaspar Corrêa (1496–1563), *Lendas da India*, seems not to have been published until the nineteenth century (4 vols.; Lisbon, 1858–66). A. Kammerer (*La découverte de la Chine* [Leiden, 1944], p. 5) mentions without citing his source that there might have been an edition of it in twelve volumes published at Lisbon in 1556 which has since disappeared. It seems highly unlikely, however, that practically all references to this work, had it been published in the sixteenth century, would likewise have vanished. It seems more probable that this excellent compendium existed in several manuscript copies in Lisbon and that these circularized to authorized persons only. It is known that shortly after his death his manuscript of 3,500 pages was taken from India to Portugal by Miguel da Gama. For those interested in India's history or the story of Portuguese expansion, Corrêa's work is an indispensable contemporary source. He spent over thirty-five years preparing it, during which time he lived and worked in the East. Corrêa clearly had at his disposal sources of information which were untapped or unknown to Barros and Castanheda. For his biography and a critical evaluation of the literary merits of the *Lendas* see Aubrey F. G. Bell, *Gaspar Corrêa* (Oxford, 1924).

Castanheda, and Barros), supplemented by the others, it is perhaps possible to determine what educated and interested Europeans of the latter half of the century could have known of India through Portuguese sources. To a degree the four authors of these works depend upon one another and upon the manuscript materials of others which probably circulated in Portugal in their day. While these four main accounts exhibit many similarities which enable the careful reader to check one against the other, they are fundamentally quite different and of varying degrees of authority. Pires and Barbosa outline their personal travels and experiences in the East and describe as well the lands, peoples, and products seen. Castanheda and Barros depend heavily at certain points upon the firsthand observations of an earlier generation. But Castanheda's *História* combines the patient research and collation of information gathered by interviewing firsthand observers with personal experience in the field. Barros' history is rich in official materials and humanistic erudition, but it lacks quite naturally much of the individualistic viewpoint and local color which he might have given his story had he had the opportunity to travel in India.

A. GEOGRAPHICAL PLACEMENT AND ADJACENT ISLANDS

A glance at the Ptolemaic map of the world or a study of its descriptions of India within and beyond the Ganges will reveal immediately that its compilers knew little about India south of the Godavari River, that they extended India's boundaries much too far to the east, and that they greatly exaggerated the size of Taprobane (Ceylon).[3] Perusal of Marco Polo brings out the fact that he saw "Seilan" (Ceylon) as "the best island of its size in the whole world" and Malabar as "the best of all the Indias."[4] Particularly important here is Polo's emphatic addition of south India to the European image of the peninsula proper; for even though the Romans had visited the Malabar Coast, no clear idea of its configuration seems to have persisted in medieval Europe. During the fifteenth century, several reports got back to western Europe, as we have seen, which confirmed Polo's generally exalted view of the wealth, trade, and Christianity of south India. Thus, from the Ptolemaic tradition, Europe had at hand before 1500 some geographical data on the Gangetic plain of the north. On the ports and kingdoms of south India there were available the Poloan tradition and the more detailed accounts of the fifteenth-century overland travelers to India. It remains

---

[3] See the maps and texts in S. M. Sastri (ed.), *McCrindle's Ancient India as Described by Ptolemy* (Calcutta, 1927).

[4] H. Yule and H. Cordier (eds.), *The Book of Ser Marco Polo* (New York, 1903), II, 312. Cf. Orta's remark about Ceylon being "the most fruit bearing and best island in the world." (Sir Clements Markham [trans. and ed.], *Garcia da Orta. Colloquies on the Simples and Drugs of India* [London, 1913], p. 135.)

now to see what the Portuguese discoveries did to round out the European conception of India's geography.

The early newsletters and private dispatches which circulated in Europe after 1500 dealt mainly with the sea route to India, trade prospects, and the Portuguese triumphs. More extensive, confirmatory detail was relayed to Europe through the *Itinerario* (1510) of the Italian Ludovico di Varthema recounting his experiences in the major cities of maritime India, principally at Calicut, from 1504 to 1506. Varthema also gives greater detail than most of his predecessors about India's eastern coastal regions. But, to the death of King Manuel in 1521, none of the Portuguese accounts of India was allowed to circulate freely. Whatever information did leak out from Lisbon to other parts of Europe was slight. The accounts of India which appear during the generation from 1520 to 1550 are all written by non-Iberians and are mainly significant as vehicles for diffusing the hazy geographical picture that was slowly emerging from the mixture of traditional and recent testimony garnered from the few available materials.

The works of Tomé Pires and Duarte Barbosa, first published by Ramusio in 1550, are organized according to large geographical areas. In writing about India, they deal first of all with the west coast and focus their discussion upon its major cities and ports. On the whole the descriptions of the west coast, especially Malabar, are far superior in detail to the cursory treatment which they give to the cities on India's eastern coast. Barbosa, however, gets inland to Vijayanagar and a few other places of which he gives an eyewitness account. Like Barros and Castanheda, Barbosa dwells at some length on Ceylon and other insular areas. Well aware of the shortcomings of his work as a geographical description, Barbosa frankly acknowledges that it was his intention to write "only a short summary of that which can in truth be ascertained regarding the chief places in India." [5] In the frame of reference of both Pires and Barbosa the "chief places" are clearly those where the Portuguese did business. Castanheda's *História*, organized chronologically in terms of Portugal's conquests, introduces geographical description mainly as incidental or introductory information to the discussion of other topics.

The first effort to produce a systematic and general description of India's geography is published in the *Décadas* of Barros. He starts off by commenting that India proper in the Ptolemaic geographies was considered to encompass only the territory between the Indus and the Ganges, the locale of the old kingdom of "Eli" (Delhi).[6] The Persians, who live adjacent to northern India, call it in Barros' words by "its proper name, Indostan."[7] The whole of India,

---

5 M. L. Dames (trans. and ed.), *The Book of Duarte Barbosa* (London, 1918), I, 177.

6 H. Cidade and M. Múrias (eds.), *Asia de João de Barros* (Lisbon, 1945), I, 153. In the fifteenth century the Delhi sultanate, which had begun establishing its power at the beginning of the thirteenth century, began to disintegrate and collapsed completely by 1526. See for discussion R. C. Majumdar *et al.*, *An Advanced History of India* (rev. ed.; London, 1958), pp. 338–90.

7 Persian for *Hindustan*, or "the country of the Hindus."

the Portuguese chronicler observes, is bounded by the Indus, the Ganges, the Indian Ocean, and the great mountains of the north called "Imaos" by Ptolemy.[8] To Barros the shape of the peninsula resembles a rhombus, an oblique-angled equilateral parallelogram, with its greater length extending in the north-south direction from the foot of the mountains to the tip of Cape Comorin. From north to south the land stretches about 400 leagues (1,600 miles); at its greatest breadth it is not less than 300 leagues (1,200 miles).[9]

Hindustan includes both "idolaters" and Muslims whose customs and rites differ quite markedly. It is divided into many kingdoms: "Maltan" (Multan), Delhi, "Cospetir" (Gajpati or a territory held by Orissa),[10] Bengal, Orissa, "Māndū" (Malwa), "Chitor" (Mewar), and Gujarat (often called Cambay after its great port city).[11] The Deccan "kingdom" to the south is divided among many lords who have the stature of kings,[12] and it is bordered by the kingdom of "Pale."[13] Vijayanagar, lying on the other side of "Pale," is a great kingdom which controls a number of minor kings; and the Malabar Coast is divided into a number of petty states, each of which is ruled by a king or a prince. These states are so bellicose and covetous toward each other that, were it not for natural boundaries, the entire region would fall into the hands of the greediest and most powerful. Great and numerous rivers, mountains, lakes, jungles, and deserts, inhabited by countless and diverse animals make communication difficult and help to frustrate would-be conquerors. Among the most conspicuous of these natural barriers in the south are a number of rivers, not connected with the Indus or the Ganges, which enfold the lands they water in

[8] "Mount Imaos (in Sanskrit, *himā*, meaning cold), a name which was at first applied by the Greeks to the Hindu-Kush and the chain of the Himalayas running parallel to the equator, but which was gradually in the course of time transferred to the Bolar range which runs from north to south and intersects them." (S. M. Sastri [ed.], *op. cit.* [n. 3], p. 35.)

[9] In the Portuguese rules of the leagues (cited in Armando Cortesão [trans. and ed.], *The Suma Oriental of Tomé Pires* [London, 1944], II, 299–301) the length of the league naturally varies depending on the point of the compass from which it is calculated. On a straight line from north to south each degree is said to equal 17½ leagues, or slightly under four statute or land miles. Hereafter, we shall use "four" as a round number to simplify calculations, but with the understanding that this will make the distances in miles somewhat greater than the Portuguese actually thought them to be.

[10] This name appeared regularly on maps of the sixteenth and seventeenth century in the area to the west of the Ganges Delta. Scholars were perplexed by it until the mid-nineteenth century when it was ascertained that "Cospetir" was the Bengali genitive of Gajpati. Hence it is now assumed that "Cospetir" was simply another name for Gajpati, and that this territory belonged to the Gajpati rulers of Orissa. See H. Yule and A. C. Burnell, *Hobson-Jobson. A Glossary of Anglo-Indian Colloquial Words and Phrases* (London, 1886), pp. 201–2.

[11] "Māndū," sometimes written "Mandou," was frequently used as the name for Malwa, though it is simply the name of Malwa's capital city. "Chitor," the capital of Mewar, was likewise used as the name for the country as well as the city. While this is not a complete list of the independent states north of the Deccan, it does give the reader a feeling for the divided condition of northern India. For further discussion see below, pp. 418–19

[12] "Five separate Sultanates arose in the Deccan, one after another, on the breakup of the Bahmanī kingdom." (Majumdar *et al.*, *op. cit.* [n. 6], p. 363.)

[13] Appears in central India on the map dated 1561 of Giacomo Gastaldi as reproduced in R. H. Phillimore (comp.), *Historical Records of the Survey of India* (Dehra Dun, 1945), Vol. I, plate xvi. Cf. the account of "Palu" in E. Thornton (comp.), *A Gazetteer of the Territories under the Government of the East-India Company* . . . (London, 1857), p. 749.

their twists and turns as they slowly make their way to the surrounding seas. There are also many inlets of salt water which penetrate the coasts so deeply that ships sail inland via them from one place to another. The most striking of the divisions imposed on India by nature is the chain of internal mountains called Ghats (or Sierras to Barros) which extend as far south as Cape Comorin. Between the Ghats and the Indian Ocean the land is flat and marshy. It is in such a lowland area that Malabar and Calicut are situated.

In Book IX of the first *Década*, Barros describes in detail the maritime regions of the Orient based on the reports funneling into Lisbon from merchants, sailors, and administrators.[14] The whole of this vast region he divides into nine parts, three of which are concerned directly with the coastal regions of India. He starts at the Indus and proceeds to list and comment upon cities, rivers, and other landmarks along the coast of India all the way around the peninsula to the delta of the Ganges and with frequent references to the distances separating one place from the other. Not all of the names he uses are readily indentifiable. It is certainly possible, however, that the majority of his identifications can be verified by anyone willing to expend the necessary time and effort.

On Ceylon, the work of Barros is particularly full,[15] probably because the Portuguese began to have important contacts with that island as early as 1505–6. He locates it across from Cape Comorin, indicates that it has an oval form, and estimates its length as seventy-eight leagues (312 miles) in a north-south direction and its extreme east-west breadth as forty-four leagues (176 miles).[16] He compares Ceylon's position in relation to India with Sicily's relation to Italy, and speculates on whether it was once united to the mainland as the Indians believe. He concludes that there is more reason to believe that Ceylon was once a part of India than that Sicily was once attached to Italy. The name "Ceilam" (Ceylon) leads him into a series of philological and historical speculations, some of which turn out to be egregious errors. After observing that the ancient Europeans called it Taprobane, Barros notes in puzzlement that by native tradition the island was previously called "Ilanare" or "Tranate."[17] The name "Ceilam," he speculates from what he has heard of the island's

---

[14] Cidade and Múrias (eds.), *op. cit.* (n. 6), I, 351–62.

[15] *Ibid.*, III, 55–61. For ready reference and helpful documentation see D. Ferguson (trans. and ed.) "The History of Ceylon, from the Earliest Times to 1600 A.D., as Related by João de Barros and Diogo do Couto," *Journal of the Royal Asiatic Society, Ceylon Branch*, Vol. XX (1908), No. 60, pp. 29–53.

[16] The actual length and breadth are 270 by 140 miles. Like the ancients, but not so grossly, Barros exaggerates the size of Ceylon. Orta (in Markham [ed.], *op. cit.* [n. 4], p. 135) underestimates the size of Ceylon, for he makes it have a length "thirty leagues by six to eight broad." Barros is much closer.

[17] "Ilanare" probably represents Tamil, "Ilan-nādu," the "country of Ceylon" (Ilan = Silam = Simhalam); "Tranate" may represent Tamil *tiru-nádu*, the "sacred country." See Ferguson (ed.), *loc. cit.* (n. 15), p. 30. Castanheda (in Pedro de Azevedo [ed.], *História do descobrimento e conquista da India pelos Portugueses* [3d ed.; Coimbra, 1928], I, 258) says that the Arabian and Persian Moors called it "Ceilão," while the Indians called it "Hibernãro" meaning "luxuriant land." For further discussion see Dames (ed.), *op. cit.* (n. 5), II, 109, n. 1.

history, dates back to the Chinese "conquest." [18] He clearly believes that the Chinese in the early fifteenth century were masters of the Coromandel coast, part of Malabar, and the entire island of Ceylon. After arguing that the name "Ceilam," the Sinhalese language, and certain Ceylonese peoples were derived from the Chinese, Barros claims that China did for Ceylon what Rome did for Portugal. In this conclusion he appears to go far beyond his evidence and contradicts what we know of these matters from other sources. [19]

Ceylon is described as being lush and fertile, especially its southwestern region. The bulk of its population is located in the rich area around Colombo where cinnamon, elephants, and precious stones are the major items of trade. For all its ancient reputation as an island rich in gold, Barros points out that iron is really the only metal actually mined on Ceylon. [20] The island is well endowed with large palm groves, good water, cinnamon, and sweet oranges. Its elephants, the tamest and most trainable to be found in India, are bred in captivity. [21] Trained elephants are often used to capture their wild relatives, and Castanheda describes in some detail how elephants are hunted. [22] Cattle and buffalo are also bred, and "ghee" (*ghī*, boiled butter used in cookery in India, as oil is in southern Europe, and also in other ways) made from their milk is exported to "many parts." [23] To Barros, who was obviously impressed by the fertility of Ceylon, "it seems as if nature had made of it a watered orchard." [24] But as Barbosa more realistically points out: "Of rice there is but little, they bring the more part of it, hither from Coromendel [Coromandel], and this is their principal diet." [25]

[18] The Chinese sources indicate that the expeditions usually associated with the name of Cheng Ho visited Ceylon, possibly as early as 1406. In the course of a subsequent voyage, the Chinese in 1411 got into a serious conflict with King Algakkōnara, defeated him, took him captive, and carried him back to Peking. A trilingual inscription (in Tamil, Chinese, Persian), evidently prepared in China ahead of time, was also set up at Galle in Ceylon to commemorate the Chinese victory. Later Chinese records include Ceylon among those states sending tribute to the Ming court. See J. J. L. Duyvendak, "The True Dates of the Chinese Maritime Expeditions in the Early Fifteenth Century," *T'oung pao* XXXIV (1939), 367–73. For a brief summary of Duyvendak's conclusions as they relate to Sino-Sinhalese relations see Luciano Petech, "Some Chinese Texts Concerning Ceylon," *The Ceylon Historical Journal*, III (1954), 227. The last tribute mission was sent in 1459 from Ceylon to China. See H. W. Codrington, *A Short History of Ceylon* (London, 1947), p. 91.

[19] Ferguson (ed.), *loc. cit.* (n. 15), p. 33. Actually the name "Ceylon," in one form or another, became common about the thirteenth century, though traces of it can even be found at much earlier dates. See Yule and Burnell, *op. cit.* (n. 10), p. 138. Castanheda in Azevedo (ed.), *op. cit.* (n. 17), I, 261, says that the Sinhalese language is derived from those of Kanara and Malabar. Barbosa (in Dames [ed.], *op. cit.* [n. 5], II, 111) says that it is "drawn partly from Malabar and partly from Coromandel." Barros (in Cidade and Múrias [eds.], *op. cit.* [n. 6], III, 57) fantastically derives Sinhalese from "Chins de Galle." Sinhalese actually has no relation to Malayālam; it is an Indo-Aryan tongue.

[20] This assertion is borne out by Robert Knox, *An Historical Relation of Ceylon* (1681), pp. 153–54, reprinted as Vol. VI (1956–57) of the *Ceylon Historical Journal* and edited by S. D. Saparamadu.

[21] Ferguson (ed.), *loc. cit.* (n. 15), p. 35.

[22] Azevedo (ed.), *op. cit.* (n. 17), I, 258–59. Also see Dames (ed.), *op. cit.* (n. 5), II, 113–15. On the training of elephants see Orta's remarks in Markham, *op. cit.* (n. 4), pp. 185–90.

[23] Ferguson (ed.), *loc. cit.* (n. 5), p. 35.

[24] *Ibid.* On the fruits of Ceylon see Duarte Barbosa's account in Dames (ed.), *op. cit.* (n. 5), II, 111; also Orta's remarks in Markham, *op. cit.* (n. 4), pp. 135–36 where he suggests: "Certainly very good profit might be made of the oranges, for they are the best fruit in the world."

[25] Dames (ed.), *op. cit.* (n. 5), II, 111–12. Ceylon still imports most of its rice.

While describing the sea coast as low, marshy, and luxuriant, Barros depicts the mountainous regions of Ceylon as forming a kind of inner oval, concentric with the generally spherical outlines of the island. This hollow oval, which he calls a corral, is flat in the interior and must be entered through passes in the encircling mountains. The mountains are heavily wooded and swift rivers flow down their sides to the sea. About Adam's Peak (elevation 7,352 feet) Barbosa, Barros, and Castanheda write at length. "Three or four principal rivers" [26] rise in this mountain which can be seen from the sea and which is located about forty-five miles east of Colombo.[27] Pilgrims make regular trips from the coast to its conical summit which is revered as a shrine. On their way to the mountain the pilgrims, clad in weeds and animal skins, often have to wade waist-deep through flooded lands and swollen rivers.[28] To climb the mountain's steep sides the pilgrims cling to ladders made of iron chains to pull themselves to its various levels. On the narrow, oblong platform at the top of the peak, there is to be found a rock that rises out of the generally flat surface. In the middle of this table-like rock, it is possible to see a hollow that resembles a man's footprint. This phenomenon is thought by the natives to be the footprint of a holy man who brought the worship of "Deunú" [29] from Delhi to Ceylon. Barros also tells the story of the holy tooth of Buddha, another sacred relic associated with "Deunú," presumably without knowing that it had been destroyed in Goa in about 1561.[30] He also comments on the distant and numerous pilgrimages made to the mountain by "jógues" (Yogis) [31] who are "like men that have left the world and dedicated themselves entirely to God." [32]

Barros reports that Ceylon is divided into nine states, each of which claims to be a kingdom. The most renowned of these kingdoms is that which produces the cinnamon and has Colombo as its chief city. Its king lives in a *Cóta* (Kotte, meaning fortress) [33] which lies nearby the city, though it is set apart from the metropolis' busy commercial life. Barbosa implies that the king's revenues are derived from his monopoly of cinnamon, elephants, and precious stones.[34] To the south of Colombo at the tip of the island is the kingdom of Galle which is bordered on the east by "Iáula" (Yāla) and on the north by "Tanavaca" (Dinavaca).[35] Its king reportedly forbids his vassals to pass on their property from one generation to the other and so discourages enterprise. The easternmost kingdom is "Batecalou" (Batticaloa) and between it and "Cande"

---

26 Ferguson (ed.), *loc. cit.* (n. 15), p. 36.

27 Barros puts it at twenty leagues (80 miles) from the seacoast, obviously an exaggeration. Castanheda and Barbosa simply place it in the middle of the island; a mistake, for it is actually located in southern Ceylon.

28 Barbosa in Dames (ed.), *op. cit.* (n. 5), II, 118–19.

29 From Sinhalese, *Diviyamsé*.

30 Ferguson (ed.), *loc. cit.* (n. 15), p. 36.

31 From Sanskrit, *yogī*.

32 Ferguson (ed.), *loc. cit.* (n. 15), p. 37.

33 Jayawardhana Kōttē, six miles from modern Colombo.

34 Dames (ed.), *op. cit.* (n. 5), II, 113–17.

35 For discussion see P. E. Pieris (trans.), *Ribeiros History of Ceilão* (Colombo, 1909), pp. 3–4.

(Kandy) lies another called "Vilacem" (Wellassea). North of Batticaloa along the coast are successively the kingdoms of "Triquinámale" (Trincomalle) and "Jafanapatam" (Jaffna). But Barros, even while listing these kingdoms, warns the reader that their frontiers cannot be defined with accuracy "for they have no other demarcations than the power of each." [36] Actually, the rulers of the Kōttē dynasty of Colombo apparently sought to hold the other states in vassalage. [37]

Castanheda indicates that Ceylon has seven major seaports. [38] Barros, who is always interested in information pertinent to Portugal's expansion, describes in some detail the location and natural defenses of the port of Colombo. All of the people in these towns are heathens except for the Moorish merchants. Priesthood and government among the heathen are but two sides of the same coin. [39] Not only do the kings work closely with the Brahmans; they themselves are superior Brahmans having secular control over the bodies of their subjects and spiritual control over their minds. The common people, while living in abject subjection, are described as being well formed, white, and devoted to good and gentle living. They go naked from the waist up and wear garments of silk and cotton called *patolas* from their hips down. They carry ornaments in their hair and suspend precious stones from their ears. A poor man may sell himself into slavery; the rich are great collectors of gold, silver, and precious stones. Ceylon boasts many talented lapidaries. [40] The Sinhalese are unskilled in war, somewhat effeminate, and apparently ignorant of firearms. [41]

The Maldive Islands, an archipelago lying in the Indian Ocean about four hundred miles southwest of Ceylon, are alleged by Barros to derive their name either from the Malabar term *mal-diva*, meaning chain of islands, or from the name of the island of "Male" (Mahal) where the king (sultan) resides. [42] Ibn Batuta, the great Arabic traveler of the fourteenth century, was the first writer to bring the Maldives to the attention of Europe. [43] The Portuguese first touched upon the Maldives in 1507, but they were acutely aware beforehand of the strategic importance of the islands in the trade of the Indian Ocean. They soon sought, but unsuccessfully, to establish control over them. Barros contends that the islands were organized into groupings called *patana* (towns). [44] Neither

[36] Ferguson (ed.), *loc. cit.* (n. 15), p. 37.

[37] For a more recent listing see Codrington, *op. cit.* (n. 18), pp. 98–99.

[38] Castanheda in Azevedo (ed.), *op. cit.* (n. 17), I, 261. Barbosa (in Dames [ed.], *op. cit.* [n. 5], II, 117) says that besides Colombo, "there are also four or five other ports . . . which are under the rule of other Lords, nephews of the King of Ceilam, to whom they owe allegiance; yet at times they rise up against him."

[39] Ferguson (ed.), *loc. cit.* (n. 15), pp. 44–45.

[40] Barbosa in Dames (ed.), *op. cit.* (n. 5), II, 115–16.

[41] Castanheda in Azevedo (ed.), *op. cit.* (n. 5), I, 261; Ferguson (ed.), *loc. cit.* (n. 15), p. 53.

[42] Cidade and Múrias (eds.), *op. cit.* (n. 6), III, 142–46. For further discussion of this name, but surprisingly without reference to Barros, see Yule and Burnell, *op. cit.* (n. 10), pp. 417–18.

[43] On this and other points see M. A. H. Fitzler, "Die Maldiven im 16. und 17. Jahrhundert," *Zeitschrift für Indologie und Iranistik*, X (1935–36), 215–56; and Albert Gray (trans. and ed.), *The Voyage of François Pyrard* . . . (London, 1890), II, Pt. II, 423–508.

[44] S. R. Dalgado, *Glossário Luso-Asiático* (Coimbra, 1919), II, 188.

Barbosa nor Barros seems to have distinguished clearly between the Maldives and the Laccadives (from *Laksha-diva*, meaning 100,000 islands). Barros apparently thought of the two groups as forming a single arc like a diadem extending from the neighborhood of Mount Deli south around India and all the way to Java.[45]

The inhabitants of these islands are described as being short, puny, and malicious, and as possessing their own language.[46] The common people are heathen, but their government is in the hands of the Moors.[47] Silk and cotton garments worn by the upper classes are often woven in the islands, even though the raw materials have to be imported. Their cloths are said to be superior to those then being woven in Bengal and Coromandel. The most important export of the islands is coir, rope made from coconut fibers, used generally in the areas bordering the Indian Ocean for stitching together the Indian and Moorish ships that were made without nails, and for cables and rigging. These ropes, Barros notes, swell and recover their freshness in salt water and so contract and stretch with the movements of the sea.[48] He remains convinced, however, that ships constructed in this manner could never survive in the stormy seas at the Cape of Good Hope. The Maldivians also export fish and cowrie shells,[49] the latter being used for buttons and especially for currency in Bengal and Siam.[50] Most interesting also is Barros' reference to their export of the Coco-de-Mer, the fruit of the *lodvicea sechellarum*, reputed to be an antidote for poison. The virtues of this huge double-coconut were renowned throughout the Orient, and, its reputation being carried to Europe, the Emperor Rudolf II (reigned 1576–1612) tried in vain to buy one that had been brought to Europe by some Dutch merchantmen early in the seventeenth century.[51]

To the north of the Maldives the Portuguese notice that the Laccadive Islands and Anjediva, which they used as stopover places and sources of fresh water, were originally inhabited by Malabar peoples who had become converts to Islam.[52] On the pearl fisheries of the Gulf of Manaar, lying between Ceylon

45 See Pyard in Gray (trans. and ed.), *op. cit.* (n. 43), II, Pt. II, p. 480, n. 2.

46 Perhaps a reference to the dialect *Gabali-Tana*, formerly in general use throughout the island. See W. W. Hunter, *The Imperial Gazetteer of India* (London, 1881), VI, 265.

47 Today the entire population is Muslim. For a more recent discussion of Maldive religion and government see *ibid.*, VI, 264–65. For more details on government see Fitzler, *loc. cit.* (n. 43), pp. 223–24.

48 Cf. Orta in Markham (ed.), *op. cit.* (n. 4), p. 141, on the subject of "coir": "Of it they make the rigging and cordage for all the ships. It is very serviceable for us, for it is very flexible and does not rot in salt water. All the ships are caulked with it, so that it serves as linen, as oakum, and as matting. These qualities make it good merchandise for Portugal, and the space it requires is small, which is the reason for so much being used." For trade in coir see Dames (ed.), *op. cit.* (n. 5), I, 197.

49 For details on cowries in European literature see Dames (ed.), *op. cit.* (n. 5), II, 105, n. 3. Barros also says that in certain years two or three thousand hundredweight of cowrie were carried to Portugal as ballast in the ships.

50 See below, p. 417.

51 See Yule and Burnell, *op. cit.* (n. 10), pp. 176–78. Barros remarks that it is said to be a more efficacious antidote than bezoar stone. Orta questions its powers. See Markham (ed.), *op. cit.* (n. 4), p. 145.

52 For Barros' description of Anjediva see Cidade and Múrias (eds.), *op. cit.* (n. 6), I, 337–38.

and the tip of the Indian peninsula, Castanheda comments at some length.[53] He reports that the people "of Calicare[54] go pearl-diving twice each year,"[55] presumably off the northwest coast of Ceylon. Two to three hundred little boats, each containing about thirty-five men, go out to the oyster banks. The divers work in pairs, one diving with a sink-stone while the other holds tightly to an attached rope. The diver stays under water as long as possible collecting oysters for his basket. The largest pearls are saved for the king.[56] Castanheda also brings out clearly the fact that the yield from the oyster beds of Ceylon varied greatly and that decline in production was a worry in his day.[57] Orta compares these pearls with those which come from the fisheries of the Strait of Ormuz, Borneo, and China.[58]

B. MALABAR

In turning to the mainland of India, we shall commence with the Malabar Coast where the Portuguese obtained their earliest footholds. Even though the Romans traded there, this southwestern coast of the subcontinent was not clearly delineated in the European maps or narratives of the prediscovery era. From the eighth century down to the advent of the Portuguese the foreign trade of Malabar and the Indian Ocean was in the hands of the Arabs. Only occasional travelers, like Cosmas Indicopleustes and Marco Polo,[59] published notices of Malabar and its place in the trade of the Indian Ocean. All the Portuguese accounts printed in the sixteenth century are exceedingly full on Malabar, but none of them excels in detail or accuracy the first one to be published—that of Duarte Barbosa.

A Portuguese official in India from about 1500 to 1516 or 1517, Barbosa was secretary of the Portuguese factory in the Malabar port of Cannanore for a number of years. Here he reputedly mastered the local language "so well, that he spoke it better than the natives of the country."[60] It is probably because of his long residence in Malabar, his official position, his acute powers of observation,

---

[53] Azevedo (ed.), *op. cit.* (n. 17), I, 259–60. Cf. the even more vivid accounts in Marco Polo (in Yule and Cordier [eds.], *op. cit.* [n. 4], II, 331–32; 337) and Orta (in Markham [ed.], *op. cit.* [n. 4], pp. 297–300).

[54] This place I have not been able to identify.

[55] Normally today they go but once each year, beginning in the second week of March. Polo has them also going in September, so perhaps Castanheda is correct. See Yule and Cordier (eds.), *op. cit.* (n. 4), II, 337.

[56] Once Ceylon was taken over by Portugal, we know that the pearl fishery was operated as a royal monopoly. See Codrington, *op. cit.* (n. 18), p. 125.

[57] Cf. for an account of the cyclical character of the production of the Ceylon reefs, G. F. Kunz and C. H. Stevenson, *The Book of Pearl* (New York, 1908), pp. 103–4.

[58] Markham (ed.), *op. cit.* (n. 4), pp. 296–98.

[59] On Malabar as described in foreign sources of the prediscovery era see W. Logan, *Malabar* (Madras, 1951), I, 245–94.

[60] In the opinion of Gaspar Corrêa as quoted in Dames (ed.), *op. cit.* (n. 5), I, xxxvi.

and his linguistic ability that Barbosa was able to write a description of Malabar customs which still is regarded as an authoritative source. When supplemented by the details given by the other Portuguese authors, we can readily see that there was available in sixteenth-century Europe a substantial amount of reliable information on Malabar. Of the other Portuguese authors, only Pires, Castanheda and Orta wrote about Malabar from personal experience, and both Castanheda and Barros seem at times to be heavily indebted to Barbosa for their descriptive material.

The "land of Malabar"[61] (the natives prefer the name Kerala) extends, according to the Portuguese, from Cambola on the Chandragiri River, or from Mount Deli, to the tip of Cape Comorin.[62] On the north, Malabar is bordered by the Hindu kingdom of Vijayanagar. Castanheda relates the native tradition which asserts that the marshy lowlands of the coast were once covered entirely by the sea and that the mountains of the interior were connected by a land-bridge to the Maldives (meaning the Laccadives presumably).[63] These mountains are so high that they prevent the winds of the Indian Ocean from penetrating into the interior.[64] Barros notes that it is possible to travel inland by water from one place to the other along the coast via the maze of waterways.[65] Aside from such general statements, the Portuguese have very few remarks to make on topography.

The southernmost of the Malabar Kingdoms, Quilon, is called "Coilam" or "Coulan" by the Portuguese,[66] an area which in modern terms corresponds closely to the state of Travancore. In ancient times, Malabar was ruled from Quilon by a single ruler. The last of the line to govern the Malabar peoples from this port city and early center of the pepper trade was Chērumān Perumāl,[67] who died more than six hundred years before the Portuguese arrived in Malabar. It was during his reign that the Moors reportedly first began to trade on a large scale in India. The proselytizing Muslims soon converted the *Perumāl* (emperor) to the law of the Prophet, and convinced him to abandon his territories and to

[61] Malabar, meaning "hill country," was probably derived by the Arabs from the ordinary Dravidian *mala* (hill) with the addition of the Arabic *bar* (country). See Logan, *op. cit.* (n. 59), I, 1.

[62] This makes the Malabar Coast about 400 miles in length, or just about the same as the north-south extension of Portugal. Pires estimates it as having a coastline of 110 to 120 leagues and as extending into the interior from 5 to 15 leagues (or 20 to 60 miles). See Cortesão (ed.), *op. cit.* (n. 9), I, 66–67.

[63] Azevedo (ed.), *op. cit.* (n. 17), I, 34.

[64] Pires in Cortesão (ed.), *op. cit.* (n. 9), I, 66.

[65] Cidade and Múrias (eds.), *op. cit.* (n. 6), I, 372. Barros uses the Arabic word *leziras*. This may be *jaza'ir*, a term in vulgar Arabic which was used to denote the rivers. See notes under the adjectival form *jazirigy* in R. Dozy, *Supplément aux dictionnaires arabes* (2 vols.; Leyden, 1881). On the rivers, backwaters, and canals of the coast as arteries of traffic see Logan, *op. cit.* (n. 59), I, 8–17.

[66] For alternative identifications see Dames (ed.), *op. cit.* (n. 5), II, 3, n. 2.

[67] Barbosa writes "Cirimay Pirençal"; Castanheda makes it "Sarrana-perima"; and Barros gives it as "Sarama Pereimal." In all cases they are certainly referring to Chērumān, the last king of the Perumāl epoch (to about A.D. 826). For traditional history see accounts in Logan, *op. cit.* (n. 59), I, chap. iii; and P. K. S. Raja, *Medieval Kerala* (Chidambaram, 1953), chap. i. Barros (in Cidade and Múrias [eds.] *op. cit.* [n. 6], I, 370–72) asserts on the basis of certain Indian writings "interpreted for us" that Chērumān's reign ended precisely 612 years before the Portuguese first arrived in India.

leave in one of their ships for Mecca.[68] Before departing on his pilgrimage, Chērumān partitioned his lands among his kinsmen[69] leaving for himself only the uninhabited coastal strip on which Calicut, his embarkation point, was later to be built. This slight territory and the emblems of his authority, the sword and "a golden lamp,"[70] he finally bequeathed to one of his favorite nephews and enjoined the other nobles, excepting the kings of Cannanore and Quilon, to regard and obey his appointee as their new sovereign. It was also from the date of his departure that the Malabars began to reckon their calendar.[71]

The division of Chērumān left three independent kingdoms in Malabar: "Coulam" (Quilon), according to Barros the seat of the Brahman faith, "Kolathiri" (Cannanore), and Calicut.[72] The Zamorin, as the heir of the *Perumāl*, was to have the exclusive right of coining money, a traditional recognition of Calicut's importance in foreign trade. With the help of the Moors the Zamorin was gradually to make himself the supreme secular ruler in Malabar;[73] over religious affairs the king of Quilon, called the *cobritim* (or pontiff) by Barros,[74] was to assume control; apparently the king of Cannanore was not to possess jurisdiction over anything outside of his own boundaries. Besides these three rulers, Barbosa notes that other great nobles "wish to be called kings" but cannot be considered so since they neither coin money nor "roof houses with tiles."[75] Most of the Portuguese stress the fact that the Zamorin's strength lay in his close association with the Muslim merchants.

In describing the individual kingdoms and towns of Malabar, Pires, Barbosa, and Barros start in the north, proceed southward along the coast, and rarely

[68] On the debated question of Chērumān's conversion and subsequent pilgrimage to Mecca see Raja, *op. cit.* (n. 67), pp. 6–8.

[69] "All available Malayālam sources agree that there was a *bhuvibhaga*, or partition of the Empire by the last Perumāl, before his abdication." (*Ibid.*, p. 8.) Also see Logan, *op. cit.* (n. 59), I, 243, and Dames (ed.), *op. cit.* (n. 5), II, 4–5, n. 1.

[70] The sword was still preserved in the Zamorin's palace in Calicut early in the twentieth century, and was seen there by Mr. J. A. Thorne who was then in charge of the Zamorin's estates. No trace of the "golden lamp" seems to be left. See Dames (ed.), *op. cit.* (n. 5), II, 3–4, n. 3. Castanheda (Azevedo [ed.], *op. cit.* [n. 17], I, 34) calls it a "tocha mourisca" or "Moorish lamp."

[71] Castanheda in Azevedo (ed.), *op. cit.* (n. 17), I, 34.

[72] Barros (in Cidade and Múrias [eds.], *op. cit.* [n. 6], I, 370–71) also points out, unlike the others, that the Arabs "according to what we hear" already had a settlement at Calicut before the abdication of the Perumāl.

[73] "Zamorin" is equated with "emperor" by Castanheda and Barros. Ordinarily it has been defined as literally meaning "sea-lord." Thorne gives an alternative analysis in Dames, *op. cit.* (n. 5), II, 260–61.

[74] In this designation Barros disagrees with Barbosa (*ibid.*, II, 6), who states that the ruler of Cannanore was called "Cobertorim" and the ruler of Quilon the "Benetady." Perhaps Barros is here repeating a tradition of the St. Thomas Christians which claims that the founding of Quilon in A.D. 825 was the work of Christian immigrants who then made it into their metropolitan see.

[75] Dames (ed.), *op. cit.* (n. 5), II, 6. In Thorne's note he observes it has traditionally been the prerogative of Malabar rulers "to forbid roofing with tiles instead of thatch without permission." The right to grant such permission is a symbol of superior status.

refer to places or events in the interior.[76] The northernmost territory is the kingdom of Cannanore: it borders Vijayanagar and has "Coticolam" (Kotta-kulam) as its northernmost outpost. This fortress is commanded by the "Warden of the Marches," a nephew of the king of Cannanore, and is situated north of the "Miraporam" (Nileshwaram) River. In the estuary of this river there is a center of trade ruled over by another of the king's nephews, who was apparently restive under Cannanore's suzerainty. Farther south, close to the foot of Mount Deli, lies the prosperous old town of "Maravel" (Madayi or Pazhayangadi) which is a center of trade and fishing. A short distance farther to the south is the fortress town of "Balaerpartam" (Vallerepattanam) located on the river of the same name where the ruler of Cannanore makes his permanent residence. Inland a few miles is the town of "Taliparam" (Taliparamba) which is an entre-pôt in the trade between Malabar and Vijayanagar.

The city of Cannanore itself is described as an international trading center which deals in goods of all sorts from the other great port cities surrounding the eastern rim of the Arabian Sea. Had the Portuguese not taken over the city, Pires believes that it would have fallen to Mohammed Ali and the Moors.[77] But since 1504, the Portuguese had a fortress, trading station, and colony there made up of Portuguese and their Christianized wives and families.[78] Castanheda, who apparently visited Cannanore, writes:

This is a large city with a fine bay, the houses being built of earth, and covered with flat stones or slates. . . . It abounds in fish, flesh, and fruits, but has to import rice from other places. The king or rajah is a bramin . . . but is not so rich as the Zamorin, or even as the rajah of Coulan [Quilon].[79]

To the south of the city of Cannanore, Barbosa identifies two rich and powerful Moorish towns, "Cragnate" (Eddakād) and "Tremopatam" (Dharmadam?), as the last places "which the King of Cananor hold against Calecut." [80] Inland and upriver from these two Moorish strongholds is the landlocked trading center called "Quategatam" (Kottayam?) whose inhabitants deal with the merchants of Vijayanagar and are traditional enemies of Cannanore.[81] Though Barbosa spent a number of years in Cannanore, he has very little to say about life there.

76 Barros (in Cidade and Múrias [eds.], *op. cit.* [n. 6], I, 356–57) treats the west coast of India from Cambay to Cape Comorin as a single area which is divided naturally into subareas by the rivers which empty into the Arabian sea. Pires (in Cortesão [ed.], *op. cit.* [n. 9], I, 73–75) and Barbosa give long lists of the seaport towns and their rulers. In the discussion which follows we shall mainly follow Barbosa.

77 Cortesão (ed.), *op. cit.* (n. 9), I, 77.

78 Barbosa in Dames (ed.), *op. cit.* (n. 5), II, 81. Beginning in 1504, the Portuguese won the support of Cannanore in their fight against the Zamorin of Calicut and thereafter began to build up a colony there. For a description of the reception given to the Portuguese in 1504, see Castanheda's account as translated in Richard Eden (trans.), *The First Booke of the Historie of the Discoveries and Conquest of the East Indies by the Portingals* (London, 1582) as reprinted in Robert Kerr (ed.), *A General History and Collection of Voyages and Travels* (London, 1824), II, 493–94.

79 Eden (trans.), *op. cit.* (n. 78), II, 425. Cf. P. K. Raja, *op. cit.* (n. 67), p. 61 on the higher social status of the *Kolattiri* (king of Cannanore).

80 Dames (ed.), *op. cit.* (n. 5), II, 82.

81 Pires in Cortesão (ed.), *op. cit.* (n. 9), I, 77.

Aside from mentioning that Cannanore produces a number of spices, the only other items that he feels inclined to discuss are the crocodiles and cobras of the country.[82]

The territory of Cannanore is described as being separated from Calicut by Moorish towns on both sides of the Anjarakandi and Tellicherry rivers. Just south of the rivers are the three Moorish commercial towns belonging to northern Calicut called "Tiramunigate" (Tiruyangad), "Manjaim" (Mayyazhi or Mahe) and "Chamobai" (Chombāla). Inland from these thriving seaports the land is heavily populated with Nāyars "who give obedience to no king," and are "divided between two lords who rule them."[83] The jurisdiction of the Zamorin of Calicut begins at the south bank of the "Pedirpatam" (Kotta) River. Between the border and the city of Calicut itself, Barbosa mentions three coastal towns: "Tircore" (Trikkodi), "Pandanare" (Pantalāyini), and "Capucate" (Kappata). Seven or eight miles south lies the Zamorin's capital, but Barbosa merely mentions it at this juncture since most of what he has to say later about Malabar in general is based upon conditions prevailing in Calicut. Along the river which runs south of the capital stands the town of "Chiliate" (Chāliyam) "where dwell many Moors, natives of the land who are merchants."[84] Barbosa then lists several other trading and fishing villages situated between Calicut and the important port of "Pananee" (Pounani) from which the Zamorin "draws a great revenue in dues."[85]

Further to the south is the river called the "Chatua" (Chittuvayi) down which comes the "greater part of the pepper"[86] grown in the area. Still further south is "another river which forms the frontier area with the Kingdom of Cochim [Cochin], on the hither bank of which is a place called 'Crangalor' [Cranganore]."[87] In this border territory live some of the native Christians of St. Thomas, and Barbosa understands that other members of this sect "dwell from here as far as *Charamandel* [Coromandel]."[88] The Malabar Christians, who are judged to be very devout, have two churches in Cranganore, one dedicated to St. Thomas and the other to Our Lady. Castanheda reports in summary what the Portuguese were told in detail by a native priest of the traditional history of the St. Thomas Christians, of their community at Cranganore, and of their religious practices.[89] Once having reached the southern extremity of the

[82] *Ibid.*, p. 83. Like any modern visitor, Castanheda was impressed by the crocodiles, reptiles, and bats of the area (in Eden [trans.], *op. cit.* [n.78], II, 425). Also see Pires in Cortesão (ed.), *op. cit.* (n. 9), I, 72–73. On the failure of the Portuguese to remark on the scenic beauty of this area see J. Gerson da Cunha, "The Portuguese in South Kanara," *Journal of the Bombay Branch of the Royal Asiatic Society*, XIX (1895–97), 251.

[83] Dames (ed.), *op. cit.* (n. 5), II, 85. The Nāyars are the warrior caste of Malabar.

[84] *Ibid.*, p. 87.

[85] *Ibid.*, p. 88.

[86] *Ibid.*

[87] *Ibid.*

[88] *Ibid.*, p. 89. Pires (in Cortesão [ed.], *op. cit.* [n. 9], I, 73) says that the Malabar Christians "live in the district from Chittuvaye to Quilon."

[89] See Eden (trans.), *op. cit.* (n. 78), II, 422–23. Cf. G. Schurhammer (trans. and ed.), "Three Letters of Mar Jacob Bishop of Malabar, 1503–1550," *Gregorianum*, XIV (1933), 62–86.

Zamorin's dominions, Barbosa comments at length on the palm tree and its multiple uses. The products of the palm are so abundant in Malabar that they are exported in dried or preserved form to Cambay and distant Dacca.[90] Pires observes that Malabar imports most of its rice and he discusses where it comes from and how it gets to the southwest coast of India from Coromandel and Kanara.[91]

Cochin, which owed its independence in the sixteenth century to Portuguese support of its ruler, is described as the land where pepper and other valuable spices grow in abundance. Castanheda, who visited the Portuguese colony there, writes that Cochin is located

... on a river [actually an inlet] close to the sea, and is almost an island, so that it is very strong and difficult of access, having a large and safe harbour. The land in its neighborhood is low and intersected by branches of the river into many islands. The city itself is built much after the same manner with Calicut....[92]

Both Barbosa and Castanheda are well aware of the fact that the "king" of Cochin is generally regarded in Malabar as a vassal of the Zamorin. They acknowledge that traditionally he did not possess the coveted rights of coining his own money or of roofing his palace with tiles. They also recognize that the Zamorin possesses rights of investiture over the rājās of Cochin, that tribute and military support are owed to Calicut, and that the vassal must always be of the same faith as the suzerain. The Portuguese (since 1503) possess a fine fortress at Cochin, and "every day" refugee Christians of St. Thomas from "Coilam [Quilon] and other places" seek sanctuary with the Europeans.[93] The Portuguese themselves, in addition to their merchandising at Cochin, use their outpost for the repairing and building of ships, "both galley and caravels in as great perfection as on the Lisbon strand."[94]

In a disputed border region separating Quilon from Cochin, Barbosa locates the small town of "Porqua" (Porakád). Living under their own ruler, Porakád's inhabitants survive on fishing and piracy. In their forays against becalmed vessels, they use light rowboats called *caturs* to surround and attack their victims. South of Porakád is the first port belonging to Quilon, the trading town of "Cale Coilam" (Kayankullam) "whither come numbers of Moors, Heathens, and Christians of the doctrine of the Blessed Saint Thomas and many of them also dwell in the inland country."[95] Immediately to the south lies the "very great city" of Quilon where trade is carried on with merchants from Ceylon and other marts as far east as Malacca. At one time, Pires contends, the foremost king of Ceylon paid annual tribute to Quilon.[96] Apparently, however, traders

90 Dames (ed.), *op. cit.* (n. 5), II, 92.
91 Cortesão (ed.), *op. cit.* (n. 9), I, 76–77.
92 Eden (trans.), *op. cit.* (n. 78), II, 419.
93 Barbosa in Dames (ed.), *op. cit.* (n. 5), II, 93.
94 *Ibid.*
95 *Ibid.*, pp. 96–97.
96 Cortesão (ed.), *op. cit.* (n. 9), I, 80.

from the north did not ordinarily come to Quilon, since Barbosa remarks that they "trade not with Cambaya [Gujarat]."[97] Of Quilon Castanheda writes:

Coulan is twelve leagues [48 miles] from Cochin, and twenty-four [96 miles] from Cape Comorin. Before the building of Calicut, Coulan was the principal city of Malabar, and the port of greatest trade on that coast. Its buildings, more especially the temples and shrines of their idols are larger and more splendid than those of Cochin.[98]

Near Quilon on a small peninsula is a great church reputedly built by St. Thomas for his Indian converts. Barbosa comments extensively on the traditions surrounding St. Thomas' part in constructing this church.[99] In the Ramusio version, Barbosa gives 7,000 households as the number of St. Thomas Christians scattered over Malabar, both on the coast and inland.[100] All of the Portuguese authors agree that the ruler of Quilon is both rich and powerful militarily, but Castanheda observes that "the men are mostly of a low stature" and that the king's palace guard consists of three hundred female archers.[101] South of the city of Quilon is the area called "Tiramgoto" (Tiruvankodu) by Barbosa and "Travancor" by Barros. Apparently it was a semi-independent state, and it was, of course, the area from which the former province of Travancore received its name. While Cape Comorin "ends the land of Malabar," the territory of Quilon is said by Barbosa to extend further eastward to "a city named Cael [Palayaka-yal]," where the rājā usually resides.[102]

Most of what the Portuguese writers have to report on the customs and political organization of Malabar is based upon the situation prevailing in Calicut. Often they generalize on the practices of Calicut and apply them to the whole of Malabar, though this is not to say that they are unconscious of variations from place to place. The kings of Malabar, Barbosa observes, are of one caste and custom,[103] with little difference between them.[104] They worship idols

97 Dames (ed.), *op. cit.* (n. 5), II, 97.　　　98 Eden (trans.), *op. cit.* (n. 78), II, 467.

99 "This ancient church is now no more, and the encroaching sea has covered even its site ..." See Rao Bahadur L. K. Anatakrishna Ayyar, *Anthropology of the Syrian Christians* (Ernakulam, 1926), p. 14.

100 Dames (ed.), *op. cit.*, II, 100, n. 1. Pires (in Cortesão [ed.], *op. cit.* [n. 9], I, 73) estimates their numbers at fifteen thousand of whom some two thousand are "men of repute," the rest being poor artisans.

101 Eden (trans.), *op. cit.* (n. 78), II, 467.

102 Dames (ed.), *op. cit.* (n. 5), II, 102, 124. Also see below, pp. 408–9.

103 The English word "caste" is derived from Portuguese *casta*, a word meaning "family," "stock," "kind," "strain," "clan," "tribe," or "race." The English words "caste" and "chaste" have the same Latin root, *castus*, which originally meant "pure." The early Portuguese writers, confronted by a social situation for which they had no precedent in their own experience or even a descriptive word, quickly begin to apply this Latin term to the various subdivisions which they observed in Indian society. They do not, however, use the term "caste" exclusively with reference to Hindu groups. Barros talks about the "caste of Moors" and others assert that the St. Thomas Christians belong to the general "caste of Christians." It was the Dutch (their word is *kaste*) and the English who seem to have taken the Portuguese *casta* for a technical social term. For further discussion see A. L. Basham, *The Wonder That Was India* (London, 1954), pp. 148–51. In what follows we use the word "caste" in its ordinary English sense as a one-word description of the approximately three thousand subdivisions within Hindu society.

104 Dames (ed.), *op. cit.* (n. 5), II, 6–7. See especially Thorne's notes on the basic similarity in customs prevailing in the Kshatriya and Sāmantan families. Most of the ruling families claim to be Sāmantan.

and they are classified as heathens by the Portuguese. In color the ruling families of Malabar are thought of as being "tawny," or brown, or "almost white," and with some being "blacker than others."[105] Generally they go about naked above the waist, but at times they wear jackets called *bajus*[106] made of cotton, silk, or rich brocades which are open in the front and come down to the middle of the thigh. The lower parts of their bodies they clothe in silk or cotton garments.[107] They tie their hair into a knot on the tops of their heads and sometimes "wear small hoods like Gallego caps."[108] They shave their beards with razors leaving short mustaches in the Turkish mode. From their ear lobes hang precious stones, and over their garments they wear broad belts decorated with jewels. Across their chests, shoulders, and foreheads they streak themselves with ashes which they put on in three stripes "according to the manner of their caste."[109]

The Portuguese, especially Barbosa, appear to have made a special study of the establishment and customs of the Zamorin. His palace is "only constructed of earth," but it is considered to be an extensive and "handsome structure."[110] On state occasions the Zamorin sits on a high platform "plastered daily with cow dung" on which "they place a very white stool" and "a coarse cloth of sheep's wool dyed black."[111] The sword mentioned earlier as part of the traditional regalia is also brought out on ceremonial occasions at which times it never leaves the Zamorin's side. Barros and Castanheda dwell at length on the richness of the Zamorin's garb and his wealth in gold, jewels, and pearls. In describing the reception of Da Gama at a special durbar, Castanheda writes that the Zamorin

lay on a sofa covered with a cloth of white silk and gold, and a rich canopy over his head. On his head he had a cap or mitre adorned with precious stones and pearls, and had jewels of the same kind in his ears. He wore a jacket of fine cotton cloth, having buttons

---

The Zamorin is a Sāmantan who is generally considered to be of Erōde background. The customs of all the royal families approximate those of the Nāyar caste. See Pires (in Cortesão [ed.], *op. cit.* [n. 9], I, 67). But Castanheda (in Azevedo [ed.], *op. cit.* [n. 17], I, 36) categorizes the Zamorin as a Brahman. K. M. Panikkar (*Malabar and the Portuguese* [Bombay, 1929] p. 11), who is himself of the Nāyar caste, states flatly that the Zamorins "belong to the Nair caste."

105 Barbosa in Dames (ed.), *op. cit.* (n. 5), II, 7.
106 Castanheda in Azevedo (ed.), *op. cit.* (n. 17), I, 36. A modern Portuguese dictionary defines *bajú* as a "kind of shift used by Indian ladies." Dames (ed.), *op. cit.* (n. 5), II, 7, n. 3 notes that "coats" were no longer worn at the beginning of the twentieth century. Yule and Burnell (eds.), *op. cit.* (n. 10), refer to the "badjoe" or "bajoo" as a Malay jacket and derive the term from Malay, *baju*. Cf. Dutch *baadje* meaning jacket.
107 For an example of his dress see the photograph of Mānavikrama Rājā, Zamorin of Calicut from 1912 to 1915, in the frontispiece to Dames, *op. cit.* (n. 5), II.
108 *Ibid.*, p. 8. Apparently the hoods were not worn any longer in Thorne's time.
109 *Ibid.* In reality these streaks of ashes indicate the religious affiliation rather than the caste of the wearer.
110 Castanheda's remarks as given in Eden (trans.), *op. cit.* (n. 78), II, 365.
111 Dames (ed.), *op. cit.* (n. 5), II, 9. This black cloth, "as large as an Alentejo cloak," called *kavim-padam* was, along with the white cloth called *vella*, part of the ceremonial apparatus still in use by the Zamorins of the twentieth century.

of large pearls and the button-holes wrought with gold thread. About his middle he had a piece of white calico, which came only down to his knees, and both his fingers and toes were adorned with many gold rings set with fine stones; his arms and legs were covered with many golden bracelets.[112]

Impressed as the Portuguese are with the wealth and display of the Malabar kings, they are even more fascinated by their peculiar system of marriage, inheritance, and succession. These "kings" (or *tamburāns*), including the Zamorin, never marry or found families in the European sense of these terms. They reportedly take as a mate "a woman of good family, of Nayre [Nāyar] descent, and beautiful for their delight."[113] The Zamorin, for example, who ordinarily resides just outside of Calicut, erects a house near his own palace for the private use of his "wife." She also has her own allowance and staff of servants, so that she may live "quite independently and well supplied."[114] If the king desires it, he may always replace her with another woman taken from the same caste. The children of such alliances are treated exceedingly well when they are young, but upon reaching maturity the Zamorin's sons "receive no more honour than comes to them from their mother's rank."[115] While the "king" often gives special presents to his sons, they remain only slightly better off than other Nāyars. They may not inherit their father's property or succeed to his kingdom. To many Europeans of the sixteenth century such a peculiar scheme of inheritance seemed almost to run contrary to nature.

The "kings" of Malabar are succeeded by their brothers, or, failing these, the throne passes to the sons of their sisters.[116] Under this matrilineal system of descent, the royal sisters never marry in the Western sense. Ordinarily the *tamburāttis* (royal ladies) take their mates from among the *Nambūtiri*, a Brahman group native to Malabar. The tamburāttis always remain in their own residences (*kovilagams*) and receive periodic visits from their mates. To Castanheda this was a rather shocking practice, for he sees the tamburāttis as "free and dissolute in their manners, choosing paramours as they please."[117] In such a system the ruler really has no certainty respecting the identity of his father—a state of affairs which the Europeans could hardly conceive of in terms of their own patrilineal background. But perhaps Barbosa reflects the attitude of the Nāyar when he asserts that they consider that the sons of their sisters "are their true sons, for they know who is their mother. . . ."[118] And, in summarizing the effects of this system, Barbosa points out that "the Kings of Malabar are always

---

[112] As translated in Eden (trans.), *op. cit.* (n. 78), II, 365. A similar description may be found by Barros in Cidade and Múrias (eds.), *op. cit.* (n. 6), I, 158.

[113] Barbosa in Dames (ed.), *op. cit.* (n. 5), II, 10.

[114] *Ibid.*

[115] *Ibid.* See also Pires in Cortesão (ed.), *op. cit.* (n. 9), I, 70.

[116] Cf. Albuquerque who asserts that "the sons of Malabar kings do not inherit; instead the king-ship usually devolves on the sons of their sisters, who are usually the mistresses of Brahmins." See Walter de Gray Birch (trans.), *Affonso de Albuquerque. Commentaries* (4 vols.; London, 1875-84), II, 71.

[117] As translated in Eden (trans.), *op. cit.* (n. 78), II, 351.

[118] Dames (ed.), *op. cit.* (n. 5), II, 10.

old." [119] He might also have added that this means that their reigns are uniformly short and usually limited in constructive effectiveness.

In considering the role of the tamburāttis, the Portuguese observe that the nieces and sisters of the rulers have their independent residences and revenues. When such a girl reaches puberty, custom requires that a young noble from outside the kingdom be called in to deflower her. He is sent money and gifts before making the journey and upon his arrival he is feted "as if it were a wedding." [120] After remaining with her for several days, he hangs a small golden jewel (*tāli*) around her neck as a token of her maturity. This ceremony being performed, the young noble returns to his own land and "thereafter she may dispose of herself according to her own desires." [121] In a word, she may then enter into more permanent relationships with men of her own kingdom who are Nambūtiri Brahmans in caste.

The Portuguese have a number of arresting and puzzling comments to make on the crucial problem of succession. Barbosa contends that if the ruler dies without heirs a council is convened to elect a successor from among the surviving relatives of the king; or, failing relatives, any "suitable" person may be chosen. [122] Castanheda asserts that it is traditional for the Zamorins to die in a temple, and that custom ordains that all Zamorins must serve the gods of this temple before death. [123] Each Zamorin therefore retires from his secular office with the death of his predecessor. In retiring from civil office to take up his religious duties the Zamorin has no choice. As an example of this procedure, Castanheda later in his account cites the events of 1504 when the Zamorin was defeated by Portuguese arms. [124] Crestfallen and despairing, the Zamorin took up religious seclusion in a *turcol* (temple). [125] There, in the company of his Brahman advisers, he was forced to spend the rest of his days in an effort to propitiate the gods. Simultaneously he yielded the government of the state to his brother. From what we know from other sources about succession practices in Calicut, it appears that Castanheda's generalization about forced retirement to the temple before death is quite incorrect. None of the other sources bears him out in his contentions about the succession. [126]

Funeral rites and mourning ceremonies also attract the attention of the

[119] *Ibid.*, p. 11.

[120] *Ibid.*, p. 12.

[121] *Ibid.* Cf. account of Castanheda (Eden [trans.], *op. cit.* [n. 78], II, 351).

[122] Dames (ed.), *op. cit.* (n. 5), II, 11. For a much more detailed discussion of practices followed in Malabar on determining the succession in the absence of a legitimate heir see the *Historia do Malavar* prepared around 1615 by the Portuguese Jesuit, Diogo Gonçalves, as published by Josef Wicki as No. 20 of the *Missionswissenschaftliche Abhandlungen und Texte* (Münster, 1955), pp. 14–15.

[123] Azevedo (ed.), *op. cit.* (n. 17), I, 36; for English translation see Eden (trans.), *op. cit.* (n. 78), II, 350.

[124] Azevedo (ed.), *op. cit.* (n. 17), I, 183–84; Eden (trans.), *op. cit.* (n. 78), II, 489–90.

[125] Used by Castanheda as a synonym for "pagode," this is probably a Portuguese rendition of Malayālam, *tiru-koyil* (temple). See Yule and Burnell, *op. cit.* (n. 10), p. 713.

[126] There was a tradition, however, which persisted until 1743 that the Zamorin deposed himself as suzerain of Malabar at the festival of *Mahamakham* (big sacrifice) which was presumably held every twelve years. See Logan, *op. cit.* (n. 59), I, 163–65 and Raja, *op. cit.* (n. 67), pp. 28–31.

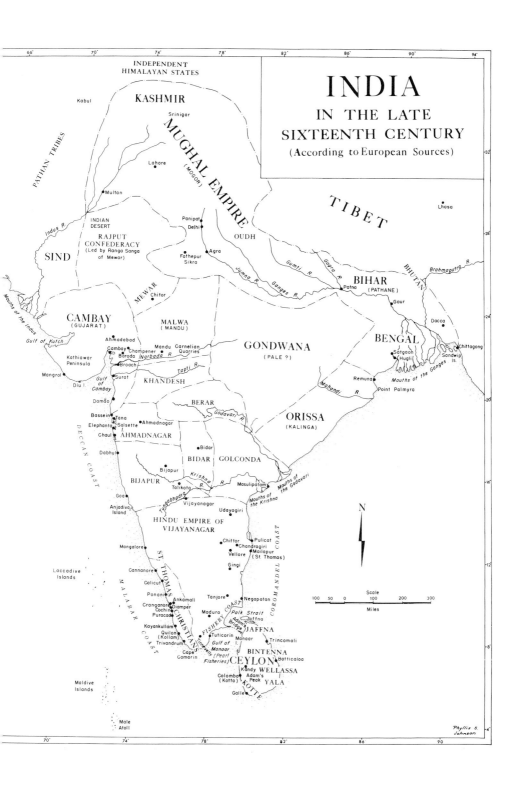

INDEPENDENT
HIMALAYAN STATES

INDIA
IN THE LATE
SIXTEENTH CENTURY
(According to European Sources)

Kabul

KASHMIR

Srinigar

PATHAN TRIBES

MUGHAL EMPIRE
(MOGOR)

Lahore

TIBET

Lhasa

Multan

Indus R.

INDIAN
DESERT

RAJPUT
CONFEDERACY
(Led by Ranga Sanga
of Mewar)

SIND

Panipat
Delhi

OUDH

Agra

Fathepur
Sikra

Jumna R.

Gumti R.

Gogra R.

Ganges R.

BIHAR
(PATHANE)

Patna

BHUTAN

Brahmaputra R.

Gaur

Dacca

Mouths of the Indus

MEWAR

Chitor

CAMBAY
(GUJARAT)

Gulf of Kutch

Ahmadabad

Cambay Champener Mandu Carnelian
Baroda Narbada R. Quarries
Broach

Kathiawar
Peninsula

MALWA
(MANDU)

GONDWANA
(PALE ?)

BENGAL

Satgaon
Hugli
Sandwip
Is.

Chittagong

Mangrol

Diu I.

Gulf
of
Cambay

Surat

Tapti R.

KHANDESH

Mouths of the Ganges

Remuna

Point Palmyra

Mahanadi R.

Damão

Bassein Tana
Elephanta Salsette Ahmadnagar
Chaul AHMADNAGAR

BERAR

Godavari R.

ORISSA
(KALINGA)

DECCAN COAST

Dabhul

Bidar

BIDAR GOLCONDA

Bijapur

BIJAPUR

Krishna R.

Tungabhadra R.

Talikota R.

Vijayanagar

Udayagiri

Masulipatam

Mouths of
the Godavari

Mouths of
the Krishna

Goa

Anjadiva
Island

HINDU EMPIRE OF
VIJAYANAGAR

N

Mangalore

Laccadive
Islands

Cannanore

Calicut

Ponani

ST. THOMAS CHRISTIANS

MALABAR COAST

Chittor Pulicat
Chandragiri
Vellore Mailapur
(St. Thomas)

Gingi

COROMANDEL COAST

Scale
100 50 0 100 200 300
Miles

Ankamali Tanjore Negapatan
Cranganore Diamper
Cochin Puracade

Madura

Kayankullam
Quilon
(Kollam)
Trivandrum

Palk Strait

Adam's
Bridge

Jaffna

JAFFNA

FISHERY COAST

Tuticorin Manaar

Gulf of
Manaar
(Pearl
Fisheries)

Trincomali

BINTENNA

Batticaloa

Cape
Comorin

CEYLON

WELLASSA

Kandy Adam's
Colombo Peak
(Kotta) KOTTE YALA

Maldive
Islands

Galle

Male
Atoll

Phyllis S.
Johnson

Cannanore at the beginning of the sixteenth century.

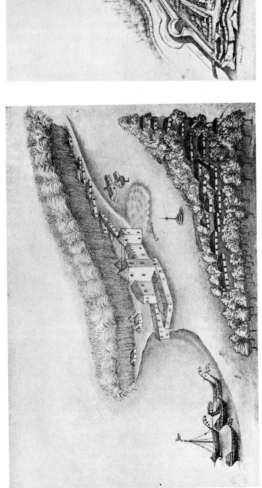

Quilon at the beginning of the sixteenth century.

Both illustrations from Agência geral do ultramar, *Fundacão do estado do India em 1505* (Lisbon, 1955).

The king of Cochin with his attendants. Woodcut in Balthasar Springer's *Meerfahrt* (published 1509) attributed to Hans Burgkmair, the famous engraver of Augsburg. Reproduced here from Franz Schulze, *Balthasar Springers Indienfahrt* (Strassburg, 1902).

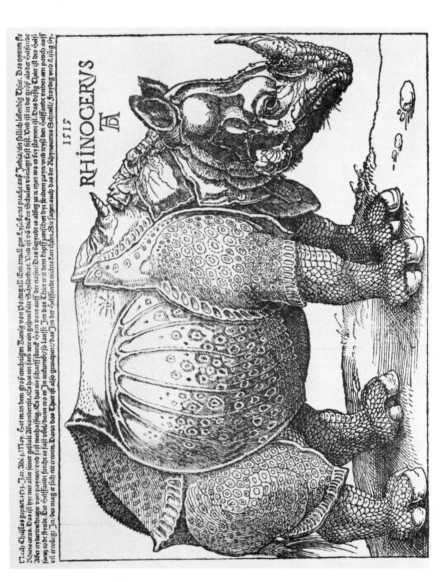

The "famous rhinoceros" of Cambay. Woodcut by Albrecht Dürer (1515). A copy of this woodcut is in the Albertina Museum in Vienna. The original drawing was based on a description sent to Dürer from Lisbon by a friend.

Mahmud III, king of Cambay (reigned 1537-54). Watercolor probably executed by a Portuguese in the East (ca. 1538-46). Original in the Biblioteca Casanatense (Rome). This and the two illustrations on the following page are from G. Schurhammer's "Desenhos orientais do tempo de S. Francisco Xavier," *Garcia da Orta*, Special Number (Lisbon, 1956).

"Reisbutos" (Rajputs) of Cambay. Watercolor.

"Baneanes" (Bānyas) of Cambay. Watercolor.

IX.

De funere in demortui cremandique Brachmani honorem inſtituto: in quo ſimul eorum vxores viuæ in rogum ardentem inſiliunt.

9

Os eſt Brachmanis, vt aliquo ex ipſis demortuo propinqui foueam parent, in quam ligna Sandali, herbas odoratas, cibaria, oriZam, ſiliginem atque oleum inflammando rogo infundant, quibus incenſis cadauer ſuperimponunt. mox procedit vidua, comitata inſtrumentis muſicis, quam cognatæ alacres exhortantur, vt virum fideliter inſequatur, quo in altero mundo cum ipſo inter mille gaudia exultet. ipſa vero animo paratiſſimo, lætabunda veſtes & clenodia depoſita inter proximas diſtribuit, mox ridens rogum inſilit viua cum mariti cadauere concremanda.

vid. cap. 36.

C 2   RITVS

Sati, or widow-burning. From Theodor de Bry, *Indiae orientalis* (Frankfurt, 1599).

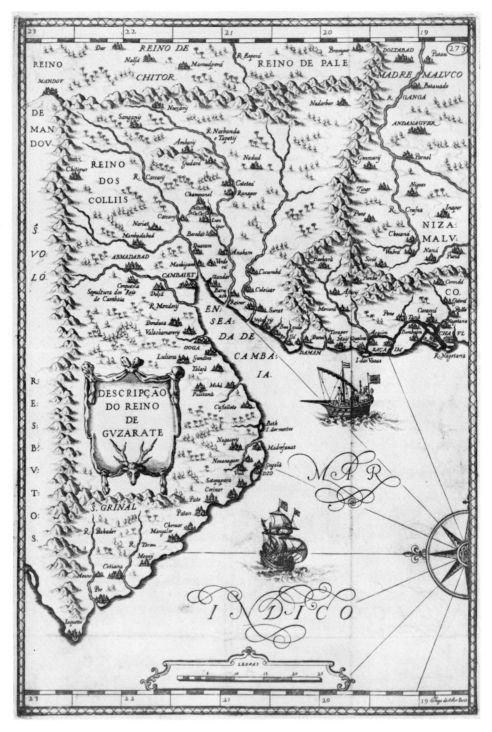

Gujarat. This and the map on the facing page are from João de Barros, *Décadas da Ásia* (Madrid, 1615). Courtesy of the Cornell University Library.

Bengal.

Juggernaut and ceremonial religious suicide in the *Rath-játra*, a Hindu procession. This and the illustration on the facing page are from G. Schurhammer's "Desenhos orientais do tempo de S. Francisco Xavier," *Garcia da Orta*, Special Number (Lisbon, 1956).

A Portuguese fidalgo in India.

Ships and boats of India. From J. van Linschoten, *Itinerario* (Amsterdam, 1596).
Courtesy of the Newberry Library.

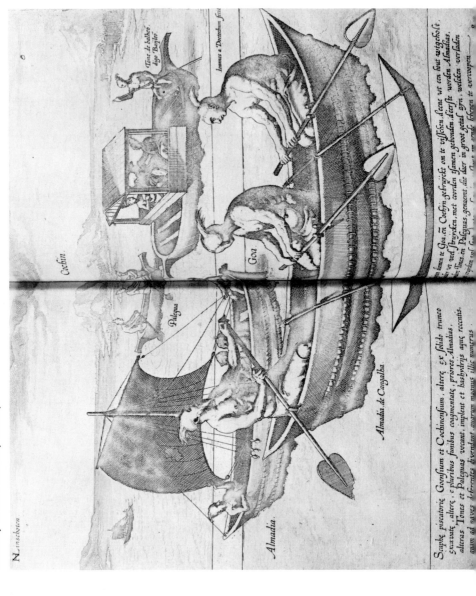

Portuguese as they deal with the rulers of Malabar.[127] On the death of a king his kinsmen, officials, and retainers assemble in an open field to observe the cremation of the body. Once the ashes are buried the mourners shave their bodies completely, "saving only their eyelashes and eyebrows," and, after cleaning their teeth, refrain from chewing betel and eating meat or fish for thirteen days. From the estate of the deceased ruler alms are distributed to fishermen, and many of the poor as well as the Brahmans are fed at his expense. In this period of official mourning, the successor of the dead Zamorin performs no official acts and is not formally installed "lest there should be someone to oppose him." The state is meanwhile governed by a regent appointed from the Nāyar nobility. At the end of the thirteen days, the new Zamorin is sworn into office before the assembled notables. In this ceremony he swears to preserve and enforce the laws, to pay the outstanding debts left by his predecessor, and to strive to regain what former rulers had lost.

While taking this oath, having his sword in his left hand, he holds in his right hand a burning candle,[128] on which is a gold ring which he touches with his finger. After this they throw some grains of rice over him, using many other ceremonies, and numerous prayers, and then they worship the sun three times. When all the *Caymales*,[129] or lords of noble birth, taking hold of the candle, take an oath to be true and faithful subjects to the new king.

While all others are released from restrictions after this investiture ceremony, the new Zamorin continues his personal mourning (the *diksha*) for a whole year.

At the end of the Zamorin's official year of mourning another ceremony (the *tírūmāsam*) takes place.[130] The heir apparent (*erālpād*), the other kinsmen, and the nobles of the realm congregate to "confirm the prince [erālpād] as heir, and the others after him, each in their degrees."[131] Once the succession has been determined, the Zamorin makes his own appointments to office. He confirms in their appointments some of those who had served his predecessor; others he removes completely and replaces them with men of his own choice. The assembly then disperses and the erālpād withdraws to "lands set apart for him, and he may come no more to Calicut as long as the King lives."[132] The departure of the heir apparent and his pilgrimage to the headquarters of the

---

[127] Dames (ed.), *op. cit.* (n. 5), II, 12–13, and Castanheda in Azevedo (ed.), *op. cit.* (n. 17), I, 36–37.

[128] Quotation from the sixteenth-century English translation of Castanheda in Eden (trans.), *op. cit.* (n. 78), II, 352. Almost identical to the description by Barbosa as translated in Dames (ed.), *op. cit.* (n. 5), II, 13. In the original Portuguese Castanheda (Azevedo [ed.], *op. cit.* [n. 17], I, 37) refers to a *candea acesa* which the sixteenth-century English translator renders as a "burning candle"; the translator of Barbosa renders the same words as a "lighted oil lamp." Both translations of the Portuguese are possible, but it is likely that a lamp is meant.

[129] Malayālam, *kaimal*, meaning a Nāyar chief. See Yule and Burnell, *op. cit.* (n. 10), p. 770. For details see Dames (ed.), *op. cit.* (n. 5), II, 13–14, n. 3.

[130] Cf. Thorne's eyewitness account of this ceremony in 1916 in Dames (ed.), *op. cit.* (n. 5), II, 16, n. 1.

[131] *Ibid.*, p. 16.

[132] *Ibid.*

erālpād is performed with great ceremony and according to rites prescribed by tradition.[133]

In connection with his description of court ceremonies at Calicut, Barbosa incidentally gives a few details on the functioning of the central authority. The regent (*mangāt achan*), who traditionally acts in place of the Zamorin during the thirteen days of general mourning, is described as having "all the laws of the Kingdom"[134] in his possession and as holding complete control over the treasury. Upon coming into power the new Zamorin makes his own political appointments. At his court he maintains a large number of secretaries who write down on palm leaves "everything connected with the King's Exchequer" and with the "justice and governance of the realm."[135] The Zamorin employs a "thousand women" of "good caste" as "sweepers of his palace,"[136] each one being a specialist in her particular job. Aside from pages and other attendants, the court of Calicut is guarded by large contingents of Nāyars who accompany the ruler whenever he goes abroad. Over the city of Calicut the Zamorin appoints a governor from the Nāyar caste who is called "Talixe"[137] and who is responsible for maintaining order and meting out justice. In administering justice, the governor is responsible to the Zamorin. Outside the city itself, the Zamorin appoints a chief justice who is called *contante carnaxies* and who has his deputies in every town.[138] Calicut obviously is outfitted with a customs office, and Castanheda comments that the Zamorin is able because of the huge revenues flowing into his coffers "to raise a force of thirty thousand men in a single day, and could even bring a hundred thousand men into the field, completely equipt for war in three days."[139] Even while allowing for conventional exaggeration in the use of figures, one gets the impression that the Zamorin's efficiency in bringing an army into existence was startling to the Portuguese.

On the administration of justice, Barbosa gives many details. He is well aware of the fact that the castes themselves take the responsibility for the misdeeds of their members, and he points out that the methods of trial and punishment differ depending on the caste of the offender or on his status as native or foreigner. Persons of the lower castes, if they confess to or are caught in the act of committing a theft, are executed summarily by beheading or impalement of the body on short stakes (*kazhu*).[140] Moors are treated in a similar fashion, except that they are executed by thrusts of a sword. If a thief so executed has stolen goods from a private person, the owner forfeits his goods to the state, presumably in payment for its execution of justice. When the thief is not apprehended, even though

[133] Cf. on these ceremonies and others connected with the succession the accounts of the installation rites of 1909 by the Zamorin of Calicut himself in *ibid.*, pp. 249–55.

[134] *Ibid.*, p. 14.

[135] *Ibid.*, p. 18.

[136] *Ibid.*, p. 19.

[137] *Kozhikkot Talachannavar*, or the Calicut Talachan. See *ibid.*, p. 27, n. 1.

[138] Identification uncertain. *Contante* is possibly a Portuguese word meaning roughly "to give account." See *ibid.*, p. 32, n. 2; also cf. Castanheda in Azevedo (ed.), *op. cit.* (n. 17), I, 37.

[139] Eden (trans.), *op. cit.* (n. 78), II, 350.

[140] Dames (ed.), *op. cit.* (n. 5), II, 27, n. 2.

the stolen goods are recovered, the authorities retain the property in question for a specified period of days, and, if the thief is not caught in the interim, all the goods less one-fourth are returned to their owner. Should an accused thief deny being guilty, they imprison him for nine or ten days under very harsh conditions. Should he still refuse to confess, the accuser is asked whether he wants the accused to be released or tried. If the decision is for trial, the accused is ritually prepared for trial by ordeal. If he is a native, he is required to testify to his innocence and then plunge the first two fingers of his right hand into a pot of boiling oil. Should his fingers be burnt, the accused is tortured to force a confession of what he has done with the stolen goods. Whether he confesses or not, he is still executed. Should the accused's fingers not be burnt, he is released and the accuser is either executed, fined, or banished. Moors are subjected to the same trials, except that their ordeal is to lick a red-hot axe with their tongues. The procedures and punishments for theft are likewise followed in cases where the individual is accused of murder, cow-killing, attacks on Brahmans or Nāyars, or of having relations with a Brahman's wife. In no case, however, is a woman ever executed by the law (she may be by her caste); if guilty, she is either fined or banished. Vagrants (all of those who have no parents, master, or employment, whether they be men or women) are wards of the state and are sold at low prices to any willing purchaser. Such an account at once raises the question whether Barbosa was not describing some modes of trial and punishment drawn from his European background which he then transposed to India and incorporated in his account to make it seem more complete and authoritative. Misgivings are not warranted, however, for Barbosa's report agrees very closely with accounts of justice in Malabar written by British official and unofficial observers in the eighteenth century.[141]

The status of the Nāyars under the law is quite different from the lower castes. No matter what crime he commits, the Nāyar is never imprisoned or fettered. If a complaint is made against a Nāyar, he is summoned to appear before the governor. Should he fail to appear, the governor issues a warrant which prescribes death for the offending Nāyar at the hands of three or four appointed Nāyars. After being hunted down, the offending Nāyar is slain by his fellows, the warrant is placed upon his breast, and his body lies exposed until it is devoured by "the fowls of the air and the jackals."[142] If the accused Nāyar responds to the summons, he is confronted by the complainant in the governor's presence and each is called upon "to say all that he knows regarding the other."[143] If the accused denies the charge, the litigants are given eight days in which "to establish clearly what each one has said."[144] Should each hold to his original position then at the end of eight days a trial by ordeal in boiling oil is decreed as for the lower castes.

---

141 See Thorne's note in *ibid*.
142 *Ibid*., p. 31. Some additional references by Castanheda to the Nāyar's status under the law may also be found in Azevedo (ed.), *op. cit*. (n. 17), I, 39-40.
143 Barbosa in Dames (ed.), *op. cit*. (n. 5), II, 31.   144 *Ibid*.

Barbosa and the other Portuguese writers are particularly intrigued by the caste system of Malabar and go to considerable pains to understand and explain certain of its aspects. None of the Portuguese is very clear on the precise relationship of the ruling families to the Brahmans. Barbosa (and who could expect a European to think otherwise) evidently thought that the ruling families, not the Brahmans, form the highest caste. Pires claims that the "best" of the Brahmans are the *Kshatriyas* and that in rank they are followed by the *Pattars* and the *Nambūtiris*.[145] Barros[146] makes the king of Quilon the leader of the Brahmans, and Castanheda[147] declares outright that the Zamorin is of the Brahman caste. All of them agree that the Brahmans are a learned and priestly caste who "all speak the same tongue"[148] and serve as courtly functionaries. Albuquerque declares that they have a "scientific language [Sanskrit] which is like our Latin."[149] The only way to be a Brahman is through being born into a Brahman's family. In Malabar, since most Brahmans were and are Nambūtiris, the descriptions of the Portuguese, who make no such distinction themselves, refer to the practices of the Nambūtiri group.[150]

The male children in a Nambūtiri family are ritually invested when seven years of age with a strip of untanned skin which they wear over the shoulder. In other Brahman groups it is customary to bestow a thread rather than a skin upon the novice who is entering the stage of life called *brahmāchāryam*. For the next seven years of his training period the young Nambūtiri must wear his strap and refrain from eating betel. The novitiate being over, the leather strip is ceremoniously removed and the Nambūtiri is invested with a three-stranded cord of twenty-seven threads as a symbol of his having attained full status as a Brahman. "Thereafter, he may eat betel, but not flesh or fish,"[151] his diet consisting of rice, milk, butter and fruit.[152] In a Nambūtiri family only the eldest son marries and he marries "only once in our manner,"[153] and he is looked upon as the successor to an entailed estate.[154] His younger brothers officially remain unmarried. Though they form alliances (*sambandhams*) with Nāyar women, "they may not sleep with any woman older than themselves."[155]

---

145 Pires in Cortesão (ed.), *op. cit.* (n. 9), I, 68.

146 Cidade and Múrias (eds.), *op. cit.* (n. 6), I, 371.

147 Azevedo (ed.), *op. cit.* (n. 17), I, 36.

148 Barbosa in Dames (ed.), *op. cit.* (n. 5), II, 33.

149 Birch (trans.), *op. cit.* (n. 116), II, 78.

150 Also known as the Kerala or Malayāla Brahmans, this group was the dominant priestly and aristocratic group in Malabar from ancient times. For a detailed exposition of their customs see L. K. Anatha Krishna Iyer, *The Cochin Tribes and Castes* (Madras, 1912), II, 170–288. There is also a sizable group of Tamil Brahmans, who are looked upon as being foreign in contrast to the native Nambūtiris.

151 Barbosa in Dames (ed.), *op. cit.* (n. 5), II, 34.

152 Albuquerque in Birch (trans.), *op. cit.* (n. 116), II, 78. For more details on diet see Iyer, *op. cit.* (n. 150), II, 284.

153 Barbosa in Dames (ed.), *op. cit.* (n. 5), II, 34, n. 3.

154 Family property is called *Brahmāswum* and every member of the family has an equal claim; in practice, however, the eldest son succeeds to the father's estate and the others receive maintenance from him. See Iyer, *op. cit.* (n. 150), II, 214.

155 Dames (ed.), *op. cit.* (n. 5), II, 35.

The eldest son keeps his wife under close surveillance; when the eldest son dies his wife never remarries. Should a wife be unfaithful to her husband, she is put to death by poison.

The Brahmans are universally revered among the natives. They live apart from others "in their own houses and cities," [156] and act as clergy in the numerous temples. Their houses of worship have three principal portals which "face the west." [157] Over the central portal of the temple in which Vasco da Gama was received there hung seven small bells.[158] On the outside of the temple, in front of the main portal, there stands a stone (*maṇḍapa*) as tall as a man with three steps leading up to it.[159] The interior of the temple houses a tower-like chapel (*srī-kōyil*) which contains the "idol" and which none may enter except the officiating Brahmans. These priests wear a "kind of petticoat of cotton" that covers them from the waist to the knees, calico patches in their armpits, and nothing on their legs, feet, and heads.[160] Twice each day the Brahmans, after performing ceremonial ablutions, take the "idol" out of the chapel and carry it around the outside of the temple (always remaining within the surrounding enclosure) in a great procession. They also wash the stone three times each day and place upon it twice each day a ritual offering of boiled rice for the crows. In the interior of the temple which Vasco da Gama visited were "many images painted on the walls" possessing "monstrous teeth" and having "as many as four arms." To Castanheda such paintings appeared "ugly," but he nevertheless comments admiringly on the temple as an edifice of "splendid workmanship." [161]

In their religious practices, the Malabars are judged to be superstitious, given to soothsaying, and prone to believe in lucky and unlucky days. They are often visited by the devil, and they believe that people are moved to behave in extraordinary ways by the gods of the temple who enter into them. Their deities are the sun, moon, stars, fire, cows, and whatever they first meet on going out in the morning. The Brahmans look upon "three" as a sacred number and they believe in a god who has three persons.[162] This god is "Bermabesma Maceru" and he is believed "to have been since the beginning of the world." [163] Of Christ they have no knowledge, but, according to Garcia da Orta, they believe in the transmigration of souls.[164]

Barbosa also notes a number of other features about the Brahmans' life. Under law they are never subject to the death penalty and ordinarily receive

[156] *Ibid.*
[157] See *ibid.*, pp. 35–36, n. 3. Incorrect. Actually the principal portals face the East.
[158] Castanheda in Azevedo (ed.), *op. cit.* (n. 17), I, 44.
[159] This stone platform could be used only by Brahmans; see Dames (ed.), *op. cit.* (n. 5), II, 36, n. 1.
[160] Castanheda in Azevedo (ed.), *op. cit.* (n. 17), I, 44.
[161] In Eden (trans.), *op. cit.* (n. 78), II, 363.
[162] *Ibid.*, p. 355.
[163] Sanskrit: *Brahma, Vishnu,* and *Maheśvara,* the three gods who are combined to make the *Trimūrti,* the triune god of Hinduism. See Dames (ed.), *op. cit.* (n. 5), II, 37, n. 1. See also Pires in Cortesão (ed.), *op. cit.* (n. 9), I, 66.
[164] Markham (ed.), *op. cit.* (n. 4), p. 291.

for their wrongdoings only a "mild chastisement" from their superiors.[165] After bathing, they always paint certain marks on their foreheads with ashes. They cremate their dead. When a husband learns that his wife is pregnant, he cleans his teeth, abstains from betel and food, and does not trim his beard until she is delivered.[166] The Brahmans serve their rulers in everything except war. They are cooks in the royal court, couriers, and emissaries to foreign lands. Even in times of war, they travel about freely and "none does them any ill."[167] They are learned in religion, possess many books on religious subjects, "believe and respect many truths,"[168] and have powers of excommunication and absolution.[169] For their learning and piety, they are held in the highest esteem by everyone, even the kings.

The Nāyars,[170] or warrior caste, particularly attracts the attention of the Portuguese writers, for it was the dominant caste of Malabar and the one which possessed social customs most foreign to Europeans. Barbosa, whose account of the Nāyars is still considered to be the most accurate Western narrative of his day, states categorically that the *fidalgos* (nobles) of this caste "have no other duty than to serve in war."[171] Pires believes that there must be 150,000 Nāyars in Malabar.[172] Armed at all times with swords, bows, or spears, the Nāyars act in periods of peace as guards for the king and other great lords. As retainers of the aristocracy, they serve their lords loyally and live at the lord's expense. Neither the king nor any other lord can create a Nāyar, since descent is the only entry to this soldierly aristocracy. Upon becoming seven years of age, young Nāyars begin to receive instruction in physical training, fencing, and the use of arms. The teachers, called "panicals" (*pannikars*),[173] are highly esteemed by people of all ages, and in the rainy season each year they give refresher courses in fencing which are compulsory for the mature Nāyar throughout his life.

Once sufficiently prepared at the school (*kalari*) in the arts of war, the fledgling soldier presents himself for investiture as a Nāyar. In Cannanore the ceremony is performed by the king; in Calicut by the youth's teacher with the approbation

---

165 *Ibid.*, p. 37.

166 Though nothing is said of this particular practice, for details on pregnancy rites among certain of the Nambūtiris see Iyer, *op. cit.* (n. 150), II, 199–201.

167 Barbosa in Dames (ed.), *op. cit.* (n. 5), II, 37.

168 *Ibid.*

169 Pires in Cortesão (ed.), *op. cit.* (n. 9), I, 68.

170 The name Nāyar is possibly the same as the Malayālam word *Nagar*, "serpent men." See K. M. Panikkar, "Some Aspects of Nāyar Life," *Journal of the Royal Anthropological Institute*, XLVIII (1918), 289–91, appendix, n. 1. Also see Dames (ed.), *op. cit.* (n. 5), II, 38, n. 1, who concludes that none of the derivations so far propounded can be considered satisfactory.

171 Dames (ed.), *op. cit.* (n. 5), II, 38. Panikkar (*loc. cit.* [n. 170], p. 256) comments that this kind of observation is "unscientific and unreliable." He feels that a historical reconstruction "is possible only after a thorough and searching study of Nāyar literature."

172 Cortesão (ed.), *op. cit.* (n. 9), I, 67.

173 For further details on military training see E. K. Gough-Aberle, "Changing Kinship Usages in the Setting of Political and Economic Change among the Nayars of Malabar," *Journal of the Royal Anthropological Society*, LXXXII (1952), 76.

of the king. The ceremony of investiture in Cannanore is naturally the more elaborate of the two. Here the youth who wants to receive initiation as a soldier presents himself at the king's palace at an appointed time in the company of his soldier-kinsmen. Upon being ushered into the royal presence, the youth makes a gift in coins to the king. He is then asked if he will uphold the laws and customs of his caste. When an affirmative answer is given by the applicant and his kinsmen, the king commands the youth to gird himself with a sword. The royal hand is then placed on the initiate's head, the king utters a prayer in a low voice, and then embraces the young man while commanding him to "Protect cows and Brahmans."¹⁷⁴ This ceremony being finished, the youth is asked to declare his name and lineage before the assemblage; this information is then entered into the king's register so that he may henceforward be on the royal payroll. The rites of initiation followed in Calicut are essentially the same, except that the teacher acts in the place of the king.

Among the Europeans the Nāyars are held in high esteem as warriors. Though they are mercenaries, they abide by their oath to die for their lords. Should a master be killed, his Nāyars relentlessly search out the slayer without regard for their own lives. The private person who hires Nāyars as bodyguards may even be able to escape the king's wrath, so great is their prestige and influence with the crown. In war they never give up until they are all slain. Certainly, the Portuguese do not look in this case, as they do in so many others, upon the Indians as being weak, effeminate, and unwarlike. Through bitter experience the Portuguese, from Vasco da Gama onward, had every practical reason for respecting the military prowess of the Nāyars.¹⁷⁵

The marriage customs and the matrilineal kinship system of this soldierly caste engage the attention of all the Portuguese writers. They contend that the Nāyars are not permitted to marry, rear families, or control property because such duties might interfere with their devotion to the military life.¹⁷⁶ The Nāyars live in their own villages in seclusion from other groups and possess their own palm trees and water tanks. Since they never "marry" in the Western sense of the word, the children never know their own fathers and a father never has a son. Three or four Nāyars customarily cohabit with the same woman at certain specified times which all members of the group (*taravad*) have agreed upon.¹⁷⁷ All members of the taravad stem from the same caste (or subcaste) and both sexes are forbidden on pain of death to cohabit with persons of a

---

¹⁷⁴ Barbosa (Dames [ed.], *op. cit.* [n. 5], II, 46) gives the king's words in transliteration as "Paje Gubramarca"; Barros (in Cidade and Múrias [eds.], *op. cit.* [n. 6], I, 375), who seems to follow Barbosa in other matters, writes this admonition: "*Paguego bramenta bisquera.*" For an effort to analyze these words see Dames (ed.), *op. cit.* (n. 5), II, 46, n. 2. Castanheda (in Azevedo [ed.], *op. cit.* [n. 17], I, 38) tells much the same story, evidently based on Barbosa, but does not attempt to give a transliteration of these words.

¹⁷⁵ Even as late as World War I, the Nāyars joined the Indian army in large numbers. See Dames (ed.), *op. cit.* (n. 5), II, 38, n. 2.

¹⁷⁶ Cf. Gough-Aberle, *loc. cit.* (n. 173), LXXXII (1952), 77, for a recent and a similar opinion.

¹⁷⁷ Based on Castanheda in Azevedo (ed.), *op. cit.* (n. 17), I, 37–38.

lower caste. Nāyar women are free to accept Brahmans as lovers. A kinsman or friend is invited by the mother to perform the ceremony of tying the *tāli* of each twelve-year-old daughter. Thereafter a young Nāyar is chosen to initiate the girl into sexual relations so that she will be "fit for association with men," [178] and will be ready to establish her own taravad.

In such a system all relationship and inheritance is necessarily based on the mother. The property of a male passes on to his brothers and to the sons of their sisters, all of whom must be born of the same mother. Even though all Nāyars receive stipends from the king, "some of them possess also estates on which they live and support their sisters for whom they have great regard." [179] To their older sisters the Nāyars show great respect and affection. Their relations with younger sisters are very distant, for they never enter the same room with them, or touch them, or even speak to them. With their brothers and other relatives the Nāyars are exceedingly respectful and courteous.

On the death of a Nāyar, his body is burned within his own compound and the ashes are cast into running water. [180] He is mourned for a stipulated period by his mother and other kinsmen. [181] The nephew, or whoever is his heir, mourns for a full year. [182] During the year of obligatory mourning, the heir does his own cooking, bathes before eating, and ceremoniously changes his clothes. He feeds crows from his own food and gives alms to the poor and the Brahmans. The Nāyars believe that "with the proper signs a man who has died may be born again of another woman." [183] They worship the sun, moon, the lamp, and cows, and are great believers in omens, tabus, and unlucky and lucky days. If a cat crosses the path of a person bent on business, he does not do it. On going out of doors, if they see a crow carrying a stick they turn back. When a person is departing, he postpones his leaving if someone in the party sneezes. The Nāyars, it is evident to Barbosa, "believe in ghosts of many kinds." [184]

The Nāyars are depicted as being even more afraid of staining their nobility by association with lower castes than are the Brahmans. They will neither touch nor eat and drink with lesser people. In walking along the road they order lower-caste people to get out of their way. Should such a person be foolhardy enough to refuse to give way, the Nāyar "may kill him without punish-

<hr/>

[178] Barbosa in Dames (ed.), *op. cit.* (n. 5), II, 42; for an account of more recent practices see Pannikar, *loc. cit.* (n. 170), pp. 268–69. On what is considered normal sexual posture in Malabar see Pires in Cortesão (ed.), *op. cit.* (n. 9), I, 69.

[179] Barbosa in Dames (ed.), *op. cit.* (n. 5), II, 53.

[180] In recent times "only the eldest members [of the Nāyar caste] are burnt; others are buried." (Panikkar, *loc. cit.* [n. 170], p. 275).

[181] Panikkar (*ibid.*, p. 276) gives the period as fourteen days.

[182] He also takes a vow (*diksha*) to lead a pure and pious life (*ibid.*).

[183] Barbosa in Dames (ed.), *op. cit.* (n. 5), II, 55.

[184] *Ibid.* Cf. this statement with Panikkar, *loc. cit.* (n. 170), p. 278. ". . . it is nothing short of marvelous to see the Nayars, who have, it must be remembered, assimilated a very great deal of the material and intellectual culture of their neighbors . . . still maintain with undiminished vigour their spirit-worship, black-magic, and demoniacal ceremonies. . . ."

ment."[185] Even if a low-caste man touches a Nāyar woman by accident, he will be killed by her kinsmen.[186] In the towns lower-caste individuals walk close to the walls to avoid touching and thereby polluting a Nāyar. Business transactions between Nāyars and the lower castes are conducted through intermediaries to avoid pollution. When a Nāyar is unavoidably polluted, he cleanses himself by bathing and changing his clothes before entering his dwelling. Ordinarily, the Nāyar women strictly avoid going into the towns. In all matters relating to pollution by lower castes the Nāyars are judged by Barbosa to be "great sticklers."[187] It is only when they go off to war that the Nāyars are relieved from worry about performing purification rites.

In their role as warriors the Nāyars are kept on the king's list throughout their lives. The mothers and nephews of Nāyars slain in battle are given a royal pension. In case a Nāyar is wounded, he continues to receive his regular stipend as well as medical care. When the Nāyar is on active duty, he receives his wages at the end of each day. Should the king fail or be unable to pay the customary stipends, the aggrieved Nāyars join together in warning the delinquent king that they will take service under another master. If he does not immediately pay them one-third of their back wages and give them a definite promise of payment for the remainder, they take employment elsewhere. Their departure constitutes an injury to the king's reputation, presumably both with his own subjects and his fellow rulers.

While the Nāyars are praised for their unswerving devotion to duty, Barbosa[188] and Castanheda[189] both observe that they seem able to bring personal and popular grievances to the attention of the crown in their role as protectors of the people. Apparently under the pressure of injustice, a Nāyar sometimes acts as if possessed. Uttering terrible threats, he appears before the king with a naked sword in his hand. While slashing himself, as a vivid demonstration of his sincerity, he asserts: "I am such and such a god, and I have come to tell you such and such a thing." Should the king doubt his words, the Nāyar keeps on shouting and slashing until the king takes heed of his complaint. Apparently, as in later times, the Nāyars were the only group who could remonstrate with the king and still expect to receive a hearing and to see justice done.[190]

On the other castes of Malabar, Barbosa is the only Portuguese writer who attempts any systematic description of them. Pires gives a partial list of the lower castes, and adds a few details not included in Barbosa's more detailed description.[191] Barros, who notes that he will talk about the castes in more detail in

---

[185] Dames (ed.), *op. cit.* (n. 5), II, 49.
[186] Cf. account of Pires in Cortesão (ed.), *op. cit.* (n. 9), I, 71.
[187] Dames (ed.), *op. cit.* (n. 5), II, 50. For the importance of ritual purity and pollution in caste-ranking see E. K. Gough-Aberle, "Criteria of Caste Ranking in South India," *Man in India*, XXXIX (1959), 115.
[188] Dames (ed.), *op. cit.* (n. 5), II, 55.
[189] Azevedo (ed.), *op. cit.* (n. 17), I, 39.
[190] On the Nāyars as political leaders see Logan, *op. cit.* (n. 59), I, 132–33.
[191] For a comparison of the two lists see Cortesão (ed.), *op. cit.* (n. 9), I, 72, n. 1.

his *Geografia* (which has never been found), observes only that the farmer is distinct from the fisherman and the weaver is different from the carpenter in a variety of ways.[192] None of the writers clearly makes the distinction commonly talked about now between the castes of the "Right-hand" (agricultural groups) and the "Left-hand" (artisan groups).

Barbosa places the "Biabares"[193] (*Vyābāri*), a caste of native merchants, just below the Nāyars, for they are "of such established lineage that the Nayres may touch them."[194] Dealers in goods of every kind, both inland and at the seaports, they are described as being an ancient and wealthy caste. Their wealth is not only in trade, but also "in land inherited from of old."[195] Like the Nāyars, they are never executed by legal process, but by members of their own group. Unlike the Nāyars, they have but one wife and her sons are their heirs. Upon death the members of this caste are cremated. The wives, even when they are widowed at a young age, never remarry; the husbands may remarry after the death of a wife.

The "Cuicavem" (probably potters, called *Kusavan*) are said to be related to but separate from the Nāyars.[196] The members of this subcaste, whose sons may adopt no other occupation, make pottery and roofing bricks. They have their own religious practices, gods, and temples. Their marital customs are the same as the Nāyars', and presumably their inheritance and related practices follow the same general pattern as those of the Nāyars. Another non-military subcaste is the "Mainatos" (*Mainattu*) "whose occupation is to wash clothes for the Kings, Bramenes and Nayres."[197] In addition to washing clothes they also run a linen supply service which daily furnishes the higher castes with clean clothes for a regular monthly fee. Finally, among the Nāyar-related groups there are the "Caletis" (*Chaliyans*), a caste of weavers of low social and economic status.[198] Many of them are the sons of Nāyars, and like their fathers they carry arms and act as soldiers. Although he does not say so specifically, Barbosa is apparently aware of the fact that Nāyars can associate with these subcastes without being polluted.

There are, according to Barbosa, eleven polluting castes. The purest of these is the "Tuias" (*Tiyans*) who cultivate and harvest the palm groves and make toddy, quarry for stone, and sometimes fight in the wars. The majority of them work as serfs on the lands of the Nāyars. They worship their own gods, live apart, and strictly avoid all contact with castes lower than their own. As with the Nāyars, their brothers and nephews are their heirs because "their women openly earn their living with their bodies."[199] The "Manens" (*Mamans*), a caste of

---

192 Cidade and Múrias (eds.), *op. cit.* (n. 6), I, 372.

193 Dames (ed.), *op. cit.* (n. 5), II, 56, n. 1.

194 *Ibid.*, p. 57.   195 *Ibid.*, p. 56.

196 Cf. *ibid.*, p. 57, n. 1 which quotes the *Malabar Gazetteer* (p. 120) as listing the *Kusavan* as "non-military classes ranking as *Nayars*." Pires (in Cortesão [ed.], *op. cit.* [n. 9], I, 71) remarks that "there are also Nayars who sell oil and fish, and many are craftsmen."

197 Dames (ed.), *op. cit.* (n. 5), II, 58.

198 *Ibid.*, p. 59, n. 1.   199 *Ibid.*, p. 60.

washermen who serve the polluted castes, are omitted from Ramusio's version of Barbosa's account, but Pires mentions them in the list which Ramusio did publish.[200] The "Canaquas" (*Kaniyans*), a polluted caste still lower on Barbosa's scale, monopolize the manufacture of bucklers and umbrellas and have astrology and fortune telling as important sidelines. The artisans he groups together (castes of the Left-hand?) as "Ageres" (*Asari*), and notes that there are subcastes of masons, carpenters, smiths, metalworkers, and goldsmiths. These groups have their own gods, their own systems of apprenticing sons in their father's trade, and a patrilineal kinship organization. The "Mogeres" (*Mogers*), most of whom "gain their living on the sea,"[201] are very few in number and of foreign origin. In addition to fishing and sailing, they work as carriers "of all things belonging to the Royal State"[202] and act as slaves to the Nāyars. They live in their own villages, possess no recognizable "marriage law," and bequeath their properties to their nephews rather than their sons. The "Monquers" (*Mukkuvans*), "who have no other work than fishing,"[203] are considered to be expert seamen, rude fellows, and shameless thieves. Though their women "sleep with anyone soever,"[204] they marry and pass on their goods to their sons. Some of them are rich landowners who seem to run the danger of having their properties confiscated by the king "whensoever he wills."[205] Still, as a caste they enjoy the privilege of not paying tax on fresh fish, although on dried fish they are required to pay a duty of 4 per cent.

Barbosa seems to descend to a lower level in his caste hierarchy (castes of the Right-hand?) when he talks of the "Betunes" (*Vettuvans*). These poverty-stricken people make salt, grow rice, and live in houses "standing by themselves in the fields."[206] An even ruder people are the "Pāneens" (*Pānans*) "who are great sorcerers and live by no other means."[207] Barbosa describes at some length the ceremonies which they follow when they are called in to help diagnose and prescribe for a sick king. They live in the hinterlands and hills, entirely apart from other people. Being good hunters and mountaineers, they live on game and wild fowl. And, at this point, Barbosa inserts a short description of the "Revoleens," a term which possibly denotes the *Eravallens*, a primitive jungle tribe.[208] Clad only in filthy rags, these poor people carry firewood and grass to the towns. While all of these low-caste people are untouchables, the group most feared by the Nāyars is the "Poleas" (*Pulayans*). These primitive people, who live in "secret lurking places"[209] or mean huts, cultivate rice with

---

[200] Cortesão (ed.), *op. cit.* (n. 9), I, 72.
[201] Dames (ed.), *op. cit.* (n. 5), II, 64.
[202] *Ibid.*
[203] *Ibid.*
[204] *Ibid.*, p. 65.
[205] *Ibid.*
[206] *Ibid.*
[207] *Ibid.*, p. 66.
[208] For a discussion of this identification see *ibid.*, p. 67, n. 1.
[209] *Ibid.*, p. 68.

buffalos and oxen. This "evil race" [210] will try at certain months of the year to take revenge upon their masters by intentionally polluting Nāyar women. The most degenerate of the lowest castes is the "Pareans" (*Parayans*) who "dwell in the most desert places" [211] and eat cow's flesh. Even though some of them are lettered men, they are thought to be so base that the sight of them will pollute the beholder.[212]

In all, Barbosa identifies eighteen upper and lower castes indigenous to Malabar with "each one separate and unable to touch others or marry with them." [213] He also identifies four immigrant castes as dwelling in Malabar. The first foreign caste on his list is the "Chatis" (*Chettys*),[214] a merchant group. The majority of the "Chatis" are rich merchants who deal in precious stones, pearls, and corals. They dress differently from the natives and possess "spacious houses in their own appointed streets." [215] They speak "a tongue [Konkani] which differs from that of Malabar [Malayālam] as it is with the Castilians and Portuguese." [216] They live outside the local law and maintain peace and order among themselves, apparently to the king's satisfaction. They have their own gods, temples, marital and burial customs, and dietary habits. Evidently they live in peace with the other foreign merchant colony whom Barbosa calls the "Guzarates" (*Gujarati banyā*), and he correctly identifies them as natives of Cambay. These Gujarati merchants dwell in great houses on their own streets "as the Jews are wont to dwell in our land." [217] The rulers of the Malabar cities look upon the Gujarati with favor because of the revenues they pay into the treasury in the form of duties.

Both Barbosa and Barros give considerable attention to the Moors of Malabar. They are described as being of two kinds: those who are natives and those of foreign origin. The mestizo group called "Malpueres" (*Moplahs*) [218] intermarry with low-caste natives. They speak Malayālam and dress like the natives except for little round caps that they wear on their heads as emblems of distinction.[219] Making their living by trade, the indigenous Moors are scattered throughout Malabar, especially in the cities, and constitute about 20 per cent of the total

---

[210] *Ibid.*, p. 69.

[211] *Ibid.*

[212] Pires in Cortesão (ed.), *op. cit.* (n. 9), I, 72.

[213] Dames (ed.), *op. cit.* (n. 5), II, 70. He actually lists only seventeen separate castes, but clearly considers that the kings form a separate caste. Though not exhaustive, Barbosa's listing "includes nearly all the castes of importance which still exist in Malabar." (*Ibid.*, n. 2.)

[214] Barros (in Cidade and Múrias [eds.], *op. cit.* [n.6], I, 372–73) calls them *chatins* and reports: "These are men who have a genius for trade and who are so sharp in their dealings that our people, whenever they desire to blame or praise a man for his subtlety and skill in bargaining, they say 'He is a *chatim*,' and they use the word *chatinar* for 'to haggle'—these words now being very commonly adopted by us." The modern Portuguese dictionary defines a *chatim* as a "crooked merchant" and *chatinar* as meaning "to deal crookedly."

[215] Dames (ed.), *op. cit.* (n. 5), II, 72.

[216] *Ibid.*, p. 73.

[217] *Ibid.*

[218] This is the name used by Barbosa (*ibid.*, p. 75); Barros (in Cidade and Múrias [eds.], *op. cit.* [n. 6], I, 373) refers to these mestizo Moors as "naiteás."

[219] They still wear these marks of identification. See Dames (ed.), *op. cit.* (n. 5), II, 74, n. 1.

population. They have a great number of mosques and generally follow the teachings of Mohammed.[220] Barbosa contends that they were so numerous and their influence so great that the advent of the Portuguese was the only thing which prevented Malabar from becoming a Moorish state.

The danger of a Muslim conquest was apparently made even more possible by the presence in Calicut and other Malabar towns of sizable communities of foreign Moors. Arabs, Persians, Gujaratis, Khorasanis, and Daquanis[221] who congregated there with their wives and families were all called "Pardesis" (*Paradēśī* or foreigners). Virtually in control of Malabar's overseas trade, the foreign Moors, like their indigenous co-religionists, enjoy a preferred position because of the substantial revenues that they bring to the towns of Malabar. They are ruled over by their own governor who acts independently except for giving "an account of certain matters to the King"[222] and administers justice according to Muslim precepts. In their keeled ships built without nails the Moors sail for the West with each favorable monsoon. The returns from their spice trade are enough to make most of them wealthy and to attract a constant stream of newcomers to Malabar. The king, ever mindful of the great returns to to be derived from trade and customs, co-operates to the utmost with the foreign traders. As soon as a new merchant arrives at a port city, he is assigned a Nāyar to protect and serve him, a Chetty clerk to keep his records, and a broker to arrange his purchases and sales. This commercial relationship between Malabars and Muslims remains thriving and mutually beneficial until the arrival of the Portuguese in India. "Now," Barbosa laconically comments about the Muslim traders, "there are, it may almost be said, none, and these that are [here] do not live independently."[223]

C. THE HINDU EMPIRE OF VIJAYANAGAR

In about 1346, a century and a half before the Portuguese arrived in India, the Hindus of the Deccan rallied to form a political and military confederation to halt the Muslim onslaught from the north. By 1400, Bukka I had consolidated Vijayanagar's control over the southern half of the peninsula and Hindu civilization hereafter seemed relatively secure in the south. Great ports like Goa, Chaul, and Dabhul were also brought under Vijayanagar's jurisdiction and Ceylon soon became a tributary state. But the northern frontiers of this last citadel of Hindu civilization, especially those fronting on the Bahmani kingdom

---

[220] They are generally Sunnites. Logan, *op. cit.* (n. 59), I, 199.

[221] Probably merchants from Dhaka (often written Dacca) in eastern Bengal, a great center of muslin weaving.

[222] Dames (ed.), *op. cit.* (n. 5), II, 76.

[223] *Ibid.*, p. 78.

in the Deccan, subsequently came under constant pressure from the Muslims as well as from non-Muslim Orissa. The rulers of Vijayanagar thereafter found that they had to be eternally vigilant to prevent their vassals in the border region from revolting and trying to aggrandize themselves by joining forces with the enemy. Still, despite the problem of the unstable northern frontier, the kingdom of Vijayanagar flourished in the fifteenth century, and the city of Vijayanagar rapidly became the economic and cultural center of south India.

The earlier European accounts, those of Conti, Nikitin, and Varthema, describe the wealth and power of Vijayanagar in colorful language if not always in great detail. In 1510, Varthema extravagantly hails the city itself as "a second paradise."[224] Pires, writing between 1512 and 1518, reports that Vijayanagar, reputed to be the largest state in India, was not as extensive as it once had been.[225] This was so because of Muslim expansion in the Deccan and the severance of Goa from Vijayanagar's control.

Viceroy d'Almeida first learned of Vijayanagar in 1505 from a native, and thereafter began to think that Portugal might have more to gain in India by trade than by conquest.[226] Albuquerque in his war against Calicut invited the co-operation of Vijayanagar, and the Franciscan friar, Luis do Salvador, was sent there in 1510 as his emissary. Later in 1510, after Albuquerque captured Goa for the second time, a mission was sent from Vijayanagar to establish friendly relations with the Portuguese and to bring to Albuquerque the written recommendations of Friar Luis.[227] Soon a treaty was concluded with Vijayanagar for the continuation of the traditional horse trade that the Hindu state depended upon so heavily for its military activities. Relations were generally good thereafter for a long time between the Hindus and Christians who were united, if for no other reason, by their common hostility to the Moors.[228]

For the re-creation of sixteenth-century Vijayanagar, the Portuguese sources are of critical importance. Pires makes a number of general comments on it based perhaps on reports which he heard from others in the marts of India. Of special significance is the account of Barbosa written around 1518; Barbosa probably visited Vijayanagar just a few years after Albuquerque's second conquest of Goa in 1510. Shortly after 1520, the Portuguese merchant, Domingo Paes, wrote a lengthy description of Vijayanagar as it was in his day. For the next fifteen years there are extant no Portuguese sources on the Hindu empire. The next important document was prepared around 1535 by Fernão Nuniz, who wrote a chronicle of Vijayanagar based on information which he acquired during three years of residence there (*ca.* 1532–35). It appears that Garcia da Orta, the physician and herbalist of Goa, might have visited Vijayanagar in 1534

---

224 J. W. Jones (trans.), and G. P. Badger (ed.), *The Travels of Lodovico di Varthema* . . . ("Hakluyt Society Publications," Old Series, Vol. XXXII [London, 1863]), p. 126.

225 Cortesão (ed.), *op. cit.* (n. 9), I, 64.

226 Robert Sewell, *A Forgotten Empire (Vijayanagar)* (London, 1900), p. 117.

227 Albuquerque in Birch (trans.), *op. cit.* (n. 116), III, 35–38. Friar Luis was shortly thereafter slain "by the hand of a Turk." (*Ibid.*, p. 38.)

228 Frederick C. Danvers, *The Portuguese in India* (London, 1894), I, 301.

while Nuniz was still there.²²⁹ And it was in these same years (*ca.* 1528–38) that Castanheda was in India. Whether or not he ever visited Vijayanagar is not clear, but it is certain that Castanheda inquired about the Hindu capital from merchants who had been there.²³⁰ Finally, it was around 1537 that the accounts of Paes and Nuniz were dispatched to Portugal, probably addressed to Barros.²³¹

Though Barros had these accounts at his disposal while working on the *Décadas*, he evidently made little use of them.²³² Paes provided a good description of Vijayanagar and Nuniz a detailed chronicle, but Barros' references to the Hindu state are relatively few and generally incidental to the development of his larger narrative. Certainly, it may be true that the Paes and Nuniz accounts were circulated in Europe as manuscripts. But, so far as I know, they were not used extensively by later authors, though Castanheda may have derived information from them. The only accounts of Vijayanagar published around mid-century were those by Pires, Barbosa (both in Ramusio's collection) and Castanheda. And, in the case of Castanheda, he repeats almost verbatim several of the eyewitness stories told by Barbosa, though it must not be concluded from these borrowings that Castanheda's account is completely dependent upon the earlier observers. In Orta's *Colloquies* there are a few additional references to Vijayanagar which substantiate and amplify the basic accounts.

The European writers, beginning with Varthema, refer to the empire of Vijayanagar as the "kingdom of Narsinga."²³³ The capital city of the empire is called "Bisinegar" as an approximation of Vijayanagar,²³⁴ then the leading metropolis of Kanara. According to Castanheda,²³⁵ Vijayanagara, the largest state in the "second India is bordered on the east by the state of *Deli*,"²³⁶ on the west by the Indian Ocean and Malabar, on the north by the Deccan "kingdom," and on the south by the "kingdom" of "Doria" (Orissa).²³⁷ Barbosa describes the country as being "high and rugged," and "very hard to cross" if one is tempted to leave the seacoast for the interior. On the western side the terrain is so difficult to climb "that it is like mounting to the sky, and so rough . . . that men can only pass through it by certain places and passes." This is, in Barbosa's view, the reason why the coastal Malabars succeeded in maintaining

---

²²⁹ Sewell, *op. cit.* (n. 226), p. 115, n. 2.

²³⁰ Cf. Azevedo (ed.), *op. cit.* (n. 17), I, 246.

²³¹ Sewell, *op. cit.* (n. 226), p. vi.

²³² His scanty comments are devoted mainly to warfare; see Cidade and Múrias (eds.), *op. cit.* (n. 6), III, 189–93.

²³³ Or "Narsyngna," "Narasinha," and "Narsin." This name was apparently derived from the name of the ruler, Vira Narasihma, who was in power until 1509. Varthema probably visited there at the end of 1504. (Sir Richard Carnac Temple [ed.], *The Itinerary of Ludovico di Varthema of Bologna* [London, 1928], p. xxv.)

²³⁴ Also "Bisnegar" or "Bijanagher." Conti, around 1420, refers to it as "Bizenegalia" and Nikitin in 1474 as "Bicheneger." See Yule and Burnell, *op. cit.* (n. 10), p. 73. On the various names under which the city was known to the people of south India see B. A. Saletore, *Social and Political Life in the Vijayanagara Empire* (A.D. 1346–A.D. 1646) (Madras, 1934), I, 112–13.

²³⁵ Azevedo (ed.), *op. cit.* (n. 17), I, 242.

²³⁶ The Delhi sultanate.

²³⁷ Castanheda is certainly misplacing Orissa which is roughly east-northeast of Vijayanagar.

their independence of Vijayanagar. But beyond the mountains on the eastern side of the peninsula, the land is reported to be "flat and level,"[238] and presumably no barrier to the spread of Vijayanagar's rule.

Vijayanagar is divided into five "provinces." The first of these political divisions is called "Talinate"[239] and it extends along the west coast from "Cintacora"[240] on the border of the Deccan in the north to the beginning of Malabar in the south, a distance of about fifty leagues (200 miles). For this coastal territory Castanheda gives a list of eleven towns all of which are said to be large and good ports.[241] Barbosa in his separate treatment of these towns indicates clearly that they enjoyed a high degree of political independence.[242] The second province, which borders on the "kingdom" of Deccan and is in the interior, is called "Teãrragei."[243] A third province, also in the interior, is named "Canarâ," and herein is located the capital city of Vijayanagar. "Choramandel" is the fourth province and it extends along the coast for almost a hundred leagues (400 miles) from the southern border of "Coulão" (Quilon) northward to the mountains called the "Udigirmele"[244] which divides "Narsinga" from "Doria." The fifth province is in the interior and is given the name of "Telingue."[245] Except for Castanheda's confusion over the location of "Doria" (Orissa), his account of the extent of Vijayanagar corresponds well with what is known from other sources.[246] His political divisions of the empire appear to be approximately correct, even if unavoidably vague.[247] Pires and Barbosa, unlike Castanheda, pay attention to the language divisions as well, and Barbosa asserts that each province has its own language;[248] in Coromandel, for instance, he knows that the prevailing tongue is Tamil.[249] Pires reports that the ruler of

[238] Dames (ed.), *op. cit.* (n. 5), I, 198–99.

[239] Talinate = Tólinate = Tulu-nāda = North and South Kanara. *Ibid.*, p. 183 n.

[240] The name of this fortress town has disappeared from modern maps, though it is shown on European maps of the sixteenth and seventeenth centuries. Evidently it was situated at the southern extremity of the mainland territory of Goa north of the Liga (now the Kalinadi) River. See note in *ibid.*, p. 171.

[241] These towns in his order are: "Ancolâ," "Manjavarrão," "Bracelos," "Mangalor," "Vdelbarrão," "Caramate," "Bacanor," "Banaverrão," "Baticalo," "Honor," and "Mergen." Similar lists, though not identical ones, are given by Barros (in Cidade and Múrias [eds.], *op. cit.* [n. 6], I, 357) and Barbosa (in Dames [ed.], *op. cit.* [n. 5], I, 182–97). For identification of many of these towns with modern places see *ibid.*

[242] Dames (ed.), *op. cit.* (n. 5), I, 182–87.

[243] Corresponds with the territory called "Danseam Rayen" by Barbosa and may perhaps be identified with modern Bankapur (*ibid.*, p. 183 n).

[244] The Udayagiri chain south of the Krishna River (*ibid.*, II, 130 n).

[245] Probably Telingāna, the area in which Telegu is spoken. This designation agrees with that mentioned in Barbosa except that the latter gives it a coastal outlet (see *ibid.*, II, 236).

[246] Under Krishna Dēva Rāyya (reigned 1509–29) the jurisdiction of Vijayanagar extended to all of India south of the Krishna River, except for the Malabar states. For further detail see T. V. Mahalingham, *Administration and Social Life under Vijayanagar* (Madras, 1940), pp. 174–77.

[247] The provinces, known as *rājyas*, had their boundaries changed from time to time to suit administrative requirements. See K. A. N. Sastri, *A History of South India from Prehistoric Times to the Fall of Vijayanagar* (2d ed.; Madras, 1958), p. 298.

[248] Dames (ed.), *op. cit.* (n. 5), I, 183.

[249] *Ibid.*, p. 184.

Vijayanagar speaks Kanarese, and that many other languages are also spoken at his court.[250]

Every one of these provinces is well supplied with rice, meat, fish, fruits, and the game of forest and field. Each is luxuriantly provided with gardens, groves, springs, and rivers.[251] The mountains are covered with forests which shelter wild boars, deer, elephants, ounces, leopards, tigers, bears, and—"certain ash-coloured animals like camels," which are "so swift that no man may kill them"[252]—antelopes. The farmers grow rice and other grains and breed goats, cows, and sheep. Oxen and asses are used as beasts of burden and for plowing. Barbosa notices rice cultivation, both by wet and dry methods, on a fertile plain near "Baticala" (modern Bhatkal). He also indicates that in plowing flooded fields the seeds are sown by a drill contained in the plowshare. After pointing out that the Indians obtain two crops a year, he gives the names of the various grades of rice produced and asserts that "each of these differs from the rest in price."[253]

In the seacoast towns of "Tolinate province" there is "traffic in goods of divers kinds."[254] Coarse, black rice grown in the valley of the "Mergen" (Gangawali) River is traded for coconut and palm products brought in from other places. At Bhatkal and other Kanara ports white rice, powdered sugar, and iron are bought by the merchants of Ormuz and Malabar to exchange for horses and pearls, and for palm products, respectively. Spices, ivory, and copper, used inland for coinage, are all traded in these coastal ports. The rice is husked, cleaned, and packed in uniformly sized bales of its own straw for shipment abroad. Although black rice is cheaper, Barbosa esteems it as being "better and more wholesome than the white."[255]

All of these, and many other more precious items, can be found in the great markets of the capital city "because all the merchants of the world are able to go there safely to buy and sell."[256] To encourage the traders, particularly those who deal in horses, the "king of Narsinga" makes it his business to see that they pass duty-free through his territories from the seaports to the capital.[257] This does not mean, however, that they are exempted from duties at the ports, quite the contrary being true. Finally, the merchants of any faith may trade freely in the city "without suffering any annoyance and without inquiry."[258]

[250] Cortesão (ed.), *op. cit.* (n. 9), I, 69.
[251] General description of Castanheda in Azevedo (ed.), *op. cit.* (n. 17), I, 242.
[252] Barbosa in Dames (ed.), *op. cit.* (n. 5), I, 199.
[253] *Ibid.*, p. 192.
[254] *Ibid.*, p. 184.
[255] *Ibid.*, p. 195 and n. 1.
[256] Castanheda in Azevedo (ed.), *op. cit.* (n. 17), I, 245. He also lists many of the commodities available in the capital, including among them the "velvet taffetas of Mecca" and "the camphor of Borneo."
[257] *Ibid.* This fact is not mentioned, so far as I know, in any other contemporary Western source. Nor is it noticed in G. S. Dixit, "Economic Conditions in the Time of Krishnadevaraya," in the *Vijayanagara Sexcentenary Commemoration Volume* (Dhaswar, 1936), pp. 220–24.
[258] Barbosa in Dames (ed.), *op. cit.* (n. 5), I, 202.

The diamonds, precious stones, and jewelry of Vijayanagar are commented upon in some detail by all the Portuguese writers. In Kanara, and also in the Deccan, diamonds of enormous size and great value are mined and brought to be marketed in the capital.[259] Orta describes the mining of diamonds as an industry from which the ruler of Vijayanagar obtains great revenue.[260] Guards are placed at the mines to supervise the work and to make certain that the largest diamonds get safely to the royal court. All diamonds weighing 30 *mangelims* or more belong to the king, and some, according to Castanheda, reach 200 *mangelims* in size.[261] The ruler of Vijayanagar entrusts his huge diamonds to skilled lapidaries and apparently manages to market the cut and polished stones at a vast profit to himself. Other semi-precious stones such as amethysts and sapphires are found in the streams and rivers of the mountainous areas.[262] Any precious stones or jewels not native to the country, such as pearls, are readily imported.[263] These, along with imported coral, gold, and copper, are made up into all sorts of jewelry and other ornamental baubles. Even some of their umbrellas, which "are so made as to open and shut,"[264] are inlaid with precious stones and covered with fine silk ornamented by gold tassels. So skilled are the lapidaries and jewelers that they fabricate a wide variety of false stones to meet the great demand for rings, earrings, nose jewels, and ornamental pieces like coral branches.[265] To put it mildly, the Portuguese were impressed by the great quantity of precious stones and fine jewelry available in Vijayanagar and never seem to tire of describing how jewels are used for personal adornment by both sexes.

The city of Vijayanagar as the entrepôt, administrative center, and royal residence occupies the center of the stage in all accounts of the empire. Situated forty leagues (160 miles) inland, the city stands in the midst of a "very level plain" between two great mountain ranges.[266] On one side of the city runs a great river (the Tungabhadrā) and in its outskirts stand low hills covered with mammoth boulders. The city itself, except for the river fort, is encircled with

[259] *Ibid.* Castanheda in Azevedo (ed.), *op. cit.* (n. 17), I, 242; Orta in Markham (ed.), *op. cit.* (n. 4), p. 345. The diamond mine of Kanara was probably at Vijrakurur, north of the Krishna and about twenty miles southwest of Gooty (Dixit, *loc. cit.* [n. 257], p. 218), or in the neighborhood of Kamul, south of the Krishna (Dames [ed.], *op. cit.* [n. 5], I, 227 n). For further confirmatory detail see Sewell, *op. cit.* (n. 226), appendix A, pp. 399–401, who says that "in their way they were the richest in the world." These mines were subsequently referred to as the fabulous Golconda centers of diamond production.

[260] Markham (ed.), *op. cit.* (n. 4), p. 235.

[261] Azevedo (ed.), *op. cit.* (n. 17), I, 246. *Mangelim*, equivalent more or less to a carat, is derived from the Telegu, *mañjāli*, or Tamil, *mañjādi*. See Dalgado, *op. cit.* (n. 44), II, 29–30. Orta himself claims to have seen a diamond weighing 140 *mangelims* and to have heard from a trustworthy informant that "he saw one in Bisnaguer the size of a small hen's egg." (Markham [ed.], *op. cit.* [n. 4], p. 437.)

[262] Barbosa in Dames (ed.), *op. cit.* (n. 5), I, 200.

[263] *Ibid.*, p. 227.

[264] *Ibid.*, p. 207.

[265] See the part of Barbosa which appears in Ramusio, but not in the extant manuscripts, as translated in *ibid.*, II, 221–22.

[266] *Ibid.*, I, 201. Castanheda (Azevedo [ed], *op. cit.* [n. 17], I, 244) places it sixty leagues (240 miles) from the coast.

strong ramparts.[267] Within the walls the city is divided into streets that funnel into great squares. The royal palaces are numerous, well built, and enclosed by courtyards. The great lords of the city likewise live in fine stone palaces and travel about the city in elegant litters. The houses of the common people are thatched, "but nonetheless are very well built and arranged according to occupations, in long streets with many open places."[268] The people of the capital are numerous beyond counting and the streets overflow with the multitude of them.[269]

In this city the "king," called "Rayen" (*rāyya* or *rājā*),[270] has his residences and he stays in them unless at war. Dwelling in great luxury, the "king" leaves the administration of the realm in the hands of his provincial governors. But should his governors or lords prove to be unworthy of trust, the royal vengeance is swift and terrible. Barbosa and Castanheda describe graphically how the rājā severely punishes those nobles who deserve it without respect to their rank, connections, or wealth.[271] Indeed, some of the nobles so disciplined are reputed to "possess more land than some kings in Europe."[272] The "king's" justice is meted out in a public hall where he holds regular audiences; his will is respected as being final and absolute.[273] Nevertheless, justice is administered with great equity "not only by the rulers, but by the people."[274]

On occasion disputes are settled by the sword. Castanheda writes: "There are many duels over women whom they love in which many men lose their lives."[275] Duels are also fought between officials who are at odds over administrative problems. Such disputants receive permission to fight a duel from the king, who assigns them a field of battle, seconds, and judges. Should they be men of position, the king himself may go to watch the duel. The combatants fight naked, except for turbans on their heads, with daggers, swords, and shields. Such combats are usually over quickly, and the king awards to the victor a golden chain (*berid*)[276] to wear on his right arm as a symbol of his valor. Custom

[267] In Castanheda's account the capital is described as having the shape of a half-moon. On this point and its symbolic significance see Saletore, *op. cit.* (n. 234), I, 121.

[268] Barbosa in Dames (ed.), *op. cit.* (n. 5), I, 202.

[269] *Ibid.* Pires (in Cortesão [ed.], *op. cit.* [n. 9], I, 64) estimates that the population is 20,000, though he apparently never actually visited the city himself. It is estimated by modern scholars that the city had a population of 500,000 in the first half of the sixteenth century. See Dixit, *loc cit.* (n. 257), p. 215.

[270] This term used by Barbosa in Dames (ed.), *op. cit.* (n. 5), I, 201; the "king" in his day was Krishna Dēva Rāyya.

[271] Castanheda in Azevedo (ed.), *op. cit.* (n. 17), I, 246; and Barbosa in Dames (ed.), *op. cit.* (n. 5), I, 208-09.

[272] Castanheda in Azevedo (ed.), *op. cit.* (n. 217), I, 246.

[273] *Ibid.* For a more balanced view of the king's role in administration and justice see Mahalingham, *op. cit.* (n. 246), pp. 9-26.

[274] Barbosa in Dames (ed.), *op. cit.* (n. 5), I, 202.

[275] Azevedo (ed.), *op. cit.* (n. 17), I, 243; for other confirmatory literature see Saletore, *op. cit.* (n. 234), II, 416-19, and Barbosa's similar account of dueling at Bhatkal in Dames (ed.), *op. cit.* (n. 5), I, 190-91.

[276] Sanskrit: *biruda*—a device or insignia of superiority or excellence in the form of an arm-bracelet or chain. See Dalgado, *op. cit.* (n. 44), I, 119.

ordains that he who possesses the golden chain must accept further challenges in order to keep it. In addition to helping settle disputes, dueling is described as a source of amusement and sport.

The Portuguese particularly delight in recounting how elegantly the rulers live, Castanheda asserting that they are waited upon with greater splendor than the "kings" of Malabar.[277] Barbosa insists that "the King and the country-people marry almost in our way, and have a marriage-law," though they may marry as many wives as they can maintain. Castanheda alleges that the "king" does not marry, though he keeps more than three hundred concubines.[278] Both agree that there are many serving women in the palace who are the daughters of the leading families in the realm. These women do all the work of the house-hold, sing and play for the king's amusement, and are well maintained at his expense.[279] Every afternoon they bathe in the numerous tanks within the palace enclosure, and on this occasion the "king" chooses the most appealing of them for his pleasure. The women of the seraglio vie with each other for the "king's" favor so intensely "that some kill others and some poison themselves"[280] when they are scorned or passed over. The first son born to any of the "king's" wives or mistresses is regarded as the heir.[281] On other data regarding succession both Barbosa and Castanheda are silent.

The wealth of Vijayanagar "is the greatest known to the whole world."[282] This is true, in part, because each king is responsible for adding to it and must not touch the accumulated treasure of his predecessors.[283] Among the most prized of the royal possessions are the elephants and horses, the king usually possessing more than 900 elephants and 20,000 horses.[284] Special kitchens are maintained by the "king" to prepare the food for his prized horses and ele-phants. Nobody is permitted to own horses for personal use. Those held by the crown are parceled out to the great lords for care and maintenance, "and they must continually give accounts of them."[285] Each knight is furnished with a horse, a groom, a serving maid, a monthly allowance, and daily supplies for the horse and groom. Horses, though well taken care of, generally do not thrive or survive very long in south India, and hence are highly valued and very expensive to buy.

The people of Vijayanagar are of tawny color and wear their black hair long and straight. "The men are of good height," Barbosa comments, "and with facial features like our own."[286] Both sexes are well formed and handsome,

---

277 Azevedo (ed.), *op. cit.* (n. 17), I, 245.

278 *Ibid.* For further details and discussion see Saletore, *op. cit.* (n. 234), II, 174–76.

279 Cf. Pires (in Cortesão [ed.], *op. cit.* [n. 9], I, 65), who alleges that the rājā has one thousand girl entertainers and four or five thousand male performers.

280 Barbosa in Dames (ed.), *op. cit.* (n. 5), I, 208.

281 *Ibid.* It appears that the heir apparent (*yuvarājā*) was not always the eldest son. For this and related matters see Mahalingham, *op. cit.* (n. 246), pp. 11–14.

282 Castanheda in Azevedo (ed.), *op. cit.* (n. 17), I, 246.   283 *Ibid.*

284 Barbosa in Dames (ed.), *op. cit.* (n. 5), I, 210.

285 *Ibid.*

286 *Ibid.*, p. 205.

the women being especially attractive.[287] The men wear girdle-like clothes, with short white shirts which are open in front and pulled down between the thighs. On their feet they wear sandals and on their heads turbans or caps. Some boast garments thrown over their shoulders like capes, and many wear rings and earrings set with precious stones and pearls.[288] The women wear white or colored wrappers of thin cotton or silk which are five yards long. These *saris* (though Barbosa does not use this word) they tie around themselves in such a way that only one arm and shoulder remain uncovered.[289] On their feet they wear embroidered shoes, keep their heads uncovered, dress their hair gathered in a knot at the top, and adorn it with flowers. In their noses and ears they wear precious stones, around their necks they hang necklaces of gold, jewels, and coral beads, and on their arms they fit costly bracelets. Lavish costumes are so common that Barbosa is led to conclude that "the more part of this people is very wealthy."[290]

Like their ruler, the majority of the people of Vijayanagar are "heathens." Most of these "idolaters" worship a god (Vishnu or Shiva) whom they hold to be "lord of everything."[291] They also believe in demons, witchcraft, and sorcery, and are tolerant of the beliefs of others. They celebrate the "Sabbath" on the sixth day, and they believe that the evil are punished and that the good go to their glory.[292] Throughout the kingdom there are many temples (*pagodes*) dedicated to their gods which receive heavy contributions from the "king" and the rest of the faithful. Great festivals are held at these temples to which people make pilgrimages from afar. As an example of their superstition, Castanheda tells the story of a ruler who when ill promised to give his weight in gold to the temple. When, after weighing himself, he gave the clothes which he wore to the priest of the temple, the latter fell dead while dressing in them.[293] Such stories they believe in, as well as in bad omens and the predictions of sorcerers. From such remarks it was clearly not possible for European readers to understand much about Hinduism and the practices associated with it.

Each of Vijayanagar's political divisions includes a substantial number of towns and cities. In the seacoast towns the Moors are especially prominent and numerous; in the interior the cities are peopled almost entirely by the "gentiles."[294] These "gentiles" are divided into three distinct classes:[295] (1) royalty, aristocracy, and soldiery; (2) Brahmans; and (3) a priestly-merchant group called "Baneanes" (*Banyā*) by Castanheda.[296] Such divisions do not correspond

---

[287] Castanheda in Azevedo (ed.), *op. cit.* (n. 17), I, 243.

[288] Barbosa in Dames (ed.), *op. cit.* (n. 5), I, 205.

[289] *Ibid.*, p. 207.

[290] *Ibid.*, p. 208.

[291] Castanheda in Azevedo (ed.), *op. cit.* (n. 17), I, 242.

[292] *Ibid.*, p. 243.

[293] *Ibid.*, pp. 246-47.

[294] *Ibid.*, p. 242.

[295] Barbosa in Dames (ed.), *op. cit.* (n. 5), I, 212.

[296] Azevedo (ed.), *op. cit.* (n. 17), I, 242. For discussion of "Baneanes" see below, pp. 378-79. For comments on this class division see Saletore, *op. cit.* (n. 234), II, 28-29.

to the caste system, but are probably the classes which seemed individually most distinct to observers from Europe. The members of this first class are distinguished by their polygamy, filial inheritance customs, and the practice of *sati*. Both Barros and Castanheda discourse on sati at length and in a similar vein. The Brahmans, "who are priests and rulers of their houses of worship,"[297] are distinguished by their adherence to monogamy, to dietary regulations which forbid their eating anything "subject to death,"[298] and to full exemption from the death penalty. As a mark of distinction, the Brahmans wear three linen threads over their shoulders. Some Brahmans live from alms, others have estates of their own, and others reside in the numerous and sumptuous temples which exist everywhere. These pagodes often have good revenues from land which are supplemented by earnings from temple prostitutes. Little girls are educated in the temples "for similar work after they come of age." The Brahmans are alleged never to work "except to feed well"[299] on a diet consisting of honey, butter, rice, sugar, pulse, and milk.

The "Baneanes" (*Banyā*),[300] who are described as similar to the Brahmans, are highly respected and looked upon as holy men. As their mark of distinction, the members of this third group wear around their necks a little cloth bag suspended from twisted cords which contains an egg-shaped stone called a *tambarane* that they believe is their god.[301] Possession of this sacred stone insures their safety wherever they go, and for this reason they are often entrusted with transporting merchandise and money and with carrying on trade in distant parts. In their dietary habits they are vegetarians; in their marital customs they are monogamous. Upon the death of a husband, the wife is buried alive.[302] Barbosa also describes, perhaps for the first time, the hook-swinging ceremony: a sacrifice which a young maiden of the class who is about to be married makes in blood to the god who has helped her win the husband of her choice.[303] He

[297] Barbosa in Dames (ed.), *op. cit.* (n. 5), I, 217.

[298] *Ibid.* This also sets them apart from the members of the first class who eat all meats excepting beef.

[299] *Ibid.*

[300] The descriptions of this group by Barbosa and Castanheda are very similar; in fact, I suspect that Castanheda "borrowed" his account from Barbosa. The greatest difference comes in Castanheda's designation of them as "Baneanes," for Barbosa does not use this term in this particular portion of his book. Ordinarily, the term "Baneanes," as used by the Portuguese writers, refers to the merchants of Gujarat (see Dalgado, *op. cit.* [n. 44], I, 93–95): on other occasions it is used to apply to merchants working in the Dravidian areas. But Damião de Góis in his chronicle published in 1566, perhaps following Castanheda, refers to the "Baneanes" of "Narsinga" (*ibid.*, p. 94) as a distinct class of Vijayanagar.

[301] Barbosa in Dames (ed.), *op. cit.* (n. 5), I, 218. In this connection *tambarane* probably refers to the linga, or phallic symbol, thought to be "Siva himself," which is often worn by members of the Lingāyat sect. For the derivation and use of the word *tambarane* see Dalgado, *op. cit.* (n. 44), II, 346–47.

[302] On this custom of the Lingāyats see Edgar Thurston, *Castes and Tribes of Southern India* (7 vols.; Madras, 1909), IV, 236–91. Barbosa (in Dames [ed.], *op. cit.* [n. 5], I, 22) gives a truncated but interesting description of this ceremony.

[303] See account and notes in Dames (ed.), *op. cit.* (n. 5), I, 220–22. For a modern description see E. Thurston, *Ethnographic Notes on South India* (Madras, 1906), pp. 487–501.

also describes a ceremony in which young girls who dedicate their maidenhood to the gods are deflowered.[304] From such descriptions of cultural traits it would seem that Castanheda's designation of this class as "Baneanes" was correct only in the sense that this was a merchant group; actually the ceremonies described seem more typical of the *Lingāyats*, the phallic worshippers of Shiva, who still live in the environs of the ruins of Vijayanagar.

The rulers of Vijayanagar "are always at war with their neighboring rulers," Castanheda reports, and so they constantly have at hand "great multitudes of men, on foot as well as on horseback, to whom they pay wages."[305] In strength this permanent army is estimated to number more than 100,000 by the most conservative of the foreign observers,[306] and all agree, no matter what figures they give, that this is an immense military establishment that the rulers of Vijayanagar regularly maintain. Fighting men of all classes and nationalities, even Muslims, are attracted to serve in the army of Vijayanagar by steady pay, good treatment, and regular work. The system of enlistment particularly attracts the attention of the Portuguese writers, for a prospective soldier apparently gets on the royal payroll only after submitting to a thorough examination.[307] The recruit, especially if a foreigner, is required to appear before four secretaries who examine his nude body to observe its physical condition and to note any distinguishing marks. They also record his name, age, color, height, creed, place of origin, and the names of his parents. Once he has satisfied these requirements, the recruit's name is entered on the royal payroll at a salary that may range from three to fifteen *pardãos* of gold, presumably depending upon the type of post to which he has been assigned. After entering the service of Vijayanagar, the foreign recruit is forbidden to leave the country but is permitted to live according to his own faith and customs. Should he leave the jurisdiction of Vijayanagar without permission, and then be captured, he may expect to be "very evilly entreated."[308] In addition to fighting men, the rulers of Vijayanagar keep on their regular payroll a large number[309] of unmarried courtesans who are allotted to the various fighting groups. For, Barbosa reports, the ruler "says that war cannot be waged where there are no women."[310] Naturally, many of these women are also attached to the royal camp whenever the king goes on a campaign. The courtesans are also credited with attracting many foreign soldiers to take service with Vijayanagar.

304 In Dames (ed.), *op. cit.* (n. 5), I, 222–23; evidently this was also a ceremony connected with the phallic worship of the Lingāyats.

305 In Azevedo (ed.), *op. cit.* (n. 17), I, 247. Barbosa qualifies this assertion somewhat by noting that they are "oftentimes" at war with the rulers of the Deccan and Orissa (Dames [ed.], *op. cit.* [n. 5], I, 223–24).

306 For comparative figures see Saletore, *op. cit.* (n. 234), I, 414–19.

307 The details are given by Castanheda in Azevedo (ed.), *op. cit.* (n. 17), I, 247.

308 Barbosa in Dames (ed.), *op. cit.* (n. 5), I, 212.

309 Four to six thousand are the numbers usually mentioned.

310 Dames (ed.), *op. cit.* (n. 5), I, 212. Castanheda asserts that these women were paid at a high rate and that with their support an army would fight six times better than without them (Azevedo [ed.], *op. cit.* [n. 17], I, 248).

The rājā rarely goes to war himself but when he does it is apparently a great spectacle and a tortuous effort. He leaves the capital accompanied by a colorful retinue and sets up camp on an open plain. Then he lets it be known throughout his realm that he will depart for the battlefield on a particular date. All the people are required at the appointed time to leave the capital with all their possessions, except for those who remain behind to guard the palaces, fortresses, and temples. Once the evacuation is complete, it is ordered that all the thatched houses of the common folk be burned [311] so that the levies will have no desire left to return home, and will fight better to protect and provide for their families. Once this horde is assembled, the camp is razed, a day's short march ensues, and then a "great town of straw" [312] is again hastily thrown up on a new camping site. Such camps are constructed with streets and open spaces, and while on the march the mass army lives in temporary quarters for three-day periods. Each time they leave the camp it is burned behind them as the motley array slowly progresses toward the battlefield.

The Portuguese give no table of organization for the army of Vijayanagar, but it is possible to conclude from their rambling accounts that the Hindus have infantry and cavalry units, a special corps of armored elephants, and all sorts of provisioning units and entertainment personnel. In this connection Castanheda remarks that whenever "they add a thousand [soldiers] to an army, two thousand [servitors] must also be recruited." [313] The camp followers are unarmed, and the serving men have no defensive armor except shields. The cavalrymen are outfitted with great padded tunics, heavy leather jackets, and helmets; they are armed with Moorish poniards, lances, and javelins. While the horse brigades are obviously numerous and well equipped, the flower of the Vijayanagar army is the terrifying elephant corps. These colossal beasts when prepared for war are covered with copper trimmings and their trunks are similarly protected. On their tusks are fastened great two-edged swords with which they kill many of the enemy by rampaging through their ranks. Wooden towers are strapped to the backs of the leading elephants from which as many as eight archers launch their arrows against the enemy. The vast army of Vijayanagar led by war elephants is, in Castanheda's words, "a very beautiful sight to behold." [314] But, despite the strength of Vijayanagar's arms, its ruler recognizes the might of Portugal and sends emissaries to deal with the viceroy stationed at Cannanore. [315]

---

[311] This may have been an interpolation by the copyist who acquired Barbosa's account for Ramusio (Dames [ed.], *op. cit.* [n. 5], I, 225, n. 1). Nevertheless, it was published in Europe and a similar account of the razing of the capital is given by Castanheda (in Azevedo [ed.], *op. cit.* [n. 17], I, 248).

[312] Barbosa in Dames (ed.), *op. cit.* (n.5), I, 227; for a word picture of a Hindu camp see Saletore, *op. cit.* (n. 234), I, 450-57.

[313] Azevedo (ed.), *op. cit.* (n. 17), I, 247.

[314] *Ibid.*

[315] *Ibid.*, p. 248.

D. THE DECCAN STATES AND GOA

Once the Portuguese became active in the affairs of south India, the Muslim states to the north, in alliance with their coreligionists from Egypt, Turkey, and Persia, prepared a counteroffensive to drive the Europeans out. The Muslim headquarters for a southern push against the Portuguese footholds were the ports of the Deccan and Gujarat, great centers in the Arabic trade with India. Even before the Portuguese arrived in India, the strategic control of Goa, one of these Deccan ports, was hotly contested by the Hindu rulers of Vijayanagar and the Muslim rulers of the Deccan. This island fortress, which is described by Pires as being "as strong as Rhodes," [316] was taken by the Muslims in 1470 and they held it until Albuquerque in 1510 brought it under the sway of Portugal. Although it was Albuquerque's hope that the taking of Goa would keep "India in repose and quiet," [317] the Portuguese quickly learned that the Bahmani rulers of the Deccan, [318] divided though they were among themselves, would nonetheless continue to be a source of trouble.

The Deccan (meaning "the south") in its broadest sense is often used to designate all of India south of the Vindhyan hills. [319] The Portuguese writers of the sixteenth century, however, consistently use the word "Decão" or "Daqué" with reference to the Muslim states which, though their jurisdiction varied greatly from time to time, generally extended inland from Chaul in the north to the Tungabhadrā River in the south. Though the earliest Portuguese travelers refer to these territories, their remarks are generally limited to the coastal towns and to matters of trade. Orta is the only one who speaks of the Deccan kingdoms from extensive personal experience. Castanheda writes of them from limited direct exposure and the reports of others. Barros, in Portugal, who gives the most connected and intelligible historical account, bases his narrative to a large extent on a "Deccan chronicle" which he had in his possession. He used this source rather than others because it conforms "much better in its chronology to the general Persian chronicle" which he refers to repeatedly as the "Tarigh" (*Ta'rīkh*) or "History." Clearly, Barros had before him, when he wrote, the translations of several Muslim histories, and this was almost a century before Ferishta (also known as Mohammed Kasim) wrote his basic Persian account of the rise of Muslim power in India. [320]

[316] Cortesão (ed.), *op. cit.* (n. 9), I, 58.

[317] Birch (trans.), *op. cit.* (n. 116), III, 259.

[318] For an excellent recent study of these rulers based on most of the available Muslim sources see H. K. Sherwani, *The Bahmanis of the Deccan* (Hyderbad-Deccan, 1953). Consult also for the general picture N. Venkataramanya, *The Early Muslim Expansion in South India* (Madras, 1942).

[319] For a discussion of the nomenclature and extent of the Deccan see H. Raychaudhuri, "Geography of the Deccan," in G. Yazdani (ed.), *The Early History of the Deccan* (London, 1960), pp. 3–4.

[320] Another basic Persian source written in about 1630 is Alî Bin 'Assîz-Ullâh Ṭabâṭabâ, *Burhân-i Ma-âṣir (History of the Bāhmanī Dynasty)*. Translated in an epitomized version by J. S. King in *Indian Antiquary*, XXVIII (1899), 119–38, 141–55, 180–92, 209–19, 235–47, 277–92, 305–23; XXIX (1900), 4–8. Where the two Persian accounts differ on dates, numismatic evidence seems to support Ṭabâṭabâ. For a general survey of the Muslim sources of Deccan history see Sherwani, *op. cit.* (n. 318), pp. 424–37.

Barros reports that in the year 707 of the Muslim calendar, or A.D. 1300,[321] the Sultan of Delhi, "Xá Nasaradim,"[322] began a campaign to conquer the Hindu states of south India. He descended upon the Hindu state of "Canarâ" (Kanara) which then extended from north of Chaul inland and southward to Cape Comorin, being bounded in the west by numerous petty kingdoms and on the east by Orissa. After pillaging and looting, "Xá Nasaradim" returned to Delhi and left in charge of his conquests in Kanara his captain named "Habede-Xá."[323] The latter, who had only a handful of men at his disposal to maintain control over the large and hostile Hindu population, was forced gradually to pull back toward the north. Finally, he consolidated his position and recruited troops from the Hindu converts to Islam, the Christians[324] and from people of varied backgrounds. He held this motley army together by paying the soldiers well, and was subsequently able over a period of twenty years to become powerful enough to found his own dynasty and to win recognition of his preponderance in the Deccan from the court at Delhi.[325]

With the death of the founder of the Bahmani dynasty, Barros reports that his son, "Mamudi-Xá"[326] (Mohammed I, 1358–75), was confirmed in his inheritance by the Sultan of Delhi[327] upon agreeing to pay more tribute than had his father. After meeting the exactions of Delhi for several years, he became sufficiently powerful in his own right to cancel further payments and to refuse to dispatch troops to aid the Delhi ruler in the war then being waged against Persia. Fearing that his recalcitrance would bring reprisals once the war was over, the Deccan ruler allied himself with the Muslim lord of Gujarat. But fortune favored Mohammed I for the Sultan of Delhi died in the war and a difficult period ensued for the northern sultanate. Taking advantage of this situation, Mohammed I declared his independence of Delhi and exalted himself Sultan of "Canarâ," renaming it the "Decão." And this name, it is said, was given to the new kingdom to represent the many different peoples inhabiting it, for in the local language *deçani* means *mestiços*.[328]

Being aged, weary of war, and fearful over the future of his dynasty,

---

[321] The Deccan chronicler, whom Barros uses, gives dates which are exactly twenty years earlier than those listed in the "established chronology" in the Appendix of Sherwani, *op. cit.* (n. 318), pp. 438–44. I have not been able to identify Barros' source, though it is clear that a number of chronicles were then available.

[322] Sultan Julāl-ud-Din. Orta puts this event "about three hundred years ago," or more than a century before it happened (Markham [ed.], *op. cit.* [n. 4], p. 69).

[323] Probably Hasan, who proclaimed himself Sultan of the Deccan in 1347 under the title Alā-ud-Dīn Bāhman Shah.

[324] The presence of "Franks" (presumably European Christians) in the armies of the Deccan is noted in Sherwani, *op. cit.* (n. 318), pp. 81–82. They, along with the Turks, probably brought gunpowder and cannon into the Deccan wars.

[325] Barros in Cidade and Múrias (eds.), *op. cit.* (n. 6), II, 193–94. On this twenty-year period from 1327 to 1347 see Sherwani, *op. cit.* (n. 318), 20–25.

[326] Mohammed I is traditionally known as the organizer of the kingdom.

[327] Probably Firoz Tughlug.

[328] As in a number of other cases, Barros (in Cidade and Múrias [eds.], *op. cit.* [n. 6], II, 195) seems to be wrong in this etymology. See Yule and Burnell, *op. cit.* (n. 10), p. 233.

Mohammed I decentralized his state by dividing its administration among eighteen[329] of his captains and appointing one of them captain-general to watch over the rest. Each captain was charged with defending his own district and with providing from local taxation for the payment of a stipulated number of infantry and cavalry. In an effort to keep these captains from becoming too independent, they were not raised to the nobility and were forbidden to marry except with their own slaves. The captains were also obliged to establish a residence in the capital city of Bīdar[330] in which they were required to live a certain number of months each year. When they were not there personally, their residences were to be occupied by a son or near relative who would perform in their stead the required daily rituals of vassalage.[331]

Barros then describes at some length the ceremonies and reverences ("salema" or *salaams*) which the vassals are required to make before the Sultan, and of how the supplicant is invested with a "Cabaia"[332] as a reward for his loyalty and services. On festival occasions the captains are not permitted to send substitutes, but have to present themselves personally before the ruler, the only excuse being serious illness or involvement in war. Failure to appear in normal times is considered tantamount to rebellion. Apparently, the Portuguese historian is not greatly impressed with this device for maintaining loyalty, because he goes on to remark that it was not long after Mohammed's time that the disintegration of the Deccan state began. With this observation he concludes his brief historical sketch and undertakes to describe the political condition of the Deccan when the Portuguese arrived in India.

Castanheda, who sees the Deccan primarily from the viewpoint of a European resident of Goa, presents a very sketchy and disconnected account of its history during the period of its "last three kings."[333] He himself was in India (1528–38) during the waning years of the Bahmani dynasty at the time when Kalimer ul-lāh ruled (1526–38) the Deccan. Of this king's two predecessors, whose jurisdictions were confined to the environs of Bīdar, Castanheda condemns the first one, possibly Ahmud IV, as "a man greatly given to all the vices of sensuality"[334] and completely incapable of governing. The next king, possibly Alā-ud-dīn Shah (reigned 1520–23), is a quite different type; he devotes himself to good living and to an effort to recover what his intemperate predecessors had lost. Believing his own people to be too unreliable and enervated, he sent to

329 He certainly founded the provincial structure of government which prevailed almost to the end of the Bahmani dynasty (*ca.* 1538), but nowhere else can I find mention of this number. For more details see Sherwani, *op. cit.* (n. 318), p. 80.

330 At this period the capital was actually at Gulbarga. It was not moved to Bīdar until 1422.

331 Barros in Cidade and Múrias (eds.), *op. cit.* (n. 6), II, 195. On Mohammed's durbars, held daily except for Fridays, see Sherwani, *op. cit.* (n. 318), pp. 77–78.

332 Barros (in Cidade and Múrias [eds.], *op. cit.* [n. 6], II, 195–96) describes this tunic of brocade, silk, or muslin in some detail, and rightly mentions that it was generally used by all the Moors "in those parts." For additional discussion see Yule and Burnell, *op. cit.* (n. 10), pp. 105–06, and Dalgado, *op. cit.* (n. 44), I, 158–59.

333 Azevedo (ed.), *op. cit.* (n. 17), I, 286.

334 *Ibid.* Cf. similar description in Sherwani, *op. cit.* (n. 318), pp. 414–15.

Arabia for mercenaries to help him regain his power.[335] The last king of the Deccan reverted to a life of intemperance and sloth, and as a consequence he was unable to control his nominal feudatories or even retain Bīdar to pass on to his son.

The divided condition of the Deccan kingdom in the sixteenth century is commented on by the Portuguese at some length. Barros notes that of the eighteen provinces created by Mohammed I in the fourteenth century a number of the stronger had taken over the weaker. Castanheda contends that twelve kingdoms had emerged from the original provinces and Barros lists six of them. Both agree that the ruler of Goa, the "Sabaio"[336] or "Cabai," was the most powerful of the Deccan rulers before Albuquerque captured Goa. The other great lords of the Deccan are entitled, according to Barros, "Nizamaluco,"[337] "Madremaluco,"[338] "Melique Verido,"[339] "Cogi Mocadao,"[340] and "Cota-maluco."[341] Orta, who gives the greatest detail on these Deccan rulers, insists that all of them are foreigners, presumably from western Muslim countries, except for his friend, the "Nizamaluco," who is said to be a native of the Deccan.[342] The "Sabaio" and the "Nizamaluco" possess between them the territory along the seacoast and inland to the Ghats.[343] All of the other provinces are in the "Ballagate," a term used by the Portuguese to mean the Ghat highlands.

On the basis of the Portuguese accounts it is impossible to learn much about the territorial holdings of the Deccan rulers. Barbosa, who describes a number of the port cities, contents himself by saying that their possessions "extend far inland,"[344] and Pires notes that there are twenty principal inland towns.[345] Castanheda describes the Deccan as one of the greatest states of India with a coastline of seventy leagues (280 miles) which borders on the north with Cambay (Gujarat) and which extends into the interior to the frontiers of Vijayanagar

---

[335] Cf. with the recruitment of Abyssinian slaves during the fifteenth century in Bengal. See below, p. 416.

[336] Probably the popular title of Yūsuf 'Ādil Khan whose capital was at Bijapur. Barros (in Cidade and Múrias [eds.], *op. cit.* [n. 6], II, 197) says that this title was derived from his native place, Sava, in Persia. For additional comment see Dames (ed.), *op. cit.* (n. 5), I, 172–73, n. 1; Markham (ed.), *op. cit.* (n. 4), pp. 73–74; and Cortesão (ed.), *op. cit.* (n. 9), I, 50.

[337] Popular title (Nizamu 'l-Mulk or "The Regulator of the State") for Burhan Nizam Shah whose capital was at Ahmadnagar. Orta (Markham [ed.], *op. cit.* [n. 4], p. 7) describes him as "being well read in his own literature" and as patronizing Turkish and Persian doctors at his court.

[338] A popular title (correctly rendered as Imad 'l-Mulk) which probably refers in this instance to Fath-Ullah 'Imad Shah whose capital was at Berar.

[339] Popular title of the princes who established themselves at Bīdar around the end of the fifteenth century.

[340] Possibly the same as Orta's "Mohadum Coja" (Markham [ed.], *op. cit.* [n. 4], p. 71) who held a number of important places in Sholapur.

[341] Popular title (correctly rendered as Kutb-ub-Mulk or the "Pole Star of the State") for the rulers of the Golconda dynasty.

[342] Markham (ed.), *op. cit.* (n. 4), p. 71.

[343] *Ibid.*, pp. 70–71.

[344] Dames (ed.), *op. cit.* (n. 5), I, 158.

[345] Of these, the largest in numbers of inhabitants are Bīdar, Bijapur, Sholapur, Raichur, Sagar, Kulbarga, and two unidentifiable places. See Cortesão (ed.), *op. cit.* (n. 9), I, 49.

and Orissa. None of the Portuguese seems to know that in 1472 Bahmani supremacy extended across the peninsula from sea to sea and included a large part of Orissa within its dominion. Orta tries to describe the holdings of a few of the rulers as they were in his day, but his remarks are very indefinite. Barros lists the names of the inland cities left to the "Sabaio" after Albuquerque's conquest of Goa, but leaves further discussion of them to his *Geografia*, which he mentions so often in the *Décadas*.

The most concrete information, as might be expected, relates to the coastal towns. Beginning in the north, the Portuguese comment in some detail on Chaul, a bustling entrepôt of the sixteenth century which exists today mainly as a memory.[346] Located at the estuary of the Kondulika River (about thirty miles south of modern Bombay), Chaul is described as lying "more than two leagues [8 miles] inside the bar."[347] It was in this roadstead that a Portuguese fleet was surprised and defeated in 1508 by an Egyptian–Gujarati contingent. Shortly thereafter the Viceroy d'Almeida proceeded northward with a fleet reinforced by new arrivals from Portugal to wipe out the Muslim fleet and its naval bases which threatened the Portuguese footholds in Malabar and the trade with India. After the Portuguese destroyed Dabhul, and defeated the Muslim fleet at Diu, the ruler of Ahmadnagar, whose only port was Chaul, was intimidated enough to agree to pay tribute to the Portuguese for the port's "defense." In 1510 a Portuguese factor arrived in Chaul, and over the following fifteen years the Portuguese built a factory and a fortress at the city as they gradually made it one of their principal trading centers north of Goa.

In 1504, before the advent of the Portuguese, Varthema visited Chaul. His narrative corresponds well to that of Barbosa, who visited Chaul after the Portuguese already had a factor in residence there. Located on "a beautiful river," Chaul is described by Varthema as being "more warm than cold."[348] The city is "extremely well-walled"[349] and its houses are roofed with thatch. Its tawny-colored inhabitants are warlike, but the ruler does not have fighting men at his disposal though he does possess artillery. Horses, cows, and oxen are in good supply, and the country round about "abounds in everything excepting grapes, nuts and chestnuts."[350] The city is populated entirely by Moors and gentiles who speak "a language which seems to be like that of the Guzerats."[351] Chaul has a "Moorish governor" who is subject to a king who is "himself a vassal of the King of Daquem [Deccan] and who accounts to him for his revenues and collects them."[352]

---

[346] Actually it now appears on maps as the village of Revadanda. For its history and decline see J. Gerson da Cunha, *Notes on the History and Antiquities of Chaul and Bassein* (Bombay, 1876). Also see Dames (ed.), *op. cit.* (n. 5), I, 159, n. 1.
[347] Barros in Cidade and Múrias (eds.), *op. cit.* (n. 6), II, 81.
[348] Temple (ed.), *op. cit.* (n. 233), p. 47.
[349] *Ibid.*
[350] *Ibid.*
[351] Castanheda in Azevedo (ed.), *op. cit.* (n. 17), I, 289.
[352] Barbosa in Dames (ed.), *op. cit.* (n. 5), I, 162.

The Portuguese bring out clearly that before they arrived at Chaul ships from Ormuz, Cambay, and Malabar traded there regularly with each other and the merchants of the Deccan. The great trading months were from December through March, and the Portuguese were evidently not long in fitting themselves into this international commercial pattern. Spices and drugs from the south were brought in by Malabar vessels to be exchanged for the grains, cotton cloths, muslins, and calicoes produced in the Deccan. Copper in quantity was also purchased by the Deccan merchants to be used in minting and in the manufacture of cooking utensils. Even after the appearance of the Portuguese, merchants from the interior bring their oxen trains loaded with goods to the outskirts of the city just as the foreign vessels continue to moor themselves along the waterfront each year at the trading season. The city itself in the trading months "is like a fair,"[353] and the taxes on this trade are very slight.[354] The Portuguese purchase at these markets many of the commodities essential to the supplying and outfitting of their fleets. A similar trade is carried on at Danda (Danda Rajpur), another Deccan town located at the mouth of a river just to the south of Chaul and also subject to Ahmadnagar.[355] But even in Pires' time it is possible to see that Chaul and other Deccan ports are beginning to decline.

Dabhul, at the time when D'Almeida sacked it in 1509, is described as being "one of the most populous and magnificent maritime cities"[356] in the East. Varthema, who visited Dabhul in 1504, likens it to Chaul in the customs obtaining there.[357] Barbosa, who probably arrived in Dabhul a few years after the Portuguese sacked the town, reports that it "is now peopled and as prosperous as before, and wealthy."[358] Located on the north bank of the estuary of the Vashishti River, Dabhul in this period is within the territory of the "Sabaio" who maintains a garrison there. Barros describes at length the fortifications of the city and the successful Portuguese attack upon them. Ships from Mecca, Aden, Ormuz, as well as from Gujarat and Malabar, regularly trade at Dabhul. The merchants from the interior bring to the port grains, copper, quicksilver, and vermilion dye.[359] The "Sabaio" of Goa is said to receive great revenues from the customs imposed on this trade.

Some of the merchants of Dabhul, "as well Moors as Heathen,"[360] are very wealthy. These men of substance live in noble houses and sumptuous edifices which are the best to be found in the region.[361] Beautiful villages and mosques line both sides of the river behind Dabhul. The surrounding countryside is

[353] *Ibid.*

[354] Castanheda in Azevedo (ed.), *op. cit.* (n. 17), I, 289.

[355] Barbosa in Dames (ed.), *op. cit.* (n. 5), I, 163; Castanheda in Azevedo (ed.), *op. cit.* (n. 17), II, 284–85; Pires in Cortesão (ed.), *op. cit.* (n. 9), I, 51.

[356] Barros in Cidade and Múrias, *op. cit.* (n. 6), II, 117.

[357] Temple (ed.), *op. cit.* (n. 233), p. 48.

[358] Dames (ed.), *op. cit.* (n. 5), I, 166.

[359] *Ibid.*, p. 165.

[360] *Ibid.*

[361] Barros in Cidade and Múrias, *op. cit.* (n. 6), II, 117.

"well-tilled, rich and fertile, with good ploughing and breeding of cattle."[362] The Portuguese, however, perhaps because they had raided the city and had formed an alliance with the rival port of Chaul, were generally on bad terms with Dabhul; as a result trade was systematically funneled into Goa and Diu, and Dabhul began rapidly to decline. Still, enough trade continued for Orta to be able to enjoy eating in his home in Goa the watermelons of Dabhul.[363]

The Europeans also comment on other smaller port towns of the Deccan, but in no case do they discuss at length the customs and beliefs prevailing in the Konkani country. The people are said to be industrious tillers and excellent soldiers.[364] Castanheda reports that the Deccanese "do not have as many idolatries and superstitions as the Malabars and are much more genteel in living."[365] Beautiful of face and well formed in their bodies, these people wear tunics of white cotton and elaborate headdresses. Although they eat all meats excepting beef, they drink no wine. The Brahmans are especially strict about their dietary habits and their religious beliefs and ceremonies. Castanheda then goes on to discuss at some length the beliefs of the Brahmans in "a single god," in numerous devils who must be propitiated, in transmigration of souls, and in paradise and hell. He clearly thinks that their beliefs resemble Christian teachings, for he alleges that "they have hints of the birth of our lord and his sufferings," venerate the picture of Our Lady, and on festival occasions wash themselves as "a kind of baptismal rite."[366] His analysis of such matters illustrates graphically how difficult it was for a Christian European of limited background and experience to comprehend alien religious practices, even though he observed them at first hand and over a fairly long period of time.

It is only when they consider Goa that we begin to get substantial accounts from the Portuguese sources. This is true primarily because Goa became Portugal's leading port in India and because it was soon elevated to be the administrative and episcopal center for the entire eastern empire. In Malabar the Portuguese held their position by force and by the policy of playing off the local rulers against each other. Their factories at Cannanore and Cochin enjoyed extraterritorial privileges, but even the most co-operative of the Malabar rulers continued to maintain the trappings and some of the substance of sovereignty. In 1510, Albuquerque, after having once been ejected from the city, managed to wrest Goa permanently away from its Muslim ruler. Thereafter the Portuguese took possession of their first real colony in Asia and were confronted for the first time with the task of ruling in India.

Under their mastery the defensive works of the island of Goa, constructed to withstand attacks from the land, were repaired and reinforced. The Portuguese then had the Goans construct some public buildings, a factory, a hospital, and a

---

[362] Barbosa in Dames (ed.), *op. cit.* (n. 5), I, 166.
[363] Markham (ed.), *op. cit.* (n. 4), p. 304.
[364] Pires in Cortesão (ed.), *op. cit.* (n. 9), I, 48.
[365] Azevedo (ed.), *op. cit.* (n. 17), I, 287.
[366] *Ibid.*, p. 288.

church. The political organization of the colony also went ahead swiftly as Albuquerque sought to develop Goa into Portugal's imperial anchor post on the west coast of India. Initially, the people of Goa seemed to prefer the Portuguese to the Muslim overlords whom the Europeans replaced. This was probably so because the financial exactions of the Portuguese were less and their attitude towards native customs and religion far more tolerant. The only native practice immediately outlawed was *sati*.[367]

Goa played host for varying periods of time to many European writers on India. Varthema touched there when the island was still ruled over by the Muslims. Pires, who visited Goa shortly after its conquest by the Portuguese, calls it "the key to the First and Second India." [368] Barbosa, who wrote shortly before 1518, evidently had only a relatively limited experience in Goa. He writes, in any case, much less about Goa than about Malabar and Gujarat. Castanheda, it seems, was based for most of a decade (1529–38) in Goa and its environs. The physician and apothecary Orta spent more than a generation (1534–*ca.* 1570) there tending the Portuguese viceroys and other officials. The scene of his *Colloquies* is laid in Goa, where he had his own house and a garden in which he grew medical herbs. Since Goa was a great crossroads of eastern trade, the Portuguese resident in the "Golden City" had splendid opportunities to become acquainted with traders and travelers from elsewhere in India and from the East Indies and the Far East. These itinerants provided the Portuguese with more than a little of their information on Asia. Camoëns, who visited with Orta in Goa in about 1561,[369] wrote in *The Lusiads*:

Goa will be taken from the infidel, and will come in time to be queen of all the East, raised to a pinnacle by the triumphs of the conquerors; from which proud eminence they will keep the idolatrous heathen, and all such as may be tempted to wage war against your beloved people, severely in check.[370]

While outfitting his fleet at Cannanore between the first and second conquests of Goa, Albuquerque wrote in 1510 to King Manuel explaining that possession of this strategic territory was in his opinion essential to the maintenance of the Portuguese position in India and a possible springboard for conquest of the Deccan.[371] Pires concurs in this estimate of Goa's importance and adds that the Muslim rulers of the Deccan and Gujarat have "a bad neighbor in Goa." [372] He describes it as a civilized trading center and "the coolest place in India." [373] Its port and trading facilities have the greatest possibilities for development. News of the conquest of Goa was relayed to Rome by the Portuguese

---

[367] Albuquerque in Birch (ed.), *op. cit.* (n. 116), II, 94.

[368] Cortesão (ed.), *op. cit.* (n. 9), I, 54.

[369] The great poet wrote a sonnet in honor of the Viceroy, Dom Francisco Coutinho, which was first published at Goa in Orta's *Colloquies* of 1563. For the text see Conde de Ficalho (ed.), *Coloquios dos simples e drogas da India* (2 vols.; Lisbon, 189–95), I, 7–9.

[370] From the modern prose translation of William C. Atkinson (London, 1952), p. 65.

[371] Birch (trans.), *op. cit.* (n. 116), III, 258–63.

[372] Cortesão (ed.), *op. cit.* (n. 9), I, 57.

[373] *Ibid.*

embassy of 1514 to the Vatican; details about the development of Goa as a colony of Portugal were not generally circulated in Europe until after mid-century.

Although Ramusio in his first volume published Pires' and Barbosa's accounts,[374] their narratives of Goa are slight and unsystematic by comparison to the descriptions of the Portuguese chroniclers. Castanheda, Barros, and Albuquerque give similar accounts of Goa's geography, history, and development under the Portuguese. These, supplemented by occasional asides from Orta's *Colloquies* and by incidental references from the other sources were sufficient to give an interested student of the mid-sixteenth century an accurate notion of what the Portuguese were doing in Goa.

The name "Goa," though it may have been used before 1510, begins to be common only after the Portuguese conquest.[375] The natives of the region, the Kanarese, call the island "Ticuari." This means "thirty villages," [376] the number of units into which the island was divided for administrative purposes when the Portuguese arrived there. "Ticuari," or the island of Goa, is "surrounded on every side with lagoons of salt water and islands." [377] Looked at from the sea side, there are two great bays, north and south of the island, into which flow two rivers: the "Pangim" [378] (now called the Mandavi) and the river of Old Goa (now called the Juari). The bays are joined together by a streamlet that separates the island from the mainland and which is fed by the numerous waters that descend from the "Gate" (Ghats) to the sea. The lofty and extensive Ghat range "hangs over Goa and the sea like an awning." [379] The eastern side of the island, where attacks from the mainland must come, is serviced by two main fords at the villages of "Benestari" (Banastarim) and "Gondali" (Gandau-lim).[380] It is said that the crocodiles make crossings at Gandaulim exceedingly dangerous, and that in times of stress the Goans throw condemned criminals and prisoners of war to the hungry reptiles to keep them congregated at the ford. Goa was also protected on its land side by towers and bulwarks mounted by artillery. The length of the island measured from Banastarim in the east to the cape is three leagues (12 miles); its width from north to south is one league (4 miles).[381]

---

[374] G. B. Ramusio, *Delle navigationi et viaggi* (Venice, 1550), I, 320 r & v on Goa.

[375] See discussion in Dames, *op. cit.* (n. 5), I, 170, n. 2. Both Castanheda and Barros note that this is what "we call it."

[376] Cidade and Múrias (eds.), *op. cit.* (n. 6), II, 189. Cf. the note in Yule and Burnell (eds.), *op. cit.* (n. 10), p. 290, in which an unnamed author writing around 1520 is quoted as saying that on the island of "Tissoury" there are 31 *aldeas* (villages). In modern transliteration it is Tisvadi (see José N. da Fonseca, *An Historical and Archaeological Sketch of the City of Goa* [Bombay, 1878], p. 111). For a list of the villages and towns see Barros in Cidade and Múrias (eds.), *op. cit.* (n. 6), II, 198.

[377] Albuquerque in Birch (trans.), *op. cit.* (n. 116), II, 92.

[378] The name used by Castanheda; Barros appears not to know it.

[379] Albuquerque in Birch (trans.), *op. cit.* (n. 116), II, 95.

[380] Barros lists five fording places between the islands and the mainland: "Pangi," "Daugi," "Gondali," "Benestari," "Agaci." See Cidade and Múrias (eds.), *op. cit.* (n. 6), II, 198–99.

[381] *Ibid.* p. 189; Fonseca, *op. cit.* (n. 376), p. 111 gives these measurements as nine and three miles respectively.

One of the few general descriptions of the island of Goa available early in the sixteenth century was written by Castanheda:

The greater part of this island is encircled with rocky cliffs and mires: the land itself is very beautiful and luxuriant with numerous and tall groves of palm trees that give much wine, oil, vinegar, and jaggery,[382] that almost tastes like sugar. It also has areca palms that give areca with which betel is eaten.[383] All this makes them much money, and now many Portuguese have large incomes from it. They have also many gardens in which they grow numerous and very singular fruits of the earth, and have many and very healthful waters. They produce much rice and other vegetables which are different from ours and all good to eat. They have a large amount of sesame from which they make a very good oil which spares our own, and it is in such abundance that they make it in presses as we do ours. They produce much livestock, cows and oxen, many pigs and hens, and much good fish, as well as numerous other foods of land and sea. There is a large population of gentiles whom they call canarins [*Kanarese*], including brahmins and other learned doctors, who possess numerous gilded edifices of their idols which they call *pagodes*:[384] and for everybody there are many large tanks made of bricks (in which one can sail boats) wherein the Moors and heathens bathe themselves.[385]

The language of Goa is Konkani, a tongue which, according to Pires,[386] does not resemble the languages spoken in the Deccan or Vijayanagar.

According to traditional history as related to the Portuguese "by the natives,"[387] the marshy territory near Goa was originally occupied by refugees from Kanara. After these first settlers had established themselves, they were subjected to the princes of Kanara and forced to conclude a perpetual contract with them. By the terms of this contract the thirty villages of the Goa area were required to pay annual tribute called "cocivarado" to the prince of Kanara.[388] Each village was obliged to contribute an annual tax according to its resources as determined by the headmen in council. The authority in charge of each village was a *tanadar*,[389] who apparently was charged with collecting revenues and making new assessments in those villages which defaulted. This "first population" founded the ancient Hindu city of Goa on the southern extremity

[382] On this and other palm products see Orta's account in Markham (ed.), *op. cit.* (n. 4), p. 140.
[383] See *ibid.*, p. 192, n. 1.
[384] This word, obscure in its origins, is often used by the Portuguese to mean the "heathen" temples of India.
[385] Castanheda in Azevedo (ed.), *op. cit.* (n. 17), II, 21.
[386] Cortesão (ed.), *op. cit.* (n. 9), I, 54.
[387] Account of Barros in Cidade and Múrias (eds.), *op. cit.* (n. 6), II, 192–93.
[388] Albuquerque and his successors honored the special constitutions of these village communities. In 1526 a register, called *Foral de usos e costumes*, was compiled of their traditional usages and privileges, and it was subsequently employed in the sixteenth century as an administrative guidebook by the Portuguese rulers of Goa. An abstract of it in English may be found in R. S. Whiteway, *The Rise of the Portuguese Empire in India* (London, 1898), pp. 215–20. For the complete text, "rearranged so as to bring together all the orders relating to the same subject," and followed by a commentary, see B. H. Baden-Powell, "The Villages of Goa in the Early 16th Century," *Journal of the Royal Asiatic Society for 1900*, pp. 261–91.
[389] Cf. discussion of this term in Cortesão (ed.), *op. cit.* (n. 9), I, 56, n. 1.

of the island and "from the appearance of its buildings" when the Portuguese arrived there, "it was a great place."[390]

Barros, who gives more details on Goa's history than any of the other Portuguese writers, is apparently not aware of the fact that the Hindu city of Goa was the capital of the Kadamba rulers until the latter part of the thirteenth century.[391] Nor does he seem to touch upon the first Muslim conquest of it in the fourteenth century. He and Albuquerque refer when they talk of Goa under its Hindu rulers to the century of Vijayanagar control from about 1370 to 1470. At this time, reports Albuquerque, Goa "was a very important place in these parts"[392] and was well staffed with troops to stand off the rising power of the Muslims in the Deccan. It had many Hindu temples "of a very good style of architecture" and remained a tributary of Vijayanagar until "about seventy years" before Albuquerque's conquest.[393] It was during these seventy years that a new city of Goa was built, according to Albuquerque, in the northern part of the island. The city was moved, he asserts, because the Juari River had become shallow and so was unable to accommodate the largest vessels. In the meantime the Mandavi had become broader and deeper and so a port was erected on its banks and Old Goa was left to die.[394]

As we have seen earlier, by this period the local rulers of the Deccan paid no more than nominal vassalage to the Bahmani sultan. The most powerful of these independent Deccan princelings in the Konkan was Yūsuf ʿĀdil Khan, the ruler of Bijapur and lord of Goa who died in 1510. To the Portuguese he was known as the "Sabaio," his familiar name in common use at the time, which, Barros says, was derived from the name of his native town of Sava in northern Persia.[395] The Portuguese chronicler also gives two different stories derived from tradition concerning the Persian's decision to remain in India.[396] The "Sabaio" was reported by Albuquerque to be so pleased with Goa's beauty and strategic position that "he determined to take up his residence therein."[397] The "Sabaio" soon began to think in terms of using Goa as a base of operations for attacks upon Malabar and Gujarat. But all of these hopes came to nothing when Albuquerque wrested away his prize possession.

That Goa before 1510 was a great emporium, an impressive city, and a center of maritime activity on India's west coast is repeated time after time in the European sources. Barros even speculates that it once may have been populated by the Christians of St. Thomas. But more than anything else, the Portuguese

390 Albuquerque in Birch (trans.), *op. cit.* (n. 116), II, 93.

391 On Goa's history see Fonseca, *op. cit.* (n. 376), pp. 83, 119–23.

392 Albuquerque in Birch (trans.), *op. cit.* (n. 116), II, 94.

393 *Ibid.*, p. 92. Seventy years before 1510 would push the end of Vijayanagar control back to 1440 rather than the date 1470 which is usually accepted. For comments see Fonseca, *op. cit.* (n. 376), p. 125.

394 Birch (trans.), *op. cit.* (n. 116), II, 93–94.

395 Cidade and Múrias (eds.), *op. cit.* (n. 6), II, 197; see also Dames (ed.), *op. cit.* (n. 5), I, 172–73, n. 1.

396 Cidade and Múrias (eds.), *op. cit.* (n. 6), II, 197. Orta claims that he was a Turk (Markham [ed.], *op. cit.* [n. 4], p. 72).

397 Birch (trans.), *op. cit.* (n. 116), II, 96.

are impressed by the revenues which the "Sabaio" derived from trade and taxation. Arabian horses from Ormuz were sold in Goa at great profit to merchants from Vijayanagar and the Deccan. From the tax on these and other commercial items the "Sabaio" received substantial revenues. Barros gives figures on the taxes collected from the thirty villages, the mainland, and other Goan possessions of the "Sabaio."[398] The "Sabaio" is also reported to have large fleets, excellent fortifications, and a sizable army. Indeed, the strength and reputation of the "Sabaio" were so great that emissaries reportedly were sent to his court from as far away as Aden and Cairo.

Still, the Portuguese allege, the natives of Goa were restive under Muslim jurisdiction because of the high taxes and the tendency of the Moors to live apart and to treat the natives cruelly. Barros describes at some length how willingly the Goans after 1510 took to the Portuguese ways of trading, governing, and living. The Kanara women, unlike those of Malabar, were apparently quite willing to form alliances with or marry the Portuguese men, especially since newlyweds were given subsidies from the treasury of the city.[399] The non-Muslim population of the city was more willing to become converted to Christianity than the Malabars. But while the Portuguese describe the general receptivity of the Goans to Portuguese rule, they fail to comment in detail upon the customs of their Goan subjects. Much of what Orta has to say in his *Colloquies* is derived from his experience in Goa, but he has practically nothing to report on the customs of its inhabitants. His digressions into history, politics, and social practices almost always deal with some other part of India. In reporting on Goa after its capture, the Portuguese generally center their attention upon their achievements in the "Golden City" and their development of it as the administrative, episcopal, and commercial center of their Asiatic empire.

E. GUJARAT (CAMBAY)

North and west of the Deccan in the territory that surrounds the Gulf of Cambay lay the maritime state of Gujarat, which had been under Muslim rule since the end of the thirteenth century.[400] In 1342, Ibn Batuta visited several seaport towns of Gujarat and subsequently described the trade, prosperity, and

---

[398] Cidade and Múrias (eds.), *op. cit.* (n. 6), II, 198–99. According to rumor, the city of Goa alone paid him 500,000 *pardãos*, principally from taxes on the importation of horses. He also received taxes from the village communities (*tanadarias*) and the islands of Divar, Chorão, and Jua, as well as tolls paid for use of the fords to the mainland, port fees, and export duties.

[399] *Ibid.*, II, 199. On the marriage of Portuguese with native women see Danvers, *op. cit.* (n. 228), I, 217.

[400] The best general study, which utilizes some of the Portuguese sources, is M. S. Commissariat, *A History of Gujarat* (London, 1938), Vol. I. See also M. L. Dames, "The Portuguese and Turks in the Indian Ocean in the Sixteenth Century," *Journal of the Royal Asiatic Society* (1921), pp. 1–28; and the supplementary article by E. D. Ross, "The Portuguese in India and Arabia between 1507 and 1517," in *ibid.*, pp. 545–62. For earlier times see L. Stembach, "Gujarat as Known to Medieval Europe," *Proceedings of the Indian Historical Congress*, VII (1956), 292–95.

strategic location of the city of Cambay. With the appearance of the Portuguese in the Indian Ocean in the sixteenth century, the rulers of Gujarat, along with their Egyptian coreligionists, were quick to realize that the Christians would eventually threaten their vital maritime connections with the West. The Gujaratis therefore combined forces with the Egyptians to prevent the Portuguese from controlling the strategic ports of Ormuz at the entrance to the Persian Gulf and of Aden at the southern portal to the Red Sea. The Portuguese, on their side, soon came to realize that their position in southern India and their freedom to sail in the Indian Ocean and farther east depended upon their ability to check or overwhelm the Muslim powers whose leading representative in Asian waters was the Sultanate of Gujarat. Thus, the issue was joined between Portugal and Gujarat before the end of the first decade of European activity in India.

The Zamorin of Calicut in 1507 requested aid of the Sultan of Gujarat to help him wage war against those who were threatening to disrupt the profitable coastal and oceanic trade so vital to both of their states. However, the Gujaratis, who had suffered at the hands of the Portuguese the year before in the defense of Ormuz, were disinclined to engage the Europeans at too great a distance from their home bases. So it was not until 1507–8, when the Portuguese moved northward to the Deccan coast, that the combined Egyptian and Gujarati fleets descended upon them without warning at Chaul.[401] To avenge this defeat, Viceroy d'Almeida in 1509 brought a great new fleet northward, plundered Dabhul, and then proceeded to the island of Diu at the entrance to the Gulf of Cambay. Here he met and decisively defeated the combined fleets in a naval battle which halted the Muslim attack.[402] Among the spoils of victory the Portuguese acquired a number of books in various languages as well as the battle flags of the Egyptian sultan. The captured banners were taken to Portugal and hung from the walls of the Templars' church in Tomar, the headquarters of the crusading Order of Christ. D'Almeida did not feel strong enough to storm the fortress of Diu, and so after his victory he returned to Chaul, intimidated the ruler of Ahmadnagar, and forced him to pay tribute.

After Albuquerque's first victory at Goa in 1510, Sultan Mahmūd I of Gujarat sent an envoy to Cannanore to request peace and an alliance with Portugal. The envoy also carried two letters from the Sultan's capital at Chāmpāner addressed to Albuquerque; one was from Christians who were captive there, and the other from Malik Gopi, the minister of the Sultan. The Portuguese commander promised the envoy he would visit Gujarat to arrange terms for an alliance, and then he proceeded to his major task of preparing for the second descent on Goa. Once Albuquerque had clearly established Portuguese hegemony over Goa, diplomatic relations with the new ruler of Gujarat, Sultan

[401] On the date of this Muslim victory (January, 1508) see Ross, *loc. cit.* (n. 400), p. 547.

[402] Information on this battle is derived solely from Portuguese, Turkish, and Arabic histories. The contemporary Gujarati historians make no mention of this defeat in their annals. See Commissariat, *op. cit.* (n. 400), I, 247–48.

Muzaffar II (reigned 1511–26), became more regular.[403] At the end of 1512 Albuquerque received from Lisbon the terms which he should insist upon as the basis for an alliance. They involved permission to erect a fortress on the island of Diu, a request that Gujarati traders deal exclusively with Goa, and the requirement that the Sultan should have no further connections with the Egyptians or Turks.

After a few tentative efforts to feel out the Sultan, the Portuguese in 1514 sent an impressive embassy to the court of Muzaffar II. Even before the envoys arrived at the Sultan's court, it had become clear that Malik Ayaz, the governor of Diu, had convinced the government of Gujarat that it should not yield to the demand for a fortress at Diu. The Portuguese envoys, armed with gifts of cloth, silver, and horses, nevertheless proceeded to the Sultan's court which was then being held at Ahmadābād. In their negotiations with the royal officials, the Portuguese were offered various sites for a fortress but not Diu. The Sultan was apparently convinced, despite the tempting bait of increased revenues from trade which the Portuguese held before him, that the Europeans might use a fortress at Diu as a bastion from which to attack the mainland.[404] Upon the failure of these negotiations, the Portuguese envoys returned to Goa accompanied by a rhinoceros, the Sultan's gift to Albuquerque. (It was this rhinoceros that was sent on to Europe in 1514, and confined in the king's menagerie at Lisbon until 1517. The animal was finally dispatched to Rome as a gift to Pope Leo X. Though it perished in a shipwreck on the Mediterranean, the carcass was washed ashore. It was subsequently stuffed and sent on to the Holy Father.)

After negotiations broke down, a stalemate developed in Portugal's relations with Gujarat. The Portuguese stubbornly persisted in demanding permission to erect a fortress at Diu; the Sultan remained adamant and proceeded to fortify the island against a possible attack. Located off the southern shore of the Kathiawar Peninsula, Diu's trading prosperity was based on ease of access, a very good harbor, and freedom from the influence of the dangerous tides, currents, and shoals of the Gulf of Cambay which menaced shipping at other Gujarati ports. From the Portuguese viewpoint, Diu, in addition to its natural advantages as a trading center, was also a potential menace as a base for Muslim (Turkish–Gujarati) attacks. It was therefore primarily on strategic grounds that the Portuguese persisted in their efforts to establish an outpost at Diu.

Though the successors of Albuquerque sought through diplomacy and sporadic coastal raids to change the Sultan's mind, the Gujarati refused to budge. Finally, in the reign of Sultan Bahādur Shah (1526–37), the Portuguese managed to advance their position in northern India at the expense of Gujarat. While preparing to do battle with the Mughul emperor, Humayun, the ruler of Gujarat tried to obtain help from the Portuguese viceroy, Nuno da Cunha (in office 1529–38). In return for a promise of aid, Bahādur, by a treaty of 1534, ceded Bassein with all its territories and revenues in perpetuity to the Portuguese.

[403] *Ibid.*, p. 293.
[404] *Ibid.*, pp. 295–96.

The following year, despite Portuguese aid, Bahādur was defeated by the Mughuls. In return for their providing him with sanctuary, Bahādur was required to permit the Lusitanians to build a fortress at Diu. After Bahādur's death at their hands in 1537, the Portuguese assumed sovereignty over Diu and took over its entire administration. Shortly thereafter, a messenger was dispatched overland to carry the good tidings to Lisbon.[405] Portuguese troubles were not over, however, because the garrison at Diu was seriously besieged in 1538 and again in 1546. The success of the Portuguese in withstanding the second siege of Diu was one of the last of their great exploits in India, for thereafter their power began to wane in Europe and India, and, as we earlier pointed out,[406] this was related to the breakdown of their spice monopoly. Still, the Portuguese managed to retain their hold on Diu, and it remained a Portuguese possession to 1962.[407] Bassein, on the other hand, was lost to the Marathis in 1729.

A number of the European writers on India visited Gujarat before the middle of the sixteenth century and they subsequently relayed to Europe a substantial amount of data about it. Varthema, who visited the city of Cambay in 1504, describes it at greater length than he does most of the other places on his itinerary. Albuquerque, who actually spent six days at Diu in 1513 while waiting for ship repairs, wrote in considerable detail on his diplomatic relations with Gujarat, and a large part of this information was published in the *Commentaries*. Pires' description of Cambay based on his travels in India during 1511–12[408] was translated and published by Ramusio in 1550 as was the account by Barbosa, who traveled in Gujarat around 1515. The latter presents in his *Book* the most reliable and interesting account of the seaports of Gujarat ever to be printed. Castanheda, who accompanied Nuno da Cunha's unsuccessful expedition against Diu in 1531, describes at some length its position in trade and strategy before the Portuguese takeover.[409] But for his general description of Gujarat, Castanheda seems to rely heavily on Pires and Barbosa. Orta, who went to Diu in 1535 with the expedition that established a Portuguese fortress there, also visited the city of Cambay and the islands of Bassein, Salsette, and Elephanta.[410] In the first three *Décadas* by Barros there are only incidental references to Gujarat, presumably because Barros felt that he could add very little to Barbosa's account.[411] The systematic discussion of Gujarat which appears in the fourth *Década* was probably the work of the continuator, and since it was not published until the seventeenth century it will not be considered here.

[405] *Ibid.*, pp. 385–86.

[406] Above, pp. 128–29.

[407] For a history of the island during its Portuguese period see A. B. de Bragança Pereira, *Os Portugueses em Diu* (Bastorá, n.d.).

[408] For the dating of his travels see Cortesão (ed.), *op. cit.* (n. 9), I, xxiv.

[409] Azevedo (ed.), *op. cit.* (n. 17), IV, 242–54; also I, 385–87.

[410] On his travels in these regions see A. X. Soares, "Garcia d'Orta, a Little Known Owner of Bombay," *Journal of the Bombay Branch of the Royal Asiatic Society*, XXVI (1921–23), 204–7.

[411] Cf. the discussion in Dames (ed.), *op. cit.* (n. 5), I, xxxiii–vii.

In addition to the general accounts, a series of works was published in Portugal in the latter half of the sixteenth century which celebrates the triumphs of the Portuguese at Diu. Diogo de Teive (Jacobus Tevius), a Portuguese Humanist trained in Paris, published in 1548 at Coimbra a book containing two poems by friends of his which salute the construction and defense of Diu.[412] In 1556 an eyewitness account of the second siege of Diu appeared at Coimbra[413]; the author was Lopo de Sousa Coutinho, a *fidalgo* of the king's household, who wrote of this dramatic defense in "a grave and excellent style."[414] Jerónimo Côrte Real, a poet who specialized in rejoicing over naval victories such as Lepanto, published at Lisbon in 1574 a series of cantos honoring the heros of the second siege of Diu;[415] and, in 1589, Francisco de Andrade had printed at Coimbra a poem commemorating the fiftieth anniversary of the first siege of Diu.[416] Though none of these works was translated into other European languages, it is apparent from their number that they helped to keep alive Portugal's interest in Diu and Gujarat.

Gujarat, which is generally called Cambay by the Portuguese as it was by the Muslim authors, is considered to be one of the "chief kingdoms of India."[417] On the interior it is bounded by two other "great and rich kingdoms," Malwa and "Sanga" (actually the territory to the east and north ruled by Rana Sanga, the leader of the Rajput Confederacy). On the north Gujarat confines with "Dulcinde" (a combination of Diul, or the seaport of Dival, with Sind). The coastal jurisdiction of Gujarat, upon leaving Sind, begins at the city of Mangalor[418] on the southwest coast of Kathiawar and extends southward almost to Chaul in the Deccan. Such a geographical description, while it differs in a few details among the several Portuguese writers, seems to be typical of those written by the Europeans who comment on Gujarat.[419]

On the history of Gujarat before their arrival there, the Europeans are not well informed though they have a few vague ideas about it. Barbosa, after hearing tales in Gujarat of the exploits of Alexander the Great and Darius of Persia, concludes that Darius once ruled over this kingdom.[420] Originally, the Gujarati territory was controlled by "heathens," especially the Rajputs, who

---

[412] Entitled *Cõmentarius de rebus in India apud Dium gestis anno salutis nostrae M. D. XLVI*. For bibliographical detail see King Manuel II, *Early Portuguese Books* (3 vols.; London, 1929–35), II, 233–41.

[413] Entitled *Livro do cerco de Diu*. See King Manuel II, *op. cit.* (n. 412), II, 486–95.

[414] Estimate of Diogo do Couto as quoted in *ibid.*, p. 493.

[415] Entitled *Sucesso do segundo cerco de Diu*. See King Manuel II, *op. cit.* (n. 412), II, 79–81.

[416] Entitled *O primeiro cerco de Diu*. See King Manuel II, *op. cit.* (n. 412), III, 280–81.

[417] Geographical description based on Castanheda in Azevedo (ed.), *op. cit.* (n. 17), II, 313.

[418] Mangrol is sometimes used instead to distinguish the northern Mangalor from the city in the southern Konkan of the same name. See Dames (ed.), *op. cit.* (n. 5), I, 127–28.

[419] For a modern map which generally accepts these boundaries see C. C. Davies, *An Historical Atlas of the Indian Peninsula* (2d ed.; Oxford, 1959), p. 39. Also see Pires' description in Cortesão (ed.), *op. cit.* (n. 9), I, 33.

[420] Dames (ed.), *op. cit.* (n. 5), I, 108. For the latest scholarship on this debatable assertion see Commissariat, *op. cit.* (n. 400), I, xiv.

acted as "knights and wardens of the land." [421] About two hundred years before the Portuguese conquest (*ca.* 1300), Muslim forces based on Delhi began to expand into Gujarat. [422] They pushed the Rajputs out of its cities and into the hinterland. The Rajputs continued for a long time thereafter to harass the Muslim invaders from bases in the back country. The Muslim sultans of Gujarat, who were in power at the time of the Portuguese advent there, are said to have been truly independent for just a short time. Originally, Castanheda remarks, [423] they were captains in the service of the Delhi emperor, and only succeeded in establishing an independent dynasty by concerting with the other captains (of "Dulcinde," "Sanga," Malwa, etc.) in overthrowing the emperor's authority. The disintegration of the Delhi empire in northwestern India was followed, according to the Portuguese, by the establishment of the separate kingdom of Cambay whose ruler in the early sixteenth century was "the fourth of his line counting as the first the one who [had] revolted." [424]

The original rebel was Mahmūd I (reigned 1458–1511), the greatest of the Gujarati sultans and the conqueror of the Rajputs of Chāmpāner in 1484. Varthema, who visited Gujarat in 1504, remarks with surprising accuracy that Mahmūd "about forty years ago . . . captured this kingdom from a king of the Gujarati. . . ." [425] The Italian observer then goes on to describe Mahmūd's manner of living and seems particularly impressed by the elephants which do reverence to him. Varthema, Barbosa, and Castanheda, incredible as it may seem, report that Mahmūd was nourished from childhood on a daily ration of poison so that he would develop an immunity to it. [426] As a result of this regime, he became so poisonous that "when a fly touched him . . . it forthwith died . . . and as many women as slept with him perished." [427] Varthema also describes the Sultan as having "mustachios under his nose so long that he ties them over his

---

[421] Dames (ed.), *op. cit.* (n. 5), I, 110.

[422] Probably a vague reference to the Muslim conquest of 1298. See Albuquerque in Birch (trans.), *op. cit.* (n. 116), IV, 106.

[423] Azevedo (ed.), *op. cit.* (n. 17), II, 316; cf. Pires in Cortesão (ed.), *op. cit.* (n. 9), I, 36.

[424] Since Castanheda is writing during the reign of Bahādur (1526–37), he is probably referring to the sultans beginning with Mahmūd I (Azevedo [ed.], *op. cit.* [n. 17], II, 316). For a detailed history of Gujarat in the early sixteenth century, based on Persian and Gujarati sources, see the fourth *Década* of Barros (Cidade and Múrias [eds.], *op. cit.* [n. 6], IV, 258–65).

[425] Temple (ed.), *op. cit.* (n. 233), p. 45.

[426] Commissariat, *op. cit.* (n. 400), I, 230–31 appears to treat this story with more seriousness than it deserves; for a more plausible appraisal of it as a piece of folklore see Dames (ed.), *op. cit.* (n. 5), I, 121–22, n. 3. Pires (in Cortesão [ed.], *op. cit.* [n. 9], I, 40) gives a similar account and adds: "But I do not believe this, although they say it is so." Castanheda (in Azevedo [ed.], *op. cit.* [n. 17], II, 316) accepts this story and relays it without comment to posterity. Garcia de Resende in his *Commentaries* (1554) ascribes similar habits to the kings of Sumatra (see passage translated in Cortesão [ed.], *op. cit.* [n. 9], I, 40, n. 2). It also eventually got into Purchas and was apparently the inspiration that moved Samuel Butler in *Hudibras* (Pt. II, Canto 1,) to write:
"The Prince of Cambay's daily food
Is asp and basilisk and toad,
Which makes him have so strong a breath,
Each night he stinks a queen to death."

[427] Dames (ed.), *op. cit.* (n. 5), I, 122.

head as a woman would tie her tresses, and he has a white beard which reaches to his girdle." [428]

Mahmūd's son, Muzaffar II (reigned 1511–26), came to the throne when he was almost forty years of age and shortly before Pires visited Gujarat. The Portuguese traveler reports that he was then at war with the neighboring princes of Malwa, Sind, and the Rajput confederacy "and to some extent with Delhi." [429] Gujarat is protected from invasions by Delhi, however, by the high Malwa plateau which separates the two states, and by the activities of a "Gujarat Jogee" who controls the only pass connecting them. [430] Muzaffar is judged as being "given to all manner of vice in eating and lechery" and of spending most of the time "among his women stupefied with opium." [431] In all other matters he is said to be "judicious." [432] The Sultan is aided in governing by "Milagobim" (Malik Gopi, a Brahman of Surat and "friend of the Portuguese"), "Chamlc-malec" (Kiwam-ul-Mulk, title of the great noble, Malik Sarang), "Asturmalec" (unidentified), [433] and "Codandam" (possibly Khush-'adam, whose title was Imad'l-Mulk). Each of these emirs has a vast retinue of mounted followers, and, as great lords native to the kingdom, they share with the sultan in the administration of justice, government, and revenues. When the ruler dies, they are said to act as "the electors of the kingdom." In addition to his noble advisers, Muzaffar is reputed to possess "up to a thousand wives and concubines" [434] of whom the leading one was apparently a Rajput woman. [435]

The sultan with his court usually resides at Chāmpāner, a fortified mountain town whose ruins stand today a short distance northeast of Baroda. Captured in 1484 from the Rajputs, it remained the royal stronghold, minting center, and capital of Gujarat until its conquest by the Mughul emperor, Humayun, in 1535. At the time when Castanheda was in India (1528–38), the city is reputed to have had 130,000 hearths enclosed within seven strong walls. The royal palaces, warehouses, and arsenals, "which occupy as much space as Evora," [436] are separated from the rest of the city by a wall that has iron gates at its three portals. The only persons permitted to go within the wall are the sultan, his wives, household officials, and tax collectors. The countryside around the city is "a land of broad plains which yield great store of food" so that "in the city

---

[428] Temple (ed.), *op. cit.* (n. 233), p. 45. For comment on this enormous mustache and the possible relationship of it to the sobriquet "Begada" (impotent) under which Mahmūd I is known to posterity see Commissariat, *op. cit.* (n. 400), I, 232–33.

[429] Cortesão (ed.), *op. cit.* (n. 9), I, 36. See below, p. 420.

[430] *Ibid.* For a more detailed account of "the king of the Ioghe" or Yogis see Varthema in Temple (ed.), *op. cit.* (n. 233), pp. 46–47. This is possibly a reference to the chief of a tribe known as the Gor khnatha Gosains (Yule and Burnell, *op. cit.* [n. 10], p. 352). None of the Portuguese who visit Gujarat after Pires remarks on this ruler.

[431] Pires in Cortesão (ed.), *op. cit.* (n. 9), I, 40.

[432] *Ibid.* Commissariat, *op. cit.* (n. 400), I, 290–92 calls him the "clement" ruler and describes his regime as "liberal and tolerant."

[433] Listed also by Albuquerque in Birch (trans.), *op. cit.* (n. 116), IV, 108.

[434] Pires in Cortesão (ed.), *op. cit.* (n. 9), I, 41.

[435] Albuquerque in Birch (trans.), *op. cit.* (n. 116), IV, 107.

[436] Azevedo (ed.), *op. cit.* (n. 17), II, 319.

there is enough and to spare of all things."⁴³⁷ In the mountains surrounding the plain there is much game, and Muzaffar II domesticates animals for hunting and collects wild animals from all over the world as a hobby. It was this ruler who sent the rhinoceros from his menagerie to Albuquerque. The *Commentaries* of Albuquerque record details on the reception accorded a Persian embassy at Chāmpāner in 1511–13 and on the difficulties which developed between the envoy's retinue and the retainers of a visiting prince from Malwa.⁴³⁸ As on the occasion of the Portuguese embassy of 1514 to Chāmpāner, the Sultan sent the Persian envoys off with a gift rhinoceros.

Because of the constant threat of war from the Rajputs and other neighboring peoples, the Sultan of Gujarat must constantly be prepared for hostilities. In addition to powerful horse and elephant units, he maintains a large standing army, recruited mostly from foreign Muslim adventurers to whom he pays high salaries.⁴³⁹ The horsemen are "so light and skillful in the saddle"⁴⁴⁰ that they play polo for recreation. When girded for war, the foreparts of the horses are protected by stiff caparisons and their riders wear coats of mail or quilted cotton jackets and carry shields, swords, and a Turkish bow.⁴⁴¹ While the horses are native to Gujarat, the elephants have to be imported at high cost from Ceylon and Malabar. Still, the ruler of Gujarat maintains a standing force of four or five hundred fighting elephants who are outfitted for battle and used in combat as is customary in other parts of India. Like the armies of the Deccan, those of Gujarat are also using imported artillery by the beginning of the sixteenth century.

The general descriptions of life in Gujarat relate to conditions in 1515 and shortly before.⁴⁴² Even Castanheda's account of social organization appears to be based on the earlier eyewitness reports of Pires and Barbosa. All the Europeans, beginning with Varthema, remark on the mixed population of the country. In the interior the majority of the people are Hindu; in the seaports the Moors and their practices predominate.⁴⁴³ The Hindus, who count for "almost the third part of the kingdom,"⁴⁴⁴ are divided into three major groups: Rajputs or the fighters, Banyā or the merchants, Brahmans or the priests. The Rajputs, who live in mountain villages, have no ruler of their own and they wage war constantly against the Sultan of Gujarat.⁴⁴⁵ In addition to being excellent horsemen and archers, the Rajputs are distinguished from other Hindus by the fact that they "kill and eat sheep and fish and other kinds of food."⁴⁴⁶

⁴³⁷ Barbosa in Dames (ed.), *op. cit.* (n. 5), I, 123–24.
⁴³⁸ Birch (trans.), *op. cit.* (n. 116), IV, 82–85.
⁴³⁹ Castanheda in Azevedo (ed.), *op. cit.* (n. 17), II, 316.
⁴⁴⁰ Barbosa in Dames (ed.), *op. cit.* (n. 5), I, 119.
⁴⁴¹ Pires in Cortesão (ed.), *op. cit.* (n. 9), I, 33–34.
⁴⁴² Commissariat, *op. cit.* (n. 400), I, chap. xx uses the reports of Albuquerque and Barbosa as the basis for his description of Gujarat immediately following the long reign of Mahmūd I, which ended in 1511. He calls (p. 254) Barbosa's "a reliable and interesting account."
⁴⁴³ Castanheda in Azevedo (ed.), *op. cit.* (n. 17), II, 314.
⁴⁴⁴ Pires in Cortesão (ed.), *op. cit.* (n. 9), I, 39.
⁴⁴⁵ Barbosa in Dames (ed.), *op. cit.* (n. 5), I, 110.   ⁴⁴⁶ *Ibid.*

The Banyā "dwell among the Moors with whom they carry on all their trade."[447] Barbosa and Castanheda describe at length the abhorrence felt by the Banyā about taking life of any sort. Actually the Portuguese writers seem to be describing practices of Jains who follow the doctrine of *ahiṃsā*.[448] Barbosa seems to delight in recounting how these devotees are forced—by Moors, beggars, and others—to ransom small birds, insects, and other living things to prevent them from being killed in their presence. But while revering life, the Banyā are still "great usurers, falsifiers of weights and measures . . . and great liars."[449] Tall, tawny, and well clothed, the Banyā restrict their diet to milk, butter, sugar, rice, fruit, and vegetables. The women, fair and dark alike, are slender, well shaped, and beautiful. Both men and women bathe twice each day to purify themselves of their sins. The men have long hair, "as women do with us,"[450] which they twist upon the head under a turban. Dressed in long cotton and silk shirts, or with short coats of silk and brocade, the men wear pointed shoes. The women, like their husbands, clothe themselves in long garments, as well as in silken bodices cut low at the back. On going outside they throw over themselves a cloak called a *chadar*. They always are barefooted and "on their heads they wear nought but their own hair well-dressed."[451] The women wear anklets of gold and silver as well as rings on their fingers and toes; the men ornament themselves with rings and earrings set with precious stones. The men do not carry arms, both out of predisposition and because the Moors protect them. A very amorous people, the women of the Banyā "are kept much at home and shut up."[452]

Certain Brahmans manage beautiful and large temples which have great revenues. Other members of the priestly caste beg for alms or act as couriers.[453] Though subject to the Moors, some of the Brahmans are among "the men who rule in the kingdom"[454] as, for example, the rich and renowned minister, Malik Gopi. Below the waist, the Brahmans wear cotton garments. They go about bare from the waist up, except that they wear "a cord of three strands [the sacred thread]" over their shoulder. Like the Banyā, the Brahmans marry just once in a lifetime, this rule applying to both men and women. Barbosa describes in some detail their wedding ceremony and the accompanying festivities. Adultery on the woman's part brings death by poisoning, "unless it be with the brothers of their husbands" with whom it is lawful to sleep.[455] The sons are the only legitimate heirs of the father's property and position, "for Brahmans must be sons of

---

[447] *Ibid.*, p. 111. For a lengthier description of the Rajputs see Pires in Cortesão (ed.), *op. cit.* (n. 9), I, 32–33.

[448] Commissariat, *op. cit.* (n. 400), I, 255.

[449] Barbosa in Dames (ed.), *op. cit.* (n. 5), I, 112.

[450] *Ibid.*, p. 113.   [451] *Ibid.*, p. 114.   [452] *Ibid.*

[453] *Ibid.*, p. 117, talks about "Pateles" who are a lower order of Brahmans who act as messengers; Pires (in Cortesão [ed.], *op. cit.* [n. 9], I, 39, 42) refers to "Pattars" (presumably also messengers) whom he calls "the more honoured Brahmans." See for discussion of this term Dalgado, *op. cit.* (n. 44), II, 186–88. It would appear that both terms are derived from Sanskrit: *Patel* = governor.

[454] Pires in Cortesão (ed.), *op. cit.* (n. 9), I, 40.

[455] Castanheda in Azevedo (ed.), *op. cit.* (n. 17), II, 314–15.

Brahmans."[456] In their creed the Brahmans attach great importance to a God in three persons, and their teachings show "many resemblances to the Holy Trinity."[457] Upon entering a Christian church, they revere the sacred images and ask for Holy Mary. From this it is concluded "that they were once Christians" who "gradually lost the faith because of the Mohammedans."[458]

Moors from all over the Islamic world congregate in the cities of Gujarat to carry on trade or to find employment as soldiers of the sultan. In addition to the native Moors and their coreligionists of Delhi, a cosmopolitan flavor "is given to life by the presence of Turks, Mamalukes, Arabs, Persians, Khurasanis, Turcomans, Abyssinians, and a sprinkling of renegade Christians."[459] In this melting pot of peoples, many tongues are spoken, including Arabic, Turkish, and Gujarati. Fair of complexion, the members of the ruling class live a luxurious life. Attired in rich clothes of gold, silk, cotton and camlets, the Moors wear high turbans on their heads and leather boots up to the knee which are decorated with dainty devices. Unlike the Banyā, the Moors carry in their girdles short swords "finely damascened with gold and silver according to the rank of the wearer."[460] Of their women, who are beautiful, white, and well dressed, they may marry as many as they can support. Since they are extremely jealous of their wives, the women are transported from one place to another in enclosed carriages which are drawn by horses and extravagant to behold.[461] Divorce is possible, and may be initiated by either husbands or wives, on the payment of a sum of money the size of which is determined and agreed upon at the time of marriage.[462]

The Sultan of Gujarat is said to have jurisdiction over sixty thousand towns,[463] large and small, both along the seacoast and scattered throughout the interior. Many of these towns are enclosed with walls, divided into streets, and built up with "high houses of stone and mortar like those of Spain."[464] Aside from the capital at Chāmpāner already described, the only other interior cities noticed by the Portuguese are "Andava" (Ahmadābād), "Varodrra" (Baroda), and "Barnez" (Broach). Over these cities rule "grand viziers or captains, men by whom the whole kingdom is governed."[465] Ahmadābād, founded by Ahmad Shah in 1411 and capital of the Gujarati sultans until the conquest of Chāmpāner,

[456] Barbosa in Dames (ed.), *op. cit.* (n. 5), I, 117.

[457] *Ibid.*, p. 115, especially n. 1.

[458] Pires in Cortesão (ed.), *op. cit.* (n. 9), I, 39; Castanheda (in Azevedo [ed.], *op. cit.* [n. 17], II, 314), who wrote a generation later and long after the Portuguese had discovered that the Hindus were not former Christians, still arrives at this same conclusion.

[459] Composite list is derived from Dames (ed.), *op. cit.* (n. 5), I, 119–20; Cortesão (ed.), *op. cit.* (n. 9), I, 34; and Azevedo (ed.), *op. cit.* (n. 17), II, 316.

[460] Barbosa in Dames (ed.), *op. cit.* (n. 5), I, 120.

[461] For further detail on these carriages see Castanheda in Azevedo (ed.), *op. cit.* (n. 17), II, 315.

[462] On women having the liberty to divorce their husbands, Barbosa may be misinformed (Dames [ed.], *op. cit.* [n. 5], I, 121, n. 2).

[463] Castanheda in Azevedo (ed.), *op. cit.* (n. 17), II, 315.

[464] *Ibid.*

[465] Pires in Cortesão (ed.), *op. cit.* (n. 9), I, 35.

is the only one of these inland cities talked about at any length by the Portuguese. Evidently the sultans, even after 1484, continued to spend a good deal of their time in the larger and pleasanter city of Ahmadābād.[466] Barbosa, in commenting upon this city, notes that the all-powerful sultan punished an official guilty of malfeasance by forcing him to drink poison.[467]

The seaport towns, both on the mainland coast and on the nearby islands of the entire region from the Gulf of Kutch around the coast of the Kathiawar Peninsula and the Gulf of Cambay as far south as the Deccan frontier which runs between Mahim and Chaul, are listed by a number of the Portuguese writers. Pires names sixteen such ports and Barbosa comments on fourteen of them. Other maritime trading centers, such as "Betexagor" (Bate-shahr on Bate Island in the Gulf of Kutch),[468] attract the attention of Albuquerque. The principal coastal cities are clearly identified by all commentators as Diu, Cambay, Surat, and Randēr. In recent times, these seaport towns of Gujarat have declined as oceanic trade has increasingly concentrated at Bombay which was little more than a fishing village in the early sixteenth century.

The most important trading center west of the Gulf of Cambay is located on the island of Diu, a point of rendezvous before the Portuguese got there for ships from East Africa, the Red Sea, and the Persian Gulf, as well as from the ports of western India. Here the Malabars are accustomed by 1515 to bring coconuts and spices to exchange for silk and cotton cloth, horses, and opium, "both that brought from Aden and that which they make in Cambay, which is not so fine as the former."[469] Goods of India and the further East are also shipped from Diu to Arabia and Persia; the traffic at Diu is the greatest "of any found in these regions" and the returns from it are so great as to be termed "astonishing." Malik Ayaz, the governor of Diu for a number of years before his death in 1522, is a subject of interest to most of the Portuguese writers. Barros avers that he was a Russian by birth who was taken into slavery by the Turks and eventually became the ward of a merchant doing business in India. On a journey to Cambay, the merchant presented the young slave to Sultan Mahmud I to add to his corps of archers. The ruler was so pleased with Ayaz's skill that he soon freed him. Little by little he won further recognition and ultimately he was given the honorary title of Malik and the post of governor of Diu.[470] Citing the *Chronicle of the Kings of Gujarat*, Barros reports that Diu was built by the father[471] of Mahmud I on the ruins of an ancient settlement to celebrate a victory which he had won at sea against some Chinese junks which

---

[466] See Albuquerque in Birch (trans.), *op. cit.* (n. 116), IV, 108.

[467] Dames (ed.), *op. cit.* (n. 5), I, 125–26.

[468] Birch (trans.), *op. cit.* (n. 116), IV, 106–7.

[469] Barbosa in Dames (ed.), *op. cit.* (n. 5), I, 129. On opium see Orta's discourse in Markham (ed.), *op. cit.* (n. 4), pp. 330–34.

[470] Cidade and Múrias (eds.), *op. cit.* (n. 6), II, 93–95. For further details see Commissariat, *op. cit.* (n. 400), I, 213–15.

[471] Cidade and Múrias (eds.), *op. cit.* (n. 6), II, 94. Probably this was the brother rather than the father, the one who became Ahmad Shah (reigned 1451–58).

were operating to the north of their factory at Cochin. When Malik Ayaz first took over, Diu was no great trading center. It only became so under his regime as he built up there a small personal empire and heavily fortified the port which held out against the Portuguese until long after his death.

In the Gulf of Cambay between Diu and the city of Cambay, there are a number of active ports "where dealings take place in many kinds of goods," [472] and where the sultan has custom houses and officials. But because of the dangerous tides in the gulf, navigation with keeled ships is very hazardous, and strangers dare not try to navigate these treacherous waters without native pilots to guide them. It is for this reason, Castanheda guesses, [473] that the small ships of Gujarat are constructed without keels. Ships approach the city of Cambay by way of "Guindarim" (Ghandar) close to the entrance of the Mahi River which flows by the metropolis.

As of 1512 the "great and fair city" [474] of Cambay is under the jurisdiction of "Sey Debiaa," a noble Moor of great repute. [475] This walled city is a great center of international trade; according to Varthema, "about three hundred ships of different countries come and go here." [476] But it is mainly the industries and crafts of Cambay which attract the eye of Barbosa. Skilled mechanics and craftsmen produce "cunning work of many kinds, as in Flanders." [477] They weave fabrics of all kinds: cotton, silk, velvets, satins, and carpets. Their artisans turn out ivory beads, bedsteads, dice, and chessmen, as well as inlaid productions of great variety. Lapidaries, goldsmiths, and counterfeiters of gems cut stones and produce finely wrought jewelry. Particularly striking is the great amount of work they do with corals and carnelians. In sum, "the best workmen in every kind of work are found" [478] in this city.

The people of Cambay are both Moors and Hindus, the tone of the city's life being set by the men of substance who have derived their wealth from trade and industry. The city boasts great buildings of stone and mortar, well laid out streets and parks, and "many fair houses, very lofty with windows and roofed with tiles in our [the Portuguese] manner." [479] The householders cultivate gardens and orchards, not only for the fruits and vegetables they produce but also for pleasure. Men and women alike wash and perfume themselves and wear jasmine flowers or other local blooms in their hair. In traveling about the city they go to visit their friends or attend functions in coaches drawn by oxen or horses, the richer coaches being enclosed like rooms and having windows decorated with silk hangings. In their coaches, as they go about the city, the

---

[472] Barbosa in Dames (ed.), *op. cit.* (n. 5), I, 136.

[473] Azevedo (ed.), *op. cit.* (n. 17), II, 315.

[474] Barbosa in Dames (ed.), *op. cit.* (n. 5), I, 139.

[475] Pires in Cortesão (ed.), *op. cit.* (n. 9), I, 35. I have not been able from other sources to confirm this statement or to identify the governor any further.

[476] Temple (ed.), *op. cit.* (n. 233), p. 46.

[477] Dames (ed.), *op. cit.* (n. 5), I, 141.

[478] *Ibid.*, p. 142.

[479] *Ibid.*, p. 140.

passengers sing and play instruments, for they are great adepts in music. These cosmopolites, who are "almost white," are "a people of great culture, accustomed to good clothing, leading a luxurious life, given to pleasure and vice."[480]

Cambay "lies in a pleasant district, rich in supplies."[481] As if to prove this assertion, Barbosa makes a short detour inland to talk about the town of Limodara on the banks of the Narbada in the vicinity of Ratanpur in the Rajput state. Here he locates the carnelian quarries and comments on the extraction and working of the stones. Dealers from Cambay buy the finished stones and market them to merchants from all over the world, even the Portuguese. Because the carnelians are plentiful, they do not bring high prices.[482] The Moors apparently believe in their power to help preserve chastity and to staunch blood.[483]

On the eastern shore of the Gulf of Cambay the town of Randēr stands on the northern side of the Tāpti estuary. Along with Damão and Surat, Randēr is within the jurisdiction of Dastur Khan, a native Moor.[484] Aside from the regular items of trade found in most of Cambay's ports, Barbosa advises "whosoever would have at his disposal things from Malacca and China, let him go to this place, where he will find them in greater perfection than in any other place soever."[485] In their houses the wealthy Moors keep on display their collections of "fair and rich porcelains of new styles."[486] The women of Randēr, unlike Moorish ladies elsewhere, go about the city freely with their faces unveiled. This departure from custom may possibly be accounted for by the fact that the Moors of Randēr, called *navāyāta* (newcomers), were Shiites from Arabia who had originally migrated to India to escape the persecutions of the numerically superior Sunnites.[487] Until the Portuguese sack of Randēr in 1530, Randēr clearly seems to have been the principal commercial center south of Broach. Surat, which was also a rich entrepôt with a customs house of its own in the early sixteenth century, outstripped Randēr in importance after 1530 as both towns strove to recover from the Portuguese onslaught.

The southernmost outposts of Gujarat bordering on the Deccan are the complex of island and mainland ports in the vicinity of modern Bombay. Barbosa, who visited the islands of Bassein and Mahim as well as the town of Tana at the head of the creek which encircles the island of Salsette, speaks of them as being active ports and fine Moorish towns.[488] He also remarks upon

[480] *Ibid.*, p. 141.   [481] *Ibid.*   [482] *Ibid.*, p. 145.

[483] Orta in Temple (ed.), *op. cit.* (n. 233), p. 360. For a more detailed discussion of Cambay's trade in semi-precious stones see A. Summers, "An Account of the Agate and Carnelian Trade of Cambay," *Journal of the Bombay Branch of the Royal Asiatic Society*, Vol. III (1851), Pt. II, pp. 318–27.

[484] Pires in Cortesão (ed.), *op. cit.* (n. 9), p. 35; also see Albuquerque, in Birch (trans.), *op. cit.* (n. 116), IV, 94–96 for a discussion of Dastur's reception at Surat of the Portuguese embassy of 1514. Malik Gopi, a Hindu noble and friend of the Portuguese, was a person of particular consequence in Surat during the reign of Sultan Muzaffar II.

[485] Dames (ed.), *op. cit.* (n. 5), I, 146–47.

[486] *Ibid.*, p. 148.

[487] Commissariat, *op. cit.* (n. 399), I, 264.

[488] Dames (ed.), *op. cit.* (n. 5), I, 151–53.

these islands and inland waterways as lairs for the pirates who prey upon oceanic and inland waterway shipping. Orta, who toured some of these islands in 1535, clearly indicates that Bassein is the leading town of the region.[489] He also describes the extensive Buddhist caves at Kanhiri a few miles from Tana on the island of Salsette with their great underground houses and temples.[490] From his visit to the island of "Pori" (Gharapuri or Elephanta) the Portuguese herbalist describes the great cave-temple, concluding that it is a sight worth seeing, and reporting that "some say that it is the work of the Chinese when they navigated to this land."[491] The island later came to be called Elephanta by the Portuguese because a huge elephant cut from rock stood on a knoll near the port when they took over. The sculptured elephant gradually crumbled over the years, and in 1864 its rocky remains were removed to the Victoria Gardens in Bombay.

Orta, who is writing around 1560, has a good deal to say about the native populations of these islands.[492] Only a few Moors, essentially those who had intermarried with the Hindus, remained in the Bassein area after the Portuguese takeover in 1535–36. The natives are described as Hindus of the non-Brahmanical castes. Those who till and sow the ricelands are called "curumbis" (*Kutumbi* or cultivators). Those named Mālīs (a gardener caste) tend the gardens, raising flowers and fruits. Clerks and accountants known as "Parus" (Parsis) are great businessmen and they collect taxes and rents both for the government and private estate-owners. There are also those whose duty it is to bear arms and, as elsewhere in Cambay, many who engage in trade. Pariahs, who are universally abhorred, exist in every locality and are employed as executioners. The Parsis, whom many Portuguese apparently thought of as Jews, are correctly described by Orta as being originally from Persia, as having "special letters of their own," and as exposing their dead. Notable by their absence from this list are the Brahmans.

While the towns of Gujarat, especially the seaports, are described in some detail, the Portuguese have very little to say about the rural inland areas or about agriculture. Pires asserts that "the kingdom of Cambay does not extend far inland";[493] however, on its luxuriant flat coastal land enough wheat, barley, millet, rice, vegetables, and fruits are produced to feed its large population, to export, and to support in addition a substantial livestock industry. Gujarat, unlike many of the Indian states, breeds and raises small horses of its

[489] Markham (ed.), *op. cit.* (n. 4), pp. 443–45.

[490] For a more recent description see J. Ferguson and J. Burgess, *The Cave Temples of India* (London, 1880), pp. 348–66. For a translation of Do Couto's account see W. K. Fletcher (trans.), "Of the Famous Island of Salsette at Bassein, and Its Wonderful Pagoda Called Canari . . . ," *Journal of the Bombay Branch of the Royal Asiatic Society*, I (1841–44), 34–40.

[491] Markham (ed.), *op. cit.* (n. 4), p. 444. This rumor, which indicates the great respect which the Portuguese had for Chinese craftsmanship, was ill-founded. For a summary of contemporary scholarship on these Hindu caves see Commissariat, *op. cit.* (n. 400), I, 548–49. Also see Ferguson and Burgess, *op. cit.* (n. 490), pp. 465–75, and Fletcher (trans.), *loc. cit.* (n. 490), pp. 40–45, for a translation of Do Couto's description.

[492] Markham (ed.), *op. cit.* (n. 4), pp. 445–46.

[493] Cortesão (ed.), *op. cit.* (n. 9), I, 35.

own, some great lords having several hundred such horses regularly in their stables.[494] Among the other natural products of the country, the Portuguese list cotton, indigo, lac, wormwood, and opium poppies.[495] From their agricultural resources the Gujaratis produce at least twenty different types and colors of cotton cloth, soap, dressed hides, leather, honey, and wax.[496] Their lapidaries, as already mentioned, cut, shape and make jewelry from the local carnelians just as their potters shape crude pottery of various kinds from their native clay.[497]

But trade, rather than agriculture or industry, is deemed to be the life blood of Gujarat. Albuquerque remarks that the Gujaratis understand the navigation of the seas east of India "much more thoroughly than any other nation on account of the great commerce they carry on in those parts."[498] The Banyā, who dominate the foreign trade of Gujarat, are as prominent in all the seaports of the region from Aden to Malacca as are the Genoese in Europe's marts.[499] When Albuquerque stormed Malacca, he found the Gujaratis resident there to be among those who held out most staunchly against him. In the ports of Gujarat itself merchants congregate from all over the East. The products of Italy and Greece reach Cambay by way of Cairo and Aden. Merchants from Ormuz bring horses to Cambay and return with the same variety of items carried westward by Gujarati merchants on their regular trading missions to Malacca. Pires sums up the relationship of Gujarat to the eastern trade before the Portuguese interrupted it. He asserts that if they are to remain rich and prosperous "Malacca cannot live without Cambay, nor Cambay without Malacca."[500] Thus, it was the Gujaratis who suffered most severely by Albuquerque's conquest of Malacca,[501] for they were the main intermediaries in the trade of south Asia with the countries of the west.

F. FROM CAPE COMORIN TO BENGAL

Portuguese ships and factories straddled the traditional commercial routes of western India from Diu south to Colombo. But with the east coast of India the Portuguese had little direct contact and accumulated information mainly through hearsay in the years when they were hastily constructing their empire. Still the Portuguese established a few footholds on the east coast to the north of

---

[494] See Castanheda in Azevedo (ed.), *op. cit.* (n. 17), II, 314; Pires in Cortesão (ed.), *op. cit.* (n. 9), I, 33, 40.

[495] Orta (Markham [ed.], *op. cit.* [n. 4], p. 333) says that most of the opium sold in Cambay originates in Malwa.

[496] Pires in Cortesão (ed.), *op. cit.* (n. 9), I, 43–44.

[497] *Ibid.*, p. 44.

[498] Birch (trans.), *op. cit.* (n. 116), III, 58.

[499] See Pires in Cortesão (ed.), *op. cit.* (n. 9), I, 42, 45.

[500] *Ibid.*, p. 45.

[501] *Ibid.*

Madras in the first years after arriving in India. Alarmed by the inroads they had made, the ruler of Orissa forced them in 1514 to limit their activities to Pippli, a small town at the mouth of the Subarnarekha River. But such early settlements seem not to have endured and prospered.[502] Even Albuquerque apparently possessed very little knowledge of the maritime region of Coromandel or the rich double delta of the Godavari and Krishna rivers though he was aware that the people of these areas traded with Malacca, Bengal, Burma, and Sumatra.[503] Once Goa was in his hands, the great conqueror, ignoring eastern India, proceeded to attack Malacca itself by following the well traveled trade route from Ceylon directly eastward. Even after definite trade connections were established with Bengal, beginning in 1517, the main Portuguese trading fleets continued to bypass the eastern coast as they sailed directly from Ceylon to the delta of the Ganges. Still, from Malacca and Colombo the Portuguese were able to extend their authority over trade in the Bay of Bengal and to plant settlements at a few points on the Coromandel coast and in Bengal.[504]

Ptolemy takes notice of the ports of eastern India,[505] but most of the other writers of antiquity and the Middle Ages are not so well informed. Marco Polo, who uses the Arabic word "'Ma'bar''" for the Coromandel coast, discourses at some length on examples of the trade, traditions, enterprises, personalities, and ports of the Tamil country.[506] The friars who visited and worked in south India during the late thirteenth and early fourteenth centuries visited the shrine of St. Thomas at Mylapore and commented on Hindu and other native customs and practices. The Italian trader, Nicolò de' Conti, who visited Vijayanagar around 1420, remarked on several of the eastern seaports of that Hindu empire. But beyond these incidental references, there was very little more until the sixteenth century when connected narratives appeared which more clearly identified the coastal towns, their relationship to one another and to more distant places, and presented a few observations on the type of life prevailing there. The only European writers among those here under consideration to travel on the east coast were Varthema, Pires, and Barbosa, and none of them seems actually to have visited Bengal. The other commentators appear to derive their information from these early travelers and numerous unspecified sources.

Barros divides the coast facing the Bay of Bengal into three major areas. Beginning just north of Cape Comorin he indicates that the coastal region for 200 leagues (800 miles) is within the jurisdiction of Vijayanagar. The next large division of 110 leagues (440 miles) belongs to Orissa, and it is followed as he proceeds northward, by a segment of 100 leagues (400 miles) belonging to

[502] N. K. Sahu (ed.), *A History of Orissa* (Calcutta, 1956), I, 178–79.

[503] See, *inter alia*, the reference in Academia Real das Sciencias, *Cartas de Affonso de Albuquerque* (7 vols.; Lisbon, 1884–1935), II, 392.

[504] See general discussion in W. H. Moreland (ed.), *Relations of Golconda in the Seventeenth Century* ("Hakluyt Society Publications," Series II, Vol. LXVI [London, 1931]), pp. xx–xxi.

[505] See S. M. Sastri (ed.), *op. cit.* (n. 3), pp. 62–72.

[506] For evaluation of Polo's account see K. A. Nilakanta Sastri, "Marco Polo on India," in *Oriente Poliano* (Rome, 1957), pp. 114–17.

Bengal.[507] Like the other European writers, Barros notices that the ports at the tip of the peninsula and those on the east coast just north of the Cape lie outside the direct authority of Vijayanagar and that the local rulers maintain some sort of vassal relationship to Quilon.[508]

Comorin itself, which the Ptolemaic writers refer to as "Komar,"[509] is shown by most of the sixteenth-century authors to have intimate geographical, cultural, and commercial relationships with Malabar, Coromandel, the Maldives, and Ceylon. Barros lists many of the ports lying within each of his larger divisions of the east coast, but does not comment in detail on any of them except Mylapore.[510] Pires describes Comorin as a separate "kingdom" bounded on the west by Travancore and on the east by "Quaile" (Palayakayal or Old Kayal in the delta of the Tamraparni River).[511] Upon the death of the ruler of Quilon the prince of Comorin is said to succeed to the rājā's place. Aside from Travancore, the land of Comorin is held to be inferior to its other neighbors and almost without palm trees. The sterility of the land at the cape, Pires attributes to the fact that it lacks the wet winds which keep Malabar fresh and luxuriant.[512]

The port of Palayakayal is important for its intermediary position on the trade route linking Bengal, Cambay, and Malacca. Though technically within the territory of Quilon, at least until 1532 when Vijayanagar took it over, this town appears to have enjoyed a measure of independence. In Marco Polo's time, "Cael" (Kayal) was considered to be the most important city and seaport on the eastern coast of India.[513] Its relative commercial importance was probably not so great in Barbosa's day, for shortly thereafter its harbor silted up and its merchants and fishers moved to Tuticorin, now the principal seaport of Tinnevelly.[514] Still, when the Portuguese first arrived at Palayakayal, it is singled out as a great center of pearl fishing. The rājā of Quilon possesses the monopoly of these fishing rights which he farms out to a Moor. The Muslim fishers, who probably came originally from the pearl fisheries of the Gulf of Ormuz, had taken over at a somewhat earlier date from the native fisher caste of Paravans. In Barbosa's time, the Muslim fishers are said to work all week for themselves except for Fridays when they hand over their catch as rent to the owner of the fishing boat. In the last week of the fishing season their catch is paid to the chief pearl farmer in compensation for their fishing rights. Though the ruler of Quilon and his armed retainers are always close by the city, the real arbiters of justice in local affairs seem to be the wealthy Moors who run the fishery.[515]

[507] Cidade and Múrias (eds.), *op. cit.* (n. 6), I, 359–60.
[508] *Ibid.*, p. 358. See also Castanheda in Azevedo (ed.), *op. cit.* (n. 17), II, 404.
[509] S. M. Sastri (ed.), *op. cit.* (n. 3), p. 55. "Komar" is short for Kanyā Kumārī, the full name.
[510] Cidade and Múrias (eds.), *op. cit.* (n. 6), I, 360–61.
[511] Cortesão (ed.), *op. cit.* (n. 9), I, 81. Pires is not entirely consistent in his account of political control. At another place in his narrative (*ibid.*, p. 66) he talks about Cape Comorin as being "in the King of Quilon's land."
[512] *Ibid.*, p. 66.
[513] Yule and Cordier (eds.), *op. cit.* (n. 4), II, 370–75. For confirmation of this assertion see R. Caldwell, "Explorations at Korkei and Kayal," *Indian Antiquary*, VI (1877), 82.
[514] Dames (ed.), *op. cit.* (n. 5), II, 122–23, n. 1.   [515] *Ibid.*, p. 124.

Northward along the Fishery Coast, close to the narrows and Adam's Bridge in the Gulf of Manaar, is the small seaport of Kilakarai.[516] This town and the surrounding country are, according to Barbosa, still within the territories of the rājā of Quilon.[517] Moorish traders come here in sampans, bringing horses from Cambay and taking out cargoes of rice and cloth for sale in Malabar. Barbosa also reports that "in this province" there is a great temple with revenue-producing estates which is large enough to have its own ruler. Every twelve years a great jubilee is held to honor the god of the temple. On these festival occasions the ruler ritually kills himself on a platform in the presence of a great throng and his intended successor. The resemblance of this festival to the *Mahāmakka* celebration of Calicut is remarkable and deserves consideration from those who categorically deny, on the basis of tradition alone that self-immolation by the Zamorin after a twelve years' reign was customary.[518]

The Coromandel coast (*Choḷamaṇḍala* or country of the Cholas) is given different limits and a variety of place-names by the Portuguese chronicles, rutters, and maps. In general, however, they place it, along with Barros and any modern Admiralty Pilot, between Point Calimere in the south and the deltas of the Godavari and Krishna rivers in the north. All of this coastal stretch, peopled mainly by Hindus, is within the jurisdiction of Vijayanagar and separated from Orissa on the interior by a range of mountains called the "Odirguale-mado" (Udayagiri, south of the Krishna).[519] Barbosa, who is the only one of the European writers to attempt a general description of Coromandel, indicates that this coastal "land of open plains" produces an abundance of rice, meat, and wheat.[520] Ships from Malabar bring in the products of the west and carry out cargoes of rice and dispose of it in rice-deficit areas. Drought and famine sometimes sweep this normally fruitful land, and in those catastrophic years the ships from Malabar bring in rice and coconuts and take away shiploads of children whom their parents out of want sell into slavery. After the Portuguese made merchandising dangerous for Muslims on the west coast of India, Barbosa reports that the Arab traders concentrated their activities on developing commerce between the Far East and the marts of Coromandel.[521]

Both Pires and Barros give extended but dissimilar lists of the individual seaports of Coromandel.[522] The trader, Pires, lists five coastal towns northward as far as Pulicat, where he seems to think Coromandel ends. Barros, the research student, lists sixteen ports as coming under the jurisdiction of Vijayanagar but has almost nothing to say about them. Negapatam, the southernmost port of

---

[516] Identification in *ibid.*, p. 120, n. 2; for a slightly different identification see Cortesão (ed.), *op. cit.* (n. 9), II, 271, n. 1.

[517] Dames (ed.), *op. cit.* (n. 5), II, 120.

[518] See above, p. 356 and Raja, *op. cit.* (n. 67), pp. 28–31.

[519] See above, p. 372; also Dames (ed.), *op. cit.* (n. 5), II, 130 n.

[520] Dames (ed.), *op. cit.* (n. 5), II, 125.

[521] *Ibid.*

[522] See Cortesão (ed.), *op. cit.* (n. 9), II, 271, and Cidade and Múrias (eds.), *op. cit.* (n. 6), I, 360–61.

Vijayanagar, was visited in 1505 by Varthema. The Italian describes it as being located in rice-producing country and "on the route to very large countries." [523] Pires mentions a famous temple of Vijayanagar in connection with Negapatam. The probability is, since no temple exists within the city antedating 1777, that he is referring to the famous and rich temple in nearby Tiruvalur.[524]

Mylapore, today practically a southern suburb of Madras, is noticed by the Europeans primarily because of the tradition that St. Thomas died there. Isidore of Seville in 636 reported that the Apostle had been killed and buried in India.[525] In Europe this report was echoed by later travelers and commentators, and in India pilgrims visited the tomb at Mylapore long before the Portuguese arrived there.[526] Varthema in 1505 heard from some Indian Christians of Coromandel that the bones of St. Thomas were nearby and were being watched over by native Christians. Meanwhile, the Portuguese in Malabar were occupying themselves with the St. Thomas Christians whom they found there, and with the restoration of the church at Mylapore. But when Barbosa arrived at this spot around 1515 the ancient city "which erstwhile was very great and fair" is described as being "almost deserted." The body of St. Thomas lies buried "in a little ruined church near the sea" in which a "poor Moor" keeps lonely vigil over the tomb.[527] In 1516, a Franciscan mission and church were built at Mylapore[528] and in the next year a group of Portuguese and Indian Christians made a pilgrimage to the tomb. By 1521 the tomb had been opened by a Portuguese expedition[529] and eventually the bones found therein became sacred relics and Mylapore was elevated by the Portuguese to a holy place.[530] So by the time when Barros wrote, he is able to comment on the restoration of the city with magnificent houses and to note that since about 1545 it has been called St. Thomas.[531] Through Nuno da Cunha, Barros also received some native writings which gave him information on the customs of the people in these parts.[532]

The most active and richest port of the Coromandel coast is Pulicat.[533] Varthema arrived in this Vijayanagar city from Ceylon early in 1505, and he observes that it is an entrepôt in the trade with Ceylon and Burma.[534] Merchants from the inland marts of the great Hindu kingdom exchange goods,

[523] Temple (ed.), *op. cit.* (n. 233), p. 72. Probably meaning the provinces of Vijayanagar. For substantiation see Castanheda in Azevedo (ed.), *op. cit.* (n. 17), IV, 277.

[524] Cortesão (ed.), *op. cit.* (n. 9), I, 91–92.

[525] L. W. Brown, *The Indian Christians of St. Thomas* (Cambridge, 1956), p. 55.

[526] *Ibid.*, p. 56.

[527] Dames (ed.), *op. cit.* (n. 5), II, 126–29.

[528] See above, p. 235.

[529] Corrêa, *op. cit.* (n. 2), II, 724–25.

[530] Brown, *op. cit.* (n. 525), p. 58.

[531] Cidade and Múrias (eds.), *op cit.* (n.6), I, 360–61.

[532] *Ibid.*, p. 361. These were "um livro da escritura dos chis [possibly Shiites] e outro dos parseos. ..." Eventually they were forwarded to Paulus Jovius in Rome on the request of papal representatives in Lisbon.

[533] Cf. remarks of Castanheda in Azevedo (ed.), *op. cit.* (n. 17), I, 458.

[534] Temple (ed.), *op. cit.* (n. 233), p. 74.

especially precious stones, with the maritime traders. The rājā has a governor at Pulicat charged with collecting the duties of the trade.[535] The colored cotton goods produced as a specialty at Pulicat are exported to pay for the rubies of Burma and the elephants of Ceylon. The customs, dress, and laws of Pulicat, Varthema asserts, "are the same as at Calicut."[536] Bellicose, even though they possess no artillery, the people of Pulicat are said to be waging war in 1505 against "Tarnassari."[537] Though the Portuguese landed at Pulicat in 1521 on their way to Mylapore, their appearances at Vijayanagar's great eastern port seem to have occurred only at relatively infrequent intervals during the first generation of the sixteenth century.[538] Of the coastal strip from Pulicat to the Krishna, often known as the Northern Sircars, the Europeans say little beyond supplying the names of seven ports.[539] Indeed, it appears that most of what they have to report about the entire east coast to the north of Pulicat is derived from the accounts of others.

Orissa, the Hindu kingdom which was being pinched between Vijayanagar and Bengal, receives a bit of attention from Pires and Barbosa. Barros reports that the seaboard of Orissa is rough and concludes therefrom that this is the reason why the kingdom has so few ports. Then he goes on to give a list of ten of them, ending up with "*Cabo Segogara* to which we give the name 'das Palmeiras' [Point Palmyras]."[540] Orissa extends far inland, and has very little maritime trade.[541] The northernmost of its ports is Remuna, the chief town of northern Orissa, where the Europeans apparently traded by way of the Burabalanga River. Orissa is separated from Bengal by a river that Barbosa and later European writers call the "Ganges" or the "Ganga," possibly confusing the Dhamura River with the authentic Ganges to the north.[542]

Ruled over by a "heathen" king, Orissa is constantly at war with one or the other of its neighbors.[543] Even though there are but a few Moors in Orissa, its Gajapati king still has a large and capable army of infantrymen.[544] Pires also indicates that Orissa's ruler pays tribute to Bengal, possibly in return for help in warding off the onslaughts of Vijayanagar.[545] While the Portuguese admit

535 Barbosa in Dames (ed.), *op. cit.* (n. 5), II, 132.

536 Temple (ed.), *op. cit.* (n. 233), p. 74.

537 *Ibid.* The editor (Temple) of Varthema appears to think that a war was being fought with Tenassêrim across the Bay of Bengal. Dames (ed.), *op. cit.* (n. 5), II, 130, considers this improbable and thinks that Varthema was speaking of Orissa.

538 For examples of these irregular contacts see Castanheda in Azevedo (ed.), *op. cit.* (n. 17), IV, 115, 116, 130.

539 Barros in Cidade and Múrias (eds.), *op. cit.* (n. 6), I, 361.   540 *Ibid.*

541 Barbosa in Dames (ed.), *op. cit.* (n. 5), II, 133.

542 *Ibid.*, pp. 133–34. Or for another interpretation of this disputed identification see C. R. Wilson, "Note on the Topography of the River Hugli . . .," *Journal of the Asiatic Society of Bengal*, LXI (1892), 112.

543 Krishna Dēva Rāyya, ruler of Vijayanagar, had as one of his primary ambitions the capture of Orissa's eastern coast. He started his major campaign in 1512 and occupied the fortress of Udayagiri during the following year. These internal wars seem to be what the Portuguese hear most about, probably through Vijayanagar.

544 Barbosa in Dames (ed.), *op. cit.* (n. 5), II, 132–33.

545 Cortesão (ed.), *op. cit.* (n. 9), I, 89.

to having no first-hand knowledge of the people of Orissa "by reason of their dwelling away from the coast,"[546] Pires unqualifiedly asserts that the best diamonds come from there and that "cowries are the current coinage."[547]

Most of what the Portuguese heard about Orissa evidently came to them through Vijayanagar and their outposts in Bengal, Colombo, and Malacca. In Malacca the merchants native to the Telugu coast were usually called "Klings," a Malay form of the territorial name Kalinga. Pires states that Orissa is within "the province of the Klings"[548] and he appears to understand that their languages (Oriya and Telugu) are different from the Kanarese spoken in Vijayanagar.[549] The "Klings," who are particularly prominent in the cloth trade at Malacca, are reported to marry their daughters at an early age to the merchants of other nationalities in the great Malay port. In the total trade of Malacca the "Klings," before the influx of the Portuguese, have a greater share than any other foreign group and live there under a special administration.[550] The generic term "Kling," as used in Malacca, probably included most of the merchants who originated in the ports of eastern India south of Bengal, and so it would seem logical to assume that those from the Telugu country constituted no more than an influential minority.

Individual Portuguese certainly got as far north as Bengal in Albuquerque's time, but no evidence exists of a Portuguese vessel arriving there before the visit of João Coelho in 1516–17.[551] This initial contact was followed by the expedition of 1518 sent from the Maldives under João de Silveira to ask for trading facilities and permission to erect a factory. Silveira landed at Chittāgong on the extreme eastern side of the delta on May 9,[552] but the ruler of Bengal, Mahmūd Shah, refused to receive the Portuguese envoy, and the governor of the city finally turned him away. Though rebuffed, the Portuguese hereafter continued annually to send a trading ship to Chittāgong.[553] It was not, however, until Nuno da Cunha's period as viceroy (1529–38) that the Portuguese renewed

[546] Barbosa in Dames (ed.), *op. cit.* (n. 5), I, 229.

[547] Cortesão (ed.), *op. cit.* (n. 9), I, 89, 94, 224.

[548] *Ibid.*, p. 4; for the relation of Orissa to the ancient term "Kalinga," see R. M. Chakravarti, "Notes on the Geography of Orissa in the Sixteenth Century," *Journal of the Asiatic Society of Bengal*, XII (1916), 34.

[549] Cortesão (ed.), *op. cit.* (n. 9), I, 64–65.

[550] *Ibid.*, p. 281. Also see below, p. 513.

[551] Early Portuguese documents indicate that ships were being sent to Bengal before 1516, but they do not tell of the success or failure of these missions. For a summary of early references see A. Cortesão, "The 'City of Bengala' in Early Reports," *Journal of the Royal Asiatic Society of Bengal* (*Letters*), XI (1945), 13, n. 2. See also J. J. A. Campos, *History of the Portuguese in Bengal* (Calcutta, 1919), p. 26. And for general historical background see J. N. Sarkar (ed.), *The History of Bengal* (Dacca, 1948). Unfortunately, the authors of this otherwise excellent history rely almost entirely upon the general secondary accounts of the Portuguese in Bengal and they do not refer to either Castanheda or Barros.

[552] Castanheda in Azevedo (ed.), *op. cit.* (n. 17), II, 441; also Barros in Cidade and Múrias (eds.), *op. cit.* (n. 6), III, 68. For a summary of the story which Silveira told about Bengal after his return to Cochin see the letter of Dom João de Leyma to the king (December 22, 1518) as summarized in S. N. Sen, "An Early Portuguese Account of Bengal," *The Calcutta Review*, LXVI (1938), 21–25.

[553] Campos, *op. cit.* (n. 551), p. 30.

their efforts to establish a trading settlement in Bengal. Attempts in 1529 and 1533 failed to establish cordial relations with the ruler of Bengal and the Portuguese suffered many losses at his hands. Largely as a result of the war in 1535–36 between Mahmūd Shah and Sher Shah, the Portuguese were able to wring concessions from the obdurate Bengal ruler. As a reward for aid rendered to Mahmūd Shah in the war, the Portuguese were permitted in 1536 and 1537 to build factories at Chittāgong and at Sātgāon in western Bengal. In both places, which they occupied almost simultaneously, the Portuguese possessed land, owned houses, and administered customs.[554] It was not until the port of Sātgāon silted up that the Portuguese in 1580 founded Hugli (or Hoogly), just a little to the southeast of their earlier settlement.

It was mainly as a result of commercial contacts in places as widely separated as Malacca, Goa, and Lisbon, that the European writers on India were able to learn about Bengal. Varthema is the only one of them who even pretends to have set foot on the soil of Bengal.[555] That part of his account which deals mainly with trade and personal relations is less valuable and more confusing than many of his other descriptions. Pires and Barbosa seem to have learned most of what they recount from reports current in Malacca and the ports of India before 1515. Castanheda is the only one of the chroniclers to publish in the sixteenth century a general description of the land and people at the lower reaches of the Ganges.[556] Barros, who clearly collected important detail on the geography and history of the delta region, is not able in his lifetime to summarize this material in print. His collection of information, like his manuscript maps, he left to be completed and published by Lavanha in *Década IV* (1613).[557] Orta confines his remarks to noticing that flax and elephants are native to Bengal.[558] It is therefore Pires, Barbosa, and Castanheda who furnish the most coherent and reliable accounts of Bengal, even though they are all based on the reports of others.

Barros, who usually revels in listing the names of ports, humorously remarks that describing the jagged and island-lined seacoast from Point Palmyras to Chittāgong is a task much more suited to the art of the painter than to that of the writer.[559] The Ganges, which empties into the Bay of Bengal (the Ptolomaic *Gangeticus Sinus*), is the overwhelmingly prominent geographical feature of the region to the Portuguese even as it had been to the Ptolemaic geographers. Though its source is unknown to Castanheda, the Ganges is described as emptying into the sea through two great mouths. In the interior its banks are

---

[554] Castanheda in Azevedo (ed.), *op. cit.* (n. 17), IV, 410–11.

[555] For an interpretation of his remarks based on the visit of 1505 see Temple (ed.), *op. cit.* (n. 233), pp. lxvi–lxix.

[556] Azevedo (ed.), *op. cit.* (n. 17), II, 439–41.

[557] Cidade and Múrias (ed.), *op. cit.* (n. 6), IV, 501–5.

[558] Markham (ed.), *op. cit.* (n. 4), pp. 54, 181.

[559] Cidade and Múrias (eds.), *op. cit.* (n. 6), I, 361. He defers this listing to his *Geografia* which has never been found. In the map of Bengal published in 1613 by Lavanha, presumably on the basis of Barros' notes and drawings, a large number of towns appear. See illustrations.

said to be lined for many leagues with towns.[560] The great Gangetic plain which covers a vast expanse is surrounded by hills. The mountainous state of Orissa borders Bengal on the south and Arakan fronts it on the east or the "Pegu (Burma) side."[561] In the interior towards Delhi it is bounded by the bellicose states of Coos and Tipura. The lords of all these surrounding territories are said to be vassals of the ruler of Bengal.[562] The principal city of the kingdom is "Bengala" (Gaur),[563] and its most important ports, when Castanheda wrote, are recognized to be Chittāgong and Sātgāon.[564]

Gaur is located on the Ganges one hundred leagues (400 miles) from the sea,[565] two days being required to make the journey upriver.[566] A city of forty thousand hearths, it is a long narrow metropolis which stretches out along the river for four leagues (16 miles).[567] Though it is located on level ground, Gaur is surrounded by rivers (the Ganges and the Mahānanda) in which seagoing vessels of four hundred tons lie anchored. That Gaur was accessible to seagoing vessels is clear from all the Portuguese accounts. On the east the city is protected by a great marsh backed up by a dense jungle populated by ferocious beasts; and because the jungle helps to protect the city from invasion, the rulers of Bengal forbid that it be cut down. Upriver more than twenty leagues (80 miles) from Gaur is a fortress town called "Gori" (Garhi) which controls the passes to the mountains separating Bihar from Bengal and was known as "the gate of Bengal."[568]

Within the city there stand many elegant mosques and fine houses. The royal residence includes many sumptuous palaces spread over as much of an area as the entire city of Evora.[569] Constructed of sun-dried bricks,[570] the

---

[560] Azevedo (ed.), *op. cit.* (n. 17), II, 439–46.

[561] Pires in Cortesão (ed.), *op. cit.* (n. 9), I, 89.   [562] *Ibid.*, pp. 89–90.

[563] On the much disputed question of the identity of the "city of Bengala" see Cortesão, *loc. cit.* (n. 551), pp. 10–14. He concludes that the writers of the early sixteenth century are talking about Gaur when they refer to "Bengala." Later, after the Portuguese actually had settlements in Bengal, they usually equate Chittāgong with "Bengala." It may be pointed out that in Bengali sources Gaur and Bengala are considered to be separate towns.

[564] Azevedo (ed.), *op. cit.* (n. 17), II, 441. For a later effort to describe the political geography of Bengal in this period see H. Blochmann, "Contributions to the Geography and History of Bengal," *Journal of the Asiatic Society of Bengal*, Vol. XLII, Pt. I (1873), pp. 209–307.

[565] Castanheda (in Azevedo [ed.], *op. cit.* [n. 17], II, 440) greatly exaggerates the distance, for it was actually only 200 miles upriver.

[566] Pires in Cortesão (ed.), *op. cit.* (n. 9), I, 90.

[567] A change in the course of the Ganges River and the pillaging of war brought Gaur to ruin and desolation in 1575. According to calculations by modern archaeologists, the city with its suburbs covered an area of from 20 to 30 square miles. The city proper, enclosed by a continuous embankment, ran about 7.5 miles in length and 1 to 2 miles in width. See Hunter, *op. cit.* (n. 46) V, 37. Barros (in Cidade and Múrias [eds.], *op. cit.* [n. 6], IV, 505) estimates its population as running as high as 200,000. For a map of Gaur see M. Martin, *The History . . . of Eastern India* (London, 1838), facing p. 72.

[568] This description by Castanheda (in Azevedo [ed.], *op. cit.* [n. 17], IV, 408) is similar to that given by certain Muslim historians (Blochmann, *loc. cit.* [n. 564], p. 213); for its identification with Garhi see Campos, *op. cit.* (n. 551), p. 38.

[569] Castanheda in Azevedo (ed.), *op. cit.* (n. 17), II, 440.

[570] Pires in Cortesão (ed.), *op. cit.* (n. 9), I, 91. For confirmation see Hunter, *op. cit.* (n. 46), V, 37, who writes: "Countless millions of small, thin bricks were used in building Gaur."

splendid houses of the city have only ground floors, are decorated in gold and blue, and enclose beautiful patios and gardens.[571] The poorer people live in palm-leaf huts.[572]

Most descriptions of life in Bengal given by the European writers appear to be based on observations made at Gaur. The population of the city includes Moors, Hindus, and many foreigners. Most Bengalis are "sleek, handsome black men, more sharpwitted than the men of any other known race."[573] The European writers denounce the Bengalis for being overly wary and treacherous, and Pires reports that in Malacca it is an insult to call a man a Bengali.[574] The women of Bengal are beautiful and clean; they live in luxury and are forced to remain indoors. Moors of the upper class have three or four wives or as many as they can maintain. It is obviously an advantage in sixteenth-century Bengal to be a Moor inasmuch as the Hindus "daily become Moors to gain the favor of their rulers."[575]

Life in Gaur is opulent and it centers around the royal residence whose occupant is esteemed to be a "faithful Muslim and much richer in treasure than any other king in India."[576] The betel he chews is mixed with camphor of Borneo which is so expensive that the royal chamberlain makes a tidy sum annually by recovering the camphor from the ruler's golden cuspidor![577] Being extremely fond of music, the ruler imports singers and musicians from as far away as Vijayanagar and Gujarat. To one of his Moorish singers he pays an enormous annual salary.[578] Husain Shāh, who was ruling when Pires wrote, is reported to have many daughters and twenty-four sons by his various wives.[579] He also maintains a large military establishment of both cavalry and infantry, for he is almost constantly engaged in war with his vassals and neighbors, especially Delhi.[580]

The government of Bengal is correctly reported to have been taken over by Muslims about three hundred years before the arrival of the Portuguese in India. Pires also contends that "for seventy-four years" before the date of his writing the succession in Bengal was systematically achieved by murder. This system, which he claims was borrowed from Pasay in Sumatra, he calls "the Pase practice."[581] Regicide was mainly the task of a Pretorian band of Abyssinians and, as a result, the Abyssinian eunuchs closest to the throne were considered

---

[571] Castanheda in Azevedo (ed.), *op. cit.* (n. 17), II, 440.

[572] Pires in Cortesão (ed.), *op. cit.* (n. 9), I, 91.   [573] *Ibid.*, p. 88.

[574] *Ibid.*, p. 93; also Castanheda in Azevedo (ed.), *op. cit.* (n. 17), II, 440. Campos (*op. cit.* [n. 551], pp. 20–21) apologetically contends that the Portuguese were giving this bad character to the rulers rather than the people of Bengal. Such a contention holds no water, because Pires clearly means for his defamatory remarks to apply to Bengali fishermen and tailors working in Malacca.

[575] Barbosa in Dames (ed.), *op. cit.* (n. 5), II, 148; also Castanheda in Azevedo (ed.), *op. cit.* (n. 17), II, 441.

[576] Castanheda in Azevedo (ed.), *op. cit.* (n. 17), II, 441.

[577] *Ibid.*   [578] *Ibid.*

[579] Cortesão (ed.), *op. cit.* (n. 9), I, 95.

[580] *Ibid.*, pp. 89–90.

[581] *Ibid.*, pp. 88–89. For a description of the practice at Pasay see Barros in Cidade and Múrias (eds.), *op. cit.* (n. 6), III, 234–35. Also see below, p. 578.

by Pires as being the real governors of the land. Though Pires' dates for the Abyssinian ascendancy may be suspect, his description of the role which they played in the late fifteenth century corresponds extremely well with what is known from other sources.[582] According to the Muslim histories, it was Bārbak Shāh (reigned 1460–74) who first maintained a large number of Abyssinian slaves as protectors of the throne. Between this ruler's death and the accession of Husain Shāh in 1493, the very names of the rulers during the interregnum proclaim that they were Abyssinian eunuchs.[583] In Bengal, Pires avers, "they are more in the habit of having eunuchs . . . than in any other part of the world."[584] Aside from the Abyssinian eunuchs at the court, it is common for eunuchs to act as harem guards and domestic servants in the houses of the wealthy.[585] Others receive administrative appointments as city governors and they are "called 'lascars' in the language of the land."[586] Traffic in young boys, taken particularly from the non-Muslims of the back country, apparently prevails in the early sixteenth century as it did in the time of Marco Polo. While many of the enslaved youths die from castration, those who survive are held in high regard and often become rich and influential in their own right.[587]

In addition to Abyssinians, Bengal plays host to other foreigners, especially merchants from Arabia, Egypt, Turkey and other parts of India. In Husain Shāh's time, however, many were said to be going elsewhere because he is antagonistic to them.[588] Still, some foreign merchants, mostly Muslims, decide to remain in Bengal because "this land is large, fruitful, and healthy."[589] Wheat, rice, and sugar are produced in great quantities. Cattle, both large and small varieties, are innumerable; sheep, horses,[590] fish, and poultry are all in excellent supply; and wild game and birds exist in profusion. The land also yields citrus and a multitude of other fruits, long pepper, ginger, cotton, and flax. But what is evidently most attractive to the foreign merchants and astounding to the Portuguese is the cheapness of food.[591]

Native industries based on the produce of the field are also numerous. From cotton and flax the Bengali men make thread on a spinning wheel. This is woven by the same men into white and colored materials for the domestic

---

582 Majumdar *et al.*, *op. cit.* (n. 6), pp. 345–46.

583 Blochmann, *loc. cit.* (n. 564), p. 286.

584 Cortesão (ed.), *op. cit.* (n. 9), I, 88.

585 Barbosa in Dames (ed.), *op. cit.* (n. 5), II, 147.

586 Castanheda in Azevedo (ed.), *op. cit.* (n. 17), II, 441. Ordinarily, as used in Luso-Indian works, "lascar" means "soldier" or "sailor" and is of Persian derivation. With reference to Bengal it roughly means "the governor of a city." See Dalgado, *op. cit.* (n. 44), I, 514–15.

587 Barbosa in Dames (ed.), *op. cit.* (n. 5), II, 147.

588 Pires in Cortesão (ed.), *op. cit.* (n. 9), I, 95.

589 *Ibid.*, pp. 140–41.

590 Castanheda (in Azevedo [ed.], *op. cit.* [n. 17], II, 440) compares the horses of Bengal in size to "the little horses of England."

591 Castanheda (*ibid.*) gives prices for cattle, poultry and rice with the obvious intention of impressing his reader with how inexpensive they are. Also see Pires in Cortesão (ed.), *op. cit.* (n. 9), I, 88.

and export markets. These cloths are especially fine for making ladies' head-dresses and turbans. Others are turned into rich canopies for beds, fancy pieces of cutwork, and tapestry-like hangings. Numerous fruits and vegetables for both domestic and foreign consumption are preserved in ginger, and sugar, and sometimes in vinegar. Sugar, since they do not know how to press it into loaves, is wrapped for export as a powder in sewn, leather parcels.[592]

The foreign trade of Bengal in the early years of the sixteenth century seems to have been concentrated at Gaur and Sātgāon. Chittāgong does not attract the notice of either Barbosa or Pires, perhaps because it was the seaport serving Gaur.[593] Sātgāon, a good port with a satisfactory entry, is a city of ten thousand hearths where many merchants concentrate.[594] Writing later on in the century, Castanheda describes Chittāgong as a kind of Venice in Bengal with its numerous waterways and bridges. A city of great commercial activity, Chittāgong is governed by a "lascar" who is a vassal of the ruler in Gaur.[595] Bengali trading vessels, both ships like those of Mecca and junks like those of China, sail annually to Malacca and Pasay.[596] In the Malay port they market Bengali cotton and muslin materials at a great profit; in Sumatra the Bengalis buy mainly pepper and silk.[597]

Ships sailing from Malacca to Bengal (presumably Sātgāon) usually depart around the first of August and arrive there at the end of the month. The merchants then stay in Bengal until the first of the following February to catch the monsoon back. In the interim they sell Borneo camphor and pepper in large quantities as well as other spices, porcelains, silks and damasks, and the swords and krises of Java. Foreign merchants trading in Bengal have to pay duties of "three on every eight."[598] Gold in Bengal is worth one-sixth more than it is in Malacca; silver is from 20 to 25 per cent cheaper. The local currency is primarily in silver, but for smaller units cowrie shells are commonly in use. In Bengal the cowries are larger than those circulating elsewhere, and are further distinguished by a yellow stripe down the middle. These special cowries originate in the Maldive Islands and are accepted as coinage in all of Bengal and Orissa, but not elsewhere. Goods are weighed in the ports of Bengal on a balance stick called a *dala* and duties are apparently assessed in terms of the weight so determined. Pires clearly feels these duties are excessive, an opinion which he probably derived from his contacts in the merchant community of Malacca.[599]

Little is reported by European writers about the Hindu population of Bengal beyond remarks to the effect that their children are sometimes sold to be

---

[592] Barbosa in Dames (ed.), *op. cit.* (n. 5), II, 146.
[593] Pires in Cortesão (ed.), *op. cit.* (n. 9), II, 13.
[594] *Ibid.*, I, 91.
[595] Castanheda in Azevedo (ed.), *op. cit.* (n. 17), II, 441.
[596] Pires in Cortesão (ed.), *op. cit.* (n. 9), I, 92.
[597] *Ibid.*, pp. 92–93.
[598] *Ibid.*, p. 93.
[599] *Ibid.*, pp. 94–95.

eunuchs, that many of them become converts to the Muslim faith, and that they constitute the majority of the population outside of the port cities. Castanheda, in talking about the Ganges, reports that for some unknown reason the "gentiles" of Bengal believe that its waters are holy and its source is in heaven. He reports that they make pilgrimages from near and far to bathe in its waters and so become cleansed of their sins. The king of Vijayanagar is said to have a cask of holy water from the Ganges brought to him each week so that he may bathe in it regularly. Orta, who claims to have proved the efficacy of its waters, records that the Bengalis go to the Ganges so that they may die with their feet in the holy river.[600]

G. HINDUSTAN AND THE AFGHAN–MUGHUL STRUGGLE FOR SUPREMACY

None of the European writers seems to have penetrated personally very far into the interior of northern India, aside from a few excursions inland from one seacoast town or the other. Gaur was probably as far into Bengal as the Portuguese merchants were ever able to penetrate in any numbers. On the west coast Portuguese adventurers from Diu went as far inland as Chitor, the leading city of Mewar, when they fought with the armies of Gujarat. It does not follow, however, that the Portuguese were uninformed about the Indo-Gangetic plain. From native informants, as well as the reports relayed to them by their own countrymen, the Portuguese writers from Pires to Barros are conscious that Delhi is the imperial city of northern India and that its ruler is an "emperor" who irregularly exacts obedience from a number of vassal "kings." Barros, as mentioned earlier, refers to the region between the Indus and western Bengal as Hindustan. South of the Himalayas, Barros includes within Hindustan the states of "Maltan" (Multan), Delhi, western Bengal, Orissa, "Māndū" (Malwa), "Chitor" (Mewar), and Gujarat, a political definition which corresponds closely to the conclusions of modern scholars working from Muslim sources.[601] But neither Barros nor the other Portuguese writers are able to comment on this entire list. Their observations on interior places are restricted to Delhi, Mewar, Malwa, and Bengal west of Gaur.

Pires and Barbosa report about the Delhi sultanate in the time of Sikander Lodi, the last ruler of the Lodi (Afghan) sultanate who died at his capital of Agra in 1517.[602] The rulers of Delhi were originally Hindus, according to the two Portuguese reporters, and about a century and a half before Vasco da Gama

600 Markham (ed.), *op. cit.* (n. 4), pp. 401–2.

601 See K. M. Ashraf, "Life and Conditions of the People of Hindustan (1200–1550 A.D.)—Mainly Based on Islamic Sources," *Journal of the Asiatic Society of Bengal (Letters)*, I (1935), 105–6. The most notable omissions in Barros' list are the Punjab and Oudh. Also see above, p. 341 and Orta in Markham (ed.), *op. cit.* (n. 4), p. 293.

602 The Lodis were Sultans of Delhi from 1451 to 1517.

arrived in Calicut the Muslims took over in Delhi.[603] At its apogee the Muslim sultanate of Delhi was clearly the greatest state of India with dominion over Sind, the Rajputs, Cambay, Malwa, and part of the Deccan. With the decline of central authority the captains of these provinces set themselves up as independent princes. In Delhi itself, which is described as a large and mountainous country far in the interior, there lived at the time of the Portuguese arrival many Hindus and Muslims. The sultans of Delhi, however, made life extremely difficult for the non-Muslims in their jurisdiction.[604] Many of the northern Hindus, especially the Yogis, emigrated to a more favorable political climate.

Barbosa reports that the Yogis, being "unwilling to stay under the power of the Moors,"[605] left Delhi and became wanderers to atone for their failure to take up arms against the invading Muslims. These pilgrims, who migrate from place to place in small bands, have no desire for property after having lost all their worldly possessions. Naked except for brass girdles, they smear their bodies and faces with ashes and carry heavy iron chains around their necks. The Yogis abide by no dietary laws, hold no pollution beliefs, and perform no purification ceremonies. Still they are held in great respect by the Hindus and even by some Moors. As they go about begging for alms, they bless their devotees by streaking them with ashes, and to the kings and lords who protect them they give antidotes against poison.[606] Orta, who evidently knew Barbosa's account, remarks a generation later that the Portuguese "are very little conversant with things in the kingdom of Delhi" and that what they know about it has come to them through the Yogis.[607]

Essentially this assertion is correct, for the Portuguese limit themselves to very general statements about life in Delhi. It is described as a cold and heavily populated country rich in horses, elephants, and food. The horses, which are born and bred there, are used mainly in war. The warriors of Delhi, Moors and Hindus alike, are good archers and well equipped with a variety of spears, swords, battle-axes, and maces.[608] Most of them carry steel quoits with razor-like outer edges called *chacora* (in Sanskrit, *cakra*) which they hurl at their enemies with skill and great effect.[609] The products of Delhi, like those of other inland states, are distributed to the outside world through Cambay.[610]

Aside from Delhi, the only other inland states of the north referred to by the

---

[603] See Pires in Cortesão (ed.), *op. cit.* (n. 9), I, 36. Possibly this is a reference to the establishment of the Khalji sultans in Delhi around 1290.

[604] Barbosa in Dames (ed.), *op. cit.* (n. 5), I, 230.

[605] *Ibid.*

[606] *Ibid.*, pp. 233–36.

[607] Markham (ed.), *op. cit.* (n. 4), p. 483. Some writers (for example, Ficalho [ed.], *op. cit.* [n. 369], II, 186) contend that Barbosa sees the Yogis as leading a Hindu reaction against the Muslim usurpation of power. In my reading of Barbosa I have not been able to discover this assertion.

[608] For confirmation and greater detail see William Irvine, *Army of the Indian Moghuls: Its Organization and Administration* (London, 1903), pp. 73–112.

[609] Barbosa in Dames (ed.), *op. cit.* (n. 5), I, 232–33. Also see the account of Varthema for a description of Yogis throwing quoits of this sort in Calicut in 1505 (Temple [ed.], *op. cit.* [n. 233], p. 101).

[610] Pires in Cortesão (ed.), *op. cit.*, I, 37.

early Portuguese writers are "Indo" (Sind), the Rajput territories, and the Muslim state of Malwa. At the beginning of the sixteenth century Sind, to the west of the Rajput country,[611] is already Muslim. Through its territories runs the Indus, "where India begins."[612] At its mouth there is a large port city whose governor is a Hindu of Sind. The products of Sind are indigo and, in small quantities, lac. Though it was once a famous kingdom, it is in Pires' day a small, mountainous, landlocked territory far removed from the centers of greatest activity in India.[613] The Rajput territories to the north of Gujarat are the homeland of Hindu warriors who obey no master and constantly prey upon their richer Muslim neighbors. To the east of Gujarat on the edge of the Vindhyan hills is the state of Malwa, whose king had but recently become a follower of the Prophet.[614] In olden times the warriors of this rocky plateau country were Amazons. And its king, in Pires' day, was said to have about two thousand women who rode out to battle with him.[615]

It is from Castanheda that Europe first learned in some detail about the Mughul advent in India, and about the subsequent struggle for supremacy between the Afghans and the Mughuls which occurred over the next generation. Upon arriving at Goa in 1528, Castanheda heard of the great victories being won by Babur in the north. The Mughul conqueror, who had spent the early years of the sixteenth century in winning dominion over central Asia, began his march from Kabul against the heart of Hindustan in 1525, after subjugating the Punjab. With the connivance of discontented nobles in Delhi, Babur proceeded against the forces of Ibrāhīm Lodi, the nominal sultan, and defeated them at Pānipāt in 1526. Routing of the Lodi forces led to the occupation of Delhi and Agra by the Mughuls, but Babur still had before him the task of pacifying the Rajputs under Rana Sanga and the provincial Afghan military chieftains. In 1527 he defeated Rana at Khanua, a town to the west of Agra, and brought an end to the Rajput national revival and the loose political confederacy led by Mewar. Then he turned eastward to hunt down the allied Afghans of Bihar and Bengal, whom he successfully defeated on the banks of the Gogra in 1529. With most of Hindustan at his mercy, Babur died at Agra in 1530 before he could organize and consolidate his conquests. Humayun, the son and successor of Babur to the Delhi sultanate, was thus confronted from the beginning of his reign with holding down hostile populations over an extended area with nothing at his command but military force. The Afghans in the east soon

---

[611] *Ibid.*, p. 37, n. 4.

[612] *Ibid.*, p. 38.

[613] *Ibid.*, pp. 37–38. In fact, it may almost be said that the Arabs and the Portuguese did not usually consider this Indus state to be within what they called India. See Yule and Burnell, *op. cit.* (n. 10), p. 634.

[614] Pires in Cortesão (ed.), *op. cit.* (n. 9), I, 37. The first Muslim king was the founder of the house of Ghori, an Afghan, Dilawar Khan, who ruled from 1387 to 1405.

[615] *Ibid.* This is a reference to the harem government which developed in Malwa and had its own army. See Ashraf, *loc. cit.* (n. 601), p. 150. Ferishta and other Muslim writers refer to Māndū, the capital, as the "city of joy" and they include in their accounts references to armed women. See Commissariat, *op. cit.* (n. 400), I, 288.

received the support of Bengal, and in the west Gujarat openly offered refuge and aid to the victims of the Mughul expansion into Hindustan.[616] When Gujarat and Bengal joined the resistance to the Mughuls, the Portuguese began to take more than an academic interest in the events transpiring in Hindustan.

Castanheda discusses at some length the expansion of the "Mogors" (Mughuls) into India and the resistance which formed against them. In connection with these discussions he also deals at greater length than the earlier writers with the states and peoples of north central India. He begins with a general account in which he describes how the Mughuls entered India from their own kingdom which borders on Persia and was called "Parchia" (Parthia) in antiquity.[617] The Mughuls, on the basis of testimony by Portuguese who had been in their company, are said to be white,[618] full-bearded, and to wear Moorish caps on their shaved heads. The nobles dress themselves in silken gowns and eat their dinners in great luxury at tables bedecked with elegant silver services and lighted by wax tapers. When traveling, camels carry their effects in large trunks and each night they pitch their own tents when they make camp. The Mughuls, who fight mainly from horseback, carry suspended from the pommels of their saddles a variety of weapons: bows, arrows, machetes, iron maces, and small axes.[619] Their cavalcades also include pieces of light artillery mounted on carts.[620] The Mughul warriors are accompanied by Tartars, Turcomans, and Khurasanis, and other peoples. The ruler of the Mughuls (presumably Babur) is highly respected by his Moorish retainers, and they salaam to him twice each day for they consider him to be holy. It is reported that he shuns women and so refrains from overly luxurious living.[621] But, even in peacetime, the Mughul ruler maintains a large personal bodyguard paid directly from his private funds and fed from his own kitchen.[622]

After Humayun became ruler of the Mughuls in 1530, Bahādur Shah of Gujarat shortly became involved in hostilities with him. The Gujarati ruler had provoked Humayun by giving sanctuary to certain Afghan refugees and by having taken advantage of the breakdown of the Rajput confederacy to annex Malwa in 1531, thus bringing to an end the Ghori dynasty which had ruled there since 1387. He then gradually made its capital city, Māndū, into a base of operations for an attack upon the Rajput fortress of Chitor. And, preparatory

---

[616] Majumdar *et al.*, *op. cit.* (n. 6), pp. 425–34. Also see Ishwari Prasad, *The Life and Time of Humayun* (Bombay, 1956), pp. 66–67.

[617] Castanheda in Azevedo (ed.), *op. cit.* (n. 17), IV, 337–39.

[618] Later European travelers use the word "Mogor" to mean white peoples. For a short summary of such references see E. Maclagan, *The Jesuits and the Great Mogul* (London, 1932), p. xxi, n. 1.

[619] On the offensive arms of the Mughuls see Irvine, *op. cit.* (n. 608), pp. 73–89.

[620] Cf. *ibid.*, pp. 133–51.

[621] Actually Babur, unlike most Muslim rulers in India, appears to have been a devoted family man, although perhaps a bit too much inclined to wine which he renounced at least twice during his career in India on the eve of decisive battles. For an account of his life see L. F. Rushbrook Williams, *An Empire Builder of the Sixteenth Century* (London, 1918).

[622] Cf. Ashraf, *loc. cit.* (n. 601), p. 154.

to the campaign against Chitor, Bahādur Shah in 1534 concluded peace with those Portuguese who had been harassing shipping in the Gulf of Cambay and enlisted their help for his inland expedition. Castanheda, who participated in the unsuccessful expedition of 1531 against Diu, acquired his information about the Gujarati war of 1534–35 from those same Portuguese and perhaps the other Europeans who accompanied Bahādur Shah. Consequently, his account relates many of their experiences and reflects their bias.

According to Castanheda,[623] Bahādur Shah assembles at the entry of Māndū in 1534 an army of 150,000 cavalrymen, of whom about 30,000 are mounted on good horses, the rest of the horses being only mediocre. Of the 500,000 infantry under Bahādur's command about 15,000 are foreign mercenaries: Fartakis from the Arabian peninsula, Abyssinians, 300 Rumes (Turks or Egyptians) including the engineer Rumi-Khan of Constantinople, 50 Portuguese, 15 captive Christians who were released to aid in the war, and 30 "Franceses" (probably Christian Europeans) who were being held at Diu on the Portuguese ship, the "Dobrigas."[624] Among the Portuguese are four artillerymen whom Nuno da Cunha, the viceroy, had sent out from Portugal. Capable gunners familiar with European guns are essential to the effective functioning of the artillery, inasmuch as Bahādur manages to assemble, so Castanheda reports, 1,000 pieces of artillery mounted on four-wheel ox carts. The final contingent is an elephant brigade of 800, all of them saddled with wooden turrets on which are mounted either short cannons or muskets. To finance this army, Bahādur fills 500 great copper coffers with gold and silver pieces which are transported in individual carts. Additional money is also forthcoming from the great lords and merchants who accompany the army.

From the city of Māndū, Bahādur set out in 1534 on the road to Chitor, a name "which means in the language of the land, 'the sombrero of the world.'"[625] Situated upon a very high mountain, Chitor is described as a fortress surrounded by strong walls and bulwarks within which there stand many sumptuous temples and dwellings. Orta, who never visited there himself, says that he is told that the city is a picture.[626] The queen, who resides in this hill fortress is a young and beautiful widow called "Cremeti" (Hadi Karmeti, the Rani [queen] and widow of Rana Sanga). Energetic as a man, she is said to have at her command 2,000 cavalry and 30,000 swordsmen for the defense of the city. Castanheda then describes the encirclement of the city in 1535, the destruction of its walls, and the final desperate sortie of the queen. Defeated, the queen flees from the city with her sons and a vassal whom she calls her friend. And the Portuguese chronicler concludes his account with the observation that Bahādur Shah,

---

[623] Castanheda in Azevedo (ed.), *op. cit.* (n. 17), IV, 355–56.

[624] On Europeans in the service of Indian rulers also see Irvine, *op. cit.* (n. 608), pp. 152–53.

[625] Castanheda in Azevedo (ed.), *op. cit.* (n. 17), IV, 355. It is also called Chattrapura, or "the city of the royal umbrella." For further comment on this derivation see Orta in Markham (ed.), *op. cit.* (n. 4), p. 462. For a different etymology see W. Crook (ed.), *Tods Annals and Antiquities of Rajasthan* (Oxford, 1920), III, 1647, n. 2.

[626] Markham (ed.), *op. cit.* (n. 4), p. 462.

being so delighted with the capture of Chitor, remarked that"nobody hereafter would wear this sombrero if he did not." [627]

While the Gujaratis besieged and captured Chitor, Humayun, en route to meet Bahādur Shah, remained strangely inactive.[628] According to Castanheda,[629] the Mughul emperor, when he departed from Delhi, had under his command 200,000 horsemen, one-fourth of whom are armored and the rest of whom are light cavalry. In addition, there are in this cavalcade many female archers on horseback. His foot soldiers are beyond count, though he possesses at least 10,000 swordsmen and 1,000 pieces of artillery. This great and mobile Mughul force occupies the road to Māndū without a fight, probably in 1535, and so places itself between Bahādur Shah and the road back to Gujarat. Three days after investing Chitor, Bahādur Shah, learning of Humayun's actions, moves his forces back towards Māndū. Arriving at a place called "Dacer," [630] Bahādur entrenches himself in a level field along the bank of a river. He encircles his camp with palisades, trenches, and much artillery to await the onslaught of the Mughuls. The army of Humayun being only seven leagues (28 miles) away, Bahādur, contrary to his usual custom of making his own decisions, consults with Rumi-Khan as to whether or not he should venture out to attack the Mughuls. On the advice of the Turk, Bahādur decides to try to extricate himself from his situation by means other than direct attack.[631] It seems that Rumi-Khan felt that with the onset of the rainy season only about a month away, rains, floods, and swollen rivers would make unlikely a victory in the field for either party. In the meantime his troops, suffering from famine and exposure, begin to desert and ultimately Bahādur himself flees from the camp at the riverside. Humayun follows him, and ultimately Bahādur takes refuge at Diu. From Castanheda's viewpoint, the defeat of Bahādur is providential because, had the Gujarati ruler won a victory over Humayun, "all his power would then have been directed against the Portuguese and he would not have let up until they had been driven from India." [632]

While Humayun overran Gujarat in 1535 and while the Portuguese were beginning to build their fortress at Diu, events were transpiring in eastern Hindustan which required the Mughuls' attention. The victory of Babur at Gogra had not resulted in the complete pacification of the Afghan chiefs in and around Bihar. Even in the reign of Sultan Nasrat Shah (1519–32) of Bengal, an alliance with the Lohani rulers of Bihar directed against the Mughuls was

---

[627] Castanheda in Azevedo (ed.), *op. cit.* (n. 17), IV, 356. For a similar account of the siege based on Persian, Sanskrit, and Rajput sources see G. N. Sharma, *Mewar and the Mughal Emperors* (A.D. *1526– 1707*) (Agra, 1954), pp. 55–57.

[628] The reason usually given is that he did not want to engage a fellow Muslim while he was fighting an infidel army. But for further discussion of this debated issue see Sharma, *op. cit.* (n. 627), pp. 51–53, and Prasad, *op. cit.* (n. 616), pp. 70–71.

[629] Azevedo (ed.), *op. cit.* (n. 17), IV, 356–57.

[630] Probably near Mandsur, northwest of Māndū, the capital city, on the bank of the Sipra River, where the two armies first made contact.

[631] Cf. account in Prasad, *op. cit.* (n. 616), p. 72, and see insert maps.

[632] Azevedo (ed.), *op. cit.* (n. 17), IV, 357.

basic to Bengali foreign policy. The anti-Mughul confederation was, however, constantly being endangered by the internal feuds of the Afghan chiefs, some of whom, probably out of self-interest, favored co-operation with the Mughuls. Among these chieftains there was one bearing the title of Sher Khan who sought to take over the leadership of the Afghan revival from the Lohanis and to check the growing influence of Bengal in the affairs of Bihar and other Afghan-ruled states. In 1533, Sher Khan defeated the Lohani–Bengali forces at Surajgarh on the banks of the Kiul River. Then, taking advantage of Humayun's preoccupation in western Hindustan, Sher Khan suddenly invaded Bengal by an unusual route and appeared at Gaur before Mahmūd Shah (reigned 1532–38) realized what was happening. The Bengali ruler immediately sued for peace, paid the Afghan tribute, and ceded him territory. As a consequence of this victory, many Afghan leaders, who hitherto had been reluctant to accept Sher Khan's supremacy, joined forces with him. While Humayun lingered in Agra, Sher Khan gathered his forces in 1537 for another descent upon rich Bengal. He besieged, occupied, and plundered Gaur in 1538 and escaped from the city with his loot before Humayun could bring it succor. Shortly after the Mughul ruler reached Gaur, Sher Khan transferred his plundering activities to the Mughul territories in Bihar and Jaunpur. Within the following two years Sher Khan consolidated his gains, defeated Humayun in two major battles, and forced the Mughul ruler in 1540 from the throne of Delhi.[633]

The Portuguese, being as involved in the affairs of Bengal as they were in those of Gujarat, followed these events closely and so were able to take advantage of Mahmūd's plight to wring concessions from him. Castanheda,[634] in particular, tells how "Xercansur" (Sher Khan Sur) seized the kingdom of the "Pathanes"[635] (Afghan kingdom of Bihar) from the grasp of Bengal in the time of "Mahumedxa" (Mahmūd Shah). The Portuguese chronicler further relates that after the Mughuls had been defeated by the joint efforts of the "Pathanes" and Bengalis, probably around 1530, the Bengal ruler occupied Bihar and seized its king. This area was then turned over to a governor, "Cotufoxa,"[636] a vassal of Bengal who maintained a large army in which the services of "Xercansur" were enlisted. It was not long before "Xercansur" deserted, raised his own army, killed the governor appointed by Bengal, and set up in his place a man of his own choice, "Sultan Halamo" (Jalal Khān). Shortly thereafter, in 1532, "Nancarote Xa" (Nusrat Shah) died, and his successor, Mahmūd, quickly instructed "Sultan Halamo" to restore the kingdom of the "Pathanes" to Bengal's control or accept the consequences. In the ensuing war of 1534, Sher Khan emerged victorious and Bihar was lost to Bengal. Though Castanheda's story is not entirely consistent with the accounts based on other sources,

---

[633] Account based upon chapters by A. B. M. Habibullah and N. B. Roy in Sarkar (ed.), *op. cit.* (n. 55), pp. 152–76, and upon Majumdar *et al.*, *op. cit.* (n. 6), pp. 434–38.

[634] Azevedo (ed.), *op. cit.* (n. 17), IV, 379–80.

[635] Derived from Hindustani, *Pathan*. See Dalgado, *op. cit.* (n. 44), II, 188.

[636] Possibly Khatif Shah.

it depicts, in their essentials, the original alliance of Bengal with the Afghans against Babur, the ensuing effort of Bengal to control Bihar, and the rise of Sher Khan as a new power to be reckoned with in eastern Hindustan.

It was as a result of the military services that the Portuguese rendered Mahmūd Shah in this campaign that they were permitted, in 1536–37, to establish their first settlements in Bengal. The Portuguese, through their emissary, Affonso Vaz de Brito, let Mahmūd know in 1538 that, all of their available forces then being involved in Gujarat, they would not be able to send the military aid which they had earlier promised him until the following year. To make certain that the Portuguese would finally live up to their promise of aid, Mahmūd held Affonso Vaz de Brito and four other Portuguese as hostages in Gaur. It was apparently from the reports of these eyewitnesses that Castanheda and the continuator of Barros were able to reconstruct the campaigns of Sher Shah and Humayun in Bengal during 1538. So far, however, no historian of Bengal has seen fit to incorporate the detail from the Portuguese chroniclers into their accounts of these wars, depending as they do almost too exclusively on the scantier Muslim sources.[637]

Castanheda's report of the crucial events of 1538 in Bengal are not so full as those published in 1613 in the fourth *Década* of Barros.[638] In his eighth book,[639] however, first published in 1559, Castanheda reports that when Affonso Vaz de Brito arrived in Gaur news was already abroad in the capital that Sher Shah with 100,000 cavalry and 300,000 infantry was advancing on the city. Mahmūd thereupon inquired at once to learn if Martim Affonso de Mello and the other released Portuguese prisoners had left the city. After hearing that they had gone, the sultan dispatched Nuno Fernandes Freire to Chittāgong with orders to acquire 1,000 "munchuas" (little boats like those of Malacca) with which he hoped to obstruct Sher Shah's advance down the Ganges. Even before the Portuguese emissary left, however, the "Pathanes" had begun to encircle Gaur, and so he was forced to make his way through their blockade in a small boat rather than in a "parão" (warship). Downriver, Nuno Fernandes Freire met the "lascar" (governor) of "Carnagão"[640] who was on his way to Gaur with 600 "almadias" (Indian rafts) loaded with provisions. When he learned from the Portuguese that the city was already under siege, the governor refused to go on; consequently there was so great a famine in Gaur that the fathers ate their children. When the "Pathanes" finally entered the city, they killed the majority of its inhabitants and Sultan Mahmūd was sorely wounded while fleeing his ravaged capital. The fugitive ruler soon met with a Mughul captain who had 40,000 cavalry at his command. This contingent, accompanied by Mahmūd,

---

637 See the comment in Campos, *op. cit.* (n. 551), p. 41n. The writers of Bengali history for this period in Sarkar (ed.), *op. cit.* (n. 551) utilize Campos and other secondary works based on the Portuguese chroniclers but they fail to exploit the chronicles themselves.

638 Cidade and Múrias (eds.), *op. cit.* (n. 6), IV, 507–34.

639 Azevedo (ed.), *op. cit.* (n. 17), IV, 486–87.

640 "Sornagam" on Lavanha's map in Barros. A river town near Dacca called "Sonagam" on D'Anville's map of 1752. Possibly identical to Sonārgāon the capital of eastern Bengal.

joined the main body of Humayun's army and immediately proceeded towards Gaur. Before they could reach the capital, Sher Khan evacuated it and escaped with all its treasure. Mahmūd meanwhile had died of his wounds and so Sher Khan immediately proclaimed himself the monarch of Bihar and Bengal. Exalted by these successes, Sher Khan then met and defeated the Mughuls, killed many great lords of the land, seized control of Delhi, Chitor, and Malwa, and established Afghan supremacy throughout Hindustan.

The profile of India as it emerges from the major Portuguese literary sources of the sixteenth century is an uneven outline resembling an artist's preliminary sketch for a monumental fresco. The west coast, especially the two maritime states of Malabar and Gujarat, stand out in bold relief, in good perspective, and with some of the shadings already suggested. The east coast is chalked out vaguely as far north as the delta of the Ganges where the representation again becomes more graphic and studied. Vijayanagar, especially its capital city, dominates the piece in the interior of India south of the Krishna River. The Indo-Gangetic plain of the north is sharply defined along its eastern and western extremities, in Bengal and Gujarat, but then the details and the firm lines fade out towards the interior. In the extreme north of the subcontinent no interior demarcations can be seen at all between Delhi and the brooding mountains which divide India from the rest of Asia. Though stark in its outlines, the basic pattern of India's geography can be clearly perceived here; it is left for subsequent generations to give it better form, substance, and tone.

The Portuguese perspective on India is distorted somewhat by the limits of the observers' experiences and by the preconceptions and prejudices which they brought with them. Concerned with trading and building an empire, the Portuguese naturally overstress the importance of maritime activities and related enterprises. And because they are also thinking of conquest, the writers tend to look at the states of India too exclusively in terms of military potential. The Europeans also persist in believing that the Hindus adhere to some early form of Christianity which they were either forced to give up or modify under pressure from the Muslims. Consequently, they seek to associate Hindu practices with Christian beliefs rather than trying to understand Hinduism for itself. Though they remark upon the religious tolerance of both the Hindus and the Moors, they categorically relegate many of the native beliefs to the limbo of super-stition. Literary conventions also make some of their comparisons pointless, as when on almost every occasion they contrast the cities of India with Evora. And being gallant Latins, the Portuguese almost always describe the women as attractive and desirable. They do not, however, express universal admiration for the men, though they do generally admit, except in the case of the Sin-halese, that the Indians make good soldiers. Nonetheless, in the final analysis, a handful of valiant Portuguese can usually overwhelm extremely large armies without suffering heavy casualties.

Like travelers of practically any era, the Portuguese record what interests them and see only those things which they are prepared to see. Except for Barbosa, they show no interest in the languages spoken in the places which they visited or heard about. Pires, Orta, and Castanheda were obviously men of education, and they clearly evince, on the basis of their Asian experiences, a consciousness of the limits of European knowledge about the East. Barros, who never visited India himself, systematically collected, checked, and collated information on India, not only from Portuguese informants and writings but also from Persian and Arabic literary sources. The simple fact that the Portuguese observers in India were intellectually curious and open-minded (or prejudiced) enough to record the obvious and sometimes the superficial gives particular value to certain of their observations. They remark, for example, on everyday activities, customs, and particularly inhuman practices which rarely appear in the Indian writings, either Hindu or Muslim.[641] And, as we have seen, when their statements can be checked against available native records, they are generally, though not unexceptionably, shown to be accurate and reliable.

2

THE JESUIT NEWSLETTERS AND HISTORIES

In an earlier chapter, we surveyed the Jesuit system of epistolary communication and observed how it systematically helped to disseminate in Europe a substantial amount of information about the East.[642] The newsletters published at intervals between 1545 and 1601 supply documentation on India for the period after 1542, or *that part of the century which is not covered by the Portuguese histories.* Both the published letterbooks and the unpublished Jesuit letters available in southern Europe also provided those sixteenth-century historians writing on the mission with some of their best primary sources. But, like most sources, the newsletters and the histories based on them must be subjected to rigorous historical criticism if they are to be used intelligently by the modern scholar. That they were designed to be letters of edification is a fact never to be forgotten. In the case of the "Indian letters" particularly, the Jesuits, soon to find that there was very little edification for ecclesiastic or layman to obtain from their arduous and disagreeable experiences in India, were not particularly inclined to view India's religions, customs, or people with the clear eye of impartiality. Nonetheless, the Jesuit letters and histories extend in time the European sources available on sixteenth-century history, and add dimensions on Indian languages and religions which the lay historians of Portuguese expansion treated only sketchily.

641 Cf. comments in Ashraf, *loc. cit.* (n. 601), pp. 121–22.
642 See above, pp. 314–28.

A. THE "INDIAN LETTERS" IN EUROPE, 1545–1601

As an example of how complicated it is to trace the evolution of the European image of India from the Jesuit sources, let us look at the publication history of Xavier's letters during the sixteenth century. Two of his general letters from Goa of 1542 were published in Paris in 1545, presumably in an effort to inspire the students in that seat of learning to volunteer for service in Asia, and these were among the first missionary letters about India to be printed.[643] In them he paints a rosy picture of the state of Christianity in India. Two personal letters of the same date addressed to Loyola from Goa did not appear in print until the end of the century, perhaps because they were less edifying and much more descriptive of the hardships recruits might expect to suffer in India; they were finally published by Tursellinus in 1596 as part of the documentation then being prepared by the Jesuits for the anticipated canonization of Xavier.[644] The Apostle's letter of October 28, 1542,[645] which was penned to Loyola from Tuticorin on the Fishery Coast, was included, at least in part, in the publications of 1545. Here Xavier, who had just barely arrived at his new post, tells of how he made conversions among the gentiles and of how the Portuguese governor had helped the Paravans in their struggle against the Muslims. His letter from Cochin of January 15, 1544 (also published in a French collection of 1545),[646] gave Europe the first of his detailed and optimistic reports on the progress of evangelizing along the Fishery Coast and in Travancore. It was this hopeful letter which was republished more frequently in the sixteenth century than any of his other dispatches.[647]

The fleet which landed at Lisbon in September, 1545, brought four letters from Xavier written in Cochin, as well as Miguel Vaz, the Vicar-General of Goa.[648] From these letters and the personal testimony of Vaz and his companions, the European sponsors of the Christian enterprise in India received the happy impression that a complete conquest for the faith was in the making if only the Portuguese rulers of India would co-operate more effectively and sincerely and if only more able recruits could be sent to gather in the harvest. Once Xavier's letters arrived at Lisbon, they were immediately dispatched to the court which was then in Evora. Simão Rodriguez opened and read them and, after making copies of the letters, had them forwarded to the Roman Fathers for local distribution. King John responded immediately to the Jesuits' appeal

[643] For the titles of these pamphlets see John Correia-Afonso, S. J., *Jesuit Letters and Indian History* (Bombay, 1955), p. 176, Appendix D. This author also notes a German translation published at Augsburg in 1545.

[644] H. Tursellinus, *Francisci Xaverii epistolarum libri quatuor* (Rome, 1596).

[645] G. Schurhammer and J. Wicki (eds.), *Epistolae S. Francisci Xaverii aliaque eius scripta* (Rome, 1944), I, 129–43.

[646] *Ibid.*, pp. 152–77.

[647] R. Streit, *Biblioteca missionum* (Aachen, 1928), IV, 126.

[648] G. Schurhammer, "Xaveriusforschung im 16. Jahrhundert," *Zeitschrift für Missionswissenschaft*, XII (1922), 130–33.

for funds and likewise acted at once to draw up directives for the authorities in India in an effort to establish better working relationships between the secular arm and the missions. Many Portuguese volunteered to join the Society to carry on the work in India, and with the fleet of the next year nine Jesuits and six Franciscans were sent to Goa.

At the Jesuit College of Coimbra, Xavier's letters of 1545 created a sensation and in the midst of the fervor the Rector wrote to Rome "that there would be no difficulty in transplanting this College to there [India!]." [649] Xavier's general letter to the brothers of Europe created a similar stir in other Jesuit centers. Copies of it were received and read at Jesuit stations as widely separated as Valencia and Cologne just one year after Xavier had penned it. At the German center additional copies were made and distributed to high ecclesiastics in the surrounding areas. A Dutch Jesuit, Jacobus Lhoost, commented after reading it that the firm faith of the Indians compensated the church for the losses suffered at the hands of Luther and Melanchthon. [650] Finally it was translated into Italian and published in pamphlet form at the Eternal City in 1546 as *Copia de una lettera. . . .* [651]

Though it was apparently not reprinted again until 1596 (Tursellinus), Xavier's general letter of 1545 awakened hopes in Europe that great progress was to be expected in India and it was even the subject of discussion at the ecumenical Council of Trent (1545–63) which was then beginning to meet. [652] After reporting that he baptized more than 10,000 people in Travancore during a single month, Xavier explains his simple method of reciting the articles of the faith to the assembled multitude in Tamil and how he considered their affirmation of them as constituting conversion. [653] Through such mass conversions, he hoped that more than 100,000 could be baptized in a year. [654] The text printed in the *Copia de una lettera . . .* contains conversion figures which far exceed in size all previous statistics, it being alleged that to 1545 there had been 635,000 conversions in the various parts of Portugal's Asian empire. [655]

Thirty-two of Xavier's letters dated from India are still extant. Of this number, twenty-two were published for the first time in Tursellinus' collection of 1596 appended to Xavier's biography. Seven of his other letters were first published at intervals between 1545 and 1570; the only ones which appeared before his death in 1552 are those published in 1545 already discussed. Of the seven letters published before 1596, just four of them were printed more than once: the two missives of 1542 (printed in 1545 in two editions) and two others of 1559 (first printed in 1569 and 1570). And most of the Xavier letters written in the last three years of his life (1549–52) have more to say about Japan and China than India. The letters printed before the appearance

[649] Schurhammer and Wicki (eds.), *op. cit.* (n. 645), I, 264.   [650] *Ibid.*, pp. 266–67.
[651] The sole surviving copy of this newsletter exists in the library of the Historical Society of Würzburg. Published in *Serapeum*, XIX (1858), 180–85.
[652] Schurhammer and Wicki (eds.), *op. cit.* (n. 645), I, 267.
[653] *Ibid.*, pp. 273–74.   [654] *Ibid.*, p. 277.
[655] See Schurhammer, *loc. cit.* (n. 648), p. 133.

of the Tursellinus collection in 1596 stress the successes of Christianity in the East and the need for more missionaries to bring in the great harvest of souls awaiting Christian enlightenment; there is no hint in them of the problems which he anticipated in India or little mention of his dissatisfaction with the secular arm. Tursellinus, eager to stress the hardships overcome by the first great Jesuit missionary, naturally has no hesitation in putting into print Xavier's more critical and pessimistic letters.

In trying to reconstruct the channels by which information subsequently filtered into Europe through the Jesuit letters, it is necessary to isolate for analysis the published writings of Xavier's successors in India. From their correspondence at least 120 separate letters were published in whole or in substantial part during the latter half of the sixteenth century. These missives were penned from the Indian stations by at least forty-seven different correspondents, some of whom are represented in the published books by just a single letter. A number of the letters, however, were printed in several different collections, and a handful of them appeared in as many as five to seven different editions. From the first published letters of 1545 to the end of the century, fifty separate collections were printed which included substantial numbers of letters from and about India and the state of the Christian enterprise there.[656] These compilations were produced mainly in the cities of Italy, Portugal, and Spain, but a few originated in the printing shops of Paris, Louvain, Dillingen, and other Jesuit centers in northern Europe. Certain of the collections were derivative, in the sense that they seem to have been compiled wholly or in part from earlier letterbooks. A substantial number of the letters which recount the trials of evangelizing in India or complain about the relationship between the Society and other agencies of church or government, were not printed at all during the sixteenth century.

In approaching the complicated problem of dealing with the printed letters, it seems best to divide them and our consideration of them into two distinct chronological periods: 1552-1570; 1571-1601. The first epoch begins with the systematic publication in southern Europe almost annually of collections of missionary letters. Normally, in this period, the letters were compiled, edited, and printed shortly after their arrival. It closes with the publication of several massive Latin collections prepared for distribution in northern Europe. The second epoch commences with a decade (1571-81) of decline in publication. It is followed by the issuing of the "true" annual letters (beginning in 1581) and concludes with the appearance of the first of the Jesuit histories (beginning in 1588). The last decade is concerned with the revival of interest in India inspired by the hope of converting Akbar, and with the publication of Tursellinus' collection of Xavier letters and Guzman's Spanish history of the Society's activities in the East.

---

[656] The list of "principal editions" compiled by Correia-Afonso (*op. cit.* [n. 643], pp. 176–79) includes just thirty-five separate items for the sixteenth century. The list of editions referred to here is longer because it includes a few items missed by Correia-Afonso and a number of editions of "Japan Letters" which contain significant Indian materials.

B. THE FIRST IMPRESSIONS, 1552–70

In the two decades of this period three great series of letterbooks were being published. At Coimbra, beginning first in 1551 or 1552, appeared those which are referred to variously as *Copia de unas cartas* or *Copia da diversas cartas*. After the initial publications, new compendiums in this series were printed in 1555, 1561, 1562, 1565, and 1570. To facilitate their circulation they were issued from Coimbra in Spanish rather than in Portuguese versions; even so, several of them were later reissued in Spain in somewhat more elegant Spanish versions. At Rome (and beginning in 1559 at Venice) the series known as *Avisi particolari* or *Nuovi avisi* also began to appear in 1552, and subsequent editions came out in 1553, 1556, 1557, 1558, 1559, 1562, 1565,[657] 1568, 1570, and thereafter. More comprehensive compilations soon began to be published in Latin. The first of these was an unauthorized collection of *Epistolae Indicae* ... published at Dillingen in 1563. Provoked to action, the Jesuits published similar Latin collections of their own at Louvain in 1566 and 1570. Occasionally one volume or the other of these three series was translated into German or French, but the trend even in this period was towards issuing the letters in the more universally acceptable Latin. The separate letters were often reproduced in more than one of these volumes, but at times the versions printed are quite different from one another. The "Indian letters" in the publications of 1552 to 1570 were all written between 1548 and 1561. For some unexplained reason there was no effort to publish the letters written from India between 1561 and 1568.[658] The following generalizations are therefore based on the letters *actually published* in the period from 1552 to 1570 (though all are dated as of 1561 or before) as we have extracted them from the versions reproduced in the first five of the critically edited Wicki volumes entitled *Documenta Indica*.

The newsletters, which began to be published in books contemporary with the appearance of the works of Ramusio, Castanheda, and Barros, are very sketchy and unorganized when compared to the secular books. Like many lay commentators, the Jesuit writers dwell on the great length, hardships, and uncertainties of the sea voyage. "The experience of traveling from Portugal to India," concludes the Provincial Dom Gonçalo da Silveira, "cannot be related except by those who have undergone it, cannot be understood or believed except by those who have observed it...."[659] The major ports of India

[657] This collection of twenty-six letters (printed in Venice), almost all of which are dated 1561, includes five from Japan, one from China, thirteen from India, one each from the Moluccas and Ethiopia, and five from Brazil.

[658] Examination of the sixth volume of J. Wicki (ed.), *Documenta Indica* (Rome, 1960), which includes letters written between 1563 and 1566, reveals that not a single one of the letters from these years was published during the sixteenth century.

[659] Letter from Cochin to Father Gonçalo Vaz de Melo at Lisbon (January, 1557) in Wicki (ed.), *op. cit.* (n. 658), III, 622.

receive little more than mere mention, though occasionally the Jesuits give approximate distances from one place to the other. The letters of Henrique Henriques give considerable detail not to be found elsewhere on the place names of the Fishery Coast and Travancore.[660] Michael Carneiro, the first Jesuit to penetrate the Serra of the Malabar Christians, gives some descriptive material on the hilly country of the interior behind Cochin.[661] Of particular interest is the account by Gonçalves Rodrigues of his overland journey in 1561 from Belgaum, inland from Goa, to the court of Bijapur. This part of the Deccan he describes as "excellent country" with "many fine streams, large towns, much livestock ... and many different foods." He goes on to make a few more specific observations:

The land ... is very black and fertile, and very flat. Seldom are stones found in the earth, and it seems to be the most fertile soil imaginable for grains, that is, if it were in the hands of our Portuguese farmers. As it is such excellent land, all foods grow abundantly with only the dews [for moisture]. The natives make poor use of the land, and many parts lie unused, for the land is too large and there is much left over.[662]

Rodrigues speaks less favorably about living conditions in the towns of the Deccan. In the five or six places he passed through on the road to Bijapur, he found the people to be living in "little huts worse than what the cows have in our country."[663] Bijapur itself is situated in a fertile plain where irrigated orchards produce fruits in splendid abundance. Though he concludes that Bijapur is larger than Goa and very strongly fortified, Rodrigues summarizes his unfavorable impression of the interior of the town by asserting that it "does not contain ten servicable houses."[664] In an earlier letter from Bassein,[665] Rodrigues, who clearly had an eye for agriculture, tells how the Jesuits bought land and houses at Trindade and Tana and started farms to give their converts employment and income.

Surprisingly, the Jesuits give only cursory descriptions of the major centers of their activities,[666] though occasionally they make revealing incidental remarks. For example, we learn that in 1550 "many parts of Pesquaria [the Fishery Coast] were barren because of drought."[667] Mortality of adults on the Fishery Coast is not abnormally high, but the children, particularly the infants, seem

[660] See especially his letter to the General from Manakkudi in Travancore (January 13, 1558) in *ibid.*, IV, 31–36.

[661] Letter from Goa to Luis Gonçalves de Câmara at Lisbon (December 24, 1557) in *ibid.*, III, 795–801.

[662] Letter from Bijapur (April 7, 1561) to Quadros in Goa as reproduced in *ibid.*, V, 138–39.

[663] *Ibid.*, p. 139.

[664] *Ibid.*, p. 143.

[665] To the Fathers in Portugal (September 5, 1558) in *ibid.*, IV, 100–104.

[666] The only effort to give brief background summaries on each of the Jesuit centers from Goa to China is contained in Barzaeus to Loyola (January 12, 1553) in *ibid.*, II, 581–600; in two earlier letters Barzaeus also gives fine descriptions of Ormuz and surrounding areas. See his letter of December 10, 1549, in *ibid.*, I, 644–47, and his letter of November 24, 1550, in *ibid.*, II, 77–79.

[667] Henriques to Rodrigues (January 12, 1551) from Cochin in *ibid.*, II, 156.

to have more trouble surviving than they do elsewhere in India.[668] Cochin is said to have "houses like those of Rome" and to be serviced by a "large river of salt water."[669] In September, 1557, Goa suffered from an epidemic of what it seems from the description of symptoms we would now call influenza.[670] And, of the places further to the East, the Jesuits report that Japan is cold and unpleasant,[671] and notice that the people of Amboina "live on high hills that can be reached only crawling up on hands and feet."[672] Scattered throughout the letters are numerous references to the names of coins, prices, and the availability of products, particularly foodstuffs, in the various localities.

A European reader of the earliest published newsletters would not receive a general perspective on Asia's political organization. Most of the missionaries are content merely to mention that the overlord is either a heathen or a Moor, and that he is either a friend or an enemy of the Portuguese. They relay some slight information on general political conditions in the *padroado* generally by references to the joint attacks of Calicut and the Turks on the Portuguese outposts in south India during 1553, to the power of the Muslims in Travancore subsequently, or to rumors of an outbreak of war between the Turks and Abyssinians in 1557.[673] Gaspar Barzaeus, who is somewhat more politically conscious than his colleagues, discusses in a letter to Loyola dated 1553 the extent of Malay political dominion in southeastern Asia and observes that China is said to include a land inhabited by Jews, to border on its land side with Germany, and to "allow no commerce except at the seaports."[674] Three years later the Jesuits from India optimistically report to Europe that the ports of China are open to trade and that a letter was received at Canton from a ruler in Japan who promised to become a Christian.[675]

On India itself the letters are most specific on events transpiring along the Fishery Coast. Beginning in 1549 the Jesuits begin to complain about the attacks of the Badagás upon Punical, the Portuguese fortress and trading center.[676] Repeatedly, Henriques complains about the meddling of the Portuguese captains in the politics of the Fishery Coast. Troubles with the Badagás and hostilities within Paravan factions leads Henriques in 1556 to act as a political mediator,[677] probably because of his abilities in both Tamil and Portuguese. Proposals were meanwhile being made in Goa suggesting that the Paravan Christians should be transplanted to the friendlier and more accessible territory

[668] Henriques to the General (January 13, 1558) from Manakkudi in *ibid.*, IV, 29.
[669] Antonius de Herédia to Loyola, from Cochin (January, 1552) in *ibid.*, II, 291.
[670] Fróis to Portuguese fathers from Goa (December 12, 1557) in *ibid.*, III, 749.
[671] For example, see Barzaeus to Loyola from Goa (January 12, 1553) in *ibid.*, II, 600.
[672] Fróis to Fathers of Coimbra from Goa (November 30, 1555) in *ibid.*, III, 716.
[673] Fróis to Fathers of Coimbra from Goa (November 30, 1557) in *ibid.*, III, 712.
[674] From Goa during January, 1553, in *ibid.*, II, 586.
[675] See especially Soveral to Coimbra Fathers from Cochin (January 20, 1556) in *ibid.*, III, 451, and Brandão to Portuguese Fathers from Goa (November, 1556) in *ibid.*, III, 579–80.
[676] Jesuits of the Fishery Coast to the Bishop of Goa written from Punical (January 19, 1549) in *ibid.*, I, 482.
[677] Henriques to Loyola from Punical (December 31, 1556) in *ibid.*, III, 595.

across the Straits of Manaar in northern Ceylon. Events going from bad to worse at Punical in 1557, Henriques, who was blamed both by the Portuguese and local factions for his political meddling, was sent to Cochin and Travancore until the situation at Punical could be brought under control. He was replaced on the Fishery Coast for a time by Father Francisco Peres who helped the Governor's agent, Francisco Alvares, to restore temporary order.[678]

Shortly thereafter the new Viceroy, Dom Costantino de Braganza, decided early in 1560 to transplant the Paravans to the territories of the ruler of Jaffna by force if necessary. This decision was apparently taken because Viśvanātha, the *Nāyaka* (viceroy) of Madura and Hindu overlord of the region, had demanded from the Christians the proceeds from one day's pearl fishing and threatened, if not obeyed, to imprison the women and children. When the Portuguese began to remove the Christians in large numbers, Viśvanātha in 1560 attacked and overwhelmed their garrison at Punical.[679] Father Pedro Mesquita was captured and taken to Madura as a hostage. With the aid of a Christian boy, he escaped in September, 1560, and arduously made his way to Henriques and the transplanted Christian community on the island of Manaar and ultimately got to Cochin.[680] Since the project of moving the Paravans to Jaffna could not be carried out successfully, they returned gradually to their former homes, particularly after the death of Viśvanātha in 1561.[681]

Conditions in Travancore are generally described as being worse for the Europeans than those prevailing on the Fishery Coast because "the Moors lord it over this coast."[682] Henriques reports that Martānda Varma, the prince of Travancore, died in 1554 and that disorders followed.[683] While in temporary exile in Travancore, Henriques comments on the hostility of the new ruler to the Christian "macuas." They cannot be protected adequately by the secular arm because the Portuguese captain at Quilon is much too far away from their centers to act effectively in their behalf.[684] Clearly, here as elsewhere in continental south India, the mission is still on the shakiest of foundations.

Little is said about the political relations between the Portuguese at Goa and Adil Khan of Bijapur until 1557, even though the Portuguese had been endeavoring for over a decade to replace Adil Khan by his brother, Meale Khan. The latter had conspired and revolted against Adil Khan in 1545, and, his plot failing, was forced to seek refuge in Goa. A series of Portuguese governors thereafter sought to use him as a political pawn in their efforts to acquire control

[678] Henriques to the General from Manakkudi on January 13, 1558, in *ibid.*, IV, 23–24.

[679] Henriques to Lainez from Manaar (January 8, 1561) in *ibid.*, V, 6–10.

[680] For the conditions of his imprisonment see Mesquita to Henriques from Madura (?) on August 29, 1560, in *ibid.*, IV, 604; for his escape see Mesquita to Coimbra Fathers from Cochin (January 16, 1561) in *ibid.*, V, 77.

[681] Probably died in October, 1561. See Henriques to Lainez from Manaar (December 19, 1561) in *ibid.*, V, 378. For further details see above, pp. 270–71.

[682] Francisco Durão to Rodrigues from Thêngâppattanam (November 22, 1557) in Wicki (ed.), *op. cit.* (n. 18), III, 695.

[683] Letter to Loyola from Punical (December 25–31, 1555), *ibid.*, III, 423.

[684] Henriques to the General from Manakkudi (January 13, 1558) in *ibid.*, IV, 32.

over the Deccan territories under Adil Khan's control. The Jesuits only begin to recount details of these enterprises beginning with the spring campaign of 1557.[685] Even then they give military and political data only as background to the conversion of Meale Khan's daughter at the end of 1557[686] and to the more repressive policies then being inaugurated at Goa to wipe out the Hindu and Muslim resistance to Christianity. Peace finally being concluded with the Portuguese in 1560, Adil Khan sent a request in 1561 to the Archbishop of Goa for the dispatch to his court of two or three learned priests.[687] The Muslim ruler, who was apparently curious about Christianity, received Fathers Gonçalves Rodrigues and Francisco Lopes in state at Bijapur in April, 1561. While accomplishing little in the way of religious instruction, the fathers interviewed the ambassador from Vijayanagar and requested him to ask his rājā for permission to let the Christians visit his domains. They also saw at Bijapur the brother of the Nizamu 'l-Mulk of Ahmadnagar whose kingdom had recently been invaded by a coalition of Bijapur, Golconda, and Vijayanagar. Particularly interesting are the identifications the Jesuits give of Adil Khan's leading advisers and of the ceremonies then prevailing at his court.[688]

The close working relationship between church and state during Dom Costantino de Braganza's term as viceroy (1558–61) was carried over to the military and diplomatic activities of the Portuguese in northwestern India. In the attack and capture of Damão and the island of Bulsar during 1559,[689] the Viceroy was accompanied by the Provincial of the Jesuits, Dom Gonçalo da Silveira, and the Vicar of the Dominicans, Friar Antonio Pegado, and a delegation of Franciscans. The Jesuit superior was accompanied by a lay brother who had in his charge some youths from the college at Goa. The enemy withdrew from Damão without a serious struggle, and when the Portuguese landed, the Provincial went to the city's leading mosque to celebrate mass. The boys from the College helped to pave the way for the capture of Bulsar, for the residents received them warmly. On this island, possibly because the Portuguese came with youths from the region, "the Viceroy found the natives to be tractable, willing to deal with and talk to the Portuguese, . . . [a quality] rarely met with in the nations of these parts."[690]

From Damão the Jesuits probed further northward to Surat by the end of 1560. Father Marcus Prancudo, a native of Valencia who was at Damão from 1558 to 1565, corresponded with the ruler of Surat, Khudāband Khan.[691] The young prince, then twenty years of age, was the son of parents who had once

685 Fróis to Coimbra Fathers from Goa (November 30, 1557) in *ibid.*, III, 708–9.
686 Celebrated as the first conversion of an aristocratic Muslim woman. For details of her conversion, see the remarkably frank letter of Fróis to the Fathers in Portugal from Goa (December 12, 1557) in *ibid.*, III, 731–35.
687 Fróis to the Fathers in Portugal from Goa (December 1, 1561) in *ibid.*, V, 280.
688 Rodrigues to Quadros from Bijapur (April 7, 1561) in *ibid.*, V, 140–43.
689 A description of this action in Fróis to the Coimbra Fathers in *ibid.*, IV, 278–80.
690 *Ibid.*, p. 280.
691 Prancudo to Fathers in Goa from Damão (February 28, 1561) in *ibid.*, V, 110.

been Christians and who had reconverted to Islam. The Jesuit apparently got in touch with him through merchants who traded at Damão and Surat. With the help of these merchants Prancudo obtained an invitation to visit the court in order to explain the tenets of Christianity to Khudāband Khan. On the trip to Surat, Prancudo was accompanied by Diogo Pereira, a Portuguese merchant and faithful friend of Xavier, and by Abraam the Jew, both of whom are described as being "great friends" of Khudāband Khan. While Prancudo failed to convert the young ruler, he was apparently satisfied that his explanations and admonitions had not fallen on deaf ears. About secular matters the Jesuit remarks only on the rundown condition of the city's fortress (probably built around 1540) and on the young ruler's comment that a war was in the offing for which Surat could accept no blame.[692]

The key to the understanding of India, the Jesuits realized, lay in the mastery of the native languages and the opening of their literatures. Only a few missionaries working in the Portuguese-controlled ports troubled to learn Konkani or Marāthī in these early years.[693] Usually at Goa and in the Bassein area they relied upon professional interpreters and native boys from the College. The problem was further complicated for them in the trading centers by the fact that they worked with people of diverse backgrounds (Muslims, Jews, and heathens) who were themselves foreigners to the local languages. This problem was sometimes met in the Portuguese centers by communicating in "pidgin Portuguese."[694] It was only in the areas outside of Portuguese control that the Jesuits successfully attacked the local languages. In Japan, the Moluccas, and in south India, including Ceylon, the Jesuits from Xavier's time onward made serious efforts to speak, read, and write the native tongues, to prepare grammars and vocabularies, and to translate Christian prayers, catechisms, and songs into them. Occasionally in this period, the missionaries also acquired literary works in the native tongues for the purpose of understanding local beliefs in order to refute them in public disputations.

The greatest progress in India was made in the Tamil and Malayālam regions at the southern tip of the peninsula. Following the lead of Xavier, the Italian, Antonio Criminale, the first superior of the Fishery Coast, had learned by 1548 how to communicate and read in Tamil (or "Malabar," as the missionaries generally called it).[695] After Criminale's martyrdom in 1549, the lead in the study of Tamil was taken over by Henrique Henriques who reports that he learned to speak it in five months by studying day and night with the aid of a native youth.[696] He learned to speak and write it correctly, according to his own claims,[697] by organizing it according to the principles of Latin grammar and

[692] *Ibid.*, pp. 115–16.
[693] Brother Francisco Anes preached in Marāthī during 1556 at Tana (*ibid.*, III, 591), but as late as 1561 Fróis wrote that only a few fathers in Goa knew enough Kanarese to listen to confessions in that language (*ibid.*, V, 274).
[694] Teixeira to Portuguese Fathers from Goa (December 25, 1558) in *ibid.*, IV, 168.
[695] Henriques to Loyola from Bembay (October 31, 1548) in *ibid.*, I, 280.
[696] *Ibid.*, p. 285.   [697] *Ibid.*, pp. 287–88.

by working out a system of transliteration by which he and others could learn to pronounce it.[698] From remarks scattered throughout his letters, it is clear that Henriques and his associates found the pronunciation and accent of Tamil to be among their knottiest problems. As a product of his own experience in learning the language, Henriques prepared by 1551 a "Malabar" grammar and some translations of prayers. He sent a manuscript copy of the grammar to Portugal and notified the fathers there that all of the missionaries on the Fishery Coast were learning the language and talking in it with one another. "We hope," he comments, "that within a few days we can make a rule that no one is to write in Portuguese, only in Malabar." [699]

For his own translations and correspondence in Tamil, Henriques soon employed an interpreter and a secretary. He wrote out his texts in Portuguese, a boy then read them aloud to the interpreter, who then dictated them to the secretary, who wrote them down in "Malabar." Henriques would read the Tamil translations over, and then correct the mistakes in the *olas* (writings inscribed on palm leaves) before completing or dispatching them.[700] Like other missionaries after him, Henriques found it particularly difficult to convey through Tamil the precise meaning of Christian words and concepts, and so he was constantly revising his grammar, vocabularies, and translations to render them more accurate. Though hampered in carrying on his linguistic work by the unsettled conditions of life on the Fishery Coast, Henriques finally completed a revision of his "Malabar" grammar, compiled a vocabulary, and translated several Christian tracts into Tamil. In 1576, Henriques' *Doutrina Christão*, a translation of Xavier's brief Catechism, was printed in Tamil characters at Quilon. In the following year his lengthier *Doutrina Christão* was printed at Cochin.[701] And, in 1586, Henriques' *Flos Sanctorum* was printed in Tamil characters on the Fishery Coast, probably at Punical.[702]

Henriques did not confine his linguistic ambitions to Tamil. He believed that with the help of an interpreter and a secretary, and by following the method used in constructing the "Malabar" texts, he could "devise a grammar for the learning of any language in these parts in less than four months, even if it be a tongue of Japan, or China, or Prester John, or any other." [703] While reveling in his naïve optimism, Henriques soon learned that even Malayālam could pose

---

[698] For the kinds of linguistic difficulties which must have faced the missionary pioneers in learning Tamil see G. Moraes, "St. Francis Xavier, Apostolic Nuncio, 1542–1552," *Journal of the Bombay Branch of the Royal Asiatic Society*, New Series, XXVII (1950), 293.

[699] Henriques to Rodriguez from Cochin (January 12, 1551) in Wicki (ed.), *op. cit.* (n. 658), II, 158.

[700] Henriques to Loyola from Punical (November 6, 1552), in *ibid.*, II, 395. Later on he remarks that he receives from four to eight *olas* each day (*ibid.*, III, 239).

[701] Anant Kakba Priolkar, *The Printing Press in India* (Bombay, 1958), p. 11.

[702] A copy of this book is in the Vatican Library. See Xavier S. Thani Nayagam, "Tamil Manuscripts in European Libraries," *Tamil Culture*, III (1954), 225. For a sample page see Priolkar, *op. cit.* (n. 701), p. 319. *The Flos Sanctorum* (*Flower of the Saints*) is the *Golden Legend* prepared by the thirteenth-century Dominican, Jacobus de Voragine. See above, p. 27.

[703] Henriques to Loyola from Punical (December 31, 1556) in Wicki (ed.), *op. cit.* (n. 658), III, 598.

problems for the unwary. During his stay at Cochin for three months (September-November, 1557), he found that he could not work effectively on the west coast without an interpreter. From this experience he concluded that Malayālam and Tamil have "many points of similarity though they differ more than Spanish does from Portuguese."[704] Tamil, he asserts, is the "better language" and is more widely spoken; Malayālam is the language of Quilon, Cochin, the St. Thomas Christians, and others.[705] Still, he persisted in hoping that persons acquainted with both languages could, in conference with the religious authorities, prepare versions of the same prayers and other Christian writings in both languages so that they could be used everywhere in south India by the missionaries. During his visit to Cochin in 1560, he continued to make arrangements for the preparation of a Malayālam grammar and vocabulary.[706] While this project of training the missionaries in the languages of south India failed to produce fruit, Henriques' concern with it highlighted for Europe the importance of studying independently each of the many languages of India. A further complication was added to the language picture by the suggestion that instructors in Chaldean should be sent to Cochin to train the missionaries to the Serra in the sacred language used in the rituals and writings of the St. Thomas Christians.[707]

Though the early Jesuits knew next to nothing about the other languages of India, they were interested enough in them to notice inscriptions, to send copies of books written in them to Europe, and to have translations of some of the sacred Hindu texts made by their Indian converts. For example, Gonçalvo Rodrigues, while visiting Bijapur, tells of seeing an inscription on a newly constructed gateway "in a language I believe to be Persian."[708] In 1549, while Barzaeus was at Ormuz, he acquired a copy of the New Testament "written in [the] Gurzi script"[709] of Persian which he sent to Europe. While trying to root out Hinduism in Goa, the Jesuits in 1558 ransacked a Hindu home and confiscated two books "which they call *Anadipurana* [*Ananta-purāna*, or the history of Vishnu]."[710] A portion of this which related to the origins and creation of the Hindu gods was translated. In the following year, a Brahman convert "with the permission of the Viceroy" went to the mainland from Goa, accompanied by two or three men, and seized the library of a Brahman who "had spent eight years in copying out and gathering together several ancient authors."[711] Among the books seized and taken to the Jesuit College were eighteen books of the epic, *Mahabharata*, attributed to Vyāsa. Translations of

---

[704] Henriques to General from Manakkudi (January 13, 1558) in *ibid.*, IV, 28.
[705] *Ibid.*
[706] Henriques to Lainez from Manaar (January 8, 1561) in *ibid.*, V, 19.
[707] Melchior Nunes Barreto to European Fathers from Cochin (December 31, 1561) in *ibid.*, V, 416.
[708] Letter to Quadros from Bijapur (April 7, 1561) in *ibid.*, V, 140.
[709] Barzaeus to European Brothers from Ormuz (December 10, 1549) in *ibid.*, I, 698.
[710] D'Almeida to Portuguese Fathers from Goa (December 26, 1558) in *ibid.*, IV, 203.
[711] Fróis to Portuguese Fathers from Goa (November 14, 1559) in *ibid.*, IV, 335–36.

this work were made for the Jesuits in Ceylon and Europe by the youths in the College. When they were dispatched to Europe, translations of some of the land grants made by the rājā of Vijayanagar to the St. Thomas Christians were sent along with them.[712]

From their informants, both heathen and Christian, and from the translations of the confiscated texts, the Jesuits learned next to nothing about Hindu doctrine. Even Henriques, who clearly had more appreciation of Tamil culture than his fellow missionaries had of the native beliefs in their areas of India, remained completely untouched by Hindu thought. "After I had begun to learn the language," he comments, "I heard many of the stories and fables of the Gentiles, and . . . I shall one day write in Malabar against their fables."[713] While he apparently was too preoccupied otherwise to carry out this intention, he like-wise never bothered to acquire and translate Tamil writings. From the transla-tions made from the *Ananta-purāna*, D'Almeida relayed to Europe (in awkward Portuguese transliterations) the names of numerous Hindu gods, the reincarna-tions (*Avatars*) of Vishnu, and the knowledge that Vishnu, Shiva, and Brahma constituted the *Tri-mūrti* of Sanskrit teachings.[714] Fróis, on the basis of the *Mahabharata*, recounts the story of the marriage of Shiva and Pārvatī (whom he calls Adam and Eve) and the birth of Ganeśa from the sweat of Pārvatī's body.[715] Such information was relayed, not for its intrinsic interest, but rather as confirmation of the assertions that the Jesuits never tired of making about the hopeless superstitions which they met in India. "[Francisco] Rodrigues under-stands something of the question," Fróis writes, "for he has many translations from their books and has preached against their religion every Sunday for about one year."[716] Teixeira puts the unbending hostility of the Jesuits into an even more somber light by his gloating admission that "sometimes we spend our time making fun of their gods, of their eating and drinking habits, and of the errors in their religion, so that they will grow less fond of them."[717]

Limited by their cultural and religious hostility to Hinduism, the Jesuits were naturally unable to penetrate beneath the surface of Hindu life. Consequently, most of their letters, even when dealing with religious questions, are concerned primarily with outer trappings. Writing from Ormuz about the "superstitions of the Gentiles," Barzaeus remarks that they worship cows who are given "*cartas d'alforia* [patents of freedom]"[718] which allow them to walk unmolested around the streets of the city. The humble Hindus of this rowdy port city on the Persian Gulf refuse to take life or eat anything which has been killed. While living austerely on vegetables and harming nobody, these people barbarically sacrifice themselves to their gods by slashing each other with razors,

[712] *Ibid.*, p. 339.
[713] Henriques to Loyola from Bembay (October 31, 1548) in *ibid.*, I, 288.
[714] Letter to Portuguese Fathers from Goa (December 26, 1558) in *ibid.*, IV, 204.
[715] Letter to Portuguese Fathers from Goa (November 13, 1560) in *ibid.*, IV, 669–70.
[716] Letter to Portuguese Fathers from Goa (December 8, 1560) in *ibid.*, IV, 801.
[717] Letter to Portuguese Fathers from Goa (December 25, 1558) in *ibid.*, IV, 171.
[718] Letter to European Brothers from Ormuz (December 10, 1549) in *ibid.*, I, 646.

hurling themselves under carts, and burning widows alive.[719] Even in the "jungles of Cambay" they sacrifice to their gods by burning offerings of sugar, butter, and silk.[720] They have many rituals for purifying themselves, and feel polluted when they have relations with Christians. Father Prancudo complains about the Hindus of Damão:

They regard us as being so accursed that if we set foot, not in their houses, but merely on the porch, they tear down the house and build another one in some place we have not touched. If they give us something to drink, they will not use that vessel again. . . .[721]

Clearly, from these and similar references, the Jesuits saw the Hindus as humble folk who irrationally esteem their gods and cows while despising Christians as being polluted and "as bearing the curse of God."[722]

The Jesuit letters are dotted with references to the adoration of the Hindus for their *pagodes*. The Christian writers use the word to mean both "temples" and "gods,"[723] and in certain letters it is used in both senses by the same author within the same paragraph.[724] The Hindu temples of Travancore are described as being "very large houses, all of stone and marble" which contain images of bulls, cows, elephants, monkeys, and men.[725] Some of the more ethnocentric Jesuits, who were plainly astonished by the massiveness and beauty of the Hindu temples, believed that they were the creations of Alexander the Great or the Romans.[726] A great temple in Cochin, where pilgrims came from as far away as Cambay, was destroyed by the Christians as early as 1550.[727] Eight years later a luxurious temple located near Tana was converted into a Christian chapel and its entrance was destroyed and replaced by a Roman archway.[728] Statues of the gods were likewise ruthlessly destroyed by the Jesuits and their converts, even though these statues were "highly honored by the people" who treated them as living beings that eat, urinate, and perform numerous miracles.[729]

The island of Divar, just north of the island of Goa, is regarded by the Hindus as a "holy land" or as something like "Rome in Europe."[730] Divar is described as a center consecrated to temples and idols to which pilgrims come from many places to obtain indulgences and forgiveness for their sins. Every year in August at least thirty thousand believers are reported to be in the habit of coming to bathe in the purifying waters of the river facing Divar, near the temple of

---

[719] *Ibid.*
[720] Teixeira to Portuguese Fathers from Goa (December 25, 1558) in *ibid.*, IV, 169–70.
[721] Letter to Portuguese Fathers from Damão (November 15, 1560) in *ibid.*, IV, 697.
[722] *Ibid.*
[723] For the very complicated history of this word see Dalgado, *op. cit.* (n. 44), II, 130–37.
[724] As an example see Nunes Baretto to Coimbra Fathers from Travancore (November 18, 1548) in Wicki (ed.), *op. cit.* (n. 658), I, 320.
[725] *Ibid.*
[726] Barzaeus to European Brothers from Ormuz (December 10, 1549) in *ibid.*, I, 648; and Gonçalves Rodrigues to Portuguese Fathers from Bassein (September 5, 1558) in *ibid.*, IV, 100.
[727] Melchior Gonçalves to Portuguese Fathers from Cochin (January 20 [?], 1551), *ibid.*, II, 184.
[728] Rodrigues to Portuguese Fathers from Bassein (September 5, 1558) in *ibid.*, IV, 100.
[729] Nunes Barreto to Coimbra Fathers from Travancore (November 18, 1548) in *ibid.*, I, 320–21.
[730] Fróis to Portuguese Fathers from Goa (November 13, 1560) in *ibid.*, IV, 671.

Sapta-nātha.[731] The Portuguese, beginning in 1557, sought by force to halt these pilgrimages. The Christian converts, supported by Portuguese arms, were sent out to pollute the holy places on the island. On one occasion, at least, they cut up a cow and threw pieces of its carcass into the river to prevent the Hindus from bathing there.[732] Roadside shrines, at Divar and elsewhere, were callously pushed over to show the Hindus the error of their ways.

The effort at Goa to force the Hindus to abandon their rites and ceremonies resulted in the publication in Europe of information about native processions and festivals. After the secular authority began to break up public celebrations, the Hindu faithful sought to follow their traditional rites covertly. The Jesuits, who took a "special interest in stopping the feasts and ceremonies," [733] obtained advance information through their Christian converts about the festival dates on which secret celebrations were almost certain to be held in private homes and at odd hours of the night. By this indirect route, we also learn that around mid-December, 1558, feasts were held in honor of the god who is variously called Ganeśa, Vighnanāśaka, and Vināyaka. These feasts were held at various locations in Goa and some of them, at least, were invaded by the Jesuits and their converts.[734] On a later occasion when Hindus from Divar wanted to celebrate the feast of Ganeśa they tried to escape the vigilance of the Christians by sending their sons to the mainland where they were apparently free to carry on their festivals in Muslim territory.[735] The feasts of "Divalli" (Divālī) and of Sita, the god of fortune, are celebrated at the same time in Goa,[736] usually during the month of October, and are attended by the most honorable in the Hindu community. In writing from the Portuguese territories outside of Goa, where the Christians were not strong enough to forbid the celebrations, the Jesuits content themselves with giving graphic descriptions of Hindu processions but without really understanding what is being celebrated.[737]

The Hindus, according to the Jesuits, have three sorts of priests: Brahmans, Yogis, and Gurus. While the letterwriters recognize that the Brahmans manage the temples and are dominant in religious affairs, they have no admiration for them unless they become converts. Repeatedly they charge them with insincerity, duplicity, and with having "no aim except to collect money" [738] from the Hindu laity. When asked why they intentionally deceive their own people, the Brahmans reply, "What can we do, for this is how we earn our living? We beg you not to reveal our affairs to the people." [739] Fróis discourses

[731] D'Almeida to Portuguese Fathers from Goa (December 26, 1558) in *ibid.*, IV, 205–06.

[732] Fróis to Portuguese Fathers from Goa (December 1, 1561) in *ibid.*, V, 279–80.

[733] D'Almeida to Portuguese Fathers from Goa (December 26, 1558) in *ibid.*, IV, 201.

[734] *Ibid.*, p. 202.

[735] Fróis to Portuguese Fathers from Goa (November 13, 1560) in *ibid.*, IV, 669.

[736] D'Almeida to Portuguese Fathers from Goa (December 26, 1558) in *ibid.*, IV, 203.

[737] See, for example, Brother Luis de Gouveia to Goa Fathers from Quilon (April 7, 1560) in *ibid.*, IV, 545–46.

[738] Henriques to Loyola from Bembay (October 31, 1548) in *ibid.*, I, 284. See also his comparison of the Brahmans and the Christian priests (*ibid.*, p. 295).

[739] *Ibid.*, p. 292.

learnedly about the sacred threads of the Brahmans which are "worn around the neck next to the skin from the age of seven onwards." This ceremonial symbol "has three strands each of which has been twisted several times with a knot covering where the ends meet." Each thread honors a particular god and the "knot which joins the ends represents the oneness of the three persons, and thus they try to claim that they have a Trinity like ours." After showing the falsity of this assumption, Fróis concludes "that they only speak of three persons [*Tri-mūrti*, Sanskrit for three forms] because they learned it from the Christians" [740] Though the Brahmans pretend to be vegetarians, Nunes Barreto believes that "in secret . . . they will eat anything." [741] The Brahmans, though they are priests, marry "as many women as they want" [742] and entice young girls to prostitute themselves for the honor and revenue of the temples.

The ascetic Yogis are men of a different sort, and the Jesuits show marked respect for their spirituality, abstinence, learning, and willingness to listen. Fróis distinguishes two types of Yogis: mendicants and hermits. [743] They seem to "obey a superior" and are "regarded as saints" by the common people. [744] Barzaeus is so impressed with the influence they wield that he suggests that he might dress like them and live with them. [745] One of those whom he converted he sent to Europe in 1551, and later on this Christianized Yogi worked at the College of Goa. Two others, who were studying in the College, are reputed to know eighteen native languages. [746] Another, converted by Henriques on the Fishery Coast, was held to have great influence through the purity of his life among the *patangatins*, the village heads of the Paravans. [747] While the Gurus are recognized as being authorities on Hindu teachings, the Jesuits have very little to say about them as a group. They are more intent upon telling about sorcerers who are able to conjure up with their incantations "five hundred phantasmagoric elephants," [748] and about "jousi" (*jyotisī* or astrologers) who tell *fula* (fortunes) [749] by attaching leaves to both shoulders of an idol and waiting to see from which side they first fall before making a prediction, [750] or about the nocturnal demons and devils which plagued the Paravans at sea until they became Christians. [751]

On social questions, the Jesuit letters concern themselves mainly with those institutions and ideas which made the problem of conversion more complex.

---

[740] Fróis to Portuguese Fathers from Goa (December 8, 1560) in *ibid.*, IV, 803–4.

[741] Nunes Barreto to Coimbra Fathers from Travancore (November 18, 1548) in *ibid.*, I, 321.

[742] *Ibid.*

[743] *Ibid.*, p. 801.

[744] Barzaeus to European Brothers from Ormuz (December 10, 1549) in *ibid.*, I, 676; see also Nunes Barreto to Coimbra Fathers (November 18, 1548) in *ibid.*, I, 321.

[745] *Ibid.*, I, 676.

[746] Melchior Dias to Miron from Goa (January 4, 1555) in *ibid.*, III, 210–11.

[747] Henriques to Rodrigues from Cochin (January 12, 1551) in *ibid.*, II, 159–60.

[748] D'Almeida to Portuguese Fathers from Goa (December 26, 1558) in *ibid.*, IV, 204–05.

[749] Possibly from Sanskrit: *phala* = fruits of an act, hence fate.

[750] Fróis to Portuguese Fathers from Goa (November 14, 1559) in Wicki (ed.), *op. cit.* (n. 658), IV, 344–45.

[751] Henriques to Loyola from Bembay (October 31, 1548) in *ibid.*, I, 290.

The caste divisions of southern India interest them particularly. In addition to giving the names of a number of south Indian castes, Henriques advised Loyola that "... it is better in India to baptize all those of one caste than different individuals taken from various castes."[752] He talks mostly about the practices common to the Paravans and of the related groups of the interior called the "Chavallacars" and the "Taquanqutes," inhabitants of the region called Thekkumkur to the east of Lake Vampanad.[753] From Quilon the Jesuits of Europe learned about the castes of blacksmiths, carpenters, tailors, coconut workers, and other occupational groups. Very little specific information is given on the castes of Goa and those of the northern settlements. Fróis, who knows a great deal about the Brahmans and several of the lower castes of Goa, condemns the cruel custom by which the rich men of India cast their slaves into the streets to die when they become too ill or too old to work. Slaves and refugees from caste discipline often found sanctuary in the convents and schools of the Christian settlements in India.[754]

Marital practices and death customs intrigue and perplex the Jesuits. Henriques writes that there are "many people married to cousins, sisters and sisters-in-law, and it would make a great scandal to separate them because there are many of them, and they have many sons and daughters."[755] Always generous himself in allowing dispensations to the natives, Henriques repeatedly asks for a papal dispensation which would permit marriage within the third and fourth degrees of affinity and consanguinity, a concession already permitted in New Spain.[756] Instead of prayers and candles at the deathbed, "they bring in a live cow to the patient and put its tail into his hands and this for them is to die in the most devout manner."[757] In Travancore, it was the custom for all men to cut their beards at the death of a king; those who refused were usually arrested or done away with.[758] On the death of a king in southern India, it was also customary for his retainers to run amuck in order to avenge his death or to die in the attempt.[759] Even the St. Thomas Christians threatened to run amuck to avenge their bishop when the Portuguese tried to capture him.[760]

At Cape Comorin the people have a diet made up mainly of rice, wheat, flour, chicken, fish, milk, butter, eggs, figs, and the coconut and its milk.[761] The adults, who walk about in semi-nudity, ordinarily wear a loin cloth of slightly over two feet in width. Their children under the age of ten usually walk about

---

[752] *Ibid.*, III, 599.

[753] Henriques to Loyola from Punical (November 6, 1552) in *ibid.*, II, 397, and Silveira to Torres from Goa (December, 1557) in *ibid.*, III, 754.

[754] Fróis to Portuguese Fathers from Goa (December 8, 1560) in *ibid.*, IV, 793.

[755] Henriques to Loyola from Punical (December 31, 1556) in *ibid.*, III, 595–96.

[756] Henriques to Loyola from Punical (November 6, 1552) in *ibid.*, II, 396–400.

[757] Fróis to the Portuguese Fathers from Goa (November 14, 1559) in *ibid.*, IV, 344.

[758] Henriques to Loyola from Punical (December 25–31, 1555) in *ibid.*, III, 420.

[759] Carneiro to De Câmara from Goa (December 24, 1557) in *ibid.*, III, 796.

[760] *Ibid.*, p. 801.

[761] Nunes Barreto to Coimbra Fathers from Travancore (November 18, 1548) in *ibid.*, I, 319–20.

in nothing at all.⁷⁶² A commonplace sign of friendship is the companionable habit of chewing betel and areca, and a royal indication of good will is the sending of a branch of figs.⁷⁶³ Whenever traveling in south India, even in hostile territory, a stranger, if accompanied by a local guide, is understood to be under the ruler's protection.⁷⁶⁴ The climate of the island of Manaar is reported to accentuate sensuality, and Henriques wrote to the Jesuit General requesting permission to take certain tranquilizing drugs commonly employed by the Yogis "to mortify the flesh."⁷⁶⁵

In the judgment of the Jesuits, the non-Christian peoples of India, even when most advanced and learned, are very inferior to the peoples of eastern Asia. The Chinese are described as being wise and just, while the Japanese are esteemed for their industry, intelligence, and cleanliness. The Malabars and Kanarese are held to be much less acute, very weak and superstitious, and completely lacking in standards of cleanliness.⁷⁶⁶ The natives of Tana are brutish and troublesome to the missionaries, but "full of astuteness and worldly wisdom . . . in looking after their own interests."⁷⁶⁷ While the lower classes in Indian society are sometimes given credit for mildness and docility, the Brahmans, unless they become converts, are criticized for their obstinacy, arrogance, and unwillingness to listen to reason.

Even the implacable foes of the Jesuits, the Moors and Jews, are accorded greater respect than the Hindus. While the Jesuits condemn them for practicing sodomy and usury, they also admire their business acumen and their understanding of the faiths of their fathers.⁷⁶⁸ They recognize that most of the Muslims are Sunnites, and complain that their "casizes" (Muslim teachers) are sometimes able to win native Christians over to the faith of the Prophet.⁷⁶⁹ While Muslim women are ordinarily kept indoors, they apparently escaped surveillance enough of the time to cause the Jesuits to attack them for their immoral association with Christian men.⁷⁷⁰ G. Rodrigues remarks that in Bijapur "the Moors are as innumerable as insects" and extends his remarks to include a description of a Muslim festival and an estimate of Adil Khan.⁷⁷¹ With regard to the Moors, in particular, the Jesuits seem to be on the defensive. "We are here on a battlefield," Barzaeus writes from Goa to Loyola, "in constant struggle with Turks, Moors, and Gentiles, and we have no peace."⁷⁷²

⁷⁶² *Ibid.*, p. 320.
⁷⁶³ Carneiro to De Câmara from Goa (December 24, 1557) in *ibid.*, III, 799.
⁷⁶⁴ *Ibid.*, p. 797.
⁷⁶⁵ To Lainez from Manaar (December 19, 1561) in *ibid.*, V, 382. For the General's reaction see his reply of December 11, 1562, in *ibid.*, p. 661.
⁷⁶⁶ Gonçalves to Portuguese Fathers from Cochin (January, 1551) in *ibid.*, II, 185.
⁷⁶⁷ G. Rodrigues to Goa Fathers from Tana (December 1, 1558) in *ibid.*, IV, 116–17.
⁷⁶⁸ For example see Barzaeus to European Brothers from Ormuz (December 10, 1549) in *ibid.*, I, 657.
⁷⁶⁹ Durão to F. Rodriguez from Thêngâppattanam (November 22, 1557) in *ibid.*, III, 694–95.
⁷⁷⁰ Barzaeus to European Brothers from Ormuz (December 10, 1549) in *ibid.*, I, 663.
⁷⁷¹ Letter to Quadros (April 7, 1561) in *ibid.*, V, 143–44.
⁷⁷² Letter of January 12, 1553, in *ibid.*, II, 589.

The embattled Jesuits were by no means uncritical admirers of their secular Portuguese cohorts in India. In commenting about the Portuguese soldiers at Ormuz, Barzaeus complains that they seem "like men without law, king, or captain—all savages, renegades, blasphemers."[773] Many Portuguese men, already married at home, contract "secret" marriages in India and refuse to have the banns of their new marriages proclaimed in church.[774] In Goa, one street was famed for its Portuguese prostitutes,[775] some of whom were sent back to Europe by the missionaries from time to time. The Portuguese, like the Moors, shock the Jesuits by their addiction to sodomy, and in 1559, as part of a strict moral and religious rehabilitation campaign a number of Portuguese were executed, exiled, or imprisoned for unnatural sexual practices.[776] Indeed, the Jesuits repeatedly charge the Portuguese with making their mission difficult and of undoing their good works by the bad moral example they set and by the injustices which they tyrannically perpetrate upon the natives.[777] Friction was probably inevitable in the settlements, since, as in Goa, the Jesuits "were so surrounded by Portuguese that it is like living in Portugal."[778]

But the picture of the Portuguese painted by the Jesuits is not completely black. Portuguese youths are praised for remaining firm in their faith even while serving "in the armies of the Gentiles along with Moors and other Gentiles."[779] Their elders contribute to the mission, take pleasure in working in the confraternities, and lend aid in the construction of churches and schools. In 1557 an "honorable" Portuguese provided the paper for printing confessional manuals so that they could be distributed free of charge in all of the settlements.[780] Many Portuguese and Luso-Indians sought admission to the Society even though the Jesuits discouraged them because proper training was not available in India.[781] Naturally exceptions were made, one of the most notable being the admission of Fernão Mendes Pinto to the Society in 1554.[782] Occasionally it seems that the Jesuits won devotion from Portuguese officials who hoped to win Jesuit support in India and Europe for advancing their careers. Barzaeus writes about a captain working in Ormuz: "He is devoted to the Company and wants to be governor of India one day. Pray for him!"[783] Or, when Henriques speaks well of a captain at Punical, the Jesuit comments: "He takes our advice on everything. . . ."[784]

773 Letter of December 10, 1549, in *ibid.*, I, 663.
774 For example, see Henriques to Loyola from Punical (December 25–31, 1555) in *ibid.*, III, 419.
775 Dias to Society in Europe (December 15, 1554) in *ibid.*, III, 158.
776 Fróis to Coimbra Fathers from Goa (November, 1559) in *ibid.*, IV, 285–86.
777 Quadros to Miron from Goa (December 6, 1555) in *ibid.*, III, 347.
778 Da Costa to Portuguese Fathers from Goa (December 26, 1558) in *ibid.*, IV, 178. At Ormuz there always were 800 to 1000 Portuguese in the city. See Brandão to Coimbra Fathers from Goa (December 23, 1554) in *ibid.*, III, 191.
779 Henriques to Loyola from Bembay (October 31, 1548) in *ibid.*, I, 297–98.
780 Fróis to Coimbra Fathers from Goa (November 30, 1557) in *ibid.*, III, 711.
781 Barzaeus to Loyola from Goa (January 12, 1553) in *ibid.*, II, 589.
782 Brandão to Coimbra Fathers from Goa (December 23, 1554) in *ibid.*, III, 178–82.
783 Letter to European Brothers (December 10, 1549) in *ibid.*, I, 673.
784 *Ibid.*, III, 419.

The first impressions summarized here are, as we have said, based on letters written from India between 1548 and 1561, and so they necessarily relate events and describe practices from the first years of the Jesuit experience in the subcontinent. In Europe all of the letters quoted were available in printed form by 1570, and these letters, as well as others which remained unpublished, were likewise circulated in manuscript. From 1554 onward, voices were raised in criticism of the published letterbooks both in Europe and India. The letterwriters were attacked, particularly by the Portuguese in India, for exhibiting bias and for not always giving all the facts relating to certain questions. It was even rumored that a book had been compiled to point out the factual errors and inconsistencies in the letterbooks.[785] Within the Society the demand was also being made for more careful and comprehensive editions of the letters and for the preparation of an official history of the mission. It was these considerations, among others, which probably help to account for the lacuna of 1561–68 in the published letters. From the perspective of today, while giving due weight to the shortcomings of the letters as historical sources, the Jesuit writings are unique among European writings for this period in the information which they give on Indian languages and literature and for the way in which they point up the disdain of the missionaries for the Indian peoples, particularly the Brahmans, and for their religions. Blinded by their cultural and religious hostility, the Jesuits contented themselves with superficial or incidental references to Hindu practices.

C. THE SECOND GENERATION, 1570–1601

Between 1570 and 1588 very little information about India appeared in Europe in published form. Though several of Xavier's letters from India were published in 1566 and 1570, they deal with the Far East and say practically nothing about India. The *Nuovi avisi* published at Rome in 1570 included five new letters from India written between 1568 and 1570. From 1570 until 1585, just nine brief letters or extracts about India got into print, the most notable of which was a notice published in the *Nouveau advis* (Paris, 1582) telling about Aquaviva's departure for the court of Akbar in 1580. The *Litterae annuae* published at Rome in 1585 includes a detailed letter from Valignano which deals exclusively with the Salsette martyrs—those five Jesuits, including Rudolph Aquaviva, who were murdered in July, 1583. The other annual letters of this decade are notable for their failure to include news from India.

Not only was there a blackout of India during these years; those letters which actually saw light contributed almost nothing to the European image

---

[785] J. Wicki, *Alessandro Valignano, S. I., Historia del principio y progresso de la Compañía de Jesús en las Indias Orientales* (Rome, 1944), pp. 36*–37*.

and are little more than letters of edification. A letter from Goa of 1568[786] stresses the dangers to the missionaries from the growing power of the Moors in the waters and seaports of India. "The Malabar nation is Muslim," it asserts, "and they are almost all pirates and hostile to the Christians."[787] While this was certainly not literally true, it brings out how seriously the Portuguese were under attack from an alliance of the Turks and Malabars.[788] The "pirates of Malabar," after the Zamorin in 1559 denounced his treaty of 1540 with the Portuguese, made the seas unsafe for the Europeans along the entire coast of western India—from Diu to Ceylon. Jesuits were killed, captured, or held for ransom. Even the Christian communities in the vicinity of Goa itself were preyed upon by plunderers from the sea. But, fascinatingly, even as the Europeans are forced on the defensive by the renewed Muslim and Malabar attacks, they begin to find that the Brahmans, whom they had so roundly condemned in their earlier letters, now come forward to help them in their hour of need.

The published reports on the status of the missions in Quilon (1569), Goa and its environs (1569), and Cochin (1570) take what must be described as a more appreciative attitude towards the Brahmans, whether converted or not.[789] The converted sons of leading Brahmans are praised for traveling about with the Jesuits and for their aid in bringing other Indians into the Christian fold. In many of the outlying territories of Goa the Jesuits are successful in converting Brahmans who are also *gancars*,[790] or members of the native councils which rule the village communities. In the attacks upon the Christians of Salsette, Brahman youths fought along with the other converts and some of the *gancars* secretly aided and gave sanctuary to the hard-pressed missionaries. In fact, the Hindu converts of all castes are described as standing sturdily beside the Europeans who are seeking to preserve their foothold in India.

These reports also give somewhat more statistical data than most of the Jesuit letters. Quilon "lies at the foot of a mountain and is back from the ocean by about 11,000 paces."[791] In its environs are twenty-three villages, all except four of which possess Christian churches. These are heavily populated places, but the necessities of life are available in abundance and the climate is healthy. Near the city of Cochin, about three thousand paces (yards) from its outskirts, there are a number of villages around Palurt, all of which are under the jurisdiction of the state of Cochin. The small principality of Porakád "which lies

[786] Organtino da Brescia to Europe (December 28, 1568). Text reproduced in German translation in Anton Eglauer (ed.), *Die Missionsgeschichte späterer Zeiten; oder, Gesammelte Briefe der katholischen Missionäre aus allen Theilen der Welt. Briefe aus Ost-Indien* (3 vols.; Augsburg, 1794–95), II, 290–309.

[787] *Ibid.*, p. 278.

[788] For a survey of these hostilities see Danvers, *op. cit.* (n. 228), I, chap. xix; also K. M. Panikkar, *A History of Kerala, 1498–1801* (Annamalainagar, 1960), pp. 116–20.

[789] J. de Gouvea to Society from Quilon (January 15, 1569) in Eglauer (ed.), *op. cit.* (n. 786), II, 313–17; Sebastian Fernandes to General from Goa (November, 1569) in *ibid.*, pp. 333–66; G. Ruis to General from Cochin (January 15, 1570) in *ibid.*, pp. 366–79.

[790] See Dalgado, *op. cit.* (n. 44), I, 416–17.

[791] Eglauer (ed.), *op. cit.* (n. 786), II, pp. 313–15.

twenty miles from here"[792] is apparently also a fief of Cochin. But while the Jesuits enjoyed good relations with the rulers of Quilon and Cochin as well as some of their vassals, the missionaries continue to rail against their blindness in refusing to accept Christianity.

Despite the obvious difficulties faced by the Europeans, the missionaries continued to make converts in the Portuguese settlements. On Salsette Island, the converts numbered 2,000 in 1568 out of a total population of 200,000.[793] In the following year Sebastian Fernandes reports a total of 3,200 conversions in the Goa area, "a smaller number than in previous years, but large enough considering how progress was limited by war and unrest."[794] The College at Goa in 1569 housed 88 Jesuits, some of whom taught in the school which had 720 students.[795] In Cochin during 1570 the two Jesuit elementary schools together had a registration of 270 students. Mass baptisms continued in all of the coastal settlements of India, and in Goa they were still celebrated with great pomp and often with the viceroy in attendance.

News of Aquaviva's visit to the court of Akbar was published in Europe by 1582.[796] Three years later it became known that he, the nephew of the Jesuit General, had dispiritedly returned to Goa and was shortly thereafter killed on the island of Salsette.[797] The other letters from these years are also full of the hardships being suffered in India, even though the missions to Akbar apparently raised hope for a time that real achievements in India were in the offing. Contrast this bleak picture to the bright successes that the Jesuits were celebrating or anticipating in the Far East around 1585, and it is no longer hard to understand why the letters from India were not more frequently printed in the letterbooks of these years.

Maffei's Latin history which appeared at Florence in 1588 includes in chronological order a systematic discussion of the Portuguese enterprise in India from Vasco da Gama to about 1557. Though often classified as a Jesuit history, Maffei's work, as it relates to India, resembles in organization and emphasis the books of Castanheda and Barros. In fact, he explains at one point that it is his object to describe "the conquests of the Portuguese, and not the manners and customs of other nations."[798] The Jesuit historian, perhaps intentionally, has relatively little to say about the missions in India, though he does laud the great successes of Xavier and refers to him as a "saint." While Maffei fails to fill in systematically the gap (1561–68) in our information on India, it is clear from his discussion of particular subjects, whenever he examines them closely, that he was

---

[792] *Ibid.*, p. 376.　　[793] *Ibid.*, p. 301.
[794] *Ibid.*, p. 364.　　[795] *Ibid.*, pp. 333–34.
[796] Extracts from his letter of 1580 from Fatehpur Sīkrī appeared in *Nouveau advis* (Paris) and in the annual letter published at Rome in 1582.
[797] Valignano's letter of January, 1584, published in *Litterae annuae* (Rome, 1585).
[798] G. Maffei, *Historiarum Indicarum libri XVI* (Florence, 1588), I, 255. Apparently, he used two documents prepared in 1568 and 1569 on the fortresses, ports, and mission stations of India. These two reports have recently been edited and published in J. Wicki, "Duas relações sobre a situação da India portuguesa nos anos 1568 e 1569," *Studia* (Lisbon), VIII (1961), 133–220.

probably acquainted with many of the Jesuit letters from India which remained unpublished during the sixteenth century, and that he used some of them as well as special reports in the preparation of his digressions on social classes and religious practices.[799]

For Maffei, the political and social organization existing in Malabar, especially in Calicut, is the norm for India as a whole. The Zamorin, who is the chief ruler or "emperor" of Malabar, governs four kinds of people: magistrates or governors called "Caimales,"[800] priests called "Brachmanes," a military aristocracy called "Naires," and a great host of artisans and farmers. In addition to his own people, the Zamorin tolerates Muslim and Jewish merchants within his realm and they derive great profits from trading in his port cities. Such a description and emphasis was obviously derived by Maffei from the secular accounts rather than the missionary letters.

In his generalized descriptions of the Brahmans, Nāyars and working classes of Malabar, Maffei combines the secular sources with material from the missionary letters and the writers of antiquity. "There are several types of Brahmans," he asserts, "those who marry and raise children and the others who profess celibacy and are today called yogis. In former times the Greeks called them Gymnophistes." He then goes on to repeat what was said about the Brahmans and Yogis by the earlier writers, including the assertion that the Yogis live under a supreme general "who enjoys great revenues and who sends certain of these imposters at particular times to preach in divers countries their impious errors and their dreams."[801] He also notes that the Yogis believe that by their renunciation of things of the flesh they will eventually be "received in great glory among the '*Abdutes*' [Avadhūtas], which is one of their Orders."[802] The Yogis, with their "spiritual exercises," monastic hierarchy and organization, and evangelizing spirit seem to remind Maffei, as they did some of the Jesuits in India, of the regular Orders of the Catholic church.

Like the letterwriters, Maffei writes in wonderment about the Hindu temples "which are able to compete in magnificence with the most superb of ancient Rome."[803] And, like his colleagues, Maffei dismisses Hindu teachings as a mass of fable and superstition. The Jesuit historian saw some of the Brahmanical translations which had been prepared in India and sent to Portugal.[804] He admits that these books show "incredible care and labor" and that their teachings are "similar in some ways to the fables of ancient Greece or the '*Augurale*' [Auguria] discipline of the old Etruscans."[805] But, the good

---

[799] In the appendix of letters at the end of Maffei's *Historiarum Indicarum* just three of those included relate to the affairs of India. Most of those reproduced were written from Japan. See below, pp. 706–9.

[800] See above, p. 375n.

[801] Maffei, *op. cit.* (n. 798), I, 255.

[802] *Ibid.*

[803] *Ibid.*

[804] *Ibid.*, p. 56. Cf., above, pp. 438–39.

[805] *Ibid.* The Etruscans were famous even in the late Roman empire for their ability to discover by signs (auguries) whether a proposed act met with divine approval.

Christian Humanist concludes that it is of "little importance to give space at this point to these bagatelles and to these tales of old." [806] It is of more importance to reflect that God in his goodness is now ready to remove the scales from the eyes of those who have so long lived in darkness.

Maffei, perhaps more than any other writer of the century, gives considerable detail on the preparation of the Nāyars for military service, their equipment, and their conduct in battle. As the hereditary warrior caste, the Nāyars are in constant training from the age of seven until death, and Maffei is clearly impressed by the rigor of their physical training program and the bodily agility which it gives them. While they previously relied upon bows, pikes, and swords, the Nāyars quickly learned how to make, burnish, and aim all the firearms, large and small, that were to be found in the arsenals of the Portuguese. Still they went almost nude into battle and without the protection of breastplate or helmet. In battle with armored Europeans the Nāyars show themselves to be less firm when meeting the shock of attack than their enemies, but much nimbler and extremely well-outfitted for hit-and-run tactics. Their ability to strike quickly and effectively and then melt into the interior while harassing their pursuers with javelins and metal quoits thrown with deadly accuracy clearly made them formidable foes to the Portuguese. Though all Nāyars pride themselves on their aptitude for war, an elite exists among them called "Amoques" who pledge their lives, family, and children to avenge their masters or their fellows. Reckless and impetuous warriors, the "Amoques" are held universally in great esteem and the strength of a king is measured by the number of "Amoques" who have pledged themselves to him. [807]

While Maffei contents himself with denouncing the marital and inheritance customs of the Nāyars, he reserves his full wrath for their impossible pride, insolence, and pollution beliefs. Artisans and farmers live most miserably, a condition which the Nāyars seem to do their utmost to maintain. Men of the working classes are unable to better their conditions by changing their jobs for better ones. Evidently he was under the impression that the individual chose his occupation and was then frozen in it. Maffei, while referring to Arrian's Greek history of India, concludes that groupings based on occupation is one of the oldest of India's customs. The Nāyars and other Indian nobles who have been responsible for maintaining this system since antiquity quite naturally hate Christianity vehemently for its emphasis on moderation and brotherly love. [808]

Certain general impressions about Portuguese India emerge from Maffei's pages. The motivation for the Portuguese enterprise is primarily trade. In India, the Portuguese ruined themselves by overindulging in the debilitating luxuries of the Orient. The Franciscan missionaries, who dominated the Christian enterprise in India until the advent of the Jesuits, are depicted as

[806] *Ibid.*

[807] *Ibid.*, pp. 56–58. For a detailed discussion of the "Amoques" consult "Amouco" in Dalgado, *op. cit.* (n. 44), I, 33–36.

[808] Maffei, *op. cit.* (n. 798), pp. 58–59.

being well-intentioned and sincere but not overly effective.[809] Maffei finds that the St. Thomas Christians exhibit similarities in rites and traditions to the Latin faith, and he seems completely untroubled by their alleged predilection for Nestorian heresies. About India itself, and on those areas beyond the Portuguese outposts, Maffei has practically nothing to say and in this regard is less informative than the secular writers. While Maffei refers constantly to the classical authors of Greece and Rome, he indicates on more than one occasion that he feels that their descriptions of India must be modified in the light of what his contemporaries learned from actually being there.[810] And, like the secular historians, Maffei interrupts his narrative of the Portuguese conquest from time to time to titillate his readers with stories—about swordfish so huge that they are able to stop a ship at sea, of venomous serpents, and of bats which possess "the snout and teeth of a fox."[811] But not everything about India is weird and unbelievable to Maffei. He also enjoys giving a somewhat imaginative description of Ceylon as an earthly paradise, the beautiful pleasure gardens of the Nāyars in Malabar, and the jewels, rich dress, and costly ceremonies prized by the upper classes everywhere.

In the last decade of the sixteenth century, there is a revival of general interest in India which the newly published biographies and letters of Xavier helped to promote in Europe. Most important to the new wave of optimism, however, was the encouraging news from India itself. The three Jesuit missions to Akbar of 1580–83, 1591, and 1595–1605 stirred hopes in Europe that the Christian conquest of the Mughul empire, the greatest kingdom in India, had finally come to be within the realm of reality. Simultaneously it should be remembered, Christian fortunes were also improving in China where the Jesuit penetration was being slowly advanced by Ricci, Valignano, and others. Though a few setbacks had been experienced by the Christians in Japan, these reverses were still outshone in Europe in the last decade of the century by the triumphal tour of the Japanese embassy of 1584–86. In the Philippines, too, progress was marked. Though the united Spanish and Portuguese empire had suffered maritime defeats at the hands of the Dutch and English Protestants, the fortunes of Philip II seemed to be improving in the non-European world, and in Asia particularly, largely through the efforts of the religious Orders. The grand work which Xavier had begun a half century before seemed to be bearing fruits in India and China, the two great Asian civilizations which the Christian Europeans had hitherto found so much difficulty in penetrating.

Information about Akbar's realm, or the land of the great "Mogor," slowly appeared in published form in Europe. A short account of the first Jesuit mission was published in Paris in 1582 based upon the letters of Father Rudolf Aquaviva and others.[812] Notice of this mission was also included in the official

---

[809] For example, see *ibid.*, II, 111–23.
[810] *Ibid.*, I, 211.   [811] *Ibid.*, pp. 78–79.
[812] *Nouveaux advis de l'estat du Christianisme ès pays et royaulmes des Indes Orientales et Jappon,* (Paris, 1582), pp. 1–4.

Litterae annuae (pp. 111–12) for 1582. Nothing further is heard in Europe about Akbar until news of the second mission of 1591 reached there. In the following year extracts from the letters of the Provincial in Goa about "Mogor" were published in Italian at Rome by the Jesuit, Father Spitelli.[813] And his compendium quickly appeared in Latin translation at Antwerp (1593) and in French at Lyon (1594). It was not, however, until three years later that a little book appeared which gave substantial data on northern India and the court of Akbar.

Giovanni Battista Peruschi (1525–98), an Italian Jesuit who apparently had never visited Asia, prepared and published a summary of what was known in 1597 about Akbar's realm. His study consisting of two parts is entitled *Informatione del regno et stato del Gran Re di Mogor, della sua persona, qualita, & costumi, & congretture della sua conversione alla nostra santa fede....*[814] The first section is based mainly upon a *Relaçam ...*[815] (Account of Akbar) prepared by Father Monserrate at Goa in 1582 shortly after his return from the first mission to Akbar's court. Monserrate had received instructions before leaving Goa in 1579 that he should keep a diary of his experiences in the Mughul empire. For the next two-and-a-half years he faithfully recorded his experiences every evening. Upon his return to Goa a summary of his diary was prepared for dispatch to Europe.[816] While Peruschi faithfully gives the substance of the *Relaçam*, he reorganized it, presented it in his own language, and modified it with materials taken from letters dealing with the second mission of 1591.[817] Following his narrative, Peruschi reproduces in his second part the texts of four letters[818] written in 1595 by the members of the third mission as forwarded to Europe by the Provincial at Goa. French translations of Peruschi quickly appeared at Besançon (1597) and Paris (1598), and in 1598 at Mainz German and Latin versions came off the press.

Several other works in Italian and French reproduced parts of Peruschi's

[813] *Ragguaglio d'alcune missioni dell'Indie Orientali e Occidentali cavato da alcuni avvisi scritti gli anni 1590 et 1591.* Extracts from the Latin version in English translation may be found in the *Journal of the Asiatic Society of Bengal*, LXV (1896), 62–63.

[814] G. B. Peruschi, *Informatione del regno et stato del Gran Re di Mogor, della sua persona, qualita, & costumi, & congretture della sua conversione alla nostra santa fede* ... (Rome, 1597). In the same year Peruschi had a revised version published at Brescia and added to it a map of India and the Far East. The imprimatur to the Brescia edition indicates that the Jesuit General, Claude Acquaviva, himself checked Peruschi's summary and published letters against the original materials possessed by the Society. Further references are to the revised Brescia edition of 1597.

[815] *Relaçam do Equebar Rei dos Mogores* existed in three manuscripts until the nineteenth century, but today the only one which is known is in the possession of the Society. An English translation of this lone manuscript was published by H. Hosten, S. J., in the *Journal of the Asiatic Society of Bengal*, VIII (1912), 185–221.

[816] Maclagan, *op. cit.* (n. 618), pp. 149–50.

[817] He cites (p. 5) just two sources: letters from "Mogor" dated 1582 and 1592 (?). One of the letters most generally quoted on the second embassy, and one of those probably used by Peruschi, is that of Pedro Martinez (November 1590 or 1591). For details of publication see Streit, *op. cit.* (n. 647), p. 282. Text is in Eglauer (ed.), *op. cit.* (n. 786), III, 112–16.

[818] These four letters are also available in German translation in Eglauer (ed.), *op. cit.* (n. 786), III, 136–68.

narrative of Mughul India before the end of the sixteenth century.[819] In 1597, the *Litterae annuae* (pp. 567–73), also summarized the progress being made by the Jesuits in northern India. Three letters from the third mission penned in Lahore were published in 1598 in a collection prepared by the Portuguese Jesuit, Amador Rebello (d. 1622).[820] One of these, written by Jerome Xavier, is similar to one reproduced in Peruschi, while a second of 1596 seems not to have been published elsewhere in the sixteenth century.[821] Rebello also provides a lengthy letter on the condition of the Indian mission from the Provincial of Goa, Francisco Cabral, to the General, written on December 16, 1596, which seems never to have been printed by another collector.[822]

Castanheda was the first European writer to comment at length on the advent of the Mughuls in northern India, and his story ends abruptly in 1540.[823] Thereafter, Europe appears to have been left in the dark about the subsequent activities of the Mughuls until the appearance of Peruschi's book in 1597. The Italian Jesuit, apparently unaware of Castanheda's earlier work, provides a systematic description of Hindustan under Akbar, exclusively from the Jesuit sources. It should by no means be assumed, however, that Peruschi or his sources are primarily concerned with religious matters. Rather the Jesuits seek quite consciously to describe methodically what they have been able to learn through native informants (including Akbar himself) and from their own experiences about the geography, organization, administration, and economy of Akbar's extended realm as it appeared around 1582, or about twenty years after the beginning of Akbar's personal rule. Naturally, they also show a profound interest in the personality and beliefs of Akbar, particularly since their missionary endeavor was aimed primarily at his conversion.

"Mahometto Zelaldim Echebar" (Akbar) in Peruschi's italianized form of his name, is the eighth descendant of Tamerlane and a native of "Chaquata" (Chaghata) which "lies between Tartary and Persia to the north, while India is more to the east of it."[824] The common language of Chaghata is Turkish but different from that spoken in Turkey; the court language is Persian which is not pronounced like the Persian of Persia. Chaghata borders on its Tartary side with the Uzbeks whose first ruler was Jenghis Khan. The Uzbek ruler in power, Abdullah Khan, is a descendant of Jenghis Khan and he governs the region from

[819] For example, *Appresso discipolo* (Verona, 1597) and F. B. Th., *Advis moderne de l'estat et grand royaume de Mogor . . . Jouxte la copie imprimée à Rome depuis un mois, par Loys Zanneti* (Paris, 1598).

[820] Amador Rebello, *Compendio de algunas cartas que este anno de 97, vierão dos Padres da Companhia de Iesu, que residim na India, & Corto do Grão Mogor, & nos Reynos da China et Japão, no Brasil, em que se contem varias cousas* (Lisbon, 1598). This large collection of letters which Streit (*op. cit.* [n. 649], p. 295) lists but neglects to analyze has not been used by the standard authorities on the Mughul mission. My references are to the copy preserved in the National Library at Madrid.

[821] Xavier's letter dated 1596 (in Rebello, *op. cit.* [n. 820], pp. 70–71) is not listed either in Streit or in the more recent list of Xavier letters compiled in A. Camps, *Jerome Xavier and the Muslims of the Mogul Empire* (Schöneck-Beckenried, 1957), p. 40.

[822] Streit, *op. cit.* (n. 647), p. 291.

[823] See above, pp. 420–25.

[824] Peruschi, *op. cit.* (n. 814), pp. 5–6.

Samarkand and Bokhara. This family of rulers, to whom Akbar is related, was originally heathen but had recently accepted Islam.

The kingdom of "Mogor," according to Peruschi, is bounded on the west by Hither India (region of the Indus) and on the northwest by Persia; on the east by Further India (region of the Ganges and eastward) which borders on China; across the mountains to the north is the great kingdom of Tartary;[825] on the southwest is the kingdom of Calicut and the sea; and on the southeast lies the Bay of Bengal. "Mogor," or the territory which Akbar rules, is not just one kingdom but many kingdoms joined together. Its principal territories which are situated between the Indus and the Ganges are Hindustan, Agra, the very ancient state of Māndū (Malwa), Lahore, Cambay, and Bengal.[826] Its chief cities are Cambay, Delhi, Lahore, Multan, Māndū, Patna, Jaunpur, and Ahmadābād. Some of these cities are as large as Lisbon, and Māndū with its great and beautiful edifices, invites comparison with ancient Rome.

The Mughul empire although powerful and vast (its area is 600 by 400 leagues),[827] is clearly not to be feared as a maritime rival. Akbar, even after conquering Gujarat in 1573, had only the southwestern ports of Surat, Broach, Kambhāyat, and Gogra for his use.[828] Hindustan is watered by eleven rivers, only some of which connect the hinterland with the harbors under Akbar's control. The Tāpti passes through Surat, the Narbada serves Broach, and the Chambal flows into the Jumna which passes into the Ganges which, in turn, empties into the Bay of Bengal. Five other rivers, the Sutlej, Biah, Ravi, Chanab, and Bihat (or Jhelam) are all identified correctly as affluents of the Indus.[829]

To the northeast, in the mountains called "Kumaon" (Himalayas) by the natives, there live a heathen people called "Botthantis" (Tibetans).[830] These people are white, have no Moors in their land, and are independent of Akbar's political control. They have no king of their own, but are ruled by sorcerers. Their livelihood is derived from the manufacture of felt, which they bring to India and sell at the markets of Negariott (Kangra) and Kalamur. Since they are snowbound the rest of the year, they come down from the mountains only from June to September. Their garments are made from felt and are worn until they rot and fall off. They never wash their hands because they believe it is improper to defile so pure and beautiful an element as water. While they live in clans, a man has but one wife and does not remarry if she dies. They fight on foot with bows, arrows, and swords. Even though their dishes and bowls are made from human skulls,[831] they are not cannibals and are charitably inclined towards outsiders. Monserrate's report on the Tibetans, as summarized by

---

825 *Ibid.*, p. 6.   826 *Ibid.*, pp. 7–8.

827 *Ibid.*, p. 14. Or 2,400 by 1,600 miles.

828 *Ibid.*, p. 13.

829 For details on these identifications see Hosten, *loc. cit.* (n. 815), pp. 206–07.

830 For identification see *ibid.*, pp. 219–20, n. 4; and also Peruschi, *op. cit.* (n. 814), pp. 10–12.

831 For a picture of a Tibetan cup made from a skull see Sir Charles Bell, *Tibet, Past and Present* (Oxford, 1924), facing p. 36.

Peruschi, is to my knowledge the first substantial information on this mountain people to be printed in Europe.[832]

Details about Akbar's appearance, personality, and interests run like a thread throughout Peruschi's narrative. He is described as being of medium height, broad-shouldered, and about forty years of age (which is correct, since he was born in 1542).

His complexion is dark, his eyes are small . . . ; his nostrils are broad and on the left one he has a small wart; he carries his head somewhat inclined to the right; with the exception of his moustache which he keeps short and trimmed, he shaves his beard completely. . . .[833]

He lets his hair grow long, wears a turban, and adorns his head with pearls and precious stones. His clothes are costly and elegant and he wears slippers of his own design. He always keeps a dagger in his girdle and either wears a sword or has one near at hand. While Akbar is described as being prudent, wise, simple, brave, and kind, he is also disposed to be grave and melancholy and is endowed with a slow but violent temper. Although he is unable to read or write, he is intellectually curious and constantly keeps men of letters in his company. While perpetually busy with affairs of state, he delights in hunting wild animals, playing polo on horseback, witnessing fights of beast against beast and man against man, and participating in dances and gymnastics. Watching jesters and trained animals are also among his favorite pastimes, and he especially likes to make pigeons fly and dance in the air.[834]

The capital, Fatehpur Sīkrī, built by Akbar six leagues from Agra, has great and sumptuous palaces in which he maintains a huge court and large numbers of servants. Prominent in court affairs are his three sons and two daughters. The eldest son is "Scieco"[835] (Salīm), the middle son is called "Pahari" (nickname of Murād), and the youngest is "Dân or Danial" (Dāmyāl). Twenty gentile kings, as important as the Zamorin, serve in Akbar's retinue; some, his vassals by conquest, are forced to reside at the court, while others are there voluntarily.[836] Many other rulers pay tribute to him even though they do not reside at court. In choosing his own officials Akbar makes use of men of talent without regard to their origins. The *kotwāl* of the court, who is similar to a chief bailiff, "was originally a fencing master," while Akbar's secretary was once a poor Mullah. Commoners elevated to high office are required to wear ensignia of their former craft or trade, possibly to keep before them a reminder of their lowly origins and of their indebtedness to the ruler. Though Akbar takes counsel with his advisers, he generally makes decisions by himself.

[832] For references by earlier European writers to Tibet see Yule and Burnell, *op. cit.* (n. 10), pp. 698–99. For the relationship of this information on Tibet to the search for Cathay and to the later Jesuit mission in Tibet see Maclagan, *op. cit.* (n. 618), pp. 335–38.

[833] Peruschi, *op. cit.* (n. 814), p. 7.

[834] For a description of the art of pigeon-flying, see Hosten, *loc. cit.* (n. 815), p. 196, n. 3.

[835] "Scieco" is also called "Sciecogiò" (Peruschi, *op. cit.* [n. 814], p. 7), the suffix "gio" being an honorific similar to "Don" which means "spirit." *Ji* or *jiu*, as it is still pronounced in northern India, means "spirit" and it is used as an honorific. See Hosten, *loc. cit.*, pp. 202–03, n. 6.

[836] Peruschi, *op. cit.* (n. 814), p. 9.

In transacting business, Akbar appears twice each day in two great squares. One of these squares is open to all people of distinction; admission to the other square is limited to his military leaders, the literati (including the Jesuits), and foreigners. The ruler settles most of this public business just by standing and talking to the people concerned. Petitioners are presented to the king by a group who might be termed masters of ceremony. When the king speaks, scribes write down his orders, presumably to keep the records straight. In more private meetings, Akbar either sits on a cushion in Moorish fashion or in a Western-type chair.[837] He administers his finances with the greatest care, but Monserrate (and hence Peruschi) avoids discussion of how this is done because it is too lengthy a matter.[838]

Much more detail is included on the administration of justice. "The King, his justices, and his magistrates govern by reason and without differences among them; they adjudicate all kinds of controversies and questions and give their decisions verbally rather than in writing."[839] In addition to ordinary magistrates, the king appoints appelate justices and bailiffs who run the court system. The king himself, when present, administers both civil and criminal justice for high and low alike. The death penalty may never be carried out, if he is available, without his permission. Those found guilty of major crimes are beheaded, impaled on sharp stakes, or trampled to death by elephants. Rape and adultery are classified as crimes worthy of impalement or beheading. Convicted robbers have their hands cut off, and those guilty of minor offenses are whipped with the lash.[840]

The Jesuits, like Castanheda earlier, are greatly interested in the composition, organization, and effectiveness of the Mughul military forces. Monserrate, the tutor of Sultan Murād, received permission to accompany his pupil on Akbar's Kabul campaign of 1581, and so was in an excellent position to study the military system of the Mughuls as well as this particular campaign.[841] Akbar's army is a mélange of different peoples (Mughuls, Persians, Turkimales, Gujaratis, Pathans, Hindustanis, Moors, and gentiles), but the king seems to have greatest confidence in his gentile troops.[842] In times of internal order and stability, Akbar has many captains who can muster from ten to fourteen thousand horses and many elephants, as well as lesser officers who can put from six to eight thousand horses and some elephants into the field. Akbar himself maintains fifty thousand elephants which are stationed at various strategic locations in his empire.[843] In addition, he has a personal army of forty thousand cavalry

[837] *Ibid.*, pp. 24–25.

[838] Hosten, *loc. cit.* (n. 815), p. 200.

[839] Peruschi, *op. cit.* (n. 814), pp. 23–24.

[840] *Ibid.*, pp. 22–23.

[841] On Monserrate's writings as a source for the Kabul campaign see Maclagan, *op. cit.* (n. 618), p. 35.

[842] Peruschi, *op. cit.* (n. 814), p. 18.

[843] This information is not in Monserrate's report (see Hosten, *loc. cit.* [n. 815], p. 210, n. 2). Peruschi (*op. cit.* [n. 814], p. 16) probably incorporated this data from the letter of Pedro Martinez (1590–91). See Eglauer (ed.), *op. cit.* (n. 786), III, 115.

and an infinite number of foot soldiers. Workmen are constantly kept busy manufacturing arms for these vast forces, and Akbar is reputed to have artillery of fine quality.

Peruschi itemizes some of the conquests of Akbar's Mughul predecessors, and recounts how early in his reign he defeated the Pathans (Afghans) and made himself master of Bengal.[844] But Akbar's control of Bengal and Cambay is seen as far from secure, for in 1582 he faces major revolts in both areas. The attack of 1581 on the Portuguese outpost of Damão is attributed to the willful and unsanctioned action of one of these recalcitrants of Cambay, Qutb-ud-dīn Khan, the Sarkar of Broach.[845] The campaign against Akbar's brother in Kabul is said by Peruschi to have begun in February, 1582, but this date is clearly incorrect and is probably a misprint for 1581.[846] It is clear that the Jesuits, while respecting the might of Akbar's arms, were very much aware of the fact that he was constantly threatened with uprisings, particularly on the distant fringes of his empire.

Possibly this state of unrest can be attributed, though Peruschi does not say so explicitly, to Akbar's method of administering conquered territories. "The king is lord of all and nobody owns anything of his own except that which is bestowed upon him."[847] Lands conquered are parceled out to selected lords and captains who receive an annual salary and who are obliged to maintain elephants, camels, and horses all of which are sent to the royal palace each year for the king to inspect. The royal vassals, who can be removed or shifted about at the king's pleasure, place the towns and villages of their territories under the command of select subordinates who administer them. When a captain dies, his estate passes to the king. From this source, as well as from his control over trade, Akbar receives great revenues.

Peruschi closes his account of the realm of "Mogor" with a historical discussion of Akbar's meeting with the Portuguese and the development of his interest in Christianity. It was Antonio Cabral's embassy of March, 1573, to Surat, when Akbar was besieging the city, that first brought the Portuguese directly in touch with the Mughul ruler. Evidently Cabral made a favorable impression upon Akbar by his courteous and correct behavior. The ruler's interest in Christianity was aroused by his hearing news of the activities of the two Jesuits who had begun working in Bengal in 1576, by the visit of Pedro Tavares, the Portuguese captain of Bengal, to Fatehpur Sīkrī in 1577, and by the visit of Julian Pereira at his court beginning in 1578. It was probably at Pereira's suggestion that Akbar sent his letter of invitation of December, 1578, to the Jesuits at Goa. Though Akbar clearly favored Christianity over Islam, the Jesuits are forced to admit that when they left him he was still in a quandary about his beliefs. They also indicate in a number of places that his Moorish

---

[844] Peruschi, *op. cit.* (n. 814), p. 14.
[845] *Ibid.*, p. 15.
[846] See Hosten, *loc. cit.* (n. 815), p. 210, n. 4.
[847] Peruschi, *op. cit.* (n. 814), p. 19.

subjects were rebellious over his hostility to Islam, and so the Jesuits seem inclined to attribute their failure to political causes rather than to Akbar's personal unwillingness to consider Christianity the only true religion. Still the Jesuits admit that he is "dubious about all types of faith and holds that there is no divinely sanctioned faith, since he finds in all forms something to offend his reason and intelligence."[848] Even with this evaluation before them, the Jesuits and their Portuguese supporters apparently continued to hope for a change of heart since they refused to ignore the second and third invitations to send missionaries to his court.

The first three letters from the third mission to appear in print in Europe deal primarily with the experiences and observations of the Jesuits while in Cambay.[849] Delayed there for more than twenty days waiting for a caravan to take them to Lahore, the headquarters of Akbar for approximately sixteen years, the missionaries, especially Manuel Pinheiro, made good use of their time to gather data on the northwestern part of India.[850] All three letters are dated 1595 and are from the pen of Pinheiro; the first was written from Cambay and the other two from Lahore. In recent histories of Gujarat these letters have been used to supplement the otherwise meager sources available on this period.[851]

The Jesuits shipped out from Goa on December 3, 1594, stopped over in Damão, and arrived in Cambay just before Christmas. Here they commemorated the Feast of the Nativity with the one hundred Portuguese residing there. Well received by the governor and some leading citizens of Cambay, Pinheiro and his colleagues set about observing the conditions of life in the city to determine how receptive its inhabitants might be to the introduction of Christianity. They quickly concluded that the majority group were heathens inclined to piety, devotion, and charity even though their beliefs were clearly in error. Such optimistic conclusions were probably unwarranted inasmuch as the Jesuits were possibly inclined to confuse curiosity and tolerance with genuine interest.[852] And, even before leaving Cambay, Pinheiro directed a letter to Nicolas Pimenta, the Provincial in Goa, to let him know that a plentiful harvest might be reaped in Gujarat.

In this letter and more especially in the two which followed from Lahore, Pinheiro describes the city of Cambay. The "first city in Gujarat is not dissimilar to Evora in Portugal"[853] and it is within the jurisdiction of Akbar. Cambay is praised for its fine streets and buildings, and Pinheiro observes that the streets are closed off at night with tight gates similar to the city gates of Europe. Water is in short supply in Cambay even though the city has great tanks in which water is stored during the winter (the rainy season). These reservoirs, like

848 *Ibid.*, p. 32.
849 *Ibid.*, pp. 41–54, 60–71; Rebello, *op. cit.* (n. 820), pp. 49–55, gives an extract from the Pinheiro letter. Also reproduced in Eglauer (ed.), *op. cit.* (n. 786), III, 136–48, 153–68.
850 But see above, pp. 395–96, for the secular accounts.
851 For example, see Commissariat, *op. cit.* (n. 400), II, 267–73.
852 *Ibid.*, II, 270.
853 Peruschi, *op. cit.* (n. 814), p. 60.

many of the great houses of Cambay, are costly and beautiful structures. Pinheiro also tells of a visit to a public hospital which was built to take care of sick and crippled birds of all kinds. Somewhat aghast by this discovery, the Jesuit ironically remarks: "So they have hospitals for birds but not for humans who are generally left uncared for to die."[854]

Cambay is a center at which faithful Hindus gather, sometimes forty thousand of them, to undertake pilgrimages to the Ganges in Bengal.[855] It is their belief that bathing in its water is sanctifying and that the fortunate individuals who drink of it at the approach of death are certain of salvation. Pinheiro met a rich heathen devotee named "Gadacham" who had once journeyed to the Ganges, weighed his mother three times in the river, once with silver, then with precious stones, and then with gold, and finally distributed all of this wealth as alms to the poor. When in Lahore, Pinheiro met a prince from Bengal who assured him that sometimes three to four hundred thousand pilgrims would congregate along the banks of the Ganges.[856]

The Jesuits were escorted about Cambay by a native called "Babausa" who acted as their interpreter. "Babausa" was very congenial to Christian teachings himself and the Jesuits visited with him in his home which was constructed along Portuguese lines. It was probably through "Babausa" that the Jesuits met and talked with several of the city's notables whom they sounded out about their beliefs and their attitudes towards Christianity. This man also assured the Jesuits that the heathen doctrines were frivolous fabrications and that Cambay was awaiting Christianity.

"Babausa" also introduced the Jesuits to a group of religious men whom Pinheiro refers to as "Verteas."[857] There can be little question on the basis of context that this term, whatever its etymology, refers to the Jains, and especially their monks (*yatis*), of Gujarat.[858] The Jesuits visited a community of about fifty *yatis* who were dressed in white, an indication that they belonged to the sect known as *Svetāmbaras* (meaning, clad in white).[859] These Jain monks wear nothing on their heads and they pluck out the hairs of their chins and heads leaving only a tuft of hair on the crown. They live in poverty and accept in

---

[854] *Ibid.*, p. 52.

[855] *Ibid.*, pp. 61–62.

[856] *Ibid.*, p. 62.

[857] On the etymology and meaning of this word see T. Zachariae, "Vertea, eine Bezeichnung der Jains," *Wiener Zeitschrift für die Kunde des Morgenlandes*, XXIV (1910), 341. He derives it from Sanskrit, *Vratin*; Hindi, *Barti*; Gujarati, *Varti*. These words mean "saint" or "devotee." Dalgado (*op. cit.* [n. 44], II, 413) derives it from *Vrātya*, a Sanskrit term applied to Hindus who are expelled from their castes for not observing the *Saniskaras*, especially the rite of investiture with the sacred thread. For an identification of the *Vrātyas* with the Jains see J. Prasad Jain, *Jainism, the Oldest Living Religion* (Benares, 1951), p. 17.

[858] For a summary of what other Portuguese writers have to say about the "Verteas" see W. Caland and A. A. Fokker, "Due oude Portugeesche verhandelingen over het Hindoeisme," *Verhandelingen der koninklijke Akademie van Wetenschappen* (Afdeeling Letterkunde, nieuwe reeks), XVI (1916), 49–50.

[859] For a recent description of this rather unorthodox and lax monastic group see H. von Glasenapp, *Der Jainismus, eine indische Erlösungsreligion* (Berlin, 1925), p. 341.

alms only what is necessary for their daily sustenance. They possess no wives. They drink only hot water, because water has a soul that will be killed if it is drunk without being heated. Since it is a great crime to kill souls, they also carry cotton brooms with which they sweep the ground before walking or sitting on it to keep from taking the life and killing the soul of some small living creature. In their midst are boys of eight and nine, dedicated at this tender age to the religious life, who look like angels and are more European than Indian in color. All of them wear a cloth four fingers in width across their mouths which is hung over their ears by slits in the cloth. This face covering is designed to keep bugs from accidentally entering their mouths and being killed.

Their supreme prelate is supposed to have one hundred thousand believers under his obedience, and every year a new prelate is elected. Jain beliefs are written down in books in the Gujarati language. From these it can be gathered that they believe that the world was created many hundreds of thousands of years ago and that during this time God sent to the earth twenty-three apostles. More than two thousand years ago, when their third era began, a twenty-fourth apostle was sent who, it seems, gave them their doctrines.[860]

Shortly after the Jesuits arrived in Cambay, Sultan Murād, Akbar's second son who was then the Viceroy of Gujarat, appeared in the city with a large army. He was on his way to make war in the Deccan against the kingdom of Ahmadnagar, and was about to join forces near Surat with another of Akbar's armies under Khanan Khan. The prince had with him a body of 4,000 to 5,000 horses (he was said to have sent 20,000 ahead), 400 elephants, 700 camels, 400 to 500 dromedaries, 4,000 oxen, and 15 large, 4 medium, and a number of smaller pieces of artillery.[861] Leaving his army outside the city, Murād stayed with his retinue in the "castle" of Cambay. As a boy, the prince had studied with Father Monserrate at Akbar's court. So, on learning of the presence of the Jesuits in Cambay, he summoned them to an audience at the citadel on Christmas eve, 1594. He received the fathers affectionately and told them that he was bound for Surat on his way to attack the Deccan. Before leaving Cambay, he bled the city with impositions through which he obtained a large sum of gold.

After Murād had traveled about one league (4 miles) away from Cambay toward Surat, he again called the Jesuits into his presence early on the morning of the Feast of Circumcision (January 1, 1595). Here he held an early durbar in his camp at which the Jesuits made their reverence to him and then retired to join his attendants "who were standing as silent as statues with their eyes fixed on him."[862] The formal assemblage being over, Murād retired into a tent

860 Pinheiro's letter from Lahore (dated from internal evidence as of January 9, 1595) containing this discussion of "Vertea" practices and teachings was published in the sixteenth century in Peruschi *op. cit.* (n. 814), pp. 52–54 and in Rebello, *op. cit.* (n. 820), pp. 53–55. Pinheiro's understanding of Jain traditions is essentially correct as far as it goes. He accurately reports the Jain tradition that the twenty-fourth apostle (or teacher), Mahavira, died around 500 B.C. (for discussion see Majumdar et al., *op. cit.* [n. 6], pp. 85–86) or about 2,100 years before Pinheiro's date of writing.
861 Pinheiro's letter from Cambay of 1595 in Peruschi, *op. cit.* (n. 814), pp. 46–47.
862 Rebello, *op. cit.* (n. 820), p. 47.

pavilion which enclosed a spacious courtyard. The sultan's tent stood in the middle of this square and was open on all sides and contained a small couch on which Murād reclined. He held a long conversation with the Jesuits and asked them many things about various lands, and whether Portugal had snow and wild animals for the hunt. At the end of the interview, Murād presented the Jesuits with a sum of money for their journey to Akbar, and to the Armenian who accompanied them he gave three carts with six bullocks and three fine horses. The prince then mounted a very large elephant and ascended from it to a still larger one that looked like a tower, and then continued on his journey. The fathers returned to Cambay to prepare for their trip with the impression that Murād was no friend of the Muslims, that he was primarily devoted to hunting and traveling, and was too much under the influence of youthful advisers who had already corrupted him.[863]

Around the middle of January, 1595, the Jesuits left Cambay, where Pinheiro had felt as at home as in Portugal, for the long trek by caravan to Lahore. They could not go through Sind as originally planned, and so were forced to take the longer route by way of Ahmadābād, Pathan, and Rājputāna. In Ahmadābād they had to remain longer than anticipated, apparently to wait for more of the caravan to assemble. Again Pinheiro used his time well by making observations in the sacred city of the Jains and capital of Gujarat with its great temples, tombs, and historical associations. Though Pinheiro had seen many Yogis performing penances, he was particularly impressed by a penitent of Ahmadābād. This Yogi had set himself up in the great square between the Bhadia towers and the Three Gates. The people who flocked to see him practice his austerities caused more commotion than was customarily to be seen on the quay of Lisbon when ships arrived there from India.[864] When Sultan Murād invited him to an audience, the Yogi had the temerity to respond that the prince should visit him. Once Murād heard this reply, he had the Yogi seized, soundly whipped, and driven out of the city. Pinheiro was impressed also in Ahmadābād by the care lavished upon the sacred cows. On one occasion he reports having seen the devout bring fresh grass for, stand watch over, and keep the flies off a dying cow. While the Jesuit was obviously disdainful and intolerant of such heathen practices, he was clearly appreciative of the architectural beauties of the city. He comments at length on some tombs outside the city which it appears from internal evidence were the tombs at Sirkej built in the middle of the fifteenth century. Pinheiro reports that he never saw anything more beautiful than these tombs and concludes that they are "a work of barbarians which is not at all barbarous."[865] In the capital of Gujarat, Pinheiro also met many Moors of both sexes who had come from deep in the interior of India and were pilgrims on their way to Mecca. He reports that since the Prophet

---

[863] Peruschi, *op. cit.* (n. 814), p. 47; Commissariat, *op. cit.* (n. 400), pp. 271–72.

[864] Peruschi, *op. cit.* (n. 814), p. 61.

[865] *Ibid.*, p. 63. Cf. the plan of the Sirkej tombs and mosque in J. Fergusson, *History of Indian and Eastern Architecture* (New York, 1899), II, 146.

ordained that no unmarried woman might make the journey to Mecca, the Muslims of India contract convenience marriages which are dissolved when the pilgrims return home.[866]

The caravan in which the Jesuits were traveling left Ahmadābād on March 23 and arrived on the evening of March 24, the day before Easter, in Pathan. Three days later, after having celebrated Easter mass and listening to confessions, the Jesuits left Pathan and began the arduous journey to Lahore where they finally arrived on May 5. Most of this part of the journey was through deserts and regions where the heat was stifling, water difficult to obtain, and foodstuffs in short supply. In the course of it they went through numerous large cities which were devastated, especially the mosques therein.[867] Since there were no rivers, water was drawn from wells so deep that it had to be raised by bullocks. When they did come across water in the open it was as salty as sea water, "a fact," writes Pinheiro, "which I would not have believed had I not experienced it myself." [868] At no time was there sufficient water for their huge caravan which included 400 camels, 80 to 100 ox-carts, 100 horse-carts, and a multitude of poor people on foot.[869] Every morning the captain of the caravan ordered the kettle drums to be beaten as the signal to break camp. On the route a scout was sent out ahead of the caravan to show the way. The entire journey from Goa to Lahore took the Jesuits five months and two days.

On the morning (May 6) after their arrival in Lahore, Akbar greeted them, spoke two or three words to them in Portuguese, and asked about the health of the king of Portugal (Philip II). Then, after this public meeting, the Jesuits were given a special audience before Akbar, his twenty-five year old son, Prince Salīm, and some of his chief retainers. The Mughul ruler then had a portrait of the Virgin brought in and he held it in his own arms to show it to the Jesuits. After the fathers had knelt in reverence before the portrait, Akbar showed them that he was also a collector of European books. Aside from two Bibles, Akbar's collection included a number of works by St. Thomas Aquinas and other eminent churchmen as well as the *Commentaries* of Albuquerque and the Constitutions of the Society of Jesus.[870] The king graciously offered to lend the books to the missionaries, and also suggested that they apply themselves to the study of Persian so that he might speak to them without an interpreter. At a second private interview on the evening of the same day, Akbar asked them questions about the king of Portugal and about the various kingdoms of Europe. He ordered that a house be provided for them near to his own palace, and urged them to look around for a suitable place. At midnight, after receiving a second admonition to learn Persian, the travel-weary Jesuits went to their quarters.[871]

A few days later, Akbar, acting through Prince Salīm, established the Jesuits

---

[866] Peruschi, *op. cit.* (n. 814), p. 64.

[867] *Ibid.*, p. 65.   [868] *Ibid.*

[869] Letter of Xavier of 1595 from Lahore in Rebello, *op. cit.* (n. 820), p. 56.

[870] List of books given in Peruschi, *op. cit.* (n. 814), pp. 65–66. For further discussion of them see Maclagan, *op. cit.* (n. 618), pp. 191–92.

[871] Rebello, *op. cit.* (n. 820), p. 58.

in certain houses on the royal grounds in which he had once lived himself. These houses were located close to the Ravi River and beneath the windows of the king's fortress. "This river," writes Xavier, "is called 'beautiful' and deserves its name; it has sweet water and is almost the same size as the Tagus."[872] The Ravi may be crossed by a bridge of boats and many vessels sail on it constantly carrying an infinity of supplies. On the opposite side of the river, a tent city stands where the merchants from other countries bring their goods to sell. In the middle of the river there is a place like an island where a great crowd of people wait every morning to see Akbar show himself at one of the windows of the fortress. After bowing to him, the crowd amuses itself by watching animals fight. "A fight between elephants," remarks Xavier, "is something to see...."[873] Fifty men who carry torches guard the bank of the river by day and the same number patrol it at night, evidently to keep intruders from entering the royal grounds from the riverside.

At their residence beside the river the fathers built a temporary chapel large enough to accommodate the Armenian Christians residing in Lahore. While all others were forbidden admission to the royal grounds, these Christians were permitted to visit the Jesuits and attend chapel there. By September, Akbar had already given the Jesuits oral permission to build a church. When they asked for this promise in writing, he answered tartly that he was a living document and that they should go ahead with their plans.[874] Prince Salīm acted as an advocate of the Jesuits in their dealings with his father and showed real personal interest in their religious activities. As a token of his regard for their well-being, he sent them a box of snow on a summer's day when it was stifling hot.[875]

While Akbar was personally congenial to the Jesuits and curious about their faith, they quickly discerned, as had their predecessors, that his personal conversion was not to be expected. After being in Lahore just a short while, Xavier wrote:

We are very confused ... when we try to find out the real intentions of the King—and we do not understand him. On the one hand he makes much over our religion as well as over the images of Christ and Our Lady and at the same time abominates Mafumede [Mohammed] and all his works; yet, on the other hand, he follows the ways of the Gentiles, adoring the sun in the morning and praying at night, and also at noon and midnight. The Gentiles have much influence over him, and ... he has himself revered as a saint. It seems that his heart cannot find peace in any religion. He seems pleased with the praises given to him as a saint, and some Gentiles call him a god. It seems that Our Lord sent him to these lands to wipe out the religion of Mafumede from the hearts of men....[876]

---

[872] *Ibid.*, p. 59. Pinheiro (in Peruschi, *op. cit.* [n. 814], p. 66) says that the houses were fifteen feet from a river which is the size of a lake. For further information on their residence see the extract from unpublished Xavier letters of 1596 in H. Hosten, "Mirza Zu-L-Quarnain," Pt. II of "Jesuit Letters and Allied Papers on Mogor, Tibet, Bengal and Burma," *Memoirs of the Asiatic Society of Bengal*, V (1916), 174.

[873] Rebello, *op. cit.* (n. 820), p. 59.

[874] Peruschi, *op. cit.* (n. 814), p. 69. [875] Rebello, *op. cit.* (n. 820), p. 61.

[876] *Ibid.*, pp. 68–69. The Muslim historians of Akbar's reign never mention the Jesuits. For discussion of the Muslim histories see Vincent A. Smith, *Akbar, the Great Mogul* (Delhi, 1958), pp. 337–44.

In Lahore the Jesuits claim that mosques were torn down or converted into stables and granaries. The public call to prayer and the Koran itself were proscribed. And Akbar, in his determination to root out the baleful influence of the infidels, is reported as going out of his way to offend the Muslims by eating publicly during their fast periods and by bringing pigs into the royal courtyard. On the other hand, Akbar apparently puzzles and troubles the Jesuits by the serious attention he pays to the "Verteas" (Jains) at his court.[877]

Akbar's vassals and the great "presents" which they make to Akbar in the summer of 1595 seem to intrigue Pinheiro. He observes that there are five or six crowned kings and twenty-six royal princes residing at the court. He describes at length the ceremony of investiture to which a petty ruler is subjected upon officially becoming one of Akbar's vassals and he itemizes the tribute paid to the Mughul.[878] Sultan Murād and the King of Bengal also brought expensive presents consisting mainly of elephants to Lahore in this summer. Especially numerous were the gifts which Akbar received on the festival of "Noresa"[879] which he had ordered to be celebrated. "Hardly a day passes," Pinheiro sighs, "on which he does not receive gifts."[880]

The four Jesuits spent most of their first year in their residence by the Ravi studying the Persian language.[881] At first they encountered some difficulty because they had no one to translate the Persian into Portuguese for them. Occasionally Akbar, when he sailed on the river, would embark or disembark almost at their door, and so the Jesuits always went out to welcome and speak with him. The Jesuits also opened a school at their riverside residence which was attended by the sons of some of Akbar's leading vassals and land administrators. Since the Jesuits were not happy with the site initially allocated to them for a church, Akbar finally ordered Malik Ali, one of his bailiffs, to find a satisfactory site within the crowded city of Lahore and to speed the work of construction. Shortly thereafter, Xavier reports: "The foundations have been laid, but the materials are coming a little slowly—but what a wonder that Moors are slowly building a church for Christians in the middle of their chief city."[882] The church was finally completed and formally dedicated on September 7, 1597, in the presence of the governor of Lahore.[883]

In March, 1596, from their riverside residence, the Jesuits were treated to the sight on the opposite shore of a great congregation of Yogis. The Christians were told that the Yogis gathered annually at this time and place. Huddled

---

[877] Peruschi, *op. cit.* (n. 814), p. 70. On the Jain spokesmen at Akbar's court at this time see Commissariat, *op. cit.* (n. 400), II, 238–39.

[878] Peruschi, *op. cit.* (n. 814), pp. 67–68.

[879] Possibly the festival of Narasimha, commemorating one of the incarnations of Vishnu. See Caland and Fokker, *loc. cit.* (n. 858), p. 80.

[880] Peruschi, *op. cit.* (n. 814), p. 67.

[881] Xavier's letter of 1596 in Rebello, *op. cit.* (n. 820), p. 69. Their teacher, according to Smith (*op. cit.* [n. 876], p. 210) was Abu-ul-Fazl, a friend to Akbar and the author of a Persian history of Akbar's reign which was written in about 1595.

[882] Rebello, *op. cit.* (n. 820), p. 72.

[883] L. Guzman, *Historia de las missiones . . .* (Alcalá, 1601), I, 268.

together in groups of ten and twenty, the Yogis filled the plain on the opposite shore as they begged Akbar for alms. The ruler, crowds from the city, and the Jesuits crossed the river to see and talk with them. After two or three days, the Yogis scattered and left as quickly as they had come. Xavier reports that they revere "Babam Adã," [884] or Father Adam, as the creator and the only god. They venerate and worship his picture and hope by blowing buffalo horns that they will somehow blow out their sins. [885]

The best general summary of the Jesuit activities in India and the East Indies is contained in Volume I (pp. 1–273) of L. Guzman's *Historia de las missiones . . .* (Alcalá, 1601). [886] At no time does he cite his authorities directly. Study of his work, however, brings out clearly that he relied only slightly upon secular histories. The materials collected for Xavier's biography, conversations with informants, and the Jesuit letters, constitute his main sources. Guzman presents in narrative form a straightforward statement of what Europe in his day knew of the mission in India on the basis of published and, to a lesser degree, unpublished materials. One of his sources most easily identified (see Guzman, pp. 240–54) is Monserrate's *Relaçam . . .* of the Mughul empire. It appears, however, from textual comparison that the version of the *Relaçam* used by Guzman was shorter and slightly different from the one used by Peruschi, or that he amended it from other materials. [887] It may be, since much of the material on Akbar is similar to the material in Peruschi's and Rebello's collections, that he had the Portuguese, if not the Italian, work on his bookshelf. This surmise is somewhat reinforced by the fact that his account of the condition of the Jesuit colleges in India seems to be derived from the annual report of 1596 prepared by Francisco Cabral, the Provincial, an extract from which is included in Rebello (pp. 4–48). But Guzman, because his account goes beyond these works both in terms of time and detail, obviously relied on other sources, most of which were probably unpublished when he wrote.

Guzman, unlike Maffei, [888] is concerned primarily with the progress of the Jesuit mission in the East and so the two authors supplement each other. The geographical description with which Guzman's first book begins is designed to provide a setting for Xavier's activities in India and the further East. He then recounts at some length the obstacles to the progress of the faith in India: native idolatry, the Moors, the hostility of the Nāyars and other high-caste groups in Malabar, and the control which the Brahmans and Yogis exercise over everyone, from kings to common people. [889] Incidental to this account he

---

[884] See Dalgado, *op. cit.* (n. 44), I, 73–74, under the listing *Baba*, meaning "father." The "Adã" is possibly a misrendering of *Aum*, which is a mystical representation in Yoga teachings of the "Divine Being." For a discussion of the sacred word *Aum* see Abbe J. A. Dubois, *Hindu Manners, Customs and Ceremonies*, trans. H. K. Beauchamp (3d ed.; Oxford, 1906), p. 533.

[885] Rebello, *op. cit.* (n. 820), p. 71.

[886] For general discussion see above, p. 328.

[887] Cf. Hosten, *op. cit.* (n. 815), pp. 187–88, who contends absolutely that Guzman did not use Peruschi's version.

[888] See above, pp. 324–26.

[889] Guzman, *op. cit.* (n. 883), I, 5–7.

naturally is forced to give at least some information about the social and religious beliefs of the Indians. This is followed by a brief description of Goa, and then he launches directly into the career of Xavier from his student days in Paris until his funeral in Malacca.[890]

The second book commences with a survey of the religious situation in Goa after the death of Xavier. Then follows a description of nearby Salsette, its sixty-six villages, and its recalcitrant hostility to the Portuguese and the Jesuits. From the Goa area he shifts his attention to the Fishery Coast and gives somewhat more space to the island of Manaar than is to be found in previous publications.[891] Especially interesting is the systematic presentation which follows of the progress and setbacks of the mission at Quilon, in Travancore, and at Cochin and Calicut. He does not disguise the fact that the Jesuits' position in these territories was closely related to the vagaries of Portugal's political relations with the native rulers. Guzman is somewhat less critical of the Portuguese in his appraisal of the northern settlements of Bassein, Damão, and Diu; he has a tendency to blame Jesuit difficulties in these places upon the Moors and the machinations of the rulers of Cambay. He follows the review of the mission stations with a thorough discussion of the work of St. Thomas in India and the relics of Mylapore, and concludes with a brief account of the Christian followers of St. Thomas in the south.

It is only when Guzman comes to deal with the empire of Vijayanagar, as it was in the late sixteenth century, that he goes beyond what had previously been published in Europe.[892] He discusses the power and extent of Vijayanagar under Venkāta II (reigned *ca.* 1586–1622) and mentions the uprisings of the *Nayakas* of Madura, Tanjore, and Jinjī against him. He describes briefly the city of Chandragiri, Venkāta's capital, as being located in the mountains, possessing a strong fortress, and boasting beautiful and rich palaces. He gives excellent detail on the visits of the Jesuits to Venkāta's court from their residences at the Portuguese outposts of St. Thomas and Goa, and of their receiving permission to build a church at Vellore. He concludes this discussion by describing a religious procession which the Jesuits saw in the city of Tiruvalur.[893] And this information, Guzman affirms, is derived from the letters of 1599, the latest received from the Jesuits in Vijayanagar.[894] He also records a few details on the mission of 1598 to Bengal of Fathers Francisco Fernandes and Domingo de Sousa,[895] another event which had previously not been known in Europe.

Guzman devotes more than thirty pages (240–71) of his third book to the three Jesuit missions to Akbar. While he adds little that is new regarding the first mission, he emphasizes, perhaps more than his sources justify, that the failure

[890] *Ibid.*, pp. 11–78.
[891] *Ibid.*, pp. 112–14.
[892] *Ibid.*, pp. 158–69.
[893] Cf. account in Saletore, *op. cit.* (n. 234), II, 390–92.
[894] *Op. cit.*, p. 169.
[895] *Ibid.*, pp. 169–71. For a summary apparently based on the same source (Nicolas Pimenta's letters) see Campos, *op. cit.* (n. 551), pp. 101.

of the Jesuits to convert Akbar was due to the baleful influence of the Moors and to political conditions within the empire.[896] In connection with the third mission he gives later data than his predecessors on events in the Mughul empire. He lists punishments which God placed upon Akbar for his refusal to become a convert, including the destruction by fire of his palace in Lahore on Easter Day, 1597. Shortly thereafter, in 1597, Akbar and Prince Salim took Xavier and Brother Benedict with them to their summer retreat in Kashmir to await the rebuilding of the palace. Kashmir, surrounded in large part by extremely high mountains, is described as one of the freshest lands in India, being watered by beautiful rivers which make it into a garden spot. Close by the principal city, Srinigar, is a mountain topped by a stone mosque which houses the throne of "Salomon."[897] According to local legend, "Salomon" from his throne drove the demons from the land and so permitted it to be fertile and thriving. In antiquity this land was inhabited by gentiles, but in the 1300's it was invaded by the Moors, possibly a reference to Timur, and since then the majority of the people accept Islam.[898] After a six months absence from Lahore, Akbar's party returned to the capital to find that Pinheiro, who had stayed behind to superintend its construction, had already completed and dedicated the Jesuit church. Towards the end of 1598, Akbar left Lahore accompanied by Xavier to assume personal conduct over his campaign against the stubborn rulers of the Deccan.[899]

In 1598, while in Lahore, Xavier met an old Muslim merchant who claimed to have lived and worked in "Xetay" (Cathay) for thirty years. This man assured his questioners that Cathay is a great land with fifteen hundred populous cities, that its people are "white," and that a majority of them profess Christianity. The king of Cathay lives in the city of "Cambalu" (Cambaluc) and his court can be reached overland by traveling through Kashmir and Tibet.[900] In the following year, while in the company of Akbar, Xavier wrote further on Cathay from Agra, and recommended that an emissary should be sent there by way of Lahore and Kabul.[901] In the meantime Matteo Ricci had been suggesting in his letters from China that the Cathay of the Middle Ages and China were one and the same place. It was in these circumstances that the Society decided to try to ascertain its identity, to reclaim the supposedly Christian population of the Asian interior for the Roman church, and to find a land-route as a substitute for the long and dangerous sea voyage to China. In 1601, both the Pope and Philip III gave their permission for the dispatch of the Cathay mission by way of India, and Benedict de Goes was entrusted with it.[902]

896 Guzman, *op. cit.* (n. 883), I, 249–51, 253–54.
897 What "Salomon" refers to, I do not know. There is a hill on the north side of the city topped with a mosque. See E. Thornton, *op. cit.* (n. 13), p. 913.
898 Guzman, *op. cit.* (n. 883), I, 267–68.   899 *Ibid.*, p. 269.
900 *Ibid.*, pp. 271–72, summarizes Xavier's letter of 1598 from Lahore.
901 *Ibid.*, p. 273, summarizes Xavier's letter of 1599 from Agra.
902 C. Wessels, *Early Jesuit Travellers in Central Asia* (The Hague, 1924), pp. 11–13. Also see below, p. 823.

3

THE ITALIAN, ENGLISH, AND DUTCH COMMENTATORS

The number of non-Iberians who actually journeyed to India increased in the latter half of the century as the Portuguese monopoly on trade gradually broke apart and as the Jesuits and the other Orders were forced constantly to go further afield in their search for capable missionaries. While Philip II sought after 1581 to maintain an Iberian monopoly in the overseas world, the rivalry between the Spanish and the Portuguese, as well as between the various religious orders favored by them, helped to open the door to Asia to the representatives of other European nationalities: Italians, Netherlanders, Germans, Frenchmen, and Englishmen. Near the end of the century even a Polish gentleman, Christophe Pawlowski, had journeyed to Goa and had sent back to his homeland an account of his adventure written in his native language.[903] Finally, the decline of Iberian power in northern Europe and on the sea made it possible for the English and the Dutch to crack the maritime monopoly of the Iberians and to proceed directly to the East in their own vessels.

The Italians were particularly prominent as participants both in the spice trade and in the Society of Jesus.[904] The Florentine merchants, agents of the Gualterotti and Frescobaldi interests, were associated with the Portuguese, and several of them had been sent as factors to India early in the century. The Venetians, who were as a rule strictly excluded from Portuguese Asia, had occupied themselves primarily in the early years of the century with spying in Lisbon and with encouraging the Turks to resist the Portuguese in the Indian Ocean. In the latter half of the century, as the Portuguese hold on the spice trade in Europe and their control over the sea lanes of Asia became weaker, and as Akbar established political control over northern India and central Asia, the Venetians from their trading stations in the Levant became constantly bolder in their efforts to revive the land route to India and to penetrate directly the marts of India and the East Indies.[905]

---

[903] Pawlowski's lengthy letter from Goa of November 20, 1596, appears in *Rocznik orjentalistyczny*, III (1925), 1–56; also see Stefan Stasiak, *Les Indes portugais à la fin du XVIe siècle, d'après la relation du voyage fait à Goa en 1596 par Christophe Pawlowski, gentilhomme polonais* (Lvov, 1926).

[904] For a summary of the Italian participation see Angelo de Gubernatis, *Storia dei viaggiatori italiani nelle Indie Orientali* (Leghorn, 1875), chap. i; Tomaso Sillani, *L'Italia e l'Oriente medio ed estremo* (Rome, 1935), *passim*; Pietro Amat di San Filippo, *Bibliografia dei viaggiatori italiani ordinate cronologicamente* (Rome, 1874).

[905] Most of those Venetians who published accounts or who were active in trade are discussed in Placido Zurla, *Di Marco Polo e degli altri viaggiatori veneziani piu illustri* (Venice, 1818); summaries and comments on Fedrici are in II, 252–58 followed by a similar treatment of Balbi in II, 258–65. When the notarial archives of Venice have been more closely examined it might be discovered that many other Venetian merchants were involved in similar enterprises. For a survey, based on the notarial archives, of the part played by Michael Stropeni and the Altan brothers in the effort to revive overland relations between Venice and India in the 1580's see Ugo Tucci, "Mercanti veneziani in India alla fine del secolo XVI," *Studi in onore di Armando Sapori* (Milan, 1957), II, 1091–1111.

In 1563, at a time when the English and Dutch were looking for a north-eastern route to Asia and when Akbar was just establishing his personal sway over the Mughul empire, a Venetian merchant, Cesare de Fedrici, boarded a vessel bound for Cyprus. Very desirous of seeing the East, according to his own testimony, Fedrici went on to Syria and then overland to Aleppo and Ormuz. For the next eighteen years, he traveled and traded in the East, finally returning to Venice in 1581. In the course of his voyage he evidently kept a diary or notebook which was then hammered into a narrative by the Venetian publisher, Andrea Muschio. Six years after his return, Muschio published the *Viaggio di M. Cesare de Fedrici, nell' India Orientale, et oltra l'India* . . . (Venice, 1587). The following year it was translated into English by Thomas Hickock, a merchant who spent his time at sea on the way back from the Mediterranean to England rendering it "into our vulgar tongue." [906] Hickock's translation was republished verbatim by Hakluyt in 1599, and, as we shall see, Fedrici's work was callously plagiarized by at least two other sixteenth-century writers.

Fedrici's *Viaggio*, which resembles in form and content the *Book* of Duarte Barbosa and the *Suma oriental* of Tomé Pires, was separately published in full during the sixteenth century, as they were not. But the Venetian's account, unlike those of his two Portuguese precursors, was not incorporated into the Ramusio collection until the appearance of the 1606 version of Volume III. Unfortunately, however, Fedrici was less careful about dates and organization than the earlier writers, including among them his compatriot Marco Polo. It is practically impossible from simply reading his account to determine exactly where he was on a given date, or how long he spent in each place about which he comments.[907] His book is nevertheless valuable for the simple and clear descriptions which he gives of the trade routes, products, and customs of the East. It also adds substantially to our narrative because he reports about a period (1563–81) for which the Portuguese and Jesuit

---

[906] My quotation is from the preface "to the Courteous Reader" in *The Voyage and Travaile: of M. Caesar Frederick, Merchant of Venice, into the East India and beyond the Indies. Wherein are conteined Very Pleasant and Rare Matters, with the Customs and Rites of These Countries. Also Herein Are Discovered the Marchandises and Commodities of Those Countreyes, as well the Aboundance of Goulde and Silver, as well Spices, Drugges, Pearles, and other Jeweles.* "Written at Sea in the Hercules of London Comming from Turkie, the 25 of March 1588. For the Profitable Instruction of Merchants and all Other Travellers for their Better Direction and Knowledge of These Countreyes. Out of Italian by T. Hickock. At London, Printed by Richard Jones and Edward White, 18 Junij, 1588." A copy of this rare work is in the Bodleian Library. Hickock acknowledges that he is not a scholar and that in his translation he has "simplie followed the Authors sence in that phraze of speech that we commonly use." E. Teza, "Il viaggio di Cesare dei Fedrici e la versione inglese dell'Hickocke," *Atti del reale istituto veneto di scienze, lettere, ed arti*, Vol. LXVIII (Ser. 8, Vol. XI, 1908–9), pp. 327–37, has compared the English translation with the original and admits that Hickock's rendition "is faithful" (p. 331) even though it contains a number of mistranslations, misprints, and omissions which he itemizes. Since Hickock's version is essentially correct in the matters which concern us and inasmuch as the Hakluyt version is much easier to consult, the following notes will refer to Richard Hakluyt, *The Principal Navigations, Voyages, Traffiques, and Discoveries of the English Nation* ("Extra Series of the Publications of the Hakluyt Society," Vol. V [Glasgow, 1903–5]).

[907] An effort has been made to work out the details of his itinerary in Jarl Charpentier, "Cesare di Fedrici and Gasparo Balbi," *Indian Antiquary*, LIII (1924), 51–54.

materials on India printed during the sixteenth century supply only scanty documentation. The travels of Fedrici took him from Venice to Malacca and back again. Without attempting to follow his Indian peregrinations in detail, it is essential to extract a few of the highlights from his observations to show the nature of his contribution to Europe's stock of information.

Like Barbosa's, Fedrici's account of India begins with Cambay.[908] The city of Diu is pictured (*ca.* 1564) as a great center of trade where merchandise from Cambay is loaded into the large vessels destined for the Persian Gulf and the Red Sea. While the owners of the freight-carrying vessels are both Christians and Moors, the followers of Islam are forced to obtain trading permits from the Portuguese authorities. The large vessels docked at Diu draw too much water to sail directly to Cambay through the Gulf of Cambay with its shoals and great tidal waves (*maccareo*).[909] Small barks of shallow draft enter and leave the Gulf of Cambay every fortnight at the time of the full moon when the waters of the Gulf are deepest and least dangerous. At Cambay it is the practice of the foreign merchants to market their wares and buy native products through gentile brokers. The broker acts as the exclusive seller and buyer for the foreign trader. He takes complete responsibility for the merchandise brought in: he makes storage arrangements for it and pays all port charges and taxes on it. The broker also provides housing for the foreign merchant and his companions. Fedrici took advantage of his own stay in Cambay to visit Ahmadābād (which he aptly compares to Cairo) and to learn something about the decline of the native dynasty of Gujarat and the gradual assumption of power by the Mughuls.

After short stopovers at Damão, Bassein, and Tana, Fedrici arrived in Chaul. The walled Portuguese city of Chaul, which commands the mouth of the harbor, he differentiates from the nearby Moorish city of Chaul governed by the Nizamu 'l-Mulk, the king of Ahmadnagar whose capital city is seven or eight days' journey into the interior from Chaul.[910] While describing the trade of Chaul, Fedrici digresses at length on the great value of the palm tree and itemizes its multiple uses. By 1566, the Venetian was in Goa where he was to visit again in 1570 and probably on one or two other occasions.[911] Ordinarily, he asserts, five or six large vessels from Portugal arrive at Goa between September 6 and 10 to disembark their cargoes. After remaining forty to fifty days at Goa, one of the vessels is sometimes loaded with goods for Portugal, but most of the return cargo of spices is reportedly taken aboard at Cochin. Ships from Ormuz, providing that they carry twenty or more horses to the port of Goa, pay no charges or duties on their entire cargo; but if trading vessels come to the

---

[908] Fedrici in Hakluyt, *op. cit.* (n. 906), V, 374–77.

[909] Etymology of this term is uncertain, but it is repeatedly used by European writers of the sixteenth century to refer to the tidal waves in the Gulf of Cambay and the Sittang estuary of Pegu. See Yule and Burnell, *op. cit.* (n. 10), pp. 402–3, and Dalgado, *op. cit.*, pp. 3–5.

[910] Fedrici in Hakluyt, *op. cit.* (n. 906), V, 378–80.

[911] *Ibid.*, pp. 380–82. See also Charpentier, *loc. cit.* (n. 907), pp. 52–54. On his return in 1570, Fedrici was caught in the siege of Goa by Adil Khan of Bijapur. It lasted for fourteen months.

capital of Portuguese India without horses they pay 8 per cent duty on everything imported. An export tax is levied on each horse sent from Goa into the interior.

In 1567, Fedrici accompanied two horse traders from Goa to the city of Vijayanagar.[912] Since he arrived there just two years after the disastrous battle of Talikota, the Venetian comments at some length on the battle and the sack of the city by the four Deccan rulers—a discourse which is one of the fullest left to posterity by a contemporary observer.[913] He also gives detail on the political condition of the Vijayanagar court prior to the battle, and of how its internal divisions contributed to the defeat of the Hindu state by the Muslim princes. Though the Deccan forces plundered the city for six months, the Muslim conquerors were unable to maintain political control over a city so far removed from their own centers of strength. Following the withdrawal of the conquerors, the Regent, "Temiragio" (Tirumala), returned to the depopulated city and began to restore its buildings and to re-establish trading relations with Goa. The Venetian remained in Vijayanagar for seven months, even though he could have concluded his business in one month, because of the disorders and raids which made travel back to Goa too dangerous to attempt. Because the house in which he lived was located near to the gate through which widows passed on their way to be burnt, we have from Fedrici's pen one of the fullest and most authoritative accounts of the Hindu practice of *sati* prepared in the sixteenth century.[914] Though he did not actually visit the diamond mines of the region, the Venetian learned about them from informants.[915]

Evidently it was towards the end of Fedrici's stay in Vijayanagar that Tirumala gave up in his effort to rebuild the city and transferred his court to Penugonda,[916] a hill fortress eight days away from the ravaged capital. Nonetheless, in Fedrici's eyes, semi-deserted Vijayanagar was still the greatest royal capital of all those he had seen in his travels and he describes its physical appearance and trade.[917] The account of his trials and tribulations on the return trip reflect clearly the disordered condition of life in the territories which were still nominally tributaries of Vijayanagar. En route to Ancolâ on the west coast, the Venetian found that each of the governors along the way was issuing his own coinage and refusing to accept any other. In his journey from Ancolâ back to Goa, the Venetian continued to suffer from the depredations of the numerous bandits who made travel unsafe in what was technically the coastal territory of Vijayanagar.

From Goa, Fedrici resumed his sea journey by embarking for Cochin. On the voyage southward he stopped at four of the intermediate Portuguese ports

---

912 Fedrici in Hakluyt, *op. cit.* (n. 906), V, 382–84.
913 See Saletore, *op. cit.* (n. 234), I, 133.
914 Fedrici in Hakluyt, *op. cit.* (n. 906), V, 384–86.
915 *Ibid.*, pp. 386–87.
916 Cf. Saletore, *op. cit.* (n. 234), I, 139–40.
917 Fedrici in Hakluyt, *op. cit.* (n. 906), V, 387–89.

and he comments on their trade and political condition.[918] His arrival at Cochin, where he visited for extended periods on at least two occasions, gives him an opportunity to talk about the pepper trade. He categorically affirms that the pepper sold to the Portuguese is inferior to that which the Moors buy for sale in Mecca. The deliveries to the Portuguese are "green and full of filthe"[919] because they pay only the low fixed price agreed upon in their treaty with Cochin, a policy inaugurated by Vasco da Gama.

Like Chaul, Cochin is divided into two riverine cities, the one nearer to the sea belonging to the Portuguese and the other which is upriver towards the "Kingdom of Pepper" being the capital of the native king. Western Christians who marry in Cochin (and thereby become permanent residents with direct personal interest in the welfare of the city) receive good posts and extraordinary privileges. These married Westerners, for example, are exempted like natives from paying duties on China silk and Bengal sugar, the two principal imports of Cochin. On all other commodities, the privileged Westerners pay but 4 per cent tax while the unmarried Westerners pay the normal 8 per cent on all imports, and this situation continues to be unchanged in Fedrici's time despite efforts on the part of the Portuguese to upset it. While the Venetian comments on the marital and inheritance practices of the Nāyars, he shows an unusual degree of interest in the way in which the members of this caste puncture their ear lobes and gradually stretch the openings into "great holes."[920]

In proceeding south of Cochin, Fedrici once again has an opportunity to show his keenness as an observer as well as his business acumen. He provides an excellent description of pearl fishing and ascertains that there are four major grades of commercial pearls: the round variety sold in Portugal, those sent to Bengal which are not round, and two inferior and cheaper types named for Kanara and Cambay respectively.[921] He also discusses the difficulties of navigation in the strait which runs between the islands (commonly called Adam's Bridge) separating the Gulf of Manaar and Palk Strait, and notes that large vessels headed for the East Indies normally go around Ceylon because they cannot pass through the narrows at Adam's Bridge.[922] About Ceylon, which he judges to be a "great deale bigger than Cyprus,"[923] Fedrici has nothing to add to the earlier accounts except his remarks on prevailing political conditions. The king (Dharmapāla) is described as a Christian convert who rules under the guidance of Portugal and whose sway has been threatened by the rebellious actions of "Madoni" (Maaya Dunnai) and his sons.[924]

Of particular interest is the Venetian's account of conditions along the east coast of India. Negapatam, which is rich in nothing "save a good quantitie of

[918] *Ibid.*, pp. 390–95.

[919] *Ibid.*, p. 392. Cf. above, p. 144 for European charges that the Portuguese pepper was inferior and adulterated.

[920] Fedrici in Hakluyt, *op. cit.* (n. 906), V, 394.

[921] *Ibid.*, pp. 395–97.   [922] *Ibid.*, pp. 397–98.

[923] *Ibid.*, p. 398.

[924] *Ibid.*, p. 399.

Rice"[925] and textiles, has declined as a port because of the uncertain political conditions produced by the defeat of Vijayanagar in 1565. The Portuguese city of St. Thomas, also within the jurisdiction of Vijayanagar, is still a great entrepôt in the trade between India and the East Indies despite its poor harbor and unstable political condition. Arriving in Orissa after a hectic voyage from Malacca, the Venetian judges it to be a "fair kingdome and trustie, through the which a man might have gone with gold in hand without any danger at all"[926] if only the Hindu ruler with his seat at "Catech" (Cuttack)[927] had not been deposed by the Pathans sixteen years before. Prior to the conquest of the Hindu state of Orissa, trade at its ports was flourishing and practically free of duty. Once the Pathans came to power they imposed a 20 per cent tax on trade. The Pathans were shortly thereafter replaced by the Mughuls in Bengal and as a result their power was likewise broken in Orissa.[928]

Like most itinerant merchants of the East, Fedrici eventually visited the emporiums at the mouths of the Ganges. From Orissa he was rowed along the shore and up the Ganges in large flat-bottomed boats which made their progress upriver with the incoming tide. Seagoing vessels, he indicates, are able to go upriver only to "Buttor" (Betor, near modern Howrah) where they unload and load at a temporary mart built of straw which is constructed and burned annually at the arrival and departure of the trading ships.[929] Fedrici remained at Sātgāon for four months and, like the other merchants, went up and down the Ganges to the numerous marts along its banks. He too observed on his river voyages how the Hindus daily entrust their dead to the sacred waters of the Ganges. In 1569 the Venetian visited Chittagōng, "the great port of Bengala,"[930] where the Portuguese were having trouble with the local authorities. It was also at this time that he landed by chance on the island of "Sondiva" (Sandwīp, northwest of Chittagōng), which he describes while commenting particularly on the abundance and low cost of food and the friendly reception received from the local authorities despite the hostility which the Bengalis then felt for the Portuguese at Chittagōng.[931]

While Fedrici was working his way back to the Levant and thence Europe in 1579, the Venetian jeweler, Gasparo Balbi, set out for India. For the next nine years, Balbi followed almost the same route to the East and back again which Fedrici had used. Two years after his return to Venice in 1588, the printer

---

[925] *Ibid.*, p. 400.

[926] *Ibid.*, pp. 401–2.

[927] Derived from Sanskrit word for camp, *kataka*. Probably a reference to the most imposing of the royal camps or headquarters, called Varanasi Kataka. See Chakravarti, *loc. cit.* (n. 548) XII (1916), 30.

[928] Fitch in Hakluyt, *op. cit.* (n. 906), V, 410. The Mughuls did not annex Orissa to their empire until 1592 but the northern part was invaded by the Pathans in 1568–69 and two years later they overran the south. See Chakravarti, *loc. cit.* (n. 548), pp. 30–35.

[929] For comment on this assertion see Campos, *op. cit.* (n. 551), pp. 49–50.

[930] Fedrici in Hakluyt, *op. cit.* (n. 906), V, 438. For the dating of this visit see Charpentier, *loc. cit.* (n. 907), p. 53.

[931] Fedrici in Hakluyt, *op. cit.* (n. 906), V, 437–38.

Camillo Borgominieri published Balbi's *Viaggio dell' Indie Orientali . . . Nel quale si contiene quanto egli in detto viaggio ha veduto por lo spatio di 9. Anni consumati in esse dal 1579, fino al 1588 . . .* (Venice, 1590). Dedicated to his noble Venetian relative, Teodoro Balbi,[932] this work is said to have been reissued in 1600 but I have not been able to find a copy of a second edition.[933] In 1600 the entire text appeared in Latin translation in De Bry's collection and ten illustrations were added depicting hook-swinging and various other ceremonies and events.[934] The part of Balbi's account relating to St. Thomas, Negapatam, and Pegu was eventually summarized in English and published by Purchas.[935]

Balbi's work, much more than Fedrici's, is a commercial handbook reminiscent of the fourteenth-century "La prática della mercatura" compiled by Pegolotti.[936] As a diarist and compiler of data, Balbi is far more accurate and painstaking than Fedrici. He is very careful to record the dates on which he visited particular places and at each stopover he carefully notes the coins, weights, and measures then in use. To the end of his diary he also appends a summary account of the trade routes customarily followed in the India commerce and a table of the monsoons.[937] With respect to India, he interlards his *Viaggio* with a few general observations on geography, manners, and customs. In a number of instances he has clearly taken whole descriptive passages from Fedrici's book and has unblushingly inserted them into his own composition.[938] Most of these plagiarized passages relating to India are those which describe cities, customs, and natural vegetation such as the palm and cinnamon trees. In the latter part of the *Viaggio*, where he deals with Pegu, Balbi's work is almost entirely original—a fact which his contemporaries probably realized when they selected only the Pegu section for publication in English. As a general description of India, Balbi's work in itself is therefore of very little value except on matters relating to trade. This is not to say that the book is utterly worthless for India. Balbi comments independently, for instance, on the cave temples of Elephanta and credits their construction to Alexander the Great.[939] But his distinctly in-

---

[932] On the Balbi family see Gubernatis, *op. cit.* (n. 904), p. 24, n. 1.

[933] See Charpentier, *loc. cit.* (n. 907), p. 51.

[934] J. T. and J. H. De Bry (eds.), *India Orientalis* (Frankfurt am Main, 1600), Pt. VII, pp. 43–126. Since the first edition is extremely rare, I consulted this translation.

[935] See the reprint of the 1625 edition of Purchas in Samuel Purchas (ed.), *Hakluytus Posthumus, or Purchas His Pilgrimages . . .* ("Extra Series of the Hakluyt Society Publications" [20 vols.; Glasgow, 1905–7]), X, 143–64. See below, pp. 549–50.

[936] See above, pp. 45–46.

[937] For comments on Balbi's merit as an observer and recorder see Zurla, *op. cit.* (n. 905), II, 258. For his possible influence on cartography see Olga Pinto, "Ancora il viaggiatore veneziano Gasparo Balbi a proposito della ristampa italiana di una Carta dell'Asia di W. J. Blaev," *Atti della Accademia nazionale dei Lincei* ("Classe di scienze morali, storiche e filologiche," Series VIII, Vol. III [Rome 1948]), pp. 465–71.

[938] Charpentier (*loc. cit.* [n. 907], pp. 57–61) has made a textual comparison of Balbi's book with the version of Fedrici which appeared in Ramusio (1606). From this comparison he is able to cite extracts which Balbi, quite in accord with the custom followed by many writers of his day, unhesitatingly plundered from Fedrici's account to extend and improve his own.

[939] Balbi in De Bry, *op. cit.* (n. 934), Pt. VII, p. 78.

dividualistic observations occur only at rare intervals, even though he lived in Goa for eighteen months. As an aside of interest, he tells of meeting the Japanese legates to Europe when they were in Goa in 1587 on their way home.[940]

In contrast to the private enterprise of the Venetian merchants, Fedrici and Balbi, stands the career in India of the Florentine Humanist and merchant, Filippo Sassetti (lived from 1540 to 1588). While the Venetians hoped to revive the direct overland trade with India, Sassetti, like other Tuscans of his day and earlier, worked harmoniously within the Portuguese system and went to India by rounding the Cape of Good Hope. As the great-grandson of Francesco Sassetti, who had been manager of the far-flung enterprises of the Medicis in the fifteenth century,[941] Filippo was descended from a notable family with numerous connections in the business capitals of Europe. And, like most aristocratic families of Tuscany, the Sassettis possessed, even after they ran into financial trouble, a vital and profound interest in affairs of the mind. So, it is not surprising to find young Filippo studying for six years (1568–74) at the University of Pisa and of being for some years thereafter an active participant in the learned societies of Florence. It was not until 1578, when Sassetti was already thirty-eight years old, that the decline of the family fortune and the growth of his immediate household combined to force the young intellectual to turn his hand to commerce, a way of life for which he personally had little taste.[942]

For four years (1578–81), Sassetti acted as a commercial agent of the Capponi interests in Spain and Portugal. While occupied with business affairs, Sassetti still found time to correspond with his academic and business associates in Florence.[943] When the Capponis decided to close down their enterprises in the Iberian peninsula, Sassetti took employment with Rovellasca, head of the syndicate which had purchased the spice monopoly.[944] He was sent out to India almost at once as factor for the Rovellasca interests. In November, 1583, he arrived in Cochin where he worked in the pepper trade as a supervisor for Rovellasca as he sought to recoup his family's fortune. He traveled both by land and water to the western Indian cities of Onor and Mangalor, and in

---

940 *Ibid.*, p. 122; also see below, p. 487.

941 Florence E. de Roover, "Francesco Sassetti and the Downfall of the Medici Banking House," *Bulletin of the Business Historical Society*, XVII (1943), 65–80.

942 For the Sassetti family see Filippo Luigi Polidori, *Archivio storico italiano*, Vol. IV, Pt. 2 (1853), pp. xviii–xxi (preface); for a general account of Filippo's career see Mario Rossi, *Un letterato e mercante fiorentino del secolo XVI: Filippo Sassetti* (Castello, 1899).

943 The standard edition which contains 111 of his letters is Ettore Marcucci (ed.), *Lettere edite e inedite di Filippo Sassetti* (Florence, 1855). A subsequent and cheaper edition came out at Milan in 1874 with a preface and a commentary by Eugenio Camirini. An edition of letters specially selected for the public, including a number from India, is Gino Raya (ed.), *Filippo Sassetti. Lettere scelte* (Milan, 1932). Sassetti's letters from India have been published separately in Arrigo Benedetti (ed.), *Filippo Sassetti. Lettere indiane* (2d ed.; Turin, 1961); the best study of his circle of correspondents is to be found in Giuseppe Caraci, *Introduzione al Sassetti epistolografo* (indagini sulla cultura geografica del secondo cinquecento) (Rome, 1960).

944 See above, pp. 135–36. For details on his own employment and of Rovellasca's part in the spice trade see letter to Francesco Valori (April, 1582) in Marcucci (ed.), *op. cit.* (n. 943), pp. 204–10.

1586 he accompanied the Portuguese embassy to Calicut to treat with the Zamorin. Unfortunately, Sassetti died at Goa in 1588 before he could realize his hope for a leisurely round-the-world return trip to Florence.[945]

During the six years of his tenure in India, Sassetti dispatched at least thirty-five letters to Florence which are full of his observations on the subcontinent.[946] A number of his other letters sent from India have been lost.[947] From perusal of his extant letters (from India and his earlier ones written from Portugal), it can readily be ascertained that Sassetti had read widely about Asia in the classical authors, in the accounts contained in the collection of Ramusio, and in the works of Barros, Orta, Cristobal de Acosta, and Maffei (in his first work published in 1571). While still in Portugal he interviewed pilots who had made the trip east. Even before leaving Lisbon, he was sent a sum of money and commissioned by Francis I, Grand Duke of Tuscany, to buy samples of exotic plants and wares, and to ship them back to Florence.[948] He was also asked by Baccio Valori, an intellectual of Florence close to the Grand Duke, to find out what he could about the alphabets of the oriental languages, especially the "hieroglyphics" of the Chinese.[949] From the extant letters it is apparent that in India Sassetti continued to study and read; he collected a wide variety of data, both by direct observation and by interviewing his fellow countrymen and natives; and he systematized and interpreted the data so collected. It also appears that Sassetti expected his friends, including Francis I, to circulate his letters among the literati of his native city. Unfortunately, however, none of his illuminating and learned letters appears to have been printed during the sixteenth century.

Though we will not examine Sassetti's letters in detail (as they were not published in our period), it should be noticed that he, and Garcia da Orta, are the only lay Humanists from Europe who, to our knowledge, observed and wrote in India during the sixteenth century. A man of Sassetti's training and interests naturally saw and commented intelligently on many matters which either escaped or seemed irrelevant to observers concerned with trade, administration, or religion. Large sections of his letters are concerned with his meteorological observations, including detailed and acute comments on typhoons,[950] seasonal

---

[945] His letter, outlining a projected voyage from Goa via the East Indies and America back to Europe, is included in Polidori, *op. cit.* (n. 942), pp. lxxviii–lxxix. For his travels on the west coast of India, see *ibid.*, pp. lxxiii–lxxvii.

[946] One hundred and fourteen of his letters are still extant. Besides appearing in the standard edition (Marcucci [ed.], *op. cit.* [n. 943], pp. 245–425), six of his most important letters from the East have been republished by Gubernatis (*op. cit.* [n. 904], pp. 187–227) along with commentaries based on them. For further analysis see Caraci, *op. cit.* (n. 943), pp. 83–110.

[947] On the lost letters see Caraci, *op. cit.* (n. 943), pp. 135–43.

[948] This was the Grand Duke who, along with his wife, entertained the Japanese ambassadors so royally on their visit to Tuscany in 1585 (see below, pp. 694–95) and who sought earlier to buy into the spice trade (see above, p. 133).

[949] See letters to Valori, of March, 1583, from Lisbon (Marcucci [ed.], *op. cit.* [n. 943], pp. 239–40), and of January 17, 1588, from Cochin (*ibid.*, p. 408).

[950] Raya (ed.), *op. cit.* (n. 943), pp. 64–65.

changes, and climate.⁹⁵¹ While he comments on ways of life and social organizations, especially of the Brahmans, he frankly admits that he can say little
about such matters because he has not himself lived according to native cus-
toms.⁹⁵² He wrote a letter, which is virtually a scientific paper, for the aca-
demicians of Florence on aspects of Indian folklore.⁹⁵³ On matters of trade and
on those trading cities of India with which he had more than a passing familiarity,
he wrote directly to the Grand Duke. About natural history and botany he
wrote to the Accademia degli Alterati in some detail. Evidently he learned
something of Indian medical lore by conversing with a Hindu physician. This
learned and agreeable scholar introduced Sassetti to certain Sanskrit texts on
pharmaceuticals, and evidently helped him to translate passages from one of
them, a document which modern scholarship holds to be the *Rāganighaṇṭu*
(a textbook of chemistry).⁹⁵⁴ From this and other evidence to be found in his
letters it is clear that Sassetti, from around 1585 until his death three years later,
was making an effort to learn Sanskrit.

In 1583, the year when Sassetti arrived in India, a trading expedition set sail
for the Levant from London headed by John Newbery, an English merchant.
Newbery, who had previously worked in the Levant, had earlier traveled
overland to Ormuz on the Persian Gulf. Like the Venetians, the English of this
period were not yet able to challenge effectively the Iberian control of the
maritime passage around the Cape of Good Hope, and as a result they had
sought on a number of occasions to reach Asia by other routes. The Newbery
expedition of 1583 over the land route of the Levant to Ormuz and thence to
India was but one of the many English efforts to circumvent the Portuguese
monopoly. Like its predecessors, it produced no tangible results in terms of
trade; it did, however, make possible the publication of the first description
of India and the East Indies by an Englishman.

Newbery was accompanied in 1583 on his overland trip to India by Ralph
Fitch (d. 1611)⁹⁵⁵ and two others. Among the papers which they carried, the
adventurers had two letters of introduction from Queen Elizabeth prepared in
February, 1583; one was addressed to Akbar and the other to the emperor of
China.⁹⁵⁶ Four days after their arrival in Ormuz, the Englishmen were accused
by Michael Stropeni,⁹⁵⁷ the Venetian merchant, of being spies for Dom António,
the pretender to the Portuguese throne, who was then residing in London.⁹⁵⁸

---

⁹⁵¹ Gubernatis, *op. cit.* (n. 904), pp. 194–200. See also Polidori, *op. cit.* (n. 942), pp. xciii–xcvi, n. 4,
in which a nineteenth-century Italian scientist writes a complimentary estimate of the observations
made by Sassetti during the sea voyage to India.
⁹⁵² Gubernatis, *op. cit.* (n. 904), p. 189. On the Brahmans see Raya (ed.), *op. cit.* (n. 943), pp. 89–103.
⁹⁵³ Raya (ed.), *op. cit.* (n. 943), pp. 142–52.
⁹⁵⁴ Gubernatis, *op. cit.* (n. 904), pp. 329–30.
⁹⁵⁵ For his biography see J. Horton Ryley, *Ralph Fitch, England's Pioneer to India and Burma* (London,
1899). For details on the last years of his life after his return from India see William Foster, *Early
Travels in India, 1583–1619* (London, 1921), pp. 7–8.
⁹⁵⁶ Text in Hakluyt, *op. cit.* (n. 906), II, 245.
⁹⁵⁷ See above, p. 468n.
⁹⁵⁸ Letter from Newbery to Leonard Poore dated Goa, January 20, 1584. See Hakluyt, *op. cit.*
(n. 906), II, 248–50.

The Portuguese captain in charge of the garrison at Ormuz acted upon Stropeni's denunciation quite readily, since the Portuguese were already outraged at Drake's audacity in sailing through their waters and firing on their ships. Once in custody, the Englishmen were sent to prison in Goa. The Jesuit Thomas Stevens and one of his colleagues in Goa acted as intermediaries with the authorities, and their activities were ably seconded by the Dutch trader Jan van Linschoten,[959] who was then attached to the staff of the archbishop. Before the end of a month, after professing to be honest merchants and good Catholics, the Englishmen were freed and given permission to set up a trading station. Shortly after their release both Newbery and Fitch wrote letters in which they tell of their first brush with the law and their rising hopes for a lucrative trade in Goa. These prospects soon dimmed, however, and it was leaked to them that the viceroy intended sending them back to Portugal with the next fleet. In response to this news, Newbery and Fitch slipped out of Goa, and, like so many other fugitives from the Portuguese, took refuge in the territory of Bijapur.

It was after their escape in April, 1584, that the Englishmen began to see something of the interior of India. The two fugitives went first to the city of Bijapur and then to Golconda, the residence of the Kutb Shāhī kings. Then they entered the Mughul empire near Burhānpur and went on to the imperial cities of Agra and Fatehpur Sīkrī, where they evidently visited the court of Akbar. It is not known whether or not they presented Queen Elizabeth's letter to Akbar, but they did decide at this point to part company. Newbery hoped to return to Europe by the land route and to come back to Bengal by sea within two years to pick up Fitch. In the meanwhile Fitch was to spend his time scouting prospects for trade in northeastern India. When Newbery failed to turn up at the agreed time (apparently he died before getting back to Europe), Fitch in 1586 extended his travels eastward to Burma and Malacca. He finally began his arduous and dangerous trip back to Europe by way of Goa, Ormuz, and Syria, arriving in London in April, 1591, after an absence of more than eight years.

The England to which Fitch returned (after being given up by his family and friends as dead) was at war with Spain. Those, like Hakluyt, who were interested in overseas enterprise, were now calling upon the government to defy openly the Spanish control of the Cape route and to sail directly to India in English vessels. Thomas Cavendish had returned in 1588 from his circumnavigation of the world. James Lancaster proved by his voyage to Penang and the Nicobars in 1591, the year of Fitch's return, that English vessels could safely defy the monopolists without pretending to be en route to America. Fitch himself, who was regarded as another Marco Polo in England, was called upon to give his advice on Eastern matters to those interested in developing trade with the Indies. It was probably his publisher, Hakluyt, who pressed him to write

[959] Cf. account in Linschoten's *Itinerario* as republished in English in *ibid.*, pp. 265–68, of their imprisonment and flight from Goa. See below, p. 487.

the narrative of his "wonderful travailes." The narrative made its world debut in *The Principal Navigations* (1599)[960] along with related materials, such as Newbery's letters.

Fitch, unlike Balbi, apparently did not keep a diary of his travels and so was forced to rely upon his memory when writing up his voyage. We conclude this because dates and exact references are conspicuous by their absence, and because the narrative of his eight long years of wandering is disappointingly brief. His lack of ready data may also help to explain why he incorporated almost word for word into his own composition Fedrici's descriptions of those places where they had both visited. Though Fitch could possibly have consulted Balbi's *Viaggio* (1590) as well, no convincing evidence exists to show that he referred to it.[961] Fitch's account, even though he depends heavily upon Fedrici for what he has to say about Portuguese India, is nonetheless original and valuable for his comments on interior places where Fedrici did not visit. Hakluyt, who published both Fitch and Fedrici in his collection, appears to rank the Englishman's account, along with those of Castanheda and Fedrici, as an important source of information on the East.[962]

Upon escaping from Goa in April, 1584, Newbery and Fitch made their way on foot to Belgaum and then went on to Bijapur. Apparently interested in learning about diamonds and other precious stones, Fitch reports that they next went to Golconda "the king whereof is called *Cutup de lashach.*"[963] The city of Golconda, which today stands in ruins about five miles west of Hyderabad, is in Fitch's eyes "a veery faire towne, pleasant, with faire houses of bricke and timber."[964] Though Fitch complains about it being hot in Golconda, he found also that the city was amply supplied with water and local fresh fruit, and well serviced with foreign products through the port of Masulipatam.[965] From Golconda, Fitch and Newbery made their way northward to the Mughul empire and Fitch notices en route a "fine countrey" which he calls "Servidore" (possibly Bīdar, an independent state).[966] From here they journeyed to Balapur in Berar and then to Surhanpur which is described as being within Akbar's territories.[967] In connection with his account of Burhānpur and its surroundings,

---

960 For easier consultation the references to Fitch which follow will refer to the version published in Hakluyt, *op. cit.* (n. 906), V, 465–505.

961 See Foster, *op. cit.* (n. 955), p. 8.

962 See the notes prepared in 1600 and attributed to Hakluyt's pen in which are listed the Portuguese, Spanish, Italian, English, and Dutch authorities on Asiatic matters. Reproduced in E. G. R. Taylor, *The Original Writings and Correspondence of the Two Richard Hakluyts* (London, 1935), Vol. II, doc. 78, pp. 467–68.

963 Fitch in Hakluyt, *op. cit.* (n. 906), V, 472. This is clearly a reference to one of the Muslim kings of the Kutb Shāhi dynasty, possibly to Ibrahim (reigned 1550–1611).

964 *Ibid.*

965 The English established their first factory on the Coromandel coast at this place in 1611. See Shah Manzoor Alam, "Masulipatam, a Metropolitan Port in the Seventeenth Century A.D.," *Indian Geographical Journal*, XXXIV (1959), 33–42.

966 See Foster, *op. cit.* (n. 955), p. 16, n. 2.

967 The Deccan kingdom of Khāndesh with its capital of Burhānpur was technically in vassalage to Akbar when Fitch was there. It was not actually annexed to the Mughul state until 1600.

Fitch comments on child marriages at some length, one of his few independent excursions into social questions.[968] On the way to Akbar's court, the two companions went through Māndū, Ujjain, and Sironj and crossed many rivers "which by reason of the raine were so swollen that wee waded and swamme oftentimes for our lives."[969]

On their arrival in Agra, the Englishmen learned that Akbar's court was now located at Fatehpur Sīkrī, a new city "greater than Agra, but the houses and streetes be not so faire."[970] Both cities Fitch considers to be much larger than London, and he marvels how the road between them (23 miles long) "all the way is a market . . . as full as though a man were still in a towne."[971] Akbar's court is housed in a "dericcan" (dārikhāna, Persian, meaning palace) and he keeps great numbers of animals in both imperial cities. None but the harem eunuch is permitted to enter the royal palace. The Mughul ruler dresses in a muslin tunic that is made like a shirt and on his head he wears "a little coloth . . . coloured oftentimes with red or yealow."[972] The capital of the Mughul empire is a great mart to which merchants come from Persia and Portuguese India. Fitch at this point inserts into his narration a short description of a vehicle common to market towns, the two-wheeled carts pulled by bullocks which carry two to three people and are "used here as our coches be in England."[973]

Leaving his companion and striking out alone after visiting Akbar's court, Fitch accompanied for five months a large fleet of merchant-boats downriver to Bengal. On his trip down the Jumna, Fitch observes many "strange customs" for he saw Hindus bathe, worship, and purify themselves in and beside the river. At "Prage" (Prayāga, now Allahābād), he tells us, the Jumna enters the Ganges which "commeth out of the northwest, and runneth east into the Gulfe of Bengala."[974] As he progresses through the Gangetic plain, Fitch notices and remarks on the numerous wild animals, fish, and birds, the naked beggars and ascetics, the islands, and the fruitfulness of the land. Benares is a great city peopled exclusively by Hindus "who be the greatest idolaters that ever I saw."[975] About the strange religious practices of the pilgrims who go to Benares to worship at its shrines and temples and to bathe in the sacred waters of the Ganges, Fitch becomes unusually detailed and interesting. The Ganges between Benares and Patna is "so broad that in time of raine you cannot see from one side to the other,"[976] and the surrounding countryside is fruitful but full of thieves. Patna, which is correctly described as having once been

[968] Hakluyt, *op. cit.* (n. 906), V, 473.
[969] *Ibid.*
[970] *Ibid.*, p. 474.
[971] *Ibid.*
[972] *Ibid.*
[973] *Ibid.*
[974] *Ibid.*, p. 476.
[975] *Ibid.*, p. 477.
[976] *Ibid.*, p. 480.

the seat of an independent king, is now within the Mughul empire. Though it "is a very long and a great towne," with wide streets, Patna's houses are very simple buildings made of dirt and covered with straw. The local governor, "Tipperdas" (Tripura Dās), is held in high esteem in this town where Fitch found a great exchange of cotton, cotton textiles, opium, and sugar. He concludes the remarks on his five-month-long river trip by talking about Tāndā, the town which had replaced Gaur as the capital of Bengal a decade or so before Fitch visited there.

From Tāndā, Fitch proceeded northwest as he penetrated to Kuch Bihar, an assembly place for trading caravans, possibly to inquire about commerce with China by way of Tibet.[977] This area he sees as peopled entirely by Hindus, and he remarks on their extended ear lobes, and the use they make of almonds as small coins.[978] The territory of Kuch Bihar is protected by a fence of sharpened canes or bamboos; in times of war the land is flooded to prevent the enemy from entering it.[979] Upon leaving Kuch Bihar, Fitch went back to the Gangetic plain and, by way of Gaur, he then went downriver to the Portuguese settlements. In his discussion of the Portuguese settlements and of the kingdom of Orissa he again returns to his earlier practice of following Fedrici's narrative. But he also gives a few comments of his own on Tippera and on the activities of the "Mugs" of western Arakan. Then, almost as an afterthought, Fitch introduces a description of the trading activities carried on in Bhutan where merchants reportedly come from China, Muscovy, Bengal, and Tibet. This fascinating summary appears to be accurate, even though Fitch probably did not visit Bhutan himself but pieced his story together from what he had learned during his stay in Kuch Bihar.[980]

From Chittāgong, the Porto Grande of the Portuguese, Fitch concluded his mercantile explorations of India by investigating parts of eastern Bengal.[981] He first stopped at "Bacola" (possibly a town on the west bank of the Titulia River) and then went on to Srīpur at the confluence of the Meghira and Padma rivers. Although Srīpur (near modern Rajabari) has long since been washed away by the shifting of the Padma, Fitch notes that it was a center of resistance in his day for those Bengalis still fighting the Mughuls. Its ruler, Chand Rai, evidently helped the enemies of Akbar to find sanctuary in the numerous islands around Srīpur from the mounted Mughuls who pursued them. Sonārgāon, the capital

---

[977] *Ibid.*, p. 481. It is conceivable that Fitch, like the Jesuits who visited Akbar's realm, heard about such a route. See above, p. 467. For a summary of the Muslim sources, see H. Blochmann, "Koch Bihar, Koch Hajo and A'sam in the 16th and 17th centuries ...," *Journal of the Asiatic Society of Bengal*, XLI (1872), 49–54.

[978] On the use of almonds as coins in India see A. B. Burnell and P. A. Tiele (eds.), *The Voyage of John Huyghen van Linschoten to the East Indies* ... ("Old Series of the Hakluyt Society," Vol. LXX [London, 1885]), I, 246, n. 6.

[979] Fitch in Hakluyt, *op. cit.* (n. 906), V, 481–82.

[980] *Ibid.*, pp. 483–84. See R. Boileau Pemberton, *Report on Bootan* (Calcutta, 1839), pp. 147–48, who quotes Fitch's account and asserts that the trade activity and the mode of dress are almost exactly what they are in his day. Also see the identifications in Foster, *op. cit.* (n. 955), p. 27.

[981] Fitch in Hakluyt, *op. cit.* (n. 906), V, 484–85.

of eastern Bengal from 1351 to 1608, was clearly not under Akbar's rule when Fitch visited there in 1586. Isa Khan, leader of the Afghans who dominated eastern Bengal, is named as "chiefe of all the other kings, and is a great friend to all Christians." [982] Evidently, the Christians were interested in Sonārgāon, located just fifteen miles east of Dacca, for its famous muslins, "the best and finest cloth made of cotton that is in all India." [983] It was from this great commercial region that Fitch started out in November, 1586, having apparently decided that Newbery would not return, for his peregrinations in Pegu and in the further East.

While Fitch traveled through the interior of northern India, Jan van Linschoten remained in the Portuguese service in Goa. The Dutchman's *Itinerario* naturally centers on Goa and he provides therein what is probably the best geographical description of the island city, the neighboring islands and peninsulas, and the relationships of one to the other and to the mainland to appear in print before 1600. Many of the details in this description may have been derived from the Portuguese map of Goa which he had in his possession, but he adds many observations to his narrative of the sort which maps ordinarily do not portray. For example, he affirms that Bardez and Salsette "are by the Kings of Portingale let out to farme, and the rents thereof are imployed to the payment of the Archbishop, Cloysters, Priests, Viceroy, and other of the Kings Officers, yearely stipends. . . ." [984] And, at another point, Linschoten asserts that freedom of conscience exists in Goa even though the public celebration of heretical and pagan rites is repressed.[985]

From this general description, Linschoten moves on to talk at some length about the relationships between the Portuguese and Luso-Indians (*mestiços*), including therein a few snide comments on miscegenation. He also digresses from his main concern to discuss the auctions (*lei-lâos*) which are held daily in Goa and the other Portuguese centers and which "resemble the meeting upon the burse in Andwarpe." [986] Ordinarily, the Portuguese of Goa who are not engaged in commerce are supported by the labors of their slaves, by lending and exchanging currencies, and by rents which they collect on palm groves, pastures, and fields. In short, aside from a few craftsmen, "the Portingales and Mesticos in India never worke. . . ." [987] The Portuguese in Goa belong to one of two groups: free citizens, defined as those who are married and residents of the city; and the bachelors, who are categorized as soldiers, whether they actually are or not. Both classes include *fidalgos* of many ranks. Though the bachelor-soldiers are not necessarily attached to a command, they are all registered and are expected to volunteer for military service whenever the need arises; they are paid according to the rank under which they are registered. Linschoten

[982] *Ibid.*
[983] *Ibid.*, p. 485.
[984] Burnell and Tiele (eds.), *op. cit.* (n. 978), I, 177.
[985] *Ibid.*, pp. 181–82.
[986] *Ibid.*, pp. 184–85.
[987] *Ibid.*, p. 187.

then goes on to detail recruitment procedures and to talk about the certificates required to authorize the return of individual soldiers to Portugal.

The proud and overweening manners of the Portuguese of Goa have been captured by Linschoten in a number of classical word portraits. For example, he reports how they walk "very slowly forwards, with a great pride and vaineglorious maiestie." One slave holds a shade over his master's head and another walks behind carrying his sword so that it may not trouble him as he walks, or "hinder . . . [his] gravities."[988] Marriages and christenings are celebrated in lavish style by the free citizens of the city in the presence of friends and relatives as well as the dignitaries of church and state. The unmarried men ("soldiers") also "goe verie gravely along the streets with their slaves,"[989] but they are forced to live in dormitories which house from ten to twelve, to dine in common on simple foods, and to share their wardrobes with one another. The majority of the bachelors, when not at war, are either supported by the amorous wives of the community or by the profits derived from engaging in commerce. Most of them, Linschoten asserts, have little concern for "the common profit or the service of the King, but only their particular profits. . . ."[990]

The native wives of the Portuguese, the Luso-Indians, and the Indian Christians likewise receive a lengthy and critical appraisal. Even though they are ordinarily kept indoors and are jealously guarded by their husbands, these women revel in finery and conspire at infidelity. Many husbands are fed *datura*, a powerful narcotic derived from the thorn apple, by their wives to put them into a drugged sleep while the ladies pursue their amours. Should the husband become suspicious of their adultery, these vile women will not hesitate to poison or kill them. Many women are also killed by their husbands who manage through connivance with their friends to escape punishment and to obtain permission to remarry. Conjugal fidelity, according to Linschoten's account, is conspicuous in Goa by its absence.

A new viceroy is sent to Goa every three years, and a few have their appointments renewed.[991] From his residence in Goa, where the viceroy has a council, tribunal, chancellery, and courts, he rules all of Portuguese India according to the laws of the motherland. Justice is in the hands of the viceroy, but civil cases may be appealed to Portugal for adjudication. Criminal cases are handled exclusively by the viceroy unless the accused is a titled person and hence outside of his jurisdiction. *Fidalgos* are normally sent back as prisoners to Portugal to be put on trial. Ordinarily the viceroy makes but few public appearances, but when he does it is in a regal procession. On the walls of the entrance hall in the viceregal palace are painted pictures of all the ships which ever set out for India, and on the walls of the council chamber hang the portraits of all the viceroys. In the last year of their tenure, the viceroys visit the settlements to the north and south of Goa "more to fill their purses . . . than to further the commonwealth."[992]

---

[988] *Ibid.*, pp. 193–94.
[991] *Ibid.*, pp. 217–22.

[989] *Ibid.*, p. 199.
[992] *Ibid.*, p. 219.

[990] *Ibid.*, p. 203.

From the crown the viceroy is given complete control over the treasury of India. Ordinarily, a new viceroy receives rich presents from the native rulers allied with the Portuguese. For a period these gifts were handed over to the Jesuits, but around 1570 the viceroys began to keep them for themselves much to the disappointment of the Jesuits. Whenever a viceroy leaves India, he takes all his possessions with him, including the last piece of furniture from the palace at Bardez. The greed and covetousness of the viceroys is attributed to the short tenure of three years; the new incumbent, according to local analysis, must spend his first year furnishing his residence and learning his way around; the second year he begins to look out for his own profit "for the which cause he came into India"; and the last year he spends in setting his affairs in order to hand over the office in good shape to his successor so "that he may returne into Portingall with the goods which he had scraped together." [993] The lesser officials, it is alleged, proceed in much the same fashion.

Aside from the Portuguese, Linschoten discourses at some length on the customs of the heathens, Moors, Jews, and Armenian Christians who do business in the capital. While he adds little that is new in his discussion of beliefs, Linschoten makes a number of acute observations on the habits of everyday life and on the purification customs of the Hindus. Furthermore, he describes at some length the natives' shops of Goa and the various streets in which the merchants dwell and sell their goods.[994] He comments in some detail on the barbers who have no shops of their own but visit their customers' homes to cut their hair, to give manicures, pedicures, and massages, and to perform other personal services. The native physicians of Goa are consulted by the highest Portuguese dignitaries who "put more trust in them, than in their own countrimen...." [995] This discussion he concludes by observing that the Indians must follow in the trades of their fathers, marry within their own occupational groups, and respect the inheritance custom which ordains that the possessions of the father are passed on only to his sons.[996]

After discussing the climate, seasons, diseases, currencies, weights, and measures of Goa, Linschoten passes on to more detailed descriptions of the practices followed by the natives, both residents and transients, in the Portuguese capital. The Brahmans, he concludes, "are the highest in rank and most esteemed nation amonge the Indian heathens." [997] They are the chief advisers of the native rulers and they occupy the highest administrative posts. At the same time they are the religious leaders and the single most authoritative group in India. In Goa and other seaports many Brahmans sell spices and drugs and are so sharp-witted and learned that they easily "make other simple Indians believe what they will." [998] Linschoten adds nothing to earlier appraisals of Brahman beliefs; he accounts for the practice of *sati* by telling the story which Fedrici recounted at an earlier date, of how the inconstant women of India often poisoned their

---

993 *Ibid.*, p. 222. 994 *Ibid.*, pp. 228–30.
995 *Ibid.*, p. 230. 996 *Ibid.*, p. 231.
997 *Ibid.*, p. 247. 998 *Ibid.*, p. 248.

husbands and of how *sati* was introduced to make them protect rather than take their husbands' lives.[999]

Many natives of Cambay, whom he divides into Gujaratis and Banyās, are reported to live in Goa and other India seaports. Linschoten portrays the Banyās as being sharper in their business practices than any other traders in India, including the Portuguese. Though he does not identify them as Jains, he recounts practices of the Banyās which are usually followed by the Jains. The Gujaratis are clearly much more concerned about the taking of life, ritual purification, and pollution through eating than are the other Indians known to Linschoten. They and their women are light in color and their features and figures are similar to those of the Europeans. A Gujarati dresses in a thin, white gown which covers him from the neck down, and on his feet he wears shoes of red leather with sharp toes that turn up, and on his head he wears a white turban. He is also clean-shaven, except for a mustache, and on his forehead he wears a mark "as a superstitious ceremonie of their law."[1000]

The Kanarese and Deccanese, many of whom are in Goa as purchasers of foreign merchandise, come from "Ballagate" (Balghat)[1001] the country to the east of Goa and the source of the capital's foodstuffs in time of peace. Aside from being merchants, many of the Deccanese are craftsmen and barbers and as a group they are almost as numerous as the Portuguese, Luso-Indians, and Indian Christians combined. In dress they resemble the Gujaratis, except that they wear hempen sandals instead of pointed, leather shoes. They wear their hair and beards long and cover their heads with a turban. Apparently, Linschoten felt that they, more than other Indians, were devoted to the cow, for he details how they treat them "as if they were reasonable creatures."[1002] He also describes the wedding ceremonies of the Deccanese and concludes that their practices are generally the same as those of the other Hindus. In the Goa area they act as tax collectors for the Portuguese authorities and gather the revenues from Bardez and Salsette. They are so well versed in Portuguese and canon law that they are able to present their own cases and petitions without aid of attorney. In order to place them under oath, they are required to stand within a circle of ashes, put a few ashes on their bare heads and, while placing one hand on the head and the other on the breast, swear in their own language and by their own gods that they will tell the truth.[1003]

Of even greater interest is Linschoten's account of life among the lower castes of Goa. He mentions the "maynattos" (*Mainattu*) as a people who "does nothing els but wash cloathes."[1004] He notices the "Patamares" (*Patemari*) who

---

999 *Ibid.*, pp. 250–51; also see above, p. 471.

1000 *Ibid.*, pp. 255–56.

1001 The "country above the passes" or the highlands of the Deccan. See Yule and Burnell, *op. cit.* (n. 10), p. 38.

1002 Burnell and Tiele (eds.), *op. cit.* (n. 978), I, 257.

1003 *Ibid.*, p. 259.

1004 *Ibid.*, p. 260. The Portuguese from Barbosa onward call them *mainatos*. See Dalgado, *op. cit.* (n. 44), II, 12–13.

serve as messengers by carrying letters overland.[1005] Linschoten shows most concern, however, for the "Corumbijns" (*Kutumbi*), an agricultural caste of Kanara whom he observed on a visit to the mainland behind Goa. While these people hold the same beliefs as the Deccanese, they are "the most contemptible, and the miserablest of India." [1006] They labor at fishing, tilling the rice paddies, and tending the palm groves which line the banks of the rivers and the seashore. In color they are dark brown and many of them are baptized Christians. Their tiny houses of straw have such low doors that they must be entered on hands and knees and are furnished only with sleeping mats and a few cooking utensils. The women deliver their own children and Linschoten writes in wonder about how quickly the new mother is up and about. Though these poor agriculturists live in exceedingly primitive circumstances, he asserts that they swim and dive well and live to a ripe old age "without any headach, or toothach, or loosing any of their teeth." [1007] Still, most of them are so thin, weak, and cowardly that the Portuguese treat them like animals without fear of reprisal.

Arabs, Ethiopians, and Kaffirs from Mozambique also walk the streets of Goa. While the Arabs are strictly Muslim in their faith, the Ethiopians are divided between those who accept the Prophet and those who are Christians of Prester John. Many of the Ethiopians, both men and women, are slaves and they are "sold like other Oriental Nations." [1008] The free Arabs and Ethiopians serve as sailors on the ships which sail from Goa eastward; they have no trouble getting berths as common seamen because even untrained Portuguese sailors set themselves up as officers for the voyages to the Far East. Linschoten gives considerable detail on the outfitting of the ships for Eastern voyages and notices that they never carry casks of water but have aboard only a square wooden cistern in the keel of the ship. The Kaffirs, some of whom are Muslims, are "as black as pitch," [1009] inclined to walk about in nature's raiment, to thrust bones through their cheeks for beauty's sake, and to sear their faces and bodies with irons. The Jesuits take no pains to missionize in the lands of the Kaffirs "for they see no greate profite to be reaped there, as they doe in India and the Ilands of Japan . . . where they find great quantities of riches, with the sap whereof they increase much and fill their beehyves, to satisfy their insatiable desires." [1010]

Linschoten, while discussing the enslavement of the Kaffirs, interpolates into his account a review of the slave trade in general. He explains that the political and cultural fragmentation of Mozambique produces a condition of almost perpetual warfare among its many petty rulers. The prisoners taken in these

---

[1005] This term is used in this sense primarily by the writers of the sixteenth century; later writers use it as the name for a lateen-rigged ship common to the west coast of India. See Dalgado, *op. cit.* (n. 44), II, 186–88.

[1006] Burnell and Tiele (eds.), *op. cit.* (n. 978), I, 260.

[1007] *Ibid.*, p. 262.

[1008] *Ibid.*, p. 265.

[1009] *Ibid.*, p. 271.

[1010] *Ibid.*, p. 272.

numerous wars are kept as slaves and marketed to the Portuguese when their ships put into the ports of Mozambique for water or other necessities. But the Kaffirs and other Africans are not the only people sold on the block in Goa. Linschoten observes that while he was in Goa a famine hit the mainland of India and as a result many of the natives brought their children to the Portuguese capital to sell in exchange for food. While he is not the first European writer to report on the sale of persons in India,[1011] he is the most graphic. He asserts: "I have seene Boyes of eight or ten yeares given in exchange for five or sixe measures of rice . . . and some came with their wives and children to offer themselves to bee slaves so that they might have meate and drinke to nourish their bodies."[1012] The Portuguese who trade at many eastern places distant from one another "make a living by buying and selling [slaves] as they doe with other wares"[1013] and presumably market them wherever the price is best.

During his residence in Goa, Linschoten met numerous fellow Europeans and other foreign dignitaries. His report of the imprisonment of Newbery and Fitch, and the efforts which were made to obtain their release, probably is the best source available on the event.[1014] He was also in Goa at the time of the arrival of the emissaries from Japan and he was still there when they returned from Europe.[1015] On their arrival from Japan in 1583 the Japanese youths were dressed as Jesuits; on their return from Europe in 1587 "they were all three apparelled in cloth of Golde and Silver, after the Italian manner. . . ."[1016] In June, 1584, legates arrived in Goa from Persia, Cambay, Calicut, and Cochin. Among other things a treaty was concluded by the representative of the Zamorin for the establishment of a Portuguese fort at Panan near Calicut, and after mentioning this agreement Linschoten digresses at length on the problem of piracy along the Malabar Coast.[1017] He further recounts how difficult the Portuguese found it in 1584 to force the erection of a custom house at Cochin against native resistance. He reports on the departure from Goa in April, 1585, of Bernard Burcherts, his associate in the archbishop's retinue, and summarizes from letters relayed to him the route which Burcherts followed overland from Ormuz to Tripoli in Syria and to his native city of Hamburg.[1018] News apparently arrived rather regularly in Goa during 1585 as travelers and mail came there over both the land and the sea routes. In May, 1586, Turkish galleons built in Egypt began to prey on Portuguese vessels in the Red Sea and so a fleet was outfitted in Goa to chase them down.[1019] Around the same time the

---

1011 Above, p. 409.

1012 Burnell and Tiele (eds.), *op. cit.* (n. 978), I, 276.

1013 *Ibid.*, p. 277.   1014 *Ibid.*, II, 158–66.

1015 For details see below, pp. 691–701. Linschoten, who refers to a "book in Spanish," apparently depends for his summary of their visit to Europe and their reception in Japan upon the compilation entitled *Breve relacion del recibimiento que en Espana i en toda Italia se hiço a tres embajadores* (Seville, 1586).

1016 Burnell and Tiele (eds.), *op. cit.* (n. 978), II, 168.

1017 *Ibid.*, pp. 169–73.

1018 *Ibid.*, p. 175.

1019 *Ibid.*, pp. 183–87.

queen of Ormuz came to Goa to be baptized after she had married a Portuguese man.[1020] In 1587, he notes that fleets were being prepared in Goa to relieve the sieges of the Portuguese forts at Colombo and Malacca.[1021]

In addition to his observations made in Goa, Linschoten is able on the basis of personal experience to comment generally on the places and peoples of Malabar. His discussion of the Nāyars and of the matrilineal system of inheritance adds nothing to the earlier accounts and is inferior to a number of them. Particularly interesting are his references to the Sephardic Jews resident in Cochin who are rich merchants and are "... the king of Cochins neerest counsellers."[1022] The Cochin Jews have their own synagogue and Linschoten knew them well enough to be permitted to see and touch the Torah. His acquaintance with the Moors of Cochin is not nearly so close and he blames them for the difficulties encountered by the Christian missionaries in their efforts to convert the Indians. His descriptions of the native temples at Elephanta and elsewhere likewise add little to what earlier writers had reported. More revealing is his account of the Portuguese theft in 1554 of the tooth of Buddha (an ape's tooth) from Ceylon, the consternation which it caused among a number of pious south Indian rulers, the heartless burning of the relic in Goa, and the subsequent "discovery" of a new tooth which was enshrined at Vijayanagar as if it were the original which had miraculously escaped the flames.[1023]

Linschoten's descriptions of the flora, fauna, and jewels of India are fascinating. He discourses on a wide variety of topics such as the elephant, the rhinoceros, the mango, and the palm tree and its uses. While he clearly depends upon the natural histories based on Orta, he interpolates many original remarks, observations, and experiences. For example, he tells about the boldness of the black crows who do not hesitate to enter houses to snatch food off the table.[1024] He records that in 1581 an elephant and a rhinoceros were presented to King Philip II in Lisbon and the two animals were then driven to Madrid.[1025] Philip was also sent a painting of a monstrous fish caught in a river of Goa while Linschoten was there. Gigantic seashells from Malacca were sent by the Jesuits to Lisbon to decorate the facade of their church.[1026] The ship on which Linschoten voyaged to India was entirely equipped with ropes and cables made in India of coir.[1027] After describing the manufacture and use of *olas* (palm leaf sheets used as paper), he remarks: "Of this paper with Indian writing upon it, you may see some at Dr. Paludanus' house, which I gave him for a present."[1028]

[1020] *Ibid.*, p. 187.

[1021] *Ibid.*, pp. 196–200.

[1022] *Ibid.*, I, 286.

[1023] *Ibid.*, pp. 292–94.

[1024] *Ibid.*, p. 302.

[1025] *Ibid.*, II, 10. Cf. reference in Mendoza (below, p. 569n) to the reception of the rhinoceros in Madrid.

[1026] *Ibid.*, p. 16.

[1027] *Ibid.*, p. 46.

[1028] *Ibid.*, p. 50. Paludanus' collection of exotic oddities was the pride of the town of Enkhuizen and often viewed by foreign visitors (*ibid.*, I, xxix).

Rhubarb, he tells us, comes exclusively from the interior of China. Rhubarb which is brought overland across Asia to Venice is better than the rhubarb which is shipped to Portugal and which deteriorates on the long sea voyage.[1029] Emperor Charles V, he comments, tried "roots of China"[1030] with good results as a cure for the gout. Mother-of-pearl ornaments and utensils manufactured in China and Bengal are imported into Portugal in large quantities.[1031] Emeralds, which are rarely found in the East, are imported from America and traded by the Venetians for the rubies of Burma.[1032] Such unconnected and incidental references are scattered like nuggets throughout his text and many of them are important enough to make a thorough mining of his book worth the effort.

Linschoten's work had a direct effect upon the Dutch and English merchants of his own day. This is plainly evident from even a cursory survey of the materials relating to their enterprises. Linschoten's routier of the East (*Reysgeschrift*), published in 1595, was actually made use of on board the ships which comprised the first Dutch armada that went directly to the East Indies (1595–97).[1033] Meanwhile, the Dutch, including Linschoten, continued persistently to believe in the existence of a northeastern passage to the Far East, though the English had long before abandoned hope of finding it. Linschoten himself sailed with and kept records of the two exploratory voyages of 1594 and 1595. These voyages, and a third one of 1596, finally convinced the stubborn Dutch that a northeastern passage was not possible.[1034] More than ever the Dutch thereafter pinned their hopes on the success of the southern expedition, only to find on its return in 1597 that little trading had been done because of strife among the Dutch commanders themselves.[1035] Still, the first fleet had got safely to Java and back again and had thereby shown that the Iberian monopoly was not effectively guarded. Almost immediately small fleets were outfitted in the ports of the Netherlands to sail directly for the East Indies. These private enterprises were finally combined under the guidance of Jan van Oldenbarnevelt into the Dutch East India Company (1602). The English quickly learned from the Dutch experience and accelerated their plans for direct and systematic voyages. In 1598, William Phillip, the translator of Linschoten,

---

1029 *Ibid.*, II, 102.

1030 *Ibid.*, p. 110; this is the *radix chinae*, the tuber of various species of *smilaceae*.

1031 *Ibid.*, pp. 135–36.

1032 *Ibid.*, p. 141.

1033 J. C. Mollema (ed.). *De eerste Schipvaart der Hollanders naar Oost-Indië, 1595–97* (The Hague, 1935), pp. 30–32.

1034 The journals of these ill-fated voyages were published by Gerrit de Veer in his *Waerachtige Beschrijvinghe van drie Seylagien, ter werelt noyt soo vreemt ghehoort, drie Jaeren achter Malcanderen deur de Hollandtsche ende Zeelandtsche Schepen by noorden, Noorweghen, Moscovia, ende Tartaria, na de coninckrijcken van Catthay ende China, so mede vande opdveninghe vande Weygats, Nova Sembla, en van't Landt op de 80 grade dat men acht Groenlandt te zijn* ... (Amsterdam, 1598). Though unsuccessful, these voyages apparently were still of lively interest to contemporaries because De Veer's work reappeared by 1600 in at least one reprinting and in Latin, French, German, and Italian translations. In 1609 it was translated into English by William Phillip.

1035 See the newsletter from Amsterdam dated August 8, 1597, in W. Noel Sainsbury (ed.), *Calendar of State Papers, Colonial Series; East Indies, China and Japan* (London, 1862), pp. 98–99, item 253.

published in London another translation of a Dutch work entitled *The Description of a Voyage Made by Certaine Ships of Holland into the East Indies, with Their Adventures and Successe . . . Who Set Forth on the Second of Aprill, 1595, and Returned on the 14 of August, 1597.*[1036] In a memorandum of 1600 by Foulke Grevil to Sir Robert Cecil, a brief rundown is given of the economic and political conditions prevailing in the Portuguese trading centers of the East which is drawn "specially out of the voyages of John Huighen [Linschoten]."[1037]

The merchant commentators reviewed in this chapter had their experiences in India during the period between 1564 and 1591. Fedrici, the first of this group to travel in India, was absent from Venice for eighteen years and he spent a far longer time in the East than any of the rest. The four other writers (Balbi, Sassetti, Fitch, and Linschoten) were all in India during the decade of the 1580's and we know from them and other sources that there were also many other non-Iberians in Portuguese India at the time. Two of the commentators (Sassetti and Linschoten) worked within the Portuguese trading system in India, and so are particularly authoritative on matters relating to the west coast and its place in the overseas empire. The other three (Fedrici, Balbi, and Fitch) are best described as commercial interlopers or private merchants who gathered their materials haphazardly and with a view to advancing the ambitions of their homelands in breaking into the spice monopoly. Fedrici's book and Sassetti's letters appear to be the product of their independent efforts. Balbi and Fitch clearly borrowed from Fedrici; and Linschoten relied upon a number of already published sources. All of their writings (except Sassetti's) appeared in book form within a brief span of twelve years (1587–99) and all of their books, except Fitch's, were translated into other languages and included in travel collections by 1600. But what is perhaps most important is the fact that these materials deal with a period in Indian history on which published Jesuit and Iberian sources were few and slight, the missionaries being more concerned with China, Japan, and the Mughul empire, and the Portuguese with the survival of their nation and empire in the last two decades of the sixteenth century.

The sixteenth-century European sources on India—Portuguese secular materials, Jesuit letterbooks and histories, and the narrative of the non-Iberian travelers—complement and supplement one another in many ways. Chronologically, they blanket every decade of the century. When the Portuguese chronicles end around 1540, the story is taken up by the Jesuit sources. When the Jesuit sources taper off in the 1560's, the story is taken up by Fedrici who first arrived in India in 1564. As the Jesuit letters become more official and less informative

---

[1036] The original work is entitled *Vehael vande Reyse by de Hollandtsche Schepen gedaen naer Oost Indien*. It was published at Middelburg in 1597. It contains much material on the strife between Houtman and Van Beuningen, and it is attributed to the pen of Barent Langenes. See G. P. Rouffaer and J. W. Ijzerman (eds.), *De eerste Schipvaart der Nederlanders naar Oost-Indië onder Cornelis de Houtman, 1595–1597* (3 vols.; The Hague, 1915–18), II, xxvii. A copy of the English version of 1598 is in the Library of Congress.

[1037] *Ibid.*, pp. 104–5, item 266.

after 1581, the unofficial writings of the commercial interlopers and Linschoten provide additional detail and give a new dimension to what was known about India in the last two decades of the century. The great weakness of the sources to 1580 is the complete dominance of the Portuguese and Jesuit official historiography. Philip II, while no more tolerant of dissent than were earlier rulers of Portugal, was forced under pressure from his own *conquistadores* and missionaries to allow modifications in the monopolistic practices of the Portuguese and Jesuits. While the monopolists resisted change as best they could, criticism of their policies in India and elsewhere were frequently heard in Madrid. Even the Jesuit letterbooks and histories take on a more polemical tone near the close of the century.

The sources, taken together, also blanket the physical scene, supplementing one another neatly. The Portuguese secular writings are best on the west coast and the trading centers of Gujarat and Bengal; at the end of the century, when there are practically no Portuguese materials being published, the narratives of the commercial travelers and Linschoten continue to maintain this emphasis while generally concentrating the fire of their criticism on Goa. The Jesuits, perhaps advisedly, have very little to say in their published writings about political and social conditions in the Portuguese-controlled towns and territories. Except for horse-traders and mercenary soldiers, very few lay Portuguese penetrated into the interior of India.

Whenever the Portuguese chroniclers deal with affairs in the interior of the subcontinent, they seem to rely on the reports of merchants, soldiers, and native informants. As a result, their accounts stress routes, entrepôts, products, and military activities, and almost completely ignore the social practices, religions, and languages of interior regions. The Jesuit writings, by contrast, dwell at considerable length on everyday events along the remote Fishery Coast, within the Serra of the St. Thomas Christians, and at the imperial headquarters of Akbar. While the Jesuits were more assiduous about learning Indian languages than any other group, they are very little impressed by native scholarship or high culture. Orta and Sassetti, the two leading secular Humanists to spend time in India, appear to show more genuine interest in and sympathy for the presuppositions of Indian civilization than the missionaries. The Jesuits of this era, like the merchants and administrators, are little disposed to understand Indian values and beliefs. Their comments on social practices, astute as they sometimes are, are clearly hostile; social practices are viewed as impediments to trade and Christianity.

In the reconstruction of Indian history during the sixteenth century too little attention has so far been given to the great chronicles of Castanheda and Barros, and to the Jesuit letterbooks and histories. Some specialists in Indian history, as for example Commissariat on Gujarat or Campos on Bengal, have utilized advantageously the works of the travelers of the early sixteenth century. The writings of the commercial interlopers and Linschoten at the end of the century have also been mined by students of Indian history. But in the general histories

of India, as for example that of Majumdar, the Portuguese appear prima.
as intruders rather than contributors and the records which they left to p
are generally slighted or ignored. Such omissions are to be deplored, because
the Portuguese and Jesuit writings are dotted with valuable and concrete data
for a period of Indian history when other sources are extremely thin or non-
existent. The Portuguese and Jesuit writers, conscious of the need to gi   -
tistics, though not always too precise about them, include figures in their
and letters on the populations of Indian cities and regions, the revenues of par
lar rulers, and the composition and size of Indian armies. Some of these st   .cs
do not appear in other sources, and even if they do, the European figures should
certainly be collated with them. Castanheda's account of Humayun's wars in
Gujarat and Bengal has so far been overlooked in most historical studies of the
early Mughuls. The descriptions of caste, matrilineal, familial and inheritance
practices, *sati*, sexual customs, and slavery have been used, and could be even
more diligently exploited, by cultural anthropologists interested in adding
historical dimensions to their studies.

To Europeans of the sixteenth century much of this material on India n.
have seemed highly exotic and questionable. Nevertheless, as shown earlier, the
Portuguese accounts were translated beginning in 1550 into other European
languages, most of them thereafter being available in whole or in part in
Ramusio's collection. The Jesuit and merchant writings of the latter half
the century also enjoyed general distribution in Europe. That information on
India was positively sought by scholars outside of the Iberian Peninsula is
attested by the efforts that Ramusio, Paulus Jovius, the Fuggers, and the
English made to acquire copies of Portuguese and Jesuit works.

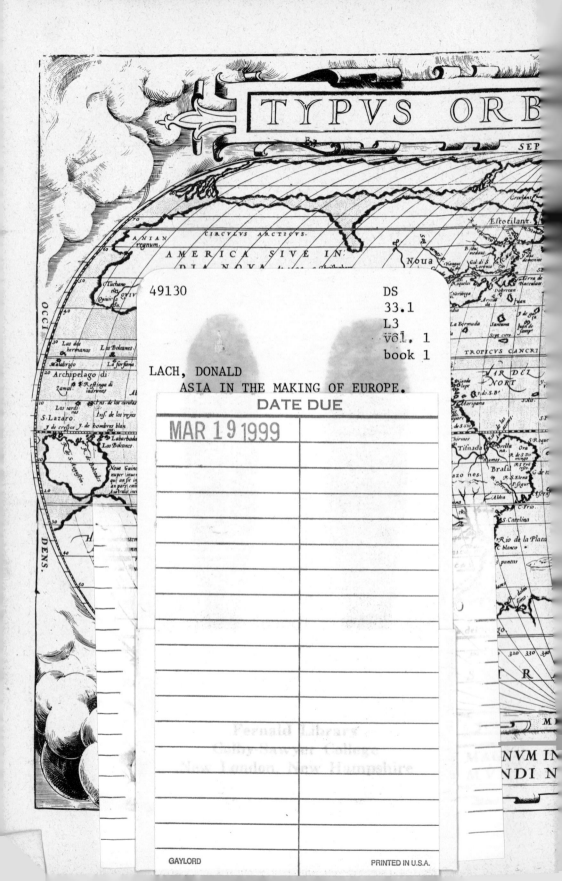

DATE DUE	
MAR 19 1999	

GAYLORD   PRINTED IN U.S.A.

TYPVS ORB